CONSULS AND *RES*

The consulate was the focal point of Roman politics. Both the ruling class and the ordinary citizens fixed their gaze on the republic's highest office – to be sure, from different perspectives and with differing expectations. While the former aspired to the consulate as the defining magistracy of their social status, the latter perceived it as the embodiment of the Roman state. Holding high office was thus not merely a political exercise. The consulate prefigured all aspects of public life, with consuls taking care of almost every element of the administration of the Roman state. This multifaceted character of the consulate invites a holistic investigation. The scope of this book is therefore not limited to political or constitutional questions. Instead, it investigates the predominant role of the consulate in, and its impact on, the political culture of the Roman republic.

HANS BECK is John MacNaughton Professor and Director of Classical Studies in the Department of History and Classical Studies at McGill University. His publications include *Central Greece and the Politics of Power in the Fourth Century* BC (2008) with John Buckler.

ANTONIO DUPLÁ is Associate Professor in the Departamento de Estudios Clásicos at the Universidad del País Vasco in Vitoria-Gasteiz, where he teaches Ancient History and Classical Reception.

MARTIN JEHNE is Professor of Ancient History in the Institut für Geschichte at the Technische Universität Dresden.

FRANCISCO PINA POLO is Professor of Ancient History in the Departamento de Ciencias de la Antigüedad at the Universidad de Zaragoza. His publications include *The Consul at Rome: The Civil Functions of the Consuls in the Roman Republic* (2011).

CONSULS AND *RES PUBLICA*

Holding High Office in the Roman Republic

EDITED BY

HANS BECK, ANTONIO DUPLÁ,
MARTIN JEHNE
AND
FRANCISCO PINA POLO

CAMBRIDGE
UNIVERSITY PRESS

CAMBRIDGE
UNIVERSITY PRESS

University Printing House, Cambridge CB2 8BS, United Kingdom

Cambridge University Press is part of the University of Cambridge.

It furthers the University's mission by disseminating knowledge in the pursuit of education, learning and research at the highest international levels of excellence.

www.cambridge.org
Information on this title: www.cambridge.org/9781107526518

© Cambridge University Press 2011

This publication is in copyright. Subject to statutory exception and to the provisions of relevant collective licensing agreements, no reproduction of any part may take place without the written permission of Cambridge University Press.

First published 2011
First paperback edition 2015

A catalogue record for this publication is available from the British Library

Library of Congress Cataloguing in Publication data
Consuls and res publica : holding high office in the Roman Republic / edited by Hans Beck... [et al.].
p. cm.
Includes bibliographical references and index.
ISBN 978-1-107-00154-1
1. Consuls, Roman – History.   2. Political culture – Rome – History.
3. Rome – History – Republic, 265–30 B.C.   4. Rome – Politics and government – 265–30 B.C.   5. Social classes – Rome – History.
6. Social status – Rome – History.   7. Power (Social sciences) – Rome – History.
8. Rome – Social conditions – 510–30 B.C.   I. Beck, Hans, 1969–   II. Title.
DG83.5.C7C67 2011
937'.02 – dc23   2011017494

ISBN 978-1-107-00154-1 Hardback
ISBN 978-1-107-52651-8 Paperback

Cambridge University Press has no responsibility for the persistence or accuracy of URLs for external or third-party internet websites referred to in this publication, and does not guarantee that any content on such websites is, or will remain, accurate or appropriate.

Contents

Preface	*page* vii
List of contributors	ix
The republic and its highest office: some introductory remarks on the Roman consulate *Hans Beck, Antonio Duplá, Martin Jehne and Francisco Pina Polo*	1

PART I THE CREATION OF THE CONSULSHIP   17

1 The magistrates of the early Roman republic   19
 Christopher Smith

2 The origin of the consulship in Cassius Dio's *Roman History*   41
 Gianpaolo Urso

3 The development of the praetorship in the third century BC   61
 Alexander Bergk

PART II POWERS AND FUNCTIONS OF THE CONSULSHIP   75

4 Consular power and the Roman constitution: the case of *imperium* reconsidered   77
 Hans Beck

5 Consuls as *curatores pacis deorum*   97
 Francisco Pina Polo

6 The *Feriae Latinae* as religious legitimation of the consuls' *imperium*   116
 Francisco Marco Simón

7 War, wealth and consuls   133
   Nathan Rosenstein

PART III SYMBOLS, MODELS, SELF-REPRESENTATION   159

8 The Roman republic as theatre of power: the consuls as
   leading actors   161
   Karl-Joachim Hölkeskamp

9 The consul(ar) as *exemplum*: Fabius *Cunctator*'s
   paradoxical glory   182
   Matthew B. Roller

10 The rise of the consular as a social type in the third and
   second centuries BC   211
   Martin Jehne

11 *Privata hospitia, beneficia publica*? Consul(ar)s, local elite
   and Roman rule in Italy   232
   Michael P. Fronda

PART IV IDEOLOGY, CONFRONTATION AND THE END OF
THE REPUBLICAN CONSULSHIP   257

12 Consular appeals to the army in 88 and 87: the locus of
   legitimacy in late-republican Rome   259
   Robert Morstein-Marx

13 *Consules populares*   279
   Antonio Duplá

14 The consulship of 78 BC. Catulus versus Lepidus: an
   optimates versus *populares* affair   299
   Valentina Arena

15 Consulship and consuls under Augustus   319
   Frédéric Hurlet

Bibliography   336
Index of persons   368
Subject index   374

Preface

This volume is primarily the result of the work carried out by an international research network, which was established in 2004 with the main purpose of studying the consulship in the Roman republic. The editors formed the core group of this network: Hans Beck (Montreal, Canada), Antonio Duplá (Vitoria, Spain), Martin Jehne (Dresden, Germany) and Francisco Pina Polo (Zaragoza, Spain), the last acting as Principal Investigator. The core group met on various occasions in Spain, and a large international conference was held at the University of Zaragoza in September 2007, where most of the papers presented in this book were delivered. These papers were significantly revised for publication. Other contributions were added as this volume took shape, to fill in the most significant gaps. The result is by no means a comprehensive study of the consulship, let alone a complete one. Rather, we look at the present volume as a contribution to an ongoing debate on Roman republican politics. That debate is more vibrant than ever. Branching out into the realms of other societies in the ancient Mediterranean, we feel that its applied models, concepts and thought paradigms are also relevant to the general discussion of elite power in antiquity.

We are grateful to the Ministerio de Ciencia y Educación of Spain for its sponsorship of two consecutive funding cycles of "Consuls, Consulars and the Government of the Roman Republic" (HUM2004–02449 and HUM2007–60776/HIST), which was vital to the work of our team. When the volume entered the publishing pipeline, Margherita Devine and Brahm Kleinman helped with the challenge of editing the work of scholars from so many different linguistic backgrounds and academic cultures. Special thanks go to them, as to Fabian Knopf, who took on the laborious task of compiling the index of persons. As so often, the editorial work took longer than anticipated, and the editors would like to thank the contributors not only for their willingness to participate, but also for their patience. Finally, we are grateful to Michael Sharp, Commissioning Editor for Classics at Cambridge University Press, for his support and guidance in bringing this publication to light.

Contributors

VALENTINA ARENA, Lecturer in Roman History, Department of History, University College London

HANS BECK, John MacNaughton Chair of Classics, Department of History and Classical Studies, McGill University

ALEXANDER BERGK, Philosophische Fakultät, Technische Universität Dresden

ANTONIO DUPLÁ, Associate Professor, Departamento de Estudios Clásicos, Universidad del País Vasco

MICHAEL P. FRONDA, Assistant Professor, Department of History and Classical Studies, McGill University

KARL-JOACHIM HÖLKESKAMP, Professor of Ancient History, Historisches Institut, Universität Köln

FRÉDÉRIC HURLET, Professor of Roman History, Département d'Histoire, Université de Nantes

MARTIN JEHNE, Professor of Ancient History, Institut für Geschichte, Technische Universität Dresden

FRANCISCO MARCO SIMÓN, Professor of Ancient History, Departamento de Ciencias de la Antigüedad, Universidad de Zaragoza

ROBERT MORSTEIN-MARX, Professor and Chair, Department of Classics, University of California, Santa Barbara

FRANCISCO PINA POLO, Professor of Ancient History, Departamento de Ciencias de la Antigüedad, Universidad de Zaragoza

MATTHEW B. ROLLER, Professor, Department of Classics, Johns Hopkins University

NATHAN ROSENSTEIN, Professor of Ancient History, Department of History, Ohio State University

CHRISTOPHER SMITH, Professor of Ancient History, School of Classics, University of St Andrews, Director of the British School at Rome

GIANPAOLO URSO, Università Cattolica del Sacro Cuore Milano

The republic and its highest office: some introductory remarks on the Roman consulate

Hans Beck, Antonio Duplá, Martin Jehne
and Francisco Pina Polo

The consulship of the Roman republic is notoriously under-researched. To be sure, the republican "constitution," and with it the consulate, have been addressed to a certain extent. Examples in English include Andrew Lintott's *The Constitution of the Roman Republic* and T. Corey Brennan's and John North's more recent syntheses.[1] In some sense, these studies provide a comprehensive summary of a long series of scholarly contributions on the republic's institutional apparatus, starting with Theodor Mommsen's contribution and explored further in the works of Ettore de Ruggiero, Francesco de Martino, Jochen Bleicken, Wolfgang Kunkel and Roland Wittmann.[2] This scholarship deals with the Roman "constitution" in general terms, and all of these essays focus, more or less, on the supreme magistracy in the republic. Furthermore, the consulship has been studied in research on Roman chronology and on the Roman nobility.[3] Republican prosopography is roughly based on the *Fasti Consulares* as a starting point.[4] In fact, without Broughton's monumental work it would be practically impossible to tackle any study on the republican period.[5] And, of course, the groundbreaking work of Adalberto Giovannini must be mentioned. Giovannini succeeded in proving the non-existence of the assumed *lex Cornelia de provinciis ordinandis*, prompted by Mommsen, and

---

[1] Lintott 1999b; Brennan 2004; North 2006.
[2] Mommsen 1887–8; de Ruggiero 1892, 679–862; de Martino 1972–5; Bleicken 1995; Kunkel & Wittmann 1995.
[3] Cf. for instance Hölkeskamp 1987; Feig Vishnia 1996; Beck 2005.
[4] Drummond 1974; Pinsent 1975; Mora 1999.
[5] Broughton 1951–86. The work of Lippold 1963 has a more limited purpose, since he analyzes the political role of the consuls in the period between the years 264 and 201, as does the work of Badian 1990b. Badian studies the prosopography of the consuls between the passing of the *lex Villia* and the beginning of the civil war, focusing on descent to analyze the importance of noble status for the recruitment of consuls.

specified the characteristics of the consular *imperium*.⁶ However, there is no book-length treatment of the office and its competences, or of the tasks performed by the consuls and their role in the government of Rome during the republic. The situation is somewhat different in other areas of constitutional research. The senate,⁷ the popular assemblies,⁸ the aedileship,⁹ the tribunate of the plebs,¹⁰ the censorship,¹¹ the dictatorship¹² and most recently the praetorship¹³ have all received in-depth treatment and works of analysis that were at times truly magisterial. In other words, virtually all republican institutions have, at some point, been the subject of extensive, although not completely updated, research. To date, the consulship is the only institution that has not received this attention.

This is astonishing, at best. The situation cannot be explained by the hazards of scholarship alone. Rather, the consulship is a nebulous office, which makes it an elusive subject of research from a constitutional point of view. While the tribunate of the plebs and the praetorship have fairly clear-cut responsibilities and spheres of authority, the consulship has only an aura of general leadership with rather blurred limits of competence. Consuls are allowed to take care of nearly everything in the administration of the *res publica*, but often their surveillance remains more or less an abstraction without much significance in everyday business. To understand Roman consuls better it is therefore necessary to determine not so much what they were allowed to do according to constitutional theory, but what they did in political practice. Or to rephrase it in a more programmatic way: the analysis of the consulship is better suited to cultural history and historical anthropology than the classical "Staatsrecht." And there is much to do in this approach.

It is precisely the study of the consulship that is the main objective of the research team formed a few years ago by the authors of this introduction. The research work has been carried out under the sponsorship of the Ministerio de Ciencia y Educación of Spain, which funded a project entitled "Consuls, Consulars and the Government of the Roman

---

⁶ Giovannini 1983. The maintenance of the *imperium militiae* by the consuls during their consular year after Sulla had already been pointed out by Balsdon 1939 and by Valgiglio 1957, esp.132–40. Girardet 2001, esp.155–61 = Girardet 2007.
⁷ Bonnefond-Coudry 1989; Ryan 1998.
⁸ Botsford 1909; Taylor 1966; Develin 1975b; Farrell 1986; Yakobson 1999; Pina Polo 1989, 1996; Laser 1997; Millar 1998; Sandberg 2001; Morstein-Marx 2004.
⁹ Sabbatucci 1954.   ¹⁰ Bleicken 1955; Lobrano 1982; Sancho 1984; Thommen 1989.
¹¹ Suolahti 1963; Pieri 1968. Cf. also the papers of Astin 1982; Astin 1985.
¹² Bandel 1910; Hartfield 1982; Hurlet 1993.   ¹³ Brennan 2000.

Republic" (HUM2004–02449 and HUM2007–60776/HIST).[14] In this context, an international conference was held at the University of Zaragoza in September 2007 where most of the papers that make up this volume were presented.

In the traditional account, the consuls are the regular supreme magistrates of the Roman "constitution" and their image is linked to the political-military management of the state from the very beginning. During the conquest of Italy and, later on, the Mediterranean, their military dimension as commanders of the army became particularly relevant. Finally, during the late republic, their political dimension is highlighted once again in the persistence of their office in the troubled times of the last century of the republic. But the republic's highest office, like the Roman "constitution" itself, should be regarded as a "work in progress," and it cannot be analyzed without taking into account the changing historical circumstances of the five centuries of republican history. Roman tradition itself, as opposed to other historical sources, highlighted the fact that the system developed with the contributions of many generations, and not as a result of the work of one particular legislator at a given time. The consulship is, in that sense, a splendid example of the elements of continuity and change that co-exist in the "constitution" of the Roman republic.

On the one hand, the picture, firmly anchored in Roman imagery, of the consuls as the immediate substitutes for the king in the change from monarchy into republic is a reflection of that continuity. The so-called *lex curiata de imperio* may well be another example of this, if the provision indeed was a genuine archaic relic that became, and continued to be, an imperative for superior magistrates, although it was reduced to a ritual formality later on. On the other hand, the various changes that affect the powers of the consuls with regards to newly created magistracies, or questions such as the date they took office or, something more essential, the transformations of the *imperium*, indicate a dramatic development and adaptation to the changing needs of each particular time. Consequently, the development of the consulship is an indication of the flexibility and creativity of Rome's ruling class in the republican period.

According to Roman traditions, Livy's narrative and his predecessors in particular, two consuls, acting as equal partners in power, replaced the

---

[14] As the main result of the research project, the coordinator of the team, Francisco Pina Polo, has published a monograph entitled *The Consul at Rome: The Civil Functions of the Consuls in the Roman republic* (Cambridge, 2011).

king as superior magistrates in 509 BC. However, Livy himself and later authors, such as Festus, also refer to a *praetor maximus*, which has led some to think of a principal magistrate at the head of the newly born republic. Reports regarding the *praetor maximus* and the annual fixing of the nail on the Capitoline temple would support that interpretation.[15] Moreover, the traditional account of the establishment of a new regime is embellished with a series of historical-literary items that render it highly implausible. The stories of Lucretia, the first consuls Brutus and Tarquinius Collatinus, the Etruscan King Porsenna, the expulsion of the relatives of the *gens* of the king, including Collatinus, the conspiracy of Brutus' sons in favor of the restoration of the monarchy and their subsequent execution, as well as other similar events, all suggest tenuous historicity.

The complexity of the many problems deriving from the reconstruction of the beginnings and of the first century and a half of the republic is enormous. There are debates over the names of the first magistrates, whether or not they had dual character, why *tribuni militum consulare potestate* existed, and whether the *Fasti* are relatively historical or totally false. The possibility of a historical reconstruction of that period is discussed, considered in the sources by both believers and non-believers. Without getting bogged down by specific problems, which are out of place in this short description of the history of the consulship, we can establish certain starting points.

After the rejection of the monarchy-tyranny, it is logical to suppose that an absolute ruler was replaced by a series of magistrates, of variable number, to ensure a better distribution of power. In an open city-state, like Rome by the end of the sixth century BC, after an oligarchic coup d'état against a monarch-tyrant, it is reasonable to argue for a joint and temporary exercise of power by the leaders of the most important clans, who were endorsed by their election-ratification at the assemblies. These superior magistrates could be elected by the *comitia centuriata*, originally the people in arms, to hold the office for a limited period of time: one year. The joint and temporary nature of the post seems to be the coherent result of a new distribution of power among aristocratic families. In fact, joint magistracies, in variable number and with limited duration of office, are recurrent in the tradition of the fifth century BC (*decemviri, tribuni plebis, tribuni militum consulare potestate*).

The essential element of superior magistrates is the *imperium*, a civil and military authority, of sacred nature, exercised *domi* and *militiae*. This *imperium* is complemented by a series of external signs of power: twelve lictors with *fasces* and *secures, sella curulis, toga praetexta*. They take turns

[15] Livy 7.3.5.

carrying the *fasces* to emphasize the joint nature of their power. Regardless of the debated historicity of the first *leges Valeriae de provocatione*, it is probable that there was, from a very early stage, some sort of right of appeal of the people against the possible arbitrariness of superior magistrates; thus the balance between *imperium* and *provocatio* is one of the defining characteristics of Rome's political system. The *intercessio* from a colleague or a tribune of the plebs was another mechanism to assure some balance of power, aimed at preventing abuses and favoring reaching consensus.

Rome's constitutional structure, certainly quite peculiar, is also well defined from the beginning in the account that sources give of the origin of the republic. A rigorous analysis of the information provided by historians and antiquarians raises many questions that cannot be answered clearly. Nonetheless, without denying those difficulties, we can outline a historical reconstruction from the retrievable elements in those sources. For example, even if we accept the possible existence of eponymous magistrates from the start, it implies the existence of lists of magistrates from a very early stage, which in turn supports the plausibility of the *Fasti*.

Indeed, it is undeniable that only after the enactment of the Licinian-Sextian laws (367/6 BC) do we have more detailed and reliable information about the consulship. The various theories about consuls or *praetor maximus* and other *praetores*, or *magister populi–magister equitum*, about the *tribuni militum consulare potestate*, give way to greater certainties. From that moment on, we have definite knowledge of a double magistracy, linked to the patrician–plebeian conflict and the plebeian demand for political parity. Fabius Pictor already pointed out the importance of this milestone in the history of the Roman constitution. After 367/6, and for over a century, there were to be three superior magistrates *cum imperio*, with closely linked powers. It is possible that the so-called *lex Licinia Sextia de consule plebeio* enabled the election of a plebeian consul and that later on (*lex Genucia*, in 342 BC), this election was made compulsory. The formation of a new patrician-plebeian ruling class, the *nobilitas*, was to be, from then on, closely linked to the exercise of the consulship, *maximus honos*, as the clearest expression of their prominence and control over the political system.

From the second half of the fourth century BC, once the direct patrician–plebeian confrontation was over and as the integration of the plebeian elite within the new Roman aristocracy was in progress, the central feature of the history of Rome is external expansion. The conquest of Italy first and later on of the Mediterranean is characteristic of this middle period of the republic, from the final few decades of the fourth century to the final decades of the second century BC. This almost uninterrupted series of military campaigns, increasingly more distant and longer-lasting, was to be the background for the leading role of consuls as generals of the Roman legions.

Military needs and the growing complexity of the Roman state brought about a series of important changes in the Roman "constitution" that affected the consulship. Its status as a supreme regular magistracy never wavered but some aspects, in particular regarding the *imperium*, did undergo some changes. In this period, almost all the consuls went to the provinces that had been allotted to them, either in Italy or beyond, after remaining in Rome just a few weeks, or at most, two or three months at the beginning of the consular year. As opposed to the more common practice in the late republic, very few remained in Rome year-round. These *consules-imperatores* were famous for their military deeds and became the essential core of the *res gestae* of the *nobilitas*, the backbone of Rome's historical narrative.

As previously mentioned, the new military demands resulted in a series of innovations in the exercise of the magistracy of the consulship. Probably the most remarkable instance was the *prorogatio imperii*, which entitled an ex-magistrate to hold *imperium* and, consequently, to continue in command of the army beyond the annual term of his office. The first instance is attributed to Q. Publilius Philo, cos. 327 and promagistrate *pro consule* the following year, within the context of the Samnite Wars. From the second half of the third century BC onwards, that *prorogatio* is increasingly more frequent. As indicated in this volume, during the Hannibalic War we know of about eight extensions of the *imperium* each year, simply by means of a decree of the senate.

The dates of the elections and of the assumption of office are also modified. In the more ancient period, the election was held upon the consuls' return from military campaigns or before their term of office expired; with Sulla, the elections were called in the summer. The date the consuls took office was March 15 between the years 217 and 154 BC. From the year 153 onwards, the appointed date was January 1, thus allowing a longer period to deal with political duties in Rome and with military reparations and requirements outside Rome.

The gradual creation of new magistracies also had an historical effect on the powers of the consulship. The censorship was created in the fifth century BC, by means of the Licinian-Sextian laws, the praetorship in the fourth century BC, and the second praetorship in the middle of the third century BC. It was probably at this point that the *cursus honorum* was established as a more or less strict sequence in the exercise of the various magistracies. The *cursus* became definitively established with the *lex Villia annalis* of 180 BC. The consulship was the highest executive rank, the supreme military command and therefore the major source of prestige. The increase in the number of praetors did nothing but reinforce the prominent status of the consulship. This pre-eminence is evident in the *res publica* through their leading role in politics and in diplomatic, military and religious matters.

Polybius, in his reconstruction of the Roman "constitution," says that the consuls, in their powers and leading roles, are similar to kings. However, Polybius himself at the same time acknowledges the absolutely central role of the senate; the balance of power between magistrates, in particular the consuls and the senate, is the key element in the stability and achievements of the Roman system in the third and second centuries BC. The break of that cohesion was a key factor in the unleashing and development of the late-republican crisis.

In the late republic, there were again changes in the sphere of power of the consuls and in their political role. We must look at, on the one hand, the appearance of the so-called extraordinary commands, and on the other hand, what Millar described as the "politicization" of the consulship.

Through the commands of proconsuls and propraetors, the *imperium* had become fragmented and separated from the exercise of the annual magistracies. At this moment, with the *imperium maius* granted to Pompey in the years 67 and 66, a new modification was introduced and along with it a precedent of immeasurable consequence was set. Socio-political and military-specific needs caused the introduction of constitutional innovations that affected the traditional hierarchy and distribution of power. A potential source of conflict between the various holders of *imperium* emerged, which contributed to the destabilization of the traditional Roman "constitution." The leading role of the popular assemblies in the granting of these extraordinary commands did nothing but exacerbate the problem.

In an increasingly conflict-ridden context from the last third of the second century onwards, another change took place regarding the direct political leadership of the consuls in the *Urbs*. Whereas in the second century the *consulares* had been particularly active in Rome's regular political life, in the first century the consuls themselves took on a central political role.

After Sulla, the consuls gradually left the city more frequently at the end of the year, after remaining in Rome for about ten months, or even remained in the *Urbs* their whole year of office. This practice was attributed by modern historiography, endorsed by the authority of Mommsen's interpretation, to a supposed *lex Cornelia de provinciis ordinandis*. A series of scholars, in particular Giovannini, have demonstrated the non-existence of that law. Once we accept the absence of any laws in this regard, we must, however, question what the reason was for this change in the patterns of behavior of the consuls. The consuls' growing participation in the politics of Rome can be observed in the *contiones*, and in the presentation of *rogationes*, in the debates of the senate. It could be asserted that this new and active leading role brought them closer to the tribunes of the plebs in their political leadership in the city. This change fits well within the overall contents of the Sullan reform, in that it limited the leadership of tribunes in the political arena. Nevertheless, whatever the cause, this was another substantial change in the traditional distribution of political roles in the "constitution" of the Roman republic.

Apart from the two main events mentioned above, that is, the extraordinary commands and the politicization, the particularly troubled circumstances of the last republican century also affected the exercise of the consulship at different stages. For example, despite the prohibition of iteration, probably set forth in the second century, we find the successive consulships of Marius, Cinna or Carbo, although all of them were certainly exceptional cases. Besides this, different measures were proposed for a better regulation of the exercise of the higher magistracies, such as a possible Sullan law on the minimum age for the magistracies. The management of the empire became one of Rome's main problems and we know of several laws regarding the government of the provinces that directly affected consuls and consulars; for instance, the Gracchan law on the allocation of provinces before the consuls take office, the *lex Iulia repetundarum* of 59 or the *lex Pompeia de provinciis* of 52, which set forth a lapse of five years between the magistracies and the government of a province.

Leaving aside all the changes, modifications or new regulations of their spheres of control and competences, the consulship always remained the ultimate ambition for any *nobilis*. Becoming a consul determined one's place in the hierarchy of the ruling class. Its joint nature was the permanent expression of the aristocratic concern to prevent an individual from amassing excessive power through higher magistracies. Pompey's consulship *sine collega* in 52, for a short period of time, is an extraordinary occurrence and the fact that it was an exception, and not a regular practice, confirms a soundly established rule.

The relevance of the consulship, from the point of view of the senatorial aristocracy, was also confirmed at various critical instances that reoccur in the last century of the republic. In those circumstances, when the senate resorts to the so-called *senatus consultum ultimum*, the consuls are mentioned in the first place in this senatorial appeal, to stress their prominence and responsibility in the restoration of order and normality in the *res publica*.

With the advent of the principate a profound change in the nature of the consular *imperium* took place. The magistracy remained as the culmination of the *cursus* but there was a substantial alteration in its nature, parallel to the gradual concentration of actual power in the hands of Octavian-Augustus. Then the "demilitarization of the consulship" occurred. However, the political system was then different from the republic, and the *res publica* was shadowed by the *princeps*.

Up until that moment and throughout five centuries, at least as it is recorded by the Roman sources, the consuls had been not only the supreme magistrates but the very personification of the republic itself.

The main purpose of this book is to begin to fill the gap in scholarship on the consulship by studying the Roman republic. The approach is by no means limited to "constitutional" questions. Instead, the predominant role of the consulship in, as well as its impact on, the political culture of the republic is investigated. As the highest magistracy of the *res publica*, the consulate was the focal point of Roman political life. Both the ruling class and the citizens of the lower social stratum fixed their gazes on the *maximus honos* – to be sure, from different perspectives and with differing expectations. While the former aspired to the consulate as the defining office of their social rank, the latter perceived it as the embodiment of the Roman state. Thus the consulship was not merely a political office, but rather prefigured all aspects of public life. The multifaceted character of the consulate invites a full-fledged investigation, and the book explores these various facets with contributions touching on the political, social, cultural, religious and also economic implications of holding the highest office. It covers the entire period of the Roman republic, from its beginnings in the fifth century until the reign of Augustus.

The fifteen chapters are arranged both in a diachronic order and clustered around broader themes. The first section deals with the much-debated question of the origin of consulship as the supreme magistracy in the Roman republic. The problem, as is well known, rests on chronologically establishing the beginning of consulship, whether it existed since the end of the monarchy or was the result of a process in which other magistracies in charge of the *civitas* could have existed previously. Ultimately, the main difficulty lies in whether or not to accept the ancient sources, which unanimously refer to the existence of the consulship from the year 509, and in particular the reliability of the list of consuls known through the *Fasti Capitolini*.

Three chapters refer to these problems and make up the first part of the book. Christopher Smith ("The magistrates of the early Roman republic") leans toward granting credibility to the list of ancient magistrates. While he is skeptical about the fact that some ancient historians may have simply invented magistrates for the initial part of the republic, in his opinion, historians and antiquarians worked simultaneously using the same lists of magistrates and the same evidence, trying to produce a coherent discourse regarding a process of creation of the republican institutions that Romans knew were the result of the work of various generations and not of one single legislator. Gianpaolo Urso ("The origin of the consulship in Cassius Dio's *Roman History*") defends the credibility of Cassius Dio as a source for the early republic. The Greek author was following a source that acknowledges an original unequal collegiality among the chief Roman magistrates. His account indicates that the consulship resulted from an evolutionary process in the first half of the fifth century, as multiple praetors possessing unequal power were finally replaced by two consuls enjoying equal power during the decemvirate of 451–450. Finally, Alexander Bergk ("The development of the praetorship in the third century BC") rejects the idea that the praetor had a minor position in relation to the consuls in the fourth and earlier third century BC. On the contrary, the three chief magistracies created in the year 367, two consuls and one praetor, were colleagues. When wars took place increasingly far away from Rome, the permanent presence of at least one magistrate with *imperium* in Rome was required. The praetor then lost his military function and the city of Rome was his usual field of action. Only then did the hierarchy of consuls and praetors emerge, and the *cursus honorum* was born.

From the time of their creation, the consuls were the chief magistrates of the Roman state and always acted in close collaboration with the senate. The consulship's *imperium* determined the consuls' powers and gave the office numerous functions, in both the military and the civil domains. In his analysis of the Roman republican institutions, Polybius describes consuls, above all, as the supreme commanders of the Roman army, and as such he claims they had absolute power on the battlefield.[16] Between the fourth and second centuries, the consuls were indeed mainly *imperatores*, and as such they left Rome year after year to go to their *provinciae*, where they commanded the legions they had previously recruited. In that period the consuls were the main persons in charge of Roman expansion, first in Italy, and later throughout the Mediterranean. Yet, as Polybius also says, the consuls carried out a great number of civil tasks, mainly, but not only, during their stay in Rome at the beginning of the consular year after taking

---

[16] Polyb. 6.12.

office, a stay that could last a few weeks or months depending on the changing circumstances of internal and external politics. The consuls were the head of Roman diplomacy and as such they had to receive foreign embassies in the *Urbs* and introduce them, if necessary, in the senate; they had legislative initiative, although the number of consular laws passed during the middle republic was relatively small and unquestionably smaller than that of tribunician laws; on occasion, the consuls were commissioned by the senate to conduct extraordinary investigations; the consuls were responsible for and promoted many public works, such as a large number of the temples erected in Rome between the fourth and second centuries, and many roads built in Italy during that period; the consuls were responsible for appointing a dictator; and finally, they presided over the elections, which in the pre-Sullan period were held at the end of the consular year.

The second part of the book deals with the powers consuls had and the functions they carried out. Hans Beck ("Consular power and the Roman constitution: the case of *imperium* reconsidered") deals with the term *imperium*, the keystone of Roman constitutional hierarchies. He starts from the observation that *imperium* gave a spatial distinction to the spheres where it was exercised. This process was related to various changes: the development of the magistracies, in both numbers and competences; the growing use of extraordinary commands, which also contributed to the inherent tensions in the relations between *imperium* holders; and finally, as the republic expanded from city-state to Mediterranean empire, the changing perceptions of the space itself in which *imperium* was exercised. In examining these changes from a diachronic perspective, Beck's chapter reveals Roman perceptions of space, political power and the nature of *imperium*.

Francisco Pina Polo and Francisco Marco Simón offer a complementary perspective concerning the religious duties and tasks performed by the consuls. As Pina Polo emphasizes ("Consuls as *curatores pacis deorum*"), religious tasks were integral to the consuls' power, as well as the Roman *civitas*: such tasks included religious ceremonies conducted in the civic realm, namely public vows, the expiation of prodigies, and the appointment of the date for the celebration of the *Feriae Latinae*, as well as presidency over the festival at the Mons Albanus, presidency over the public games, and especially responsibility for the proper performance of a *ver sacrum*. Such tasks were obviously of a religious nature, but they should also be considered as political functions, because consuls, as supreme magistrates, acted on behalf of the state with the ultimate purpose of preserving the *res publica*, thus adopting the role of *curatores* of the *pax deorum*. Marco Simón

("The *Feriae Latinae* as religious legitimation of the consuls' *imperium*") stresses the dual importance of the *Feriae Latinae*, a ceremony that was held for over a thousand years. This ritual, celebrated on the Mons Albanus, a space of augural nature, expressed the differentiated identity of Rome and its supremacy within the Latin league; additionally, compulsory attendance at the annual ceremonies, where the consul acted as high priest of the city, worked to legitimize consular authority.

This part ends with the chapter by Nathan Rosenstein "War, wealth and consuls," which analyzes the close relation between the role of the consuls as *imperatores* and the supply of funds to the *aerarium* due to the wars of expansion directed by them. Rosenstein starts from the difference between *praeda* and *manubiae* and goes on to propose a series of questions on the extent to which the spoils generated by consular victories were a boost to Rome's public economy, fueled her military expansion by funding future wars and could be a source of personal wealth for consuls.

As supreme magistrates of the *civitas* the consuls were at the core of the political scene. They were the top executors of the orders of the senate and the leaders of Rome's government. At the same time, as supreme commanders of the army, both Rome's survival and her capacity to expand rested in their hands. Thus, the consuls were the primary, visible authority in Roman society during their term of office, but their reputation went beyond the magistracy itself and automatically turned the ex-consuls, the *consulares*, into individuals whose *auctoritas* granted them influence in the senate and in society as a whole. The consuls represented Rome before the rest of the world and they had to be role models for their fellow citizens. On the other hand, the Italian aristocracies created a vast network of friendships and personal relations between cities. Roman aristocracy was obviously aware of this behavior. It was important for them to promote these relations with Italian notables as much as possible, as it was convenient for the latter to have connections with the families who had decision-making capacity in Rome. In this context, the reputation of the consuls and the consulares no doubt served to attract the attention of many Italian aristocrats willing to maintain ties with them and their families. These questions are dealt with in the third section of contributions.

The paper by Karl-Joachim Hölkeskamp ("The Roman republic as theatre of power: the consuls as leading actors") presents the consuls as leaders in the republican "theatre of power," and explores the symbolic role of the consulship within Roman society. Consuls personified institutionalized power through their protagonistic participation in civic rituals and public spectacles, for instance in the different political and social processions that took place in Rome throughout the year, namely the inauguration ritual at the beginning of the consular year and the procession on the day of consuls' departure to their provinces.

Good and bad *exempla* were decisive in the creation of the collective memory of the Roman citizens and its historiographical reflection. Matthew B. Roller ("The consul(ar) as *exemplum*: Fabius *Cunctator*'s paradoxical glory") emphasizes how consuls were the figures most likely to be presented as *exempla* in the Roman tradition, since they were the chief magistrates, supreme military commanders, and, consequently, the most visible members of the Roman aristocracy, at least during their year in office. Roller specifically analyzes the tradition around Q. Fabius *Cunctator*, elevated to a model to later generations of Romans for preserving Rome with his delaying tactics during the Hannibalic War.

Martin Jehne's paper ("The rise of the consular as a social type in the third and second centuries BC") deals with the political role played by the *consulares*. The rank of *consulares* at the top of the senate seems to have been established only in the late third or early second century. From that point on, the military career of a Roman senator usually culminated in the consulship, with rare exceptions such as Marius, so *consulares* were free to care for the *res publica* in the *Urbs* as senators. Thus, senatorial activity compensated for the loss of army commands, while the individual influence of *consulares* depended on the senate's influence as an institution and on the regular opportunity to decide on the significant problems facing the community. The new position of the *consulares* in Roman politics explains how some sort of common and stable foreign policy was achieved, despite the frequent changing of generals each seeking spectacular military action.

Current scholarship revisits the relationship between Rome and the allied communities in Italy, questioning the Mommsenian teleology that it was Italy's destiny to become a part of the greater Rome. In his paper, Michael P. Fronda ("*Privata hospitia, beneficia publica*? Consul(ar)s, local elite and Roman rule in Italy") modifies the old view (cf., for instance, Münzer) that wealthy families throughout Italy came to Rome and bound themselves to great patrician clans through marriage and other alliances, in order to gain political and social influence in the *Urbs*. Fronda approaches Roman–Italian aristocratic relations from a different perspective, focusing not on how Italian elites sought to integrate themselves into the Roman political system, but rather on how their local status was confirmed by private and public associations with Roman aristocrats.

During the first century BC, the main change in the consulship as a magistracy was the fact that the consuls remained in Rome much longer than in the previous centuries. Those who left for their provinces while being consuls always did so, except in extraordinary cases, very late in the year. Many others, such as Pompey in the year 70, Cicero in 63 and Caesar in 59, remained in the city throughout their term of office as consuls. Some of them even expressly renounced their consular provinces, as was the case of Cicero. This substantially changed the operations of the consulship. Whereas up until then the consuls had dedicated most of their time to military duties, their presence in Rome now made them much more actively involved in everyday politics. The consuls constantly took part in debates in the senate or before the people, and they had to openly state their opinion on topical questions. They were, in short, politicians. The last part of the book deals with the participation of the consuls in the political confrontations of the late republican period, emphasizing the possible support for the two ideological trends defined by Cicero as that of the *optimates* and that of the *populares*.

Starting from Sulla's appeal to his army in 88 and Cinna's similar action in 87, Robert Morstein-Marx ("Consular appeals to the army in 88 and 87: the locus of legitimacy in late-republican Rome") promotes the thesis that political legitimacy in late-republican Rome had no single institutional source. In the cases of the consuls Sulla in 88 and Cinna in 87 the character and role of the consulship were a central issue in the civil conflicts of those years. Both episodes show the reverence of Roman citizens, and perhaps especially soldiers, for the consul and the consulship, and help us to understand the meaning of the consulship in republican political culture.

In Cicero's matrix of politics, politicians of the late Roman republic could be characterized as either *populares* or *optimates*, and the significance of these terms in relation to the consulship is examined in the papers of Antonio Duplá ("*Consules populares*") and Valentina Arena ("The consulship of 78 BC. Catulus versus Lepidus: an *optimates* versus *populares* affair"). The first collects and analyzes the sources on *consules populares* in order to understand the different historical circumstances and source traditions concerning the definition of the word *popularis* as applied to consuls all through the Roman republic. In particular Duplá focuses on some late-republican consuls. The political and socio-economic measures undertaken by the so-called *consules populares* (agrarian laws, laws concerning new colonies, or the full restoration of the tribunician *potestas*) also offer new insights into the failure of the social and political consensus of the last republican century in Rome. The existence of consuls who can be related more or less directly to the *populares* would have widened the divisions within the ruling class.

Arena argues that there was not just one idea of *optimates* in the republic, but rather multiple concepts were in circulation. Some of these concepts were based on conscious re-elaborations on the part of individual thinkers (such as Cicero, in the *pro Sestio*), some on the absorption of Greek political and ethical philosophy, and some on the simple use of the term in daily political discourse. In particular Arena states that Stoicism provided the basis for many of the conventional ethical assumptions held by the Roman *optimates*, but was also actively present in the real political conflicts of the time. Arena focuses her attention on the example of the political career of Catulus, especially his consulship in the year 78, when he confronted his colleague Lepidus.

The establishment of the principate under Augustus meant an end to the republic and the foundation of a real monarchy with a republican façade, under the banner of restoration of the *res publica*. Certain republican institutions remained in force, adjusting themselves to the new political regime. What happened to the consulship? Frédéric Hurlet ("Consulship and consuls under Augustus") tries to find the answer in the closing chapter of the book. First, there was continuity with the republic, as no argument proves decisively that the consulate underwent one or more institutional modifications under Augustus. One should not, however, ignore the fact that the Augustan principate accelerated certain developments that had emerged toward the end of the republic. In particular, the consuls were *de facto* deprived of the possibility to exercise an *imperium militiae*. As a matter of fact, the consulship suffered an undeniable devaluation under Augustus, but the competition for the consulship certainly persisted and consular rank remained the key criterion for a high-ranking position in the hierarchy of Rome's strictly stratified society.

PART I

The creation of the consulship

CHAPTER I

The magistrates of the early Roman republic

Christopher Smith

Two separate but interrelated issues arise whenever one addresses the topic of the early Roman magistrates: first, the reliability of the lists of early magistrates, and second, the mechanisms through which the accounts of the magistracies' origins may have been produced. For some scholars, the likelihood of widespread corruption or falsification is so great that the lists can be ignored as evidence for anything other than the fact of their spurious creation, but even this position requires a view of the mechanisms for such creation, and the rationale. Although a slightly less sceptical position has begun to win a degree of support, the case still needs to be made and tested.[1]

In addressing this issue, I also try to make better sense of the contribution of what we sometimes call antiquarian thought to Roman historiography and knowledge of the past. Whilst the problem of the *Fasti* is often addressed from a historical perspective, the impact of the list, or, as is far more probable, lists, on the way that Roman history was constructed demands our attention, especially as it contributes to an understanding of the obscure methods of the now-lost antiquarian writers. In this account, I will return repeatedly to the problem of the *praetor maximus* as an example of the difficulty of rewriting annalistic history through the insights of antiquarian research. After establishing some of the basic approaches to the *Fasti*, and examining in some detail the charges, ancient and modern, against various named and unnamed individuals held to have falsified the *Fasti*, I will offer some thoughts on how antiquarians and annalists may have approached the complex issues surrounding the origins of Roman magistracies.

We should start by reflecting briefly on the current and recent shape of the debate about the *Fasti*. The two fundamental pieces of evidence are the

---

[1] Cornell 1995 remains the most persuasive and careful account, but see also Forsythe 2005; older but helpful analyses also in Ridley 1980, 1983.

narrative accounts in Livy and Dionysius of Halicarnassus, primarily, and the list of consuls which was originally displayed in the Roman Forum, and is currently preserved in the Capitoline Museum.[2] The congruence between the two has been commented on, though since the *Fasti* are to some extent supplemented by the historians, that may be a slightly false impression, but to a large degree they represent a fairly fixed list of two consuls a year, with some problematic years, and a period of time in which military tribunes with consular power were elected. Most of the problems arise from the years before the decemvirate; a number of scholars have discredited the evidence of consuls at least for that period.[3] Another argument is based on Roman claims that the sack of Rome by the Gauls destroyed the relevant documentation.[4] A third argument claims that the lists are hopelessly interpolated with spurious office-holders, and is based on Roman testimony about the insertion of false ancestors.[5] A fourth argument questions the very existence of consuls before the Licinian-Sextian legislation, and argues that the kings were replaced by a single officer, a *praetor maximus*.[6]

These possibilities inevitably raise questions about the mechanism of transmission of the names of the chief magistrates, and for that we turn to a source which is now missing, but which has sometimes been thought absolutely crucial to the historical tradition: the so-called *Annales Maximi* of the *pontifices*. We know that an annual record was compiled and kept at the house of the *pontifex maximus*, until the time of P. Mucius Scaevola, *pontifex maximus* from 130 to *c*. 115 BC, and that at some stage a version was published in eighty books. A published and readable form may not have emerged, however, until the Augustan period, in other words contemporary with the *Fasti* themselves, and the absence of reference to the *Annales Maximi* in Cicero, for instance, suggests that the work was either so well known as to be already fully incorporated into the work of historians or antiquarians, or else of limited actual use. The pontifical record is better evidence of the possibility of archival material than of the complete reliability of the consular lists.[7]

---

[2] Rich 1998; Feeney 2007.
[3] Werner 1963; Gjerstad 1953–73 makes this later date fundamental to a now discredited typology of the archaeological evidence.
[4] Livy 6.1.2; Claudius Quadrigarius began his history, it appears, in 390 BC; cf. Plut. *Num*. 1.1 on a Clodius who argued that the Gallic sack had destroyed all the relevant records.
[5] Cic. *Brut*. 62; Livy 8.40.4–5, both discussed below; cf. for example Münzer 1891; Wiseman 1979; and Farney 2007, for an account of the political use of different ethnic origins, many of which depend on spurious ancient genealogical thinking.
[6] Beloch 1926; Hanell 1946; discussed at more length below.
[7] For a full and challenging account of the *Annales Maximi*, see Frier 1999; cf. Bucher 1987.

I begin with the Capitoline *Fasti*, because we may reasonably reckon that the construction of these kinds of lists, and the calendrical *Fasti* with which magisterial *Fasti* are sometimes co-located,[8] are the product jointly of historical and antiquarian research. The Capitoline *Fasti* are of Augustan date and therefore at the end of a historical tradition. That list of magistrates, fortuitously surviving in epigraphic form, cannot be taken as anything other than the product of an historical development of complexity and ingenuity.[9]

We cannot be sure that in its form it reflected a traditional layout or was innovative. Take an analogous problem, the map of Agrippa. This is another poorly known product of the early imperial period; Pliny the Elder refers to *commentarii* which were used in the construction of some great geographical monument at the Porticus Vipsaniae, but we do not know if it was a map, or a vast inscription with distances from one place to another. Yet it is likely to have brought known information into a new setting. This raises the question of whether, like the reorganization of Italy into regions, the refinement of the calendar, changes to the nature of the census, and the substantial innovations involved in Augustan transmarine colonial activity are all parts of the development of new mechanisms of organizing knowledge in ways which hint at the new political and imperial realities. This relationship between empire and mechanisms of knowledge has been the subject of much recent attention, and the Capitoline *Fasti* and potentially the publication of the pontifical annals might be added to the list.[10]

Certainly, we now know from Feeney's insightful study of the *Fasti* as a text that the Augustan presentation had profoundly changed the character of the list of magistrates. Feeney notes the insertion of an AUC date to the left of the names. This calculation runs alongside, and subverts, the different kind of time reckoning of the *Fasti*, if we are right to see a "Capitoline" time, as Purcell describes it, which begins with the consulship of Brutus and the foundation of the republic.[11] It also challenges the previously authoritative principle of eponymity. Similarly, the presentation of the censorship, which we find already in republican *Fasti*, is changed by Augustus to mark the number of *lustra*, and thus we can calculate with ease that the censorship began before the republic, and explicitly with Servius

---

[8] Gildenhard 2003; Feeney 2007, 170.   [9] Taylor 1946, 1950, 1951a; Degrassi 1947.
[10] Plin. *HN* 3.17; Brodersen 1995, 268–87, whose argument that pictorial maps did not exist has been challenged; on empire and knowledge, see Wallace-Hadrill 1997; Carey 2003; Murphy 2004.
[11] Purcell 2003.

Tullius.¹² How old was this conception? We cannot tell – it is a short step from the anachronistic beliefs about the Servian reforms to the developed account of the five different classes, which had at least some history before Augustus.¹³ The point, however, raises problems similar to those regarding the *Annales Maximi*. At some point, unless we disbelieve the evidence of the *Origo Gentis Romanae*, records of the regal period were inserted into what otherwise might have been expected also to reflect Capitoline – that is, republican – time.¹⁴ It is too long an argument even to recount the options here, but something similar happens, possibly at the same time, in the conscious linking of the regal past to the republic. If that time is Augustan time then there are obvious motives and inferences.

The Augustan *Fasti*, then, represent an important stage in the manipulation of the evidence for the sequence of consuls at least, and the *Fasti Triumphales* which were exhibited nearby may represent an even more extreme version of the repackaging of information. At the same time, we know that there were pre-Augustan lists of consuls, such as the partially surviving example of the *Fasti Antiates*. So another question is whether there is anything intrinsically implausible about the contents of the list, and unfortunately for the believer, the presence of *cognomina* looks highly problematic. Clearly, it is highly likely that there has been some degree of subsequent filling out of the early *cognomina*.¹⁵ The next question is to what degree one is prepared to assume that this kind of revision occurred.

One major reason for scepticism is the known gaps in the evidence. The so-called dictator years, for instance, point to quite different approaches. On four occasions the Capitoline *Fasti* alone give a year to a dictator and *magister equitum*, and it is generally believed that this, together with an extended period of five years of anarchy associated with the attempts to pass the Licinian-Sextian legislation, is the result of problems in the numbers of colleges of magistrates.¹⁶ Clearly sources have inserted or excluded

---

¹² Cf. Livy 1.44.1–2, derived from Fabius Pictor; Dion. Hal. 1.74.5 for the lists held by censorial families; Brunt 1971, 26–7 for scepticism.
¹³ Thomsen 1980; the Servian classes are already found in Polybius.
¹⁴ On the *Origo Gentis Romanae* itself, see Cameron 2004; Smith 2006a; on the regal sections of the *Annales Maximi*, see Frier 1999.
¹⁵ Smith 2006b, 17–20. The earliest epigraphically attested *cognomen* is from the early third century BC, and consequently the likelihood of *cognomina* existing and being preserved from around 500 BC onwards is slight. It is possible that quite a lot of the insertion of families into the *Fasti* is associated precisely with efforts to identify branches of wider familial units.
¹⁶ Drummond 1978, for dictator years.

years, and the reasons may have been based on all sorts of extraneous considerations, including spurious synchronisms.[17]

Gaps are somewhat different from wholesale readjustments, and Fabio Mora has of course made a very substantial attack on the whole structure. Mora has identified a whole series of supposed problems, such as the suspicious occurrence of individuals from the same family at generational intervals and the distribution of office across *gentes*. However, the problems seem to me to be less difficult than the proffered solution, which is an inexplicably complicated readjustment and invention of both the names and the order of the names of the magistrates to justify genealogical claims in the later republic.[18] For me the most challengingly radical position remains that of Hanell.[19] Hanell argued that a list of the eponymous magistrates began in 509 with the dedication of the Capitoline temple. This officer was the *praetor maximus*. After the collapse of the decemvirate, which was itself an aspect of the fall of the kingship, the army was led by colleges of two, three or more men, known either as *consules* or as *tribuni militum*, with the addition of the words *consulari potestate*. In 366, two consuls, usually one patrician and one plebeian, became the normal pattern of office, largely as a result of the Struggle of the Orders.

The importance of Hanell's reading, and others like it, is that they offer a completely different way out of the problems of the *Fasti*, by suggesting that the difficulty lies less with the names and more with the offices. Once one has determined that the sequence of offices may be inaccurately represented, then it is possible to use the admittedly confusing array of titles and offices to reinvent the sequence and nature of early Roman history, justifying this approach by arguing that what the Romans wrote was a combination of ignorance and self-justification.[20] This approach is not, however, without its own problems methodologically – historians crucially assume that from the wreckage of our knowledge of the ancient world, and even more the archaic world, precisely the correct and sufficient pieces of information survive which, once wrested from their context, may be rejoined to produce a coherent and accurate picture of reality.

Hanell's reading, for instance, requires the invention of one magistrate every year until the middle of the fourth century. Beloch had earlier

---

[17] Gallia 2007, for a sophisticated argument about the development of synchronisms between Roman and Sicilian and Greek Southern Italian chronologies. Cf. Feeney 2007 for the concept more generally.
[18] Mora 1999. [19] Hanell 1946; Taylor 1951b.
[20] For an example of this tendency, see Mitchell 1990.

suggested that the chief magistrate was the dictator and the second name was his *magister equitum*, thus preserving the inequality of the two chief magistrates, but avoiding the need for the invention of one of the names; but this is a suggestion usually dismissed on the grounds that, in every source we have, the dictator is presented as an emergency magistrate.[21] In any case, Hanell's failure to explain where the other name came from remains to my mind highly damaging to the case. It may be pertinent that Dio, to whom we will return, clearly sees 445 as the date at which the shift in the nomenclature of office took place.[22] The arguments for the change coming in the fourth century are no stronger than those for a change in the fifth; and predicating the changes on the reforms of the army is an instance of explaining the obscure through the more obscure.

Another attempt to remedy some of the difficulties was made by Bunse, who also argued that the *praetor maximus* was the chief magistrate after the fall of the kings.[23] Furthermore, the *praetor* was *maximus* because there were two other *praetores*, and each led one of the three archaic tribes.[24] This denies the Servian tribal reorganization, and rests heavily on the factual existence of the early tribes, which do seem to have had some role in structuring early Roman society; whether they survived the territorial expansion of Rome seems more problematic, and there may well have been subsequent elaboration of their centrality.[25] These praetors were supplemented in the colleges of military tribunes (so there is no change but simply a growth in the numbers; note again Dio's placing of the shift of nomenclature quite early); and the changes in 366 were the entry of the plebeians into the magistracy; the gradual differentiation into two consuls with military power, and one praetor with urban and legal jurisdiction; and the development of a concept of collegiality, which became a more important concept than annual office (hence the permission to prorogue *imperium*). Interestingly, Corey Brennan's more conservative interpretation, in which two consuls (called praetors) led Rome, with a period where consular tribunes distributed unequally the insignia of royal power until the praetorship was recreated in 367, is based on an argument that subordination of one *imperium* to another was explicitly not permitted at Rome. It is subordination, not collegiality, which is the change

---

[21] Beloch 1926, 235–6. [22] Cass. Dio 5.19.
[23] Bunse 1998, 44–61. [24] Cf. de Sanctis 1956–67, I, 404–6.
[25] Oakley 1997–2005; on Livy 10.6.7; the tribes are very important in the reconstructions in Carandini 1997; for the tribes more generally see now Rieger 2007.

in 367, and the consular tribunate is an awkward first step towards that achievement.[26]

Thus for Corey Brennan, two consuls and an initially patrician praetor form a rationalized consular tribunate, and one very important element in his reconstruction is that the praetor is not fundamentally a legal officer, and that Livy's indication that the office was about law (6.42.11) is anachronistic. The argument can thus be said to hinge on whether Rome replaced a king with a single dominant annual magistrate and lesser colleagues, and developed the concept of collegiality, or replaced the king with two annual magistrates and developed a concept of subordination.[27] Lintott interestingly argues that the Romans were not particularly strong at either, and tried to resolve potential conflict through the concept of the *provincia*.[28]

The final argument against the reliability of the early *Fasti* to which I will refer is that the early consuls include families subsequently plebeian; the implication of the later legislation is that they must all be patrician at the outset. This argument, as has often been pointed out, though by a rather small number of people, rests to a large extent on assumptions about a simple duality in Roman society which is probably the most obvious product of the influence of the Struggle of the Orders on Roman historiography.[29] What seems least plausible about the argument that the early *Fasti* are a fake because they contain names which should not be there is that it implies that the faker was an idiot, or a committee of idiots. To create a forgery which is transparently silly would be self-defeating. So one might argue that the prohibition on plebeians holding the consulship was a later invention, or came into force later in the fifth century – in which case the objection to the names would fall – or that those who invented the names did so with absolutely no compunction about producing nonsense.

The problem was in fact sufficiently clear in antiquity. Dionysius of Halicarnassus knew there was a problem with the first consul being a Junius, because subsequently they were a plebeian family, but his answer was to shrug it off.[30] The name had a reliability for him which the legal

---

[26] Brennan 2000, 1, 49–54. The literature on the consular tribunate is substantial; see Ridley 1986, with previous bibliography.
[27] Practical differentiation on Corey Brennan's model comes from differentiation of the *auspicia* under which some offices (*magister equitum*, consular tribunes) campaigned. On *auspicia* generally see Linderski 1986.
[28] Lintott 1999b, 99–102; cf. Stewart 1998, 97–111.
[29] Important first steps in Momigliano 1967; the argument is fully developed by Cornell 1995, 242–71.
[30] Dion. Hal. 5.18.

problem could not shake. Moreover, Cicero's important statement in the *Brutus* is of precisely the same character:[31]

> Nevertheless, the historical record of our deeds has been rendered more false by these laudations. For many things are written in them which never happened; false triumphs, an exaggerated number of consulships, even invented family relationships and transitions to the plebs, when men of lowly birth are insinuated into another family of the same name, just as if I claimed to be descended from Manlius Tullius, who was a patrician consul alongside Servius Sulpicius ten years after the expulsion of the kings.

What Cicero clearly implies is that plebeians who happened to have the same name as patrician predecessors invented mechanisms by which to establish relationships which were false. Cicero believes clearly that Manlius Tullius was a consul; what he does not believe is that it would be legitimate for him to associate himself with that Tullius. As Lily Ross Taylor argued, Cicero should here be taken as evidence of a belief in the reliability of the names in the *Fasti* rather than the opposite.[32]

To summarize, the arguments against the reliability of the *Fasti* are most successful when they point to the implausibility of total accuracy, and expose the difficulties of transmission.[33] It might be argued that for a variety of reasons there is more uncertainty about the period before the decemvirate, but we need to be cautious that the arguments here are not especially strong; certainly if the issue about plebeian names is removed then a great deal of what opposes belief in the earliest *Fasti* is impressionistic, or derived from the palpable sense of a restart after the decemvirate. That there were gaps seems indisputable. We tend always to assume that annual magistracies (newly begun each year for one year) were standard. More radically, we might wonder if magistrates were appointed for tasks, some of which may have been more irregular; certainly that is the case for dictatorships, and it was perhaps more widespread. We then also must consider the question of the nature of the mechanisms which produce the lists which do survive, and which, despite the transparent problems of transmission from the early period, show only slight variations between the existing sources, a point Oakley makes most clearly.[34] If one believes this

---

[31] Cic. *Brut.* 62: *quamquam his laudationibus historia rerum nostrarum est facta mendosior. multa enim scripta sunt in eis quae facta non sunt: falsi triumphi, plures consulatus, genera etiam falsa et ad plebem transitiones, cum homines humiliores in alienum eiusdem nominis infunderentur genus; ut si ego me a M'. Tullio esse dicerem, qui patricius cum Ser. Sulpicio consul anno x post exactos reges fuit.*
[32] Taylor 1951b.
[33] For other accounts of this thorny area see, for instance, Ridley 1980; Cornell 1995, 215–41.
[34] Oakley 1997–2005, 1, 38–108.

to be a spurious unanimity, the usual culprit, again derived from Cicero's account in the *Brutus* already cited, and a key passage in Livy, coupled with claims about the Roman funeral and its tradition of *elogia*, is family history.[35]

Yet, as Badian once pointed out, family histories may have provided genuine identifications, and we can perhaps push this a little further.[36] Let us suppose, as Badian did, that there was at least a version of the list of chief magistrates, and for the sake of argument let us assume that, before the consular tribunate, there were two magistrates a year. What mechanisms can we imagine permitted the construction of a list which included false names? Why, how and when did the pontifical college collate the presumably conflicting accounts into a single authoritative list, if that is what underlay the pontifical records which eventually produced the *Annales Maximi*? Any answer must make sense in the context of the degrees of competition and co-operation between elites within the republic. It is also worth noting that whilst we find it inconceivable that one should date events by something as apparently awkward as the eponymous magistrates, as Feeney has well reminded us, the Roman way of thinking was different.[37] Events are associated with the magistrates under whose *auspicia* and *imperium* they took place, and indeed with the magistrates entering office at different points in time we cannot even map the magistrates onto a year. Yet although we cannot think about the succession of consuls as a primarily chronological tool, as Feeney rightly reminds us, nonetheless it was what drove the narrative of Roman history from Fabius Pictor on, since annalistic history in the Roman sense is not conceivable without a consular list. With the exception of Cato the Elder, who chose a different way of presenting history, Roman historians and Greeks who followed them used the succession of consuls as their organizing principle. As the fundamental grid against which the development of the Roman state was to be measured, the idea that this list was open to unrestrained falsification, certainly after the commencement of formal historiography, is itself problematic.

One area where clarity is essential is the issue of whether we assume that individual historians ruthlessly promoted the interests of their own families, or whether the assumption that the characteristic of one individual was shared by all in his family was exploited to expand Roman historiography. Wiseman, for instance, argued that positive or negative pictures of the Claudii were utilised quite late in the republic to give a dramatic twist to

---

[35] Blösel 2003, for a good recent account; on funerals, see Flower 1996.
[36] Badian 1990a.   [37] Feeney 2007, 138–66; cf. Purcell 2003 on varieties of time.

the early years, whereas other scholars have tended to assume that every appearance of a Valerius or a Licinius in early Roman history was the product of the historian of that name glorifying his ancestry.[38] The two are not exclusive. The development of the centrality of a few *gentes* could precede the systematic working up of the dramatic picture of an individual *gens*. Is this how ancient historiography worked?

As we consider this, we must bear in mind the possibility that the degree of falsification was greater for officers other than the consuls. Take the tribunes of the plebs, for instance; the original number of tribunes was disputed in antiquity. It may be that at some point in time the plebeians started to maintain a more secure list of their officers, and it may be that this happened quite early, but of course there are issues over the survival of these lists, even if one excludes the Gallic sack as a major destructive episode. Certainly it is striking that Licinii are named amongst the wretchedly thin references to the early tribunes.[39] Yet it is equally interesting that Macer, of all Roman historians, went out of his way to legitimate his ideas by reference to his discovery of the Linen Books.[40]

Licinius Macer is perhaps the best-known example of a historian credited with falsifying the ancient record to support his own family's reputation, and so we should consider the case against him with some care, as indicative of the mechanism of falsification in ancient historiography.[41] Livy explicitly states that Macer sought to cast glory on his own family (7.9.7), and he is repeatedly cited as presenting a position which no one else agreed with and which modern scholars have found unpersuasive. Yet he is unlikely to have invented the Linen Books, though he may have been misled by them, and we can identify three key mistakes.

First, he attributed suffect consuls rather than consular tribunes to 444, claiming to have seen them also in a treaty with Ardea (emphasis added).

Titus Quinctius Barbatus as interrex appointed Lucius Papirius Mugillanus and Lucius Sempronius Atratinus consuls. Under these consuls the treaty with Ardea was renewed; and this is evidence that those consuls – who are recorded neither in old annals nor in books of magistrates – **held office in this year.** (11) I believe that, because there were military tribunes in office at the beginning of the year, the names of these suffect consuls were passed over, as though the military tribunes

---

[38] Ogilvie 1965 demonstrates this tendency at length. Cf. Wiseman 1979.
[39] Two in 493 (Livy 2.33, Dion. Hal. 6.89); 481 (Livy 2.43–4, but note Dion. Hal. 9.1.3 gives Sicilius)
[40] Linen Books: Walt 1997, 75–85; Macer's praise of his family: Walt 1997, 184–91; Macer's politics: Wiseman 2002.
[41] I use the translations by Oakley from the forthcoming new edition of the fragmentary Roman historians; emboldened text marks the fragment; in all instances they are reports of what Macer wrote, not verbatim quotations.

had been in office for the whole year. Licinius Macer is my authority that **the names of these consuls were found both in the treaty with Ardea and in the linen books in the temple of Moneta**. Both abroad (despite the neighbouring peoples having paraded so much to fear) and at home there was quiet. (1) This year, whether it had only tribunes or also suffect consuls in place of tribunes, was followed by a year in which **Marcus Geganius Macerinus (for the second time) and Titus Quinctius Capitolinus (for the fifth time) were** without doubt **consuls**.[42]

But the individuals are also the censors for the following year, and indeed the first such magistrates. Macer's choice makes a difference to who was the first plebeian consular tribune, though Macer may simply not have thought that Atilius, the more usual candidate, was a plebeian.

Second, Macer claimed that the consuls of 435 were also in post in 434, though Aelius Tubero also cites the Linen Books for a different position.

In Licinius Macer I find that **the same consuls were reappointed for the following year, Julius for the third time, Verginius for the second time**. Valerius Antias and Quintus Tubero state that Marcus Manlius and Quintus Sulpicius were consuls for that year. However, even though their statements differ so much, both Tubero and Macer claim **the authority of the linen books**, but neither hides that **old writers had recorded that there were military tribunes in this year**. Licinius does not hesitate to follow **the linen books**; Tubero is rather less certain of the truth.[43]

The peculiarity of both authors using the same source for an entirely different solution, coupled with the problem of iteration, makes this a very difficult passage. Ogilvie states bluntly that 'Licinius is wrong' but it looks rather as if the records were something of a mess at this juncture, specifically on the matter of whether there were consuls or consular tribunes, so that we may have more names than the ancients knew what to do with.

---

[42] Macer F13 (Peter) Livy 4.7.10–8.1: *T. Quinctius Barbatus interrex consules creat L. Papirium Mugillanum L. Sempronium Atratinum. his consulibus cum Ardeatibus foedus renovatum est; idque monumenti est consules eos illo anno fuisse, qui neque in annalibus priscis neque in libris magistratuum inveniuntur. (11) credo, quod tribuni militum initio anni fuerunt, eo perinde ac si totum annum in imperio fuerint, suffectis iis consulibus praetermissa <nomina>. nomina consulum horum Licinius Macer auctor est* **et in foedere Ardeatino et in linteis libris ad Monetae inventa**. *et foris cum tot terrores a finitimis ostentati essent, et domi otium fuit. (1) hunc annum, seu tribunos modo seu tribunis suffectos consules quoque habuit,* **sequitur annus** *haud dubiis* **consulibus, M. Geganio Macerino iterum T. Quinctio Capitolino quintum.**

[43] F14 Peter = Livy 4.23.1–3: **eosdem consules insequenti anno refectos, Iulium tertium, Verginium iterum,** *apud Macrum Licinium invenio: Valerius Antias et Q. Tubero M. Manlium et Q. Sulpicium consules in eum annum edunt. (2) ceterum in tam discrepanti editione et Tubero et Macer* **libros linteos auctores** *profitentur; neuter* **tribunos militum eo anno fuisse traditum a scriptoribus antiquis** *dissimulat. (3) Licinio* **libros** *haud dubie sequi* **linteos** *placet: Tubero incertius veri est.*

Finally, Macer is confused about Cornelius Cossus, though it is at least reasonable to say that he was not the only one, then or now. This is not unconnected with the previously cited passage; Licinius Macer has a different sequence of magistrates in what we call the late 430s and early 420s from the standard account, and as is well known, everything about Cossus is confused by Augustus' intervention regarding whether or not he won the *spolia opima*.

All may make up their own minds as to what kind of mistake there is in this matter, namely that such old annals and the books of magistrates which were made of linen, and which Licinius Macer adduces again and again as his authority, have **Aulus Cornelius Cossus consul ten years later together with Titus Quinctius Poenus.**[44]

That there is a mistake seems quite possible, but that it was malicious or self-serving is hard to demonstrate.

What about the crucial passage at Livy 7.9.3–6? I quote the passage:

It is generally agreed that in this year **Titus Quinctius Poenus was dictator and Servius Cornelius Maluginensis master of the horse.** (4) Macer Licinius writes that **Quinctius was appointed to hold the elections and nominated by the consul Licinius, because it was necessary to stand in the way of the base desires of his colleague, who was in a hurry to place the conduct of the elections before the war in order to continue as consul.** (5) The credit sought by Licinius for his own family makes him an authority of lesser weight than others; and since I find no reference to this affair in older histories, I am more inclined to think that the dictator was appointed because of the Gallic War. (6) However, it is certain that in this year the Gauls pitched camp at the third milestone on the Via Salaria across the bridge over the Anio.[45]

A Licinius was consul, either Calvus or Stolo, and perhaps the former since Macer called his own son Calvus. A dictatorship was held. All other sources make it a dictatorship for the purpose of the war against the Gauls. Macer alone has it as the first dictatorship for holding elections, and claims that

---

[44] F15 Peter = Livy 4.20.5–11: *quis in ea re sit error quod tam veteres annales quodque magistratuum libri,* **quos linteos in aede repositos Monetae** *Macer Licinius* **citat identidem auctores, decimo post demum anno cum T. Quinctio Poeno A. Cornelium Cossum consulem habeant,** *existimatio communis omnibus est.* For this very controversial episode see Rich 1999 and Flower 2000.

[45] F16 Peter = Livy 7.9.3–6: **dictatorem T. Quinctium Poenum eo anno fuisse** *satis constat et magistrum equitum Ser. Cornelium Maluginensem.* (4) *Macer Licinius* **comitiorum habendorum causa et ab Licinio consule dictum** *scribit,* **quia collega comitia bello praeferre festinante ut continuaret consulatum, obviam eundem pravae cupiditati fuerit.** (5) *quaesita ea propriae familiae laus leviorem auctorem Licinium facit: cum mentionem eius rei in vetustioribus annalibus nullam inveniam, magis ut belli Gallici causa dictatorem creatum arbitrer inclinat animus.* (6) *eo certe anno Galli ad tertium lapidem Salaria via trans pontem Anienis castra habuere.*

his ancestor did so to prevent Sulpicius Peticus presiding over his own re-election. Sulpicius Peticus is an interesting figure.[46] First consul in 364 alongside a Licinius again, in 355, 353 and 351 he held the consulship in all-patrician colleges. The one in 351 was the product of his own interregnum, for there were dictators for holding elections in 351, 350 and 349, and the dictators of 353 and 352 tried to hold elections. The unrest relates to the failure to appoint a plebeian consul regularly, and a substantial degree of indebtedness which led to the unusual appointment of *quinqueviri mensarii* in 352 BC.[47] Macer may well have pushed a particular line through the agitation of the 350s, and seen Sulpicius Peticus as a particular example of the patrician neglect of the Licinian-Sextian legislation. Livy, whose attitude towards popular unrest was distinctly chilly, may have found in Macer an excessive disregard for the value of noble leaders to the community, and criticized him for it. Perhaps, however, we should ask what it is that Macer invents, if he is so obviously inventing here. All we can genuinely allege, it seems to me, is the intervention of a consular Licinius against the machinations of a patrician, who undoubtedly dominated office to the detriment of the plebeians now entitled to serve, and the dating of the formal office of dictator for holding elections by a decade, when in fact dictators held or tried to hold elections in this period.

This is important because this is the passage on which the whole argument for Licinius' false insertion of his family into the history of Rome is based, and all told, it seems to me that Licinius is inaccurate, and perhaps tendentious, but not evidently for the sole purpose of falsifying or actively inventing the *Fasti*. Moreover, it is precisely because Livy disagrees that we have this account, and implies that an alternative version existed, not that single interventions could transform the sequence of magistrates. One is left with precious little on which to base the wholesale distortion of the *Fasti* by the author most directly accused of doing so.

The argument I have made thus far has tended to place more emphasis on the fundamental reliability of the list of chief magistrates than others do, and to take with a degree of scepticism the claim that one historian in particular deliberately invented offices. I have not denied Cicero's annoyance about the false claims of various families to a long ancestry, or Livy's famous worry about the same process, but I have wanted to delimit the scope of the criticism. I will turn now to the distribution of office.

---

[46] Sulpicius Peticus: Mil. Tr. c. p. 380; cos. 361, 355, 353, 351; dictator 358; contextualized in Hölkeskamp 1987, 44–90.
[47] Storchi Marino 1993.

I recently argued that the fact that no two individuals of the same *gens* ever held office contemporaneously is a significant indicator of something important about the construction of Roman society and about the *gens* itself.[48] This is even more the case when one considers the relatively small number of *gentes* represented in the *Fasti*. There is a clear difference between the consulship and the consular tribunate, where there are instances of the same *gens* holding more than one office. Here, as elsewhere, the key determinant appears to be the distribution of the highest office.[49]

There is, in other words, no instance where one *gens* was able to dominate in any year, and we know that laws were passed later in the republic to insist on distribution of office in the priesthood on exactly these grounds.[50] I find it extremely difficult to believe that this distribution was either fortuitous or planned after the event. There was no bar in the early republic on iteration, and no bar even on iteration within a *gens*. My own understanding of this phenomenon depends on the interaction I perceive between the ambitions of individuals and their family groupings and the society in which they existed. Rome achieved a system whereby office was annually distributed by the assemblies between the competing familial groups. If we turn to the magistracies as a whole, we see something similar.

Establishing beyond doubt that there was a principle of collegiality in Roman magistracy is impossible, because it depends on inference from the lists of magistracies, and on arguments about the nature of Roman magistracy, which, as we have seen, are based on highly fragmentary evidence.[51] However, we must at least acknowledge that it is difficult to find any early Roman magistracy which is not collegiate, in the simple sense of being comprised of more than one individual. Even the dictatorship, the least collegiate of all Roman offices, is both inextricable from the office of the *magister equitum*, and circumscribed by various restrictions. The praetorship after 367 would stand out here, although not if regarded as inextricably linked with the consulship.

Bunse's sustained attack on collegiality as a principle brings us back to the issue of the *praetor maximus*. If this was Rome's chief magistracy, and the consuls were merely added to it in 366, replacing the previous praetors who were connected with the so-called Romulean tribes, perhaps here,

---

[48] Smith 2006b.
[49] Stewart 1998 offers a range of additional comments on distribution of office and also distribution of province.
[50] North 1990b.
[51] Though it is thought that both censors had to agree the list of excluded senators; Lintott 1999b, 100.

as with – again perhaps – the dicator or dictator amongst the Latins, we might have evidence for a single principal magistracy succeeding the *rex*. However, we must again look hard at the sources. First, Livy's account is based on an old law, in old letters:

> There is an old law, written in the earliest letters and grammar, that whoever is *praetor maximus* on the Ides of September should hammer in a nail; the law was fixed on the right side of the temple of Jupiter Optimus Maximus, on the side where the temple of Minerva is. That nail was said to have marked the number of years, because letters were rare at that time, and the law was said to have been on Minerva's temple because number was Minerva's invention. At Volsinii too nails are fixed in the temple of the Etruscan deity Nortia as indications of the number of years, as the author Cincius declares, who is a careful authority for such monuments. M. Horatius the consul dedicated the law and the temple of Jupiter Optimus Maximus in the year after the kings were expelled; afterwards the ritual of fixing the nail was transferred from the consuls to the dictators because their *imperium* was greater. Then when the custom had lapsed, the matter was seen to be important enough in itself for a dictator to be appointed for the purpose.[52]

We owe to scattered references in Festus another reference to the term *praetor maximus* (though here in the context of later multiple praetors): that consuls were previously called *praetores* (from the evidence of praetorian doors in camps) and that in joint commands with the Latins, the Roman commander was called a *praetor*.[53] The whole business might not be more reliable than a derivation from Varro's etymological equation of *praetor* with *praeire*, to go before in law and war.[54] Can we argue legitimately from this that there was a single leading Roman magistrate in the aftermath of the kings? Livy's muddled passage, with its odd digression on Volsinii, and peculiar struggle to get from the consul Horatius through the *praetor maximus* to the occasional dictator, is not definitive; apart from the usual issues of distance from original events, difficult sources, and Livy's erratic interest in and grasp of constitutional history, it makes little sense in its own terms. I continue to support the view that in the crucial passage of Livy, the reference to the *praetor maximus* only refers to the chief magistrate

---

[52] Livy 7.3.5–8: *lex vetusta est, priscis litteris verbisque scripta, ut qui praetor maximus sit idibus Septembribus clavum pangat; fixa fuit dextro lateri aedis Iovis optimi maximi, ex qua parte Minervae templum est. eum clavum, quia rarae per ea tempora litterae erant, notam numeri annorum fuisse ferunt eoque Minervae templo dicatam legem quia numerus Minervae inventum sit. Volsiniis quoque clavos indices numeri annorum fixos in templo Nortiae, Etruscae deae, comparere diligens talium monumentorum auctor Cincius adfirmat. M. Horatius consul et lege<m et> templum Iovis optimi maximi dedicavit anno post reges exactos; a consulibus postea ad dictatores, quia maius imperium erat, sollemne clavi figendi translatum est. intermisso deinde more digna per se visa res propter quam dictator crearetur.*
[53] Fest. 152L; 249L; 276L; see Oakley 1997–2005, II, 77–80.
[54] Varro, *Ling.* 5.80 *praetor dictus qui praeiret iure et exercitu.*

amongst several.⁵⁵ The process by which this reference might have been produced is what will occupy the remainder of my paper.

There are a variety of important accounts of the development of the Roman magistracies. Livy is usually our most significant narrative source, but there are contributions from antiquarian sources too. Urso has recently reminded us of the interest which Cassius Dio's sadly mutilated text has for us, and the case he makes for an antiquarian book on magistrates underpinning that account is persuasive.⁵⁶ Each magistracy has its own origin. One of the intriguing aspects of the account of the early republic is that it is not produced as a complete system. This remains the sort of account given of Romulus, where for instance Dionysius of Halicarnassus was persuaded to give a remarkably coherent picture of a once-for-all foundation, with senate, magistracies in the *curiae*, and assembly.⁵⁷ But the Roman story of their republican foundation is rather more accretive and gradual, and whilst it cannot be used to prove authenticity, it is a striking account. At Athens we tend to hear of sequential revolutions, at Sparta of the absence of change even when we can discern it happening. Is there another ancient city-state which has taken such pride in a sequential development of a particular form of government over such a long period?

The annalistic account begins of course with the consulship, but more importantly, it stresses degrees of continuity rather than rupture. The republic is re-founded with a greater emphasis on *libertas*; there is no essential break with the Romulean constitution, but a rebalancing away from the tyranny of the last king. As we have seen, the annalistic account pushes the identity of the foundation of the consulship, the dedication of the temple of Jupiter Optimus Maximus, and the beginning of a certain form of time-telling – *post reges exactos*. From here on, the account becomes very messy. The two developments which affect the consulship, the move towards a military tribunate with consular power, and then the opening of the consulship to plebeians, were both controversial, and the first in particular caused Livy difficulties as he struggled to choose between a political and a military explanation.

Quaestors for 509 are attested by Plutarch, but there are different kinds of quaestors, and Tacitus believed them to be a regal office, revitalized after the decemvirate fell.⁵⁸ The first dictator was a matter of controversy, and the office seems to have also been called *magister populi*, thus mirroring the *magister equitum* who was the indispensable accompaniment, but it is

---

⁵⁵ Brennan 2000, I, 22–3.   ⁵⁶ Urso 2005, and this volume.   ⁵⁷ Dion. Hal. 2.12–14.
⁵⁸ Latte 1960; Tac. *Ann.* 11.22 (regal origin) and Zonar. 7.13.

also important to note that the title is used for a number of other, more irregular offices.[59] The tribunes of the plebs emerge from the first secession of the plebs; born of conflict, they are the key office in what has often been called the state within the state.[60] The aediles are supposed by Dionysius of Halicarnassus to have been put in place in 492, and notably plebeian, and continue to be so until the patricians beg a position in the 360s. Yet the differentiation between patrician and plebeian offices breaks down almost immediately. Already in antiquity there was dispute about the sacrosanctity of the plebeian aediles, and Cato the Elder had an opinion on the matter.[61]

The aftermath of the decemvirate requires the almost mutual restarting of the consulship and the tribunate. The military tribunes begin in 444 (slowly) and the censors begin in 443.[62] Then there is a long gap to the awkward 360s, when the praetorship – or if one prefers, the consulship – is invented, and the consular tribunate disappears. About the same time, patrician curule aediles are introduced. It is intriguing that the first example of prorogation takes place in 326 (if we dismiss as we surely should some early fifth-century fictions), and there are subsequent clusters in times of military crisis.[63] A number of other magistracies grew up over time – these would include the moneyers and the *tresviri capitales* amongst others.

This story is well known and fascinating, but the point I would like to draw out is about the historiography of offices. For the annalists, as far as we can tell, the account develops through the back-and-forth arguments of the Struggle of the Orders; and there is a balance which is achieved in the totality of the account and indeed in individual parts of the account. This is already to some extent part of the complex picture which Polybius gives us at a more theoretical level, but it is equally rooted in the question of how to tell the story of the development of the Roman constitution, and the very fact that the story is so developmental tells us that the Romans conceived of the republic as a collective work of generations, precisely the

---

[59] Dion. Hal. 5.70–7; Livy 2.18; Cic. *Rep* 1.63 (*magister populi* according to augural books), 2.56; *Leg.* 3.9; Fest. 216L. Livy 2.18 for T. Larcius in 501 BC; cf. dictators for elections (351, Livy 7.22.10–11); nail-fixing (363, Livy 7.3.4); quelling sedition (368, Livy 6.39.1 with F. Cap.); festival (344, Livy 7.28); Latin festival (257, F. Cap.).
[60] First college in 493 (Asc. 77 C; Livy 2.33.3; 58.1; Dion. Hal. 6.45–89; Plut. *Cor.* 7.1; Cass. Dio fr 17; Zonar. 7.15). They recommence after the decemvirate in 449 (Livy 3.54.11–13). Niccolini 1932; I have also benefited from reading the doctoral theses of Sampson 2005 and Kondratieff 2003.
[61] Dion. Hal. 6.90.2–3; Gell. 17.21.10; Fest. 258–9L; Zonar. 7.15.10 (elected with tribunes); Livy 3.55.7–9, 29.20.11; Fest. 422L (Cato the Elder); Dion. Hal. 7.26.3, 35.30–4; Plut. *Cor.* 18.3–4 against sacrosanctity, derived from a reading of the Valerio-Horatian laws. Curule aediles first in 367/6: Livy 6.42.14, 7.1; cf. Polyb. 10.4.1–2 on continuing tradition of patrician aediles.
[62] Livy 4.8.2–7, Dion. Hal. 11.63.1–3 (443 BC); Suolahti 1963. [63] Develin 1975a.

message of Livy's Alexander digression.[64] I have written elsewhere of the rather interesting fact that the Romans allowed the co-existence of different assemblies.[65] Rome displays its constitutional history pretty clearly; and there are repeated references to this aggregation of experience as opposed to the Greek model of a single founder.[66]

For an example of how the characterization of the various offices is inseparable from the Struggle of the Orders, let us look at the consular tribunate. Ogilvie argued that Livy's notice in 5.12.9 suggested that Licinius Calvus was the first plebeian consular tribune (and this takes us back to Licinius' removal of Atilius from the office in 444, but does not explain the case of Antonius Merenda in 422). This, Ogilvie suggested, showed that Licinius Macer was the origin of the political interpretation of the consular tribunate.[67] Even if Macer was central to this, he is unlikely to have been the first to argue a political point from the fact that the plebeian consular tribunes came as close as they did to the *auspicia*. It is wholly plausible that this was a point made forcibly in the fourth century BC. We cannot reconstruct the rhetoric of the earlier periods of the republic, but there must have been some form of argument which explained the change from the consular tribunate to the shared consulship. This argument is constructed in our sources entirely around the narrative of the plebeians' struggle for access to office.

What, though, of the antiquarian approach? Can we answer questions about which came first and how they differed? Urso argues that Dio's account of the origins of the magistracies as transmitted through Zonaras has a number of features: a gradual change from kingship, with the consulship only clearly starting in 449. There are hints that the previous magistracy was unequal and that the concentration on the first magistrates after the decemvirate is mirrored in the way that Polybius set up Book Six. There is also a discussion of the sacrosanctity issue in relation to the tribunes.[68]

Urso is surely correct to see the source as an account of magistracies, and there are a few to choose from, none of which survives. As early as Sempronius Tuditanus, towards the last quarter of the second century BC, we find such accounts. Trying to establish what they actually looked like, however, has been difficult, but the new French edition of John Lydus'

---

[64] Morello 2002. [65] Smith 2006b.
[66] On Rome as the accumulation of individual contributions see especially Cic. *Rep.* 2.1–3.1 (deriving from Cato the Elder); cf. Polyb. 6.10.12–14; Livy 9.17–19.
[67] Ogilvie 1965, ad loc. [68] Urso 2005.

Byzantine account of the magistracies reminds us that we may have a rather good example to consider.[69]

This extraordinary work owes a great deal to antiquarianism of the late republic, which John cites frequently, including, interestingly, Cato the Elder.[70] Written in the sixth century AD, it comes from an author who appears to have substantial access to works we have now lost. He cites a tremendous range of authors, and he does have genuinely unusual things to say. What is particularly interesting here is what happens when a source takes some of the same evidence as Livy has, for instance, and reproduces it in a different kind of order and with different intentions. If this work is anything to go by, then antiquarian sources categorized by magistracy, and looked diachronically at development to some extent, whilst also looking for fundamental characteristics by reference to etymologies and similar research methods. The involvement of a substantial amount of chronography is interesting; John Lydus states when the first magistrate was appointed, and then indicates a number of crisis moments when change takes place in the constitution (such as the decemvirate). More ideas and facts are allowed – the most obvious one, which Lydus supports, is costume, but this is not irrelevant because, for instance, the dictator's insignia are directly compared to those of the kings. Thus costume can reveal the essence just as a name can.[71]

The regal period is important too. As with Macrobius, who also derived information from the antiquarian tradition, finding the beginning of an institution is as much of a preoccupation as it was for some historians to 'start at the beginning'. Junius Gracchanus, Trebatius and Fenestella (an antiquarian, a jurist and a historian) all date the introduction of the quaestors to the regal period, and although John Lydus has some awareness of the different kinds of quaestors, it is possible that one consequence of the antiquarian tradition may have been to encourage an argument for the evolution of offices which originally shared no more than a name.[72]

The antiquarians are more or less contemporary with the historians, and the genres bled into each other. Both John Lydus and Livy managed a stray digression on the introduction of drama to Rome;[73] Lydus and Cassius Dio, and to a degree Livy, all wrote about the origins of office. Cato the Elder even gave a speech about the sacrosanctity of aediles.[74] Annalists and

---

[69] Dubuisson and Schamp 2006.
[70] On antiquarianism see now Sehlmeyer 2003; Stevenson 2004; Rawson 1985 remains valuable.
[71] Lydus, *Mag.* 1.37.   [72] Lydus, *Mag.* 1.24.   [73] Lydus, *Mag.* 1.40; Livy 7.2.   [74] Fest. 422L.

antiquarians differed greatly in the way they used material and presented it; whether the conclusions differ is less clear. It seems to me that each was using the other. The Linen Books were the kind of resource any writer could claim; the antiquarians had a range of different resources such as etymology and cross-cultural comparison, but the annalists could incorporate antiquarian research into historical writing, as Livy does throughout Book One.[75]

Yet the chronographical aspect is integral to both. John lengthily recounts when certain offices were first filled; one unusual aspect of Dio's account is the linkage of a specific chronological moment with a specific office. In both instances that chronological moment cannot be dissociated from an individual in office, because, to return to Feeney's point, there was no alternative mechanism.

The antiquarians therefore explicitly drew upon the lists of magistrates as well as the other resources they could use. Historians too relied on a picture of the evolutionary development of the Roman magistracies, within the context of collective assemblies. Much of the presentational aspect of this could be derived from the way that the Romans construed and developed a story about the Struggle of the Orders, but much of it was arrived at by analysis of the sources. One area where analysis of the roots of Roman exceptionalism met the realities of Roman behaviour was in the expectation of the distribution of office, and this relates to the way the Romans saw their polity as a collective achievement over generations – this was itself an intellectual achievement of some magnitude.

In order to give an indicative model for this development, let us return one last time to the complex of arguments about the *praetor maximus*. Livy and Festus drew from the antiquarian Cincius a statement about an old law relating the driving in of a nail at the temple of Jupiter Optimus Maximus by the *praetor maximus*. Festus preserves a clear reference to praetors as generals, and Varro, at least, explained it through etymology. Festus also knows of a discussion of the mechanism for one praetor to be superior to another, which is reminiscent of the complex passage on *imperium maior* and *minor* in Gellius from Messala; this passage also has references to Tuditanus, who as we recall wrote on magistracies.[76]

The antiquarian account of the chief magistracy, as we can see it through Cincius, is the more challenging because of the strange account of the nail, which is subsequently the infrequent responsibility of a formally appointed dictator; but the annalistic account also has an explicit suggestion

---

[75] Liou-Gille 1998 gathers the material. [76] Gell. 13.15.

of a change after the decemvirate, and implies that the praetorship lapsed until 367, unless one follows Bunse in seeing some sort of continuity through the consular tribunate. Yet all accounts give us a multiplicity of magistrates. If one accepts a plural number of chief magistrates from the beginning of the republic, first called praetors, and then consuls, the antiquarians' contribution was to claim to have discovered that Capitoline time was initially marked by the magistrates we call consuls, as well as by the names of the magistrates themselves, and to establish, and perhaps to speculate upon, the etymologies of both praetors and consuls. The consultative functions of the consuls, inherent in their name, point to the two institutions strengthened in the aftermath of the decemvirate, the assemblies and the senate. The antiquarians focused on function; the contribution of the annalists was to turn this research into history.

At least one possible concern emerges, if this has any resemblance to reality: that the antiquarians' concentration on function might have tended to conflate offices with different titles and purposes into a single magistracy. It may have been no more than an assumption that the *praetor maximus* who hammers in the nail is the same kind of praetor who was later called a consul. The differences between Dio's account and the normal version require some form of explanation, but the explanation seems to me as likely to be that an antiquarian retrojected the more complex forms of subordination which subsequently characterized the praetorship as that it was an original fact, which was simply overlooked. In other words, the complex tissue of hints and references in Cincius and Festus, which one can interpret as an explosive proof that the beginnings of the republic looked completely different from the standard narrative account in Livy and Dionysius, may be nothing more than a grouping of assumptions and guesses which mistakenly ironed out the evolution of the office of praetor, and sought by the dubious mechanisms of etymology and comparison to make sense of a single old law. This law referred to a specific chronographical function which seems to have been worryingly intermittent, and does not necessarily imply anything about the absence of the consuls from the early republic.

To conclude, this paper has argued that there are relatively weak grounds for believing that the lists of names of early magistrates were substantially invented, or indeed could have been. The fact that some contemporary historians said that it was terribly difficult to know things about the distant past is not a reason to assume they had made it up, or knew that others had; the expression of the difficulty of knowing the past is a trope with more nuance than that. Moreover, it appears as if both antiquarians and annalists were working from the same lists and the same sorts of evidence. Some of the complexities of the transmitted account may reveal the difficulties and consequences inherent in the methodologies and assumptions of the ancient investigators, and by looking at the one 'book of magistrates' we have, I argue that we can get some sense of the range of material which was brought to bear, and begin to think about the different tendencies of annalists and antiquarians.

In terms of methodology, and in the field of archaic Roman constitutional thought, the capacity of the stray antiquarian fact to trump the generally accepted narrative, and thereby to render the lists of names which we have untrustworthy (as opposed to mildly unreliable), requires a defence which can only stem from a clearer understanding of the nature of Roman antiquarianism. Where we do see antiquarianism at work, for instance in the case of the *praetor maximus*, or in whatever underlies Dio's variant account, we should instead be prepared to see something that may be tremendously sophisticated and yet surprisingly wrong. Yet when we consider the activities of antiquarians and annalists alike, the emphasis some modern scholars place on the determined falsification of the records seems at odds with the expressed desire to unearth, describe and defend the realities of early Rome, a trope itself not without its own subtlety but whose importance must be reinforced against the sceptical line.

CHAPTER 2

The origin of the consulship in Cassius Dio's Roman History

Gianpaolo Urso

For the Roman upper class in the late Republic the institution of the annual dual consulship, in which two colleagues with equal powers formed the chief executive of the state, was synonymous with the republican system of government. Since it ensured the sharing of power, it was a bulwark against domination by an individual and for the elite at least a fundamental guarantee of their collective and personal political liberty. Yet the uniform ancient view that such a dual magistracy was established immediately after the overthrow of the monarchy has often been challenged, usually in the belief that a single chief magistrate (with or without subordinates) was essential for effective government. The arguments adduced to support such a position are for the most part, however, a priori.[1]

This statement is quoted from the second edition of the *Cambridge Ancient History* and seems to be fully correct. Nevertheless there is an "argument" that has not attracted particular attention so far: at least one ancient source denies that "such a dual magistracy was established immediately after the overthrow of the monarchy." This source is Cassius Dio's *Roman History*. Dio's reconstruction of the origin of the consulship is rather different from the traditional one and seems to be, at its core, more ancient as well. Before coming to the point, in order to better appreciate the value of this unconventional tale, it is worth dwelling briefly on the circle of Severan jurists whom Dio knew well, on Dio's attention to the pre-Livian tradition and on his interest in the history of Roman institutions.

PRELIMINARY REMARKS

A distinguishing characteristic of Cassius Dio's *Roman History* is its strong interest in the history of Roman institutions and magistracies, already pointed out in the early twentieth century by Cary ("he excels the other historians of Rome in the attention paid to constitutional and administrative

[1] Drummond 1989b, 187.

matters") and Vrind.² De Sanctis passed similar judgment, though adding a negative comment on Dio's reliability as a whole: "Superiore d'assai per intelligenza pratica delle cose politiche e per cognizione dell'organismo dello Stato romano a Livio e a Dionisio, i suoi tentativi però non approdarono che ad alterare ancora la tradizione già sì alterata che era pervenuta fino a lui."³ Hinard has recently come back to the topic: "On n'a pas assez remarqué que Dion prêtait une attention particulière aux questions institutionnelles et que c'est probablement dans ce domaine qu'il est le plus utile;"⁴ sometimes "c'est Dion qui donne les indications les plus précises, les autres sources ne servant qu'à recouper ces informations."⁵ At the same time the severe opinion that made Cassius Dio "le plus prodigue en renseignements, vulnérable aux critiques"⁶ has given way to more cautious judgments ("if the work is not a masterpiece, its author deserves attention and respect")⁷ and even to real eulogies: "In using his *Roman history*... we tend to slight or pass by the solid contributions he often makes to our knowledge. Greater alertness to his virtues as an historian, to the valuable, sometimes unique interpretations and data he provides is needed to achieve a more balanced perception of Cassius Dio's work;"⁸ "Dion est bien un historien qui n'était pas dépourvu de talent et qu'on aurait tort de négliger parce qu'il avait une immense culture et qu'il a travaillé avec intelligence et une indiscutable compétence, du moins pour la période républicaine."⁹

Dio's interest in Roman public law is not at all surprising: the age of the Severans was not only the peak (and the end) of classical jurisprudence, but it was also the period when jurists were involved in the very government of the empire[10] and two of them, Papinianus and Ulpianus, became praetorian prefects. Ulpian's fragments form about a third of the whole *Digesta*:

---

² Cary 1914, XVI; Vrind 1923, 1: *apparet igitur Dionem et cognitionis iuris publici studiosum fuisse et instituta Romana praesertim aetatis imperatoriae optime cognoscere potuisse*.
³ De Sanctis 1956–67, 1, 46.   ⁴ Hinard 1999, 431.
⁵ Freyburger-Galland, Hinard & Cordier 2002, LI. Cf. also L ("On comprend que, dans ces conditions, Dion s'intéresse particulièrement au fonctionnement des institutions"), LVIII ("Le récit de Dion se montre toujours très précis dès qu'il aborde un point de droit public") and *passim*; Freyburger-Galland & Roddaz 1994, XXX: "C'est précisément à propos de certaines magistratures que Dion s'étend plus longuement qu'il ne conviendrait au récit historique;" Hinard 2005, 264: "C'est sur la question des magistratures que les notations sont les plus nombreuses. Ce qui ne signifie pas qu'elles soient toutes très originales; mais au moins nous permettent-elles de vérifier que l'information de Dion est d'excellente qualité en ce qu'elle confirme ce qu'on peut savoir par ailleurs"; 272–3: "La fréquence des notations institutionnelles ne relève pas d'une curiosité d'antiquaire, mais... ces notations déterminent à la fois le cadre et l'enjeu de la lutte politique qui s'est alors livrée, ce que prouve le fait qu'elles s'accompagnent presque toujours d'indications permettant de comprendre comment les dites institutions ont été tournées ou faussées, et que, par conséquent, elles sont une des clés d'interprétation des derniers livres républicains."
⁶ Béranger 1953, 97.   ⁷ Millar 1964, 72.   ⁸ Reinhold 1986, 213.   ⁹ Hinard 2005, 262.
[10] Crifò 1976, 711, 781; Schiavone 1992, 57–8.

he wrote, among other works, *De officio proconsulis libri* x, *De officio consulis libri* iii, *De officio consularium, De officio quaestoris, De officio praefecti urbi, De officio praefecti vigilum, De officio curatoris rei publicae, De officio praetoris tutelaris*.[11] The tasks of Roman magistrates are a typical topic of Severan jurisprudence: not only in the case of Ulpian, but for Iulius Paulus too.[12] Even Aemilius Macer[13] showed deep interest in public law and in the *officia* of town magistrates, praefects and provincial governors.[14] Ulpianus was not only interested in the normative aspects of the legal system; he was a real historian of Roman law, "tanto nel senso di avere cercato e indicato cause e sviluppi degli istituti e delle dottrine che egli espone nelle proprie opere quanto nell'altro senso, che ci pare di grande rilievo e modernità, di avere usato la storia come argomento."[15] The fragments of his works are rich in quotations (about two thousand) from earlier jurists, his writing "è spesso costruit[o] attraverso lunghe catene di citazioni della giurisprudenza precedente."[16] In a sense the two characters integrate and complete each other: on the one hand we have the historian who pays attention to juridical facts; on the other, the jurist who does not ignore the diachronic perspective.

Both of Greek origin, Dio and Ulpian are the only contemporary authors known to us who refer to Caracalla's universal grant of citizenship[17] and were "the key figures in the absorption of Roman history and law into the culture of the Greek East."[18] They also shared several opinions, perspectives and ideas about the "ideology of Empire."[19] For example, Ulpian's principle *princeps legibus solutus est* (*Dig.* 1.3.31) is evidently recalled, if not quoted, by Dio (53.18.1: "For they have been released from the laws, as the very words in Latin declare; that is, they are free from all compulsion of the laws and are bound by none of the written ordinances");[20] another passage

---

[11] Crifò 1976, 754–5; Millar 2005, 36–7.
[12] Paulus was a member of the *consilium principis* of Septimius Severus and Caracalla, assessor to Papinianus as praetorian praefect, *magister memoriae*. He wrote, among other works, *De officio proconsulis libri* ii, *De officio praefecti urbi liber singularis, De officio praefecti vigilum liber singularis, De officio adsessorum liber singularis, De officio praetoris tutelarii liber singularis* (Maschi 1976, 685–6).
[13] Author of the book *De officio praesidis*.
[14] Bretone 1982, 35 (who quotes also Ulpius Marcellus and Venuleius Saturninus, of the mid-second century AD).
[15] Crifò 1976, 713.
[16] Schiavone 1992, 58. On Ulpian's sources cf. Honoré 2002, 128–44 (first-hand sources), 145–8 (collections of lawyers' opinions), 148–51 (sources cited second-hand), 152–7 (imperial sources).
[17] Millar 2005, 18 – though we must add Marius Maximus if he was, as is probable, the source of SHA *Sev.* 1.2 (Zecchini 1998, 351–2).
[18] Millar 2005, 40. [19] Marotta 2000, 165.
[20] Λέλυνται γὰρ δὴ τῶν νόμων, ὡς αὐτὰ τὰ Λατῖνα ῥήματα λέγει· τοῦτ' ἔστιν ἐλεύθεροι ἀπὸ πάσης ἀναγκαίας νομίσεώς εἰσι καὶ οὐδενὶ τῶν γεγραμμένων ἐνέχονται (Magdelain 1947, 106;

from the same book (53.17.1: "In this way the power of both people and senate passed entirely into the hands of Augustus, and from his time there was, strictly speaking, a monarchy"[21]) seems to be a reference to the other well-known norm *quod principi placuit, legis habet vigorem* (*Dig.* 1.4.1.pr.), and more exactly to Ulpian's explanation.[22] There is some resemblance between "Maecenas'" words "But make all the appointments yourself"[23] (Dio 52.20.3) and Ulpian's statement *princeps . . . ei magistratum dedit* (*Dig.* 42.1.57);[24] and there is a similarity between the tasks of the *praefectus urbi* in "Maecenas' speech" (Dio 52.21.1–2)[25] and those described in Ulpian's *De officio praefecti urbi* (*Dig.* 1.12.1), which could perhaps be identified as Dio's source.[26]

Cassius Dio, to put it simply, worked in an epoch when the recovery and transmission of the most ancient juridical texts was promoted and encouraged, and it would have been possible for him to find alternative traditions on the origins of the consulship. Dio's time, the political circles he worked in, the people he came into contact with and even his juvenile practice of law[27] (Dio 74.12.2) provided the context in which Cassius Dio could search, find and re-employ some republican writings on *ius publicum*.

This research into the ancient (and rare) traditions on the origin of the Roman consulship is consistent with what we know of Dio's methods, which have been studied and clarified in many respects in the last few decades. In particular, Dio's independence from Livy, pointed out by Schwartz in the books dealing with the early republic, emerges also in the middle- and late-republican narrative. Klotz, in his study of Dio's sources

---

Millar 1964, 96; Crifò 1976, 777–9; Noè 1994, 155; Rohr Vio 1998, 10, 15–16). Cf. Cass. Dio 53.28.2. I do not come here to the heart of the exegesis of Ulpian's words, which has been discussed among scholars. Cf. Urso 2005, 178. Here and after I have reproduced the translation by Cary 1914, except where indicated (cf. nn. 44, 46, 47 and 61).

[21] Οὕτω μὲν δὴ τό τε τοῦ δήμου καὶ τὸ τῆς γερουσίας κράτος πᾶν ἐς τὸν Αὔγουστον μετέστη, καὶ ἀπ' αὐτοῦ καὶ ἀκριβὴς μοναρχία κατέστη.

[22] *Utpote . . . populus ei et in eum omne suum imperium et potestatem conferat.* Cf. Bretone 1982, 30.

[23] Αὐτὸς μέντοι σὺ πάντας αὐτοὺς αἱροῦ.

[24] Millar 1964, 112: "His recommendation that the Emperor should appoint all the magistrates himself corresponds with the plain statement of a contemporary jurist, ignoring whatever antiquarian fictions were still mantained." Cf. also Reinhold 1988, 190. Meister 1994, 138 points out the anachronism without citing Ulpian.

[25] Πολίαρχος δὲ δή τις ἔκ τε τῶν προηκόντων καὶ ἐκ τῶν πάντα τὰ καθήκοντα προπεπολιτευμένων ἀποδεικνύσθω, οὐχ ἵνα ἀποδημησάντων που τῶν ὑπάτων ἄρχῃ, ἀλλ' ἵνα τά τε ἄλλα ἀεὶ τῆς πόλεως προστατῇ, καὶ τὰς δίκας τάς τε παρὰ πάντων ὧν εἶπον ἀρχόντων ἐφεσίμους τε καὶ ἀναπομπίμους καὶ τὰς τοῦ θανάτου τοῖς τε ἐν τῇ πόλει, πλὴν ὧν ἂν εἴπω, καὶ τοῖς ἔξω αὐτῆς μέχρι πεντήκοντα καὶ ἑπτακοσίων σταδίων οἰκοῦσι κρίνῃ.

[26] Marotta 2000, 175–6: "Individuare, nell'opera del giurista, la fonte utilizzata, in questo specifico contesto, da Cassio Dione, non è inverosimile." On the anachronisms in Dio's description of the *praefectus urbi*, cf. Mommsen 1887–8, 1, 1065; Bleicken 1962, 449; Reinhold 1988, 191.

[27] Marotta 2000, 86.

for the Second Punic War, had already demonstrated that in the history of Cassius Dio an anti-Scipionic source had converged with a Scipionic one, these being respectively identified with Coelius Antipater and Valerius Antias. Dio used them directly, that is, without the mediation of Livy.[28] Other recent studies have challenged the theory that holds that Dio was a "Livian" for the second–first century BC; Lintott for the late republic,[29] Zecchini for the years of the Gallic War,[30] Berti for the war between Caesar and Pompey,[31] Manuwald for the Second Triumvirate and the age of Augustus;[32] Roddaz too has repeatedly discussed this subject.[33] More recently, returning to the First Punic War, Bleckmann has convincingly demonstrated that Dio used, without Livy's (or even Polybius') mediation, some very ancient material: "eine ältere römische Tradition... die sicher nicht systematisch der polybianischen Darstellung vorgezogen werden kann, gleichwohl aber prinzipiell mit ihr gleichrangig ist;" a tradition "spätestens im zweiten Jahrhundert geformten."[34] In short, it has been widely demonstrated that Cassius Dio cannot be defined as a "Livian" source. There are on the contrary many clues that reveal a sort of "anti-Livian" attitude: Dio "si impegnò a riscrivere la storia di Roma, ricercando e risalendo ad autori preliviani, alla grande annalistica dimenticata del I sec. a.C., alla storiografia che l'opera di Livio aveva oscurato."[35]

In light of all these considerations, it is worth having a closer look at some passages of Dio's *Roman History*, relating to the first decades of the republic.

THE αρχων AND HIS συναρχων

For the events of 509 BC,[36] Cassius Dio's account corresponds on the whole to the tradition, but it includes some particulars that need attention. We do not have the original text, but only the epitome of Zonaras (7.12.1):[37]

---

[28] Klotz 1936, 68–116. Cf. Zecchini 2002, 99–103.   [29] Lintott 1997, 2519–21.
[30] Zecchini 1978, 188–200 (probably Q. Aelius Tubero); Zecchini 1979, 85–7 (two pre-Livian sources, one in favour of Cato, the other against him, perhaps respectively Tubero himself and C. Asinius Pollio). Cf. Sordi 1971, 167–83.
[31] Berti 1988, 7–21.   [32] Manuwald 1979, 168–272.
[33] Roddaz 1983, 67–71; Freyburger-Galland & Roddaz 1991, XII–XXIII.
[34] Bleckmann 2002, 35–56 (50, 55). La Bua 1981, 253 had stated that Dio directly used Cincius Alimentus, in which he found Philinus' version. Other scholars too accepted that Dio ultimately derived from Philinus, but the majority of them supposed the mediation of a late annalist (Klotz 1952, 330; de Sanctis 1956–67, III.1, 229–33; de Sensi Sestito 1974, 30, 38; de Sensi Sestito 1977, 205–6, 212–13; Frézouls 1980, 966).
[35] Zecchini 1979, 86–7. Cf. Zecchini 1978, 199.
[36] The margin between "Varronian" and "real" chronology is unimportant in this case.
[37] Most of the texts I am citing in this paper are taken from Zonaras, but we shall see that Zonaras reproduces accurately (at least on this topic) Dio's terminology. For Zonaras' passages, I have added

ὁ μὲν οὖν Ταρκύνιος πέντε καὶ εἴκοσι τυραννήσας ἐνιαυτοὺς οὕτως ἐξέπεσε τῆς ἀρχῆς, οἱ Ῥωμαῖοι δὲ πρὸς τὸν Βροῦτον ἀπέκλιναν καὶ αὐτὸν εἵλοντο ἄρχοντα. ἵνα δὲ μὴ ἡ μοναρχία βασιλεία δοκῇ, καὶ συνάρχοντα αὐτῷ ἐψηφίσαντο τὸν τῆς Λουκρητίας ἐκείνης ἄνδρα τὸν Κολλατῖνον Ταρκύνιον, ὡς ἀπεχθῶς πρὸς τοὺς τυράννους πιστευόμενον ἔχειν διὰ τὴν βίαν τῆς γυναικός.

[Thus Tarquin was deprived of his power, after ruling twenty-five years; and the Romans turned to Brutus and chose him ruler. In order, however, that the rule of one man might not suggest the kingly power, they elected also, as joint-ruler with him, the husband of Lucretia, Tarquinius Collatinus. He was believed to be hostile to the tyrants because of the outrage done his wife.]

This piece of information is very short and is restricted to the essentials: L. Junius Brutus and L. Tarquinius Collatinus take power (ἀρχή) instead of Tarquinius Superbus, Brutus becomes ἄρχων and Collatinus συνάρχων. The conciseness of the passage would not be a problem, but for the presence in the following chapters of some detailed excursuses describing each new magistracy: that is why the lack of a first excursus on the consuls causes surprise.[38] In a sense this passage is more interesting for its omissions than for its contents and particularly for the absence of the name of the office. Of course we would expect to find ὕπατοι, but we have here neither this word nor any other specific term;[39] in a few lines we have instead the substantive ἀρχή and its compound μοναρχία, the correspondent verb ἄρχειν and its compound συνάρχειν. The terminology is not only repetitive, but also generic.

Zonaras undoubtedly reproduces Dio's exact terminology. Zonaras could have inserted ὕπατοι (the ordinary word he found in Plutarch, his other source) instead of Dio's rather vague expressions, but he is totally unlikely to have found ὕπατοι (or any other specific term) in Dio and replaced it:[40] it seems therefore that the lost original text was particularly ambiguous in its terminology. In my opinion this ambiguity has a definite meaning. First of all we can observe that the terms ἀρχή/ἄρχειν indicate in the same context both the powers of the king (οὕτως ἐξέπεσε τῆς ἀρχῆς) and

---

the numbering of the paragraphs as printed in Boissevain's edition of Cassius Dio (with the obvious exception of n. 66, where Zonaras' passages are taken from Plutarch).

[38] This incongruity could be explained on the one hand by Zonaras' cuts, on the other by the use of two sources for chapters 12–13 of Zonaras' seventh book: Cassius Dio and Plutarch's *Life of Publicola* (on Zonaras' sources, Schmidt 1875, xxiv–xxxix; Ziegler 1972, 726). The use of Plutarch may have induced Zonaras to cut off a good portion of Dio's text, perhaps including a first excursus on the consuls.

[39] Cf. Libourel 1968, 212.

[40] Here I do not agree with Vrind 1923, 50. The topic is not discussed by Freyburger-Galland, 1997 54–5, 154.

those of the new magistrates (αὐτὸν εἵλοντο ἄρχοντα ... συνάρχοντα αὐτῷ ἐψηφίσαντο). The transition from monarchy to republic does not seem particularly traumatic, because the first magistrates are invested with the powers of the king, and these powers are progressively eroded as new magistracies are created. This statement is certainly not a novelty,[41] but the shift seems more gradual in Cassius Dio than in the other sources, if only because he does not even mention the name of this new office.

There is another interesting omission: strictly speaking, we do not find here the plural term ἄρχοντες, because Brutus is called ἄρχων and Collatinus συνάρχων. The passage is undoubtedly too short to allow any deduction: but this same terminology is also used shortly after (Zonar. 7.12.4–5) for P. Valerius Publicola, elected συνάρχων after Collatinus' exile. We would expect συνάρχων Βρούτου, or even just ἄρχων. On the contrary, Dio seems to use συνάρχων absolutely, without specifications.[42] And it is noteworthy that the plural ἄρχοντες does not appear in this passage either:

ἀλλὰ τοῦτο μὲν οὐκ ἐποίησαν, τὴν δ' ἀρχὴν ἠνάγκασαν αὐτὸν ἀπειπεῖν. εἵλοντο δὲ ἀντ' ἐκείνου συνάρχοντα Πόπλιον Οὐαλέριον, ὃς Ποπλικόλας προσωνομάσθη· δηλοῖ δ' ἡ κλῆσις ἐξελληνιζομένη δημοκηδῆ ἢ δημοτικώτατον.

[However, they did not do this,[43] but forced him to resign his office. In his place they elected as colleague[44] Publius Valerius, whose cognomen was Publicola; this appellation, translated, means Friend of the People, or Most Democratic.]

This same terminology is employed in a fragment of Dio (13.2), taken from the *Excerpta Constantiniana de sententiis* and concerning Publicola himself:

ὅτι Οὐαλέριον, τὸν συνάρχοντα [corr. Mai; ms. ἄρχοντα] Βρούτου, καίπερ δημοτικώτατον ἀνδρῶν γενόμενον, ὅμως αὐτοεντίᾳ μικροῦ ὁ ὅμιλος κατεχρήσατο· ἐπιθυμεῖν γὰρ αὐτὸν μοναρχίας ὑπετόπησαν.

---

[41] Cf. e.g. Polyb. 6.11.12; 6.12.9; Cic. *Rep.* 2.32.56; *Leg.* 3.3.8; Dion. Hal. 4.76.1; 4.84.5; 5.1.2; 7.35.5; Livy 2.1.7; 8.32.3; Val. Max. 4.1.1; and Kübler 1901a, 1118; Dyck 2004, 456–7. A sort of continuity between monarchy and republic is suggested by the controversial statement of Livy about Servius Tullius' *commentarii* (1.60.4), which seems to represent the transition "come un evento istituzionalmente semplicissimo" (Giovannini 1993, 75; cf. Bernardi 1952, 17; Heurgon 1969, 261), even without refusing the nucleus of the tradition on the violent fall of the Tarquins (cf. Mazzarino 1945, 170–3).
[42] *Maior consul* or *prior consul* are widely attested in an utterly formal meaning (Cic. *Rep.* 2.31.55; Val. Max. 4.1.1; Plut. *Publ.* 12.4; Gell. 2.15.4–8; Fest. 154L; cf. Lintott 1999b, 100): here Dio could refer to such a distinction, which does not imply a disparity of powers.
[43] Shortly before Dio/Zonaras says that "they all but slew him [*scil.* Collatinus] with their own hands." This detail is not attested to elsewhere (Hose 1994, 404).
[44] Cary translates "Brutus' colleague," but in the original Brutus is not mentioned.

[Valerius, the colleague of Brutus, although he had proved himself the most democratic of men, came near being murdered by the multitude with their own hands; for they suspected him of being eager to become sole sovereign.]

Here we still have the terms ἀρχή, συνάρχειν, μοναρχία and Publicola is called συνάρχων.⁴⁵ The *excerptum* in particular is important, because it confirms that Dio's terminology is correctly reproduced by Zonaras.

The ambiguities of our historian are not finished yet. We find again συνάρχων attributed to Maenenius Agrippa, "consul" of 503 (Zonar. 7.13.9):

τὸν Ποστούμιον ἐκάκωσαν τὸ δεύτερον ὑπατεύοντα· καὶ εἷλον ἂν αὐτὸν πανσυδί, εἰ μὴ Μενήνιος Ἀγρίππας ὁ συνάρχων αὐτῷ ἐπεκούρησε.

[[The Sabines] discomfited Postumius when he filled the consulship for the second time. And they would have captured him with his entire force, had not Menenius Agrippa, his colleague, come to his aid.]⁴⁶

Here Zonaras employs the participle ὑπατεύων,⁴⁷ not the substantive: still we do not find the corresponding name (ὕπατοι or any other specific term), or the plural ἄρχοντες, which seems to be strangely avoided. As far as we can judge from Zonaras and from the extant fragments, ἀρχή and its nominal and verbal derivatives were the only terms used to indicate, in Cassius Dio, the first republican magistrates. If we compare the certainty of the ancient tradition (which regularly mentions *consules* or ὕπατοι) and the uncertainties of many modern studies that outline a much more problematic picture,⁴⁸ the ambiguity of our source on the definition of these magistrates is significant.

---

⁴⁵ In the *excerptum* we find συνάρχοντα Βρούτου, but the genitive Βρούτου could even be a supplement by the anthologist, who often expands the opening sentence to make it intelligible. On similar alterations of Dio's original text, see Boissevain 1901, 767–75; Millar 1964, 1–2 (and cf. Pittia 2006, 116–17, on the *excerpta* from Appian).

⁴⁶ Cary translates: "... Postumius when he was for the second time consul..."

⁴⁷ We find the same verb in Zonar. 7.13.3, regarding the designation of the first quaestors (καὶ τὴν τῶν χρημάτων διοίκησιν ἄλλοις ἀπένειμεν [*scil.* Ποπλικόλας], ἵνα μὴ τούτων ἐγκρατεῖς ὄντες οἱ ὑπατεύοντες μέγα δύνωνται.) Shortly after, the year 502 is indicated (7.13.10) with Σπούριός τε Κάσσιος καὶ Ὀπιτώριος Οὐεργίνιος ὑπατεύοντες, perhaps a transcription of Livy 2.17.1 (*secuti consules Opiter Verginius Sp. Cassius*). It is significant that in this passage Zonaras refers to the members of the three "consular" colleges of 502, 501 and 500, without even using the word ὕπατοι (μετὰ δὲ ταῦτα Σπούριός τε Κάσσιος καὶ Ὀπιτώριος Οὐεργίνιος ὑπατεύοντες τοῖς Σαβίνοις ἐσπείσαντο. Καμέριον δὲ τὸ ἄστυ ἑλόντες τοὺς μὲν πλείους ἀπέκτειναν, τοὺς δὲ λοιποὺς ζωγρήσαντες ἀπέδοντο, καὶ τὴν πόλιν κατέσκαψαν. Ποστούμιος δὲ Κομίνιος καὶ Τίτος Λάρκιος δούλους τινὰς ἐπὶ καταλήψει τοῦ Καπιτωλίου συνωμοσίαν θεμένους συλλαβόντες ἔφθειραν. Σερουίος τε Σουλπίκιος καὶ Μάρκος Τούλλιος ἑτέραν αὖθις συνωμοσίαν δούλων καὶ ἄλλων δή τινων συστάντων αὐτοῖς προκατέλαβον, ἀγγελθεῖσαν αὐτοῖς πρός τινων τῶν τῆς ἐπιβουλῆς μετεχόντων.)

⁴⁸ The ancient tradition about the immediate shift from the monarchic to consular system has often been judged unreliable (for the bibliography cf. Mazzarino 1945, 83–97; Wesemberg 1954, 1583–7; Staveley 1956, 90–101; de Martino 1972, 233–9; Richard 1978, 555–72; Valditara 1989, 318–22): as

FROM στρατηγοί TO ὕπατοι

Our magistrates are finally called by a specific name in a passage (Zonar. 7.14.3) about the rising of the plebs in 494. The term is not ὕπατοι but στρατηγοί, that is, "praetors":

κατὰ τῆς βουλῆς καὶ τῶν στρατηγῶν ἐστασίαζον. Πολέμου δὲ αὖθις ἐπενεχθέντος οἱ μὲν στρατηγοὶ χρεῶν ἀποκοπὰς ἐψηφίζοντο, ἠναντιώθησαν πδ' ἕτεροι.

[[They] made an uprising against both the senate and the praetors. But upon the outbreak of another war the praetors decreed a cancelling of debts, though others opposed this measure.]

It is well known that some modern hypotheses on the origin of consulship are based on a few isolated passages, remains of a more ancient tradition according to which the chief magistrates of the early republic were called "praetors" instead of "consuls."[49] No source explains when the change of terminology took place: Livy (7.3.5) alone inserts the piece of information into a narrative context,[50] even if he neither dwell upon the *praetor maximus* nor adds any comment;[51] on the other hand we deduce from Pliny (*HN* 18.3.12) and Aulus Gellius (*NA* 11.18.8) that "praetors" was the definition of the chief magistrates at the time of the Twelve Tables.[52]

As for the adoption of the title of "consuls", Livy gives a *terminus post quem* in the description of the *leges Valeriae Horatiae* of 449: stating that then the name "consuls" was not yet used (3.55.7–12), our source refutes an opinion of *interpretes iuris* on one of these laws[53] on the inviolability of some magistrates:

fuere qui interpretarentur eadem hac Horatia lege consulibus quoque et praetoribus, quia eisdem auspiciis quibus consules crearentur, cautum esse: iudicem

---

stated by Beloch 1926, 232, "die constitutionelle Entwickelung macht keine Sprünge." According to some scholars, the powers of *rex* were limited to the religious sphere and a *praetor maximus* became chief magistrate, assisted by several praetors *minores* (Hanell 1946, 179–80; Werner 1963, 254; Heurgon 1967, 110) or by only one praetor (Pareti 1952, 361–3); according to others, the place of *rex* was immediately taken by the dictator (*magister populi*, who is sometimes identified with the *praetor maximus*), with the *magister equitum* subordinated to him, then the *par potestas* gradually established itself and dictatorship became an extraordinary magistracy (Ihne 1868, 107–19; Kornemann 1915, 205–6; Beloch 1926, 231–6; Mazzarino 1945, 169–91; Alföldi 1965, 43; Valditara 1989, 307–65); others scholars have supposed a *magister populi* with the same powers of *rex*, replaced after the decemvirate by a *praetor maximus* subject to *provocatio* and by a *praetor minor* subordinate to him (de Martino 1972, 234–5).

[49] Cic. *Leg.* 3.3.8; Livy 7.3.5; Plin. *HN* 18.3.12; Gell. 11.18.8; Fest. 249L.
[50] Cf. Urso 2005, 21.   [51] Poma 1984, 60; Forsythe 2005, 152–3.
[52] Bernardi 1988, 422 *contra*.
[53] According to Mazzarino 1971, 444, here Livy recalls a controversy of contemporary *interpretes iuris*, against earlier jurists.

enim consulem appellari. Quae refellitur interpretatio, quod iis temporibus nondum consulem iudicem sed praetorem appellari mos fuerit. (3.55.10–11)⁵⁴

[There were some who taught that by this same Horatian law the consuls also were protected, and the praetors, inasmuch as they were created under the same auspices as the consuls; for the consul was called "judge." But this interpretation is refuted by the fact that it was not yet the custom in those days for the consul to be called "judge", but "praetor".]

If Livy gives a *terminus post quem*, Dio (and Dio alone) gives an exact date (Zonar. 7.19.1):

οἱ δ' ὕπατοι (τότε γὰρ λέγεται πρῶτον ὑπάτους αὐτοὺς προσαγορευθῆναι, στρατηγοὺς καλουμένους τὸ πρότερον· ἦσαν δὲ Οὐαλλέριος καὶ Ὁράτιος) καὶ τότε καὶ μετέπειτα τῷ πλήθει προσέκειντο καὶ μᾶλλον αὐτοὺς ἢ τοὺς εὐπατρίδας ἐκράτυναν.

[Now the consuls (it is said that this is the first time they were styled consuls, having been previously called praetors; and they were Valerius and Horatius) both then and later favoured the populace and strengthened their cause rather than that of the patricians.]

As one can easily infer from the context, this piece of information refers to 449, the year of the fall of the decemvirs and of the so-called restoration of the consulship. It is noteworthy that Dio is the only ancient source that tells us when the name "consuls" started being used: his statement is particularly interesting, at least for its uniqueness. But there are two other issues: (1) it is striking that this problem, which (as far as we can judge) the ancient tradition pays little attention to, is attributed to the same year by two sources that finally solve it in a quite different way; (2) both Livy and Dio refer to the year 449, even though in opposite ways: according to Dio this was just the year when the terminology changed; according to Livy in 449 the consuls were still called "praetors." This cannot be accidental and needs an explanation.⁵⁵

---

⁵⁴ For this use of *iudex* see Cic. *Leg.* 3.3.8; Varro, *Ling.* 6.9.88 (cf. Dyck 2004, 457–8; Urso 2005 22–3).
⁵⁵ In his wide synopsis of Dio, Livy and Dionysius, Schwartz 1899, 1692–3 strangely omits this passage; the comparison between Livy and Zonaras is in Jones & Last 1928, 438, according to whom Zonaras' passage "suggests that the term *consul* was not to be found in the Twelve Tables" (but shortly afterwards they assert that "the title *consul* is implied in the *consularis potestas* conferred on the Decemvirs in 451 B.C."); Hanell 1946, 162, thinks that Livy and Zonaras reflect the same tradition "in etwas verschiedener Form" (cf. also Bernardi 1952, 36); de Sanctis 1956–67, I, 390–1, quotes Livy and Zonaras to confirm that in 450 the term "praetors" was still employed and does not take the divergence into consideration; Sealey 1959, 528 thinks that Livy "seems to refute Zonaras' statement" (implicitly admitting the derivation of Zonaras' [or rather of Dio's] passage from a pre-Livian source); Heurgon 1969, 271, states that "le changement de nom ne semble être intervenu qu'au lendemain du Décemvirat, en 449" (he quotes Livy, Festus and Zonaras without noticing

The origin of the consulship

We could suppose that Dio has used Livy, totally misunderstanding him and reversing the meaning of his words; but we must rule out this hypothesis, because it is evident that at least on this point Livy's statement would be clear to even the shallowest reader. We could instead suppose an error of Zonaras, but such a hypothesis would remain impossible to demonstrate. Most of all, the structure of the sentence introduced by λέγεται shows that Dio drew his reader's attention to an important fact, which he probably did not get from the same source employed in the context: an error on the part of Zonaras seems to be an unlikely possibility.[56] In my opinion, Dio's information is derived from that same source that Livy (or Livy's more immediate source) rejects but that Dio accepts as reliable.

We obviously cannot identify this source for certain, but Livy gives an indication mentioning *interpretes iuris* and using in the same context the terms *interpretari* and *interpretatio*, whose technical meaning is here evident. As I have tried to demonstrate elsewhere, I think that Dio employed at least one juridical source for his digressions on the magistrates (one book *de magistratibus*, written perhaps between the 50s and the 40s of the first century BC)[57]: it is probably from this source that our historian has derived the information on the original terminology and on its change. But as we shall soon see, it was not a mere matter of terminology.

Dio's mention of the change of terminology is not isolated, but it is part of a consistent reconstruction of early republican history. In this respect we must consider Zonaras' account from 494 to 449. This account, even if very concise, is interesting for its terminology, because Zonaras regularly employs στρατηγοί instead of ὕπατοι, with only three apparent exceptions: Kaesus Fabius, Spurius Furius' colleague, is again called συνάρχων

---

that only Zonaras provides the precise date – so even Richard 1982, 21; Richard 1990, 775); the change of terminology after the decemvirate is maintained also by Ferenczy 1976, 35 (who does not quote the sources); Livy and Zonaras are mentioned on several occasions by Valditara 1989, but always separately (Livy: 311, 336; Zonaras: 324, 326, 335, 344); cf. also Lintott 1999b, 104; Dyck 2004, 455 (who quote Zonaras without expressing their opinions on his reliability). The comparison is correctly formulated by Oakley 1997–2005, II, 78–9 (Zonaras is "independent of L., but also relating to 449"), according to whom nevertheless "it is just conceivable that the view of Zonaras that the change in name occurred in 449 went back to reliable testimony"; Oakley concludes that the decemvirs were immediately followed by the *tribuni militum* and later (from 366) by the consuls. The discussion remains open, not so much because Dio's chronology is in itself unreliable, as because Dio leaves another problem unsolved: if the *praetores* were called *consules* from 449 on, what relationship have they to the praetor elected according to the *leges Liciniae Sextiae*?

[56] As we shall see, Dio's account of the decemvirate provides a picture consistent with the adoption of the name "consuls" in 449.

[57] Urso 2005, 163–93.

(Zonar. 7.17.2);[58] and the term ὕπατος is used twice – but adding, in both passages, the "correct" στρατηγός.

The name ὕπατος first appears in Zonar. 7.17.1. The way the term is introduced is interesting: χρόνῳ δέ ποτε ὑποτοπήσαντές τινες τὸ πραττόμενον, οὐκ εἴων καὶ ἄμφω τοὺς ὑπάτους ἢ στρατηγοὺς ὑπὸ τῶν δυνατῶν ἀποδείκνυσθαι, ἀλλ' ἤθελον καὶ αὐτοὶ τὸν ἕτερον ἐκ τῶν εὐπατριδῶν αἱρεῖσθαι ("But after a time some persons began to suspect what was going on, and would not permit both of the consuls (or praetors) to be appointed by the nobles, but desired to choose one of them themselves from the patricians"). This first occurrence of ὕπατος is immediately followed by the correction ἢ στρατηγούς, and this is very significant: Dio did not confine himself, as the other sources did, to a vague mention of the terminological problem but recalled it in his whole narration. Here he corrects the terminology of his narrative source (or sources), using another source that dwelt on the issue and that Dio judged as more reliable (στρατηγούς has more emphasis than ὑπάτους):[59] this means that Dio was perfectly aware of the problem. It is worth remarking also that the passage about the consuls of 449 shows the same parenthetical structure (cf. above): Dio used a source that was particularly interested in the archaic *praetores*, with which he corrected the statements of his main sources.

There is a second occurrence of ὕπατος, in the description of a battle against the Etruscans (Zonar. 7.17.2): ἔπεσε δὲ καὶ ὁ εἷς τῶν ὑπάτων ὁ Μάλιος. ὁ δὲ ὅμιλος στρατηγὸν τὸ τρίτον τὸν Μάλιον [sic] εἵλετο[60] ("One of the consuls, Manlius, likewise fell; the populace chose Manlius praetor for the third time"). In this case too the *facilior* term (ὕπατος) is immediately followed by the *difficilior* one (στρατηγός).

Apart from these passages, the chief Roman magistrates are called στρατηγοί in two fragments (20.3[61] and 21.3[62]) and in two other

---

[58] Οἱ δὲ τῷ συνάρχοντι αὐτοῦ Φαβίῳ Καίσωνι συνεξελθόντες οὐ μόνον οὐκ ἐρρώσθησαν....

[59] Vrind 1923, 50 supposed that Zonaras had employed "utriusque suis fontis vocabulum," but it is more probably an intervention by Dio himself than a correction by Zonaras (who has employed Plutarch for chapters 12–13, but here is following Dio alone).

[60] The second "Manlius" is actually Kaeso Fabius, consul of 479.

[61] Οὕτω γοῦν ὑφ' ἑκατέρου παρωξύνθησαν ὥστε καὶ τὴν νίκην ἔνορκον τοῖς στρατηγοῖς ὑποσχέσθαι· πρὸς γὰρ τὴν αὐτίκα ὁρμὴν κύριοι καὶ τῆς τύχης εἶναι ἐνόμισαν.

[62] Καὶ Τίτου Μενηνίου τοῦ στρατηγοῦ (ἐπὶ γὰρ τούτου τὸ πάθος ἐγένετο) κατηγορηθέντος ὕστερον ἐν τῷ δήμῳ ὅτι μήτ' ἐκείνοις ἤμυνε καὶ μάχῃ μετὰ τοῦθ' ἡττήθη, κατεψηφίσαντο. In fr. 18.3, referring to Coriolanus, Dio uses the verb στρατηγεῖν: ὁ αὐτὸς στρατηγῆσαι θελήσας καὶ μὴ τελεσθεὶς ἠγανάκτησε τῷ ὁμίλῳ. In Plutarch (*Cor.* 14.1) we find instead ὀλίγου δὲ χρόνου μετῄει μὲν ὑπατείαν ὁ Μάρκιος.

passages from Zonaras (7.17.5[63] and 7.17.6[64]): the fragments are particularly important, because they confirm Zonaras' terminological fidelity. And a conclusive piece of evidence on this point comes from the analysis of the whole of Zonaras' text, which derives not only from Dio, but also (in chapters 12–13) from Plutarch's *Life of Publicola* (which is the source of about 60 percent of these chapters; Dio is the source of the remaining 40 percent).[65] In the parts derived from Plutarch, the nouns ὕπατος and ὑπατεία and the verb ὑπατεύειν (and συνυπατεύειν) recur thirteen times, with neither doubts nor explanations.[66] In those derived from Dio, the use

---

[63] Here the word στρατηγός is used twice. No doubt Dio is referring to the consuls, given the mention of Appius Claudius "consul" of 471: τραπόμενοι δ' ἐπ' ἀλλήλους ἔπραξαν πολλὰ καὶ δεινά, ὡς μηδὲ τῶν στρατηγῶν ἀποσχέσθαι τὸ πλῆθος. τούς τε γὰρ ὑπηρέτας αὐτῶν ἔπαιον καὶ τὰς ῥάβδους κατέκλων, αὐτούς τε τοὺς στρατηγοὺς ὑπ' εὐθύνην ἦγον ἐπὶ πάσῃ προφάσει καὶ μείζονι καὶ ἐλάττονι. Ἄππιον οὖν Κλαύδιον καὶ παρ' αὐτὴν τὴν ἀρχὴν ἐς τὸ δεσμωτήριον ἐμβαλεῖν ἐβουλεύσαντο, ὅτι τε αὐτοῖς ἠναντιοῦτο εἰς ἅπαντα καὶ ὅτι τοὺς συστρατευσαμένους αὐτῷ ἐδεκάτευσεν, ἐπειδὴ τοῖς Οὐολούσκοις ἐν μάχῃ ἐνέδοσαν.

[64] Κἄν τις ἐπ' αἰτίᾳ τινὶ παρὰ τῶν στρατηγῶν προστιμηθῇ, ἔκκλητον ἐπὶ τούτοις τὸν δῆμον δικάζειν ἔταξαν.

[65] We still have the whole *Publicola*, so it is very easy to divide, in Zonaras' text, what is derived from Plutarch and what from Dio.

[66] a) Zonar. 7.12: ἔλαθεν οὖν ἔνδον ὢν οὐκ ἐκ προνοίας ἀλλὰ τυχαίως οἰκέτης ὄνομα Οὐινδίκιος, καὶ κατακρυφθεὶς ἐκεῖ θεατής τε τῶν δρωμένων ἦν καὶ τῶν βεβουλευμένων ἐπήκοος· ἅπερ ἦσαν, τοὺς ὑπάτους ἀνελεῖν... < Plut. *Publ.* 4.1–2: ἔλαθεν οὖν αὐτοὺς οἰκέτης ὄνομα Οὐινδίκιος ἔνδον κατακρύψας ἑαυτόν, οὐ κατ' ἐπιβουλὴν ἢ προαίσθησίν τινα τοῦ μέλλοντος, ἀλλ' ἔνδον ὢν ἔτυχε καὶ προσιοῦσιν αὐτοῖς μετὰ σπουδῆς ὀφθῆναι φοβηθεὶς ὑπέστη, λάρνακα κειμένην πρὸ αὐτοῦ ποιησάμενος, ὥστε καὶ τῶν πραττομένων θεατὴς γενέσθαι καὶ τῶν βουλευμάτων ἐπήκοος. ἔδοξε δ' αὐτοῖς τοὺς ὑπάτους ἀναιρεῖν...
b) Zonar. 7.12: ἀντεξῆγον δὲ καὶ τοὺς Ῥωμαίους οἱ ὕπατοι. ἀρχομένης δὲ τῆς μάχης Ἄρρων ὁ Ταρκυνίου παῖς καὶ Βροῦτος ὁ Ῥωμαίων ὕπατος ἀλλήλοις περιπεσόντες ἐμάχοντο. < Plut. *Publ.* 9.1: ἀντεξῆγον δὲ τοὺς Ῥωμαίους οἱ ὕπατοι... ἀρχομένων δὲ αὐτῶν συνάγειν εἰς χεῖρας Ἄρρων ὁ Ταρκυνίου παῖς καὶ Βροῦτος ὁ Ῥωμαίων ὕπατος οὐ κατὰ τύχην ἀλλήλοις περιπεσόντες.
c) Zonar. 7.12: ἐθριάμβευσε δὲ Οὐαλλέριος Ποπλικόλας πρῶτος ὑπατεύων. < Plut. *Publ.* 9.5: ἐθριάμβευσε δ' ἀπ' αὐτῆς Οὐαλλέριος εἰσελάσας τεθρίππῳ πρῶτος ὑπάτων.
d) Zonar. 7.12: ὁ δὲ Ποπλικόλας τὸ τρίτον ὑπατεύων τότε προὐκαλεῖτο συνεχῶς τὸν Ταρκύνιον ἐπὶ δίκῃ. < Plut. *Publ.* 17.1: Ποπλικόλας δὲ τὸ τρίτον ὑπατεύων... (cf. 18.1).
e) Zonar. 7.13: ἐκείνων δ' ἐξωσθέντων τῆς βασιλείας ὕπατοι, ὡς εἴρηται, παρὰ τῶν Ῥωμαίων ᾑρέθησαν. ὧν εἷς ἦν καὶ Πόπλιος Οὐαλλέριος, ὃς τετράκις ὑπάτευσεν, ὁ καὶ Ποπλικόλας ἐπικληθείς. οὗτος οὖν μόνος ἄρχων καὶ μὴ συνάρχοντα εἰληφὼς Ῥωμαίοις προσέκρουσε, λέγουσι μὴ τῆς τοῦ Βρούτου κληρονόμον ὑπατείας εἶναι. < Plut. *Publ.* 10.1: Βροῦτος... οὐκ ἠξίωσε μόνος ἄρχειν, ἀλλὰ καὶ πρῶτον αὐτῷ συνάρχοντα προσείλετο καὶ δεύτερον. "Οὑτοσὶ δ'," ἔφασαν, "εἰς αὑτὸν ἅπαντα συνενεγκάμενος οὐκ ἔστι τῆς Βρούτου κληρονόμος ὑπατείας...". (ἐκείνων... ἐπικληθείς derives neither from Plutarch nor from Dio; it is a summary by Zonaras: cf. Boissevain 1895, 40).
f) Zonar. 7.13: αἱρεθεὶς δὲ καὶ αὖθις ὕπατος ὁ Ποπλικόλας ἔσχε συνυπατεύοντα Τίτον Λουκρίτιον. Μετὰ δὲ ταῦτα Σαβίνων ἐμβαλόντων εἰς τὴν χώραν ὕπατος ἀνεδείχθη Μάρκος Οὐαλλέριος ἀδελφὸς Ποπλικόλα καὶ Ποστούμιος Τούβερτος. < Plut. *Publ.* 16.2: Ποπλικόλας δ' ᾑρέθη μὲν ἀπὼν ὕπατος τὸ δεύτερον, καὶ σὺν αὐτῷ Τίτος Λουκρήτιος. / 20.1: μετὰ δὲ ταῦτα

is very different, until 449: after this date our source will only employ ὕπατοι and the word στρατηγοί will disappear. The choice of words is not accidental but seems to follow a specific criterion.⁶⁷

To summarize, Cassius Dio did not just claim that the original title of the first Roman magistracy was "praetors," not "consuls," but stated it repeatedly and consistently. He is the only preserved source that clearly indicates when the terminology changed and shows a particular interest in this topic. Dio did not use Livy, but a source that Livy knew and that itself knew the *interpretes iuris*: a pre-Livian source that preserved a reconstruction of the early republic that was no longer common knowledge in the Augustan age (this tradition would be totally erased even by the extant juridical sources such as the long fragment from Pomponius' *Enchiridion* on the history of the magistracies, in *Dig.* 1.2.2).⁶⁸

But there is more. Cassius Dio (or his source) was not interested in the mere terminological problem, but tried also to resolve the ambiguities surrounding the powers of the first Roman magistrates and the difference between *praetores* and *consules*. We can find a trace of these reflections in his account of the decemvirate.

THE TWO COLLEGES OF DECEMVIRS

The creation of the new college of magistrates is described as follows (Zonar. 7.18.2):

διὰ ταῦτα τοίνυν οἱ Ῥωμαῖοι καὶ διά τινα σημεῖα εὐλαβηθέντες, τῶν τε πρὸς ἀλλήλους ἀπηλλάγησαν ἐγκλημάτων, καὶ τὴν πολιτείαν ἰσωτέραν

    Σαβίνων ἐμβαλόντων εἰς τὴν χώραν ὕπατος μὲν ἀπεδείχθη Μάρκος Οὐαλλέριος, ἀδελφὸς Ποπλικόλα, καὶ Ποστούμιος Τούβερτος.
  g) Zonar. 7.13: τῷ δ' ἑξῆς ἔτει πάλιν ὑπάτευε Ποπλικόλας. < Plut. *Publ.* 21.1: τῷ δ' ἑξῆς ἔτει πάλιν ὑπάτευε Ποπλικόλας τὸ τέταρτον.
  h) Zonar. 7.13: ἀγαγὼν δ' ἐπὶ τῇ νίκῃ θρίαμβον, καὶ τοῖς μετ' αὐτὸν ὑπάτοις παραδοὺς τὴν πόλιν, εὐθὺς ἐτελεύτησε. <Plut. *Publ* 23.2: ὁ δὲ Ποπλικόλας τόν τε θρίαμβον ἀγαγὼν καὶ τοῖς μετ' αὐτὸν ἀποδειχθεῖσιν ὑπάτοις παραδοὺς τὴν πόλιν, εὐθὺς ἐτελεύτησεν.

⁶⁷ The change of terminology is particularly clear in Zonaras' passage (7.19.2–5) on the consuls of 449, Lucius Valerius and Marcus Horatius, and on the creation in the following year of the *tribuni militum consulari potestate* (ὕπατοι ὑπάτευειν is repeated ten times). It is undeniable that the subject itself requires the use of ὕπατοι, but its frequency seems here even superabundant.

⁶⁸ Freyburger-Galland 1997, 154 tackles this problem briefly, without going over the mere conjecture ("il est possible que pour les premiers temps de Rome, il se soit conformé à l'usage romain et ait parlé de 'préteurs'"). According to Vrind 1923, 50, "ante 449 a.C. Dio semper στρατηγός στρατηγία στρατηγεῖν scripsisse videtur... Non raro autem apud eum ὕπατος ὑπάτευειν... Veri simile est talibus locis Zonaram aut Dionis narrationem contraxisse atque suis verbis reddidisse, aut quod plerumque factum esse puto, praeter Dionem etiam habuisse ex alio fonte qui plerumque est Plutarchus."

ποιήσασθαι ἐψηφίσαντο. καὶ τρεῖς ἄνδρας εἰς τὴν Ἑλλάδα διὰ τοὺς νόμους καὶ τὰ παρ' ἐκείνοις ἔθη πεπόμφασι. καὶ κομισθέντων αὐτῶν τάς τε ἄλλας ἀρχὰς καὶ τὰς τῶν δημάρχων κατέλυσαν, καὶ ἄνδρας ὀκτὼ ἐκ τῶν πρώτων ἀνθείλοντο, καὶ Ἄππιον Κλαύδιον Τίτον τε Γενούκιον ἀπέδειξαν κατὰ τὸν ἐνιαυτὸν ἐκεῖνον στρατηγοὺς αὐτοκράτορας.

[For these reasons, accordingly, and because of certain portents, the Romans became sobered, dismissed their mutual grievances and voted to establish the rights of citizenship on a fairer basis. And they sent three men to Greece to observe the laws and the customs of the people there. Upon the return of the commission they abolished all the magistracies, including that of the tribunes, and chose instead eight of the foremost men, and appointed Appius Claudius and Titus Genucius praetors with absolute power for that year.]

While the first part of this passage corresponds to the tradition from many points of view,[69] the second is remarkably different.[70] According to Dio, eight of the most illustrious citizens were chosen (ἀνθείλοντο)[71] as members of the college, while Claudius and Genucius were elected (ἀπέδειξαν) στρατηγοὶ αὐτοκράτορες. The distinction could be due to the fact that Claudius and Genucius were the *consules designati* of 451 (Livy 3.33.4; Dion. Hal. 10.54.4; 56.2; *Fast. Cap.*),[72] but I wonder whether Dio is suggesting here the existence of a hierarchy among the decemvirs, an unequal collegiality.[73] This hypothesis seems to be excluded by all the other sources and in particular by Livy and Dionysius, who mention all the decemvirs together (Livy 3.33.3; Dion. Hal. 10.56.2), even if both Livy and Dionysius repeatedly lay stress on Claudius' pre-eminence.[74] Only Ioannes

[69] The agreement between patricians and plebeians (Livy 3.31.7–8; Dion. Hal. 10.52); the sending of ambassadors to Greece (Livy 3.31.8; Dion. Hal. 10.51.5; 10.52.4; 10.54.3); the reference in the same context to the *aequitas* requested by the plebeians (Livy 3.31.7: *legum latores... qui utrisque utilia ferrent quaeque aequandae libertatis essent*; Dion. Hal. 10.55.1: παύσασθαι στασιάζοντας τοὺς πολίτας ὑπὲρ τῶν ἴσων) and reminiscent of the Thucydidean expression τὴν πολιτείαν ἰσωτέραν ποιήσασθαι (Thuc. 8.89.2: ... ἀλλὰ τοὺς πεντακισχιλίους ἔργῳ καὶ μὴ ὀνόματι χρῆναι ἀποδεικνύναι καὶ τὴν πολιτείαν ἰσαιτέραν καθιστάναι). Finally, the σημεῖα could coincide with the pestilence of 453 (Livy 3.32.1–4; Dion. Hal. 10.53).
[70] Schwartz 1899, 1693 also notices it, but does not comment.
[71] Cf. Dion. Hal. 10.55.4; Flor. 1.24.1.
[72] Mommsen 1887–8, II, 720 supposed that this piece of information had been inspired by the eight praetors appointed by Sulla, and subordinated to the consuls. But in my opinion this hypothesis (accepted by Vrind 1923, 38) is an unconvincing scholarly construction. In a passage below we will see the real explanation for this distinction.
[73] Libourel 1968, 213–15 rightly states that "Dio probably meant that Appius and Genucius possessed an *imperium* greater than that of their eight colleagues." In his opinion this version is "a rationalistic invention by an annalist who wished to account for Claudius' predominance among the decemvirs in the traditional accounts." But this interpretation is not convincing: it does not explain Genucius' role, or the different structure of the second college of decemvirs, which we will discuss.
[74] Livy says that Claudius held the chairmanship of the college (3.33.7: *regimen totius magistratus penes Appium erat*) and that in 449 Claudius and Quintus Fabius were "chief among the ten"

Lydus mentions a real hierarchy (*Mag.* 1.34: "The people appointed ten men to take charge of the republic, the first of whom was called 'the guardian of the city,' called in our day 'prefect of the city'"):⁷⁵ the mention of a "first" (πρῶτος) among the decemvirs, with a specific title, is interesting and significant, even if this title is inaccurately rendered as τῆς πόλεως φύλαξ (that is *praefectus urbi*).⁷⁶

Unequal collegiality was apparently not alien to archaic public law: we have prudently supposed that Dio retained a somewhat confused recollection of it, in the repeated use of the term συνάρχων, even in the absence of the corresponding ἄρχων, to indicate one of the early chief magistrates. In light of these remarks and of the clues given by Livy, Dionysius and especially Lydus, I think that the piece of information about the first college of decemvirs, which distinguishes Claudius and Genucius from "the other eight," means a real hierarchic relation: the title of στρατηγοὶ αὐτοκράτορες is attributed only to them⁷⁷ and two different verbs are employed (ἀπέδειξαν and ἀνθείλοντο), hinting perhaps that Claudius and Genucius after their election co-opted the other eight.⁷⁸ The term στρατηγοί is used again with its original meaning and gives the idea of a continuity, in spite of the abolition of the other magistracies: at the same time the title of αὐτοκράτορες and most of all the distinction between Claudius and Genucius and "the other eight" reinforce the impression that Dio is using

---

(3.41.8: *principes inter decemviros*), though in the same context he mentions the agreement among the decemvirs on the command of the war against Aequi and Sabines (3.41.7: *inter se decemviri comparant, quos ire ad bellum, quos praeesse exercitibus oporteret*). And Dionysius often connotes Claudius as the "chief of the decemvirs," even if he seems to allude to an actual fact, not to a real hierarchy (*Ant. Rom.* 10.57.3; 10.58.3; 11.4.3; 11.9.2; 11.22.4; 11.28.3). Cf. de Martino 1958, 246: "la direzione della magistratura era presso Appio Claudio sulla base del favore della plebe."

⁷⁵ Δέκα προεβάλετο ὁ δῆμος ἄνδρας ἀνθεξομένους τῶν πραγμάτων, ὧν ὁ πρῶτος τῆς πόλεως φύλαξ προσηγορεύθη, ὁ καθ' ἡμᾶς πολίαρχος. Translation by A. C. Bandy.

⁷⁶ Perhaps Lydus' misunderstanding derived from a wrong interpretation of his Latin source (if not from Livy 4.36.5, where an Appius Claudius, son of the decemvir and *tribunus militum*, is left in Rome by his colleagues just as *praefectus urbi*).

⁷⁷ Στρατηγοὶ αὐτοκράτορες is clearly predicative of ἀπέδειξαν (Mommsen 1887–8, II, 720; Cary 1914, 169; Vrind 1923, 38; Freyburger-Galland 1997, 203). Kübler 1901b, 2258, seems to attribute it to all ten of them, but he is wrong. A similar title is in Cicero, who assigns it not to Claudius and Genucius, but to the whole college (*Rep.* 2.36.61: *decemviri maxima potestate*; cf. Pompon., in *Dig.* 1.2.2.4); and the adjective αὐτοκράτωρ is also in Dionysius, but in a different context, that is, in the description of the college of 450 (*Ant. Rom.* 10.58.1: ἵνα ἑκόντες τε καὶ ἄκοντες ἐν αὐτοῖς μένοιεν, ἐδόκει δή τινος ἀρχῆς αὐτοκράτορος δεῖν). Dio's use is different.

⁷⁸ According to Ogilvie 1965, 452, it is not clear whether Claudius and Genucius came into office and then co-opted eight *legati* or whether there was a total suspension of the "constitution," followed by the appointment of the decemvirs. Ogilvie thinks that the first hypothesis is supported by Cicero (*Rep.* 2.36.61) and by the *Fasti* (*Ap. Claudius Ap. f. M. n. Crass(us) Inr[i]gill(ensis) T. Genu[cius L. f. L. n.] Au[gu]rinus Sabin(us) II abdicarunt ut de[ce]mviri consular[i imperio fier]ent*): but neither Cicero nor the *Fasti* mention a co-optation, while in a sense Cassius Dio (here ignored by Ogilvie) suggests something like that.

a source that is foreign to the annalistic tradition,[79] probably a pre-Livian source.[80]

At this point Zonaras' synthesis continues, referring to the activity of the first college (7.18.3):

καὶ νόμους αὐτοῖς συγγράψαι ἐπέτρεψαν, μηδεμίαν τε δίκην ἐφέσιμον ἀπ' αὐτῶν γενέσθαι προσεψηφίσαντο· ὃ πρώην οὐδενὶ τῶν ἀρχόντων πλὴν τῶν δικτατόρων ἐδέδοτο. ἦρξάν τε οὗτοι ἐφ' ἡμέραν ἕκαστος, ἐναλλὰξ τὸ πρόσχημα τῆς ἡγεμονίας λαμβάνοντες. καὶ νόμους συγγράψαντες εἰς τὴν ἀγορὰν ἐξέθηκαν οἳ ἐπεὶ πᾶσιν ἤρεσαν, ἐς τὸν δῆμον εἰσήχθησαν, καὶ κυρωθέντες σανίσιν ἐνεγράφησαν δέκα· ὅσα γὰρ φυλακῆς ἐκρίθησαν ἄξια, ἐν σανιδίοις ἐθησαυρίζοντο.

[They empowered them to compile laws, and further voted that no appeal could be taken from them – a power granted previously to none of the magistrates except the dictators. These men held sway each for a day, assuming by turns the dignity of rulership. They also compiled laws which they exposed to view in the Forum. When the laws were found acceptable to all, they were brought before the people, and after receiving their ratification were inscribed on ten tables; for all records that were deemed worthy of safe-keeping used to be preserved on tables.]

The account substantially agrees with the tradition, particularly with Livy.[81] The statement that they held power "by turns" (ἐναλλάξ) could be seen to be in contrast with the concept of unequal collegiality suggested shortly before. The definition of this hierarchy remains up to now rather confused: this confusion can be imputed to Zonaras' synthesis or better yet to the use, on the part of Dio, of badly combined sources. But the following passage (Zonar. 7.18.4) about the college of 450[82] seems to corroborate my hypothesis on the unequal collegiality of the first decemvirs:

---

[79] Poma 1984, 219, thinks that Zonaras "ci riporta, attraverso Cassio Dione, alla tradizione liviana." Poma quotes the passage in full, but interrupts it abruptly (cf. p. 260).
[80] See above.
[81] The decemvirs were *sine provocatione* (cf. Livy 3.32.6; 3.33.9; Cic. *Rep.* 2.31.54; 2.36.61; Pompon. in *Dig.* 1.2.2.4); they wielded their power in turn, one day each (cf. Livy 3.33.8; Dion. Hal. 10.57.1–2); their laws were at first exposed in the Forum, then voted in the *comitia* (Livy 3.34.6; cf. Dion. Hal. 10.55.5; 10.57.6–7). Two details are not testified elsewhere: the comparison with the dictators and the mention of the habit of transcribing on tables (σανίδες, that is, "wooden tables") what was worth retaining.
[82] The tradition about this second college already existed in the second century BC, when L. Cassius Hemina (*HRRel*.18) and C. Sempronius Tuditanus (*HRRel.* 7) mention it (cf. Macrob. *Sat.* 1.13.21). Its historicity is disputed: cf. Beloch 1926, 242; Siber 1951, 112; Ogilvie 1965, 452–3, 461–2; von Ungern-Sternberg 1986, 84; Drummond 1989a, 114; Drummond 1989b, 230. Some modern scholars have singled out possible allusions to the age of Sulla (Ogilvie 1965, 464, 467), or to the first (Klotz 1938, 46) or the second triumvirate (von Ungern-Sternberg 1986, 95) – but cf. Cornell 1995, 275, 452.

ἐκεῖνοι μὲν οὖν τὸν ἐνιαυτὸν ἀνύσαντες ἀφῆκαν τὴν ἀρχήν, ἕτεροι δ' αὖθις αἱρεθέντες δέκα, ὥσπερ ἐπὶ καταλύσει τῆς πολιτείας χειροτονηθέντες, ἐξώκειλαν. πάντες γὰρ ἅμα ἀπὸ τῆς ἴσης ἦρχον, καὶ νεανίσκους ἐκ τῶν εὐπατριδῶν θρασυτάτους ἐκλεξάμενοι πολλὰ δι' αὐτῶν ἐποίουν καὶ βίαια. ὀψὲ δέ ποτε ἐπ' ἐξόδῳ τοῦ ἔτους ὀλίγα ἄττα ἐν δύο σανίσι προσέγραψαν ἐς πάντα δὴ αὐτογνωμονήσαντες. ἀφ' ὧν οὐχ ὁμόνοια, ἀλλὰ καὶ διαφοραὶ μείζους Ῥωμαίοις γενήσεσθαι ἔμελλον. αἱ μὲν οὖν λεγόμεναι δώδεκα δέλτοι οὕτως τότε ἐγένοντο.

[The above-mentioned magistrates surrendered their office at the expiration of the year, but ten more chosen anew – for the overthrow of the state, as it almost seemed – came to grief. For they all held sway on equal terms, and chose from among the patricians some most brazen youths, through whose agency they committed many acts of violence. At last, toward the end of the year, they compiled some few additional statutes written upon two tables, all of which were the product of their own arbitrary judgement. From these not harmony but greater disputes were destined to fall to the lot of the Romans. The so-called twelve tables were thus created at that time.]

This passage is also somewhat muddled: the expression ἕτεροι δέκα is contradicted shortly after, when Appius Claudius appears as a member of this college too. This is another example of confusion, probably deriving from the use of different sources. It is worth noting that, unlike in the passage on the first college, the word στρατηγοί is not employed any more. But most of all we have to pay attention to a particular: according to Dio, the decemvirs of 450 held power together (ἅμα), a statement that corresponds to the tradition and to the ἐναλλάξ of 451; but ἀπὸ τῆς ἴσης has a proper meaning ("on equal terms") that is consistent with the interpretation we have given of the college of 451 and its unequal collegiality. The strange distinction, in the first college of decemvirs, between the two στρατηγοὶ αὐτοκράτορες and "the other eight" becomes clear in light of this "on equal terms." Cassius Dio (or Dio's source) seems to know of a new conception of the collegiality introduced just in 450: among the decemvirs of 451 there were two αὐτοκράτορες and eight *collegae minores*. Among the decemvirs of 450 this distinction has been abolished.

In this respect Cassius Dio differs totally from all of the other sources,[83] giving a *difficilior* version that in my opinion is derived from a very ancient

---

[83] Libourel 1968, 216–17 comes to diametrically opposed conclusions: "Aside from calling the magistrates 'praetors' rather than 'consuls' Dio in no way differs from the conventional annalistic tradition that the office was set up at the beginning of the republic and consisted of two colleagues of equal *imperium*. In other words, he furnishes no support for the various modern theories that the highest magistracy at Rome in its oldest form consisted of three colleagues or that it was held by a single supreme officer – either called 'praetor maximus,' 'dictator,' or 'magister populi' – possibly in conjunction with a subordinate colleague, or that the highest magistracy was a continuation of an office

tradition, the same that called the first Roman "consuls" στρατηγοί instead of ὕπατοι. Or rather, in Dio we find both traditions. According to the first, the colleges of decemvirs were different because the first was composed of ἄνδρες ὀκτὼ ἐκ τῶν πρώτων καὶ στρατηγοὶ αὐτοκράτορες [δύο], the second of ἕτεροι δέκα, ἀπὸ τῆς ἴσης [ἀρχῆς]. According to the second tradition the difference consisted in the fact that in 451 the decemvirs held power ἐφ' ἡμέραν ἕκαστος, ἐναλλάξ, while in 450 πάντες ἅμα ἦρχον. The suspicion arises that the version according to which the decemvirs of 450 ruled no longer "one day each," but "together" (a tradition that Cicero himself does not seem to know of),[84] originated from an incorrect interpretation of this earlier version, whose meaning was probably already unclear at the end of the republican period.

CONCLUSION

The distinction between the unequal collegiality of 451 and the equal collegiality of 450 is quite consistent with the piece of information about the institution of the "consulship" instead of the "praetorship" in 449. Cassius Dio is following a source that acknowledges an original unequal collegiality among the chief Roman magistrates. Apart from his reliability, Dio's source reveals the existence of an ancient debate on this topic. After some hesitation about the last years of the sixth century, this source regularly mentioned "praetors" instead of "consuls" from about 500 to 450; it identified the second college of decemvirs as the end of this original hierarchy; it used the term "praetors" in its archaic meaning for the last time just for the decemvirs of 451 (and for only two of them) and not for the decemvirs of 450. According to this source, the two magistrates elected in 449 did not have the same powers as their colleagues elected before 451, because equal collegiality had been introduced. This in turn justified the change in their title.

In the end we should add that the *rogatio Terentilia* of 462, generally considered to be among the origins of the decemvirate, had asked for "the appointment of five men to write out the statutes pertaining to the consular power" (Livy 3.9.5).[85] We find nothing on this subject in the tradition concerning the Twelve Tables: but the innovations made, according to

---

which had existed under the kings. It is evident that Dio, despite his researches into the history of the Roman constitution and his access to much material unavailable to modern scholars, found no reason to reject the conventional tradition."
[84] He does not mention it in *Rep.* 2.36.61.
[85] *Ut quinque viri creentur legibus de imperio consulari scribendis.*

Dio, between 450 (introduction of equal collegiality) and 449 (election of the first *consules*) seem to be a response to the demands attributed ten years before to Terentilius Harsa, whose substantial historicity is highly probable.[86] In the traditional version of the narrative these demands are not really satisfied, so they have perplexed modern scholars quite a lot.[87] Dio's account furnishes a possible answer to these perplexities.[88]

---

[86] This *rogatio* was never turned into a *lex*. Its memory "si giustifica solo con il suo collegamento stretto con le vicende che determinarono il decemvirato; del resto *C. Terentilius Harsa* è personaggio oscurissimo il cui nome compare nei fasti dei tribuni della plebe solo in questa occasione" (Poma 1984, 177).

[87] According to Mommsen 1887–88, II, 703, "hat er [*scil*. Livy] die Formel missverstanden" (cf. *contra* already Kübler 1901b, 2258). Cf. also Baviera 1925, 23–5 (the decemvirs had the task of reconciling patricians and plebeians through constitutional laws); Arangio Ruiz 1957, 57; de Sanctis 1956–67, II, 41 ("queste discrepanze mostrano... che nulla si sapeva del contenuto della rogazione Terentilia"); Humbert 1990, 263–4; Forsythe 2005, 202. Further bibliography in Poma 1984, 208–9.

[88] Cf. de Francisci 1959, 751: "E come si spiegherebbe il potere uguale e collegiale dei *decemviri legibus scribundis* e dei *tribuni militum consulari potestate*, in confronto a quello ineguale dei *praetores*?" Cassius Dio seemingly gives an explanation.

CHAPTER 3

The development of the praetorship in the third century BC

Alexander Bergk

There are two opposing views in modern scholarship on the Roman *praetura*. According to our sources the praetorship was established in 367 BC by the Licinian-Sextian Laws. One camp of scholars accepts this basic picture, the other group criticizes it strongly. Two questions are particularly contentious: if the picture of the sources must be revised, how do we place the two consuls, and what were the original duties of the praetor?

The most prominent proponent of the first school of thought is Theodor Mommsen. In his *Staatsrecht*, Mommsen developed the theory of *imperium*, which the consuls inherited from the kings and which conferred authority in three fields: military, political and legal.[1] The one-year limitation of the term and the potential rivalry of a second consul tended to mitigate the overwhelming power of the office. Establishing new magistracies also helped to relieve the consuls. The assignments of censor and praetor were derived from the authority of the consuls without the consuls actually ceding this authority: the consuls could always prevail over all the other magistrates, thanks to their superior *imperium*. In this perspective, the detailed report of Livy[2] and the additional hints in other authors[3] can claim some credence.

This interpretation is still very popular. I spare my readers the names and titles of all the scholars and handbooks who accept it. But from the beginning, there were also other voices. Alfred Heuss criticized Mommsen's theory and emphasized the military origins of the *imperium*, while doubting its civilian competences.[4] However, if this is true, what was the task of the praetor after 366? R. Gilbert argued in 1939 that the peregrine praetorship was established for military action,[5] and Oliver Brupbacher has now made

---

For the translation I would like to thank Christoph Lundgreen and Dr. Rene Pfeilschifter.
[1] Mommsen 1887–8, 1, 6f., 22–4, 116–36.   [2] Livy 6.42.9–11.
[3] Plut. *Cam.* 39.1; 42.7; Flor. 1.17 [= 1.26.1–4]; *De vir. ill.* 20.1; Pompon. *Dig.* 1.2.2.26; Zonar. 7.24.4.
[4] Heuss 1944, 57–133.   [5] Gilbert 1939, 50–8; similarly Serrati 2000, 115–33.

the case that jurisdiction was not among the main tasks of the praetor in the fourth and early third centuries.[6]

T. Corey Brennan[7] provides an extensive assessment of the praetorship in his monumental two-volume set. He rejects Livy's report of the early praetor exercising legal functions in lawsuits between citizens. Not once in the first ten books of *Ab Urbe Condita* does the praetor act as a judge. On only one occasion does he make a law, but he does so when away from Rome and more for political than for administrative reasons.[8] Moreover, Livy mentions the praetor only when he is acting outside of the city (which happens regularly),[9] and he never speaks of a *"praetor urbanus"* in his second pentad.[10]

While modern scholarship tends to emphasize the military duties of the praetor, there is still no consensus about the relationship between praetor and consuls. In 366, was the praetor subordinate to the consuls, or was he a colleague of equal rank? If the latter is true, when and why did the consulship rise above the other office? Robert Bunse, who has investigated this problem in several publications,[11] thinks that there was a collegium of three praetors after 366.[12] Only in the first half of the third century were the consuls distinguished from the praetorship.[13] In Bunse's opinion, the

---

[6] Brupbacher 2006, 107–51. For the military etymology of the noun "praetor" cf. van Leijenhorst 1986, 176–83.

[7] Brennan 2000.

[8] Livy 9.20.5: *Eodem anno* (318) *primum praefecti Capuam creari coepti legibus ab L. Furio praetore datis, cum utrumque ipsi pro remedio aegris rebus discordia intestina petissent.* This must have been a *lex data*. For another *lex data* in 317, we do not know anything about the identity and office of the persons involved (Livy 9.20.10). Later *leges datae* from 212 (Livy 25.40.4), 204 (Cic. *Verr.* 2.123), 197 (Livy 34.57.1), 167 (Livy 45.17–18; Just. *Epit.* 33.2.7) and 146 (Polyb. 39.4; Paus. 7.16.9) were all given by proconsuls in accordance with a senate commission. It seems that in the fourth century praetors exercised duties on a regular basis that were later reserved for persons with proconsular *imperium*.

[9] An overview of the activities of the praetor outside of Rome is given by Mommsen 1887–8, II, 1, 233 n. 4. A law barring the praetor from leaving Rome for more than ten days (Cic. *Phil.* 2.31) dates perhaps only from the Sullan age, because the *praetor urbanus* P. Cornelius Lentulus was sent to Campania in 165 (Gran. Lic. 28, 29–37 [Criniti]); cf. Kunkel & Wittmann 1995, 296 n. 6 against Mommsen 1887–8, II, 1, 195 n. 3; cf. also Scardigli and Berardi 1983, 38f.

[10] Brennan 2000, I, 61.

[11] Bunse 2001, 145–62; Bunse 2002a, 416–32; Bunse 2002b, 29–43.   [12] Bunse 1998, 189.

[13] The earliest epigraphic evidence for the term *consol*, in the *elogia* of L. Cornelius Barbatus and his son (*CIL* I² 6/7), is important. The *elogia* must have been written after the death of the son in the second half of the third century. For the chronological conundrum, cf. Saladino 1970; Till 1970, 276–89; Coarelli 1972, 36–106; Wachter 1987, 301–42. A milestone from Sicily which may be from earlier speaks of the consul C. Aurelius Cotta (cos. 252); cf. de Vita 1955, 10–21; de Vita 1963, 477–88. Some corroborative evidence for the theory that the early consuls were called *praetores* exists. But the fragmentary inscription breaks off in the middle of the decisive word, much to the desperation of historians: *C. Cenucio Clousino prai (----)*, first published in Cristofani 1986, 24–6. The person mentioned is without a doubt the consul of 276 and 270, C. Genucius L. f. L. n. Clepsina. Is *prai (----)* to be read *praitor* or *praifectus* (cf. Crawford 1996a, 979–81)? If *prai(tor)* is correct and

par potestas of the consuls came into being only after 366, while no system of equal power-sharing ever existed among the praetors. The superiority of the *praetor urbanus* was thus not challenged until the end of the republic.[14] Unfortunately Bunse has nothing to say about the respective positions within this hierarchy of the praetor and consuls.

Hans Beck, in his book about career and hierarchy,[15] also argues for a collegium of three superior magistrates, pointing to the priority of military tasks and the close links between praetor and consuls.[16] The *Fasti Praetorii* lend some credence to the theory that in a period in which prorogation was still a rare phenomenon, the praetorship was often sought immediately after the consulate or between two consulates to guarantee the continuing possession of *imperium*.[17] Beck emphasizes the strong dynamics of the development: there were two praetorships in 242, four in 227 and six in 197. Beck sees military necessities and the rapid growth of the empire as the rationale behind this. The increase in positions – from 227, twice as many as the consulships – was the prerequisite for the tightening of the *cursus honorum* after the chaos of the Hannibalic War.

I hope this short summary of recent scholarship has shown that there are still gaps in our picture of the praetorship between 366 and 218, the beginning of Livy's third decade. I will now try to provide an outline of the relationship between praetor and consuls from 366 until the end of the Samnite Wars and analyze the reasons for the rise of the consulate. In the rest of the paper I shall approach my subject in three consecutive steps. First, I will explain the position and role of the praetor after 366. I will then argue that the praetorship underwent what I call a metamorphosis, something that was closely connected with the overall development, the change in the military situation from that of a city-state with wars close to home to a mighty power with wars far away in Italic territory. Third and

---

the list of Clepsina's *cursus honorum* starts with his highest office (as in the perhaps contemporary Barbatus inscription (*CIL* I² 6)), we would have proof for three *praetores* as the highest magistrates. But see Naso 1986, 191–8 and Torelli 2000, 141–76, who argues for the reading *prai(fectos)*.

[14] Bunse 2002a, cf. also Plut. *Brut.* 7; App. *B Civ.* 2.112(= 466). It is not clear if the *praetor urbanus* was also *praetor maior* in relation to the other praetors (Fest. s. v. maiorem consulem 154L).

[15] Beck 2005, 63–70.

[16] Beck 2005, 64. Beck's judgment is slightly mistaken when he argues that the praetorship conferred less prestige than the consulate because it was filled very early by a plebeian (Q. Publilius Philo, praet. 336). But this happened thirty years or one generation after the last of the other major offices (consulate, dictatorship, censorship) was first given to a plebeian. So it seems on the contrary that the praetorship was the last bulwark of the patricians; cf. the negative reaction of C. Sulpicius Longus, who presided over the voting assembly when he heard that Publilius was running (Livy 8.15.9). The senate's defeatism is best explained by the small chance of preventing Publilius' election.

[17] Beck 2005, S. 65f.

last, I will try to outline what were in my view the final steps after the First Punic War that eventually led to the well-known hierarchy of praetorship and consulship.

First I will analyze the "compromise" of 367, for a better understanding of the place of the praetorship in the so-called *Konsulatsverfassung*. The annalistic tradition emphasizes the *leges Liciniae Sextiae* as a turning point in the development of the Roman magistracies. Scholars have speculated a great deal about the *lex Licinia Sextia de consule plebeio*.[18] It may be that this was not a *lex* but a *plebiscitum*, because decisions of the *concilium plebis* did not bind the patricians before the *lex Hortensia* of 287.[19] In addition, the compromise between patricians and plebeians did not last: patricians filled both positions in 355, 354, 353, 351, 349, 345 and 343.[20] But we know from a fragment of Fabius Pictor[21] that the first Roman historian was already well aware of the importance of the decisions of 366 and saw them as an important turning point in Roman history.[22] But the fragment does not say anything about the character of the compromise. If the plebiscite of C. Licinius Stolo and L. Sextius was not valid for the patricians, if it was only a statement of plebeian will, and if the patricians were not ready to accept a plebeian consul, how could the plebeian L. Sextius have been elected consul? It may help to take a closer look at the presiding magistrate.[23] Livy

---

[18] Livy 6.42.9–11; Diod. Sic. 12.25.2 (in the year 443); Plut. *Cam.* 42.3–8; Gell. 17.21.27; Flor. 1.17 (1.26.1–4). The other Licinan-Sextian laws, especially the *lex Licinia Sextia de modo agrorum*, are not relevant here; cf. Flach 1994, 294–7 with bibliography and Bringmann 1985.

[19] Cf. the commentary in Flach 1994, 294–7 with bibliography.

[20] Hölkeskamp 1987, 62–109 is groundbreaking, with bibliography. It is possible that 321 was another year with two patrician consuls (T. Veturius and Sp. Postumius). The defeat at Caudium discredited a purely patrician consulship once and for all; cf. Shatzman 1973, 65–77.

[21] Gell. 5.4.3 (F 6 HRR Peter = F 33 Jacoby = Beck & Walter 2005/2004, I, n. 23).

[22] Cf. the commentary in Beck & Walter 2005/2004, I, no. 23. But see von Ungern-Sternberg 1990, 92–102, who does not see a break in the Roman constitution around 366. The Romans saw the Republic as completed after the decemvirate; cf. Scipio Aemilianus' sentence in Cic. *Rep.* 2.63: <maio> *res nostros et probavisse maxime et retinuisse sapientissime iudico*. It may actually be true that in Roman eyes the decemvirate marked a more important event for the formation of the Republic.

[23] It may be true that the presiding magistrate did not wield much influence and was restricted to formal tasks in the second century; cf. Rilinger 1976. The reason for this was both the consensus of the senate, which at this time had already developed into the central institution of the Republic, and a certain indifference on the part of the magistrate. Things were different in the fourth, third and partly also in the second century. There is the interesting example of the aedile Q. Fulvius Flaccus in 184. After the *praetor urbanus* C. Decimius Flavus had died, Flaccus decided to run for the office in a by-election. The consul presiding over the assembly was wavering, and the senate could not persuade Flaccus to withdraw. So the senate was forced to cancel the by-election (Livy 39.39.1–15). It seems that it was perfectly within the consul's authority to decline an application as long as he was assured the solidarity of his peers. On the other hand, the senate was simply not able to stop a single nobleman as long as he was decisive enough. Fulvius' ambition to prevail against the will of the senate and to force the allegedly omnipotent institution to settle for an emergency solution did not damage him permanently. He was elected praetor in 182, became consul for 179 at the first

reports that Furius Camillus resigned as dictator in 368 because a mistake was made in taking the auspices;[24] P. Manlius succeeded as *dictator seditionis sedandae et rei gerundae causa*.[25]

Manlius appointed the plebeian Licinius, who was related to him by marriage, as *magister equitum* and thus conferred upon him a curule office.[26] It was possible to appoint a dictator not just to deal with domestic uprising[27] but also one *rei gerundae causa* if war was imminent.[28] So it may be that there was an overlap between Manlius' dictatorship and Camillus' next appointment to the dictatorship for the war against the Gauls.[29] It seems probable that Manlius not only appointed a plebeian Master of Horses but also presided over the elections for 366.[30] In this assembly L. Sextius was elected, which did not imply new and valid long-term regulations. Camillus, newly arrived in Rome, urged the patricians to accept the status quo.[31] This means that the admission of plebeians to the consulate was less a formal matter than a result of the identity of both the patricians presiding over the voting assembly and the plebeians running for the office.

Proof of this is in the nature of the small plebeian group that shared the consulship with the patricians between 366 and 361.[32] It is not entirely

---

attempt (which was not the norm) and finally rose to the censorship in 174. His ambition only came at the wrong moment, and the senate did not hold grudges but decided according to the necessities of the moment. For the possibilities of the presiding magistrate, cf. Hölkeskamp 1987, 62–74.

[24] Livy 6.38.9–12; *Inscr. Ital.* XIII, 1.32–3: [*post edictu*]*m in milites ex s* (*enatus*) *c*(*onsulto*) *abdicarunt*.

[25] Livy 6.39.1–4. Only the *Fasti Capitolini* give this form (*Inscr. Ital.* XIII, 1.33).

[26] *Inscr. Ital.* XIII, 1.32–3: [*C. Licinius C. f. P. n. Calvus pr*]*imus e plebe*. Manlius rejected some patrician protests, pointing out that *magister equitum* was a lesser office than consular tribune – a position that had already been filled by plebeians (Livy 6.39.4). For the hierarchy of magistracies, cf. *lex Bantinae* (*CIL* I² 45; Crawford, 1996b, I, 200) line 15: *dic., cos., pr., mag. eq., cens., aid., tr., pl., q., IIIvir cap., IIIvir d. a., ioudex ex h. l. plebive scitus*; cf. also the *lex repetundarum* (*CIL* I² 58; Crawford, 1996b, I, 65) line 8: *dic., cos., pr., mag. eq., aid.* . . . ; cf. Mommsen 1887–8, I, 561f.

[27] Cic. *Leg.* 3.3.9. It may be that Cicero's suggestion was an innovation following Sulla's example; cf. Lehmann, 1980, 36–44. But the *princeps* Claudius expresses the same thought when he says in a speech before the senate: *dictaturae hoc ipso consulari imperium valentius repertum apud maiores nostros, quo in a*[*s*]*perioribus bellis aut in civili motu difficiliore uterentur* (*CIL* XIII 1668 line 28f.).

[28] Kunkel & Wittmann 1995, 685. The dictatorship of M. Fabius Buteo for the refilling of the senate in 216 is evidence that there could be two dictators at the same time provided one of them had only to fulfill civilian duties in Rome (Livy 23.23.1–7). The other magistrate was the *dictator rei gerundae causa* M. Iunius Pera, who commanded the troops in Campania. Nevertheless this was an extreme emergency, and it is this that Livy's Fabius Buteo points out (Livy 23.23.1–2).

[29] Livy reports only the election of six consular tribunes between the two dictatorships (Livy 6.42.3; *Inscr. Ital.* XIII, 1.33; Diod. Sic. 15.61.1). We don't know anything about their activities.

[30] Siber's (1952, 57) suggestion.

[31] According to Plut. *Cam.* 42 Camillus presided over the elections, although another dictator is mentioned (without a name).

[32] L. Genucius Aventinensis (cos. 365, 362), his brother Cn. Genucius Aventinensis (cos. 363) and C. Licinius Calvus (?) (coss. 364, 361). The patricians were L. Aemilius Mamercinus (coss. 366, 363), Q. Servilius Ahala (coss. 365, 362, 342) and C. Sulpicius Peticus (coss. 364, 361, 355, 353, 351); cf. Broughton 1951–86, I, 114–18.

clear why the Genucii and the Licinii filled all the plebeian positions. But both *gentes* had already produced consular tribunes as proof of their *Regimentsfähigkeit*.³³ The compromise of 367 seems to have been a temporary solution intended to integrate some top plebeians finally into the patrician-dominated upper class. There was still a long way to go until the Struggle of the Orders was settled.³⁴ More important was the final decision for the so-called "consular constitution," which fixed the number of the major magistrates (without it being clear how much of a change this was from the situation before 366).³⁵ From 366 on only three major office-holders were elected, one of whom could be a plebeian. This brings us to my second point: the relationship between the three magistrates.

There is an often-quoted passage of the Augur Messala, transmitted in the *Noctes Atticae* by Gellius, in which we read about the similar nature of the auspices of consuls and of the praetor. But he then goes on to make a distinction between the *imperium* of the consuls and the praetor, the former being *maius*.³⁶ In an article about "römische Amtsgewalt,"³⁷ Jochen Bleicken has argued that it was the auspices that led to a hierarchy between Roman magistrates. In his view, the authority of Roman magistrates was exercised by and based on the right and ability to communicate with the gods.³⁸ And it is precisely this mediation between the gods and the people that the patricians always claimed as their special privilege³⁹ – again according to the annalistic tradition. This monopoly of auspices can be traced back even to the late republic. We have only to think, for example, of the interrex. Things look different, however, with *imperium*.⁴⁰ At the

---

[33] A certain Cn. Genucius was consular tribune in 399 and 396. One of his ancestors, T. Genucius Augurinus, was even a *decemvir consulari imperio legibus scribundis*. For the Licinii, P. Licinius Calvus was elected to the consular tribunate in 400; cf. Bronghton 1951–2, 1² for the respective years, and Pinsent 1975, 13f.
[34] Hölkeskamp 1987, 90–109 shows that the plebeians had to prevail again and again in every election, without the possibility of enforcing formal claims.
[35] For this see Bunse 1998, 213–18.   [36] Gell. 13.15.4.
[37] Bleicken 1981, 257–300; cf. also Linderski 1986, 2146–312, esp. 2177–180, and Linderski 1990, 34–48.
[38] Bleicken 1981, 262: "daß das *auspicium* alles das umfaßte, was staatliche Gewalt damals bedeutete bzw. was sich als solche ausdrücken ließ."
[39] Cf. the speech by App. Claudius Crassus in the year 368, Livy 6.41.4–8. On the *superbia* of the Claudii, cf. Wiseman 1979, 57–112.
[40] In Cic. *Att.* 9.9.3; 9.15.2 Cicero discusses Caesar's intention to let a praetor preside over the consular *comitia*. He, as an augur well informed in these matters, declines the plan because of the *imperium maius* of the consuls; cf. the analysis in Stewart 1998, 98f. Cicero had to consult some books (Cic. *Att.* 9, 9, 3), but only the *imperium* is decisive; *iisdem auspiciis* do not matter. Messala, augur for more than fifty-five years (Macrob. *Sat.* 1, 19, 14), also voiced a negative opinion according to Gellius (n. 36). There exists an analogy in an event of the year 217. After the battle of Lake Trasimene, one consul had died and his surviving colleague was far away from Rome. The senate decided to let the people elect a dictator and a *magister equitum*; Polyb. 3.87.6 and 9; Livy 22.8.5–7; Plut. *Fab.* 4.1; App.

beginning it simply relates to the authority every commander exercises over his troops, and it is not before the end of the fourth century that it becomes synonymous with Roman might and power. Still, it seems to be rather a term of special military authority, which eventually in later times led to a finer definition of distinctions between magistrates – while the authority in principle was based on *auspicia*.

This seems, however, to be an artificial construction, which does not reflect the real relationship between the consuls and the praetor. In Livy there are actually many examples that quite clearly show the equal rights of the magistracies. Thus it seems to me convincing that in 297 BC the two patricians and rival candidates for the consulship, Quintus Fabius Rullianus and Appius Claudius Caecus, did not wait for the assembly to decide between them, but rather made a compromise – that Appius should first become praetor and consul only a year later – without any hint that Appius would get something less desirable or less honorable as a praetor.[41]

Also, if one thinks of the military tasks accomplished by praetors from the Twelve Tables onwards and still later than 366 BC, it is not that easy to picture the praetorship as being mainly concerned with civil functions. Down to the outbreak of the Second Punic War, we count eight military praetorian *provinciae*.[42] Given the loss of Livy, it is obviously hard to suggest here a possible development in the third century. The often-mentioned fact, however, that the praetor acted only in the vicinity of Rome is less significant than one might think, because this is true for virtually everyone with *imperium* – at least until the beginning of the Third Samnite War, which is the last big conflict covered in Livy's first decade.

If one maintains the idea of three powerful magistrates possessing basically (or nearly) equal powers in the second half of the fourth century BC and the beginning of the third century BC, one should, of course, ask why one of them in later times became more and more responsible for the city of Rome and at the same time became subordinated to the other two magistrates. First, one should ask why one magistrate should stay in Rome at all. Regarding the conduct of war, one has to take into account that the so-called "military campaigns" of the period were mere raids. Given the distance and power of the enemies involved, the tradition of large-scale

---

Hann. 11 (= 48); Cass. Dio fr. 57.8. It must have been the *praetor urbanus* M. Aemilius who presided over the assembly. Livy calls the elected dictator Fabius Maximus only *pro dictatore*, an astonishing example of Livy's working method. He designs new structures and emergency regulations for events that run contrary to his perspective on Roman constitutional life; cf. also Lesiński 2002, 144f.
[41] Livy 10.22. For this election, cf. Rilinger 1976, 80 and Taylor 1966, 153 n. 21.
[42] Kunkel & Wittmann 1995, 296 n. 3.

wars and military operations is not to be believed. The alleged "Great War" against Veii was merely a ten-year-long conflict against a neighbor, just seventeen kilometers away from Rome.[43] A Roman army could arrive there within a day in order to steal some cattle or imprison some shepherds.[44] The same holds true, it seems, for the war against the Latins. The war against the Samnites, even the very beginning of it, was, however, quite different. Livy begins his narrative:

> Wars of greater magnitude, in respect both of the forces of our enemies and of the remoteness of their countries and the long periods of time involved, now fall to be related. For in that year [343] the sword was drawn against the Samnites, a people powerful in arms and in resources; and hard upon the Samnite war, which was waged with varying success, came war with Pyrrhus, and after that with the Carthaginians. How vast a series of events! How many times the extremity of danger was incurred, in order that our empire might be exalted to its present greatness, hardly to be maintained![45]

Unlike modern scholarship, ancient historiography draws no distinction between the wars against the Samnites, against the South Italians and, indeed, against Pyrrhus, but instead regards all of them as belonging to one epoch in Roman history.[46] It is important to note what Livy says not only about the new types of enemies but also – and even more importantly – about the now greater distances between the battlefields and the city of Rome, which led also, according to Livy, to a change in the conduct of war. The fact that a magistrate had to travel further away from home and stayed abroad for a longer period of time inevitably had consequences for the development of the Roman constitution. Alongside the invention of prorogation, it was the praetorship that underwent changes.

Since a magistrate in the field could no longer return to Rome quickly if necessary, the need became obvious for a magistrate with *imperium* to stay in Rome permanently. Thereby the praetorship became closely connected with a *provincia*, in this case the city and the surroundings of Rome. The importance of this development can hardly be overestimated. Since nearly every year both consuls left Rome in order to conduct war in distant places, the praetor was the only magistrate with *imperium* in Rome. He was the only one to summon the senate, to summon and preside over the

---

[43] Hantos 1997, 127–48.
[44] For warfare in the early Republic, cf. Versnel 1980, 97–150; Timpe 1990, 368–87; Versnel 1997, 177–200; Rawlings 1999, 97–127.
[45] Livy 7.29.1f. Trans. B. O. Foster, Loeb edition.
[46] Cf. the summary of scholarship in Cornell 2004, 115–21. For the development of Roman warfare at the end of the Samnite Wars, cf. Fronda 2006, 406f.

assemblies, and therefore he was also the only one – we are still ahead of the *lex Hortensia* of 287 – who could introduce a bill. He was probably the only one to receive embassies, although that seems to be of minor importance in the third century. In sum, the functions just mentioned gave him a unique position in the political hierarchy, and his position was most certainly not less important than that of the consuls.

This leads us to the question of why, during the course of the third century, the praetor gradually became subordinated to the consuls. From my point of view, this question cannot be answered by recourse to Roman constitutional law, but should rather be examined in relation to development of the consulship as well as in relation to Roman expansion during the third century. Even though this development surely was not monocausal, I would still like to highlight one aspect that from my point of view has been neglected by current research. In the course of expansion into Magna Graecia the Romans encountered exceedingly wealthy peoples; a fact that clearly gave booty and its material value a whole new significance.[47] This can be illustrated with a few brief examples.

After an armistice in 308, the Etruscans delivered to the Romans the pay for soldiers for a year and two tunics per soldier.[48] Similarly, the Hernici in 306 were able to negotiate an armistice through the payment of pay and corn for two months as well as one tunic per soldier.[49] So much for the significance of booty in the fourth century. Gains rose significantly during the height of the Samnite Wars as well as in the course of the battles against the Greek *poleis* in Magna Graecia. In 295, for instance, 1,740 Samnites were sold for 310 asses each, a total of 539,400 As.[50] As early as 293 BC the consul L. Papirius Cursor carried with him on his triumph in Rome 2,533,000 pieces of *aes grave* and 1,830 lb of silver.[51] There was only a small chance of capturing works of art like precious bronze. It was the talk of the town when Camillus reserved two bronze doors of the booty taken from Veii for himself and attached them to his house.[52]

Sixteen years later, in 380, the dictator T. Quinctius captured a statue of Iuppiter Imperator in Praeneste; he erected it on the Capitol.[53] Obviously the Romans did not take impressive amounts of booty in those days.[54]

---

[47] Cf. Harris 1979, 54–104.   [48] Livy 9.41.7.   [49] Livy 9.43.7.
[50] Livy 10.31.3f.   [51] Livy 10.46.3–6.
[52] Plut. *Cam.* 12.1; Plin. *HN* 34.13. It is said that Camillus was convicted for misappropriation of booty. It is more likely that the doors were removed from a temple, since it is not probable that even in rich Veii a private person could afford doors made of bronze for the entrance of his house. Removing them was a sacrilege, something the Romans never took lightly. But this assumption cannot be more than speculation due to our poor knowledge of the events.
[53] Livy 6.29.8–9.   [54] Cf. the compilation in McDonnell 2006b, 68–90.

This was to change when the republic expanded into Magna Graecia. Two statues of Alcibiades and Pythagoras were brought to the Forum, allegedly when the Delphic Oracle advised the Romans during the Samnite Wars to put up statues of the bravest and wisest Greeks in a busy place.[55] Pliny was wary of this explanation because he thought Socrates and Themistocles would have been the obvious choice. In fact, there must have been other reasons for the dedication of the statues. They may have been booty from the sack of Croton, a Greek city that was conquered by P. Cornelius Rufinus in 277.[56] Pythagoras spent some time in Croton,[57] so it seems plausible that the Romans learnt in this way of the great philosopher.[58] The conqueror of Croton was a few years later expelled from the senate – he possessed (or had bought)[59] ten pounds of silver.[60] And as we learn from Florus, following the conquest of the camp of King Pyrrhus in 275 BC, the people of Rome were able to catch a glimpse of gold and crimson, as well as various works of art and other treasures from Tarentum, during the triumph in Rome. The sheer amount of the booty from so many wealthy people was of such dimensions that the Romans could hardly believe the extent of their victory. A rather amused Florus notes that before this day the Romans had not been able to catch sight of anything except the cattle of the Volscians, the herds of the Sabines, the carriages of the Gauls and the broken weapons of the Samnites in their triumphs.[61]

If we now take a closer look at the allocation of offices at the end of the fourth and the beginning of the third century, we still meet men like M. Valerius Corvus, six times consul, Q. Publilius Philo, four times consul, L. Papirius Cursor, five times consul, or Q. Fabius Rullianus, five times consul. There is no sign in any of the sources that these permanent iterations led to any resistance. After the beginning of the profitable wars against Etruria and especially against Greek *poleis* in southern Italy, this situation quickly changed. Even though after the first half of the 290s multiple iterations were not uncommon, with the exception of the time of the Second Punic

---

[55] Plin. *HN* 34.26; Plut. *Num.* 8.20.21.   [56] Frontin. *Str.* 3.6.4; Zonar. 8.6.
[57] Pythagoras had fled to Croton from Samos when Polycrates established his tyranny there (Porph. *Pyth.* 9; Iambl. v. P. 88); the philosopher became famous in his new home city (Just. *Epit.* 20.4).
[58] Cf. Sehlmeyer 1999, 88–90.
[59] Hölkeskamp 1987, 147 n. 26 thinks this, not the pure possession, was the real reason for the removal.
[60] Dion. Hal. 20.13; Gell. 4.8; 17.21.39; Livy, *Per.* 14; Ov. *Fast.* 1.208; Plin. *HN* 18.39; 33.142; Plut. *Sull.* 1.1; Sen. *Vit. Beat.* 21.3; Val. Max. 2.9.4.
[61] Flor. 1.13.25–8: *et tanta de opulentissimis tot gentibus spolia, ut victoriam suam Roma non caperet. Nec enim temere ullus pulchrior in urbem aut speciosior triumphus intravit. Ante hunc diem nihil praeter pecora Volscorum, greges Sabinorum, carpenta Gallorum, fracta Samnitium arma vidisses; tum si captives aspiceres, Molossi, Thessali, Macedones, Bruttius, Apulus atque Lucanus; si pompam, aurum purpura signa tabula Tarentinaeque deliciae.*

War, there were never more than three consulships per person. Thus the possibility of election to four or even five consulships clearly was a thing of the past. Since this happened at the same time as the *lex Hortensia* was passed and the alleged reconciliation of the orders took place, it has been frequently explained as an increasing modulation of the appointment of offices, which was vital for the creation of a meritocracy.

More important than the discussion of Roman constitutional rules, however, is the fact that in these years war was waged against an enemy whose wealth exceeded by far that of any prior enemies. Henceforth, holding the consulship and doing it successfully could imply not only the *maximus honos* but also substantial material gain, exceeding by far the income of other aristocrats. This did not necessarily lead to further complications within the social hierarchy as was the case in the second and first century, but it certainly led to an obvious and considerable gain in prestige.

What did this development imply for the praetorship, the only magistracy with *imperium* that was very closely linked to Rome? Actually, its status did not change much. The praetorship continued to be a distinguished and prestigious office that – given the absence of the consuls – was politically the most important one in Rome. However, the consulship became more and more attractive: every successful battle, every glorious triumph back in Rome and, last but not least, the material wealth that could be earned in a campaign made the consulship more popular. I maintain therefore that there was no real subordination of the praetorship but an increase in the significance of the consulship. This was not problematic as long as only former consuls (*consulares*) took up the office of the praetor. But what if some ambitious *nobiles* were to climb up to the praetorship and then imagine themselves as having status equal to that of the consuls?

Sometimes we are lucky in our recorded history, so we indeed know of such a case: of the consuls of 242 BC, C. Lutatius Catulus and A. Postumius Albinus, the latter was forbidden to leave the city because of his religious duties as *flamen Martialis*. The election to the consulship of someone who had to observe these kinds of religious taboos may be surprising, but it is by no means totally unusual. Unique, however, is the role played by the praetor of that year, Q. Valerius Falto, who went abroad together with the other consul. It seems that his presence in Rome was no longer needed, since there was still one magistrate with *imperium* left: the consul and *flamen* Postumius Albinus. The senate and the praetor himself seem to have had this view; at least, there is no evidence to the contrary, which is an indication that the presence of one magistrate with *imperium* was regarded as sufficient – no matter whether he happened to be consul or praetor – since a functional specialization between these two offices had not yet come into existence.

When the consul Lutatius was injured during the battle of Drepanum, it was the praetor Valerius who won the decisive and strategically important naval victory around the Aegetes Islands that in the end forced the Carthaginians into peace negotiations with Rome. Back home, however, after this glorious victory, a dispute arose between the consul Lutatius and the praetor about who was to be given the right to celebrate a triumph. In this conflict the famous former consul Atilius Calatinus (according to Cicero the most distinguished citizen of his time)[62] acted as an arbitrator. We find the dialogue between Calatinus and the praetor Valerius in Valerius Maximus:

"Tell me, Valerius, if you two had disagreed as to whether battle should be joined or not, taking opposite views, which would have counted more, the Consul's orders or the Praetor's?" Valerius replied that he was not disputing that the Consul would have taken precedence. "Next now," said Calatinus, "since I have taken it upon me to adjudicate between you about command and auspices and you acknowledge that your opponent was superior in both, I can have no further doubts. Therefore, Lutatius, though you have said nothing so far, I give judgement in your favour." All credit is given to the judge for not letting time be wasted in a clear case. More commendations are given to Lutatius for stoutly defending the rights of the highest authority. But no blame is placed upon Valerius for seeking a reward for a gallant and successful action, not undeserved though not legally due.[63]

In my view, this clear and seemingly unambiguous decision is striking. The relationship, or more precisely the hierarchy among the military commanders, simply cannot have been so easily determined, otherwise the very discussion (as well as any arbitration) would not have been necessary. It is also interesting to see what Valerius Maximus does not tell us. Only one day later, the praetor celebrated a triumph of his own *ex Sicilia navalem*.[64] Leaving out this detail, Valerius Maximus' argument about a clear hierarchy between the consul and the praetor seems to be overdone.

Even if one doubts the exact wording in this episode, it does give us some indication as to how the Roman political system worked: different

---

[62] Cic. *Pis.* 14; *Planc.* 60; *Tusc.* 1.110; *Nat. D.* 2.165; *Rep.* 1.1; *Leg. agr.* 2.64.
[63] Val. Max. 2.8.2. Trans. D. L. Shackleton Bailey, Loeb edition.
[64] *Inscr. Ital.* XIII, 1.22: Q. *Valerius Q. f. P. n. Falto pro pr(aetore) a* DXII *es Sicilia navalem prid. non. Oct.* Itgenshorst 2005 and Engels 2001, 139–69, here p. 160f, emphasize the strong link to the time of Valerius Maximus. Octavian too was sick during Actium, and it was Agrippa who actually commanded the fleet. But Octavian counted the battle as his victory when celebrating three triumphs in 29.

The development of the praetorship 73

developments lead to a process of growing functional specialization by which in the end the two offices are distinguished from each other. When a conflict of hierarchy arises, an informal but respected judge makes a decision, which is accepted at least by the following generation. From then on, the one praetor remains *collega consulis*, but with inferior prestige. As Hans Beck put it colorfully: "ein Orbital, das um das Konsulat kreiste."[65]

This clearly problematic situation had to be brought to an end by the Romans sooner or later. In a fragment of the author Censorinus (from the third century AD) we find that a *lex Plaetoria* conferred upon the *praetor urbanus* the jurisdiction between citizens.[66] This information is hard to date. Censorinus wrote a small book in AD 238 about different ways of reckoning time and dedicated to his patron, a certain Caerellius. In the passage cited he speaks about the divisions of the day: the so-called *suprema*,[67] which from the Twelve Tables[68] on defined sunset as the end of the day, was changed by a *lex Plaetoria*. Up to this year, an *accensus consulum* announced the end of the day. From now on the praetor ordered two of his lictors to make this announcement and end any public business for the day.[69] Pliny says the former routine was maintained until the First Punic War.[70] Censorinus casually mentions that the *lex Plaetoria* also conferred the jurisdiction *inter cives* upon the praetor. This is a hint that Censorinus' source had more to say about the tasks of the praetor, but unfortunately Censorinus abbreviated this information as irrelevant to the divisions of the day.[71]

---

[65] Beck 2005, 64.
[66] Cens. 24.3: *sed postea M. Plaetorius tribunus plebiscitum tulit, in quo scriptum est: praetor urbanus, qui nunc est quique posthac fuat, duo lictores apud se habeto isque <usque> supremam ad solem occasum ius inter cives dicito*. On these old names for the times of day, cf. Macrob. *Sat.* 1.3.12–16.
[67] On *suprema*, Varro, *Ling.* 6.5: *Supremum summum diei, id ab superrimo. Hoc tempus XII Tabulae dicunt occasum esse solis; sed postea lex Plaetoria id quoque tempus esse iubet supremum quo praetor in Comitio supremam pronuntiavit populo.*
[68] Twelve Tables 1.6 (Gell. 17.2.10): *Sole, inquit, occaso. Sole occaso non insuavi vetustate est, si quis aurem habeat non sordidam nec proculcatam; in duodecim autem tabulis verbum hoc ita scriptum est: "ante meridiem causam coniciunt <o>; {c}<t>um perorant<o> ambo praesentes, post meridiem praesenti litem addicito, si ambo praesentes, sol occasus suprema tempestas esto."*
[69] For the authenticity of the two lictors, cf. the dialogue of the slaves in Plaut. *Epid*. 25. The *praetor urbanus* was always accompanied by two lictors even in the late republic; cf. Cic. *Leg. agr.* 2.34.93.
[70] Plin. *Nat.* 7.212: *XII tabulis ortus tantum et occasus nominantur, post aliquot annos adiectus est et meridies, accenso consulum id pronuntiante, cum a curia inter Rostra et Graecostasin prospexisset solem; a columna Maenia ad carcerem inclinato sidere supremam pronuntiavit, sed hoc serenis tantum diebus, usque ad primum Punicum bellum.* For the *graecostasis* see Varro, *Ling.* 5.155; Cic. *Q Fr.* 2.1; Plin. *HN* 7.212; *LTUR* II, S. 373. For the location of the *columna Maenia* and of the other buildings cf. *LTUR* I, fig. 182.
[71] Mommsen 1887–8, I, 384 n. 2; Broughton, 1951–86, II, 472; Meyer 1961, 510 n. 23; Kunkel & Wittmann, 1995, 121 n. 67; Crawford, 1996b, II, 731–3; Elster 2003, 159 n. 71.

It would thus be possible to assume that the last part of Censorinus' sentence could have included a description of the duties attributed to the *praetor peregrinus*.[72] With the *lex Plaetoria* the jurisdiction would have been assigned for the first time to the praetors.[73]

To summarize: the creation of three chief magistracies in 367 did not, in my view, enforce any hierarchy between them. According to augural law all three of them were colleagues. Similarly, the annalistic tradition does not indicate an internal distinction between them. And indeed, no conflicts arose between them in their various military activities. With the beginning of Roman expansion, however, in the third century BC, things began to change. The conduct of war far away from Rome made the permanent presence of at least one magistrate with *imperium* in Rome necessary. But the growing amount of booty in the wars against the Greeks raised the prestige of the army leaders, whereas the magistracies back home became less important or at least less visible in the political process and therefore less desirable as positions. This whole development led eventually to a conflict – solved in an informal agreement, which became an *exemplum* for later times. From then on, new duties and responsibilities were specified by laws that would not interfere with the hierarchy between the magistrates but that would simply try to avoid possible conflicts: *praetor non collega consulis est*.

---

[72] Elster 2003, 161.
[73] Kunkel & Wittmann 1995, 326 suggests this. In this way, during a military crisis both *provinciae* could indeed be ascribed to one person. This happened in the year 213, when the *praetor urbanus* M. Atilius took over the responsibilities of the *praetor peregrinus* M. Aemilius, who was entrusted with the command of the two legions near Luceria (Livy 24.44.2f.). Particularly interesting is the fact that the absence of one praetor did not imply the automatic transfer of his *provincia* to his colleague. The unification of both spheres of activity under a single magistrate illustrates the extent to which the collegiality of the praetorship, understood as mutual control, was in fact not so relevant; in this regard see Bunse 2002b.

PART II
Powers and functions of the consulship

CHAPTER 4

Consular power and the Roman constitution: the case of imperium *reconsidered*

Hans Beck

"Why was it," Plutarch asks in *Roman Questions* no. 80, "that when [the Romans] gave a public banquet for men who had celebrated a triumph, they formally invited the consuls and then sent word to them requesting that they not come to the dinner?" It was "because it was imperative that the place of honor at the table and an escort home after dinner should be assigned to the man who had triumphed. But these honors can be given to no one else when the consuls are present, but only to them."[1] Plutarch's *Roman Questions* are a hotchpotch of distinct cultural practices and traditional codes of behavior. Throughout long sections of the work, it appears to be a random collection of curiosities rather than a treatise that is geared toward a stringent analysis of typically Roman customs and socio-political institutions. But this does not undermine the work's value as a historical source.[2] Beyond the actual information related (sparse as it may be, at times), the *Roman Questions* shed light on the silent assumptions of Roman political life. In his attempt to familiarize his readership with select political or social practices, Plutarch alludes to the very basic implications of those practices.[3] Question no. 80 illustrates the case: the practice of inviting consuls to triumphal banquets and then telling them not to come appeared to be a peculiarity and hence was deemed worthy of relating. But it also discloses some of the most vital features of Roman political culture. It operates on the assumption that the consuls were the highest magistrates

---

Project "Consuls, Consulars and the Government of the Roman Republic" (HUM2004–02449 and HUM2007–60776/HIST) funded by Ministerio Educación y Ciencia, Gobierno de España. *FRH* = Beck & Walter 2005/2004; *MRR*= Broughton 1951–86.

[1] Plut. *Quaest. Rom.* 80 = *Mor.* 283a.
[2] A systematic study would be worth the effort. For a first introduction, see Boulogne 1992.
[3] See, most eminently, *Quaest. Rom.* 27 (inviolability of the city wall); 43 (procedures regarding foreign ambassadors); 58 (addressing some senators as conscript fathers); 63 (restrictions for the *rex sacrorum*); 79 (bones of triumphators); 81 (tribunes' dress); 82 (lictors' rods); 91 (banishing patrician homes from the Capitoline); 98 (taking office of censor); 113 (*flamines*' privileges as consolation for exclusion from public office-holding).

not only in the field (*militiae*) but also at home, within the sacred boundary of the city (*domi*). Whenever present, they were to be included in public events and preside over them. Moreover, while the consuls claimed the right of highest honor, the story makes it clear that there were other distinctions, such as a triumphator's rights and privileges, which under certain circumstances challenged the superior power of a consul, whether present or not.[4] And third, Plutarch reveals that if such a conflict between authorities arose, the Romans were not shy about practical solutions that enabled them to navigate around the provisions of their constitution without actually abandoning it. The messenger sent to the consuls was a go-between that kept everyone's honor intact – at least as long as everybody played along.

The main distinction of a consul who occupied the *maximus honos*, the highest honor and office, was his *imperium*. Not only did the consular *imperium*, or "command," outrank that of other magistrates *cum imperio* ("with imperial command"), but its inherent capacities provided its holder with far-reaching, if not unlimited, competences that governed the exercise of communal power at home and abroad. It encompassed both civil magisterial capacities and the military command, although the latter was not transferred automatically; it required the ratification of a *lex curiata de imperio* to grant it solemnly to the consul when he entered office.[5] *Imperium*-holders were empowered "to investigate, to punish, to administer justice, and to make (legal) decisions." This is only an abridged extract of their competences as attested in the famous pirate law from Cnidus that dates toward the end of the second century BC.[6] To be sure, in the civil sphere or *domi*, the functions of a consul were subject to public law and performed in conjunction with the senate as well as the people's assemblies.

---

[4] The various privileges of triumphators are assembled by Itgenshorst 2005; cf. also Beard 2007. Gaius Duilius (cos. triumph. 260) was granted the right to be guarded by a band of flute-players and torch-bearers every time he attended a banquet: *Inscr. Ital.* 13.3.13 = *CIL* I² 193 no. 11 = VI.8.3 40952; cf. also Livy, *Per.* 17; Cic. *Sen.* 44; Flor. 1.18.10; Val. Max. 3.6.4; Sil. *Pun.* 6.667. This symbolic perpetuation of his famous naval triumph may well have been in contradiction of the consuls' exclusive right to an escort.

[5] Both the procedure of passing a curiate law and its precise provisions are notoriously debated. The practice was believed to constitute one of the oldest legally binding decisions by the nebulous curiate assembly, but the contents can hardly be deduced from later sources, e.g. Cic. *Leg. agr.* 2.30–1; *Rep.* 2.25; Livy 1.17.8–9. Kunkel & Wittmann 1995, 96–103 offers a good summary of the debate and highlights what Kunkel asserts as "das einigermaßen Sichere" (97); cf. also Mommsen 1887–8, I, 609–15; Bleicken 1981, 15–21; Lintott 1999b, 28–9 and *passim*. The notion of imperial power at home, within the sacred boundary of the city (see below), has recently been challenged by Drogula 2007, who argues that *imperium*, under normal circumstances, did not exist within the *pomerium*, "but rather that it was a strictly extra-mural military power" (419). I find this general conclusion unconvincing, but it should be acknowledged that Drogula's argument is too refined to be dismissed with a single stroke of the pencil. The issue is open for future consideration.

[6] Crawford 1996b, I, no. 12, Cn. IV, lines 31–9.

For instance, in the third and second centuries a set of *leges* was (re-)enacted that banned the capital punishment of a Roman citizen without prior reference to the people's assembly (*provocatio*).[7] These and other provisions were antithetic to a consul's *imperium* because they restricted his power to prosecute citizens.[8] As a consequence, the balance between *provocatio* and *imperium* became characteristic of Roman politics, with a certain privilege of the former over the latter, especially in the realm of *domi*. Yet this did not undermine the consul's authority as supreme magistrate, or prevent him from coercing citizens or conducting public inquiries (*quaestiones*) that might eventually lead to capital punishment in the civil sphere.[9] The consuls held the highest magistracy and honor. Attempts to curb their power by means of law and public resolutions may indicate a growing self-confidence on the part of the common people; however, at the same time these attempts attest to the extensive and pre-eminent power vested in the office with *summum imperium*.

Again, *imperium* denotes a higher magistrate's power at home and in the field. Long ago Theodor Mommsen suggested that it also embodied a theological underpinning that placed it at the very center of Roman politics. Mommsen's views on *imperium* have been rebutted in more recent scholarship, but few can deny that his assessment continues to have a great influence upon modern conceptualizations. Therefore, despite the many objections, it is worthwhile to revisit what has famously been called his "theology of *imperium*."[10] Mommsen argued that *imperium* and public auspices (*auspicia publica*) expressed one and the same idea from different points of view, namely that the political power of the highest magistrates was complemented by their religious competence to request and observe the signs of the gods.[11] Both *imperium* and *auspicium* were thought to

---

[7] Livy relates a so-called *lex Valeria de provocatione* under the year 300 (10.9.3–6 = Elster 2003, no. 45; Bauman 1973a), whose contents are identical with a provocation law mentioned in Cic. *Rep.* 2.53 from 509. Cicero's evidence, in turn, resembles Livy's evidence for a *lex Porcia de provocatione* from *c.* 195 (Elster 2003, no. 142). The tradition is highly charged, since the very principle of provocation laws was considered to be the ideological flagship of Roman liberty (which partly explains why it is such a mess), e.g. Cic. *De or.* 2.199: *provocationem, patronam illam civitatis ac vindicem libertatis*. The impact on Roman political culture has now been demonstrated by Jehne 2002, but Bleicken 1959, Martin 1970 and Lintott 1972 remain fundamental.

[8] Most eminently, the so-called *lex Porciae*. Whereas the *leges Valeriae* applied to the realm *domi* up to the first mile around the *pomerium*, the Porcian laws extended the principle into the field (*militiae*), which implied a restriction on flogging or killing (*verberare aut necare*: Livy 10.9.4) a Roman soldier. See Elster 2003, no. 142 (comm.); Brennan 2004, 37–8; cf. Daubner (2007).

[9] Kunkel & Wittmann 1995, 143–5.   [10] Brennan 2004, 36.

[11] Mommsen 1887–8, I, 76; cf. I, 90: "Daher sind Zeichenschau und Beamtengewalt, auspicium und imperium nichts anderes als Bezeichnungen desselben Begriffs nach verschiedenen Seiten, jene des himmlischen, diese des irdischen Verkehrs."

have derived from the regal period, which, by implication, made the early republican exercise of *imperium* a quasi-regal power. Vested in a republican magistrate, it embodied the supreme authority of the new community.[12] *Imperium* and *auspicium* thus appeared as ideological presumptions that provided order and meaning to the Roman constitution.[13] More than that, they prefigured later constitutional changes and modifications. According to Mommsen, the increase in magistracies with distinct competences (for instance provincial praetorships, on which see below) was a redistribution into small parcels of an originally unique authority.[14] Although the multiplication of magistracies appears as a dilution of the quality of *imperium*, it is important to note that its universality was actually reinforced by such an increase, since *imperium* effectively evolved from a holistic regal power to a recognized point of reference that determined the hierarchy of the republic's political institutions.[15] Thus, in Mommsen's systematization, *imperium* interconnects and structures the various branches of the Roman constitution and society.

The most profound reassessment of this doctrine as laid out above came from Jochen Bleicken.[16] Interestingly enough, Bleicken's analysis culminated in conclusions that turned Mommsen's model upside down. For Bleicken conceived of early republican *imperium* as a purely military command. As the republic grew, so did its need to regulate the relations between its citizens and, more generally, to govern its affairs at home and abroad.[17] The vexed process of state formation and stratification of power further instigated institutional changes; they required the creation of new offices and domains – legal, judicial, administrative – some of which did and some of which did not necessarily embrace *imperium*. According to Bleicken, the various profiles of public offices with or without *imperium* thus did not derive from the regal period. Instead, they resulted from the diversification of state action. Only in the late republic did the *imperium* of a consul denote the unity of his military and civil power, the so-called

---

[12] Mommsen 1887–8, I, 10, 22–3; II.1, 14–17.
[13] It will become clear to the reader, I think, that I use the term more or less in a Polybian sense, emphasizing the processual development of the constitution and its potential to govern the conduct of politics between traditional norms and legal practices.
[14] Mommsen 1887–8, II.1, 93; cf. also Mommsen 1902, 310: "Der dem ursprünglichen römischen Staatsrecht mit dem Begriff des Oberamts unvereinbar erscheinende Begriff der begrenzten Beamtengewalt oder der Kompetenz brach allmählich sich Bahn und zerfetzte und zerstörte den älteren des einen und unteilbaren Imperium."
[15] Mommsen 1887–1888, I, 25; cf. I, 7 on the systematization of Mommsen's approach.
[16] Bleicken 1981; cf. also Bleicken 1967 and 1975, 115–21.
[17] Bleicken 1981, 33–40, which draws heavily on Heuss 1944.

total *imperium*.¹⁸ However this too was a response to gradual development, since it was triggered by the persistent expansion of the republic and the growing power of its commanders in the field.

To structure the dependency of magistracies and determine their hierarchy, the senate drew on the principle of *potestas* ("power" or "faculty"), which defined the authority of a public office in relation to other offices: magistrates would take on a *maior potestas* (e.g. the aedileship being *maior* to the quaestorship), a *par potestas* (two consuls with the same power), or a *minor potestas* (the power distributed from the bottom to the top).¹⁹ Accordingly, Bleicken noted that public offices were conceived of in relational rather than absolute terms, with *potestas* serving as a measuring stick that indicated the competences, and limitations, of each office's powers. While holding the highest office, the *imperium* of a consul was subject to the same principle of stratification as that of a praetor. In Bleicken's view, this process did not correspond to a gradual carving up of unique (regal) authority, but rather was related to Roman state formation and its dynamics of institutional diversification.²⁰

Therefore despite its lasting conception as executive power, the capacity of a magistrate *cum imperio* (consul, praetor, dictator and *magister equitum*) underwent profound changes. These include the development of the magistracies themselves, in both numbers and competences; the growing implementation both of universal and of extraordinary commands, which in turn contributed to inherent tensions between the commands of *imperium*-holders; and, as the republic expanded from city-state to Mediterranean empire, the changing perceptions of the space in which *imperium* was exercised. As mentioned before, the impact of any of these on the nature of imperial power is explained differently: previous scholarship presents *imperium* either as a partially reallocated command that derived from an originally unique authority or, alternatively, as one that expanded over time. As the complexity of state action grew, so did *imperium*. These approaches are incompatible, but it is noteworthy that they share the same belief in *imperium* as a normative force that lies at the very heart of Roman republican institutions. Indeed, this is how the writers of the first century BC and the early imperial period describe it, when they praise the incontestability of *imperium* and its lasting nature from the era of the kings to their own time: *imperium*, "without which no military affair can be

---

¹⁸ Cf. Heuss 1982, who forcefully rebutted Mommsen's concept of a total *imperium* under the kings.
¹⁹ Bleicken 1981, 24–33. ²⁰ Bleicken 1981, 41–2.

administered, no army held together, no war waged."[21] Such notions notoriously raise suspicions, even more so when time-honored traditions are invoked. As far as I can see, the idea of an inherent normative force of *imperium* has never been questioned in modern scholarship. However, in light of more recent discoveries that highlight the great degree of fluidity and change in Roman politics, it may well be noteworthy to consider whether the starting assumption that *imperium* is the decisive normative force in Roman politics is indeed viable. Rather than subscribing to a normative perception, the following sections focus on the developments, changes and turning points in the history of imperial command. The various areas of change are closely intertwined, but it is best to examine them separately. The goal is, it is hoped, to disclose the impact of these changes on the republican concept of *imperium* and its very nature.

THE NUMBERS GAME

Little is known about the nature of the republic's executive prior to the inauguration of the consular constitution, most likely in 367/6 BC. Now this does not mean that the picture is altogether clear once "one of the consuls was elected from the ordinary people," as Fabius Pictor put it in a celebrated fragment of his work.[22] Fabius' reference to the *leges Liciniae Sextiae* implies that, beginning in 367/6, plebeians were admitted to the consulate as of that year. But there is reason to believe that this measure was accompanied by a more profound reshaping of the higher stratum of offices. In the course of this, the higher magistracies seem to have been modeled along the lines of a triangular executive. From now on, *imperium* was assigned to the executive of two consuls and one praetor, whose powers were closely interconnected.[23] While the praetor was subordinate to the consuls in the sense that he was outranked by the consular *imperium*, his general claim to *imperium* made him *collega consulis*, imperfect as this collegiality may have been.[24] The collegiality between both magistracies was also reflected by

---

[21] Cic. *Phil.* 5.16: *sine quo res militaris administrari, teneri exercitus, bellum geri non potest*; cf. also references to the sovereignty (*maiestas*) of the Roman state, which phrase this in terms of the *imperium populi Romani*: e.g. Cic. *Font.* 1; or. 30.

[22] *FRH* 1 F 23: *Quapropter tum primum ex plebe alter consul factus est duo et vicesimo anno post Romam Galli ceperunt.*

[23] This is admittedly an orthodox view on what happened in or around 367, which was already established by Wilhelm Ihne in 1847. I find this the most plausible scenario. Cf. also the paper by Christopher Smith in this volume.

[24] Messalla in Gell. 13.15.4: *imperium minus*. Cf. Lintott 1999b, 107; Brennan 2000, 1, 58–69; Masi Doria 2000; Bunse 2002b.

their appointment *iisdem auspiciis*, under the same auspices, in the course of one and the same voting assembly.[25] This triangular arrangement remained in place for 120 years or so; at least, this is what the political arithmetic implies, since a new praetorship was only added *c.* 244 (see below). What the numbers do not reveal is that, despite the seemingly stable arrangement, the institutional hierarchy between these offices was by no means written in stone. The few cases that attest to the actions of praetors in the period prior to the First Punic War indicate that the praetorship was held either before or, more frequently, only after its incumbents had already served as consuls.[26] Hence, the office of praetor may best be described as *honos* that revolved around the consulate.[27] Equipped with full military command and the power to give specific orders, the praetor complemented the *imperium* of the consuls. Often highly decorated generals who had already held a successful consulship were elected to the post of praetor, which again points to a close collaboration, and in fact complementation, of the *imperia* of consuls and praetors.

This chapter in the history of offices with military command came to an abrupt end toward the conclusion of the First Punic War. Around 244, a second praetorship was established that profoundly altered the picture.[28] It has been noted that this first increase in the number of offices *cum imperio* came from the increasing need for commanders to fight independently at different military fronts in the war with Carthage.[29] This explanation deserves consideration since it accounts for the role of the new praetorship as an office with full military authority. But the extension also seems to have induced an institutional separation of two distinct types of praetorships, the *praetor urbanus* and a so-called *praetor peregrinus* (the designation for the latter stems from a later period), whose powers were characterized mostly by judicial rather than military competences. Such a separation was most likely motivated by the growing requirements of state action, but in this case it is difficult to see why a magistrate confined to the affairs between foreigners at Rome would be vested with military authority. Perhaps the

---

[25] Livy 8.32.3; Gell. 13.15.6; cf. Stewart 1998, 182–3.
[26] See the relevant section in the *Fasti Praetorii* compiled by Brennan 2000, I, App. B, with the modifications by Beck 2005, 65. From the end of the Third Samnite War to the end of the First Punic War, only a handful of praetors are attested by name. With the exception of one (Q. Valerius Falto, pr. 242, cos. 239), the praetorship postdates the consulate in that era: L. Caecilius Metellus, cos. 284, pr. 283; M'. Curius Dentatus, cos. I 290, pr. 283; C. Genucius Clepsina, cos. I 276, pr. 273; A. Atilius Caiatinus, cos. I 258, pr. 257; L. Postumius Megellus, cos. 262, pr. 253.
[27] Cf. Beck 2005, 64.
[28] Livy, *Per.* 19; Lydus *Mag.* 1.38; Pompon. *Dig.* 1.2.2.28. Cf. Lintott 1999b, 107; Brennan 2000, I, 85–9; Bunse 2002b, 30–1.
[29] Cf. Brennan 2000, I, 85–9; Serrati 2000.

motives of responding to military demands and of state action at home were not mutually exclusive.³⁰ The most prominent implication of the addition of a new *imperium*-holder was, however, the change it fostered in the traditional three-tier structure of the republic's executive. For the measure almost certainly disconnected the praetorship from the consulate, since it effectively bolstered a new office, the competences and duties of which were separated from those of the consuls. Confining praetors to areas of authority that were explicitly urban, peregrine, judicial or the like, the measure formulated implicit limitations that governed the exercise of their command.³¹

It is not surprising that the motion to add a second praetorship had an immediate impact on the patterns of office-holding. The prosopographical information available is scarce, but from the little that has survived it is possible to extrapolate a new *cursus* pattern after c. 244. For once the new position was added and none of the known praetors had served as consuls before entering office. No consul seems to have run for the office of praetor after the introduction of the second post.³² It has been suggested that this may have been due to a provision that the praetorship henceforth should become a step on the career path to the consulate.³³ But it is worth remembering that such a regulation would actually not have prevented consulars from (re-)running for the praetorship. The reason why they did not must have had something to do with the outlined downgrading of a praetor's *imperium*. The measure clearly made the authority of praetors inferior to that of the consuls, which, in turn, made the office less attractive for candidates who had already held the consulate. Under such circumstances, the *honos* of a consular may well have been reduced, if not harmed, by a praetorship that followed after his consulship. As a consequence, the gap between consuls and praetors widened significantly; the link between their *imperia* vanished. The measure of c. 244 can thus be understood as the moment of birth, as it were, of the *cursus honorum*, with its well-defined sequence of offices *cum imperio*, clear provisions for career advancement, and the hierarchization of the social prestige that was associated with these

---

³⁰ Brennan 2004, 39–40; Beck 2005, 35–6.
³¹ On this, cf. the more detailed discussion in Beck 2005, 63–7.
³² With the exception of the Hannibalic War, this holds true for the history of the praetorship from c. 244 through to the fall of the republic. Cf. Brennan 2000, 1, 94; Beck 2005, 67.
³³ The career pattern may have become compulsory only in 196. For the aftermath of the Hannibalic War, several consuls with no previous praetorship are attested: L. Cornelius Lentulus, aed. cur. 205, procos. 205–200, cos. 199; Sex. Aelius Paetus, aed. cur. 200, cos. 198; T. Quinctius Flamininus, propr. 205–202 (?), cos. 198; C. Cornelius Cethegus, procos. 201–200, aed. cur. 199, cos. 197.

magistracies. It was induced when a new post with *imperium* was added that altered the traditional triangular executive.

Less than two decades later, most likely in 227, the number of praetors was once again increased. After the recovery of Sicily and Sardinia in the aftermath of the First Punic War, two positions were added, which made for a total of four.[34] Only one generation later, the year 197 witnessed yet another increase, when the praetorship grew from four to six posts.[35] Now this increase in the number of offices with *imperium* no doubt corresponded to the foreign expansion of the republic and its need to assign generals with military command to conquered territories. It is easy to calculate the numbers: note that the praetorship increased sixfold in only two generations. But it is not quite so easy to grasp how this accelerated change affected the exercise of *imperium*. For one thing, the development of conquered territories that evolved from vague areas where a magistrate exercised military command to domains with fixed borders subject to the authority of an annual praetor significantly altered the Roman perception of space and power. The concept of *imperium*, too, was affected by this development (see below). Second, the growing number of new, geographically restricted offices *cum imperio* helped to structure the relation between the higher magistracies and their inherent *potestates*. For the increase of praetorships clearly widened the gap between the authority of consuls and that of praetors. Of the four annual praetors after 227 (six after 197) only two were able to rise to the consulate. In light of the new arithmetic, their office had become more remote from the *maximus honos* than in the earlier decades of the third century.[36]

At the same time, the relations between praetors grew increasingly complex. When Macedonia and Africa were organized as provinces in 146, the senate refrained from creating additional praetorships. This decision served not to aggravate the already fierce competition among praetors for the consulate,[37] but it also made it impossible for all provinces to be governed by annual magistrates. Consequently, the patchwork of praetorian *imperia* grew to an even greater extent: some praetors held an *imperium* that was confined to a certain province (but not all provinces were covered by this procedure). Others functioned, in the absence of the consul, as chief

---

[34] Solin. 5.1; cf. Livy, *Per.* 20. Cf. Brennan 2000, 1, 91–9 and n. 97 on the date; Kunkel & Wittmann 1995, 297–8; Lintott 1999b, 107; Bunse 2002b, 33; Beck 2005, 35.

[35] Cf. n. 34.

[36] The number long remained at six, but when Sulla increased it to eight in 81 (Vell. Pat. 2.89.3; cf. Cic. *Mil.* 39 with *Att.* 4.1.6; *Pis.* 35; Brennan 2000, 1, 391), the gap widened again. The ultimate disconnect came with sixteen praetors under Caesar.

[37] Cf. Beck 2005, 36 and 55–7.

magistrates at Rome and were, as such, in charge of the legal administration. Yet if necessary both the urban and peregrine praetors were dispatched at the head of an army and, hence, could make free use of their power during military campaigns, a privilege that could easily lead them to provinces that were left unassigned. This variety of assignments makes it evident that the *imperium* of praetors lacked a clear frame of reference. The one shared quality was that they were elected in the same centuriate assembly as the consuls. As magistrates with *imperium* they were entitled to certain *potestates* – anything from military to civil and judicial commands, be they at home or abroad – as well as to corresponding symbols of power.[38] Furthermore, from the early second century, their office provided them with the legal prerequisite to run for the consulship.[39] Beyond this distinction, it is hardly justified to speak of a uniform exercise of praetorian *imperium*.

Before returning to the *imperium* of the consuls, it should be noted that this fragmentation of praetorian assignments also had an impact on the cohesion of their *collegium* in general. In the later republic, praetors never used their *imperium* to veto the action of their colleagues, not even in the domain of civil law. If a praetor's decision was met with resistance, litigants appealed to a tribune of the plebs or sometimes a consul, and not to another praetor. This, too, indicates that praetors hardly ever developed an *esprit de corps* among their college, nor was there a monolithic praetorian *imperium* that governed their command.[40]

MORE DISTORTIONS

The consular *imperium* underwent a different development. It is a truism to note that the political arithmetic never changed, even after the office itself had lost its most profound defining qualities. But this does not mean that relations between holders of the *maximum imperium* were static, nor were they easy. In fact, Roman tradition is loaded with stories that relate conflicts and at times clashes between consuls over strategies, the use of spoils or the claim to victory. The use of collegial intercessions here, too,

---

[38] E.g. the *toga praetexta* as well as the *sella curulis* as official insignia, and six lictors (two for civil jurisdiction): Kunkel & Wittmann 1995, 120–1.

[39] As of 196: Astin 1958, 27; Brennan 2000, I, 168–9.

[40] Note, however, the notorious case of 67, when the college of praetors caused a work slowdown for almost their entire term of office after one of the consuls had smashed a praetor's ceremonial chair for not rising in his presence: Cass. Dio 6.41.1–2. This indicates some group solidarity, but the incident is too short-lived to alter the general picture. See also Brennan 2004, 42–4, who discusses the lack of evidence for intra-collegial obstruction.

was rare,[41] but there were many ways, to be sure, to bother a colleague. Since consuls exercised a *par potestas* and since a strict collegiality was applied, the use of consular *imperium* was vulnerable to distinctly uncollegial behavior.[42] So whereas the *maximus honos* clearly implied a *maximum imperium*, the actual power grid was more complex. This, too, fascinated Roman writers, who eagerly embarked on long-winded discourses on the powers vested in a consul and the areas where these might be contested. A well-known incident was reported by Claudius Quadrigarius and several authorities after him. When the consul of 213, Quintus Fabius Maximus, arrived at the Roman camp in Apulia, there he unexpectedly met his father, the renowned Fabius Maximus "Cunctator," cos. IV in 214 and now proconsul. Since neither made a move to dismount from his horse, the consul asked the proconsul: *quid postea*, "what thereafter?" ("so what now?" or maybe in a more pressing sense of "what arrogation comes next?"). The latter dismounted immediately and praised his son for maintaining the "*imperium*, which belonged to the people (*quod populi esset*)."[43]

The episode is widely cited to illustrate the inherent contradiction between *imperium* and *patria potestas*.[44] While, from the perspective of private law, Fabius son was under the jurisdiction of Fabius father (and, hence, obliged to pay him respect and dismount from his horse), the son held the *maximum imperium*, which embodied the *maiestas populi Romani*, the sovereignty of the Roman people. Praising his son and his defense of time-honored hierarchies, Fabius the elder acknowledged the superiority of *imperium* over his own *potestas* as father. The episode served to celebrate the incontestability of consular *imperium*. As such, it was a powerful reminder that the consular power symbolized the ultimate *maiestas* at Rome.

Roman exemplary accounts are often dubious, and this story is no exception. For under certain circumstances even a consul's *imperium* was subject to subordination. For instance, when a dictator was appointed during a state of emergency, the supreme power of his office placed him above the consuls – if their powers were not annulled altogether. This is also true for the *magister equitum*, who outranked the consuls. Since the dictator was

---

[41] See Kunkel & Wittmann 1995, 209 with n. 381. Roman tradition stresses the principle of collegial intercession between consuls, especially with regard to the early republic (Livy 2.18.8; 2.27.2; 3.36.6), but authentic examples are virtually non-existent. Cf. also de Libero 1992, 29–48.
[42] Mommsen 1887–8, I, 27–36, who sees an inherent contradiction between collegiality and *imperium*.
[43] Claudius Quadrigarius *FRH* 14 F 56, from Gell. 2.2.13; cf. Val. Max. 2.2.4a–b; Livy 24.44.9–10; Plut. *Fab.* 24. For an exhaustive discussion and much bibliography, see Masi Doria 2000, 240–1 and *passim*.
[44] Kunkel & Wittmann 1995, 571; Masi Doria 2000; cf. Lacey 1986, 130–2.

usually nominated by an *imperium*-holder following the senate's authorization, it was understood that consuls restrained themselves and limited their power by giving way to an extraordinary commander-in-chief.[45] But the episode of the Fabii invites more, and more profound, criticism. By the time of Claudius Quadrigarius' writing, in the late republic, the concept of *imperium* had significantly changed. This was mostly due to the creation of proconsular and propraetorian commands respectively, which soon added their own facet to an increasingly colorful mosaic of *imperium*. A brief sketch of the history of those powers is in order.

As early as the Samnite Wars, the senate began prolonging the military power of commanders so that they would not be removed from the battlefield toward the end of their term. The impulse was a practical one – that is, the removal of experienced generals in the midst of an ongoing campaign posed a significant disadvantage to the Roman forces – and so was the senate's response to it.[46] But the repeated prolonging of *imperium* also implied a separation between the higher magistracies and their inherent powers. Although the former maintained their character as annual offices with distinct duties and competences, these powers could also be exercised by individuals who had held public office in the preceding year and acted as if, or on behalf of, a genuine magistrate (*pro consule*). After a somewhat slow beginning in the late fourth century, the growing need for magistrates with *imperium* produced more and more prorogations. The Hannibalic War alone witnessed 139 prorogations, *c.* eight prorogations of *imperium* per year. The principle became a routine measure that soon required merely the decree of the senate.[47] Tellingly, the relation between consuls and proconsuls was one of equals: both were assigned twelve *fasces* that symbolized the equal weight of their *potestas*.[48] In terms of *auctoritas*, the consul prevailed over the promagistrate, who, by definition, held no regular office.

Their relation was remodeled only in the age of Sulla, when an ambitious legislative program to reform Roman administrative practice was stipulated. In their course, the Cornelian laws of 81 and 80 BC also targeted the exercise of *imperium*. Among the most eminent changes, Sulla

---

[45] Cf. Kunkel & Wittmann 1995, 665–74; Lintott 1999b, 109–13.
[46] The first attested case is Q. Publilius Philo in 326 (cos. II 327), on which see Hölkeskamp 1987, 137. The unorthodox view that prorogations prior to the Hannibalic War were designed as triumphal prorogations exclusively (Develin 1975a) has become obsolete.
[47] Cf. Kloft 1977; Kunkel & Wittmann 1995, 305–6. Figures for the Hannibalic War: Beck 2005, 109–10.
[48] Cic. *Verr.* 5.142; Plut. *Aem.* 4.2; cf. Staveley 1963, 472; Kunkel & Wittmann 1995, 121.

increased the numbers of praetors from six to eight, regulated the *cursus honorum*, streamlined the system of *quaestiones*, and reorganized the relations between *imperium*-holders in the field. It is likely that this reorganization was conceived of by its author as a uniform and integrated whole. But the surviving sources present much piecemeal that makes it difficult to determine the precise spirit of the *leges Corneliae*.[49]

This is also true for what seems to have been another innovation: it was henceforth understood that the curule magistrates stayed in Rome during most of the actual term of their office. While the consuls had no special *provinciae* in the city, the praetors were to staff the urban and peregrine jurisdictions as well as the various criminal courts. Only in the following year, after their term had come to a close, were these magistrates to govern provincial commands at the rank *pro consule*. Sulla thus generalized grants of consular *imperium* to all provincial commanders.[50] According to the traditional interpretation, which was promoted so forcefully by Mommsen,[51] the measure was intended to separate the civil magistracy from military *imperium*, so that the higher offices lost most of their competences in the field to the promagistracies. In other words, the *summum imperium* of consuls at home and in the field (*domi militiaeque*) was disrupted. In its place, a more complex governance of *imperium* came into being, which included a more institutionalized and also a symmetrical use of *imperia pro consule*. Yet this *lex Cornelia de provinciis ordinandis* continues to raise suspicions, and its historicity has been rejected on good grounds, especially with regard to a formal deprivation of an *imperium militiae* from the consuls. For it has not gone unnoticed that consuls were, at times, allotted *provinciae* early in their consulship and led military campaigns. On other occasions they left for their assigned territories before their term expired.[52]

Such observations are to the point. But they should not obfuscate the more general notion that Sulla's legislation hit the powers of provincial commanders, which consequently added to a reinterpretation of the relation between consular power and proconsular *imperium*. With this reinterpretation came a continuous emancipation of proconsular commands, which

---

[49] The best discussion now is Brennan 2000, I, 388–402.
[50] Cf. Brennan 2000, I, 394–8, who highlights the aspect of the uniform commands of provincial commanders.
[51] Mommsen 1887–8, II.1, 94–5.
[52] Cic. *Att.* 1.16.8; 1.19.2; 4.13.2; *Sest.* 71–2; *Prov. cons.* 36–7; cf. *MRR* II on years 78 and 74; Balsdon 1939 and, most eminently, Giovannini 1983, 97–101, and Girardet 2001, esp. 155–8, who argued successfully for the non-existence of this assumed *lex Cornelia*. Lintott 1999b, 212, too, declares that Sulla's intention of defusing the danger of long-term military commands by legislation is "a chimera."

henceforth took the form of a generalized consular *imperium* for all promagistrates. This development clearly came at the expense of *imperium*-holders in regular offices, which, among other things, seems to have triggered future attempts to aggrandize the *imperium* of consuls during their term of office.

The volatile nature of politics that became so characteristic of the following decades witnessed a series of motions that further targeted the relation of consular and proconsular commands. Sulla's legislation was revised after 79 and again modified by Caesar's *lex Iulia repetundarum* (59).[53] In 52, Pompey fixed a compulsory five-year interval between magistracy and provincial government.[54] These measures were instigated by the current political constellation, and they were clearly designed to harm the opponents of their rogators rather than embody the result of visionary approaches toward a reorganization of *imperium*. But the general trend is clear. While the regular offices of the higher magistracies were increasingly concerned with legal affairs and political administration, appointments at the proconsular or (after Pompey's legislation of 52) propraetorian rank gradually developed into separate spheres of institutionalized power, each of which was empowered with a particular form of *imperium*.

Let us revisit the encounter of Fabius father and Fabius son in Apulia for a moment. Claudius Quadrigarius' episode is engaging, and it may even be authentic. But it teaches little about the lasting nature of *imperium*. Quadrigarius suggests a holistic quality of consular power, in the sense that it prevails everywhere and over everyone, even the *potestas* of a father. Yet, since Fabius the elder was not only a father but also proconsul, it might be worth considering that, in the late republic, he most likely would not have met with the consul in the first place. With proconsuls stationed in the field and consuls mostly confined to the domestic sphere of the city, Fabius son would not have traveled to Apulia. And if he did, the relation between his consular *imperium* and the *imperium pro consule* of his father was unclear. It is difficult to decide which of the two would have been required to dismount from his horse and acknowledge the superiority of the other. Both men carried the same number of *fasces* in front of them, and both had a consular command power under their belt. By the time of the Second Punic War, the consular *imperium* of the son probably surpassed his father's *imperium pro consule*. A century and a half later, the tide had turned somewhat. In areas outside the city, the proconsuls exercised the command power, while the consuls dominated the political arena at Rome. If anything, Claudius Quadrigarius' incident illustrates that the exercise of

---

[53] Kunkel & Wittmann 1995, 107–8; Lintott 1999b, 160.   [54] Brennan 2000, I, 402–3.

imperium was determined by nuances of time and space that make a holistic approach difficult.

Imperium in space

The term *imperium* had a geographical connotation when it referred to the territory in which it was exercised. As mentioned above, a magistrate's command power was sanctioned by the passage of a curiate law. After taking special auspices, he then crossed the sacred boundary of the city (*pomerium*) and changed into military garb. The formula *domi militiaeque*, "at home and in the field," highlights this juxtaposition of the civic and the military realm. It is also the most fundamental spatial dichotomy that governed the exercise of *imperium* in distinct geographical spheres. The connection between military command and its spatial anchoring became characteristic of the exercise of *imperium* and, more generally, the Roman ordering of the world.

If a magistrate with *imperium* crossed back over the boundary of the city, his military command lapsed and had to be renewed once he re-entered the sphere of *militiae*. Additionally the *imperium* of a promagistrate expired for good upon crossing the *pomerium*.[55] It is worth remembering that this spatial differentiation between "at home" and "in the field" remained intact throughout the republic, despite the many changes to the constitution of both realms over time. The main evidence for this comes from the one notorious exception to the rule, that is, the *imperator*'s right to retain his military command in the augural realm of the city for a single day so as to celebrate a triumph.[56] In the late republic, some commanders waited outside the *pomerium* for periods of almost five years hoping the senate would grant them the triumph they had requested. If they did not want to bury their hopes forever, the spatial regulation regarding their *imperium* demanded that they wait outside the city until the senate had come to a decision.[57]

But the distinction between *domi* and *militiae* became formative for the exercise of *imperium* in other respects as well. In the civic sphere,

---

[55] E.g. Cic. *Verr.* 2.5.34. The classic treatise is Mommsen 1876. Drogula 2007, 435–51 offers a critical examination, but a full-fledged re-evaluation continues to be highly desirable.
[56] See e.g. Livy 45.35.4; Beard 2007, 202; Drogula 2007, 442–51.
[57] Note the case of C. Pomptinus, who returned to Rome in 59 after a successful campaign in Gaul as promagistrate in 62 and 61. He did not triumph until 54. Cf. *MRR* II under years 62, 61 and 54, and see Itgenshorst 2005, no. 259. Other examples include Licinius Lucullus and Caecilius Metellus Creticus (Itgenshorst 2005, nos. 256 and 257), who triumphed only three years after their campaigns in 66 and 65.

the exercise of magisterial power was curbed by the *lex provocationis* that saved Roman citizens from capital punishment without prior reference to the assembly of the people.[58] At some point in the second century, this privilege was extended to the realm of *militiae* and applied to the growing number of provinces. The so-called *leges Porciae*, a series of laws that seem to have been rogated and renewed by various Porcii, stipulated that Roman citizens abroad were granted the right of appeal in capital cases, and thus were safeguarded from the coercing powers of a consul or promagistrate.[59] Part of this legislation was the *lex Porcia de provinciis*, which limited the movements of promagistrates and their staff. Without previous authorization, commanders were barred from leading military expeditions outside their *provincia*. In addition, they were expected to prevent their tribunes and other officers from doing so as well.[60] A few decades later, Sulla's *lex Cornelia de maiestate* went so far as to make it a state offense to leave a province with an army or wage war without previous approval.[61]

Such limitations added to geographical notions of *imperium*, since they tied the exercise of imperial power to certain territories and confined magisterial action to these territories alone. The growing number of provincial commanders added then, it would seem, to a further fragmentation of *imperium*. As the republic expanded from city-state to Mediterranean empire and new provinces were inaugurated, the inherent qualities of *imperium* were reinterpreted. Consider the word *provincia*. The term traditionally referred to the sphere where a magistrate was to exercise his *imperium*. Only toward the second half of the third century did such spheres evolve from vague areas assigned to the command of a consul to spatial domains of civil administration with, more or less, fixed borders – hence *provinciae*.[62] From there, the history of *imperium* developed along two distinct lines. The first trajectory points toward fragmentation and limitation. The increase in new provincial commands added to the number of *imperium*-holders whose authority was limited to a certain region. Those regions were often accessible only by crossing through areas that were assigned to another commander with *imperium*. For instance, the land route to Bithynia and Cilicia did not necessarily require one to cut across the province of Asia, but such a march was certainly the most convenient one. As far as the Spanish provinces were concerned, the

---

[58] See above.   [59] See above.   [60] Crawford 1996b, 1, no. 12, Cn. III, lines 1–15.
[61] Cic. *Pis.* 50; Kunkel & Wittmann 1995, 310; Lintott 1999b, 212.
[62] Cf. Kunkel & Wittmann 1995, 337–8; Girardet 2001, 161 with n. 25.

trip demanded crossing two Gallic provinces, at best.⁶³ In such instances, conflicts between the regionally encoded commands of praetors or promagistrates were endemic, with, at times, dreadful consequences. Since commanders all aimed for military glory and personal distinction (the fierce competition between praetors for the consulship has already been mentioned, and both praetorian and consular promagistrate would strive for distinction to obtain a triumph), non-co-operation between *imperium*-holders and reluctance to fight joint campaigns were not unusual. The geographical embedding of *imperium* thus not only limited the exercise of imperial power, but also fueled potential conflicts between commanders.

In a sense, this almost invited attempts to override a colleague's powers. This is the second trajectory in the spatial development of *imperium*. As early as the Second Punic War, the senate decreed that an *imperium*-holder might operate beyond the limitations of his assigned *provincia* "if he thought this was in the interest of the republic."⁶⁴ Moreover, the time restrictions governing office appointments were sometimes suspended. When P. Cornelius Scipio's African command was prorogated for 203 BC, it was stipulated that his *imperium* lasted for the entire duration of the war and "until he was recalled by the senate."⁶⁵ While Scipio's promagistrature of that year originated in his consulate of 205 (prorogated in 204), his earlier career was notorious for its exceptional character and special arrangements, most notably the exercise of a private *imperium pro consule* in the years from 210 to 206. The details have been treated at length elsewhere and need not be discussed here.⁶⁶ It should be noted, however, that *imperium* was governed with a maximum degree of flexibility and adaptability. Throughout the Second Punic War, the exercise of *imperium* indicates that its defining characteristics – its geographical and temporal restrictions as well as its anchorage in public office-holding – became increasingly blurred, if not altogether unrecognizable.

The aftermath of the Hannibalic War witnessed various attempts to reinforce those characteristics and once again subordinate military commanders to the control of the senate.⁶⁷ But the clock was not to be put back. The common features that determined the communication between *imperium*-holders were acts of non-co-operation, the seeking of distinction vis-à-vis one's colleagues or successors, or the blunt quest for an enhanced command that overrode that of other magistrates. The late republic provides the best

---

⁶³ Cf., on these examples, Brennan 2004, 43. ⁶⁴ Livy 28.45.8.
⁶⁵ Livy 30.1.10, with Beck 2005, 349. ⁶⁶ Beck 2005, 328–67.
⁶⁷ This is treated excellently in Eckstein 1987; cf. Beck 2005, 51–61, 106–14, 354–93.

examples of this, but the picture appears to be exceptional only in quantity. In 67 BC, the *lex Gabinia* granted Pompey an *imperium proconsulare* over any province within fifty miles of the sea, which, effectively, gave him power over almost every province for the next three years.[68] In the following year, Pompey received the command of the war against Mithridates and Tigranes, and the provinces of Bithynia and Pontus and Cilicia, which implied an unprecedented accumulation of imperial power.[69] The creation of such a super-*imperium* through a plebiscite was in sharp contrast to the ubiquitous fragmentation and regional limitation of proconsular and propraetorian commands. In its desire to promote popular candidates, the people's assembly notoriously assigned *imperia* to individuals that countermanded the executive powers of others. Hence, the uniformity that defined the exercise of *imperium* disintegrated, and the unifying character of magisterial power evaporated. As the Roman republic came to a close, the command chain of its Mediterranean empire was shaped more than ever by exceptions and extensions.

Imperium *as elite ideology and social capital*

It is time to sum up. Throughout the history of the Roman republic, the notion of magisterial *imperium* was exposed to profound changes. The number of *imperium*-holders was steadily increased and their competences redefined; relations between magistrates *cum imperio* were constantly renegotiated, a process that was also shaped by the rise of new imperial commands that could not be easily streamlined into the hierarchy of public office-holding (promagistracies, extraordinary commands); and finally, the geography of *imperium* was altered both conceptually and in its application to specific regions. In the last generation of the republic, the major protagonists deliberately tampered with this spatial component of *imperium* so that it suited their goal of self-aggrandizement and autocracy. Thus, on the previous pages, it was argued that *imperium* underwent a dramatic and, at times, a dramatically accelerated dynamic that constantly altered its guiding principles. In light of this diversity, it should not be forgotten that *imperium* continued to possess a persistent state quality as an overall structuring force on the republican constitution. How do we bridge this

---

[68] *Lex Gabinia*: references in *MRR* II 144–6, and see the recent discussion by Girardet 2001, 171–6 (with much more bibliography), who dismisses the orthodox view of an "*imperium maius*"; the *triennium*: App. *Mithr.* 94; Cass. Dio 36.23.4; 36.34.3.
[69] *Lex Manilia*: *MRR* II 153–5; Kallet-Marx 1995, 320–9; Girardet 2001, 176–87; Brennan 2000, I, 404–6.

hiatus between continuity and dynamic change? What was the core of imperial command?

The quest for uniformity is a red herring. To reiterate, this is not to deny that *imperium* had in fact a binding quality, one that distinguished itself by a validity over time and through space. In all periods of republican history, the *imperium* of a magistrate denoted his authority to exercise military power. The religious connotation of declaring war and leading campaigns asked for ritualized practices, all of which clustered around the use of supreme military power: the obtaining of auspices, the passing of a *lex de imperio* and the recognition of the sacred division between the realms of *domi* and *militiae*. These practices never changed, and it is their rigid observation that surrounded *imperium* with the aura of a religiously sanctioned force.[70] But the capacity to lead an army and fight sanctioned campaigns hardly suffices to circumscribe the nature of *imperium*. At times, military contingents were detached to confront the enemy in the absence of an *imperium*-holder under the command of military tribunes or other senior officers. Such operations were carried out under the auspices and *imperium* of a commander who, despite his absence, was fully responsible for, and credited with, the outcome of the event.[71] The latter well hints at another key aspect of *imperium*, one that is best described as a consequence of it, rather than an inherent quality. For *imperium* allowed magistrates to fully capitalize on their military success and turn it into social prestige. The right of celebrating a triumph was only one, yet the most outstanding, honor that enabled commanders to perpetuate their *fama* beyond the terms of office. More permanent visual signs of honor were practices such as the dedication of temples, erection of statues or victory monuments that served as powerful reminders of a commander's *dignitas*, *honos* and *gloria*. But the prerequisite for all of these and other strategies of capitalizing on victory was that it was won under one's own *imperium*. In other words, the gain of prestige was inextricably linked to *imperium*, which opened the gates to social distinction. Without *imperium*, those gates remained closed. Thus, the granting of *imperium* was at the very core of the senate's strategies for superimposing a collective control mechanism that governed the rank, status and prestige of its members. While the traditional offices of the *cursus honorum* were increasingly jeopardized by new forms of institutionalized power such as promagistracies and extraordinary commands (and also by

---

[70] On this, see the magisterial work of Rüpke 1990.
[71] Thus, Cicero's famous characterization of *imperium* from *Phil.* 5.16 (see above) is based on a holistic approach to military campaigns, in the sense that it subsumes all actual fighting under the auspices of the commander with *imperium*.

the sheer increase of offices themselves), elite competition almost naturally shifted toward *imperium* as the most profound mode of distinction. It is in this particular environment of the last generation of the Roman republic that *imperium* developed into an elite ideology that dominated, almost exclusively, the ambitions and aims of that elite's main protagonists.

The institutional framework of command power changed significantly over time. But whereas offices grew in number and magisterial duties and hierarchies were redefined, the principal link between *imperium* and social hierarchy was never questioned. The power to command was closely related to the constitutive norms, conventions and traditions that governed the public conduct of Rome's ruling elite. In fact, it became the driving force behind those conventions in the sense that it provided order and meaning to the defining principles of the elite. And like these conventions, it was a lively principle that depended on reassurance, consensus and adaptability. If anything, this is what Plutarch's episode teaches. Why was it again "that when they gave a public banquet for men who had celebrated a triumph, they formally invited the consuls and then sent word to them requesting them not to come to the dinner?"[72] The consuls were invited because they were the highest magistrates who *ex officio* presided over state banquets. But to avoid a clash between their *imperium* and that of a triumphator at proconsular rank, they were best kept apart by a go-between who told the consuls not to attend. This solution operated on the unspoken agreement that it allowed for each of the involved parties to have their *imperium* unchallenged, while the constitution remained overall intact. When this silent consensus among the Roman elite failed, the "dreadful and mighty power"[73] of magisterial command turned *imperium* into a dangerous and indeed destructive force.

---

[72] Plut. *Quaest. Rom.* 80 = *Mor.* 283a.
[73] Cic. *Leg. agr.* 2.45: *grave est enim nomen imperii, atque id etiam in levi persona pertimescitur, propterea quod vestro, non suo nomine, cum hinc egressi sunt, abutuntur.*

CHAPTER 5

Consuls as curatores pacis deorum

Francisco Pina Polo

In his reflections on the republican constitution, Polybius[1] emphasizes the power of the consuls as typical of a monarchical government. According to the Greek author, consuls were, on the one hand, commanders-in-chief of the Roman army with full decision-making powers, and as such, spent long parts of the year away from Rome. On the other hand, during their stay in Rome, before taking command of the legions, the consuls were the heads of the Roman administration.[2] In this sense, Polybius mentions a series of tasks assigned to them involving both the senate and the people. Paradoxically, Polybius does not mention the religious duties performed by the consuls, despite the fact that some of these functions were compulsory for them and that their fulfilment was, according to Roman belief, of great importance to the welfare of the community.[3]

In fact, the religious duties performed by the consuls during the first few weeks in office were among their most important functions. Roman religion was national and civic, and its practice was a political issue since it concerned the entire *civitas*.[4] Most religious activities were performed in public, according to stringent rules, and their main purpose was to maintain or to restore the *pax deorum*. There were experts grouped into various priestly *collegia* who served as essential, qualified advisers, but the management of religious affairs was in the hands of the senate and the maintenance of the direct relationship between the community and the gods was assigned to the magistrates, particularly to the consuls as supreme magistrates of the *civitas*.[5]

Project "Consuls, consulars and the government of the Roman Republic" (HUM2004–02449 and HUM2007–60776/HIST) funded by Ministerio Educación y Ciencia, Gobierno de España.
[1] Polyb. 6.12.
[2] Cf. Mommsen 1887–8, II, 74–140; de Ruggiero 1892; Kunkel & Wittmann 1995, 311–37; Lintott 1999b, 104–7.
[3] Mommsen 1887–8, II, 135–7; de Ruggiero 1892, 742–7.   [4] Cic. *Flac.* 69. Cf. Scheid 1985, 20.
[5] Scheid 1985, 29–34; Beard 1990, 31–4, emphasizes the leading role of the senate in Roman religious life.

The first public ceremony conducted by the consuls consisted of visiting the temple of Jupiter in the Capitolium to make their vows, pleading to the supreme divinity of the Roman pantheon for the welfare of the community. The vows taken by the consuls on the day when they assumed their duties must be seen as *vota publica*. The exact content of the vows is not known, nor whether there was a fixed formula set out by the senate or by a priestly college, in particular by the *pontifices*. However, it seems apparent that consuls did not act as individuals but as supreme magistrates and that, as a result, they did not plead in their *votum* for the success of a specific venture that they might have to undertake, but for the welfare and safety of the Roman state in general during their term of office.[6]

In the same manner that the consular year started with the rituals at the Capitolium, the stay of consuls in Rome before leaving for their respective *provinciae* was ended by their delivery of new *vota publica* in the same place, wearing their military uniforms.[7] Between both actions, as guarantors of the *pax deorum*, they had to perform some habitual religious duties.

THE EXPIATION OF *PRODIGIA*

The main religious duty of the consuls upon taking office was to deal with the expiation of all the prodigies that had occurred in Rome and in Italy during the previous months. To the Roman mentality, *prodigia* included all phenomena considered supernatural or unearthly. They were perceived as an earthly expression of the wrath of the gods.[8] Thus, the prodigy generally meant that the *pax deorum* had been breached by some inadequate human action, or expressed a warning for the future.[9] The misdemeanours committed or the mistakes made by citizens were not solely of a private nature. On the contrary, they had an impact on the community and imperilled its very existence. It was therefore necessary to re-establish the appropriate relationship between the *civitas* and the gods of Rome by means of suitable expiation ceremonies. Such a task could only be performed by the magistrates who were the representatives of the citizens and who could thus rightfully and legitimately act on their behalf.

Prodigies could be observed by any individual, whether a simple citizen, a priest or a magistrate. In principle, since it meant an alteration in the normal course of events, a *prodigium* represented a danger.[10] But

---

[6] Cf. Orlin 1997, 36–8.   [7] Livy 21.63; 41.10; 45.39.11.
[8] About *prodigia* in Rome, Wülcker 1903; Luterbacher 1904; Händel 1959; Bloch 1963; Liebeschuetz 1979, 7–18; MacBain 1982; Sacchetti 1996; Rosenberger 1998; Rasmussen 2003; Engels 2007.
[9] Engels 2007, 44–7.   [10] Cf. Bloch 1963, 86.

the mere observation of a phenomenon considered as supernatural was not enough for it to be automatically considered a *prodigium*. For that purpose it was essential for the senate to recognize it as such and for its expiation to involve the state. For this reason, all of the alleged *prodigia* that occurred during a given year were compiled so that one of the new consuls, either on the first day he took office or immediately thereafter, could bring a list of prodigies before the senate.[11] The consul produced his report on behalf of the people, and it included all of the details collected on each of the phenomena. If he deemed it convenient, he could even complement the *relatio* with the introduction before the senate of eyewitnesses to the occurrence.[12] Senators would then decide whether the events described could indeed be considered as omens sent by the gods, that is, as *prodigia*.

Once the deliberations were over, the senate issued the corresponding decree. Only then did the presumed divine signs officially become *prodigia*. The *senatus consultum* also included the answer to be given to the gods by the *civitas*. If the prodigies were already known or even if they were frequent and considered to be not too important, senators would straight away order expiatory ceremonies. These were entrusted to the consuls, who could then decide on the specific form of the rituals to be celebrated in honour of the gods, as Livy sometimes emphasizes.[13] However, if the prodigies were unknown, or if they were considered to be particularly serious, the senate would decide to consult the experts: pontiffs, augurs, persons in charge of the Sibylline Books or haruspices – the senate went either to only one of these priestly colleges or to two of them jointly. Upon receiving an answer, the senate met again to deal with the question and then commissioned the expiation ceremonies that had been recommended. As in the previous case, the consuls were in charge of the sacrifices.[14]

In the *procuratio prodigiorum* there was, therefore, a clear division of roles: any citizen could report or give a warning; only the senate could decide if it was in fact a case of divine omens worthy of being taken into consideration and thus determine how to react; only the consuls could then provide the appropriate response required by the divinity in order to achieve the pacification of the relationship between gods and Romans.[15]

According to Livy, the *procuratio prodigiorum* took place at the beginning of the consular year and the expiation ceremonies were celebrated, in any

---

[11] About the *procuratio prodigiorum* see Mommsen 1887–8, III, 1059–62; Luterbacher 1904, 33ff.; Händel 1959, 2290–5; Bloch 1963, 120–3; Beard 1990, 31; Beard *et al.* 1998, 37–9.
[12] Livy 22.1.14.   [13] Livy 31.5.3; 32.1.13–14.
[14] Livy 24.10.13; 24.44.9; 30.2.13; 31.12.10; 34.55; 38.44.7; 41.16.6; 42.2.6–7.   [15] Livy 22.2.1; 32.9.4.

case, before the consuls left Rome for their provinces. Elisabeth Rawson questioned the information provided by Livy in this respect, claiming that, if this was indeed the case, many prodigies would have been left waiting for months before they could be presented by the new consuls to the senate.[16] In her opinion, this would have meant an unnecessary danger to the *civitas*, given that any potential *prodigium* meant a breach of the *pax deorum*. According to Rawson, the Roman religious logic would have demanded expiation as soon as possible and would not have accepted a delay of several months. The report of prodigies provided at the beginning of each year in *Ab Urbe Condita* would thus be the product of a literary arrangement made by Livy, the result of composition technique rather than historical fact.

There is, nevertheless, a plausible explanation for the chronological positioning of the *procuratio prodigiorum* at the beginning of the year, closely linked to the essential presence and involvement of the consuls in the process.[17] Until the dictatorship of Sulla, the consuls would spend most of their year in office away from Rome, commanding their legions. Except in particular cases, they stayed in the *Urbs* only during their first few weeks in office, apart from the usual short stay of one of the consuls to conduct the elections at the end of the consular year. Since it was the consuls (or at any rate, one of them) who had to present the *prodigia* to the senate and had to preside over the prescribed acts of expiation, it was necessary to wait until the new consuls took office in order to proceed. At this point the appeasement of the gods was carried out as soon as possible. Other functions performed by the consuls during their time in Rome could be delegated to the *praetor urbanus* in their absence.[18] It is clear, however, that this was not the case for the expiation of prodigies, which was apparently an exclusive religious responsibility of the consuls. For that reason, the task had to be attended to at the beginning of the consular year, before the consuls left to go to war. The act of undertaking a military command and participating in an armed conflict involved the obvious contamination of the person put in contact with death, as would be inevitable in a war. This contamination required the performance of the ceremonies of *lustratio* that the traditional Roman calendar had strategically placed at the beginning and at the end of the months that in archaic times were the appointed periods for military campaigns. The expiation of prodigies thus had to take place while the consuls were ritually clean, before they suffered the

---

[16] Rawson 1971.   [17] Cf. Mommsen 1887–8, III, 1059.
[18] Cf. Brennan 2000, 2, 601, 607–8 (in particular on the religious duties of the *praetor urbanus* 123–5).

contamination that would prevent them from carrying out the appropriate rituals to restore the *pax deorum*.

In this respect, the events of the year 292 were significant.[19] A plague was having devastating effects on the population of Rome. Given the extreme seriousness of the situation endured by the city, which was obviously seen as a divine punishment, the Books were consulted to find a solution that might restore the *pax deorum*. However, nothing could be done immediately, since the consuls were engaged in a war. The example of such behaviour in a situation of great urgency would seem to indicate that it was standard practice to wait for the consuls to expiate all *prodigia* jointly at the beginning of the consular year. In the same way, in the year 208, when the praetors had already left for their assigned *provinciae*, the new consuls were detained in Rome in order to complete the sacrifices required for the expiation of *prodigia*. In that context Livy states that the safety of the *res publica* depended on the religious responsibilities of the consuls, taking precedence over emergencies arising at that time due to the Hannibalic War in Italy and Hispania.[20]

Wissowa considered the expiation of *prodigia* in Rome above all to be a ceremony of *lustratio*, which would involve a procession under the presidency of the consuls in which the animals to be sacrificed were carried.[21] Livy's account does not include the specific details of the expiation ceremony performed. He usually refers to sacrifices of animals but does not mention that the ritual involved a procession through the city. However, the concept of *lustratio* does appear occasionally in his description of the events. The consuls of the year 186 conducted the sacrifices of expiation, and with them '*consules urbem lustraverunt.*'[22] This too would account for the fact that the expiation of prodigies was placed at the beginning of the year, as a rite of purification involving the renewal of the community.

The religious rituals performed by the consuls varied depending on the prodigies and on the decisions previously taken by the senate. The most typical involved the simple celebration of sacrifices. In fact, in Livy's account, mentions of the consular *relatio* of prodigies, the decision of the senate to carry out sacrifices as a means of expiation, and the subsequent application of the senatorial decree by the consuls practically become a repeated

---

[19] Livy 10.47.6–7.
[20] Livy 27.23.1; 23.4. Something similar occurred in the year 186 when the consuls, engaged in the repression of the Bacchanalia, had not been able to recruit new troops after having been in office for some time, but had not neglected the sacrifices of expiation (Livy 39.22.4).
[21] Wissowa 1912, 391. Rosenberger 1998, 140, sees the rituals with an apotropaic function as a means to lustrate the frontiers of the *Urbs*. Cf. Luc. 1 592–604.
[22] Livy 39.22.4.

formula, although the intervention of the consuls is not always specifically mentioned.[23] But the expiation could require further and more complex rituals: *lectisternia*,[24] *supplicationes*[25] and in exceptional cases *ludi*.[26]

In most of Livy's references to the expiation of *prodigia*, he mentions the consuls in the plural as executors of the rites. Only rarely does he specify that one of the two magistrates was in charge of performing them individually. This is the case of Cn. Servilius in the year 217, who had to deal on his own with all of the religious tasks since his colleague Flaminius had left Rome in a hurry, presumably without even taking the auspices.[27] Something similar happened in the year 191, when the consul Scipio Nasica conducted the expiation rituals when his colleague Acilius had already left for war.[28] On both occasions the participation of only one of the consuls was justified by the other's absence. However, in the year 200, Aurelius seems to have been the person in charge of the sacrifices to placate the gods according to the recommendations of the *decemviri*, while his colleague P. Sulpicius Galba was also in Rome.[29] In conclusion, although it seems that the custom was that both consuls participated in the appeasement of the gods, the requirement for joint action may not have been of such a compulsory nature as to invalidate the process if the rituals were not carried out in such a manner.

Livy does not usually provide precise information on how long it would take for consuls to perform the rites commissioned by the senate. In the year 212, he says, they dedicated nine days to sacred matters,[30] and in 207 they also needed nine days to perform a task which was considered a priority and had to be carried out prior to the *dilectus*, at the height of the Second Punic War.[31] In any event, the consuls acted as quickly as possible for two reasons. First, they acted for the public interest, since the pacification of the gods eradicated all danger to the community and made it possible to restore normal life in the *civitas*. Second, they acted out of personal interest, since they could not leave Rome for their provinces without having performed the required rituals. The longer it took them to carry out the prescribed sacrifices, the longer their stay in the *Urbs* would be.[32]

---

[23] Livy 24.10.6–13; 28.11.5–7; 30.2.13; 31.12.10; 40.45.4–5; 41.16.6; etc.
[24] Livy 7.2.2; 36.1.1–3; Händel 1959, 2292–3 thinks that *lectisternia* were not related to the expiation of prodigies. Cf. Rosenberger 1998, 146–7.
[25] Livy 22.1.14–15; 32.9.4; 34.55; 35.21.2; 37.2.2–5; etc. About *supplicationes* as a means for the expiation of *prodigia* see Rosenberger 1998, 143–5.
[26] Livy 27.11.1; 11.6. [27] Livy 22.1. [28] Livy 36.37.2–6.
[29] Livy 31.12.10. [30] Livy 25.7.7–9. [31] Livy 27.37.1; cf. Livy 36.37.5.
[32] In his account, Livy sometimes establishes a direct link between the end of the acts of expiation and the departure of the consuls for their provinces (Livy 32.9.4; 36.37.6; 41.9.8).

THE FERIAE LATINAE

The second compulsory religious task that was performed by the consuls every year was the celebration of the *Feriae Latinae*.[33] This was an annual festival whose date of celebration varied, so upon taking office consuls had to designate the starting day of the celebration that year.[34] The organization and presidency of the festival celebrated in honour of Iuppiter Latiaris at the Mons Albanus were intended to represent the Roman state. In fact, the Roman *civitas* was represented at the festival by all its magistrates, with the consuls at the head. That is why in their absence from the *Urbs* a *praefectus urbi feriarum Latinarum causa* was appointed to take over the government of Rome.[35] The importance accorded by the Roman state to the *Feriae Latinae* is demonstrated by the fact that the consuls were not entitled to leave Rome to take control of their provinces until the festival had been suitably celebrated under their presidency.[36] Just as in the case of the expiation of *prodigia*, the fulfilment by the consuls of their ancestral religious duties was given priority over their military duties. This rule was always observed, even during times of special emergency for Rome, such as the Hannibalic War.[37]

The requirement that the consuls not take command of the troops in their *provinciae* until the *Feriae Latinae* had been celebrated allows us to draw some conclusions concerning the period of time when they stayed in Rome during the course of the consular year in the cases where ancient sources provide a definite date of celebration, which is rarely the case, and only occurs from the Hannibalic War onwards.[38] In general, we must presume that the consuls fixed the earliest possible date for the celebration of the Latin festival, always taking into consideration their other duties in Rome, as well as the *dilectus*, since in this way they could go to their provinces as soon as possible. Nevertheless, many internal political issues influenced the decision, as shown by the diversity of dates known. On the

---

[33] About the *Feriae Latinae* see Werner 1888; Wissowa 1912, 124–5; Scullard 1981, 111–15; Sabbatucci 1988, 305–8; Liou-Gille 1996, 85–97; Baudy 1998. See also the paper by Francisco Marco Simón in this volume.

[34] The *Fasti Feriarum Latinarum* are very fragmentarily preserved and very seldom do they provide the date of celebration of the festival for a given year. Cf. *CIL* I² 1, 57–8.

[35] *CIL* VI 1421; Cass. Dio 49.42.1; 53.33.3. See a list of *praefecti Feriarum Latinarum* in Werner 1888, 41ff. Cf. Brennan 2000, I, 34–8.

[36] Livy provides various examples indicating that only when the consuls were 'liberated' from their obligation of presiding over the Latin festival were they authorized to go to their provinces: Livy 38.44.8; 43.15.3; 44.22.16.

[37] Livy 21.63; 22.1.5–7 (year 217, consul Flaminius).

[38] Livy 25.12.1: 27 April (year 212); Livy 42.35.3: Kalends of June (year 171); Livy 44.22.16: 31 March (year 168).

other hand, we must take into account the fact that the dates for the *Feriae Latinae* in the year 212 and between 171 and 168 were determined by the ongoing wars, which is the reason why Livy highlights them in his account. It is therefore reasonable to presume that the common procedure was to act with less haste and therefore the festival would usually have taken place later on, perhaps preferably in May. In fact, this is supported by the data provided by the *Fasti Feriarum Latinarum*, even during the Hannibalic War, for the years 217–212.[39] Although it is not possible to establish the exact date of celebration due to the degree of fragmentation, it is plausible to assert that the festival took place around the Nones of May in the year 214, around the Kalends of the same month in the years 213 and 212 (the latter, as we have already seen, is supported by Livy's report, which gives as the exact date the fifth day before the Kalends of May), some time in May or a little before in the years 217 and 216, and finally in June or a little earlier in the year 215.

Naturally this presumption applies only to the period of time between the Hannibalic War and the year 153, when we know that the consuls took office on the Ides of March and therefore the *Feriae Latinae* were celebrated in spring. From the year 153 onwards, the *Feriae Latinae* must obviously have been celebrated at an earlier date in the year, closer to the Kalends of January, when the consuls and the other magistrates took office. From that time onwards it was probably a winter festival. Before the Second Punic War, the festival would have taken place later in the year, since the consuls seem to have taken office in May or even later in the cases where we have exact details.[40] In that case it could have been a summer festival or one held later in the year.[41]

THE *SACRA* OF LAVINIUM

Two late texts indicate that Roman supreme magistrates had to perform annual sacrifices jointly in the city of Lavinium in honour of Vesta

---

[39] *CIL* I² 1, 57.

[40] Mommsen 1859, 100–9, believed that, during the period between the war against Pyrrhus and the end of the First Punic War, the consular year started in the Kalends of May. Ancient sources provide many different dates for the consuls' taking of office during the fifth and fourth centuries BC, generally in the second half of the year: year 493: Kal. Sept. (Dion. Hal. 6.49.1); 476: in Sextilis (Dion. Hal. 9.25.1); 463: Kal. Sext. (Livy 3.6.1); 462: III Id. Sext. (Livy 3.8.2); 451 and 450: Id. Maias (Livy 3.36.3, 38.1); 443: full moon in December (Dion. Hal. 9. 63.1); 423: Id. Dec. (Livy 4.37.3); 401: Kal. Oct. (Livy 5.9.8); 329: Kal. Quinctilis (Livy 7.20.3). Cf. Broughton 1951–86, II, 637–9.

[41] At the beginning of the fourth century, the *Fasti Feriarum Latinarum* support the date of celebration of the festival in the years 396 and 395 in the months of November and September respectively. Cf. *CIL* I² 1, 57.

and the Penates.⁴² In his commentary on Virgil's *Aeneid*, Servius states the following: 'Thus, the question here is whether Vesta is also part of the Penates or is considered as their companion, for when the consuls, the praetors or a dictator leave their magistracies they worship the Penates of Lavinium and Vesta at the same time.'⁴³ On the other hand, Macrobius writes: 'He [Virgil] also used the same name to refer to Vesta, who, in all probability as part of the Penates, is clearly their companion, so that when the consuls, praetors and dictators take over their magistracies, they worship the Penates of Lavinium and Vesta at the same time.'⁴⁴ Clearly, the two texts are very similar, but there is one significant difference that causes some uncertainty as to when exactly the ceremony took place. According to Servius, the sacrifices performed by Roman magistrates in Lavinium were carried out at the end of their term in office (*'cum . . . abeunt magistratu'*), whereas, on the other hand, from Macrobius' text it can be deduced that the ceremony was celebrated when the magistrates assumed office (*'cum adeunt magistratum'*).

To resolve the question raised by the divergence of the two texts several propositions have been put forward. Latte, implicitly basing his theory on the fact that Servius' work (fourth century AD) was previous to Macrobius' (fifth century AD), suggested that *'abeunt magistratum'* was the correct version, and considered Macrobius' text to be a copyist's mistake.⁴⁵ Weinstock, on the other hand, was inclined to consider both readings acceptable, which led him to believe that the sacrifices were celebrated both upon the taking of office and at the end of the magistrates' term in office.⁴⁶ Alföldi, however, believed Macrobius' text to be the correct one, holding that Servius' reading was the result of a mistake of a later copyist. Macrobius would have had access to Servius' correct version, from which he gathered the information, but subsequently a copyist would have misspelled *'adeunt'* and written *'abeunt'* in the transcription of Servius' text.⁴⁷ This theory is further supported by another passage from Servius in which the

---

⁴² See de Ruggiero 1892, 745; Wissowa 1904; Alföldi 1965, 258–65; Radke 1975; Dubourdieu 1989, 355–61.
⁴³ Ser. *Aen.* 2.296: *hic [Vergilius] ergo quaeritur, utrum Vesta etiam de numero Penatium sit, an comes eorum accipiatur, quod cum consules et praetores sive dictator abeunt magistratu, Lavini sacra Penatibus simul et Vestae faciunt.*
⁴⁴ Macrob. 3.4.11: *eodem nomine appellavit [Vergilius] et Vestam, quam de numero Penatium certe comitem eorum esse manifestum est adeo, ut consules et praetores seu dictatores, cum adeunt magistratum, Lavini rem divinam faciant Penatibus pariter et Vestae.*
⁴⁵ Latte 1960, 295 n. 5.
⁴⁶ Weinstock 1937, 428. Cf. Radke 1975, 611: 'Die röm. Beamten mit *imperium* opfern seit alters her in Lavinium beim Amtsantritt bzw. *in provincias ituri* den Penates und Vesta.'
⁴⁷ Alföldi 1965, 261. Dubourdieu 1989, 357 shares this opinion.

grammarian explicitly states that the sacrifice in Lavinium was carried out when the *imperatores* were on their way to their provinces.[48]

In my opinion, from what is known about consular activities throughout the year, it can be concluded that Alföldi was right, and therefore it is much more likely that the sacrifices in Lavinium were celebrated at the beginning of the consular year, at least in the period prior to Sulla. Once the consuls had departed for their provinces, one of them would usually return to Rome at the end of the year to preside over the elections, if the situation made it possible. The other consul would return to the *Urbs* only once his term in office had ended. As consuls, they did not jointly carry out any further civilian tasks or celebrate any other religious ceremonies after leaving Rome. On the contrary, the religious duties involved in the consulship were always fulfilled, as we have already seen, at the beginning of the consular year. Included among them could be the annual sacrifices celebrated at Lavinium.

A possible reference to the sacrifices to Vesta and the Penates comes from Cato's *Origines*. According to the preserved text, the oxen that ought to have been sacrificed in Lavinium escaped into the forest.[49] If this passage refers to the annual sacrifices in Lavinium, it would be the oldest documented reference to the ceremony, dating back to the beginning of the second century.[50] The most direct reference is to be found in a passage from Valerius Maximus, in which he claims that the consul C. Hostilius Mancinus, on his way to Hispania in the year 137, wanted to celebrate a sacrifice in Lavinium but could not perform it because the chickens that were to be sacrificed had escaped into a nearby forest and could not be found. This is reminiscent of Cato's text.[51] What happened was perceived as a *prodigium*. Most probably, the case mentioned by Valerius Maximus referred not to a private sacrifice but to the state sacrifice that the Roman magistrates had to perform in Lavinium, which must have taken place at the beginning of the consular year. According to the Latin author, the events occurred when the consul was preparing to set off for his province. As can be appreciated, it was the *prodigia* which occurred on both occasions that drew the attention of Cato and Valerius Maximus to the ceremony of the *sacra* in Lavinium.

---

[48] Ser. *Aen.* 3.12: *quos [Penates] inter cetera ideo magnos appellant, quod de Lavinio translati Romam bis in locum suum redierint: quod imperatores in provincias ituri apud eos primum immolarint.*

[49] Cato: Beck & Walter 2005/2004, 1, 188 = fr. 55 Peter. Cf. Engels 2007, 719–20: 'Die Annahme Alföldis, es handele sich hier um ein jährliches Staatsopfer an Vesta und die Penaten in Lavinium, muß daher ebenso hypothetisch bleiben.'

[50] Cf. Alföldi 1965, 262 n. 2.   [51] Val. Max. 1.6.7; cf. Livy, *Per.* 55. Engels 2007, 540–1.

A final question makes the solution to this issue even more complicated. Livy reports that, from the year 338, the *foedus* between Rome and Lavinium was renewed every year and that this happened '*post diem decimum [feriarum] Latinarum*'.[52] Did the ceremony of renewal of the treaty coincide with the sacrifice to the Penates in Lavinium? No ancient text, and especially not Livy, our main source of information, seems to connect the two events. However, Wissowa and Alföldi assumed that it was the same ceremony,[53] and they were probably right. It is unreasonable to presume that the Roman magistrates went to Lavinium twice every year, once to renew the *foedus* between both cities and again to celebrate the sacrifices. On the contrary, it is more logical that both ceremonies were conducted simultaneously, since, in fact, the worship of the Penates had historically linked both communities. Should this be the case, the sacrifices to the *sacra* ought to be located at the beginning of the consular year, immediately after the celebration of the *Feriae Latinae*.

However, the greatest difficulty is that the ceremony in honour of the *sacra* in Lavinium is never mentioned by Livy in any historical period, which makes the confirmation of these theories impossible. Only once does Livy make a vague reference to the sacrifices in Lavinium in the times of Romulus, also reported by Dionysius of Halicarnassus and Plutarch.[54] Although it is obvious that this information is not credible in itself, it is true that it indirectly confirms the existence of such a tradition. However, the fact that Livy does not mention it again prevents us from knowing any further details about the ritual. In the books that have been preserved, Livy makes no reference to the sacrifices either before or after the *Feriae Latinae*, and the celebration of the festival on the Mons Albanus is presented on various occasions as the final event of the civilian activities conducted by the consuls prior to their departure for their provinces. Obviously, Livy does not always report all the events that took place in every year but it seems strange that, in this case, he never refers to a possibly annual solemn ceremony where the highest-ranking Roman magistrates had to act on behalf of the state.

There is no reason to presume that the antiquarian information collected by Servius and Macrobius is false; the sacrifices must have existed. But the lack of references in the surviving portions of Livy's work makes it difficult to accept that the ceremony was habitually attended by the

---

[52] Livy 8.11.15.
[53] Wissowa 1912, 518; Alföldi 1965, 262–3. Dubourdieu 1989, 360–1 is sceptical on this question.
[54] Livy 1.14.2; Dion. Hal. 2.52.3; Plut. *Rom.* 23.

consuls.⁵⁵ After the compulsory journey to the Mons Albanus, situated about thirty kilometres from Rome, the act of attending the sacrifices in Lavinium, located at a similar distance from the *Urbs*, would have further delayed the journey of the consuls to their provinces. In this regard, it must be recalled that, according to Servius and Macrobius, the ceremony had to be conducted by a magistrate with *imperium*, which means that it could also be celebrated by praetors or by a dictator. Although there is certainly no information regarding the matter, it is possible that the consuls normally entrusted this task to one of the praetors, the *urbanus* or the *peregrinus*, and that only on exceptional occasions did one of the consuls go to Lavinium, as Hostilius Mancinus may have done in the year 137.

PRAESIDES LUDORUM

Apart from the usual religious duties specifically performed by the consuls, they had, on occasion, to carry out others that did not fall within their exclusive jurisdiction and could be performed by other magistrates with *imperium*, including praetors and dictators. Included among these duties was the task of taking, by order of the senate, the *votum* of *ludi publici* and presiding over the games, if they were still in Rome.

The *ludi* always retained their original religious nature within Roman society. Throughout the republican period the *cura ludorum* was one of the functions officially assigned to the aediles in the *Urbs*, whose names were linked to the celebration of the corresponding games in historical accounts. However, the duty of presiding over the *ludi Romani* that the aediles had organized was reserved for the higher magistrates, since they were invested with *imperium*.⁵⁶

This conclusion can be drawn from a passage from Livy, in which he claims that the presidency of the chariot races during the *ludi Romani* was an '*imperii ministerium*'.⁵⁷ Dionysius of Halicarnassus similarly refers to a passage from the work of Fabius Pictor.⁵⁸ The picture would presumably

---

⁵⁵ However, Alföldi 1965, 32: 'The consuls had to provide for the welfare of the Roman State by the three religious acts just mentioned: the *votorum nuncupatio* on the Capitol, the performance of the *Latiar* on the Alban Mountain, and the state sacrifices in Lavinium.'

⁵⁶ Salomonson 1956, 58–61; Bernstein 1998, 58–63. Bernstein (61–2) considers that the exclusive responsibility for the taking of *auspicia publica* belonging to the higher magistrates is the reason why the *ludi Romani* had to be presided over by one of them, since the games were dedicated to *Iuppiter Optimus Maximus*, the supreme divinity of the Roman pantheon. Cf. Mommsen 1887–8, I, 245; II, 136; II, 518; Kunkel & Wittmann 1995, 504 n. 120.

⁵⁷ Livy 8.40.3. Cf. Mommsen 1887–8, I, 413, n. 3.

⁵⁸ Dion. Hal. 7.71–73.4. Cf. Beck & Walter 2005/2004, I, F 20, 110–17.

correspond to the games celebrated in the year 490, but the account of Dionysius of Halicarnassus seems to imply that Fabius Pictor was providing a description of the ceremonies from his own time.[59] Before the beginning of the games, the traditional *pompa circensis* took place. The procession went from the Capitolium to the Circus Maximus, through the Forum. According to Dionysius, at the head of the *pompa circensis* were 'those who had the supreme power' in the community, while at the end of the parade were statues of the gods carried on men's shoulders.[60] Obviously, this statement cannot refer to the aediles organizing the games and it must be understood that it was the supreme magistrates, that is, the consuls, who presided over the civic procession[61] and that it was they who would, therefore, preside over the *ludi*.

A passage from Ennius, recorded by Cicero in his *De divinatione*, should be understood in similar fashion.[62] Ennius poetically describes the expectations that existed among Romans about which of the two brothers, Romulus and Remus, should govern and after which one of them the new city would be named. The same expectation, says Ennius, exists among the crowd surrounding the consul when he is at the Circus about to give the signal for the beginning of the chariot racing from the *carceres*, dropping a white cloth.[63] Ennius uses the past tense ('*exspectabat populus*') to refer to the time of the mythical founders of Rome, whereas he uses the present tense ('*exspectant*') to describe the giving of the signal by the consul. This would seem to indicate that he refers to an action taking place in his own time, at the beginning of the second century BC. From this passage it can be clearly deduced that the consul is the person in charge of giving the starting order to the participants in the race, which means, once again, that it was the consul who was presiding over the *ludi*.

Finally, a passage from Livy confirms without any doubt the consular presidency over the *ludi Romani*.[64] In the year 168, when the second day of the *ludi Romani* was being celebrated, a *tabellarius* arrived in Rome with news of the victory of the Roman army at Pydna. The courier delivered the dispatches to the consul C. Licinius Crassus, just when he was about to give the signal for the start of the quadriga race in the Circus. The consul then showed the letter to the crowd, who immediately forgot the games,

---

[59] Dion. Hal. 7.71.1. Cf. Beck & Walter 2005/2004, I, 116.
[60] Dion. Hal. 7.72.1. Cf. Beck 2006, 144–51. [61] Beck 2006, 147.
[62] Cic. *Div.* 1.107–8: *Exspectant veduti consul cum mittere signum / volt, omnes avidi spectant ad carceris oras, / quam mox emittat pictis e faucibus currus: / sic exspectabat populus atque ora timebat / rebus utri magni victoria sit data regni.*
[63] Cf. Skutsch 1985, 228; Humphrey 1986, 153–7. [64] Livy 45.1.6–7.

given the importance of the news. After that, Licinius Crassus summoned the senate, read the message and, finally, officially announced the victory in Macedonia to the people.

From the passages mentioned above we can deduce that one consul played the role of *praeses ludorum*. Dionysius uses the plural form to refer to the magistrates leading the *pompa circensis*. But from the text of Ennius and especially from that of Livy, it may be inferred that the effective presidency of the games was assigned to only one of the two consuls; the one who was in Rome at the time or, when both consuls were present within the city, the one who had been invested with command over the state at that particular moment. In the case of the year 168, it is obvious that Licinius Crassus was the only consul present in Rome. He had been assigned Italy as his *provincia*, and he had to deal in particular with the recruiting and provisioning of the soldiers intended for Macedonia.[65] It was his colleague L. Aemilius Paulus who conducted the war in Macedonia.

Other ancient records confirm the double role played by the consuls, as presidents over the games and as promoters of the celebration of the *ludi magni*, seen as extraordinary votive games celebrated in honour of Jupiter in the case of a crisis in Rome.[66] In fact, the two duties were closely linked. The *votum* taken on behalf of the *civitas* always had to be formulated by a magistrate with *imperium*. Likewise, the fulfilment of the *votum* was assigned to a magistrate invested with *imperium*. In both cases, this right belonged first to the consuls, as supreme magistrates, and they could be replaced by the praetors or, exceptionally, by a dictator.[67]

One of the consuls had to carry out the *votum* of the games, always following the senatorial decrees, and according to the instructions of the *pontifex maximus* concerning the suitable ritual.[68] For this reason, although the *decemviri* had prompted the *votum* of *ludi* in the year 172, it was necessary to wait a few months for the consul Popilius to return from his province to celebrate the elections, in order for him to pronounce the vow.

---

[65] Livy 44.17.10; 19.5; 21.11; 22.5.
[66] Cf. Bernstein 1998, 142–57. Livy 34.44.6 refers to *ludi magni* as *ludi Romani votivi*. Livy never calls the games celebrated following a *votum ludi Romani*. Quinn-Schofield 1967, 102: 'The position appears to be that the *ludi magni* or *ludi maximi* were always games vowed or decreed for a special purpose.'
[67] Cf. Eisenhut 1974, 965; Bernstein 1998, 148–9. In the year 360, the senate ordered the dictator to perform the *votum* of *ludi magni* dedicated to Jupiter before leaving Rome to lead the army (Livy 7.11.5). In 208, the *praetor urbanus* was ordered by the senate to present a law by which the *Ludi Apollinares* would become an annual event, and it was he who carried out the vow under those terms (Livy 27.23.7).
[68] Livy 36.2.2–5; 40.45.6; 42.28.8–9.

The *votum* was pronounced on behalf of the state and for that reason the senate was responsible for its fulfilment. This can clearly be seen, given that it was the responsibility of the senators to determine the amount of money that could be spent on the organization of the *ludi*, as occurred in the years 200, 191 and 172.[69] The state, through the senate, must therefore have been the source of funding for the games. In the same manner, given that the consul acted as the state's representative in the formulation of the *votum*, it was also the responsibility of a consul to put the vow into practice, undoubtedly by presiding over the *ludi*. Nevertheless, according to the available information, it can be deduced that the designated consul also played an active role in the organization of the games.

We find an example of the celebration of *ludi magni* at the beginning of the year 203. After the consuls had assumed office, their *provinciae* were assigned to them in the usual fashion and the troops were recruited. The senate then ordered the praetors to go to their assigned provinces, but instructed the consuls to preside over the *ludi magni* that had been vowed by the dictator Manlius Torquatus in the year 208,[70] before leaving the *Urbs*. Livy then informs us that the consuls carried out the usual sacrifices for the expiation of *prodigia* reported that year, after which they left for their provinces. However, he does not specifically report that the *ludi* took place.[71] The same episode was repeated the following year. Once again the senate commissioned the consuls to celebrate the games vowed by Manlius Torquatus. Although in this case Livy does not give any information on the development of the *ludi*, he does state that, within the context of the *votum* pronounced by the dictator in the year 208, some victims were sacrificed to the gods.[72]

In all probability, the celebration of the *ludi magni* can also be connected to the consuls in the year 194. Once the consuls of that year had taken office and *provinciae* had been assigned to them – both received Italy as their province – and the recruiting had taken place,[73] the senate decreed that the *ver sacrum* vowed by the praetor A. Cornelius Mammula in the year 217[74] was to be celebrated again, along with the *ludi magni* that had been vowed at the same time.[75] In fact, by senatorial order (see below), the *ver sacrum* had already been celebrated, apparently in 195, under the presidency of the consuls of that year.[76] But one year later, the *pontifex* P. Licinius informed the senate that the ritual had not been properly conducted. Therefore the senate demanded that it be repeated under the supervision of the pontiffs.

---

[69] Orlin 1997, 41–3. [70] Livy 30.2.8. [71] Livy 30.2.13 and 3.1. [72] Livy 30.27.11.
[73] Livy 34.43.3–9. [74] Livy 22.9.10–10.6. [75] Livy 34.44.1–6. [76] Livy 33.44.1–2.

Livy does not explicitly say that the consuls had to preside over the *ver sacrum* and that one of them had to preside over the *ludi magni*. However, since they were in charge of that rite in the year 195 and since the senatorial decree of 194 links the two events, it seems likely that they did so. The Latin author confirms later on that both the *ver sacrum* and the *ludi magni* were celebrated in the year 194.[77] However, Livy also states that the *ludi* had been vowed by the consul Servius Sulpicius Galba. There is no consul by that name until the year 144. This is undoubtedly a mistake. Livy confuses him with P. Sulpicius Galba Maximus, who was consul in the year 200 with Macedonia as his province.[78] Indeed, before setting off for Greece to lead the war against Philip, Sulpicius Galba was asked by the senate to carry out the *votum* of some *ludi* in honour of Jupiter, which he eventually did despite the opposition of the *pontifex maximus*.[79] Those were the *ludi magni* that had to be celebrated in the year 194, since those promised in the year 217, along with the *ver sacrum*, had already been conducted in the year 208.[80]

It may thus be concluded that the responsibility of presiding over all of the *ludi publici* was officially assigned to the consuls, but that their presence at them must have been exceptional, since both would normally be absent when most of the games were celebrated throughout the year. This would usually leave the presidency in the hands of the *praetor urbanus*, and exceptionally of a dictator, appointed for such a purpose.[81] In any case, the presidency of the *ludi* was an exclusive responsibility of the magistrates with *imperium*. In fact, unlike other tasks assigned to the consuls (expiation of prodigies, *Feriae Latinae*, etc.), whose fulfilment is systematically attributed to the annual consuls by ancient sources, the consuls are rarely mentioned in conjunction with the presidency of the *ludi Romani*, no doubt because their presence must have been exceptional.[82]

VER SACRUM

There is only one recorded incidence in historical times of the celebration of the ritual known as the *ver sacrum* in Rome.[83] Livy informs us about it in

---

[77] Livy 34.44.6.   [78] Cf. Münzer 1931, 805.
[79] Livy 31.9.10.   [80] Cf. Bernstein 1998, 156 n. 208.
[81] Livy 8.40.2–3; 27.33.6.   [82] Cf. Mommsen 1887–8, I, 416; II, 136.
[83] The only ancient definition of *ver sacrum* is from Festus, s.v. *ver sacrum*, 519 L. = 379 M.: *Ver sacrum vovendi mos fuit Italiae. Magnis enim periculis adducti vovebant, quaecunque proximo vere nata essent apud se, animalia immolaturos. Sed quum crudele videretur pueros ac puellas innocentes interficere, perductos in adultam aetatem velabant atque ita extra fines suos exigebant.* About the *ver sacrum* as institution, see Eisenhut 1955; Heurgon 1957 (in particular about the Roman *ver sacrum* 36–51);

some detail, within the context of the defeats suffered by the Roman state at the beginning of the Hannibalic War. In the year 217, after the debacle suffered by the Roman legions at Trasimene, the newly appointed dictator Q. Fabius Maximus summoned the senate on the same day he took office. In the senate, he blamed the consul C. Flaminius for the military disasters, not so much because of his lack of skill as *imperator*, but because he had not fulfilled the duties to the gods that his position as a higher magistrate required and was thus guilty of impiety.[84] His behaviour would thus have earned the wrath of the gods, according to the dictator, resulting in the punishment of the Roman *civitas* by military defeats. Fabius suggested directly addressing the gods, and the senate agreed that the *decemviri sacris faciundis* should consult the Sibylline Books to that end. After doing so, the priests advised carrying out a series of expiatory actions to restore the *pax deorum*. Among these was the suitable renewal of the *votum* to Mars, the celebration of *ludi magni* in honour of Jupiter, the construction of various temples, the celebration of a *lectisternium* and of *supplicationes*, as well as the *votum* for a *ver sacrum* to Jupiter.[85] All these actions had to be performed if the wars against Carthage and the Gauls were to result in success for the Roman *res publica*.

Praetor urbanus M. Aemilius was entrusted with the fulfilment of the sacerdotal recommendations, due to the absence of the other consul, C. Servilius Geminus, and the need for Fabius to dedicate all his efforts to the war. As a result, the temples that the *decemviri* had recommended were vowed by different magistrates. So too were the *ludi magni*, while the *supplicationes* and the *lectisternium* were celebrated.[86] The exceptional nature of the *ver sacrum* made the praetor consult the pontiffs on the process he should follow to carry out his *votum*. The *pontifex maximus*, L. Cornelius Lentulus, decided that the *votum* for the *ver sacrum* could not be performed without the consent of the people ('*iniussu populi voveri non posse*').[87] The performance of the *ver sacrum* would involve the sacrifice of livestock born in the next spring and thus would result in damage for many citizens who owned the animals. Therefore, it was logical that

---

Eisenhut 1975; Radke 1980, 110–16; Aigner Foresti 1995; Scheid 1998; de Cazanove 2000; Hermon 2001, 84–6.

[84] Livy 22.9.10.
[85] Livy 22.9.11. Heurgon 1957, 39 points out the fact that the *votum* for the *ver sacrum* was addressed to Jupiter and not to Mars, as was common among the Sabines, or to Apollo, as was usual for the Mamertines. Heurgon believes that this could be explained not only by the nature of Jupiter Optimus Maximus as a national Roman god, but also by the Latins' habit of keeping the first fruits of each year for this deity.
[86] Livy 22.10.9–10.   [87] Livy 22.10.1.

the people be consulted before he could acquiesce.[88] For this reason, the praetor presented to the popular assembly a *rogatio*, undoubtedly inspired by the *pontifex maximus*, which specified in great detail the procedure to be followed for the sacrifice of the animals affected by the *votum*, in order not to make mistakes during the rite that might invalidate it.[89] The text of the *rogatio* is clear in that the vowed *ver sacrum* referred only to animals, and did not involve the consecration of human beings or the subsequent ritual emigration of Roman young men, as had happened in 'sacred springs' promoted by other Italic peoples.[90] The purpose was to consecrate to Jupiter the livestock produced in one year, specifically, pigs, sheep, cattle and goats. Once the *rogatio* was approved by the people, the *votum* for the *ver sacrum* was conducted by the praetor of Sardinia, A. Cornelius Mammula.[91]

The *votum* referred to the following quinquennium and therefore expired in the year 212. However, the wars against the Carthaginians and the Gauls to which the *votum* referred went on much longer. Only by the year 195 did the senate commission the consuls L. Valerius Flaccus and M. Porcius Cato to celebrate the vowed *ver sacrum* before setting off for their provinces.[92] The choice of that particular year was probably due to the fact that at that time the senators considered the survival of the *res publica* to be guaranteed according to the terms of the contract pronounced in the *votum* of the year 217. It is likely that, as Heurgon pointed out,[93] the final senatorial decision was a direct result of the recent celebration of a triumph *de Galleis Insubribus* by the consul of year 196, M. Claudius Marcellus, which would have been considered as the real end of the war against the Gauls.

Livy does not mention the completion of the *ver sacrum* until a year later, within the context of the beginning of the consulship of Scipio Africanus and Ti. Sempronius Longus in 194. Once it was decided that Italy would be the *provincia* for both consuls, and after carrying out the *dilectus*, the *pontifex maximus*, P. Licinius Crassus Dives, explained that the *ver sacrum* had not been properly conducted the previous year ('*non esse recte factum*'). The senators decided consequently that it had to be celebrated again under

---

[88] Scheid 1998, 420–1.
[89] Livy 22.10.2–6. Cf. Plut. *Fab*. 4.4: according to the Greek author, the *votum* may have been pronounced by the dictator Fabius, who might have included in it everything that nature offered in the following year, 216, including not only animals, but also mountains, plains, and rivers in Italy. About the *rogatio*, see Elster 2003, 195–7.
[90] Heurgon 1957, 39; Radke 1980, 115; Scheid 1998, 421, n. 26; de Cazanove 2000, 257 and 260. Briscoe 1989, 332: 'In this case the human element is lacking entirely.'
[91] Livy 33.44.1–2.   [92] *Ibid*.   [93] Heurgon 1957, 42. Cf. Scheid 1998, 424.

the supervision of the pontiffs ('*arbitratu pontificum*').[94] Livy informs us in this passage that the *ver sacrum* was inappropriately conducted in the year 195, yet he does not provide any details on what the irregularities may have involved.

The new decree from the senate in the year 194 did not specify who should be in charge of the celebration of the *ver sacrum*, but it can be presumed that, as in the previous year, it had to be conducted by the consuls. Nevertheless, Livy does not provide any further information on its celebration in 194; he simply indicates that it was conducted along with the *ludi magni*.[95] In any case, the *ver sacrum* celebrated in the year 194 seems to have been considered appropriate, because there are no further references to it or to any other in the following years and decades.

To summarize, among the civilian functions that consuls had to or could carry out, religious tasks had enormous qualitative significance, not only as a portion of the duties of the magistracy but also as an important aspect of the Roman *civitas*. The consuls had to take the public vows on the first day in which they held office, pleading to the gods for the welfare of the community during the consular year. It was the consuls who had to perform the prescribed rites to expiate the prodigies reported in the previous months. The consuls also had to select the date for the celebration of the *Feriae Latinae* as well as preside over the festival at the Mons Albanus. No other magistrate could replace the consuls at such ceremonies. At the same time, no consul could leave Rome to take command of the army in his *provincia* without having properly completed all of these rituals. Likewise, it is also possible that, at least occasionally, the consuls presided over the ceremonies involved in the *sacra* of Lavinium in this Latin city. Besides this, the consuls had to preside *ex officio* over the *ludi*, although they could only preside over the games if the celebration took place while they were still in Rome. Exceptionally, in the only case in which sources mention the celebration of a *ver sacrum* in Rome, the consuls were responsible for ensuring that the ritual was properly performed. All of these tasks were obviously of a religious nature, but they should not be considered as sacerdotal tasks. Rather, they were political functions, because the consuls, as supreme magistrates, acted on behalf of the state with the ultimate purpose of preserving the *res publica*, thus adopting the role of *curatores* of the *pax deorum*.

---

[94] Livy 34.44.1–3. About the celebration of the *ver sacrum* in 195–194, see Briscoe 1981, 22–3.
[95] Livy 34.44.6.

CHAPTER 6

The Feriae Latinae *as religious legitimation of the consuls'* imperium

Francisco Marco Simón

Apart from the offering of the *vota publica* in the Capitoline temple, and the expiation of prodigies (*procuratio prodigiorum*) in the name of the community, the setting of the date for the celebration of the *Feriae Latinae* was among the unavoidable duties of the consuls in Rome at the beginning of their time in office. Unless they carried out this ritual properly, the consuls could never leave the *Urbs* to undertake any military campaign. In doing otherwise, they would expose themselves to failure in their endeavours, as was the case with C. Flaminius in 218[1] or the consuls of 43 BC, Aulus Hirtius and Vibius Pansa.[2] However, while it is clear why the offering of public ex-votos and the expiation of prodigies were necessary conditions for maintaining or restoring the *pax deorum*, it is not so evident, at least at first sight, why the celebration of the *Feriae Latinae* was an unavoidable duty for the consuls in the context of the conquering republic. The following reflections are aimed at understanding the reasons why, after so much time, this consular intervention in the Latin festival is still perceived as one of the *fundamenta rei publicae*.

The *Feriae Latinae* were annual rituals which the Latin League celebrated in honour of *Iuppiter Latiaris* next to his sanctuary on the summit of the Mons Albanus – the present-day Monte Cavo, situated about 27 km to the southeast of Rome. This was a movable feast (*feria conceptiva*[3]), whose exact date would be set by the consuls immediately after taking office. A series of literary sources underline the enormous political relevance of this ritual and its importance when setting the sacred calendar of Rome, as well as its exceptional longevity and the fact that it was celebrated up until the end of the fourth century AD. The decision to announce publicly the celebration of the *feriae* (specifically, on the third day, when the *sacrificium*

---

[1] Livy 21.63.5–9; 22.1.4–7.   [2] Cass. Dio 46.33.4.
[3] Varro, *Ling.* 6.25: *Similiter Latinae feriae dies conceptivus, dictus a Latinis populus, quibus in Albano monte ex sacris carnem petere fuit ius cum Romanis, a quibus Latinis Latinae dictae.*

Latinarum was celebrated)[4] was taken in the senate after the consuls took office, and it was expressed via a *senatus consultum*.[5]

The *Feriae Latinae* involved the combined journey of the Roman community as represented by all its magistrates, headed by the consuls, its priests and a part of its population[6] to the Mons Albanus along the Sacra via and the Via Latina, and the same applied to the other participating Latin cities.[7] During the feast, all hostilities were suspended,[8] and a young nobleman was appointed *praefectus urbi feriarum Latinarum causa*[9] to run the activities held in Rome.[10] Thus this was a very old Latin federation ritual which annually reinforced the links between Rome and the rest of the cities.

The consuls' religious duties as holders of the *auspicia* and the *imperium* were not only confined to the Latin Feast, but also included the regular ceremonies that had to be held in Lavinium, the mythical city founded by Aeneas, the holy city of the *primordia*, the seat of the *sacra principiorum p(opuli) R(omani) Q(uiritium) nominisque Latini, qua apud Laurentes coluntur*.[11] The consuls and other magistrates *cum imperio*[12] were required to make a pilgrimage to this city ten days after the *Feriae Latinae*[13] to make sacrifices to the Penates and Vesta.[14] In fact, Livy says that the sacred

---

[4] According to Werner (1888, 23) and other authors, the ancient festival would have been reduced to one day, increasing to two following the expulsion of the kings and three after the *foedus Cassianum* (Grandazzi 2008, 584).
[5] Cic. *Fam.* 8.6.3: *Consules autem habemus summa diligentia; adhuc s.c. nisi de feriis Latinis nullum facere potuerunt.*
[6] Even the tribunes, who could not usually leave Rome, attended Monte Cavo (Dion. Hal. 8.87.6; Livy 22.1.6; Alföldi 1965, 32). On the Latin festival, see Werner 1888; Samter 1909a; de Ruggiero 1922; Wissowa 1912, 40, 124ff.; Sabbatucci 1988, 305ff.; Pasqualini 1996; García Quintela 2007, 88–96; Grandazzi 2008, 517–729.
[7] On the layout of the Alban route see the reconstruction by Lugli 1923.
[8] Dion. Hal. 4.49.2; Macr. *Sat.* 1.16.16ff. [9] *CIL* VI 1421; Cass. Dio 49.42.1; 53.33.3.
[10] Cicero says that the two days after the Latin festival were *religiosi* (*Q. Fr.* 2.4.2), and in another passage (*Rep.* 1, 14), he claims that Scipio Aemilianus spent the Latin holidays in his country villa (*in hortis*) conversing with his friends and acquaintances. We do not know, although it was probably so, whether in the other Latin cities the solemn day of the celebration on Monte Cavo was equally followed by some days of rest. Everything indicates that a break from work was observed throughout the city, and the ludic moment of the festivity culminated in a chariot race in the Campidoglio, its winner being presented with a drink of *absynthium* (Plin. *HN* 27.45). The very little information existing (Malavolta 2006, 258) permits us to see in the *Feriae Latinae* an archaic prototype of all the important festivals included (unlike the *Feriae Latinae*) in the Roman calendar and accompanied by the celebration of games.
[11] *CIL* X 797 = *ILS* 5004.
[12] The *pontifices* (Ser. *Aen.* 1.239; Schol. Veron. *Aen.* 1.260) and the *flamines* (Ser. *Aen.* 8.664) also participated in the retinue of the magistrates.
[13] Livy 8.11.15: *Cum Laurentibus renovari foedus iussum. Renovaturque ex eo quotannis post diem decimum Latinarum.*
[14] Macr. *Sat.* 3.4.11; Ser. *Aen.* 2.296.

ancestral traditions decreed that sacrifices should be held on the Mons Albanus and in Lavinium – an essential duality that was underlined in the *primordia sacra*[15] – and it is probable that this would have been an obligation of the kings before. As in the case of the consuls in the Latin Feast, the *imperatores* could not leave for their provinces without first having sacrificed to the Penates of Lavinium.[16] This obligation is a clear example of the importance of the sacerdotal functions of the *imperatores*, who, according to Cicero, would even consecrate themselves before the immortal gods for the benefit of the state.[17]

It is particularly interesting that minor triumphs of generals who were denied such honours on the Capitoline site were celebrated on the Mons Albanus.[18] According to the *fasti*, the first triumph *in monte Albano* was celebrated by C. Papirius Maso on 5 March 231 BC[19] as an act of protest against the senatorial denial of a triumph on the Capitol,[20] although it is possible that such a ceremony was an updated version of an archaic Latin *ritus*, as some authors in the wake of Niehbur have argued.[21] This ritual of the Alban triumph, of which no instances are reported by the sources after the celebration of C. Cicereius in 173, unquestionably casts new light on the competition of the senatorial elite in the crucial decades of the Roman expansion.[22]

Most of the information available contains references to the origin of the Feast, the participants and the ceremonies, with Dionysius of Halicarnassus' account being the most thorough.[23] Although the rituals were not fully described, the ceremony was a *lustratio*, a purification ritual which included a procession with the sacrificial animals and the objects offered to the god. The consuls – certainly after the Latin League's dissolution in

---

[15] Liou-Gille 1996, 86.
[16] Ser. *Aen.* 3.12: *Quos (Penates) inter cetera ideo magnos apellant, quod de Lavinio translati Romam bis in locum suum redierint; quod imperatores in provincias ituri apud eos primum immolarint.*
[17] Cic. *Nat. D.* 2.10: *Tum enim bella gerere nostri duces incipiunt, cum auspicia posuerunt; at vero apud maiores tanta religionis vis fuit, ut quidam imperatores etiam se ipsos dis inmortalibus capite velato verbis certis pro se republica devoverent.* On the *auspicia* and the grounds of the power of *imperatores*, see Levi 1932; Rivero Gracia 2006.
[18] Versnel 1970, 165–6, 192–3; Brennan 1996; Itgenshorst 2005, 219–23; Beard 2007, 62–3.
[19] Val. Max. 3.6.5; Plin. *HN* 15.126; Degrassi 1947, 78: *de Corseis Primus in monte Albano.*
[20] These Alban triumphs, although exclusively celebrated *iure consulare potestatis* (Livy 33.23.3) and *sine publica auctoritate* (Livy 42.21.7), were included in the triumphal *Fasti* to all effects; they probably involved the ascent of the *imperator* on a triumphal quadriga; and they had the advantage of not being subject to the tribunal *intercessio*, for the right of veto of this magistrate ended at the first mile from the *Urbs* (Brennan 1996, 321).
[21] Partly due to the Latin origin of the *gens Papiria*, which had a special relationship with Roman state religion, as recalled by Goell (references in Brennan 1996, 332 n. 34). The extreme position was held by Alföldi (1965, 45 and 391–2), for whom the ancient Alban triumph may have been the genuine prototype of the Roman triumph. See also Grandazzi 2008, 735. *Contra*, Brennan 1996, 321–2.
[22] Brennan 1996.   [23] Dion. Hal. 4.49; 6.95; Plut. *Cam.* 42.5; Str. 5.3.2.

338 BC – first sprinkled the sacred area with milk, not wine, in what appears to have been a fertility and prosperity ritual (Cicero himself performed the *lustratio* during his consulship in 63 BC[24]).

According to Dionysius of Halicarnassus,[25] King Tarquinius Superbus established the Feast in a sanctuary shared by the Romans, Latins, Hernici and Volsci, on a mountain situated roughly in the middle of these peoples (*en meso málista tôn ethnôn*), when he proclaimed a law that established the annual contribution to be made by each of the 47 cities for the sacrifices to *Iuppiter Latiaris*, and the share that they would receive of the collective banquets (*synestíasis*) that followed straight afterwards. Some cities contributed lambs, others cheeses, others milk and others similar offerings characteristic of a pastoral culture. All the cities made a common sacrifice (*koinos hypo pason*) of a bull (originally white[26] and then red), and each would receive their due share (*moîra, méros; caro*[27]), in a highly formalized distribution in accordance with the established hierarchy under the control of the Roman magistrates.[28]

The hierarchic layout displayed at the communal banquet thus reflects the existing hierarchy in the Latin league, of a Laurentine origin on the mythical level and an Alban origin on the ritual plane.[29] Romans would conduct these sacrifices on behalf of all. At least on one occasion, a sudden change in the weather conditions interrupted the ceremonies.[30] The successful completion of the rituals was marked by a great sacrificial nocturnal fire at the top of the mountain, which could be seen from a great distance.[31]

Tarquinius' part in establishing the ritual, as claimed by Dionysius' text and by pseudo-Aurelius Victor,[32] is not to be found in other authors who, however, underline the Latin origin of the Feast.[33] In fact, there are Bronze

---

[24] Cic. *Div.* 1.11.18. The formula *Latinas condere* contained in a recently discovered epigraph, comparable to the formula *lustrum condere* (Ogilvie 1961), likewise indicates the purifying nature of the *Feriae*, in which, as senior magistrates, the censors would have been present (Grandazzi 2008, 612).
[25] Dion. Hal. 4.49.   [26] Arn. 2.68.   [27] Varro, *Ling.* 6.25.
[28] The expression *carnem petere* used by Varro (*Ling.* 6.25) or by Cicero (*Planc.* 9.23) to refer to the portion reclaimed by the various Latin cities underlines this subordination. And it might be considered, given the example of the *Fratres Arvales*, that the consuls might have offered – between the *praefatio* and death of the victim – a 'universal prayer' for the *nomen Latinum* as a whole (Grandazzi 2008, 594).
[29] Liou-Gille 1996, 87.   [30] Livy 40.45.2.
[31] Luc. 1.550; 5.403: *vidit flammifera confectas nocte Latinas*.   [32] *De vir. ill.* 8.2.
[33] See Varro, *Ling.* 6.25, or a scholium of Cicero: Schol. Bob. *Ad Cic. Pro Planc.* 23, 154–5 Stangl: *Nam Latinae feriae a quo fuerunt institutae, dissentiunt plerique auctores. Alii ab Tarquinio Prisco, rege Romanorum, existimant, alii vero a Latinis Priscis. Atque inter hos ipsos causa sacrificii non convenit. Nam quidam id initum ex imperato Fauni contendunt, nonnulli post obitum Latini regis et Aeneae, quod ii nusquam compaverunt.* The role of the consuls would have been performed in earlier times by a federal magistrate, perhaps the *dictator Albanus* mentioned in the epigraphy (Grandazzi 2008, 574).

Age remains on the Mons Albanus.[34] The lack of wine (a drink dedicated *par excellence* to Jupiter[35]) in the Alban rite could be an indication in dating the ritual to the pre-Orientalizing period,[36] and the lack of the *flamen Dialis* amongst the epigraphically attested priesthoods,[37] as opposed to the case of Lavinium,[38] Lanuvium[39] or Tivoli,[40] could be another indication that Jupiter was not present in the original cultic complex of the Latins, but that this was an innovation of the new Roman ruling class.[41] The expression *Latiar*,[42] regarding the festivals carried out on the Mons Albanus, seems to be another good indication of the ritual's ancient origin.[43] Additionally, Servius calls Latial Jupiter *deus antiquissimus* (*Aen.* 12, 135).

Awareness of the extremely old Latin identity, for which we have documentation *ante quem* from the middle of the seventh century with the appearance in the Etruscan epigraphy of the ethnic as a demonym for the Latins who were settled there,[44] is particularly expressed in the celebration of the *Feriae Latinae*. The problem lies in determining when those primitive ritual reunions to honour the national deity acquired a political nature. Whereas some authors hold that the Plinian list of the communities[45] which *carnem accipere* on the Mons Albanus may be already conveying the existence of a federation with political connotations, as an embryo of the future Latin League, others hold that it shows an archaic phase of the Alban cult – but without the political-military nature that it was to have when acting against the Roman intention of dominating Latium – already in existence before Tarquinius Superbus, with the political and religious centres in the territory of Aricia (the *lucus Ferentinae* at the foot of the Mons Albanus, and the sanctuary of Diana Nemorensis, respectively[46]).

Tarquinius' leading role in the Feast would therefore represent an intervention in an already existing ritual, perhaps with the building of a temple, in the context of Roman expansionist policy towards the end of the regal

---

[34] Cavo Chiarucci 1996.   [35] Dumézil 1986, 87–97.   [36] Colonna 1988, 447.
[37] The references of Pirro Ligorio to two presumed inscriptions (*CIL* XIV 124 and 126) which appeared 'presso la porta dell'Amfiteatro di Alba' mentioning Alban *Diale*s are not reliable and the inscriptions seem to be fake.
[38] *CIL* X 79 = *ILS* 5004; *CIL* XIV 4176.   [39] *CIL* XIV 2089.   [40] *CIL* XIV 3596 = *ILS* 1158.
[41] Pasqualini 1996, 240.   [42] Cic. Q. Fr. 2.4.2; Macrob. *Sat.* 1.16.16.
[43] Its suffixation also appears in the *Palatuar* (Fest. s.v. *Septimontio*, 474–6 L), an archaic sacrifice celebrated in the Palatine during the *Septimontium*.
[44] In Caere, the inscription *mi latinnas* is documented around the year 650, and in Veyes, *mi tites latinnes* towards 625 (Martínez-Pinna 2004, 44, with references).
[45] Plin. *HN* 3.69: *carnem in monte Albano soliti accipere populi Albenses: Albani, Aesolani, Accienses, Abolani, Bubetani, Bolani, Cusuetani, Coriolani, Fidenates, Foreti, Hortenses, Latinienses, Longani, Manates, Macrales, Munienses, Numinienses, Olliculani, Octulani, Pedani, Poletaurini, Querquetulani, Sicani, Sisolenses, Tolerienses, Tutienses, Vimitellani, Velienses, Venetulani, Vitellenses.*
[46] Martínez-Pinna 2004, 45–6, 53–6.

period. Thus Tarquinius would have reformed the Latin ritual, opening it up to members who did not belong to the *Latini Prisci*, by establishing new bases for participation in the organization, and for the system of distributing the sacrificial meat.[47] The process, which could represent a genuine show of force on the part of Rome, can be considered to have concluded with the presidency of the consuls over the Latin Festival. It is possible that Rome assumed the management of the celebration of this ancient Latin ritual after the signing of the *foedus Cassianum* (c. 493), in the middle of the fifth century; in fact, the list of the Roman *praefecti urbi* of the *feriae Latinae* begins in 451.[48]

A passage by Cornificius Longus – a friend of Catullus and Virgil, author of a work *De etymis deorum* and correspondent of Cicero – appears to be of great interest with regard to the mythical origin of the festival. While Dionysius of Halicarnassus[49] reports the death on the battlefield of King Latinus, the eponymous name for Latium, Cornificius points out that Latinus became *Iuppiter Latiaris* and was worshipped as such on the Mons Albanus. In the rituals of the anniversary of this apotheosis, participants simulated the search for him swinging in the air (*oscillantes*).[50] A scholium by Cicero indicates almost the same act on the anniversaries of the deaths of Latinus and Eneas, with the participants searching for their souls in the air.[51] This ritual of the *oscillantes* could thus evoke the apotheosis of Latinus.[52]

A particularly remarkable element in Christian sources (from Justinus to Paulinus of Nola)[53] is the practice of a human sacrifice at Rome during the *Feriae Latinae*, usually interpreted as part of a denigrating strategy by Christian authors from the second century onwards in order to take back these nefarious practices to the very origins of Roman religion in its Latial context. However, recently some authors have defended the authenticity of this information, based on Porphyry's confirmation thereof[54] and on the absence of response from the supporters of the traditional religion to these charges.[55] A text by Florus refers to the fact that the plotters in the *Bellum*

---

[47] Liou-Gille 1996, 92.   [48] Alföldi 1965, 31; Brennan 1996, 321.
[49] Dion. Hal. 1.64.3.   [50] Fest. 212 L.
[51] *Schol. In Cic. Orat. Bobiensia*, ed. Hildebrandt, 1907, 128–9. The formula *quaerere in aere*, which appears in Servius as well as the Bobbio scholia, seems to refer to Varro as its source (Grandazzi 2008, 648).
[52] Pasqualini 1996, 222–4.
[53] A statue of *Iuppiter Latiaris* was ritually sprinkled with blood by one of the most senior figures of the state (references in Grandazzi 2008, 653 and n. 582).
[54] Porph *Abst.* 2.56.9.
[55] Grandazzi 2008, 653ff. A comparable elusiveness is shown by the sources towards rituals which, like the burying alive of victims in the Foro Boario, were classed as being *minime romano sacrum* (Marco Simón 1997).

Sociale intended to murder the consuls during the *Feriae Latinae*, and the terminology used is clearly sacrificial.[56] The designation of *Iuppiter Latialis* given to Caligula, who wished to re-establish the rule of the *rex Nemorensis*, could make much more sense from this perspective.

This human sacrifice is an element which could underline the enormous antiquity of the Alban ritual, as well as libations of milk rather than wine in a symbolic context that gave prevalence to the colour white (bull, milk, cheese, Alba, the colour of the sow of Lavinium, Albula as the ancient name of the Tiber[57]).

The sharing out of the meat of the sacrificed white bull confirmed Roman hegemony,[58] since the representatives of the Latin communities had to ask for their share,[59] and Livy[60] says that their delegates had to formulate a prayer to *populo Romano Quiritium*. Non-compliance with this latter requirement by the magistrate of Lanuvium was precisely the reason that the ceremony (*instauratio*) had to be repeated in 176 BC. As the ritual could not be performed again until 11 August, the consuls could not leave for their provinces until this late date.[61]

We have other examples of the need for scrupulous compliance with the ritual in accordance with ancestral customs: for example, the representatives of Ardea[62] or Laurentum[63] protesting in 199 BC because they had not received their due portion of the sacrificed animal. This incorrect division of the meat was seen as a rupture in the social hierarchy, which was supposed to be confirmed and re-established every year through the meat's division and distribution.

The studies carried out by Detienne and Vernant (1979) have shown how sacrifice and conviviality established, in Greece, the relations which

---

[56] Flor. 2.6.8: *Primum fuit in Albano monte consilium, ut festo die Latinarum Iulius Caesar et Marcius Philippus consules inter sacra et aras immolarentur. Postquam id nefas proditione discussum est.*

[57] De Simone 1975, 152–7.

[58] Dion. Hal. 4.49.3. Walter Burkert (1962) compared the story of the dismembering of Romulus' body (as told by Plutarch, *Rom.* 27) with the sharing out of the meat of the white bull in the *Feriae Latinae* (see also Coarelli 1981, 183ff.; Cecamore 2006, 59), and also (like Puhvel 1975) in connection with the Indo-European mytheme of a cosmogony through the dismembering of a primordial being, such as Purusha in Sanskrit texts (references in Lincoln 1986, 1–40), with the difference that what the Roman version gives is a sociogonic myth (Lincoln 1986, 43).

[59] *Carnem petere*: Varro, *Ling.* 6.25; Cic. *Planc.* 23.   [60] Livy 41.16.1.

[61] Livy 41.16: *Latinae feriae fuere ante diem tertium nonas Maias, in quibus quia in una hostia magistratus Lanuvinus precatus non erat populo Romano Quiritium, religioni fuit. Id cum ad senatum relatum esset senatusque ad pontificum collegium reiecisset, pontificibus, quia non recte factae Latinae essent, instaurandae essent, hostias praebere. Accesserat ad religionem, quod Cn. Cornelius consul ex monte Albano rediens concidit et, parte membrorum captus ad Aquas Cumanas profectus ingravescente morbo Cumis decessit... Consul Q. Petilius cum primum per auspicia posset, collegae subrogando comitia habere iussus et Latinas edicere, comitia in ante diem tertium nonas Sextiles, Latinas in ante diem tertium idus Sextiles edixit.*

[62] Livy 32.1.19.   [63] Livy 37.3.4.

The Feriae Latinae *as religious legitimation* 123

underpinned the state under the control of the gods. Likewise, in Rome, the distribution of the flesh of the victim and its consumption gave rise to a distinction between the social and political elements of the state, starting from the federal sacrifice on Monte Cavo[64] *en meso málista tôn ethnôn.*[65] At the communal banquet (*synestíasis*) the part (*moîra, méros*) for each city was established. Although the Latin term *particeps* is related in some texts to the distribution of booty, in others it refers to the distribution of the sacrifice,[66] and the institution of sacrifice was the 'conceptual forge which supplied the Roman state with the most important models of value'.[67] The sacrifice-banquet illustrated the basic social transactions, and the sacrifice in the Mons Albanus symbolically resumes the *maiestas populi Romani* in the privileged horizon of Latium.

The very few archaeological remains found on Monte Cavo have failed to complement reliably existing information from literary sources. As a result of the construction of a convent at the beginning of the eighteenth century, a great number of marble blocks, fragments of two statues and numerous votive offerings made of clay and bronze were found. Cassius Dio's references[68] to a statue of Zeus on the site are no guarantee of the existence of a temple as such, although a *fistula* was found there, mentioning a *CVR(ator) AED(is) S(acrae)*.[69] What have been found on the summit of Monte Cavo are the *Fasti* of the *Feriae Latinae*,[70] specifically fragments bearing the names of the magistrates who presided over the ceremony. The oldest of them belong to the decemviral period,[71] when the consulate was restored after the resignation of the second college. Presided over by the consuls Marcus Horatius Barbatus and L. Valerius Potitus, the *Feriae Latinae* were celebrated three times, in January, February and May in 449.[72]

---

[64] Scheid 1984.   [65] Dion. Hal. 4.49.
[66] For example, Livy 10.38.9: *admovebatur altaribus magis ut victima quam ut sacri particeps*. The Roman census system would reproduce the share-out of the sacrifice. The *principes* are 'those who take the first share, the first rank' (Fest. 62 L), and the *adsidui* 'those who sit at the sacrificial table' (Fest. 8L).
[67] Scheid 1984, 956.   [68] Cass. Dio 47.40.4; 50.8.6.
[69] Cecamore 2006, 56. Although it has been believed that the inscription *CIL* XIV 2227 alludes to a temple at the top of the Mons Albanus, the text, as pointed out by Grandazzi (2006, 203) must be read *Ioui Latia(ri) (uo)tum*.
[70] *CIL* I 1, 55; Mommsen 1871, 379–85. The displaying of the *Fasti*, together with a probable restoration of the sanctuary, would have been the result of an intervention by Augustus, which ended with his visit there some days before the Kalends of July (Grandazzi 2008, 600).
[71] 304, 305 and 306 AUC.
[72] <*M. Horatio M. f. L. N. Barbato L. Valerio*> *P. f. P. n. Putito cos / L(atinae) f(uerunt) IIII EID IAN / <ite>rum L(atinae) f(uerunt) III NON FE<B>R / <tert(ium)> L(atinae) f(uerunt) K MAI* (Mommsen 1871, 380). Maybe the repetition of the ritual was due to flaws incurred during its celebration (Liou-Gille 1996, 96). Mommsen (1871, 382), who held that this celebration ought to

Most of the *Fasti* fragments are from the latter years of the republic and the beginning of the principate,[73] but there are others from the time of the Second Punic War; these are the ones that tell us that the Feast was then held in the second fortnight in April or the beginning of May, and it was then, in 217 BC, that the consul C. Flaminius began his activities in his province without first having seen to his religious obligations, as a *priuatus*.[74] These activities culminated in the famous disaster at Lake Trasimene. Even so, the accusation against Flaminius seems to be more of a reflection on the skill of his adversaries than on the impiety of the consul, since there are examples of how the assistance of one of the consuls was sometimes enough to ensure legally the celebration of the *Feriae*.[75]

It is reasonable to think that the consuls would have wished to celebrate the Feast as soon as possible, in order to put behind them the constraints that the ritual imposed. In fact, a passage from Cicero[76] referring to the snowy peaks of the Alban Hills in the context of these rituals would suggest, in view of the low altitude of these hills, that it was celebrated at the beginning of the year.[77] Nevertheless, literary and epigraphic sources indicate that most of the celebrations were held – on the Ides, Nones or Kalends, or on the eve of those days – between April and August, with the predominance of May and only four instances of celebration in winter.[78]

The unavoidable performing of the ceremonies by the consuls on the summit of Mount Cavo seems to be one of the true elements that bestowed authority on the highest magistrates of the Roman state.[79] Any anomaly

be considered as an action of gratitude towards the gods for the restoration of the *res Romanae* after the troubled period, proposes the following restitution of Livy's corrupt passage: *(In triduum supplicationes decrevitur Latinae dictae a consule sunt in ante IIII et IIII et pr. Id. Nob.): In triduum supplicationes decrevit. Iterum Latinae edictae a consule sunt in a.d. III et III et pr. Et id. Nov.* (cf. Liou-Gille 1996, 96).

[73] There is documentary evidence of the personal presence of, among others, Camillus (in 396 BC), Caesar (49 and 44 BC), Agrippa (27 BC), Augustus (23 BC), Claudius (AD 47 and 48) and Nero. The last inscription is dated AD 109, but it is almost certain that the *Feriae* continued right up to 394, when they were celebrated for the last time by Nicomachus Flavius (Grandazzi 2008, 569–70).

[74] Livy 21.63: *privatus clam in provinciam abiit.* See Caltabiano 1976.

[75] As occurred in 169 BC, when one of the consuls was in Macedonia (Livy 45.3.2), and in four of the consulates of Augustus (Grandazzi 2008, 578 n. 221).

[76] Cic. *Div.* 1.11.18: *Tu quoque, quum tumulos Albano in monte nivalis lustrasti et laeto mactasti lacte Latinas... quod ferme dirum in tempus cecidere Latinae.*

[77] Liou-Gille 1996, 91.

[78] The fact that most of the dates mentioned by the epigraphic *Fasti* were *dies comitiales* would explain the Roman wish not to have these ceremonies coincide with their own festivals (Brind'Amour 1983, 61 and 84).

[79] Livy 21.63.5 and 9; 22.1.6 and 7; Nic. Dam. 5.13; Cass. Dio 46.33.4. This would have been more by way of a customary rule (*mos*) than a *lex*; 'a confirmatory act', as Mommsen termed it (Grandazzi 2008, 575 and 577).

in the election of consular magistrates or the ritual setting of dates for the *Feriae* and the carrying out of the sacrifice would give rise to prodigies – such as the sudden rise in water level of Lake Alban – which needed to be atoned for.[80] Literary sources document the presence on the Mons Albanus of not just the principal altar but others, including one dedicated to Vesta or attended by the Vestal Virgins, whose flames signalled the end of the festival.[81] The existence of accommodation on the mountain to house the consuls is suggested by information supplied by Cassius Dio.[82] It is fairly safe to assume that the consuls would have spent the night in this house on the eve of the sacrifice, in view of the fact that the sacrifices were normally performed in the morning after consulting auspices.[83] And it is also fairly safe to assume that after the *auspicia urbana* in the ceremony on the Capitol that inaugurated his power over the Roman *res publica*, the new consul would have carried out a second *auspicatio* on the Mons Albanus to inaugurate his *imperium* over the *ager Latinus*, the territory that for so long symbolized the outside world for the *Urbs*.[84]

In the wake of Radin's (1936) proposal of considering the initial *triumphus in monte Albano* as a royal investiture ritual which was perpetuated through the investiture of the *dictator Latinarum feriarum causa*,[85] García Quintela[86] has proposed seeing the ascension to the Mons Albanus as a 'chemin de souveraineté et de celebration du royauté' similar to the 'federal' ritual of the *Daidala* feasts celebrated in Boeotia by Platea and other cities[87] to confirm the bonds that linked them, according to the 'political' explanation by Rocchi.[88] From this perspective, it might not be coincidental that Dionysius of Halicarnassus refers to the heritage of royal attributes (purple tunic, ivory chair) when describing the organization of the *Feriae Latinae*,[89] that Caesar made explicit his aspirations to kingship after celebrating such a ritual in 44 BC,[90] or that Augustus left the consulship, held from the year 31 to 1 July

---

[80] Livy 5.17.2 (397 or 392 BC): *ad prodigii Albani procurationem ad deos placandos . . . : inventumque tandem est ubi neglectas caerimonias intermissumve sollemne di arguerent: nihil profecto aliud esse quam magistratus vitio creatos Latinas sacrumque in Albano monte non rite concepisse.*
[81] Luc. 549–52: *Vestali raptus ab ara / ignis et ostendens confectas flamma Latinas / scinditur in partes geminoque cacumine surgit / Thebanos imitata rogos.*
[82] Cass. Dio 54.29.7: in 12 BC, after the death of Agrippa, a bolt of lightning struck the house which the consuls went down to.
[83] According to Festus (474.7 and 474.35L), it was the consul's duty that: *post mediam<noctem auspi>candi causa ex lectulo suo si<lens surr>exit*, and that: *mane surg<ens auspicandi gratia evigi>lavit.*
[84] Grandazzi 2008, 610.   [85] Mentioned by the *Fasti Capitolini*, *CIL* I 58, in 257 BC.
[86] García Quintela 2007, 96–7.   [87] Paus. 9.2.7; 9.3.1–8.   [88] Rocchi 1989, 323.
[89] Dion. Hal. 6.95.3–4.   [90] Plut. *Caes.* 60.3.

23 BC, on the occasion of a solemn ceremony performed on the Mons Albanus.[91]

The growing importance of the festival in later times shows that the consuls were accompanied to the summit of the Mons Albanus by the other higher magistrates, and in the late republic the consuls still considered it to be of great importance. For example, in a sarcastic letter to Cicero in 50, Caelius writes that the consuls were in frenzied activity, as they had only presented one motion to the senate: the setting of the date for the *Feriae Latinae*.[92] A year later, in 49, Caesar, who had hurriedly returned from Hispania and was anxious to leave for Greece to fight Pompey, had to remain in Rome for eleven days, at least one of which he had to devote to celebrating the Alban ritual.[93]

As Pasqualini has pointed out,[94] the feast in honour of *Iuppiter Latiaris*, symbolic preface to any subsequent expansion of Roman power, finally acquired all its imperialist connotations under Caesar, who, as dictator, tried to legitimize his monarchical tendencies by using myths that suggested the sovereignty of Alba, of which the *gens Iulia* was the keeper and custodian. One member of this *gens* had been the 'Alban' Julius Proculus, an eyewitness of the deification of Romulus. Having celebrated the *Feriae Latinae*,[95] Caesar entered Rome on 26 January 44 BC and was the subject of an unusual, original *ovatio*, recalling the style of the *adventus*, or rather the 'epiphany', of the eastern monarchs.[96]

Augustus, loyal to his self-representation as a *restaurator rei publicae*, deposited a list of all the magistrates who had celebrated the festival at the top of Monte Cavo, and these *Fasti* continued during the imperial era. Some fragments even show that Augustus, when consul, wanted to carry out this task, which he could not do on two occasions because of illness (in 27 and 24 BC), and on another two occasions because he was in Hispania leading the operations against the *Cantabri* and the *Astures* (in 26 and 25 BC). Finally, in 23 BC, *imperator Caesar in monte fuit*.[97]

All this information is best understood if we look at the importance of the *auspicia* in the definition of *imperium*[98] and the augural nature of the Mons Albanus. It has been suggested[99] that the element which generated

---

[91] Cass. Dio 53.32, as Syme (1939 [1985], 333–6) pointed out. See also Jullian 1899; Santi 2000, 222–4.
[92] Cic. *Fam.* 8.6.3.
[93] Caes. *B Civ.* 3.2. The fact that the festival was celebrated in December points to a second celebration (Cass. Dio. 41.14; Luc. 1.550) due to a deficient development of the first, or to Caesar being honoured with the right to celebrate some special festivals (Scullard 1981, 249 n. 144, with references).
[94] Pasqualini 1996, 251. [95] Cass. Dio 43.43.2. [96] Weinstock 1971, 320–1.
[97] Degrassi 1947, 143ff. [98] Levi 1932; Rivero Gracia 2006. [99] Grandazzi 1986, 77ff.

in ancient authors the need to imagine an urban centre as a 'metropolis' of the Latin cities could be seen in the effective ritual of the *Feriae Latinae*, and in this respect I would like to refer to a final aspect of the space where the Latin festival was celebrated: its augural nature.[100]

Not only is Monte Cavo the highest point (950 m) in the central volcanic mass of *Latium Vetus*, the federal sanctuary of the *nomen Latinum*, but it was also the sighting point taken by the augur in the Roman observatory – the Capitoline *arx*[101] – to define the axis of the heavenly regions. The *Forma Urbis Marmorea*, from the time of Severus, but started during the time of Augustus, has the Capitol at the centre and a transversal axis (*spectio auguralis*) which goes straight to the Mons Albanus, following the straight line of the Via Latina, and measures exactly eight times the length of the marble plan of the *Urbs*.[102] This condition of Monte Cavo as the core of the augural *spectio* seems also to be confirmed in the case of the city of Norba,[103] and it is possible that this very role may have been played by Monte Cavo in other Latin cities, since in Campania cities such as Pompeii and Nuceria positioned their urban layouts depending on highly visible peaks with sanctuaries on them.[104]

This correspondence between the two axes of the augural *spectio*, the Alban and Capitoline *arces*, almost certainly shows the relationship between the two manifestations of Jupiter, the Latial and the Capitoline. There is a set of elaborate and complex correlations between the two sacred

---

[100] Coarelli (1981; 1983, 195–6) had already suggested that the existence of an *auguraculum* in the *collis Latiaris* of Rome was not mere topographic coincidence, but ought to imply the existence of another on the Mons Albanus.

[101] Called *auguraculum* in the past because it was the site where auspices were taken: Fest. 17 L: *auguraculum appellabant antiqui, quam nos arcem dicimus, quod ibi augures publice auspicarentur*. A direct link between *auguraculum* and *ager* is made in Varro (*Ling.* 6.53). The same author points to a clear connection in this regard with the Mons Albanus: (*Ling.* 5, 32); that is, alongside the augural functions of the *arx Albana* there are also the commitial functions of the *nomen Latinum*, as a precise parallel of the functions of the *Comitium* and the *Campus Martius* in Rome (Cecamore 2006, 64).

[102] Rodríguez Almeida 2003, 10–11 and fig. 4; Coarelli 1983, 101 arguing for the existence of an *auguraculum* on the Mons Albanus, which would also be proved by the cognomen of *arx Albana* with which Monte Cavo is officially designated in inscriptions (Grandazzi 2008, 609). The Via Latina is the only road out of the *Urbs* that has no anthroponymic epithet, which seems to indicate that it was the processional route that climbed the *Latiar*, where the *Feriae Latinae* were celebrated (Radke 1973). It also seems significant that the *porta Capena* – from which the *Via Latina* started – gave its name to the first of the fourteen urban regions, and referred to the toponym *Cabum* and the *Cabenses* of the Monte Cavo (Coarelli 1996), while the legend that situates the city of Alba Longa on this mountain would be merely an aetiological explanation for the augural nature of the *arx Albana* situated thereon.

[103] Quilici Gigli 2003, 321–2.

[104] Details in de Cazanove 2005.

mountains, that of Rome – the Campidoglio – and of Latium – the Mons Albanus – that seem to be not contradictory,[105] but complementary:[106] this seems to be borne out by Pliny's mention[107] of Spurius Carvilius Maximus, the victorious commander in the Third Samnite War, setting up an enormous statue of Jupiter on the Capitol, which was so big that it could be seen from the Latial Jupiter. At any event, this duality expresses an essential component in the semantization of the landscape: the topography as an essential element to back up memory in oral societies. The *mnemotopos*, a place with memory, played the same role as ritual reiteration. The view of certain elements in the landscape revived both memory and identity: this seems to be the case of the Mons Albanus as an extreme of the *spectio auguralis* from the heart of the *Urbs Roma*. And the institution of the Alban triumph by C. Papirius Maso – who was a pontiff – in the year 231 BC[108] may have been an antiquarian operation based on sources from pontifical archives and potentially recalling the triumph of the Latin federal chieftains and the expansion of the dominion of the Tarquinians, who would come out to thank their Jupiter along the triumphal path towards the Mons Albanus.[109]

Two inscriptions from the imperial era[110] refer to an *arx Albana*; these have traditionally been considered to be purely antiquarian, not referring to a specific geographic reality (most recently, Granino Cecere 2006, 307). However, Grandazzi (2006, 200–) has suggested, with good arguments, that it should be identified not with the imperial villa of Castel Gandolfo but with Monte Cavo, the venue of the *sacra Albana*,[111] and *Alba* was the name given to Monte Cavo by several authors.[112]

Epigraphic evidence also shows testimonies of cultic specialists linked to the 'Alban nodule'.[113] In the very centre of Tusculum a new inscription has

---

[105] Grandazzi 1986, 130: 'Dieu de la Ville contre dieu de la ligue latine: dans cette opposition fondamentale reside la clef du devenir historique de Rome.'
[106] Pasqualini 1996, 243.   [107] Plin. *HN*. 34.43.
[108] Plin. *HN* 15.26; Val. Max. 3.6.5; cf. Degrassi 1947, 78ff.
[109] Versnel 1970, 281ff.; Pasqualini 1996, 244.   [110] *CIL* VI 2172 and XIV 2947.
[111] According to Livy 1.31.3, a divine voice ordered the Albans to sacrifice following their national rites: *ut patrio ritu sacra Albani facerent*.
[112] Luc. 1.198 (*residens celsa Latiaris Iuppiter Alba*); 3.87 (*Latiis ad summam fascibus Albam*, on the route followed by consuls when celebrating the Latin festivals; Valerius Flaccus, 2.304–5; Plut. *Caes.* 60.3, confirmed by Suetonius (*Iul.* 79.3: *in sacrificio Latinarum reuertente eo*)) regarding the return of Caesar. Martial evokes the *Iuleo monte* (13.109.2), that is, the city founded by Ascanius-Iulus on that mount, and Juvenal says that Iulus preferred this mountaintop – whose name comes from the white sow – to that of Lavinium (12.70–3: *tunc gratus Iulo / Atque novercali sedes praelata Lauino / Conspicitur sublimis apex, cui candida nomen / Scrofa dedit*).
[113] This is the case of Salian priests and Vestal Virgins (Grandazzi 2008, 898–9).

been found dating from the first century AD[114] which documents that an unknown person held the post of *accensus velatus*. The find is important since it proves the participation of the city in the *Feriae Latinae* in the imperial period. As definitively demonstrated in Di Stefano Manzella (1994), the *accensi velati* were *apparitores ad sacra*, specifically in charge of assisting the consuls in their religious duties and, in particular, in the celebration of the *Feriae Latinae*, as seems to be expressed by an inscription of the city of Ficulea[115] dedicated to a Marcus Consius Cerinthus who is an *apparens consulibus in monte Albano ferias Latinas condentibus*. The discovery of the new Tusculan inscription might show the persistence, residual as it may be, of a *communio sacrorum* with Rome on the part of the cities of Latium, whereby the *accensi velati* could have been chosen from amongst the members of Latin origin.[116]

The priests called *Kabanoí* by Dionysius of Halicarnassus[117] and *Gabienses in monte Albano* by Pliny[118] almost certainly correspond to the *Cabenses sacerdotes feriarum Latinarum montis Albani* on a third-century honorific inscription to an emperor whose name is illegible,[119] perhaps Decius,[120] and on three funerary epigraphs, dating from between the first and mid-second centuries, to C. Antistius, C. Nonius Vansa and C. Nonius Iustinus.[121] These are equestrian priesthoods related to the *sacra* of the ancient communities of *Latium vetus*, such as the *Caeninenses, Laurentes Lavinates, Lanuvini, Tusculani*, whose ritual roles are not known.[122]

According to Cicero, '*Consules ... nisi de feriis Latinis nullum facere potuerunt.*'[123] The performance of the ceremonies on top of the Mons Albanus was an essential element on which the authority of consuls as supreme magistrates of the *res publica* was based, and in this ritual the consul did truly act as the celebrant of the sacrifices.[124] He represented

---

[114] Gorostidi Pi (forthcoming), 397–8. [115] *CIL* XIV 4013–14.
[116] Gorostidi Pi (forthcoming), 195–6. [117] Dion. Hal. 5.61.3.
[118] Plin. *HN* 3.64. [119] *CIL* XIV 2228.
[120] Granino Cecere 2006, 278. [121] *CIL* VI 2174–5; Granino Cecere 2006, 279.
[122] Granino Cecere and Scheid 1999. Mommsen (1861) had already pointed out a linguistic relationship between the current oronym Cavo and the *Cabenses*, in connection with a habitat of the *Cabum type, which could be placed not at the top, but in the modern town of Rocca di Papa, attached to the mount like a buttress (Grandazzi 2006, 209). On the *Albani* priests: Granino Cecere 2006, 284–316.
[123] Cic. *Fam.* 8.6.3.
[124] On rare occasions, the *Feriae* were presided over by one consul, but normally the two magistrates were present, and several literary or epigraphic texts clearly state this (details in Grandazzi 2008, 581 and n. 235).

the hegemonic community within the Latin League, in a Romano-Latin 'essential duality' – inherent to the *sacra prodigiorum* of the *Urbs* – that would continuously re-emerge in the future through the double Roman and Latin horizon that defined the privileged legal position of municipalities and colonies in the conquering republic and in the period of the empire up to Caracalla.

In a space shared by men and gods, such as the city, the magistrate was entitled to act not only with men but also with gods, whereas priests acted only with gods; hence the superiority or 'temporal supremacy'[125] of magistrates over priests. In this sense, the religious basis of the magisterial power of the consuls cannot be stressed enough: their election takes on a charismatic nature;[126] it is sanctioned by the supreme deity, Jupiter, thanks to the successful accomplishment of the compulsory ritual, a legitimizing key to their *imperium*, and that is why consuls could not set off for the battlefield without having previously charismatically endorsed their power by means of the rituals on Monte Cavo. Thus Latial Jupiter guaranteed the *imperium iustum* for the consuls.[127]

In the same manner as for the *rex* – primal and exclusive holder of the *imperium*, invested with *auspicium* and high priest of the city[128] – so the holistic concentration of functions found in the consul-priest in the *Feriae Latinae* seems also to be attested in other spheres of archaic Latium. Such is the case of Tusculum, a city where the presence of *aediles lustrales* or *quinquennales* may not, in my opinion, reflect a duality between a civil and a religious magistracy,[129] but rather the supreme magistrates of the city, the aediles, exercising their sacerdotal functions on the occasion of the solemn *lustratio populi*, celebrated every five years as in Rome or in other parts of the Italic world such as Teanum, Ficulea, Ostia or Interamna Nahars.[130]

---

[125] Scheid 1989, 65.   [126] De Francisci 1970, 30–1.
[127] Livy 22.1.6–7; Cass. Dio 46.33.4.   [128] Ser. *Aen.* 3.80.
[129] According to Rosenberg's theory (1913), very recently recovered by Gorostidi Pi (forthcoming), 86–93.
[130] As held by Leuze (1914, 118–19) and Wissowa (1915, 19). To the former, the *aedilis lustr(alis)* was but the *aedilis quinquennalis* acting as a magistrate in charge of performing the *lustrum* every five years, whereas Wissowa pointed out that the adjective *lustr(alis)* referred to the religious functions of the civil *aedilis*, something which is epigraphically documented for other municipal magistracies – not priesthoods: 'Den *praef(ectus) sacr(orum)* in *Tusculum* und in *Vicus Martis Tudentium*; vgl. auch den *praef(ectus) rebus divinis* in *Teanum*... für eine Priester zu halten, haben wir weder Veranlassung noch Berechtigung. Wer in jedem Würdertrager, dessen Titel einen hinweis auf *sacra* enthält, einen Priester sieht, vergisst, dass auch der Magistratur sehr ehrebliche sakrale Befugnisse zukommen, und dass ein magistrate dadurch, dass ihm im Laufe der Zeit aus einem führer grössem Kreise von Obligenheiten (man vergleiche den *praef(ectus) iur(e) dic(undo) et sacris faciendis* von *Ficulea*, XIV, 4002) nur die sakralem geblieben sind, noch nicht zum Priester wird; das ist wichtig für die richtige Beurteilung der *Praetores* und *Aediles sacris Volkani faciendis* in Ostia und des *Praetor sacrorum* in

The *Feriae Latinae as religious legitimation* 131

The rituals of the *Feriae Latinae* had played a very important role in the life of Rome from the earliest times until the end of the fourth century: even then, a *praefectus* and *consul designatus* 'de Ioue... Latio voluit sperare salutem', although he was to die of dropsy before taking up office.[131] It was, predictably, the Emperor Theodosius who banned the festival.

It is hard not to admit that an extremely ancient ritual which had been celebrated for over a thousand years had decisive importance in the shaping of Roman identity. Having converted the former festival of purification and fertility that was old *Latiar* into a symbol of Roman sovereignty, opening out to the outside world and a desire to dominate it, the *Feriae Latinae* became the temporal, spatial, religious and legal metaphor for the integrating abilities of the *imperium Romanum*.[132]

Jan Assman[133] has made a distinction between communicative memory, which includes the group's memories of the recent past, and which goes no further back than the fourth generation (the Roman *saeculum*), and 'cultural memory', which may be defined as the *foundation memory*, which includes the *origins of the community*. While the former is spontaneous and unstable, not attached to the institutions, cultural memory revolves around the mythical past: its purpose is to give meaning to the present by addressing the origin (mythical and sacred), which is updated and perpetuated through ritual and feasts. Thus the role of religion is essential in this cultural memory, much more stable than communicative memory (even in the absence of the written word) because of the fact that its transmission is strictly controlled and takes on the meaning of an institutionalized message.[134] By means of the rite, the circulation of the ancestral knowledge which binds the community together is secured, thus enabling the participation in the cosmic order which serves to place and *explain* the social group as such.

All of this is best exemplified by the complex ritual of the *Feriae Latinae*. Study of the available documentation, though scarce and asystematic, clearly proves the importance of these ceremonies in the formation of the Roman identity from the starting point of the *nomen Latinum*. The strict performance of the rituals on Monte Cavo, a *lieu de mémoire*,[135] was perceived as an essential element of the *arcana imperii* which had to be

---

Interamna Nahars auch der *Aediles* und *Praetores Etruriae*' (Wissowa 1915, 6–7 n. 3). Regarding the *lustrum* as a ritual of social integration, see Marco Simón 2006.
[131] He was possibly Symmachus the Elder (data in Pasqualini 1996, 253 n. 155).
[132] Grandazzi 2008, 905. [133] Assman 1995; 2006, 1–30.
[134] Rodríguez Mayorgas 2007, 17. [135] Yates 1974; Halbwachs 1997; Ricoeur 2000.

preserved in order to secure the perpetuity of the *Urbs*. By means of their ascent of the Mons Albanus and of their presidency over the ceremonies, the new consuls received the divine sanction of their charismatic *imperium* from the divine patron of the state and, alongside it, the legitimizing of their campaigns to reach the *imperium sine fine* promised by Jupiter, while they secured the continuity of successful communication with the divine world.

CHAPTER 7

War, wealth and consuls

Nathan Rosenstein

That war was a consul's primary road to riches seems beyond question.[1] Ideological and legal impediments precluded direct aristocratic involvement in commerce and finance while the profits in commercial agriculture were surprisingly slim.[2] Despoiling the republic's provincial subjects had by the first century become an important means of aristocratic self-enrichment. But even here, the money to be made could pale in comparison to the spoils of war. Pompey returned from his eastern conquests "richer than Crassus," indeed the richest Roman ever, at least until Caesar began plundering Gaul.[3] But Pompey and Caesar were exceptional in this regard as in so many others, and the question is rarely posed, "How much money did ordinary consuls typically make out of successful wars?" Put in these terms of course the question is unanswerable. We lack even the most basic data out of which to begin formulating an answer. But it may be possible to approach the problem from a somewhat different angle by asking, "What were the limits on a consul's or proconsul's ability to profit from the wars he waged?"

The existence of such limits is no longer in doubt, despite the long-standing belief that generals were free to help themselves liberally to that portion of the spoils termed the *manubiae* and to use it as they pleased: to build monuments in fulfillment of vows to the gods for victory, to present games as acts of thanksgiving to the deities, to distribute donatives to their soldiers when they celebrated a triumph, or simply to line their own purses and those of their favorites. However, while it is clear that the Romans drew a distinction between the *praeda* generally, which was whatever the

---

I would like to thank Robert Morstein-Marx and Gregory Pellam for salutary criticism and advice as well as the editors for inviting me to contribute a paper to this volume and suggesting the topic. Regrettably, the papers in Burrer and Müller 2008 and Müller 2009a came to my attention too late to be taken into account in this study.

[1] E.g. Harris 1979, 74–93.   [2] On the limited profits from commercial farming: Rosenstein 2008.
[3] Badian 1968, 81–2, 89–90; Shatzman 1975, 348–58, 391–2.

soldiers looted and which belonged to them, and the *manubiae*, Churchill has argued persuasively against Shatzman that generals did not "own" the latter.[4] Churchill draws attention to a passage from Polybius praising Scipio Aemilianus' behavior at the sack of Carthage in 146. Scipio, the historian notes, "took absolutely nothing from it [i.e. the booty] for his own private use, either by purchase or by any other manner of acquisition whatever" and he "not only abstained from the wealth of Carthage itself, but refused to allow anything from Africa at all to be mixed up with his private property."[5] As Churchill points out, the fact that Polybius believed that Scipio would have had to resort to purchase or unspecified "other means" to acquire anything out of the spoils from Carthage is completely at odds with the notion that, as the victorious general, Scipio in any sense "owned" the *manubiae* from his victory. Likewise, the distinction Polybius draws between Scipio's personal property and "anything from Africa" strongly implies that spoils from that country did not already belong to Scipio by virtue of their status as *manubiae*. The difference between *manubiae* and a general's personal property is further emphasized in an exchange between Aemilianus' great uncle, Scipio Nasica, and the senate during the latter's consulship in 191. Nasica asked the *patres* for funds to celebrate games that he had vowed as praetor three years before in connection with a victory in Spain. To this demand the senators responded that Nasica should fund the games from his *manubiae*, if he had kept back any money for this purpose; otherwise he himself should pay for them at his own expense.[6] Again, it is difficult to make sense out of this episode if the *manubiae* from Nasica's victory were identical with his personal property.

Churchill's argument that the *manubiae* were not "owned" by the general under whose command they were taken similarly permits a much simpler interpretation of several well-known episodes in which magistrates or promagistrates were brought to trial for misappropriation of booty. Two tribunes accused M. Acilius Glabrio in 189 because money and certain items said to have been captured in the camp of Antiochus following the victory at Thermopylae two years earlier had neither been displayed in Glabrio's triumph nor brought into the treasury. While the accusation was unquestionably motivated by politics, such charges presume at the very least that Glabrio was not within his rights to appropriate booty and keep it out of the public view.[7] Rather, they imply an expectation of public

---

[4] Churchill 1999; cf. also Bona 1960; Shatzman 1972.
[5] Polyb. 18.35.9–11; cf. Churchill 1999: 95–7.   [6] Livy 36.36.1; cf. Churchill 1999, 99–100.
[7] Livy 37.57.9–.58.2; cf. *ORF*[4] Cato fr. 66. On the politics see Gruen 1974, 71–2.

accounting for what had been captured in the camp. Such an expectation is difficult to reconcile with the notion that this booty became Glabrio's personal property, but it is quite comprehensible if the *manubiae* were considered to belong to the republic. In 105 another general faced charges stemming from the "disappearance" of booty: Q. Servilius Caepio was prosecuted in connection with the theft of the gold taken from Tolosa. He claimed that the treasure had been stolen from him, but the very fact that he had to mount such a defense belies the assumption that the treasure belonged to him as *manubiae*.[8] Finally, Pompey faced trial on charges of theft of public property following the death of his father, Strabo. The property in question was booty from Strabo's sack of Asculum in 89, which Strabo had not turned in to the treasury.[9] Again, the charges are difficult to comprehend on the theory that what Strabo had captured belonged to him, but they make perfect sense if the money and other items in question were considered to be public property.

The critical distinction here is between ownership and possession. Churchill argues that the cases cited above as well as other evidence indicate that *manubiae* were public property but that they remained under the control of the general who had captured them. He was required either to deposit his booty in the *aerarium* or document what he was not turning in and deposit this record in the treasury.[10] What was not turned in was to be used for some public purpose and might remain in the general's possession for many years awaiting such a disposition.[11]

Nevertheless, it is clear from Polybius' references to "any other manner of acquisition" and Scipio's refusal to co-mingle the booty from Africa with his own property, as well as the praise in various sources accorded to upright commanders who refused to enrich themselves with the plunder from their victories, that there were various surreptitious and illicit means through which a general might do just that. And in view of the growing wealth of the senatorial class as its members conducted the conquests that won the republic its empire, one cannot but suspect that many consuls

---

[8] On the prosecution: Cic. *Nat. D.* 3.74; Cass. Dio fr. 90; Oros. 5.15.25; cf. Churchill 1999: 105–6. Caepio was apparently either acquitted or fined: Alexander 1990, 33–4, but was later tried and condemned in connection with his conduct in the Roman disaster at Arausio: cf. Rosenstein 1990, 124–8.
[9] Plut. *Pomp.* 4.1–3; cf. Oros. 5.18.29; Churchill 1999, 106–7.
[10] Cf. Cic. *Verr.* 2.1.57; Churchill 1999, 101–9.
[11] Churchill 1999, 108. However, the construction of temples vowed by generals was not financed by *manubiae* but rather from funds authorized by the senate and drawn from the *aerarium* (which might of course have been enriched by that portion of the *manubiae* that a general chose to hand over to the treasury): Orlin 1997, 127–61.

and proconsuls availed themselves of them. Yet if so, then we are left with a problem. If *manubiae* were public property that generals were illegally appropriating for themselves, why do we see so few prosecutions for *peculatus* in connection with generals' handling of their booty? To take only two egregious examples, Lucullus and Pompey each became enormously rich following their victories in the east. Lucullus faced charges that were soon dropped; Pompey escaped prosecution completely.[12] Of course such trials always involved politics, and both Lucullus and Pompey were *pesci grossi*, capable of mobilizing such imposing resources and support that they could escape conviction or even deter prosecution altogether. But what of the smaller fry? The victories most consuls won were nothing like so rich, nor were the victors themselves as deeply ensconced in powerful networks of supporters. Possibly there was something like a "gentleman's agreement" to turn a blind eye to self-enrichment by victorious generals on the understanding that those who overlooked such peculations now would benefit when it came to their turn. But this seems scarcely plausible. Rivalry among republican aristocrats was constant, political combat often intense, and prosecution a time-honored means to ruin an opponent and increase one's own prominence. Indeed, the paucity of prosecutions of generals for misappropriation of booty is perhaps the strongest argument for the theory that the *manubiae* were their personal property, which they were free to dispose of in any way they saw fit. If, however, this was not so, if generals were not free to help themselves to the loot and yet military command was the pre-eminent source of aristocratic self-enrichment, how can we explain the rarity of consuls brought to trial on such charges despite a deeply competitive political milieu?[13] A solution requires us to begin by understanding something about how the republic financed its wars.

While the spoils from previous victories often enabled the *aerarium* to fund the costs of initiating and sustaining wars, and although wars sometimes could be made to pay for themselves, the financial bedrock on which the republic's military strength rested was until 167 the *tributum*. It enabled Rome to pay its legionaries, provide food to its *socii*, and meet all the other expenses associated with mounting and sustaining a campaign. For many years, scholars viewed the *tributum* as an annual tax on citizens' wealth as assessed in the quinquennial census, usually assumed to have

---

[12] On Lucullus' wealth: Shatzman 1975, 378–81; on Pompey, see above, n. 3. On Lucullus' trial: Plut. *Cat. Min.* 29.3–4; *Luc.* 37.1–3.

[13] Apart from the cases noted above, only the consul of 74, M. Aurelius Cotta, was accused and convicted on charges of *peculatus* arising from his sack of Heracleia Pontica: Cass. Dio 36.40.3–4; Memn. 39 = *FGrH* 3B.366–7; Alexander 1990 no. 188.

been collected at the rate of one mil, that is, one as per thousand asses of property. However, Nicolet has argued persuasively that the *tributum* was much more akin to the liturgies of classical Athens than a tax in the modern sense: it was an ad hoc levy to meet a particular public expense rather than a regular source of public income.[14] Every year, the senate would determine the military needs of the republic and their cost. That sum would then be divided by a figure representing the total wealth of the *assidui* that the previous census had established. The resulting percentage then became the basis for determining each *assiduus'* individual tax liability. So, for example, if the wars in the coming year were going to require an outlay of 30,000,000 asses, and the total wealth of the citizenry stood at 50,000,000,000 asses, the *tributum* would be collected at a rate of three-fifths of an as per thousand asses of assessed value. The key point here is that the amount raised through collection of the *tributum* could vary significantly from year to year. Obviously, when the republic's annual military establishment was comparatively small, as it was throughout much of the third century when Rome typically fielded four legions in any year, costs would have been much smaller than during the second century, when the average annual levy comprised eight or nine legions.[15] And obviously the value of the *tributum* could vary over a shorter term, depending on the senate's perception of the extent of the military challenges facing the republic in the coming year and what additional forces it would take to meet them. On the other hand, the *tributum* could also decrease if other funds, such as booty from a captured city or spoils deposited in the *aerarium* from earlier victories, were available. And as is well known, it was suspended altogether following the capture of the Macedonian royal treasury in 168.

However, another characteristic of the *tributum* requires emphasis in this context. Rather than a tax in the modern sense of the term, the *tributum* was in effect a loan (albeit a compulsory one) from the *assidui* to the *res publica*. And as such, it was a debt that the *res publica* was obligated to repay when circumstances permitted.[16] This fact emerges clearly in Livy's report of the triumph of Cn. Manlius Vulso in 187. Manlius' friends were able to prevail upon the senate to decree that whatever money the citizens had contributed toward military expenses in prior years and that was still owing to them should be repaid out of the rich spoils from Manlius' triumph. The urban quaestors therefore paid out $25\frac{1}{2}$ asses per thousand (Livy 39.7.4–5). The

---

[14] Nicolet 1976a, 19–26; cf. Nicolet 1980, 149–69.
[15] On the number of legions in the middle and late republic: Brunt 1971, 423, 432–3, 449, 545.
[16] Cf. Kondratieff 2004, 21–6.

principle that the *tributum* represented a debt on the part of the *res publica* owed to those who had funded a war is likewise reflected in earlier examples, even if the veracity of the events portrayed in some of them is questionable. So in 503, Dionysius of Halicarnassus notes that following a victory over the Sabines and the sale of the booty, the citizens' contributions to the war were repaid to them (*Ant. Rom.* 5.47.1). Perhaps somewhat more credence can be given to the boast, reported in a speech of C. Fabricius Luscinus, consul in 282, following a victory over a force of Samnites, Bruttians and Lucanians, that he had not only enriched his soldiers from the spoils but "returned to the citizens the property tax they had advanced for the war" (Dion. Hal. 19.16.3). Some forty years later, at the climax of the First Punic War when the treasury lacked funds to construct a new fleet, the senate resorted to loans from the leading citizens "on the understanding that they would get their money back" if the war ended in victory (Polyb. 1.59.7). In all likelihood they did, for a generation later, following Rome's victory in the Second Punic War, the senate scrupulously repaid in three installments monies that the richer citizens had contributed in 210 to pay for a fleet, although neither of these contributions was technically *tributum*.[17] The notion that the profits of victory should be returned to the citizens in some way is likewise reflected in the inscription on the *columna rostrata* that C. Duilius erected following his naval victory over a Carthaginian fleet in 260, which proclaimed that the consul *[Triump]oque navaled praedad poplom [donavet]*.[18] The same practice also turns up in Plautus' parody of a general's victorious return: *praeda atque agro adoriaque adfecit populares suos* (*Amph.* 191). Notable, too, in this regard is the Elder Pliny's remark, apropos of a statue of Q. Marcius Tremulus erected in the Forum, that his victories over the Samnites as consul in 306 had freed the populace of the need to pay *stipendium* (*HN* 34.23).

In agitating for his booty to be used to repay the citizens, Manlius' *amici* were aiming to win favor for him with the *populus*, something of which he stood in considerable need in view of the senate's resistance to awarding

---

[17] Livy 26.35.2–3; 29.16.1–3; 31.13.1–9; 33.42.2–4.
[18] *CIL* 1² 2.25 line 17 = *ILLRP* 319 = Inscr. Ital. 13.3.69. The authenticity of the Duilius inscription has long been controversial, especially in view of Mommsen's assertion that the text is the work of a forger in the Augustan age. However, Degrassi and others have been inclined to accept the text as a fundamentally genuine artifact of the third century, although recopied in connection with a restoration of Duilius' *columna rostrata* during the reign of Augustus. Bleckmann (2002, 116–25) has recently strongly defended the authenticity of the text and convincingly accounted for its anomalies, as has, more briefly, Kondratieff (2004: 10–14), who also argues (26–32) that several issues of *aes signatum* were the means by which Duilius distributed his booty to the citizens. Cf. Beck 2005, 220 n. 17; Östenberg 2009, 58. Note also the consuls of 270, who distributed the booty from their conquest of Rhegium to the citizens: Dion. Hal. 20.17 with Kondratieff 2004, 24.

him a triumph and the popular antagonism that had been aroused against him.[19] That a general could garner substantial popularity by seeing to it that money contributed as *tributum* was repaid to the *assidui* from booty is also implicit in Fabricius' boast and the other examples noted above. On the other hand, Livy highlights the resentment of the plebs when the spoils from Papirius Cursor's victories in 293 did not go to alleviate the burden of the *tributum*.[20] Moreover, the political capital that could accrue from repaying the *assidui* was all the greater because of the way in which the republic assessed and collected the *tributum*. As noted above, how much each *assiduus* paid depended on the value of his property. The tax was progressive: richer citizens paid more than poor ones. And in order to collect the *tributum*, the republic depended on the *tribuni aerarii*.[21] Citizens so designated constituted an *ordo* of wealthy men ranking just below the *equites*. Their role was to serve as proxies for those liable to the *tributum*. In a state that had very little in the way of an administrative apparatus, the *tribuni aerarii* advanced the sums required to fund military expenses and then collected what was owed them from their fellow *assidui*. Obviously, these were men whose political importance was considerable. They voted in the first class centuries and socially their background will not have differed much from citizens enrolled in the equestrian centuries or even many of the senators. Further, it is not clear to what extent they recouped the money that they had advanced. Nicolet suggests that, like the *summoriai* at Athens, they may often have been unable to do so or may have voluntarily refused to collect from the other citizens in order to acquire a reputation for generosity. In either event, a general whose booty enabled the treasury to reimburse the *tribuni* for their contributions will have earned considerable gratitude from the members of this influential and politically potent *ordo* as well as from citizens in the higher census classes generally, upon whom the *tributum* bore most heavily. The support of both groups could be invaluable in advancing his own political ambitions or those of his relatives and friends.

Any consul contemplating how to apportion his booty will certainly have been aware of the political capital that could accrue from repayment of the *tributum* that had financed his victory. Possibly even more credit will have been gained from obviating the need to collect *tributum* or draw funds from the treasury in the first place. Cato in Spain in 195 forbade the purchase of grain to feed his army, proclaiming that "the war will feed itself."[22] How

---

[19] Livy 38.44.9–50.3; 39.6.3–6. On the dispute over his triumph see Pittenger 2008, 213–30.
[20] Livy 10.46.6; cf. Oakley 1997–2005, 4, 448. [21] Nicolet 1976a, 46–55; Nicolet 1980, 161–4.
[22] Livy 34.9.12: *bellum inquit se ipsum alet*.

often consuls and proconsuls were able to realize this ideal in practice is unclear. Q. Fulvius Flaccus managed to do so, announcing to the senate at the beginning of 180 that following his victories in Spain there was no need to send the usual *stipendium* or supply of grain to the army that year (Livy 40.35.4). What is beyond doubt is that the costs of waging war were substantial. *Stipendium* alone for a single legion's legionaries amounted to some 607,050 denarii per year in the late third century, following the reform of the coinage *c.* 211. This figure increased to 701,717 denarii in the second century and 713,550 denarii in the first.[23] The annual cost of *stipendium* for a typical force of four legions in the later third century prior to Hannibal's invasion will have been the equivalent of over two million post-211 denarii. An eight-legion force in the second century will have needed nearly five million denarii a year for the soldiers' pay. Since allied communities in Italy furnished the money to pay the *socii*, the republic's treasury and *assidui* were spared the cost of at least half (and often more) of its annual military establishment. The extension of citizenship to the Italians in 90 and 89 BC eliminated this economy, however. Pay for twenty legions in the first century would have entailed the expenditure of about 13 million denarii.

In addition to the *stipendium*, the republic supplied grain to allied troops at no cost to them during the second century and probably the third as well. If allied troops equaled the number of legionaries levied annually, third-century cost for grain might have been the equivalent of around 648,000 post-211 denarii, assuming an average price of HS 3 per modius of wheat.[24] If the *socii* outnumbered legionaries by three to two, the cost would have

---

[23] Calculations are based on Polyb. 6.39.12. The *stipendium* remained unchanged until Caesar doubled it: Suet. *Iul.* 26.3. Third-century figures: (4,140 legionaries @ 1 denarius every 3 days × 355 days of a pre-Julian Roman year = 489,900 denarii) + (60 centurions @ 1 denarius every 2 days × 355 days = 10,650 denarii) + (300 cavalry @ 1 denarius per day × 355 days = 106,500 denarii) = 607,050 denarii. For the second century: (4,940 legionaries @ 1 denarius every 3 days × 355 days = 584,567 denarii) + (60 centurions @ 1 denarius every 2 days × 355 days = 10,650 denarii) + (300 cavalry @ 1 denarius per day × 355 days = 106,500 denarii) = 701,717 denarii. First century: (5,940 legionaries @ 1 denarius every 3 days × 355 days = 702,900 denarii) + (60 centurions @ 1 denarius every 2 days × 355 days = 10,650 denarii) = 713,550 denarii; cf. Walbank 1957–79, 1,722; Crawford 1974, 624. However, Crawford's figures for the expense of a legion (1974, 696–7) cannot be relied upon since the evidence he adduces in support fails to demonstrate his claims. On the size of the legions in each period: Brunt 1971, 671–6, 687–93. As Brunt notes, however, these figures represent only typical troop strengths; the actual manpower of legions could vary depending on circumstances. On the reform of the coinage *c.* 211: Crawford 1974, 28–35. Absolute costs prior to this date will have been equivalent but expressed in fewer asses since these were considerably heavier than those minted after 211.

[24] 18,000 *socii* × 4 modii/month (Polyb. 6.39.13 with Foxhall and Forbes 1982, 62 n. 72) × 12 months = 864,000 modii × 3 sestertii = 2,592,000 sestertii/4 = 648,000 denarii. This calculation does not, however include the higher rations for allied cavalrymen. HS 3 per modius: Duncan-Jones

been the equivalent of 972,000 post-211 denarii.[25] Tribute from Sardinia and the Roman province of Sicily supplied much of this grain, so its cost to the republic will have been nil. And in fact this tribute will have permitted a significant saving, since the cost of the legionaries' grain was deducted from their *stipendium*. However, we should be careful not to overestimate the savings that this source of food for the armies represented. As Erdkamp has noted in his analysis of republican armies' food requirements during the second century, the 50,000–75,000 Roman and Italian soldiers and sailors in the east in 190–189 BC consumed "not only the double tithe-corn of Sicily and the major part of the Sardinian double tithe-corn as well, but in addition to this also consumed at least 1,3 million modii of wheat from Africa, and contributions from Pergamon, Macedon, and other allies."[26] The fact that a double tithe of grain from Sicily and Sardinia could not feed the Roman forces fighting Antiochus in the early second century makes it difficult to believe that a single tithe from Sardinia and the more limited (and less productive) portion of Sicily that Rome controlled in the third century would have been sufficient to meet all of the food requirements for the armies of that era, which will have numbered between 33,600 and 42,000 Roman and allied infantry alone. The republic will have had to buy grain to make up the difference. When Rome's military effort expanded dramatically following the outbreak of the Second Punic War and then during the republic's subsequent expansion, grain purchases naturally were required.[27] Rome even had to purchase the second tithes it demanded from Sicily and Sardinia in 190–189, albeit at a price the senate set.[28] In addition, Rome bore much of the cost of transporting its soldiers, their equipment and their food and other supplies through contracts with private shipowners, teamsters, and muleteers.[29] No evidence permits us to quantify the expenditures that that transport entailed, but they will not have been negligible, particularly since so much of the task of furnishing a constant supply of food to the troops necessitated moving large amounts of grain

---

1982, 42, 145–6; cf. Cic. *Verr.* 2.3.163, 188–9; Frank 1933, 193, cf. 402–3; Hopkins 1978, 38 n. 50, 56 n. 79.

[25] 27,000 *socii* × 4 modii/month × 12 months = 1,296,000 modii × HS 3 = HS 3,888,000/4 = 972,000 denarii. This calculation does not, however, include the higher rations for allied cavalrymen.

[26] Erdkamp 1998, 90.

[27] Purchases for the army from Etruria in 212 and 210: Livy 25.15.4, 20.4, 27.3.9, and cf. Polyb. 9.11a.1 for a report of grain purchased from Egypt. In addition, note purchases of grain from Numidia and Carthage in 191: Livy 36.3.1, and cf. 4.5–9; from Calabria and Apulia in 172: Livy 42.27.8; from Epirus in 169: Livy 44.16.2. Spanish armies, too, were fed in part by purchased grain: cf. Cato's refusal to allow it to be purchased for his army, noted above, which indicates what would ordinarily have been the case: Livy 34.9.12, and cf. Richardson 1986, 93.

[28] Erdkamp 1998, 112.   [29] Erdkamp 1998, 46–83, esp. 59–60.

overland. The costs of funding the acquisition of an empire bore heavily on the treasury and the taxpayers, and naturally they will have wanted to have their contributions refunded to them whenever possible.

The *aerarium* and the *assidui* back home were not the only ones with a strong claim on the profits of conquest, however. Generals also had to contend with another powerful constituency clamoring for a share of the loot. Citizens went to war in full anticipation that they would benefit materially from any victory they won. Thus in 264 the voters in the *comitia centuriata* readily ratified a proposal to aid the Mamertines once the consuls pointed out to them the great plunder they could expect.[30] In 249 the consul P. Claudius Pulcher found his soldiers eager to volunteer for his ill-fated attack on Drepana because of the all but certain prospect of booty in their minds (Polyb. 2.49.5). Nearly twenty-five years later, on the eve of the battle at the city of Telemon, the formidable appearance of the Gallic warriors terrified the legionaries who faced them, but the sight of the golden torques and armlets the Gauls wore and the prospect of winning them fired the Romans' eagerness for the coming battle.[31] Once the victory had been won, the consul collected the spoils and sent them to Rome but returned the booty that the Gauls had taken to its owners. Then he led his forces into the land of the Boii and let them pillage to their hearts' content (Polyb. 2.31.3–4). When an army was being levied for the Third Macedonian War, volunteers eagerly came forward to serve because they had seen the soldiers who had fought in earlier wars in the east come back rich (Livy 42.32.6). The prospect of an equally rich haul undoubtedly inspired the many citizens who rushed to enlist when the final war against Carthage was getting under way (App. *Pun.* 75). Those eager to accompany Marius to Africa in 107 imagined themselves returning victorious and wealthy from all the booty they would win (Sall. *Iug.* 84.4).

Generals were expected to see that their soldiers' hopes were not disappointed. Fabricius boasted that his conquests had not only repaid the taxpayers but had enriched his soldiers as well (Dion. Hal. 19.16.3). Good generals turned the *praeda* over to their troops in Livy's narrative of the Second Samnite War.[32] Cato prided himself on the same point: "I have never divided the *praeda* or what was taken from the enemy or the *manubiae*

---

[30] Polyb. 1.11.2 with Walbank 1957–79 ad loc. On this episode, see Hoyos 1984; *contra*, however, Eckstein 1980.

[31] Polyb. 2.29.7–9, from Fabius Pictor: Walbank 1957–79, I, 204. Interestingly, at least some of the torques wound up in the hands of the consul, who used them to decorate the Capitoline rather than to enrich his soldiers: Polyb. 2.31.5. On such decisions by generals see further below. Note also Livy's portrayal of P. Decius Mus' men's enthusiasm for continuing their campaign in 296 once he held out the prospect of rich plunder: 10.17.5–9.

[32] E.g. Livy 10.17.10; 19.22; 20.16; 31.4; 45.14; 46.14.

among a few friends of mine, taking it away from those who captured it."[33] Better, he proclaimed, for many to go home with silver than a few with gold (Plut. *Cat. Mai.* 10.4). His contemporary, Ti. Sempronius Gracchus, consul in 177, similarly proclaimed on a tablet he placed in the temple of Mater Matuta that he had brought his victorious army back from Sardinia "safe and sound and stuffed full with booty."[34] Lucullus distributed 800 drachmas apiece to his men from the spoils of Tigranocerta apart from what they had gained in plundering that city (Plut. *Luc.* 29.3). Pompey's distributions to his soldiers in the east were even more lavish.[35] And of course Caesar's generosity to his soldiers was legendary.[36]

Loot made soldiers loyal and enthusiastic in the field.[37] Disappointed expectations, on the other hand, could create problems for a commander. In 293 Livy asserts that the failure of the consul Papirius Cursor to satisfy his legionaries' expectations for a share of the booty aroused ill-feeling at his triumph.[38] And famously the troops of L. Aemilius Paullus came close to denying him a triumph for his victory over Perseus following the army's return to Rome in 167. Significantly, their anger was not due to his having denied them an opportunity to plunder. The sack of seventy Epirote towns had been ordered by the senate in part to satisfy the soldiers' demands for booty. Rather, what drew their ire was the fact that Paullus had prevented them from enriching themselves from the royal treasures of Macedon as much as they felt they deserved.[39] Lucullus's troops, too, obeyed him as long as they believed the spoils they obtained were a fair recompense for the dangers and toil they incurred, but once the latter outweighed the former in their minds, discipline vanished (Cass. Dio 36.16.3).

As noted above, the booty from a Roman victory fell into two categories, *praeda* and *manubiae*. *Praeda* was a general term for what had been captured, while as Churchill has argued *manubiae* constituted that part of the *praeda* that belonged to the *res publica* but that a general controlled and kept temporarily in his possession. For our purposes, the critical question is how the two were distinguished in practice, for no hard and fast rule seems to have created a bright line demarcating one from the other.[40]

---

[33] *ORF*[4] Cato fr. 203: *Numquam ego praedam neque quod de hostibus captum esset neque manubias inter pauculos amicos meos divisi, ut illis eriperem, qui cepissent.*
[34] Livy 41.28.9: *exercitum salvum atque incolumem plenissimum praeda domum redit.*
[35] Shatzman 1975: 391.
[36] E.g. App. *B Civ.* 2.31, and even earlier, during his command in Spain in 61–60: Plut. *Caes.* 12.2.
[37] Cf. Cass. Dio fr. 94.1 where, following the victory at Aquae Sextiae, Marius *sells* the plunder to his troops at a nominal price to encourage and reward them, a unique occurrence, if true. The tradition on the disposal of the booty from this victory is confused, however: Plut. *Mar.* 21.2–3.
[38] Livy 10.46.6; cf. Oakley 1997–2005, 4,448.
[39] Livy 45.34.1–7; 35.5–36.7; Plut. *Aem.* 29.1–3; 30.2–31.1.   [40] *Contra* Tarpin 2000.

Rather, generals had to lay claim to that portion of the *praeda* that they wished to treat as *manubiae*. So M. Claudius Marcellus, in anticipation of releasing his troops to sack Syracuse in 211, sent a force of trusted soldiers under an officer to take possession of the royal treasury and keep it under guard while the looting was going on.[41] Lucullus appears to have taken similar steps in 69 when he seized Tigranocerta (Plut. *Luc.* 29.3). Cicero in Cilicia proudly announced to Atticus that he had granted the whole of the *praeda* except the captives to his soldiers when he captured Pindenissum, clearly implying that he would have been within his rights as commander to exclude some portion of the spoils from the general plundering (Cic. *Att.* 113 [5.20].5). Despite Polybius' idealized description of an orderly system of looting that followed a Roman army's capture of a city, the reality, as Ziolkowski has shown, was far different.[42] The soldiers were turned loose by their commander to engage in a mad scramble to pillage, murder and rape, every man for himself. The fact that Marcellus believed guards were necessary to protect the treasury at Syracuse strongly implies that without them the legionaries and *socii* would have felt entitled to plunder those riches, too. A general had to make a decision about what he would let his soldiers get their hands on during the sack, and when in their eyes their commander failed to apportion what they considered their fair share, trouble could follow, as Paullus discovered. But of course the more of the spoils that went to the soldiers, the less remained for the *manubiae*. As Livy notes, if Paullus had let the soldiers have free rein in plundering the royal treasures of Macedon, nothing would have been left to deposit in the Roman treasury (45.35.6).

Generals therefore could find themselves pulled in several different directions in dealing with their booty. The treasury and in many cases those liable to *tributum* will have wanted to be reimbursed for the money they had advanced for the costs of the war, and these repayments will have come out of the *manubiae*. Generals were under pressure therefore to claim as much of the spoils as *manubiae* as possible. The greater the *manubiae*, however, the less *praeda* remained for the soldiers, who had gone to war in large part to enrich themselves. To some extent the distribution of a donative from the *manubiae* at a triumph might help to redress any lingering resentment among the troops that they had not received a large enough share of the loot. But not every victory eventuated in a triumph, so withholding booty to hand out later entailed a degree of risk. And of course generals expected to gain in important, non-monetary ways from the *manubiae*. The senate awarded the funds needed to construct a temple

---

[41] Livy 25.31.8–9; cf. Plut. *Marc.* 19.3.   [42] Polyb. 10.15.4–16.9; Ziolkowski 1998.

vowed in return for victory, and obviously a general whose spoils enriched the treasury could expect a claim on it for such a purpose to receive a favorable hearing.[43] Games, too, in honor of the gods' support in a war were apparently funded out of *manubiae*.[44] Both investments paid dividends to a general, in the one case by creating a permanent physical memorial to his victory and in the other by producing an immediate burst of popularity. And if a general expected to fill his purse as well, that money, too, would have to come from the *manubiae*.

The seriousness of the dilemma in which these conflicting demands placed a general will, however, have varied significantly over the course of the middle and late republic as well as from one case to another. Table 1 (pp. 153–8) attempts to offer some sense of the pressures these conflicts might have entailed. It attempts to address the question, "How often did a general's victory pay for itself?" by reimbursing the treasury for the costs incurred. Unfortunately, the data available on the financial aspects of Roman wars make a satisfactory answer to this question unattainable. We have only two relatively secure bits of information to work with, namely how much money a legion at full strength might have required for its annual *stipendium* and the amount of booty that our sources, mainly Livy, report that victorious generals in the period between 200 and 167 BC carried in their triumphs or ovations or in a few cases simply turned in to the treasury.[45] However, the impression that this evidence conveys is highly suggestive. While it is well known that many of the victories the republic's armies won during these years were spectacularly rich, more than 50 percent of them, 16 out of 31, did not return enough money to cover the legionaries' pay for the period during which the winning general was in command.[46] If we could gauge the additional costs of these campaigns for transport and other expenses, the percentage of victories that turned

---

[43] See above, n. 11.   [44] E.g. Livy 36.36.1–3.
[45] These two categories overlapped but were not identical, since the former included that part of the *manubiae* that a general retained in his possession while the latter did not: Churchill 1999, 103–4. Beard 2007, 159–73, however, doubts the veracity of the amounts listed in Table 1 as well as other specific figures for money and other items that Livy and other ancient authors report were displayed in Roman triumphs. Her skepticism seems unwarranted in view of the "meticulous detail with which warriors kept lists of their achievements in war": Oakley 1997–2005, III, 596, and cf. generally III, 596–9 for further discussion and sources. The Duilius inscription (see above, n. 18) offers strong, contemporary confirmation not only of this general practice but of the specific commemoration of the money a general captured in his victory. Moreover, a number of the sums Livy reports were carried in the triumphs listed in Table 1 seem surprisingly small. It is difficult to believe that a general or later annalist intent on glorifying his achievements would not have confected more impressive totals.
[46] This percentage omits naval triumphs in 190 and 167 since the cost of paying sailors cannot be determined, but does assume that P. Scipio Nasica's victory over the Gauls in 191 paid for itself: see Table 1 note f.

a profit would probably drop even lower. And of course Table 1 considers only the *stipendium* required to fund the campaigns of the generals who actually won the victories rather than the expenses incurred during the tenures of their predecessors whose operations often paved the way for these victories. Were these earlier expenses factored in, the number of victories that returned more in booty than the cost of winning them would again have to be reduced. Finally, that figure would shrink even further if the *stipendium* and additional expenses of all the legions that were mobilized in these years rather than only those responsible for a victory were included in the reckoning.

Table 1 of course is not intended to argue that Rome's conquest of an empire in the early second century did not ultimately pay for itself. The vast hauls of loot from victories in the Hellenistic east undoubtedly offset the costs of many of the republic's other wars. And Rome had other sources of funds to draw on.[47] Rather, the table offers a useful point of departure for thinking about those wars whose spoils go unreported in our sources and about how the conflicting claims upon them might have affected generals. Consider Rome's wars in Italy during the third century prior to Hannibal's invasion. Few of its conquests in this era are likely to have produced victories that, like Fabricius', both enriched the soldiers and repaid the taxpayer – to say nothing of yielding spoils at all comparable to those won in the east after 200 – to judge by the fact that at most only one victory in northern Italy during the first quarter of the second century produced enough booty to offset the money expended to pay for the *stipendium* of the legions that won it.[48] Conquests in Sicily during the First Punic War may have been richer, but few large cities were captured, and when they were it is important not to overestimate the money that could be realized from the spoils. Frank, for instance, takes the 2 minas (= 200 post-211 denarii) that 14,000 citizens of Panormus paid as ransom to the Romans at the fall of that city in 254 BC to avoid enslavement as an indication of how much money each of the remaining 13,000 residents would have fetched when the Romans sold them into slavery.[49] Even assuming, however, that the price a person might pay to avoid enslavement would not have been very much higher than what he or she would fetch on the auction block,

---

[47] Although Frank's estimates of the republic's income and expenses for the first half of the second century are at best merely impressionistic, the sources of income he describes are accurate: Frank 1933, 127–45. Note, too, the ad hoc levies of money to support Roman forces in Spain, finally regularized in 179: Richardson 1986, 72–3, 115–16. See recently Ñaco del Hoyo 2005 on second-century provincial taxation.

[48] Nasica's victory in 191: Table 1 with note f.   [49] Frank 1933, 67; cf. Diod. Sic. 23.18.5.

Frank's claim ignores the fundamental law of supply and demand. This will have dictated that when so many slaves came onto the market all at once the price of slaves would drop precipitously.[50] That was precisely what happened during Lucullus' march through Galatia in 73, when the army had taken so much booty that a slave sold for as little as 4 drachmas (= 4 denarii) in camp (Plut. *Luc.* 14.1).

Two and a half centuries earlier, Livy reports, the republic's armies captured a total of about 69,000 prisoners during the final phase of the Second Samnite War, 297–293, an average of 13,800 in each of these five years.[51] This is certainly an impressive figure. However, the cost of paying for the four legions Rome deployed to capture them totaled the equivalent of about two million post-211 denarii each year.[52] The sale price of each prisoner thus will have had to average the equivalent of about 145 post-211 denarii in order simply to recoup the cost of the legionaries' *stipendium*. So high a price seems very optimistic with such a glut of captives coming onto the market within the space of a very short time, particularly since in a number of instances the captives will have included women, children and the elderly, whose value will have been less than an adult man's. For what it is worth, Livy claims that on one occasion in 295 the Romans allowed 1,741 Perusini prisoners of war to ransom themselves for 310 asses each, the equivalent of a mere 31 post-211 denarii.[53] One can only imagine the fire-sale price that the 350,000 Aduatuci captives went for when Caesar sold them in 57 in a single lot following the fall of their city (Caes. *B Gall.* 2.33.6–7).

Moreover, war captives had to be disposed of quickly, since feeding them consumed food that either had to be paid for or taken from stores that otherwise would provide the army's commissariat, while adding a large number of prisoners to the baggage train would only slow the army's progress.[54] So Cicero in 50 sold his Pindenissian captives within three or four days following their surrender (Cic. *Att.* 113 [5.20].5). The need for a quick sale would have tended to weaken further the bargaining position of a general seeking to profit from the sale of prisoners and to reduce the

---

[50] Compare Scheidel's analysis of slave prices: Scheidel 2005b, esp. 15–16 for the republican eras, and cf. Scheidel 2008, 124–5.
[51] Oakley 1993, 24–6 for a list of numbers of captives with references and a discussion of the reliability of Livy's figures.
[52] See above, n. 23.
[53] Livy 10.31.3. If this episode is genuine and the ransom accurately reported, the price will originally have been expressed in libral asses, which Roman annalists converted to the more familiar sextantal asses by multiplying by ten: Rathbone 1993, 125, 133–4.
[54] Cf. Livy 10.17.5–10.20.16.

price that buyers were willing to pay. And finally, the demand for slaves and hence the prices captives will have fetched will scarcely have been as great in third-century Italy as it became two centuries later – and recent studies have forced a radical revision downwards of our estimates of the numbers of slaves in Italy even in the later second and first centuries.[55]

The sale of prisoners of war during the First Punic War therefore is unlikely to have yielded anything close to the sums that Frank estimates, while to judge by the numbers of captives taken following battles or the captures of towns that Livy preserves for the years 297–293, victories in Italy during the third century will have brought far fewer slaves onto the auction block.[56] Certainly, other spoils from this era will not have been negligible, as the unprecedented spate of monumental construction in the early third century demonstrates.[57] But the need to bring funds into the treasury in order to finance these monuments, coupled with the soldiers' demands for booty and the expectation of the *assidui* for repayment of the *tributum*, will have left generals with little room to divert a substantial portion of the loot into their own purses.

The situation may have improved somewhat in the wake of Rome's victory in the First Punic War. Peace terms required Carthage to pay 3,200 talents in war reparations over ten years or 320 talents per year (Polyb. 1.62.8–63.3; 3.27.5). That sum may have met the cost of a decade's *stipendium* for the four legions that were the republic's typical annual military establishment in the interwar years.[58] However, it should also be remembered that the war had been extraordinarily expensive. The treasury had been unable to fund the construction of the fleet that ultimately defeated Carthage and had been forced to rely on loans that had to be repaid (see above, p. 138). How much of the Carthaginian indemnity would have gone to repay earlier outlays not only for ships but for *tributum* and how much would have been available for future military expenses we cannot therefore say.

The republic's balance sheet was much worse following the conclusion of the Hannibalic War. Although Scipio Africanus had imposed a crushing

---

[55] Scheidel 2005a, 64–71; de Ligt 2004, 745–7.   [56] See above, n. 51.
[57] Oakley 1993, 27, 33–5, and add M'. Curius Dentatus' construction of the *aqua Anio Vetus* out of the *manubiae* from his victory over Pyrrhus in 275: Frontin. *Aq*. 1.6
[58] The uncertainty is due to the fact that we do not know the rate of legionary pay prior to the currency reforms of *c*. 211. On the assumption, however, that the rate of pay prior to that date will have been equivalent in purchasing power, *stipendium* for a single legion in the third century cost 607,050 post-211 denarii: see above, n. 23. That sum is the equivalent of 7,227 Roman pounds of silver or 2,342 kg: see Table 1 note c and Crawford 1974, 590–2. Four legions thus cost the treasury some 9,368 kg of silver per year while an annual income of 320 talents represented 8,275 kg of silver. The additional indemnity of 1,200 talents imposed on Carthage (Polyb. 1.88.12; 3.27.8) in 238 will have corrected the shortfall and created a surplus.

indemnity of 10,000 talents on Carthage, this was payable at a rate of only 200 talents a year for fifty years.[59] This sum represented the cost of the yearly *stipendium* for only two legions while the republic's military establishment in these years typically hovered between eight and nine. The annual indemnity that Philip V was forced to pay following his defeat in 197 was fifty talents a year, the cost of half a year's pay for a legion.[60] Despite the massive booty Africanus had brought back from Carthage – 133,000 Roman pounds of silver according to Livy – at the outset of the Second Macedonian War in 200 the treasury could barely meet the expenses of the army and fleet it was sending to Greece.[61] And as noted above, *tributum* was still in arrears almost fifteen years later (Livy 39.7.4–5).

The stupendous hauls of booty that resulted from the victories of Acilius Glabrio, Cn. Scipio, Fulvius Faccus and Manlius Vulso in the east improved the condition of the treasury dramatically, and even more so did the thirty million denarii Aemilius Paullus brought back as spoils from the defeat of Perseus, a sum so vast that the senate felt it could suspend collection of *tributum* indefinitely.[62] It was this step that greatly altered the financial relationship between a general and the *res publica*, for while the treasury still bore the cost of Rome's wars the *tributum*-paying *assidui* no longer stood behind the *aerarium*. The public and particularly the *tribunii aerarii* henceforth ceased to have a direct and personal financial stake in those wars and consequently in the disposition of the booty they generated. Generals now had only their peers in the senate and their soldiers to answer to, limiting public scrutiny and giving them at least to some extent a freer hand to turn the *manubiae* to their own profit.

Still, this development did not necessarily inaugurate a period of wholesale self-enrichment on the part of generals. In 157, only ten years after Paullus had added Macedon's thirty million denarii to the *aerarium*, its surplus stood at about twenty-five million (Plin. *HN* 33.55). The intervening decade had been one of relative peace for Rome, meaning few opportunities for plunder but a continuing need to maintain a somewhat reduced military establishment. In the years that followed, the destruction of Carthage produced only 4,370 Roman pounds of silver (Plin. *HN* 33.141) but the booty from the sack of Corinth must have been rich: the senate in 144 could authorize the outlay of HS 180 million (= 45 million denarii) for the *aqua Marcia* (Frontin. *Aq.* 1.7.4). However, the wars in Spain that ensued cannot have yielded much in view of Lucullus' disappointment at obtaining no gold or silver from the surrender of Intercatia, and of

---

[59] Polyb. 15.18.7; Livy 30.37.5; App. *Pun.* 54.   [60] Polyb. 18.44.7; Livy 33.30.7.
[61] Livy 30.45.3; 31.13.1–9.   [62] Cic. *Off.* 2.76; Plin. *HN* 33.56; Val. Max. 4.3.8; Plut. *Aem.* 38.1.

the paltry donative of 7 denarii that Scipio Aemilianus gave to his troops following his triumph over the Numantines.[63] Most of the accumulated wealth there had probably been looted long ago. The *patres* must have watched with concern as the surplus in the treasury dwindled. Pressure on generals to hand over as much of their spoils as possible will not have abated, therefore. And although the victory over Jugurtha produced over twenty million denarii, similar successes were rare before 101 BC.[64] Much of the fighting in these years was against tough, poor enemies. Table 1 suggests that not many of these wars will have generated enough spoils to repay the treasury, satisfy the soldiers, provide for monuments or games, and still leave plenty left over from which a general could enrich himself.[65]

The condition of the treasury improved considerably with the acquisition of the Attalid bequest in 133 and Gaius Gracchus' legislation in 122 regularizing the collection of tribute from the province of Asia, although the increase in the public revenues that resulted was probably not as great as is sometimes believed.[66] Still, there is little evidence that the wars of the later second century placed an intolerable strain on the republic's finances. The Social War, however, drained the public fisc, and straitened conditions persisted down to Pompey's victories in the east, which more than doubled the republic's annual revenues.[67] But with the defeat of Mithridates, the looting of his kingdom and other cities in Asia by Lucullus and Pompey and the latter's provincial settlement in the east, a milestone was reached. No individual victory, it might seem, could make much of a difference to the republic's balance sheet, while neither the *aerarium* nor the *assidui* were on the hook any longer for the cost of Rome's wars. And so generals should have found themselves much freer to pocket a large portion of the booty and the age of military rapacity begun in earnest, fueled by the staggering rise in the level of expenditure required to maintain a standard of living appropriate to a member of the senatorial elite And yet how are we to explain the great wealth some generals acquired following their victories

---

[63] App. *Hisp.* 54; Plin. *HN* 33.141.
[64] Sall. *Iug.* 62.5: 200,000 lb of silver (= 16,800,000 denarii) handed over to Metellus; Plut. *Mar.* 12.4: 3,007 lb of gold (= 2,525,880 denarii), 5,775 lb of silver (= 485,100 denarii), and 287,000 denarii in Marius' triumph over Jugurtha.
[65] Note in particular the paucity of temple dedications in this period resulting from war compared to the first decades of the second century: Orlin 1997, 201–2.
[66] Kallet-Marx (1995, 109–20) arguing that the senate's settlement following the defeat of Aristonicus left a substantial number of the cities of Asia Minor free and so not subject to taxation; see now the "Apollonius Decree" from Metropolis, adding further support to this argument: Dreyer and Engelmann 2003, lines 14–15; cf. Jones 2004, 480–1.
[67] Crawford 1974, 636–8 for sources and discussion.

but the lack of accusations of *peculatus* against them in the highly competitive late-republican political arena if, as Churchill has argued, they were not entitled to enrich themselves from the *manubiae*?

Unquestionably, Lucullus, Pompey and many other generals returned from their wars rich, but perhaps our long-standing assumptions about a commander's ownership of his *manubiae* have led us to jump to the conclusion that this must have been the principal source of their sudden wealth. Caesar, for example, left for Spain following his praetorship in 62 heavily in debt. While in that province, he won victories against bandits in the northwest, captured the city of Brigantium, enriched his soldiers, sent back a large sum to the treasury, and returned to Rome with enough money to satisfy his creditors.[68] Although scholars commonly assume that plunder was the source of Caesar's newly found cash, no source explicitly says so. Rather the reverse: Suetonius reports that certain authors claimed that Caesar "got money that he had begged from the allies to help with his debts."[69] While this testimony could well derive from hostile sources, the slander may consist only in the characterization of the money as gotten by begging rather than in the form of "gifts" voluntarily offered by provincials eager to win the proconsul's favor. For Pompey, too, received lavish "gifts" while commanding the republic's forces in the east.[70] And we know from the letters of that other *imperator* in the east, Cicero, that after turning the rest of the *praeda* over to the soldiers following the capture of Pindenissum the money he realized from the sale of his prisoners was meager, perhaps no more than 30,000 denarii.[71] The real profits, as his other letters make clear, would have come from the administration of justice, the "gifts" that provincials customarily offered their governors, and a variety of other less than savory sources, had Cicero been a less scrupulous magistrate.[72] Yet even he managed to accumulate 550,000 denarii *salvis legibus*, probably derived in the main from the funds the senate had granted to him for his ordinary expenses.[73] And of course a governor far less concerned with upholding his principles than Cicero had a wide array

---

[68] Cass. Dio 37.52.1–53.4; App. *B Civ.* 2.8; Plut. *Caes.* 12.1–2; Suet. *Iul.* 54.1.
[69] Suet. *Iul.* 54.1: *quidam monumentis suis testati sunt in Hispania pro consule et a sociis pecunias accepit emendicatas in auxilium aeris alieni.*
[70] Shatzman 1975, 391–2.
[71] Cic. *Att.* 113 [5.20].5: HS 120,000, with Shackleton Bailey's note ad loc.
[72] Summarized in Mitchell 1991, 213–18, 224.
[73] HS 2,200,000: Cic. *Fam.* 128 [5.20].9, although in the event, Cicero foresaw his need to repay a loan from Caesar as depriving him of the use of these funds to pay for his anticipated triumph: *Att.* 131 [7.8].5. Cf. the lavish *vasarium* that Clodius' legislation bestowed upon L. Calpurnius Piso in 57: Cic. *Pis.* 86, and note Cicero's claims that generals sold appointments of centurions and left the sums issued to them for the conduct of their campaigns at Rome to be lent at interest: *Leg. Man.*

of methods at his disposal for extorting money from the provincials subject to his *imperium*, as Cicero catalogues in his enumeration of Verres' crimes against the Sicilians.⁷⁴ Indeed, *res repetundae* is the characteristic crime of late-republican provincial administration, not *peculatus*, and there is no reason why generals with armies at their disposal should have been any less ready to practice it than governors of peaceful provinces.

Indeed, the fate of M. Aurelius Cotta, consul in 74 and the only late-republican general to suffer conviction on charges of *peculatus*, may have deterred potential imitators.⁷⁵ He returned to Rome from Bithynia in late 70 or 69 to great acclaim for his siege and capture of Heracleia Pontica (although the city was in fact taken by a legate of Lucullus) along with great spoils. The senate awarded him a triumph and the cognomen Ponticus for his achievement. Then it all fell apart. Charges that he had sacked the city simply to enrich himself roused popular antagonism, and his enormous wealth provoked jealousy. Hoping to defuse the hostility, Cotta deposited much of his booty in the treasury, but this step failed to mollify his detractors, who suspected that he had handed over only a small portion of a much larger haul. The senate ordered the prisoners Cotta had brought from Heracleia to be set free. Then C. Papirius Carbo further inflamed public sentiment in a series of speeches, and a tearful demonstration by the freed Heracleians only increased popular outrage. Cotta was brought to trial and condemned for misappropriation of the booty, expelled from the senate, with his place and rank therein awarded to his accuser, Carbo, and narrowly escaped condemnation on a related charge of *maiestas*, which would have carried a capital sentence.

Apart from the spectacular opportunities for enrichment afforded by a few exceptional wars like that against Mithridates or Caesar's conquest of Gaul, most consuls and proconsuls interested in filling their purses therefore may well have preferred to govern a peaceful province rather than go on campaign. A peaceful province meant no army clamoring for a share of the plunder, no need to hand over any *manubiae* to the treasury on his return, and no jealous rivals eager to raise accusations of theft. But when a war did have to be waged, one may suspect that generals left the *praeda* and *manubiae* mainly to the soldiers and the *aerarium* and concentrated instead on the kinds of graft that fell within the scope of the laws against extortion rather than *peculatus*.

---

37. Most praetors sent to Asia, he alleges, grew rich from public funds while achieving nothing militarily: *Leg. Man. 67*.
⁷⁴ Badian 1972, 108–9.
⁷⁵ Dio 36.40.3–4; Memn. 39 = *FGrH* 3B.366–7; on the trial and fate of Cotta, see Linderski 1987 (1995).

Table 1 *Profits of Roman victories vs. some of their costs, 200–167 BC*

Date	Commander	Province	Years in command	No. of legions	Booty	Cost of stipendium	Sources	Profit?
200	L. Cornelius Lentulus	Spain	5	1	43,000 lbs[a] silver 2,450 lbs gold (= 24,500 lbs silver[b])	41,800 lbs[c]	Livy 31.20.7	Yes
200	L. Furius Purpurio	Gaul	1	2	101,500 denarii 320,000 asses (= 32,000 denarii)	1,404,000 denarii	Livy 31.49.2	No
199	L. Manlius Acidinus	Spain	6	1	1,200 lbs silver 30 lbs gold (= 300 lbs silver)	50,160 lbs	Livy 32.7.4	No
197	C. Cornelius Cethegus	Gaul	1	2	79,000 denarii 237,500 asses (= 23,750 denarii)	1,404,000 denarii	Livy 33.23.7	No
197	Q. Minucius	Gaul and Liguria	1	2	53,200 denarii 254,000 asses (= 25,400 denarii)	1,404,000 denarii	Livy 33.23.9	No
196	Cn. Cornelius Blasio	Spain	3	1	20,000 lbs silver 1,515 lbs gold (= 15,150 lbs silver) 34,500 denarii	25,080 lbs silver (= 2,106,000 denarii)	Livy 33.27.2	Yes
196	L. Stertinius	Spain	3	1	50,000 lbs silver	25,080 lbs silver (= 2,106,000 denarii)	Livy 33.27.4	Yes
196	M. Claudius Marcellus	Gaul	1	2	320,000 asses (= 32,000 denarii) 234,000 denarii	1,404,000 denarii	Livy 33.37.11	No
196	M. Helvius	Spain	1	0 (*socii* only)	14,732 lbs silver 17,023 denarii 119,439 Oscan denarii	0	Livy 34.10.4	Yes
196	Q. Minucius Thermus	Spain	1	0 (*socii* only)	34,800 lbs silver 73,000 denarii 278,000 Oscan denarii	0	Livy 34.10.7	Yes

(*cont.*)

Table 1 (cont.)

Date	Commander	Province	Years in command	No. of legions	Booty	Cost of stipendium	Sources	Profit?
194	M. Porcius Cato	Spain	1	2	25,000 lbs silver 1,400 lbs gold (= 14,000 lbs silver) 123,000 denarii 540,000 Oscan denarii	16,720 lbs silver (= 1,404,000 denarii)	Livy 34.46.2	Yes
194	T. Quinctius Flaminius	Greece	4	2	18,270 (43,270?) lbs silver 3,714 lbs gold (= 37,140 lbs silver) 84,000 tetradrachmas (= 336,000 denarii)[d] 14,514 gold Philippics (= 348,336 denarii)[e] 114 gold crowns [50 talents/year × 8 years] [50 talents/year × 10 years]	66,880 lbs silver (= 5,616,000 denarii)	Livy 34.52.5–8; cf. Plut. *Flam.* 14.1–2	Yes
191	M. Fulvius Nobilior	Spain	2	1	12,000 lbs silver 127 lbs gold (= 1,270 lbs silver) 130,000 denarii	16,720 lbs silver (= 1,404,000 denarii)	Livy 36.21.11	No
191	P. Cornelius Scipio Nasica	Gaul	1	2	2,340 lbs silver 247 lbs gold (= 2,470 lbs silver) 234,000 denarii 1,471 gold torques	16,720 lbs silver (= 1,404,000 denarii)	Livy 36.40.12	?[f]
190	M. Acilius Glabrio	Greece	1	2	3,000 lbs silver 113,000 tetradrachmas (= 452,000 denarii) 249,000 cistophori (= 747,000 denarii) 45 gold crowns a great amount of silver	16,720 lbs silver (= 1,404,000 denarii)	Livy 37.46.3–4	Yes

190	L. Aemilius Regulus	fleet	1	fleet	34,200 tetradrachmas (= 136,800 denarii) 132,300 cistophori (= 96,900 denarii) 49 gold crowns	?	Livy 37.58.4 ?
189	Cn. Cornelius Scipio Asiagenus	Asia Minor	1	2	137,000 lbs silver 224,000 tetradrachmas (= 896,000 denarii) 321,070 cistophori (= 963,210 denarii) 140,000 gold Philippics (= 3,360,000 denarii) 1,423 silver vases 1,023 gold vases [1000 Euboic talents/year × 12 years]	16,720 lbs silver (= 1,404,000 denarii)	Livy 37.59.3–5	Yes
187	M. Fulvius Nobilior	Greece	2	2	83,000 lbs silver 243 lbs gold (= 2,430 lbs silver) 112 lbs gold crowns (= 1,120 lbs silver) 118,000 tetradrachmas (= 472,000 denarii) 12,322 gold Philippics (= 295,728 denarii) [50 Euboic talents/year × 6 years]	33,440 lbs silver (= 2,808,000 denarii)	Livy 39.5.14–15	Yes

(*cont.*)

Table 1 (*cont.*)

Date	Commander	Province	Years in command	No. of legions	Booty	Cost of stipendium	Sources	Profit?
187	Cn. Manlius Vulso	Asia Minor	2	2	220,000 lbs silver 2,103 lbs gold (= 21,030 lbs silver) 127,000 tetradrachmas (= 508,000 denarii) 250,000 cistophori (= 750,000 denarii) 16,320 gold Philippics (= 391,680 denarii) 212 gold crowns	33,440 lbs silver (= 2,808,000 denarii)	Livy 39.7.1–2	Yes
185	M. Manlius Acidinus	Spain	2	2	26,300 lbs silver 212 lbs gold (= 2,120 lbs silver) 52 gold crowns[g]	33,440 lbs silver (= 2,808,000 denarii)	Livy 39.29.6–7	Yes?
184	C. Calpurnius Piso and L. Quinctius Crispinus	Spain	2	4	24,000 lbs silver 166 gold crowns	66,880 lbs silver (= 5,616,000 denarii)	Livy 39.42.4	No
183	A. Terentius Varro	Spain	2	2	9,320 lbs silver 82 lbs gold (= 820 lbs silver) 67 gold crowns	33,440 lbs silver (= 2,808,000 denarii)	Livy 40.16.11	No
181	L. Aemilius Paullus	Liguria	2	2[h]	25 gold crowns	34,880 lbs silver (= 2,929,933 denarii)	Livy 40.34.8	No[i]
180	Q. Fulvius Flaccus	Spain	2	2	31 lbs gold (= 310 lbs silver) 173,200 Oscan denarii 124 gold crowns	33,440 lbs silver (= 2,808,000 denarii)	Livy 40.43.5	No
180	P. Cornelius Cethegus	Liguria	1	2	0	17,440 lbs silver (= 1,464,966 denarii)	Livy 40.38.9	No

Year	Name	Region				Source	
180	M. Baebius Tamphilius	Liguria	1	2	0	Livy 40.38.9	No
179	Q. Fulvius Flaccus	Liguria	1	2	0	Livy 40.59.2	No
178	Ti. Sempronius Gracchus	Spain	2	2	40,000 lbs silver	Livy 41.7.2	Yes
178	L. Postumius Albinus	Spain	2	2	20,000 lbs silver	Livy 41.7.3	No
177	C. Claudius Pulcher	Histria and Liguria	1	2	307,000 denarii 85,702 victoriati (= 64,277 denarii)	Livy 41.13.7	No
174	Ap. Claudius Centho	Spain	1	1	10,000 lbs silver 5,000? lbs gold (= 50,000? lbs silver)	Livy 41.28.6	Yes
167	L. Anicius Gallus	Illyria	1	2	19 lbs silver 27 lbs gold (= 270 lbs silver) 13,000 denarii 120,000 victoriati (= 90,000 denarii)	Livy 45.43.4	No

					17,440 lbs silver (= 1,464,966 denarii)		
					16,720 lbs silver (= 1,404,000 denarii)		
					33,440 lbs silver		
					33,440 lbs silver		
					1,404,000 denarii		
					8,360 lbs silver		
					16,720 lbs silver (= 1,404,000 denarii)		

(*cont.*)

Table 1 (cont.)

Date	Commander	Province	Years in command	No. of legions	Booty	Cost of stipendium	Sources	Profit?
167	Cn. Octavius	fleet	2	0	0	?	Livy 40.42.2	?
167	L. Aemilius Paullus	Greece	1	2	30,000,000 denarii[j]	1,654,300 denarii[k]	Livy 45.40.1	Yes

[a] All pounds are Roman pounds of 324 grams: Crawford 1974, 590–2.
[b] This assumes a 1:10 ratio of gold to silver: Polyb. 21.32.8; Livy 38.11.9; cf. Crawford 1974, 626 n. 1.
[c] The cost of *stipendium* for one legion for one year is rounded to 702,000 denarii for convenience in Table 1: see above, n. 23. This sum is equivalent to 8,357 Roman pounds of silver at 84 denarii to the Roman pound: Crawford 1974, 594–5, rounded here for convenience to 8,360 pounds.
[d] Although Livy 34.52.6 gives the value of a tetradrachma as 3 denarii, this is unlikely to be correct for this date: Thompson 1957–61, II, 139–42; cf. Crawford 1974, 28 n. 4. Here and throughout Table 1, the tetradrachma is valued at 4 denarii. On the equation of the drachma with the denarius, see Crawford 1985, 146–7.
[e] One gold Philippic was worth 24 drachmas = 24 denarii: Head 1911, 222–3.
[f] The weight of the torques is unknown. If they weighed on average 0.62 (Roman) pounds each, then Nasica's campaign will have "broken even"; if they were heavier, it will have turned a profit.
[g] If the crowns weighed, on average, 10 (Roman) pounds each, Manlius will have "broken even." If they weighed more, he will have turned a profit.
[h] The legions of Paullus, Cethegus and Tamphilius each contained 5,200 infantry in this year: Livy 40.1.5, 18.3.
[i] To make a profit, each gold crown will on average have had to weigh almost 150 pounds.
[j] Cf. Polyb. 18.35.4; Plin. *HN* 33.56; Diod. Sic. 313.8.11; Vell. Pat. 1.9.6; Plut. *Aem.* 32.5–33.2 for other figures; most are similar to Livy.
[k] Paullus' legions contained 6,000 infantry and 300 cavalry in this year: Livy 44.21.8. On the full cost of the war, see now Müller 2009a.

PART III
Symbols, models, self-representation

CHAPTER 8

The Roman republic as theatre of power: the consuls as leading actors

Karl-Joachim Hölkeskamp

> How could communities,
> Degrees in schools and brotherhoods in cities,
> Peaceful commerce from dividable shores,
> The primogenitive and due of birth,
> Prerogative of age, crowns, sceptres, laurels,
> But by degree, stand in authentic place?
> Take but degree away, untune that string,
> And, hark, what discord follows!
> Shakespeare, *Troilus and Cressida*, I, 3, 105–12

Roman culture was always a culture of spectacles – in the concrete as well as abstract or metaphorical sense of the concept.[1] To begin with, the religious calendar was packed with regular rituals and ceremonies, processions, games, festivals and other truly 'spectacular' occasions of all kinds – such as the run by the *Luperci* around the Palatine in mid-February and the carnival fight between Subura and Sacra via over the tail of the *equus October* (October Horse). The spectacular splendour of the *ludi* – in the late republic, the six most important of them, the *ludi Romani*, *Apollinares*, *Megalenses*, *Plebei*, *Ceriales* and *Florales* alone lasted for no less than 57 days every year – gave Livy reason to observe that by his own day this splendour had turned into utter craziness that would be hard to bear even for rich royalty.[2] This culture revolved around, or was defined

---

Special thanks are due to Spanish colleagues, namely Francisco Marco Simón and Francisco Pina Polo, for the invitation to the conference on which this volume is based and for their generous hospitality; I should also like to thank the other participants, especially Antonio Duplá, and (as always, last but not least) Elke Stein-Hölkeskamp for comments, criticism and encouragement.

[1] Definitions: Flower 2004, 322, 324, 338; cf. also Nicolet 1980, 343ff. (whose conceptualization of spectacles as 'alternative' – as opposed to 'regular', i.e. formal decision-making – 'institutions', however, is no longer tenable); Dupont 1985, 19ff.; Kyle 1998, 8ff. and *passim*; Bergmann & Kondoleon 1999, 10ff.; Beacham 1999, 1ff.; Bell 2004, 7ff., 24ff., 151ff.; Hölkeskamp 2006a, 318ff. with further references.

[2] Livy 7.2.13; cf. on these festivals e.g. Dupont 1989 (1992), 199ff.; Hopkins 1991, 479ff.; and on the *ludi* in general Clavel-Lévêque 1984, 23ff. and *passim* (with the discussion by Gunderson 1996, 118ff.); Bernstein 1998 and now Flaig 2003, 232ff.; Sumi 2005, 25ff.

by, 'spectacles' as 'ritualized performances that communicated, restored, consolidated, and sometimes helped change the communal order'[3] of the *populus Romanus* and their *res publica*.

Roman culture was also a visual culture, a culture of seeing and being seen, both on special occasions and in everyday public life, but this is too simplistic: this culture was characterized and indeed defined by a specific kind of theatricality as it was based on what I have termed the imperative of immediacy, an intensified degree of visibility, personal presence, public performance and sheer physicality that determined the whole scale of practices and patterns of behaviour – for this reason I will regularly and deliberately use metaphors of theatre, stage and performance. This particular theatricality is best illustrated by the dramatic structure of rituals and festivals such as the Lupercalia and the festival of the October Horse, mentioned above. The festivals were always accompanied by a special kind of romp that involved different groups of the ordinary people at large, both young women and the inhabitants of certain quarters of the *urbs* – the presence, and in fact the active participation, of the audience was part and parcel of these dramatic performances themselves, or, to put it in a more (post)modern phrasing, the actual physical 'co-presence' and participation were inscribed in the syntax of these rituals. This is also true of many other public spectacles: the man in the Roman street was always more than a mere 'spectator' in the narrow sense of the concept – he was regularly an 'integral interlocutor in the community's ritual dialogue',[4] even a 'co-actor', or perhaps, to phrase this in another postmodern sort of whimsical word-play, a '(spect-)a(c)tor'. The Roman culture of spectacles developed a complex system of sets and stages, leading and supporting roles, in which actors and audiences permanently interacted and, in a way, even changed roles in a play about Rome, her gods and great men, her history, present and future, about 'Romanness' and (or rather: as) greatness – about being a Roman, about living and acting as a Roman.[5] To quote a much-quoted (though poorly documented) phrase, also attributed to the great bard of Stratford: 'Little, or much, of what we see, we do; / We're all both *actors* and *spectators* too.'[6] Romans would certainly have had a very special and keen understanding of the meaning(s) of these two lines and their interconnected complexity.

---

[3] Kyle 1998, 9; cf. Muir 1997, 6; Flaig 2003, 9ff. and *passim*; Sumi 2005, 7ff.   [4] Bell 2004, 173.
[5] Cf. also Gunderson 1996, 119ff., on 'the spectators as part of the spectacle' (133).
[6] Cf. the documentation in Schanzer 1968.

This brings me directly to the sub-system of the republican political culture – by this category,[7] I mean to define the conceptual system of social values and views of the world, of self and other, of mutual and shared expectations of behaviour in public roles and of the semantics of politics in general that underlie the surface of power and interests, politics and political decision-making. First, I include within this concept the 'symbolic dimensions of social action'[8] in the 'public' sphere of politics and the concomitant communicative system of symbols, images and their language, shared (or at least understood) by the political community at large. Second, this concept serves to denote an 'ensemble of texts, themselves ensembles'[9] – in concrete terms, the whole range of rituals, ceremonies and other spectacles which, as 'ensembles', make up the specific repertoire of ways, means and media which serve to affirm, reproduce, modify, criticize or otherwise negotiate the system of values, norms and conceptual codes of a given culture. It is this repertoire or 'ensemble' which in turn complements, as well as overlaps and intersects with, yet another 'ensemble' with its own 'text', namely the institutions and formal procedures of politics as a decision-making process.[10] The complex interconnectivity of these dimensions is best illustrated, and indeed typically represented, by a central 'institution' of the Roman republican political system, recently discussed in this new light. The specific 'ensemble' of the *contio* as formal 'procedure' and ritual 'rhetoric', 'performance', public 'stage' and meaningful 'text' played a particularly important part in the republican socio-political structure as a communicative system uniting the *populus Romanus* and its elite.[11]

In this system, commensurate with its culture of personal presence, visibility and physical performance, a particularly sophisticated 'ensemble' of civic rituals took centre stage. Every single ritual is a peculiar hybrid of dramatic and ceremonial elements, derived from different sources, with a specific syntax, taxonomy or 'text' of its own. As a systemic 'ensemble', civic rituals constitute a symbolic language and serve as a medium for a

---

[7] Cf. for modern discussions of the meaning and dimensions of the concept 'political culture' e.g. Hunt 1984, 10ff.; cf. also Sharpe 1993, 853ff.
[8] Geertz, 'Thick Description: Toward an Interpretive Theory of Culture', in Geertz 1993, 3–30, quotation on p. 30.
[9] Geertz, 'Deep Play: Notes on a Balinese Cockfight', in Geertz 1993, 412–53, quotation on p. 452.
[10] Cf. Hölkeskamp 2004b, 57ff.; 2007, 38ff. for the underlying concept of 'political culture'.
[11] Cf. now the 'thick description' and fundamental analysis by Morstein-Marx 2004, 7ff. and *passim*; cf. also Pina Polo 1996, *passim*; Bell 1997, 1ff.; Bell 2004, 201ff., 217f., 235f. etc.; Hölkeskamp 2004a, 234ff. and 256; Hölkeskamp 2004b, 70ff., 88f. with further references; Sumi 2005, 17ff.

continuous discourse among the constituent groups of the political community, in this case between the political class and the *populus Romanus*, but also among the political class itself.[12] This particular sub-genre of rituals is specifically designed not only to stage and thus reveal, but also to constitute and continuously reconstitute an exclusively Roman civic ideology and a sense of collective indigenous identity based upon a broad consensus about political and social values – such as the *pompa funebris*. The demonstratively public funeral ritual of the great *gentes* was designed to enhance their respective accumulated symbolic capital by symbolically staging the return of the ancestors into the Forum Romanum as a central civic space and onto the *rostra* as the most prominent stage of public appearance. This ritual must be read as an implicit appeal to a universal consensus between members of the *gens*, dead or alive, as actors on the one hand and their peers and the people as co-present audience on the other. It is an ideological consensus about individual and familial contributions to Rome's greatness in the shape of outstanding accomplishments in politics and war; these accomplishments were the only legitimate origin and foundation of honours and *honores*, reputation, rank and membership in the political elite.[13] The ideology of commitment and reciprocity and its regular ritual representation, which is particularly impressive and effective through the constant repetition of key concepts and principles in the *laudationes* as well as through the use of the same symbols and the implementation of the same basic syntax, is an important symbolic source of a shared sense of unity and coherence, which in turn is a prerequisite for the exercise of authority.[14]

Moreover, civic rituals are commentaries on the city, not only on its internal dynamics, but also on its relationship with the outside world – such as the *pompa triumphalis*. This particularly splendid spectacle was designed to stage not only the ceremonial return of the victorious commander-in-chief into the city, but also the ritual completion of the subjugation of yet another foreign tribe or nation under Roman rule and the symbolic appropriation of yet another distant part of the world by the *populus Romanus*, partly co-present as awe-inspired 'civil' as well as 'civic' audience and partly co-acting in the procession of the ordinary soldiers following the triumphal chariot. It was a discourse about power in the shape of

---

[12] My definition of the concept 'civic ritual' closely follows Muir 1981, 5; cf. also Trexler 1980, xix; Hopkins 1991, 484ff.; Bell 1997, 2f.; Muir 1997, 1ff., 232ff.; Bell 2004, 7ff., etc.
[13] Cf. Flower 1996; Beacham 1999, 17ff., 38f.; Bodel 1999; Blösel 2000, 37ff.; Blösel 2003, *passim*; Flaig 2003, 49ff.; Flower 2004, 331ff.; Walter 2004b, 89ff.; Sumi 2005, 41ff.; Flower 2006, *passim*; Hölkeskamp 2006a, 347ff., 355ff., with further references.
[14] I follow the conceptual reflections by Hunt 1984, 14.

conquest and control over the world – and thus yet another aspect of the ideological consensus between *populus Romanus* and its ruling class and again a symbolic source of unity and coherence.[15]

Civic rituals illustrate the valid and legitimate arrangement of human relationships – and, in the case of the Roman republic, these relationships are by definition and indeed by nature hierarchic, characterized by a steep asymmetry of authority and power.[16] Hierarchy permeates not only all formal and informal relationships between the political elite and the ordinary people of the *populus Romanus* at large as constituent classes of the Roman political community as well as between an individual senator as patron and priest, consul and commander and the man in the Roman street as ordinary citizen, client and soldier. Hierarchy is also the omnipresent ruling principle that defines the complex network of relationships within the senatorial elite itself. It was based on the hierarchical ordering of offices in the *cursus honorum*, the consolidation of which was a prolonged, conflict-ridden and complex process – a process practically identical with the consolidation of the patricio-plebeian meritocracy as such.

To summarize, and to use the precise concepts coined by the famous historian of early modern Europe, Edward Muir, to characterize Renaissance Venice, its 'serene society' and inheritance of myth and ritual:[17] 'government by ritual' in the Roman 'republic of processions' was based on a repertoire (or 'ensemble') of civic rituals (themselves 'ensembles') that was intricately interconnected by a rich texture of symbols, images, meanings and messages, revolving around the omnipresence of, and complex correlation between, concepts of power and hierarchy. In a culture of spectacular visibility, the language or 'poetics' of power is necessarily visual.[18] That means that it is simply not enough to exercise power by pulling strings behind the scenes – power only becomes real when and if it is seen to be exercised, it needs publicity and performance, that is, in theatrical terms, actors, a 'text' (in both senses of the concept), a stage and a 'co-present' audience. And the same is true for hierarchies: they are not just in place, defining and reproducing themselves – they need to be acted out in public to reproduce

---

[15] Cf. Flower 2004, 326ff.; Itgenshorst 2005; and earlier, Marshall 1984, 123ff.; Beacham 1999, 19ff., 39ff.; Sumi 2005, 29ff.; Hölkeskamp 2006a, 339ff., 352ff.; Hölkeskamp 2006b, *passim*; Beard 2007, *passim*; Hölkeskamp 2007, 58ff; Hölkeskamp 2008, *passim*. See also for a different reading of this ritual Flaig 2003, 32ff.
[16] Cf. for the fundamental importance of hierarchy, authority and power, not only with respect to *familia* and *domus*, Saller 1994, 102ff. and generally the important book by Flaig 2003.
[17] Muir 1981, 183, 185ff., cf. 7; Muir 1997, 229ff.
[18] Hunt 1984, 19ff., has coined the term to cover the 'rhetoric' and 'imagery' of revolution and radicalism as well as the 'symbolic forms of political practice'.

and affirm themselves. This is particularly true in a city-state system in which rule and the most important acts of ruling are executed not only publicly, in the presence and literally under the eyes of those who are being ruled and are thus explicitly or implicitly the addressees of these acts. This co-presence and, even more so, the different supporting roles of a co-acting citizenry in many civic rituals generate a specific Roman kind of 'complicity' which the 'exercise of authority' in this political culture depended on and were therefore part and parcel of a typical city-state government as a 'process' shared between rulers and ruled.[19] It is exactly this variant of rule in, and through, face-to-face communication which necessarily has a particular need for special forms and media of symbolic interaction in the shape of civic rituals.[20] They structure and channel the interaction between rulers or ruling classes – or rather their representatives physically present in a given situation – and the ruled as co-present audience and addressees. Last but not least, these rituals render the situation, in which power is (seen to be) exercised in the shape of performative acts of ruling, calculable and foreseeable in its results, thus providing the kind of dependability which is the prerequisite of stability, continuity and legitimacy.

At long last, I have arrived at the point where the consuls enter the stage – and immediately take centre stage as leading actors in a variety of public spectacles, punctuating the daily life of the city.[21] Indeed, any public appearance of magistrates in high office, in different places, social and institutional contexts, ritual as well as other formal roles – and these things are all true for the consuls – is staging a spectacle of its own, regularly and continuously throughout their year in office. The very first day of that year is invariably filled with the highly ritualized spectacle of the consuls solemnly taking office.[22] In the morning, according to a time-honoured tradition, the new incumbent takes the auspices and puts on the purple-bordered *toga praetexta* as robe of his new office. The equally symbolic next act is particularly revealing: the twelve lictors of the new consul have to 'raise the *fasces*' (*fasces attollere*) – and it is only then that the consul leaves his private house and appears in his new capacity for the first time in the full view of the public. With friends and followers, probably including senators and *equites*, in attendance and with the

---

[19] Sharpe 1993, 854; cf. Bell 2004, 11ff.
[20] Cf. e.g. Althoff 2003, 31, and other recent studies on rituals, ceremonies and other forms of 'symbolic communication' in pre-modern city-states: Schlögl 2004; Goppold 2007, 30ff.
[21] Cf. Nippel 1995, 4ff.; Bell 1997, 10ff.; Bell 2004, 218ff.
[22] Ov. *Fast.* 1, 79ff.; *Pont.* 4.4.25ff.; cf. Livy 21.63.7–11. Cf. Mommsen 1887–8, I, 615ff., with further references.

co-present *populus* wearing 'the colour of the festal day',[23] the consul proceeds through the city, its streets and public places and probably across the Forum to the Capitol, with his lictors walking before him in single file and at a dignified, measured pace. It is here, in the religious centre of *urbs* and *imperium*, in front of the temple of Iuppiter Optimus Maximus, that the consul – now together with his new colleague – takes his seat for the first time, that is, the *sella curulis*. His first official duty is to perform another time-honoured, solemn religious ritual in order to guarantee the eternal continuity of divine protection: he thanks Iuppiter Optimus Maximus for preserving city and *imperium* during the previous year. In fulfilment of the vow taken by his predecessor at the beginning of his term of office, he presides over the sacrifice of white cows and then in turn vows the same sacrifice for the following year. The next stage of the inauguration ritual consists of the new consuls taking the chair in the first meeting of the senate, which regularly takes place in the temple of Iuppiter and is devoted to religious business. The final act is their return to their private houses – notably in the same order of procession as the initial appearance.

The inauguration ritual is indeed another variant of a civic ritual in the concrete shape of a procession in the full sense of the concept. Like rituals in general, it follows a specific normative order with a particular pattern, structure and imagery encoding its particular semantics of symbolic meanings that need to be recognizable for, and actually recognized by, actors and audience – in this case, the special status, the public role and the particular 'power' of a holder of *imperium*. Just like the *pompae* mentioned above, this procession is a participatory civic ritual whose syntax is especially defined by its inscription in the urban space of the *urbs Roma*, which provides the stages for the actors as well as the auditorium for the co-present and co-acting audience. This space encompasses the complex politico-religious topography centred on the Forum Romanum, Comitium and Capitol and the routes that link them, such as the Sacra via and Clivus Capitolinus, Vicus Tuscus and Iugarius.[24]

To the Roman '(spect-)a(c)tors' of all ranks, this topography itself was above all a landscape of memory thronged with monuments of power and superiority, symbols of Rome's glorious past and present of imperial grandeur – and it was a museum of might and the mighty conveying the same meanings and messages of superiority based on hierarchy. This museum was literally thronged with statues of the stern, *imperium*-holding and power-wielding figureheads such as the famous Fabius

[23] Ov. *Fast.* 1.80.   [24] Cf. Hölkeskamp 2004a, 169–98; Flower 2004, 323.

Maximus 'Cunctator', whose imposing equestrian statue – intimidating because of its prominent placing on the Capitol as well as its elevated position on an impressive pedestal[25] – could not but be read as a vivid visualization and symbolization of the principle of distance and hierarchy. The same impression was certainly generated by the imposing architecture of temples with their roof sculptures, triumphal paintings and exhibitions of representative pieces of war booty, most of which were also placed high above the heads of the passers-by. Many prominent personalities of the great past – the very same republican heroes who now and then might even have, as it were, come to life in a *pompa funebris* of one of the great *gentes* – were, in a way, permanently positioned in high places in the shape of statues of *togati* in the 'magisterial' pose of the orator addressing the people. These and other honorific column portraits would invariably show them in the public roles that constituted their 'high place' – as consuls, commanders and holders of *imperium*. And at last, I may indulge in another play with words: the arch-Roman form of a monument is perhaps the most immediate representation of the asymmetry of high and low. Arches like the archetype of the *fornix Scipionis* at the Clivus Capitolinus on the Capitol, the *fornix Calpurnius* in the same prominent area, and the *fornix Fabianus* overarching the Sacra via at the entrance to the Forum Romanum and adorned with the busts of memorable members of the *gens*[26] are much more than aspirations and ambitions of prominent and therefore highly 'visible' families of the political elite – they are expressions and affirmations of a collective vision of order through hierarchy deeply inscribed in Roman culture. To put it concisely again: the 'intense monumentalization of the republican city', which had already begun at the turn of the fourth century and ended with truly 'monumental' projects like the *theatrum Pompei* and the *Forum Iulium*, produced 'a kind of city in the sky', in which the whole spectrum of monuments literally and visually 'gave high place to the highly placed'.[27]

The spatial setting and ceremonial choreography of the new consul's inauguration anticipate and encapsulate the performative patterns and the symbolic syntax of any public appearance throughout his year of office. First, the set of rules in which the discharge of official duties by the consuls (and also the praetors as holders of *imperium* and magistrates presiding over the courts) is regularly embedded was geared to creating hierarchy through

---

[25] Plut. *Fab.* 22.8; Plin. *HN* 34.40. Cf. Sehlmeyer 1999, 125f. and *passim* for detailed descriptions of all known honorific statues of the republic.
[26] Cf. Chioffi 1995; Coarelli 1995a, 1995b; Sehlmeyer 1999, 124f., 168ff.
[27] Kuttner 2004, 320, 318, cf. 312, 318ff., *passim*.

distance and vice versa. It includes the assembling of a *tribunal* on which the *sella curulis* was placed.²⁸ Only after the consul or praetor has sat down on this seat in an elevated position does he begin to act in his magisterial capacity and, in a very concrete sense, 'hand down' justice (or, more often than not, 'rough justice', at least in the provinces) – that is, physically as well as metaphorically and symbolically, *de loco superiore*.²⁹ The *sella curulis* on the *tribunal* thus becomes a particularly strong symbol of 'magisterial' power (once again, I deliberately use this word here because of the double entendre) because it emphatically stages the particular kind of pointed distance combined with hierarchy that characterizes the relationship between consul and citizen.

Second, the lictors holding the *fasces* are omnipresent in a special sense of the concept.³⁰ The *fasces* are the *imperii*, *potestatis* or *dignitatis insignia* in the full technical as well as metaphorical meaning of these multifaceted concepts:³¹ these visual symbols express *imperium* as power and the special rank and quality of the person that holds *imperium* and may wield the concrete power enshrined in it, at least potentially anywhere, at any time and under any circumstance. For non-Romans in the provinces, these *virga imperiosa* are more than just potentially menacing: to put it in Livy's words, the praetor – as governor of the province – 'presides at the *conventus*; the people summoned by [and perhaps also: under] his *imperium* assemble; they see him in his lofty place' – that is, obviously, the *tribunal* – 'handing down arrogant judgments, with lictors around him', whose 'rods threaten their backs' and whose 'axes their necks'.³²

Conversely, leaving the *fasces* behind means for a magistrate that he foregoes his *dignitas* and quality of magistrate; losing them to the enemy in battle is particularly shameful,³³ and the breaking of the rods is a highly charged symbolic act – either as a ritual signalling the formal deposition of a magistrate or as a similarly symbolic and demonstrative way to deny

---

²⁸ Cf. on the *tribunal* and its functions Lammert 1937 and Weiss 1937, with full references; Schäfer 1989, 158ff. Cf. on the *sella curulis* Kübler 1923 and now Schäfer 1989, 46ff., with references.
²⁹ Cic. *Verr.* 2.2.102; 2.4.86; *Fam.* 3.8.2 etc.; cf. Mommsen 1887–8, I, 400.
³⁰ Cf. on the lictors, the *fasces* and their (concrete as well as symbolic) functions Mommsen 1887–8, I, 373ff.; Samter 1909b; Kübler 1926; and more recently Gladigow 1972; Marshall 1984; Schäfer 1989, 196ff.; Nippel 1995, 12ff.; Goltz 2000.
³¹ Cic. *Rep.* 2.55; Q. *Fr.* 1.1.13; *Verr.* 2.5.97; *Rab. Post.* 16; *Clu.* 154; Sall. *Cat.* 36.1; Livy 1.8.2; 2.7.7 etc.; Val. Max. 2.7.7; Sil. *Pun.* 10.563. Cf. for further references Kübler 1926, 508; Marshall 1984, 130ff., 136ff.
³² Livy 31.29.9; cf. the vivid description of the *fasces* and axes as ominous symbols of the absolute power of the king (Dion. Hal. 3.61.2–62) and tyrannical regime of the *decemviri* (Livy 3.36.3f.; Dion. Hal. 10.59.3ff.).
³³ Cf. for references Kübler 1926, 511; Marshall 1984, 135.

the authority of a magistrate and reject his orders by a crowd of citizens in revolt.[34]

The constitutive importance of the symbolic function of the *fasces* underlies a whole set of rules. To begin with, the lictors carrying the *fasces* accompany the consul and attend on him whenever he steps out of his private house onto the stage of the public – and not only when he heads for the Forum, Curia, Comitium or Capitol on official business, but also when he visits the theatre or even a public bath. Both before the consul enters a private house to pay somebody an informal visit and when he returns to his own home, his lictors announce his arrival – according to Livy, *ut mos est* – by knocking on the door with their *fasces*.[35] As long as the consul stays there, the lictors wait for him in the *vestibulum*, while their *fasces* are put up at the door to make his presence known to all passers-by. To put it in more general terms: even in the most informal or 'private' of contexts, the consul is not only not a *privatus*, he is never a 'private' person in any circumstance. In other words: his person must always and everywhere be surrounded by symbols that physically and symbolically separate him from any 'ordinary' person. He is set apart and above any *privatus* by an awe-inspiring aura of aloofness and authority.

This separation becomes most visible in certain rules of behaviour regarding the consul – rules to be strictly observed and, if need be, to be rigorously enforced by the lictors: nobody – with the notable exception of the consul's own minor sons – is allowed to approach the consul in such a way as to step between him and the line of lictors – that is, into the space behind the *lictor proximus* walking immediately before the consul.[36] And whenever the consul proceeds through the busy streets and crowded places of the city, the lictors literally make way for him by bodily removing those standing or walking in the consul's path by orders, by force of the magisterial authority that they represent or even by physical force: this is yet another way of putting citizens in their place (in the metaphorical as well as concrete sense of the phrase), at a respectful distance by reserving space around the consul, an act which is aptly circumscribed by the metaphor *summovere* (*plebem, turbam vel sim*).[37] After this, it is obvious that when the consul appears on the scene, the lictors give ordinary citizens the order to stand up when seated or dismount when on horseback – even if the *privatus* and addressee

---

[34] Cf. for references Kübler 1926, 511; Marshall 1984, 138.
[35] Livy 6.34.6; cf. Oakley 1997–2005, I, ad loc. with further references, e.g. Flor. 1.17.26; Plin. *HN* 7.112; Mart. 8.66.4f.; *De vir. ill.* 20.1.
[36] Val. Max. 2.2.4, cf. Livy 24.44.10; Mommsen 1887–8, I, 375f.
[37] Livy 3.45.5; 48.3; 6.38.8; 8.33.4 etc.; Kübler 1926, 512.

of such an order is the father of the consul and himself a former holder of *imperium* as consul and even dictator.[38] To summarize again: it is the main function of the lictors (or rather their supporting role to the consul's own part) symbolically to demonstrate, describe and comment on the leading role of the consul himself by verbally and ritually demanding respect, obedience and submission to *imperium* as well as to the person presently vested with this power, and by visibly and indeed physically enforcing the distance that is created by and at the same time symbolically reproduces and emphasizes this person's position of superiority within a strictly hierarchical order.

Hierarchy as the fundamental ordering principle governing the internal structure of the political – or perhaps rather: 'magisterial' – class was also demonstratively and publicly made visible. A lower-ranking magistrate who meets a magistrate of higher rank has to show deference to the superiority of the concrete person as well as respect for the abstract principle of universal order by having his *fasces* lowered and the axes removed.[39] And according to tradition, a consul who is summoned to appear before the dictator even has to dismiss his lictors with his *fasces* – just as if he resigned his office and was demoted to the status of *privatus*.[40]

Another time-honoured tradition was the *fasces summittere*: when the consul appears with his lictors before the *populus Romanus*, the *fasces* also must be lowered – *nota bene*, certainly not before any informal gathering, let alone the usual crowd in the Forum, but only before the people in formal assembly, in *contio* or *comitia*, called and presided over by himself, another magistrate or tribune of the plebs. The introduction of this ritual of deference to the *maiestas maior* of the Roman people as sovereign – that is, in the words of L. Licinius Crassus, consul in 95, to 'you all whom we can and must serve'[41] – was not surprisingly attributed to the legendary consul of the first year of the republic and popular icon of civic *libertas* P. Valerius Publicola. So too was the other popular symbolic gesture, the removal of the axes as threatening symbols of capital coercion from the *fasces* when publicly produced within the perimeter of the *pomerium*.[42] The power of the consul is thus not excluded or banned from the city, let alone abolished altogether – it is symbolically taken back to a certain

---

[38] Livy 24.44. 9f.; Val. Max. 2.2.4.
[39] Dion. Hal. 8.44.3f.; Vell. Pat. 2.99.4; Plut. *Pomp.* 19.8.22; App. *B Civ.* 1.65.298; Cass. Dio 3.13.2.
[40] Livy 22.11.5f.; Plut. *Fab.* 4, cf. Cic. *Planc.* 98; Val. Max. 2.7.7; App. *Mith.* 52.
[41] *ORF*[4] 66 fr. 24 (= Cic. *De or.* 1.225); cf. Cic. *Leg. agr.* 2.15f.; *Red. pop.* 4 etc.; cf. Bell 1997, 16ff.
[42] Livy 2.7.7; Dion. Hal. 5.19.3; 10.59.5; cf. Cic. *Rep.* 1.62; 2.53 and 55; Val. Max. 4.1.1; Plut. *Publ.* 10.7; Quint. *Inst.* 3.7.18 etc.; Kübler 1926, 513.

extent, but in the shape of the *fasces* reduced to the rods, it still remains visibly present *domi*. To put the principle underlying the practice in more general terms: hierarchy as an asymmetrical social relation between persons of different rank and status is conceptualized as power relation not in an abstract way but in concrete terms, in a permanent, explicit demand for deference, obedience and discipline, personally and individually addressed and thus personalized. This demand is in turn conceptualized or rather symbolically made visible in an equally permanent, direct and thus again personalized, if only implicit and conditional, threat with sanctions in the shape of corporal punishment of individuals.

The underlying principle is mirrored in the symbolic function and concrete modes of application of *provocatio* under the *leges Valeriae* and *Porciae* – the first of which was once again invariably attributed to the legendary Publicola – and the other *praesidia libertatis* such as tribunician *auxilium*, which were originally also confined to the city.[43] In terms of ritual and theatricality, *provocatio* and *auxilium* are to be described as affirmations of civic privileges from case to case that need to be actively asserted in performative forms – either by appealing to the people at large or by the 'intercession' of the tribunes. The common syntax of these rituals emphasizes the visible, concrete protection of an individual against a specific, equally concrete and isolated act of the application of *imperium* in a particular case and in the actual presence and co-presence of all parties involved – consul and lictors, appealing citizen, people and tribunes. This is crystallized in the traditional and unalterable rule that the tribune had to be physically present when granting a citizen *auxilium* on appeal against a magistrate's coercive action by exercising – or rather: visibly performing – *intercessio* with his person protected by the collective oath of the plebs under the *lex sacrata*. To put it in more general terms again: the hallowed *praesidia libertatis* were explicitly designed to protect the *civis Romanus* against the unlimited, unrestrained and unconditional application of a magistrate's *imperium*, which in principle remained in place and was never called into question, let alone substantially diminished – on the contrary: the modes of actual application of *provocatio* by appeal and *auxilium* by *intercessio* reflect, and respond to, the concrete performative forms of making power and coercion visible and thus, in a kind of drama of inversion on the stage of the theatre of power, implicitly serve to affirm the validity of *imperium*, power and coercion as such.

[43] Cic. *De or.* 2.199; *Rep.* 2.54f.; *Rab. perd.* 11ff.; Livy 3.45.8; 55.4ff. etc. Cf. Bleicken 1955 (1968), 5ff., 74ff.; Bleicken 1959; Fuhrmann 1962, 1593f.; Lintott 1972; and now Jehne 2002, with further references.

To return to the rituals that composed the Roman republican theatre of power: as soon as the consul left *domi* to assume command *militiae*, the axes were immediately and automatically put back into the *fasces*. This self-explanatory symbolic act, performed by the lictors, is an integral part of the procession of *profectio* – a specific 'ensemble' whose 'text' is focused on the crossing of the sacral borderline between *domi* and *militiae*.[44] At least in the middle republic, this spectacular ritual must have occurred almost as regularly as the annual inauguration ceremony and it indeed mirrors certain essential elements of the inauguration procession. In the early morning on the day of his departure, the consul is obliged to perform the typical religious rites on the Capitol – these rites invariably include taking the auspices and solemn vows to Iuppiter Optimus Maximus to be honoured in case of victory. The next step is a ritual change of dress, the meaning of which is evident: the consul as well as his lictors exchange the official civic dress of the *toga praetexta* for the military garb of the red *paludamentum*.[45] To the sound of horns – another military signal – the consul leaves the Capitol and proceeds through the city, once again, just as during his inauguration, attended by friends, followers and, in this case, *tribuni militum* and other officers as well as, once again, the man in the Roman street as co-present audience.

It is the complex role of the citizen audience in this spectacle that Livy describes in a surprisingly sensitive, if highly imaginative passage on the *profectio* of P. Licinius Crassus, consul 171: 'Such an occasion is always indeed conducted with great *dignitas* and *maiestas*... It is not only care in paying their respects, but also eagerness for the spectacle (*studium spectaculi*) that brings people together to see their leader to whose *imperium* and *consilium* they have entrusted the whole welfare of the *res publica*.' Interestingly, Livy explicitly emphasizes the implicit role of the co-present *populus* as co-actor having elected the consul in the *comitia centuriata* and thus conferred *imperium* on him. He proceeds to ponder the collective expectations, hopes and fears of the '(spect-)a(c)tors' in the audience in dramatic terms:

Thereupon there steals over their minds a thought of the calamities of war, and how uncertain is the outcome of fortune and how impartial the god of war ... Who of mortal men knows which kind of mind and fortune belongs to the consuls whom they are now sending to war? Shall it be soon in triumph that we shall see him,

---

[44] Livy 42.49.1ff., cf. 21.63.9ff. Cf. Mommsen 1887–8, I, 63f.; Marshall 1984, 121f.; Feldherr 1998, 9ff., 51f.; Sumi 2005, 35ff.

[45] Varro, *Ling.* 7.37; Livy 31.14.1; 41.10.5 and 7; 45.39.11. Cf. Mommsen 1887–8, I, 430ff.; Sauer 1949, 281f.; Marshall 1984, 122f.

ascending with a victorious army to the Capitol towards those very gods of whom he is now taking leave?[46]

Rather surprisingly, Livy shows a keen sense of the interconnectedness in terms of the symbolic elements and ritual syntax that link up the processions of *profectio* and of victorious return in the shape of the *pompa triumphalis*: within a kind of closed ritual sub-system or comprehensive 'ensemble' this represents – or rather: theatrically stages – the cycle of war.

The lictors demonstratively sporting the 'full' *fasces* from the outset of the consul's *profectio* convey yet another implicit symbolic message to the co-present citizenry: the legal restrictions on the consul's power are themselves subject to a restriction: the full range of *praesidia libertatis* is operative only within the urban perimeter of the *pomerium* itself. Outside this narrowly defined, confined space – and that is not only the *imperium* of the Roman people, vast and indeed *sine fine* though it may be, but the rest of the world – a Roman consul by right of his *imperium* is entitled to wield power, including his full unlimited rights of coercion. And even when in the wake of the *leges Porciae*, Roman citizens formally came to enjoy the right to *provocatio* outside Rome herself, the privilege could easily turn out to be rather precarious when a power-conscious and arrogant magistrate and an ordinary citizen met anywhere else, especially in the provinces. In his accusations against Verres, Cicero dwells on this sensitive topic and makes a considerable rhetorical effort to turn it into a particularly monstrous as well as revealing aspect of Verres' contempt for the time-honoured and hallowed foundations of civic liberty, which renders his regime in Sicily so utterly detestable.[47]

Even if Cato Censorius, as well as Gaius Gracchus, complained about the imprudent, arbitrary and humiliating maltreatment of prominent citizens and even office-holders of towns not only in the provinces, but even in Italy, Roman magistrates were accustomed to staging their power over non-citizens by ordering and presiding over their public subjection to corporal punishment[48] – and neither Cato nor Gracchus nor Cicero could deny their right to do so in principle. When in the year 51, the consul Marcellus ordered a prominent citizen of a town in the Gallia Transpadana to be flogged in public before his fellow citizens, it was a deliberate, demonstrative and highly symbolic act that was as provocative as it was well directed and

---

[46] Livy 42.49.2ff.; cf. 27.40.1ff.; 44.22.17; 45.39.11.
[47] Cic. *Verr.* 2.1.14 etc., especially 2.5.140ff., 147ff. and 158ff. (on the case of P. Gavius); cf. also the reading of this passage by Gell. 10.3.6ff. and 12ff.; Quint. *Inst.* 4.2.113f.
[48] *ORF*⁴ 8 fr. 58 (= Gell. 10.3.17) and *ORF*⁴ 48 fr. 48 (Gell. 10.3.3) and the whole chapter Gell. 10.3.

could easily and immediately be decoded by all parties involved, explicitly or implicitly. The town and its inhabitants did not enjoy the most important 'civic' *praesidium libertatis* because the consul did not recognize them as *cives Romani*. In this case, however, they – and the poor man in particular – were not the only and not even the main addressees of the message. Rather, it was no less than a thinly veiled announcement of enmity to C. Iulius Caesar, who as proconsul had been generous (for reasons of his own) with the bestowal of citizenship to individuals and communities in Cisalpine Gaul. Marcellus thus made it crystal clear that he denied not only the legality of Caesar's concrete acts but also his right to bestow this special sort of privilege, and thus denied the legitimacy of his position as proconsul and governor.[49]

Most importantly, the *praesidia libertatis* of the Roman citizen are immediately and automatically suspended as soon as he enters service in the legions. As the role of the citizen as soldier is an ideologically constitutive role of Romanness for the often-quoted man in the Roman street, an ethos of military discipline, subordination and absolute obedience to the consul as holder of *imperium* and, by virtue of this power, as commander-in-chief is at the heart of a civic ideology that underpins a concomitant civic code of behaviour. This code, shared by the *populus Romanus* as a whole, is centred on obedience, deference and the acceptance of hierarchical order, the superiority of the ruling class and the authority of its individual members in their constitutive role as elected holders of *imperium* – and it includes the ideological axiom that military discipline is the basis of a collective Roman claim to power, glory and superiority over the rest of the world. This is in turn the central aspect of the ideological consensus that underpins the acceptance of hierarchy.[50] In the words that Livy puts into the mouth of an icon of virtue and ideal representative of this class, Scipio Africanus, *summi imperii maiestas* on the one hand and *militiae disciplina* on the other were enshrined in *mos maiorum* as complementary and equally indispensable principles.[51] Another legendary, if somewhat less uncontroversial figurehead of Romanness, T. Manlius Torquatus, is credited (perhaps already by Ennius) with the dictum that it was military *disciplina* 'whereby the Roman state has stood to this day unshaken'.[52]

---

[49] Plut. *Caes.* 29.2ff.; App. *B Civ.* 2.26.98ff.; cf. Cic. *Att.* 5.11.2.   [50] Cf. Nippel 1995, 30ff.
[51] Livy 28.27.12. The concept of *mos* (*maiorum*) as such as well as its concrete meaning and contents are notoriously elusive (and therefore much discussed): cf. Blösel 2000; Hölkeskamp 2004a, 183ff.; Walter 2004b, 17f., 55f., 65ff. and *passim*, each with further references.
[52] Livy 8.7.16 (perhaps alluding to the famous line Enn. *Ann.* 156 Skutsch: *moribus antiquis res stat Romana virisque*); cf. Oakley 1997–2005, II, ad loc.

That is why there can never be mercy when it comes to imposing sanctions against any breach of discipline – and the relentless rigour of the 'ancestral law and custom' is not only to be applied when it comes to the demonstrative punishment of serious crimes such as treason, defection and desertion, as in the case of the *cives Romani* of the *legio Campana* who had forfeited their rights as citizens and were summarily executed *in medio foro*.[53] And a Roman citizen failing to answer when called up for service could face the hardly less serious consequence of social death – if he was denied *auxilium* by the tribunes, he could be sold into slavery by command of the consul presiding (once again, *nota bene*, certainly *de loco superiore*) over the levy.[54] According to the rigid rules, any disobedience left unpunished would have irreversible and fatal consequences, it would result in the utter 'abrogation' of the consular *imperium*; and, in the words of another *exemplum*[55] of unwavering and uncompromising *severitas*, once *disciplina militaris* was thus put aside, the established order of hierarchy and, in the final analysis, the auspices, all respect for gods and men would be lost for *omnia saecula* to come[56] – and that is also how to interpret this message to the '*milites* or *Quirites*', directly addressed by the consul, that they should not even think of having sympathy with the perpetrator of such a deed, let alone dream of doing anything similar. To paraphrase the words of a famous, if fictional, Oxonian amateur historian and aristocratic sleuth, Lord Peter Wimsey: admitting the principle necessarily entails that the consequences must follow.[57]

Interestingly, these 'magisterial' statements are embedded in highly rhetorical passages, centred on elaborate speeches by the protagonists, dealing in considerable detail with the exemplary way of asserting and enforcing the principle in the face of actions of subordinates that put its validity to

---

[53] Pol. 1.7.12 and 10.4; Dion. Hal. 20.16; Livy 2.55.4ff.; *Per.* 15.28.2ff.; Val. Max. 2.7.15; Frontin. *Str.* 4.1.38. Cf. Mommsen 1899, 43. Characteristically, it is exactly here, in the Forum Romanum, that the legendary first consul of the republic and icon of republican *libertas*, L. Iunius Brutus, allegedly ordered his sons to be executed for treasonably plotting to restore the dynasty of the Tarquins and the monarchical regime – and exactly according to the time-honoured ritual to be discussed below: Livy 2.3.5–6, 8; Dion. Hal. 5.8.1ff.; Plut. *Publ.* 3–6; cf. Verg. *Aen.* 6.819ff.; Flor. 1.3.5 etc.

[54] Val. Max. 6.3.4, cf. Livy, *Per.* 14; Frontin. *Str.* 4.1.20 (with Livy, *Per.* 55). Cf. Mommsen 1899, 43f.

[55] The concept of *exemplum*, its precise definition, contents, functions (and the very character of 'exemplarity' in Roman culture), poses the very same difficulties as the concept of *mos maiorum* mentioned above, because they are inseparably interconnected: cf. for the best systematic treatments now Walter 2004b, 42ff. and Bücher 2006, 152ff.; for particular aspects Stemmler 2000; Hölkeskamp 2004a, 180ff.; Roller 2004, 4ff. and *passim*; Walter 2004a.

[56] Livy 8.34.7ff. – in *oratio obliqua* attributed to the dictator L. Papirius Cursor (see below). Cf. also the collection of (Roman) *exempla* illustrating different ways, means and contexts of demonstratively restoring *disciplina militaris* by *severitas*: Frontin. *Str.* 4.1.1f.; 4–7; 13–16; 18–46.

[57] Dorothy L. Sayers, *Gaudy Night* (London: 1935), London: 2003, 544.

the test. Proceeding in chronological order, beginning with the legendary Manlius with the telling cognomen 'Imperiosus': in a famous *exemplum* of rigid *severitas*, with the words quoted above, the consul, according to Livy, was addressing his own son who had done no more (or no less) than disobey the consuls' strict order prohibiting single combat by engaging and vanquishing an enemy who had challenged him.[58] In this context I should mention another *exemplum*, standing out because of a similar degree of rhetorical elaboration (and being probably unhistorical as well), which also emphasizes the absolute validity of the principles of hierarchy and strict obedience to orders within the ruling class itself – even when it comes to humiliating a prominent *nobilis*, heir to a great name and second-in-command in war. Q. Fabius Maximus Rullianus, who later became consul no fewer than five times, allegedly escaped the fate of young Manlius only by the skin of his teeth.[59] It was only after a series of entreaties on the part of his father, the whole senate, the tribunes of the plebs and finally the *populus Romanus* at large that the stern dictator L. Papirius Cursor could be persuaded to abstain from having his *magister equitum* Fabius executed, because the latter had also disregarded strict orders and joined battle with, and brilliantly defeated, the enemy forces.

To return to Scipio: he had to quench a serious mutiny among the legions in Spain[60]; and, according to Livy once again, it was not only the impertinence of the rank and file, their *libido, licentia*, contempt for traditional *modestia militaris* and established *disciplina* and the disregard of the orders of the military tribunes, who were – Scipio being absent (and believed to be dead or seriously ill) – their superiors on the spot. First and foremost, it was the monstrous presumption of the ringleaders of the mutiny, a certain C. Albius from Cales and a C. Atrius from Umbria, who, being mere ordinary soldiers, dared to usurp the supreme command by arrogating *fasces securesque*, the *insignia summi imperii*, for themselves. Although this symbolic act of perverting the legitimate hierarchy and order and indeed of turning the time-honoured Roman world upside down created, according to Livy, nothing but a vain delusion or *vana imago imperii*, it was at least as outrageous as the mutiny as such and called

---

[58] Livy 8.7.8ff.; Zonar. 7.26; cf. Cic. *Sull.* 32; Sall. *Cat.* 52.30f.; Dion. Hal. 2.26.6; 8.79.2; Gell. 9.13.20; Frontin. *Str.* 4.1.40f.; Verg. *Aen.* 6.824f.; Flor. 1.8.14; *De vir. ill.* 28.4. Cf. Oakley 1997–2005, II, 436ff.; Feldherr 1998, 108ff.; Walter 2004a, 421ff., each with further references and detailed discussion. The same *severitas* for the same offence was attributed to A. Postumius Tubertus, dictator in 431 BC: e.g. Livy 4.29.5f. (rejecting the tradition); Diod. Sic. 12.64.3; Val. Max. 2.7.6; Gell. 17.21.17.

[59] Livy 8.30.1–35, 12; Val. Max. 2.7.8; Frontin. *Str.* 4.1.39; cf. Livy 22.25.13 and 27.3; *De vir. ill.* 31.1–32, 1. Cf. on this episode Oakley 1997–2005, II, 704ff; Beck 2003, 81ff.; Walter 2004b, 242f.

[60] Pol. 11.25.1–30, 5; Livy 28.24.5–29, 12; App. *Hisp.* 34–6; Zonar. 9.10.

for retaliation in the shape of reprisals in an equally symbolic form on the part of the 'true and just power' (*vera iustaque potestas*). That is exactly the way in which Livy describes the grisly fate that was in store for the perpetrators, who had not been aware that the rods and axes they had usurped threatened their own backs and necks and that they thus would invariably and inevitably meet with these *insignia* again in most gruesome circumstances.[61]

Typically enough, the absolute binding force of *disciplina militaris* is once again conceptualized in terms of a code of severe sanctions against breaches of any kind and the consequent, indeed uncompromisingly relentless, execution of these sanctions – and, typically again, in highly ritualized spectacles that follow an established performative syntax characterized by a rigidity of its own.[62] First of all, the procedure has to take place in the light of day and in full view (*in conspectu*) of the whole army or the people – executions by night and in secret are by definition under the suspicion of being illegal.[63] Therefore, the praetor, consul or dictator makes himself demonstratively present in person by taking his elevated seat on the *tribunal* erected in the central place of the camp and has the army summoned by trumpet to an (informal) assembly there.[64] The co-presence and indeed complicity of the citizen army are instrumental for implicitly ambivalent reasons – on the one hand, they are witnesses to the legitimacy of the severe verdict as well as to the strictly correct application of the rules of the ritual, and on the other, they are addressees of a message affirming the validity of an order based on hierarchy and power, discipline and subordination – and therefore they contain a silent threat against anyone daring to challenge this order.

The next act of the drama consequently consists in producing the delinquent, presenting him to the assembled public and establishing his guilt with this public as collective witness.[65] The following ritual unfolds with deadly consequence: the lictors demonstratively unbind the *fasces* and produce the rods and axe – the ominous meaning of *virgas et secures expedire* is evident.[66] The delinquent is forcibly stripped naked (*spoliare*) and bound to a stake (*deligare ad paludem*), which had previously and again demonstratively been put up in full view of the consul, the audience and the

---

[61] Livy 28.24.14, cf. 25.2 and 29.11.
[62] Cf. the treatment by Mommsen 1899, 915ff.; Kübler 1926, 513.
[63] Sen. *Controv.* 9.2.10; 14; 16; 22; 25; 28; cf. also Livy 8.33.21; 9.24.15.
[64] E.g. Livy 8.7.14ff.; 32.1ff.; 28.26.12ff.; Polyb. 11.27.5; Dion. Hal. 5.8.2ff.; App. *Hisp.* 35; cf. also Livy 2.5.8; Sen. *Controv.* 9.2.10; 14; Sen. *De ira* 1.16.5.
[65] Livy 8.33.21; Dion. Hal. 20.16.2; cf. e.g. Cic. *Verr.* 2.1.75f.; Gell. 10.3.3.
[66] Livy 2.55.5; 3.36.5; 45.7; 8.32.10; 9.16.17f., cf. Cic. *Verr.* 2.5.161; *De vir. ill.* 31.4.; Livy 2.55.5; 29.9.4.

delinquent, who now finds himself 'on the receiving end' in the full sense of the term: he is flogged with the rods.[67] By depriving the delinquent of the typical dress of the Roman citizen soldier, by exposing his completely naked body in public[68] and by subjecting him to corporal punishment in the presence of his former peers, he is being degraded step by step, expelled from the army as well as the citizen body and finally reduced to a mere 'body' without civic status – or rather, as it were, to a 'no-body' in a particular sense to be illustrated by yet another word-play. If, according to Florence Dupont's pointed definition, the Roman citizen consists of 'a name and a body'; if 'the body of a citizen' is actually 'the man himself', that is, the 'embodiment' of his character and status; and if this 'body' that the citizen as citizen puts 'on display should be clothed in appropriate dress, the *toga* or military dress', and 'under control' of the citizen himself'[69] – the delinquent is by this stage of the drama entirely deprived of the last remnants of his former 'civic' status as a member of the 'citizen body'.

It is only now that, in the most extreme case, the consul orders the lictor to perform the final act and execute the delinquent by beheading him with the axe – interestingly enough, by saying: 'Lictor, act according to the law' (*age lege*).[70] This is the climactic point of the syntax of this ritual as a whole, which is focused on the consul as leading actor performing the central role of holder of the supreme disciplinary power over life and death. From the initial summoning of the army onwards, through the whole sequence of ritual interactions with the lictors in a complementary supporting role, it is the consul who has to give the active part and lead the ritual from stage to stage – by giving orders to the lictors in fixed formulae aptly characterized as *legitima verba*.[71]

To put it in more general terms of theatricality and performance again: this extreme and symbolically most powerful drama (once again, I am deliberately playing on the ambivalent meaning of the words) encapsulates several fundamental functions of a coherent cultural sub-system or 'ensemble' which serves as medium or 'text' of negotiation in the permanent and omnipresent 'dialogue about and for authority',[72] hierarchy and the concomitant patterns of socio-political power relations. This drama is about

---

[67] Livy 2.5.6ff.; 8.7.19ff.; 33.21; 26.15.8; 28.29.11; Dion. Hal. 20.16.2; Plut. *Publ.* 6.2; cf. also Polyb. 11.30.1f.; Cic. *Verr.* 2.5.161f.; Dion. Hal. 5.8.5; 9.39.1; Sen. *Controv.* 9.2.21; Val. Max. 2.7.8; Gell. 10.3.3; 11; 17 etc. Cf. generally Fuhrmann 1962, 1590f.
[68] Cf. Cordier 2005, 164ff., 173ff. [69] Dupont 1989 (1992), 239ff. (quotations on pp. 239 and 240).
[70] Sen. *Controv.* 9.2.22; cf. 9.2.25; Livy 26.15.9; 26.16.3; Dion. Hal. 5.8.5; Val. Max. 3.8.1; Sen. *De ira* 1.16.5; Plut. *Publ.* 6.3f.
[71] Sen. *Controv.* 9.2.10 and 21. [72] Sharpe 1993, 853.

the consular *imperium* as an absolute power that is – as the abstract idea of an institutionalized and legitimate function – vested in an office and visibly in the person actually holding it. In a culture of visibility, direct interaction and 'dialogue', the holder of this power is necessarily and demonstratively surrounded by an awe-inspiring aura in the shape of the *fasces* as symbols of the unlimited potentiality of this power – and it is this potentiality that needs to be acted out here and there to retain its full efficiency, or rather to remain meaningful in the 'dialogue'. This drama fulfils this function by ensuring that *imperium* is seen and spelt out through the imposition of coercive measures in the shape of the corporal punishment of individuals as the exemplary execution of sanctions[73] (yet again in the full meaning of both concepts) against any form of insubordination or other sort of challenge of the authority of the consul as holder of *imperium*. Its absolute character is not only affirmed by enforcing it demonstratively at all costs and with the utmost rigidity; specifically by means of (capital) punishment. Above all, *imperium* is made visible as power over individuals, their social status as well as their 'bodies' and physical existence: the ritual is directed at individuals that are degraded, marginalized and ultimately removed from the citizen body. In this respect of symbolic meaning and message, as well as with regard to its performative syntax as a drama, this ritual is obviously closely connected with, and indeed mirrors, the other notoriously brutal 'spectacles of death'[74] ranging from the 'murderous games' of gladiatorial shows to *summa supplicia* in the arena and (later on) ritualized public executions in the shape of elaborate 'fatal charades'.[75]

However, the acting out of absolute power is only one aspect of the hidden agenda of the ritual as it moves from stage to stage, by order and under the direction of the magistrate and executed by his lictors. At the same time, the insistence on proceeding according to a normative syntax or code of rules dramatically emphasizes the legitimacy of the consul's action. Last but not least, it is the physical (or perhaps: 'bodily') 'co-presence' of the citizens/soldiers (or citizen-soldiers) as a collective 'body' which is, in more than one respect, instrumental in the ritualized reimposition and reaffirmation of order by such a performative acting-out of power and hierarchy. As audience, they are obviously witness to the ritual as such, to its legitimacy in the concrete case and to its effect – the expulsion of an individual citizen from their own midst. Implicitly, the *populus Romanus* (in

---

[73] Cf. on the symbolic dimensions of corporal punishment Saller 1994, 134ff.
[74] Cf. Kyle 1998, 53ff., 91ff. and *passim*.
[75] Hopkins 1983, 1ff.; Coleman 1990; Kyle 1998, 54f., 243ff.; cf. also Clavel-Lévêque 1984; Gunderson 1996; Futrell 1997; Flaig 2003, 242ff.

military garb) in attendance is also the addressee of this particular message in the shape of a 'magisterial' monologue in the 'dialogue' for and about the character of this power. And at last, in this as well as in many other civic rituals, there is their institutional supporting role as collective 'co-actor' and complementary part in another typical interactive ritual. The role of the citizen body as electorate in a procedure which, under the direction of a previous consul, led to the investiture of the present incumbent, and leading actor in the actual concrete performance on the stage of the republican theatre of power, is always on the hidden agenda of the 'dialogue'. My contention is that it is this kind of interconnected, complex 'complicity' of the *populus Romanus* at large which is a fundamental basis of the ascendancy of its ruling and (therefore) office-holding class, or perhaps rather: office-holding and (therefore) ruling class.

CHAPTER 9

The consul(ar) as exemplum: *Fabius* Cunctator's paradoxical glory

Matthew B. Roller

INTRODUCTION

> Unus homo nobis cunctando restituit rem.
> Noenum rumores ponebat ante salutem.
> Ergo postque magisque viri nunc gloria claret.
> Ennius, *Annales* fr. 363–5 Skutsch

> One person, by delaying, restored the commonwealth for us.
> He did not set people's criticisms (sc. of him) before safety.
> Therefore it is afterward, and more, that the hero's glory now shines out.

These three hexameter verses, composed probably in the 170s or early 160s BC, come from Ennius' historical epic, the *Annales*. They constitute the earliest surviving reference to Q. Fabius Maximus Verrucosus "Cunctator," one of the leading Roman politicians and generals of the Second Punic War.[1] This description of Fabius was among the best-known passages of Ennius' poem in antiquity, to judge from the frequency with which later authors quote or allude to it. Its earliest such appearance dates to 59 BC, when Cicero quotes the first verse in a way that shows it was already proverbial;[2] Cicero also quotes all three verses in a pair of texts dating to 44 BC – our only sources for the entire set.[3] In subsequent authors there are numerous further quotations, paraphrases, or echoes of the first or second verse.[4] Scholars have observed that these verses are already in the business of mythmaking, of manufacturing Fabius and his strategy of "delay" as

---

[1] Consul 233, 228, 215, 214, 209; censor 230; dictator II 217. On the date of Ennius' *Annales*, see Rebuffat 1982; Skutsch 1985, 4–6.
[2] Cic. *Att.* 2.19.2; discussion below.   [3] Cic. *Sen.* 10; *Off.* 1.84; discussion below.
[4] The first verse is recognizable in Livy 30.26.9; Verg. *Aen.* 6.846; Aug. *apud* Suet. *Tib.* 21; Ov. *Fast.* 2.242. These authors, like Cicero, certainly read the *Annales*. It also appears in Sen. *Ben.* 4.27.2; Ser. *Aen.* 8.645; Macrob. 6.1.23; and Serenus, *Med.* 1094, who may not have read Ennius directly but found the verse in Cicero, Virgil or another intermediary. Looser paraphrases or fainter echoes, especially of the first verse, are about as numerous. Readers will disagree, however, whether a given passage constitutes an "echo," and if so, how close: for lists of candidates, see e.g. Stanton 1971, 52–6; Skutsch 1985, 529–30; Elliott 2009, 533.

an *exemplum* for subsequent Roman aristocrats. For the speaker of these verses places Fabius' "delaying" in the past, and compares its reception by Fabius' contemporaries with its reception in later eras. The second verse, in particular, hints at a conflict of values and evaluation: Fabius pursued safety (*salus*) and disregarded criticism (*rumores*), presumably propagated by contemporaries who opposed his approach. The third verse, however, indicates that the later view of Fabius' deeds was positive: it is "now" (*nunc*, in the speaker's present time), and "later" (*post*, after Fabius' deeds), that the "glory of the hero" (*viri... gloria*, both words conferring praise) "shines forth the more" (*magis... claret*). These claims, in turn, explain and corroborate the approbative declaration of the first verse, that Fabius "restored the commonwealth for us," where *nobis* indicates the importance of Fabius' achievement for the speaker and his generation.

Whether this speaker is "Ennius" the epic narrator, or (perhaps more likely) a Roman general who appears as a character in the poem and adduces Fabius to justify his own circumspection,[5] it is these verses' overtly exemplifying aim that interests me here. During the middle republic, an ethos of service to the commonwealth (*res publica*) was pervasive in the Roman aristocracy and manifested itself in intense competition for status and honor through actions performed in the civic sphere. Under such conditions, it is inevitable that the consulship (along with the dictatorship, and a few other posts held by consulars) emerged as the institution *par excellence* for generating exemplary social actors. As the chief regular magistrates of the *res publica*, consuls were automatically leading actors in the military, legislative, judicial, electoral and other political arenas that constituted the civic sphere. Since warfare was the most valorized arena of civic performance and aristocratic competition in this era, consuls – along with dictators and ex-consuls whose commands had been extended – were objects of especially intense interest in their role as military commanders. Their performance in preparing and leading troops into battle was observed, evaluated, commemorated and subsequently invoked as a standard that later commanders might strive to surpass, or against which they might be measured. The wide array of commemorative media to which claims of military success were entrusted – military decorations, triumphal processions, honorific

---

The manuscripts of Cic. *Sen.* and *Off.* read *non enim* at the start of the second verse; Lachmann's restoration of *noenum* (metrical and Ennian) for Ennius himself tends to be cautiously accepted by modern editors. If this conjecture is correct, it remains unclear whether the corruption stood already in Cicero's text of Ennius (hence *non enim* is the correct Ciceronian reading) or occurred later, in the Ciceronian manuscript tradition: discussion by Skutsch 1985, 531 and Powell 1988, 125.

[5] For these verses' possible original contexts, see Stanton 1971, 52; Rebuffat 1982, 157–65; Skutsch 1985, 530–1.

statues and nomenclature, dedications of spoils, the erection of temples or other structures paid for by spoils, the narration of pertinent achievements through oral performance (as in a funeral *laudatio*) or in written form (funerary epitaphs, historiography, epic poetry) – all attest the ardent desire to spread positive representations of a general's prowess far and wide among contemporaries and posterity, and to establish him as a model or standard (an *exemplum*) in the present and for posterity.

The figure of Fabius is in some respects a typical product of this "exemplary" discourse.[6] In his first consulship, the tradition reports, he defeated the Ligurians and celebrated a triumph. Virtually no information is transmitted regarding his second consulship, though his iteration as consul after just five years suggests that his contemporaries esteemed him highly. His selection as dictator in 217, following the Roman military disaster at Lake Trasimene, was likely due – at least in part – to his prior military success, as well as to his seniority and experience as a two-time consul.[7] In his third and fourth consulships, during the darkest days of the Second Punic War, he supposedly enjoyed modest military successes in the struggle against Hannibal. In his fifth consulship he recaptured the important city of Tarentum, which had defected to Hannibal several years earlier; for this victory he received a second triumph. A figure known to contemporary and later Romans as having held five consulships, two dictatorships (one extremely crucial), two triumphs, a censorship and other notable honors as well makes for an exemplary Roman *exemplum*.[8]

At the heart of the Fabian *exemplum*, however, is an unusual moral ambiguity, and it is this aspect that Ennius' verses (and much of the subsequent tradition) address. For during the six months of his dictatorship in 217, according to the tradition, Fabius confronted Hannibal not by looking to initiate a large-scale set battle, but by avoiding it: he merely shadowed Hannibal's movements, thus "delaying" a major confrontation. In purposefully not pursuing what would ordinarily be considered a golden opportunity to lead Roman troops into battle and defeat a particularly fearsome and dangerous enemy, he deprived himself and his soldiers of the chance to display valor in battle, collect spoils, celebrate a triumph, win military decorations and gain the associated renown. He was consequently accused of lacking the virtues and capacities required in a commander. The Ennian passage,

---

[6] On exemplarity as a discourse, and on its characteristics, see Roller 2004, 1–7 and *passim*.
[7] On the significance of early iteration, see Beck 2005, 280–1. Fabius had also previously been appointed dictator – probably in 221 to conduct elections – but abdicated due to an ill omen: Val. Max. 1.1.5.
[8] Indeed, this enumeration of Fabius' achievements largely replicates Augustus' own list, as given in the Forum Augustum *elogium* – a text overtly out to exemplify its honorand: see below. Recent discussion of Fabius' early career in Beck 2005, 275–81 and Feig Vishnia 2007 (alternative view).

as noted above, alludes to contemporary criticism in the word *rumores*. Yet it quickly avers that "our" (later) verdict on Fabius is positive. Built into the tradition from its beginning, then, is the supposition that Fabius' actions admitted and received conflicting, even contradictory, moral evaluations from contemporaries and posterity. Moreover, the tradition holds that Fabius justified his unorthodox actions and strategy by criticizing conventional military values and action, and invoking an alternative set of values instead. The collective judgment upon him supposedly changed as his contemporaries, initially dismissive of Fabius' novel ethics, in time swung around to his viewpoint.

In this paper I examine the moral complexities of the Fabian tradition. I trace the representation of his "delaying" strategy, of its contemporary and subsequent reception, and of the competing value discourses and ethical paradoxes by which it is articulated, in a variety of republican and Imperial texts. My analysis is "synchronic" in that I move thematically through the constituent elements of the discourse about Fabius, juxtaposing texts from all eras in my discussion of each thematic element. Certainly different texts, which have different rhetorical aims, emphasize different aspects of this discourse.[9] Yet almost all crucial elements are already present, explicitly or implicitly, in the three verses of Ennius quoted above, and I cannot discern any systematic chronological development or shifts within this discourse as manifested in surviving texts. Moreover, the debates represented in our sources possibly bear no relation to the debates that actually took place among Fabius' contemporaries regarding his strategy; I make no claims for their historical correctness. I am interested, rather, in the ways Romans of later eras imagine those debates to have played out, and in the value conflicts that these (imagined) debates put on display. It is precisely, I suggest, these conflicts of value and judgment at the heart of the Fabius legend that make him a useful *exemplum*; these offer Roman social actors for centuries thereafter a touchstone with which to think about the value conflicts of their own worlds.

THE ETHICS OF DELAY

Late in June of 217 BC, the story goes, the awful news reached Rome that a consular army had been crushed at Lake Trasimene and that the consul C. Flaminius had been killed. In the wake of this disaster Fabius was

---

[9] See, for instance, Ridley 2000, 29–31 on the divergent representations of Fabius by Polybius and Livy (citing work by Wilhelm Hoffmann that I have not been able to consult). On Plutarch's representation see Beck 2002, 477–80 (and *passim*); on distinctive aspects of Silius, see below, n. 65.

appointed dictator and M. Minucius Rufus master of the horse,[10] with instructions to secure the city against Hannibal's advance. Fabius ordered a consultation of the Sybilline Books, offered games and sacrifices and vowed a "sacred spring" (*ver sacrum*).[11] Then he took command of the remaining consular army, raised fresh troops and marched off in pursuit of Hannibal, who by then had moved into southern Italy. Once in contact with the enemy, Fabius began to implement his distinctive strategy of non-engagement. As Hannibal's army pillaged and burned, Fabius neither offered nor accepted set battle, and the tradition contains divergent accounts of the extent to which he intervened even to protect Roman and allied property from Hannibal's depredations. The tradition is unanimous, however, in asserting that he kept his own soldiers in camp, apart from well-organized foraging parties and raids on enemy foraging parties that took inadequate precautions. He limited himself to shadowing Hannibal's movements, pitching camp always within sight of the enemy, yet in the hills to evade the cavalry.[12] This strategy, pursued throughout the six months of his dictatorship, earned Fabius the nickname *cunctator*, "delayer."

The tradition justifies Fabius' strategy in a variety of ways. The overarching justification, manifesting a widespread Roman idea about the fickleness of *fortuna* in war, is that Hannibal's good fortune and the Romans' bad fortune (i.e. Hannibal's victories over three different Roman armies and commanders in consecutive battles) are bound to change; therefore, it makes sense to look for evidence that this change is at hand – a particularly advantageous situation, for example – before engaging him. Other, more pragmatic explanations, though varied, tend to support and underpin this overarching justification. For instance, several texts ascribe to Fabius the view that his inexperienced army can best be trained up through skirmishing and micro-engagements; the implication is that Fabius does not believe his raw recruits can (yet) win a set battle against Hannibal's hardened veterans. This idea is encapsulated in widespread assertions that Fabius wanted, above all, to keep his soldiers safe, and not to lose any more than absolutely necessary. This aim finds its *mise-en-scène* in the story of Fabius saving the legions commanded by his then co-dictator Minucius, after the latter disastrously fell into a Hannibalic trap and his soldiers faced

---

[10] On the unusual constitutional circumstances of these appointments, already probed by Livy (22.8.5–7; 22.31.8–11), see Hartfield 1982, 495–6; Lesiński 2002; Beck 2005, 284–6.
[11] Livy 22.9.7–11; Plut. *Fab.* 4.4–7; Sil. 7.74–89; on the *ver sacrum* see below.
[12] Livy 22.12.3–10; Polyb. 3.89–90; Plut. *Fab.* 5.1–3; Sil. 7.90–5, 123–30.

annihilation.[13] Moreover, several texts ascribe to Fabius the view that, while his own army was well-provisioned and supported, Hannibal's would weaken and degrade for want of money and supplies, as well as from the small but consistent losses that accompany endless raiding and skirmishing. This view presupposes – as the tradition asserts – that no Roman allies were yet going over to Hannibal, hence that his supplies had to be procured through raiding. Indeed, several texts assert that, at certain points during Fabius' dictatorship and thereafter, Hannibal was so pressed for supplies that he feared he could not defend his own camp, or was compelled to attempt ever more risky ruses in hopes of escaping the Roman noose, or contemplated withdrawing from Italy altogether.[14] All of this tells for the long-awaited shift in the fortunes of the war: the Romans' chances are improving, and the Carthaginians' are worsening, as Fabius' strategy plays out. By the end of his six-month term as dictator, he can be represented as having all but defeated Hannibal despite never having come to blows, and the following year – when he holds no command – he can be imagined as saying to the consul Aemilius Paullus that Hannibal will wither away or leave Italy provided nobody offers him battle that year.[15] The explanations of Fabius' strategy thus bifurcate into two broad alternatives: that Fabius "delays" joining battle because he awaits an advantageous opportunity; or, that his very avoidance of battle stands to defeat Hannibal in and of itself.[16] Whether any such explanation is historically correct is, again, uncertain.[17] What is certain is that, as the Romans elaborated the Fabian *exemplum* in

---

[13] Waiting for a change in fortune: Livy 22.12.2, 10; Sil. 7.9–11, 90–3, 234–47. Training and encouraging his soldiers through skirmishing: Polyb. 3.90.4; Livy 22.12.10; Sil. 7.90–5. Not confident that his soldiers can defeat Hannibal's: Polyb. 3.89.5–8; Polyaenus 8.14.1; Zonar. 8.25. The idea that the safety of soldiers and commonwealth was Fabius' overriding concern is already implied in the Ennian *salutem* (fr. 364 Sk.); it is spelled out and thematized in Polyb. 3.89.2; Livy 22.12.8–10; 22.25.15; Val. Max. 3.8.2; Sil. 6.619–26; 9.52–5 (and *passim*); Frontin. *Str.* 4.6.1; Cass. Dio fr. 57.9–10. This "safety" is contrasted with Minucius' rashness at Livy 22.30.3; Sil. 7.396–400, 705–45; Plut. *Fab.* 10.7; 13.7 (see below for "safety" in relation to "the good of the commonwealth").

[14] Polyb. 3.90.2–3; Livy 22.15.2; 22.24.9–10; 22.32.1–3; 22.40.7–8; 22.43.2–4; Frontin. *Str.* 1.5.28; Sil. 8.11–15; App. *Hann.* 12.49–13.56; Plut. *Fab.* 5.1, 4; *Mor.* 195C–D; Zonar. 8.26.

[15] Livy 22.39.13–15; Plut. *Fab.* 14.6.

[16] In Beck's formulation (2000, 80), the question is whether Fabius becomes the *cunctator* through "delaying" an eventual, conventional military performance, or whether his "delaying" is itself the performance. While the traditional justifications of Fabius' strategy admit both views, the latter strand – linking Fabius with the idea of never, on principle, joining battle – predominates. See below on "winning without fighting."

[17] Erdkamp (1992, 132–6) and Beck (2000, 86–7) point out that the rich Campanian countryside should have furnished Hannibal with abundant provisions, and that a lack of local allies should have mattered little in this respect. Erdkamp is also skeptical about Livy's claim that the Roman cavalry effectively harried the Carthaginians (1992, 129–31 – though Erdkamp's grounds for preferring Polybius over Livy in general are unacceptable).

later years, they applied their own ingenuity and capacity for sympathetic historical imagination to make sense of what could, at first sight, seem a quite un-Roman way of confronting a formidable enemy.

Indeed, the tradition asserts that Fabius' contemporaries heavily criticized his strategy. A review of the Roman economy of social prestige is helpful for understanding the terms of this criticism. In general – and especially outside of philosophical contexts – moral values at Rome are ascribed on the basis of actions performed before an audience of witnesses, whose judgments transmit the moral views of the community at large. These witnesses consider how consequential an action is for the community, then assign it positive or negative value in one or more moral categories that they deem relevant to the circumstances of the performance.[18] Warfare, of course, is an arena in which actions carry weighty consequence for the community. In military contexts, from at least the middle republic onward, the moral/ethical category of *virtus* is central: aristocratic officers and cavalrymen, as well as lower-status legionary soldiers, seek to have this value, above all others, ascribed to themselves. *Virtus* is associated primarily with displaying aggression in combat. One seeks to be observed and acknowledged by one's fellow soldiers and officers, and if possible by members of the broader community, as fighting with great physical courage. Military decorations monumentalize spectacular deeds of valor, along with the collective positive evaluation accorded to the warriors who perform them. The high social value associated with *virtus* reflects how closely military success is linked with collective welfare in this period. *Gloria*, meanwhile, is the positive reputation one gains from having *virtus* and/or other positive moral values ascribed to oneself: it is the praise that circulates within the community when one is judged to have performed outstandingly in one or another ethical category. The more glorious one is, the greater one's social value and prestige. This economy of social prestige, especially as it involves *virtus* and military achievement, was itself an important driver of Roman warfare and imperialism during the middle and late republic, as scholars have long noted.[19] Yet it also accounts for the perceived problem

---

[18] On this aspect of Roman moral discourse, see Roller 2004, 1–10 (and *passim*).

[19] McDonnell (2006a, 12–71) shows how military achievement is conceptually and ideologically central to the moral category *virtus* (though his discussion conflates conceptual/ideological priority with temporal priority). For the display, attribution and place of *virtus* in the economy of social prestige among aristocrats, see Roller 2001, 20–5, 97–108; for its place in the honor-community of (non-elite) Roman soldiers, see Lendon 1997, 243–52. On the link between individual military achievement, social prestige and Roman militarism in the republic, see the classic discussions of Earl 1967, 11–43 and Harris 1979, 9–53. On the sources of *gloria* (chiefly military) in the middle to late republic see

with Fabius' strategy. By avoiding significant military clashes, he sharply limits opportunities for legionary soldiers, as well as aristocratic officers and cavalrymen, to display *virtus* and gain *gloria*; thus the traditional signposts to the accumulation of social value are pulled up and thrown away.

What to make of waging war in such a manner? One way Fabius' contemporaries respond, the tradition asserts, is to label his refusal to pursue military *gloria* in the expected way as cowardice, the vice opposed to *virtus*. From the very outset, the tradition asserts, Fabius' strategy found critics: Polybius writes that Fabius was at first generally despised and reputed to be cowardly and dumbstruck in the face of danger, while Polyaenus alleges similar ill-repute among his fellow senators. Plutarch adds that Fabius' own soldiers spoke ill of him, and the enemy too considered him cowardly – all except for Hannibal, who alone understood how formidable Fabius was proving himself to be.[20] Minucius, Fabius' master of the horse, favors a more conventional strategy of aggressive pursuit and risking battle. He and his supporters in Rome feed the prevailing discomfort with Fabius' strategy by stigmatizing him as mean and cowardly, contrasting this with Minucius' own desire to display and vindicate traditional military values. This contrast is merely strengthened by Minucius' success in a skirmish he conducts, contrary to Fabius' express orders, while Fabius is away.[21] At this point a tribune in Rome, Metilius, proposes elevating Minucius to the unprecedented rank of co-dictator; Livy gives Metilius a speech in which he develops further the contrast between the two commanders and their strategies. Metilius argues that the soldiers, along with Minucius himself, had been held by Fabius as if in detention or captivity, and that their weapons had been all but taken away from them. Only upon Fabius' departure did they break out and rout the enemy. Fabius is implied to be virtually the enemy himself, imprisoning Roman soldiers to prevent them from displaying their military valor and dispatching Hannibal. Metilius and Minucius thus hold that Roman soldiers are capable of and eager for

---

Harris 1979, 18–34; for the word's semantics, Thomas 2002, 28–31, 38–42. Habinek (2000, 267–77) discusses the "zero-sum" quality of *gloria*. The impression that *gloria* is chiefly an aristocratic concern (Harris 1979, 30; Habinek 2000, 267) may be due to the elite orientation of most of our texts: but see Caes. *B Civ*. 2.39.3; *B Gal*. 7.50.4; [Caes.] *Hisp*. 23.8 for its attribution to centurions and other non-elite soldiers; also Plaut. *Stich*. 281 for its (parodic) attribution to slaves.

[20] Polyb. 3.89.3; Polyaenus 8.14.1; Plut. *Fab*. 5.3. The gibe that Fabius was Hannibal's "pedagogue" (Plut. *Fab*. 5.5; Diod. Sic. 26 fr. 3.1) turns on a stereotyped image of the child-minder, a slave, following and observing his young master. Yet at Plut. *Marc*. 9.7 Hannibal says he *fears* Fabius because, like a pedagogue, he keeps him from doing harm: another way in which Hannibal is portrayed as understanding Fabius' effectiveness, even when Romans do not.

[21] Minucius' views and words about Fabius: Livy 22.14.14; App. *Han*. 12.51–2; Polyb. 3.90.6 (where Minucius' desire to "risk battle," διακινδυνεύειν, contrasts with the "risk," κίνδυνος, that Fabius, in his concern for safety, seeks to avoid: cf. Cass. Dio fr. 57.11); Polyb. 3.94.10.

victory, if only Fabius would allow it.[22] At any rate, Minucius' elevation to co-dictator is usually represented as the people's rebuke to Fabius for manifesting the wrong values, and its reward to Minucius for displaying the right ones.[23]

A second criticism, related to but distinct from the question of military values, is that Fabius' strategy is dishonorable. By leaving the property of colonists, Italian allies and others at Hannibal's mercy to plunder and burn as he moves without hindrance through Italy, the Romans lose face and forsake their obligations. Indeed, Hannibal is said to inflict great losses and suffering on allied cities and colonies during Fabius' dictatorship, among them Beneventum, Telesia and Sinuessa, though for the moment all colonies and allies remained loyal.[24] In Livy, Minucius makes a speech lamenting that the army has come only to watch the slaughter and fiery destruction of the allies and Roman colonists at Sinuessa; his invocation of the *pudor* the soldiers should feel for the city's suffering implies the moral discredit that accrues to their failure to intervene.[25] Plutarch gives Minucius similar remarks in shorter compass.[26] In Minucius' and his supporters' view, then, Roman honor demands that the army be seen to be trying to protect Italy from Hannibal. This requires military confrontation, aggression, daring and risk – the very qualities that distinguish men of valor, such as himself, from cowards. The tradition ultimately rejects the accusation of cowardice against Fabius (as we will see below). The question of honor, however, seems more troublesome to the authors who narrate Fabius' dictatorship. Perhaps with an eye toward this problem, some texts credit Fabius with doing his best in this regard, insofar as difficult conditions allow: Polybius, in his own voice, says Fabius wanted the allies to think he was not abandoning the countryside, while Appian avers that Fabius kept Hannibal from besieging any cities or ravaging the countryside.[27] Dio, too, reports that, when the people appointed Fabius dictator, they were looking to their own survival and gave the allies no help, though later took consideration

---

[22] Livy 22.25.6–9. Cf. Sil. 7.504–10. In Plut. *Fab.* 8.4, Metilius accuses Fabius of treason (προδοσία) as opposed to cowardice (μαλακία/ἀνανδρία); likewise Zonar. 8.26. In Polyb. 3.103.2, the Romans conclude that the problem is not cowardice (ἀποδειλίασις) by the soldiers, but over-caution (εὐλάβεια) by the commander.

[23] Polyb. 3.103.1–4; Livy 22.26.5; Sil. 7.511–18; App. *Han.* 12.51–2; Plut. *Fab.* 10.1; Zonar. 8.26. Indeed, Fabius' own self-justification is cast in his face in Plut. *Fab.* 7.3. After Hannibal escapes a Fabian trap by the stratagem of tying torches to the horns of cattle, Fabius is mocked for being bested in the one arena where he claimed superiority, namely judgment and foresight (γνώμη, πρόνοια). Likewise Nep. *Han.* 5.2.

[24] E.g. Polyb. 3.90.7–14.   [25] Livy 22.14.4–5, 7–8; cf. 22.13.10–11.

[26] Plut. *Fab.* 5.6.   [27] Polyb. 3.92.6; App. *Han.* 12.50; 13.57.

for their safety and hence loyalty.[28] Thus certain texts seek to mitigate the charge that Fabius' strategy is dishonorable, even if they cannot conjure from it a full-scale defense of Italy. The objections to Fabius' strategy, then, are fundamentally moral and social. Judging audiences evaluate his actions negatively in regard to the city's honor, his own *virtus* and the *virtus* of his soldiers and officers; thus they diminish his social standing relative to other social actors advocating more aggressive strategies that more easily or "obviously" admit positive evaluation in these categories.

Yet moral grounds can also be invoked in defense of Fabius' strategy. I noted earlier that, standing above the assignment of value to particular performances within particular moral categories (e.g. determining where someone's performance in battle should be placed on the spectrum of "cowardly" to "valorous"), is the overarching criterion of "consequentiality for the community." Rather than worry about how his immediate performance is evaluated by contemporary judging audiences in terms of *virtus* and what sort of *gloria* he gains directly from it, Fabius is said to be looking always to the overarching criterion: does a performance benefit the commonwealth, or not? Whereas valor displayed by Roman soldiers in battle ordinarily benefits the commonwealth, Hannibal's recent success in pitched battles opens a gap between the ultimate good of the commonwealth and the particular approach – aggressive military confrontation – that is normally the means to this end. For if aggressively confronting Hannibal entails losses on a scale that put the very survival of the commonwealth at risk, then opportunities to display *virtus* must be sacrificed in the interest of commonwealth.

The concern for "safety" commonly ascribed to Fabius finds its moral justification in precisely this reckoning of the collective interest: "safety for the good of the commonwealth" can even be represented as his guiding principle. In Cicero's *De Senectute*, the principal speaker, Cato the Elder, says that as a youth he ardently admired the much older Fabius; he reports that Fabius, who was an augur, once declared that "whatever was done

---

[28] Cass. Dio fr. 57.8; Zonar. 8.25. Livy 22.8.7 attributes similar motives to the senate. Rambaud (1980, 120–1) suggests that Fabius' strategy embodies a "patrician" interest in protecting Rome and the legions, with no care for Italy, while Minucius, along with C. Terentius Varro (cos. 216), have a "plebeian" desire to defend Italy. But it is surely incorrect to see such divergent patrician and plebeian interests within the nobility of this era. More reasonable is Beck's (2000, 87) suggestion that Minucius' argument simply makes strategic sense: it is risky to abandon the allies and colonies to their fates; therefore a more interventionist, active strategy is needed.

After Cannae, when the Romans' capacity to aid allies was even further reduced, some did defect (Livy 22.61.10–12), and others who appealed to Rome for aid were told to take counsel for themselves, as no resources existed to assist (e.g. Livy 23.20.4–10). Yet even then we hear of efforts to lend aid: immediately after Cannae, a fleet is sent to Sicily at Hieron's request (Livy 22.56.6–8).

with the safety of the commonwealth in view was done under the best of auspices, and whatever was contrary to the good of the commonwealth was inauspicious."[29] The "delaying" strategy itself is purportedly motivated by this concern for safety. The Ennian fragment asserts that delaying was the means by which Fabius set the commonwealth back up on its feet (*cunctando restituit rem*), and implies that this strategy emerged from his concern for "safety" (*salus*), notwithstanding the carping (*rumores*) of others.[30] Valerius Maximus echoes and expands this terse Ennian sentiment.[31] And in Silius' representation, Minucius' troops, once they are saved by Fabius' troops following their rash assault on Hannibal, hail Fabius as their "salvation" and "father" (*salus, parens* – i.e. they owe their lives to him); Minucius himself acclaims Fabius as the "fatherland" and as the walls of the city.[32] As everyone would agree that the city (i.e. the fatherland) needs a defensive wall for its safety, this metaphor compactly encapsulates the "safety for the good of the commonwealth" theme and ties it to Fabius (more on these ameliorative re-presentations of Fabius' strategy below). One imagines that Fabius' opponents could have found ways to invoke "the good of the commonwealth" in support of an aggressive strategy. But they never do so in the tradition as it survives to us: the moral arguments allowed to them are only those couched in terms of courage versus cowardice and honor versus dishonor; Fabius is given a monopoly on the larger *pro re publica* argument.

Finally, Fabius' prioritizing of "safety for the good of the commonwealth" is also visible in the *ver sacrum* he vows upon assuming the dictatorship. As Livy describes the motion put to the people for approval, the condition for performing this sacrifice is "if the commonwealth survives the next five years in these wars."[33] It is entirely characteristic of Fabius to enlist the gods to the Roman cause through this vow, rather than through the more conventional, even banal, channel of vowing a temple before or in the heat of battle. The vow in battle is a wager on the *virtus* of the current soldiers and officers, a bet that they will display sufficient valor to secure victory in the immediate battle. No representation about the long-term welfare of the commonwealth is made, though victory now is no doubt assumed to

---

[29] Cic. *Sen.* 11: *dicere ausus est optumis auspiciis ea geri quae pro rei publicae salute gererentur; quae contra rem publicam ferrentur, contra auspicia ferri.*
[30] Fr. 363–4 Sk., quoted above.
[31] Val. Max. 3.8.2: *numquam a consilii salibritate ne parvi qvidem certaminis discrimine recessit... ita hic non dimicando maxime civitati nostrae succurrisse visus est*, in contrast to Scipio Africanus, who helped by fighting.
[32] Sil. 7.743: *hic patria est, murique urbis stant pectore in uno*; cf. 7.734–5.
[33] Livy 22.10.2: *si res publica populi Romani Quiritium ad quinquennium proximum... salva servata erit hisce duellis.*

benefit the commonwealth in the longer term. The *ver sacrum*, by contrast, is a wager on the medium- to long-term survival of the commonwealth, and makes no representations about what commanders and soldiers must do in the short term. Hence there is no explicit privileging of performance in battle, and the door is opened to alternative approaches.

THE PARADOXES OF DELAY

The competing judgments about Fabius' strategy are encapsulated, in typically Roman style, in several paradoxical formulations that are spread widely through the tradition. These paradoxes relate to Fabius' nickname *Cunctator*, to claims about "winning without fighting," and to expressions about the sources of *gloria*. I survey these formulations in turn.

The application to Fabius of the verb *cunctor*, along with its associated nouns *cunctatio* and *cunctator*, allows these moral paradoxes to be formulated with particular point. This word's ethical versatility results from its apparent lack of a strong positive or negative connotation of its own, allowing it to be contextually reoriented so as to revalue Fabius at will.[34] In *De viris illustribus*, the label *cunctator* is said to have been bestowed by Fabius' critics (14.6: [sc. *Fabius*] *Cunctator ab obtrectatoribus dictus*), implying that it was "originally" intended as a reproach.[35] Indeed it is so used in various contexts. Livy's Minucius hurls this word against Fabius on two different occasions. While the army follows Hannibal toward Campania without intervening to prevent the devastation of the Italian countryside, Minucius laments the "delaying and indolence" (*cunctatio et socordia*) that has allowed an enemy from so far away to storm into the very heart of the Roman confederation; thanks to this delaying (*cunctatio*), it was for Hannibal that our ancestors saved Italy.[36] The ascription of this whole sorry state of affairs to the commander's (in)action, as well as the explicit glossing of *cunctatio* with the unambiguously negative term *socordia*, ethically blackens the word and makes it a term of reproach. Later, after being elevated to co-dictator, Minucius is made to say that he will follow his own counsel

---

[34] For what follows, see the helpful observations of Elliott 2009, 532–5. Elliott regards *cunctari* as "originally" pejorative (535), until redeemed by Ennius and/or its Fabian associations. This supposition is possible but unverifiable, as we have insufficient access to a pre-Fabian or even pre-Ennian stage of Latin (the two Plautine occurrences of *cunctor* are not illuminating). Hence I prefer to say that both pejorative and approbative connotations are always available, but must be constructed contextually.
[35] Similarly Zonar. 8.25: διὸ καὶ παρὰ τῶν πολιτῶν αἰτίαν εἶχεν, ὡς καὶ μελλητὴς ἐπονομασθῆναι.
[36] Livy 22.14.5–6, 10: *Poenus advena, ab extremis orbis terrarum terminis nostra cunctatione et socordia iam huc progressus? tantum pro degeneravimus a patribus nostris... quam* [sc. *Italiam*] *vereor ne sic cunctantibus nobis Hannibali ac Poenis totiens servaverint maiores nostri.*

"if the dictator persists in that delay and sloth (*cunctatio ac segnities*) that has been condemned by the judgment of both gods and men."[37] Here again, it is the generally reproachful context, as well as the coupling of *cunctatio* with the pejorative "synonym" *segnities*, that casts the word in a negative light and seeks to pin it to Fabius as a reproach.[38]

Cunctatio may also, however, be rendered approbative through similar strategies of contextualization. Livy, in his authorial voice, says that Minucius "abused Fabius as being not a delayer (*cunctator*) but slothful (*segnis*), and not as cautious (*cautus*) but as fearful (*timidus*), imputing vices adjacent to his virtues." Here Livy implies that the words *cunctator* and *cautus* – which he personally ascribes to Fabius – indicate virtues, but says that Minucius maliciously called Fabius *segnis* and *timidus*, which are the corresponding vices.[39] With this description Livy undercuts in advance the criticisms he later puts in Minucius' mouth: for Minucius does, later, apply the word *cunctatio* to Fabius, glossing it with *socordia* and *segnities* so as to render it a vice (as discussed above).[40] Minucius is thus shown to misunderstand this word's true value and meaning – previously vouched for by Livy himself – when he deploys it to characterize his colleague. Livy also vindicates *cunctatio* as a virtue when he asserts that Fabius' "clever delaying" (*sollers cunctatio*) gave Italy a brief respite from its disasters;[41] the emphasis here on the benefits of the strategy, and the presence of the ethically positive modifier *sollers*, makes *cunctatio* approbative. This *cunctatio* also appears in Silius, who writes that Fabius "surpassed the splendid achievement of his ancestors [sc. the famous 300 Fabii] by delaying... and matching Hannibal in generalship."[42] That *cunctatio* can bring such

---

[37] Livy 22.27.4: *si dictator in cunctatione ac segnitie deorum hominumque iudicio damnata perstaret.*

[38] Similar "reproachful" usages: Livy 27.21.2, where a tribune accuses the nobility of *cunctatio* and *fraus* in allowing Hannibal to linger in Italy; also Sil. 9.52–5, where Aemilius Paullus replies to Terentius Varro's criticism that Fabius is *cunctator et aeger* (feeble): at least Fabius' soldiers are now present to take up arms, in contrast to Flaminius'; also Cass. Dio fr. 57.11, from a speech of Fabius: ἔγκλημα γοῦν ἔχω... ὅτι βραδύνω καὶ ὅτι μέλλω καὶ ὅτι τῆς σωτηρίας ὑμῶν ἰσχυρῶς ἀεὶ προορῶμαι.

In non-Fabian contexts too, *cunctatio* can be presented as a vice or failure of a general, soldier or statesman. One side's *cunctatio* can bring disgrace or danger, or encourage and embolden the other side: Sall. *Hist.* fr. 1.77.17M (*Or. Philippi*); Livy 7.23.10; 8.15.5; 34.46.6; 35.35.17; 37.34.2; 42.57.3; Curt. 4.6.13; Frontin. *Str.* 2.8.4, 8. It may also cause one's own side to miss an opportunity: Caes. *B Gal.* 3.23–4; Val. Max. 3.2.17. But cf. below, n. 45, for *cunctatio* as a general's virtue.

[39] Livy 22.12.12: *pro cunctatore segnem pro cauto timidum, adfingens vicina virtutibus vitia, compellabat.* Similarly 22.39.20.

[40] Livy's description of Minucius' criticisms at 22.12.12 looks most directly ahead to 22.14.14, where Minucius says *audendo atque agendo res Romana crevit, non his segnibus consiliis quae timidi cauta vocant.* Here Minucius "misapplies" the terms *segnis, timidus* and *cautus* exactly as Livy has foretold.

[41] Livy 22.23.1.

[42] Sil. 6.638–40: *pulcherrima quorum / cunctando Fabius superavit facta ducemque / Hannibalem aequando.*

competitive advantage – with it he outstrips past heroes – marks it as a desirable quality. And while *De viris illustribus* asserts that Fabius received the nickname *Cunctator* from his detractors (as noted above), Florus implies quite the opposite: he says, "Fabius thought up a novel way to defeat Hannibal, namely by not fighting; hence his novel *cognomen*, beneficial to the commonwealth, *Cunctator*."[43] Florus seems to imagine that this designation originated as an honorific *cognomen* (so he expressly calls it), one that adverts to Fabius' military success as well as to the safety he conferred upon the commonwealth (*rei publicae salutare* – safety, again, being a leitmotif of Fabius).[44] Indeed, Florus' phrase *rei publicae salutare Cunctator* may simply paraphrase Ennius' *cunctando restituit rem*, with *restituit* interpreted as *servavit*, "saved" (which Florus then transforms into its adjectival form *salutare*, "beneficial" or "safety-bringing"). At any rate, both Florus and Ennius render *cunctatio* a positive quality by stressing its utility to the *res publica*.[45] We see, then, that *cunctatio* and its cognates can be enlisted on both sides of the debate about the ethics of Fabius' strategy. Through glossing and contextualization, these words can be positioned as approbative or pejorative, as designating a virtue or a vice, depending on the author's or speaker's viewpoint and the rhetorical needs of the immediate context.[46]

---

[43] Flor. 1.22: *Fabius... qui novam de Hannibale victoriam commentus est, non pugnare. hinc illi cognomen novum et rei publicae salutare Cunctator.*

[44] On *cunctator* as a descriptive appositive noun, a "nickname," and/or a *cognomen*, see Rebuffat 1982, 165 n. 32, and Stanton 1971, 49–52. According to Stanton, the view that *cunctator* constituted a "formal" *cognomen* for Fabius emerges fairly late (not before Florus); previously it seems to have been regarded as merely descriptive.

[45] Seneca's paraphrase of the Ennian line (or its then-conventional sentiment) likewise stresses Fabius' utility to the collective: *quo alio Fabius adfectas imperii vires recreavit quam quod cunctari et trahere et morari sciit...?* (*De ira* 1.11.5). Here, not only the verb *cunctor*, but also *trahere* and *morari*, are vindicated as military virtues under the criterion of "good of the collective" (here called *imperium* rather than *res publica*). Examples of the approbative use can be multiplied: e.g. Livy 28.40.7 (some label Fabius' *cunctatio* as *metus*, "fear," and *pigritia*, "sluggishness" – until his approach is shown to be better); 22.15.1 (*cunctatio* misunderstood as a vice); Val. Max. 7.3(ext.).8 (*saluberrimis cunctationibus*, "exceptionally wholesome delays"); Frontin. *Str.* 1.3.3 (Fabius' reputation as leading general connected with receiving the name *Cunctator*); Sil. 7.126 (*sollers cunctandi Fabius*, "Fabius, skilled at delaying"); Quint. *Inst.* 8.2.11; Ampel. 46.6.

In non-Fabian contexts, *cunctatio* can be presented more generally as a general's virtue. Tactical delays may improve the chances for victory, even when the soldiers object: Livy 10.29.8; Frontin. *Str.* 1.11.1; Tac. *Hist.* 3.20; cf. Livy 44.38–9; Val. Max. 4.1.2. Yet delaying battle for tactical reasons is not the same thing as refraining from battle in principle: this "strong" Fabian sense of *cunctatio* seems to be unparalleled. Cf. above, n. 38, for *cunctatio* as a general's vice.

[46] *Cunctatio* being a leitmotif for Fabius, two authors explore the paradoxical, even droll, idea that he is rash or hasty. Seneca (*Ben.* 4.27.2) discusses the orthodox Stoic position that all men who are not "wise" (that is, all men in the real world) are afflicted by every possible vice. An imagined critic of this position says, "What, Achilles is fearful? Aristides is unjust? And Fabius, who 'restored the state by delaying,' is rash?" (*et Fabius, qui cunctando restituit rem, temerarius est?*). Seneca then defends the orthodox position against this imagined critic by explaining that not all vices are equally prominent in all men. Silius too depicts a "hasty Fabius" following Cannae: *celer omnia*

A second set of paradoxical formulations asserts that Fabius "wins without fighting." In these formulations the ethical stance is always approbative: it is accepted that Fabius did "win," at least in the sense of successfully defending the commonwealth – but without aggressive warfare, hence without displaying the *virtus* that is normally the means to victory. The earliest surviving articulation of this paradox is in Cicero's *De Senectute*. Here Cato the Elder says that Fabius "softened Hannibal by his patience/endurance/self-possession" (*Hannibalem... patientia sua molliebat*). Cato then quotes the Ennian fragment to authorize his assessment of Fabius' achievement; Cato/Cicero seems to believe that the paradox is already latent there (perhaps in *cunctando restituit rem*).[47] Varro, early in his dialogue *Res Rusticae*, has one interlocutor, Agrius, cite what he calls an old proverb (*vetus proverbium*), namely, "The Roman conquers by sitting still" (*Romanus sedendo vincit*). The reference is presumably to Fabius, who alone could be considered proverbial in this way; also, the ablative gerund *sedendo* cannot help but recall the Ennian formulation.[48] Indeed, a handful of additional passages deploy *sedendo* apparently as a synonym – perhaps simply as variation – for *cunctando*. In Livy, as Fabius urges the next year's consul Aemilius Paullus to carry on with the delaying strategy, he asks, "Do you doubt that we will overcome him [sc. Hannibal] by sitting still, since he grows weaker by the day?"[49] And in Silius, Hannibal laments that "while he restrains himself and we are worn away by inactivity, a type of winning has been contrived."[50] The "novelty" that Silius' Hannibal perceives in Fabius' strategy is brought out elsewhere as well. Florus, as noted above, says that Fabius owes his nickname *cunctator* to devising a "novel" way of defeating Hannibal, by not fighting.[51] Again, examples of

---

lustrans / clamitat attonitis Fabius: 'Non ulla relicta est, / credite, cunctandi ratio. adproperemus (10.593–5). Thus he forswears his leitmotif.

[47] Cic. *Sen.* 10. Cicero/Cato also imposes a distinction in age, with Hannibal youthful (*Hannibalem iuveniliter exultantem*) and Fabius aged, though fighting like a younger man (*hic et bella gerebat ut adulescens, cum plane grandis esset*). The age theme is appropriate to the treatise *De senectute*, of course, but is not present at all in the Ennian fragment adduced to support the claim. For this virtuous form of *patientia*, whose paradoxical effect is to "soften" the enemy, see Kaster (2002, 136–8), under "proposition two" in his taxonomy.

[48] Varro, *Rust.* 1.2.2. Further discussion of this Varronian passage below.

[49] Livy 22.39.15: *dubitas ergo quin sedendo superaturi simus eum qui senescat in dies...?*

[50] Sil. 7.151–2: *inventum, dum se cohibet terimurque sedendo, / vincendi genus*. It is unclear whether *sedendo* refers to Fabius' strategy, or to the inactivity reciprocally imposed upon Hannibal – perhaps both understandings are available. Elsewhere, *sedendo* clearly applies to Fabius: see the passages of Varro and Livy just quoted, along with Sil. 8.12–15 on the success of Fabius' "science of inactivity" (*ars sedendi*), and 16.673–4, where Scipio gives Fabius credit: *peperitque sedendo / omnia Cunctator*.

[51] Flor. 1.22: *Fabius... qui novam de Hannibale victoriam commentus est, non pugnare.*

formulations that ring changes on the "winning without fighting" paradox – often, though not always, with an ablative gerund – can be multiplied.⁵²

One particular formulation of this paradox warrants special mention: the phrase "broke by delay" (*mora fregit*), along with minor variations, which conveys the entire paradox with extreme brevity. For the violent, destructive activity often connoted by *frangere* ("break, smash") sits incongruously with the hesitant passivity of *mora* ("delay, hesitation"); the paradox is that the latter is the means to the former. The relatively wide distribution of this phrase and its variants in the tradition may cause one to suspect that it – like the other widely distributed Fabian keywords *cunctor* (etc.), *res* (*publica*), *salus* and *gloria* – derives from an expression in Ennius.⁵³ Indeed, Propertius declares that among the themes Ennius sang were the "victorious delays (*morae*) of Fabius."⁵⁴ This is the earliest surviving "Fabian" occurrence of the word *mora*, and the passage may echo Ennian words as it describes Ennian themes. A generation later Manilius, enumerating the heroes whose souls reside in the Milky Way, includes "Fabius unconquered thanks to (?) his delaying,"⁵⁵ and much later the author of *De viris illustribus* says that our hero's nickname derived from his having "broken Hannibal by delay."⁵⁶ Florus expands the formula so as to make the paradox even more patent: he writes, "Fabius ... wore Hannibal out to such a degree that he who could not be broken by valor (*frangi virtute*) was pulverized by delay (*mora comminueretur*)."⁵⁷ Thus Florus asserts not only that *mora* was the way to victory, but that *virtus* was not and could not be. This point is always

---

⁵² E.g. Forum Augustum *elogium* (as below, n. 95): *Hannibalem ... subsequendo coercuit*; Plin. *HN* 22.10: [sc. *Fabius*] *qui rem omnem Romanam restituit non pugnando*, a slight expansion and rewording of the Ennian phrase; Val. Max. 7.3.7: *Fabius ... cui non dimicare vincere fuit*; Sil. 7.15: *lento Poenum moderamine lusit*; 7.91–2: *Fabius ... procedens ... arte bellandi / lento similis*; 7.124–5: *domat exultantia corda / infractasque minas dilato Marte fatigat*. Some formulations of the paradox merely credit Fabius with not being defeated, or with preventing Hannibal from winning. All such instances relate to Scipio, as if making room for Scipio to do something further. At Livy 28.40.14 Fabius, addressing the senate regarding Scipio's plan to invade Africa, says, *vincere ego prohibui Hannibalem ut a vobis quorum vigent nunc vires etiam vinci posset*; similarly Sil. 16.672–6; Polyaenus 8.14.2; cf. Val. Max. 3.8.2. For the ablative gerund in Ennius, in the Fabian tradition and elsewhere in Latin historiography, see Elliott 2009.

⁵³ Rebuffat (1982, 162 and n. 21) notes the frequent occurrence of *mora* in the tradition, and hints that it may have stood in Ennius; I would go further and suggest that Ennius somewhere used *mora* in conjuction with *fregit* (or some form of *frangere*) referring to Fabius. *Frango* is a good Ennian word (*Ann.* frr. 177, 395 Sk.), though *mora/moror* is unattested (unless it lurks in the corruptions at *Op. Inc.* fr. 2 Sk. and *Trag.* v. 391 Jocelyn).

⁵⁴ Prop. 3.3.9: *victricisque moras Fabii*.   ⁵⁵ Manilius 1.790: *invictusque mora Fabius*.

⁵⁶ *De vir. ill.* 14.6: *Fabium ... qui Hannibalem mora fregit, cunctator ab obtrectatoribus dictus*.

⁵⁷ Flor. 1.22: *itaque* [sc. *Fabius*] *... sic maceravit Hannibalem ut, qui frangi virtute non poterat, mora comminueretur*.

subsumed, but seldom expressly stated, in the paradox of Fabius "winning without fighting."[58]

The third set of paradoxes in which the competing judgments about Fabius' strategy are crystallized involve claims about *gloria*: which grounds for positive renown are valid and which are invalid; on what basis praise of one's actions should circulate in society; whether social value is distributed correctly. The issue here, as will already be clear, is that the *gloria* in question normally derives from displaying *virtus* in battle, which would also normally benefit the commonwealth. But Fabius holds that, under current circumstances, joining battle puts the commonwealth at mortal risk. Given this novel separation of end from means, to which should *gloria* attach? The Fabian position, of course, is that it should always attach to the end, namely the good of the commonwealth. Those who derive *gloria* only from *virtus* displayed in battle have confused the end with the means – an extremely dangerous confusion under current circumstances, when joining battle harms rather than benefits the commonwealth.

Earlier we examined the objection that Fabius' strategy is cowardly. The circulation of such criticism constitutes the bad reputation, the inverse of *gloria*, that Fabius incurs for not leading his soldiers into battle. Additional texts, however, reflect on the sources of Fabius' *gloria*, and respond to precisely the accusation of cowardice. Livy says that, when Minucius is elevated to co-dictator to reward his daring, Fabius informs the senate that "having preserved the army is more glorious than having killed many thousands of enemies."[59] Thus Fabius explicitly rejects the basis upon which Minucius' current *gloria* – the grounds for his promotion – depends. For Livy has already reported that Minucius' victorious skirmish with Hannibal cost 5,000 Roman soldiers against 6,000 enemy, a negligible difference.[60] Instead, Fabius says, the safety of Roman soldiers (*servasse exercitum*, and by extension, the *res publica* too) is the proper footing for *gloria*; the number of enemy dead, a proxy for the *virtus* of one's own soldiers, is the wrong basis at least for now. A fragment of a similar speech is found in Dio. Here Fabius remarks that he is reproached for his delaying and concern

---

[58] Other occurrences of *mora fregit* or the like: Ampel. 18.6; 46.6; Amm. Marc. 29.5.32–3 (on which see below). At App. *Han.* 13.53 the phrase ἐκτρύχειν Ἀννίβαν τῷ χρόνῳ looks like a direct translation of *frangere mora*. But note that ἐκτρύχειν picks out from within *frangere*'s semantic range a specifically grinding, wearing activity (e.g. *OLD* s.v., senses 3, 7), while Florus' gloss *comminuere* (see above, n. 57) picks out the violent shattering or breaking activity (e.g. *OLD* s.v., senses 1, 2).
[59] Livy 22.25.15: *servasse exercitum quam multa milia hostium occidisse maiorem gloriam esse*.
[60] Livy 22.24.14.

for safety, rather than for (as he implies *should* be the basis for reproach) rushing into battle and losing many soldiers, provided he can kill many enemies, in the quest to be acclaimed *imperator* and win a triumph.[61] Thus, he suggests, the traditional route to glory, and the monuments associated with such glory, ought rather to be a ground for criticism, while his own approach ought to accrue praise rather than blame. Later in the same fragment Dio inflects this thought somewhat differently: "Fabius wanted the commonwealth to be safe and victorious, but not that he himself be of good renown."[62] The point is not that Fabius despises a good reputation in principle, but that he rejects glory bestowed on the "wrong" basis – any that he deems incompatible with the safety of the commonwealth. In Plutarch, when Fabius is criticized by Minucius and the soldiers, he says that fear on behalf of the fatherland is never shameful, and that one who holds high office should never be perplexed by his reputation among men, or by their slanders and blame.[63] Thus he concedes feeling fear, as his critics allege – but since it is felt exclusively for the commonwealth, it brings no shame. Later, after Minucius is elevated to co-dictator, Fabius remarks that his colleague may fall into disaster, being "mad with empty renown and prestige."[64] It is "empty," presumably, because it derives from Minucius' (and others') mistaken valuing of valor displayed in combat above the good of the commonwealth. Again, examples of such paradoxical formulations can be multiplied.[65] Their point, however, is always the same: to indicate that a gap has opened between two bases for *gloria* that are normally coherent – indeed, under normal circumstances they may not even be

---

[61] Cass. Dio fr. 57.11: ἔγκλημα γοῦν ἔχω οὐχ ... ὅτι διὰ κινδύνων στρατηγῶ, ἵνα πολλοὺς μὲν τῶν στρατιωτῶν ἀποβαλὼν πολλοὺς δὲ καὶ τῶν πολεμίων ἀποκτείνας αὐτοκράτωρ τε ὀνομασθῶ καὶ τὰ ἐπινίκια πέμψω.

[62] Cass. Dio fr. 57.16: τὸ γὰρ κοινὸν σώζεσθαι καὶ κρατεῖν, ἀλλ' οὐκ αὐτὸς εὐδοξεῖν ἤθελεν. Cf. fr. 57.21.

[63] Plut. *Fab*. 5.7–8. [64] Plut. *Fab*. 10.4: ἐκμανεὶς ὑπὸ κενῆς δόξης καὶ ὄγκου.

[65] Cicero (*Off*. 1.84; see below) contrasts Fabius with the figures of Callicratidas and Cleombrotus, Spartan generals who put their fatherland at risk by pursuing military glory for themselves. These figures stand as Greek versions of Minucius, or – in Fabius' later representation – Scipio, who Fabius claims is doing the same thing (Livy 28.41.1). Cf. Livy 24.9.11; 27.40.8; 44.22.10 for other inflections of this paradox. It is formulated very compactly at Livy 22.3.8 and Val. Max. 3.8.2, where the *speciosa* ("good to look at," i.e. superficially praiseworthy) are contrasted with the *salutaria* (beneficial or "safety-bringing"); similarly Livy 28.40.7 (*speciosiora ~ meliora*).

Silius, uniquely, makes more limited ethical claims for Fabius. At 7.396–8, Fabius concedes to Minucius that laying the enemy low is glorious, but says that he himself will seek a "triumph" from a different source, namely preserving the army. Here he does not assert that the conventional bases for allocating *gloria* are wrong in general, or even in this case, but merely that he himself is doing something different. Similarly 16.672–6, where *gloria* is said to come either from Fabian not-being-defeated or from Scipionic aggressive confrontation.

recognized as two distinct bases – but for the moment are in conflict: the question whether a performance is courageous or cowardly (the *virtus* criterion, requiring battle), and the question whether the performance benefits the commonwealth (the *pro re publica* criterion).

POST, MAGIS, NUNC: FABIUS REVALUED AND EXEMPLIFIED

The most detailed exposition of the alternative forms of glory is found in the speech Livy gives to Fabius, where Fabius encourages Aemilius Paullus (cos. 216) to follow his example and adopt the strategy he pioneered as dictator the previous year: "The matter stands thus: the only method of waging war against Hannibal is the one I employed."[66] For just as Fabius had to contend with Hannibal as well as his *magister equitum*/co-dictator Minucius, Fabius notes that Aemilius will face opposition from his consular colleague M. Terentius Varro no less than from Hannibal. "But you will withstand them," says Fabius, "if you stand firmly enough against [sc. bad] reputation and people's criticisms, and if neither your colleague's empty glory nor your own false ill-repute troubles you."[67] This, of course, is exactly Fabius' own approach, despising as false the *infamia* that was heaped upon him and deeming his colleague's *gloria* to be "empty" (*vana*) – both reputations, in his view, standing on illegitimate grounds. Most striking, however, is the sententious conclusion, two sentences later, that "he who spurns <empty> glory will have the real thing."[68] This assertion confidently predicts that the current linking of *gloria* with displays of *virtus* in battle will eventually be recognized as incorrect and hence be abandoned, while the Fabian pursuit of safety for the good of the commonwealth will ultimately be judged the "correct" basis for *gloria*. This shift, indeed, is essential if Fabius is to become a positive *exemplum*: his strategy, and its associated values, must come to be accepted as correct and valid. The difficulty is that performance in battle can be observed and evaluated immediately; this kind of *gloria* is quickly, decisively and visibly won or lost. But the *gloria* associated with enabling the state to survive can only be assessed in a longer time frame. In waiting out the necessary lapse of time, it is almost inevitable that one who takes this approach will incur infamy of the "false" sort, precisely because he refuses to join battle.

---

[66] Livy 22.39.9: *ita res se habet: una ratio belli gerendi adversus Hannibalem est qua ego gessi.*
[67] Livy 22.39.18: *resistes autem, adversus famam rumoresque hominum si satis firmus steteris, si te neque collegae vana gloria neque tua falsa infamia moverit.*
[68] Livy 22.39.20: *<vanam> gloriam qui spreverit veram habebit.* Muretus' supplement <*vanam*> creates a neat parallel with *veram*, but it is not necessary to the sense – the meaning must be the same with or without the adjective – and most editors reject it.

The tradition insists, however, that Fabius won this ethical and ideological battle – that his contemporaries and successors did finally revalue his actions and dispositions as morally positive, and those of his detractors as negative, at least under the conditions that then held. The idea that *gloria* (of the "true" variety) later came to him is already present in the Ennian fragment. Here the speaker says that Fabius made *salus* his top priority, and that therefore (*ergo*), in the speaker's own day (*nunc*), which is after Fabius' day (*post*), Fabius' *gloria* "shines out the more" (*magis... claret*).[69] Other texts indicate even more explicitly that such a revaluation occurred. When Polybius introduces Fabius and his strategy for the first time, he immediately remarks that the initial unpopularity of this approach later turned to admiration.[70] Polybius indicates more precisely the circumstances of this revaluation in narrating how Fabius saved Minucius and his soldiers from Hannibal's trap. He says that observers of the battle saw that Minucius had been rash and reckless, while disaster was only avoided thanks to Fabius' caution, foresight and so on – thus Minucius' characteristics are revalued (by these observers) as vices, and Fabius' as virtues.[71] However, the *dénouement* of Fabius' conflict with Minucius is not the only such moment. For, as noted above, this conflict is replayed the following year in the conflict between the consuls Aemilius Paullus and Terentius Varro. Its catastrophic outcome – the defeat at Cannae – spurs yet another affirmation of Fabius' approach as virtuous rather than vicious. Plutarch relates that what had previously been regarded as cowardice and sluggishness in Fabius was deemed after Cannae to be a sort of divine intelligence, and no mere human calculation, that could foresee this future disaster.[72] Therefore, he says, the Romans now placed themselves entirely in his hands.

The broadened moral perspective among Romans that results from the revaluation of Fabius enables them to assess potential commanders more acutely. Henceforth, a general who was notably eager for battle

---

[69] Enn. *Ann.* fr. 364–5 Sk.   [70] Polyb. 3.89.3.
[71] Polyb. 3.105.8: τοῖς μὲν οὖν παρ' αὐτὸν γενομένοις τὸν κίνδυνον ἦν ἐναργὲς ὅτι διὰ μὲν τὴν Μάρκου τόλμαν ἀπόλωλε τὰ ὅλα, διὰ δὲ τὴν εὐλάβειαν τοῦ Φαβίου σέσωσται καὶ πρὸ τοῦ καὶ νῦν· τοῖς δ' ἐν τῇ Ῥώμῃ τότ' ἐγένετο φανερὸν ὁμολογουμένως τί διαφέρει στρατιωτικῆς προπετείας καὶ κενοδοξίας στρατηγικὴ πρόνοια καὶ λογισμὸς ἑστὼς καὶ νουνεχής. For similar sentiments, Livy 22.29.8–9; 22.30.7; Polyaenus 8.14.1; Plut. *Fab.* 13.2. At Livy 28.40.7, Fabius says that others' plans have often seemed more attractive at first sight (*speciosiora primo aspectu*), but his are shown by experience to be better (*usu meliora*). The change in valuation over time is implied in the contrast between first-sight attractiveness and the lessons of experience.
[72] Plut. *Fab.* 17.5: ἡ γὰρ πρὸ τῆς μάχης Φαβίου δειλία καὶ ψυχρότης λεγομένη μετὰ τὴν μάχην εὐθὺς οὐδ' ἀνθρώπινος ἐδόκει λογισμός ἀλλὰ θεῖόν τι χρῆμα διανοίας καὶ δαιμόνιον, ἐκ τοσούτου τὰ μέλλοντα προορωμένης.

could either be admired for his valorous actions or disposition, or be suspected of harboring the vice of recklessness. Livy says that during the elections for 207 the senate and people selected consuls whose *virtus* they deemed "safe" (*tuta*) from Carthaginian trickery. For both consuls of 208 had fallen into traps and died in their "overeagerness to join battle" (*nimia cupiditate conserendi*). Indeed, the people now held that overhasty, hot dispositions in commanders had been "destructive" throughout the war – destructive, presumably, to the armies and the *res publica* above all.[73] Fabius is not mentioned here, but his influence is felt in this depiction of the *populus Romanus* deliberating under a moral perspective that has now been broadened to include the values he championed. There is no suggestion that the people reject "performance in battle" altogether as a basis for conferring value: rather, they (at last) simply recognize that "the good of the commonwealth" is a distinct and legitimate moral basis, notwithstanding its lesser immediacy and tangibility. Furthermore, they recognize that judgments passed on these two bases often coincide, but may also diverge. In this case, the consul M. Claudius Marcellus' undoubted martial courage (he displayed *virtus*) resulted in his death, leaving his army perilously exposed and leaderless (bad for the commonwealth). In such cases, the people now recognize, the "good of the commonwealth" criterion must take precedence. The Romans' newfound capacity to make such distinctions and judgments is the fruit of their revaluation of Fabius.

Sometimes this revaluation is expressed in specifically military terms. In Silius, Minucius changes his tune after being saved by Fabius: he declares, "here is our fatherland: the city's walls stand in this one breast."[74] The metaphor of Fabius being, or containing, city walls confers a specifically military validity upon his strategy, since everyone would agree that a city needs a protective wall. Thus the key Fabian aim of "safety," previously damned as cowardly, is repackaged in militarily legitimating terms that reverse its ethical valence. Another legitimating military metaphor links Fabius with Claudius Marcellus: Fabius is sometimes called the "shield" of the Romans while Marcellus is the "sword."[75] This metaphor again picks out the defensive, protective aspect of Fabius' approach to warfare, but without devaluing it relative to Marcellus' more aggressive approach. For

---

[73] Livy 27.33.9–10: *cum toto eo bello damnosa praepropera ac fervida ingenia imperatorum fuissent*.
[74] Sil. 7.743: *hic patria est, murique urbis stant pectore in uno*.
[75] Plut. *Fab.* 19.4; *Marc.* 9.7 (citing Posidonius as his source for this metaphor); Flor. 1.22. Cic. *Rep.* 5.10 fr. 1, which reads (in its entirety) *Marcellus ut acer et pugnax, Maximus ut consideratus et lentus*, belongs to the same ideological stratum of presenting the two approaches as contrasting yet complementary, as opposite but equally necessary and valid manifestations of military virtue.

just as a soldier requires both shield and sword as basic, essential equipment, this metaphor suggests that the two approaches are complementary, compatible, equally legitimate and indeed essential to Rome's military success. Finally Pliny the Elder, in a discussion of herbs, remarks on the "grass crown," also called "siege crown," that soldiers bestowed upon a commander who had liberated them from a siege. Among the recipients Pliny enumerates, Fabius is deemed especially outstanding because the crown was awarded – Pliny expressly declares – not by Minucius' army after he saved it, but by all of Italy, after Hannibal was driven from the peninsula. Thus the general who refused to fight is granted the highest military honor.[76]

The tradition reports other miscellaneous honors, which collectively indicate the high value later accorded to Fabius and his strategy – the *gloria* he won, paradoxically, for spurning *gloria*; the fruit of his revaluation from coward to hero. For instance, when Livy weighs the odd constitutional circumstances of Fabius' appointment as dictator (see above, n. 10), he concludes that Fabius was actually appointed "acting dictator" (*pro dictatore*) but was wrongly remembered as being a full-fledged dictator due to "his magnificent achievements and outstanding glory as general." That the wrong office was ascribed to him, Livy suggests, reflects the honor, however inadvertent, paid to him by people who assume that the loftiest achievements require the loftiest position. The mistake itself thus indicates the high value later ascribed to Fabius and his deeds.[77] In a different vein, Plutarch reports that Fabius' son was elected consul for 213 BC, as an honor to his father – as if he could not have been elected in his own right.[78] In the census of 209, Livy reports, Fabius was selected as the leading member of the senate (*princeps senatus*) over a rival with greater seniority as censor, the traditional criterion for granting this highly honorific title. The current censor Sempronius argued for Fabius, against the objections of his traditionally minded colleague Cornelius, by asserting that Fabius "would win out as the leading man in the state, even in Hannibal's judgment." The

---

[76] Plin. *HN* 22.10. Gellius, who briefly discusses this crown at 5.6.8–10, specifically names only Fabius as a recipient, as if his achievement towered above every other. See also Maxfield 1981, 67–9, 118–19.
  Several passages simply assert that Fabius was an outstanding general: Cic. *Off.* 1.84, mentioning Hannibal and Fabius as *callidi duces*; similarly Nep. *Han.* 5.2. The Forum Augustum *elogium* (as below, n. 95) declares him *dux aetatis suae cautissimus et rei militaris peritissimus*; Quint. *Inst.* 8.2.11 refers to his *plures imperatorias virtutes*; Frontin. *Str.* 1.3.3 speaks of his *nomen . . . summi ducis*; cf. Frontin. 1.8.2; Plut. *Fab.* 23.2.
[77] Livy 22.31.11: *res inde gestas gloriamque insignem ducis . . . ut qui pro dictatore <creatus erat, dictator> crederetur facile obtinuisse*. Livy may be wrong, and Fabius was quite possibly appointed simply as dictator (see above, n. 10). But the logic of Livy's argument is what matters here, not the correctness of his conclusion.
[78] Plut. *Fab.* 24.1.

implication is that Fabius' achievements in the current war have won him prestige that overshadows senators senior to him.[79] And Valerius Maximus says that the entire *populus* contributed money for Fabius' funeral, to make it as grand and showy as possible. Valerius relates this story under the rubric "On those who display gratitude" (*de gratis*), for he asserts that the Roman people were thanking Fabius "for his five consulships discharged with such concern for the safety of the commonwealth."[80] Plutarch also mentions these funerary contributions, saying that Fabius was regarded as "father of the people." This characterization also implies gratitude, since parents – those who give the gift of life – are quintessentially the persons to whom gratitude is owed.[81]

Turning at last to exemplarity proper, we find various texts in which Fabius' "delaying" performance and its associated values are invoked as normative – that is, as a model for subsequent social actors to imitate or avoid, or as a moral standard by which subsequent actors' performances can be evaluated. Earlier we saw how, in Livy, Fabius presents himself to Aemilius Paullus as a model of how to wage war against Hannibal. When Aemilius falls at Cannae, he avers that he lived and now dies mindful of Fabius' precepts.[82] Even before this, however, the consuls who succeeded Fabius late in 217, after his dictatorship expired, continued to wage war according to his precepts.[83] And even during Fabius' dictatorship, according to Livy, Hannibal himself was at times reduced to employing the "Fabian arts" of delay and inaction.[84] Thus the Fabian strategy is depicted as an effectual model that others follow in waging this war. More interesting, perhaps, are later instances where the example of Fabius is adduced to justify or condemn some course of action. Describing the events leading up to the battle of Pydna in 168, Livy portrays Aemilius Paullus, the consul and eventual victor, as operating in a Fabian mold. Rebuffat notes how Aemilius explicitly

---

[79] Livy 27.11.11: *Q. Fabium Maximum quem tum principem Romanae civitatis esse vel Hannibale iudice victurus esset.* Five years later he was renewed in this status, according to the Forum Augustum *elogium* (as below, n. 95: *princeps in senatum duobus lustris lectus est*).

[80] Val. Max. 5.2.3: *quinque consulatibus salutariter rei publicae administratis.*

[81] Plut. *Fab.* 27.4: ὡς πατέρα τοῦ δήμου. On gratitude owed to parents, see Roller 2001, 188–9, 249–50.

[82] Livy 22.49.10; also Plut. *Fab.* 14.7; 16.8–9.

[83] Livy 22.33.1–3; Cass. Dio fr. 57.21. Fabius' six-month term will have expired in late December, but in this era new consuls entered office on March 15. In the interval, the elected consul Cn. Servilius Geminus resumed command, along with the suffect M. Atilius Regulus.

[84] Livy 22.24.9–10: *Hannibal... artibus Fabi, sedendo et cunctando, bellum gerebat.* Conversely, when Fabius takes Tarentum by treachery in 209, Hannibal declares that the Romans have found their own Hannibal, for they retook the city by the same deceitful means they had lost it (Livy 27.16.10; Plut. *Fab.* 23.1). Thus the two great generals follow one another's example.

invokes Fabius when speaking to the people, and demonstrates additional thematic and verbal echoes that leave the impression that Aemilius instantiates Fabian wisdom and cunning.[85] Indeed, Rebuffat suggests that Livy's depiction of Aemilius as a new Fabius derives ultimately from Ennius' *Annales*: in his view, the famous fragment comes from a speech Ennius puts in Aemilius Paullus' mouth before Pydna, a speech in which Aemilius justifies his own cautious strategy. Such a context would perfectly suit the fragment's retrospective, admiring invocation of the Fabian model.[86]

In Varro's dialogue *Res Rusticae*, the interlocutor Agrius invokes Fabius with tongue firmly planted in cheek. On the occasion of the Sowing Festival (*Feriae Sementivae*), Agrius, Varro and several others have gathered in the temple of Tellus (Earth) for a feast, at the temple-keeper's invitation. The keeper himself, their host, has not arrived yet, so Agrius suggests that the company put into practice the old proverb, "the Roman conquers by sitting," and sit on a bench to await his arrival.[87] This comparison of great things with small – suggesting that the guests should imitate Fabius not in order to save the state by delaying, but to obtain their dinner by *literally* sitting and waiting – is clearly humorous. Yet the leisure time so created, in the temple of Tellus during an agricultural festival, provides a highly suitable occasion for the dialogue on agriculture that follows.[88]

Cicero, too, employs Fabius as a model of comportment and standard of evaluation. Reporting to Atticus in 59 BC on the political situation in Rome, Cicero writes, "Bibulus is in heaven [i.e. in high esteem or honor] – I don't know why, but he's praised as though he were the 'one man' who, 'by delaying, restored the commonwealth for us.'"[89] Consul along with C. Iulius Caesar that year, M. Calpurnius Bibulus (in)famously stayed at home and watched the heavens for ominous signs, seeking to obstruct his colleague's agrarian law and other initiatives. For this, Cicero says, he was praised to the skies, though Cicero himself doubts the praise is deserved. Whether the Ennian verse represents the actual terms of that praise

---

[85] Rebuffat 1982, 157–8; Livy 44.22.10.
[86] This argument entails that Ennius' poem included (or ended with?) the battle of Pydna, which in turn entails that the poet lived at least until mid-168 – controversial views. See Rebuffat 1982, 158–61 on this matter, and 163–4 on Fabius as an *exemplum* for the Aemilii.
[87] Varro, *Rust.* 1.2.1–2: *voltis igitur interea vetus proverbium, quod est "Romanus sedendo vincit," usurpemus dum ille venit?... ad subsellia sequentibus nobis procedit.*
[88] In the end, however, the Fabian model fails them; they do not "win by sitting." For book one, and the dialogue it contains, ends (1.69.2–3) with the arrival of a weeping freedman who announces, shockingly, that the temple-keeper has just been stabbed to death by an unknown assailant. The guests/interlocutors thus depart without receiving dinner or meeting their host.
[89] Cic. *Att.* 2.19.2: *Bibulus in caelo est, nec qua re scio, sed ita laudatur quasi <qui> "unus homo nobis cunctando restituit rem."*

("people are seriously comparing him to Fabius!"), or rather represents Cicero's own ironic commentary on the whole situation ("as if, by such nonsense, he were saving the commonwealth à la Fabius"), is unclear. In either case, however, the Fabian model of delaying in the service of the commonwealth, as articulated by Ennius, is being deployed, seriously or ironically, as a canon of comparison and evaluation for Bibulus, whose truculence also purports to be in the service of the commonwealth.[90] Fifteen years later, in *De Officiis*, Cicero invokes the Fabian *exemplum* in a more general context. He says that the Spartan generals Callicratidas and Cleombrotus sacrificed the good of the state in pursuit of personal military glory. But Fabius did much better, as Ennius shows – and here Cicero quotes the three Ennian verses.[91] Thus he adduces Fabius as the (morally positive) counterexample to the two Spartans – a general who is praiseworthy because he willingly incurred ill-repute in his unwavering pursuit of the collective good. Then Cicero extends the Fabian example from the military arena to the civic one: he writes, "This type of error [i.e. worrying more about one's own reputation than about the common good] must be avoided in civic affairs too. For there are people who don't dare say what they think, however excellent it is, for fear of incurring ill-will." That is, the Fabian predicament – the reckoning of personal reputation against the common good, when the two do not coincide – may confront orators or magistrates who speak in the forum or senate or courts, no less than generals who fight in the field.[92]

In the next generation, the emperor Augustus likewise exploited the exemplarity of Fabius. According to Appian, Augustus often recalled the Fabian precept that one should join battle with a military genius only under dire necessity. For Augustus was not reckless, and preferred craft to daring in battle – like Fabius.[93] Augustus also cast his adopted son Tiberius in a Fabian mold, as a letter quoted by Suetonius indicates. Hearing of Tiberius' care in arranging a summer camp for his army, under difficult circumstances and while being in disfavor with his own soldiers, Augustus praises his prudence and declares that the famous verse could, by general consensus, be

---

[90] On Bibulus' obstruction of Caesar in 59, see still Münzer 1897; relevant texts listed in Broughton 1951–86, II, 187–8.

[91] Cic. *Off.* 1.84: *quanto Q. Maximus melius! de quo Ennius: "unus homo..."* (etc.).

[92] Cic. *Off.* 1.84: *quod genus peccandi vitandum est etiam in rebus urbanis. sunt enim qui quod sentiunt, etsi optimum sit, tamen invidiae metu non audent dicere.* Yet Cicero apparently regarded Bibulus' obstructionism in 59 BC as a misapplication of the Fabian model to the civic sphere.

[93] App. *Han.* 13.56: οὗ δή [sc. πρὸς ἄνδρα τεχνίτην μάχης ἕνα καιρὸν εἶναι τὴν ἀνάγκην] καὶ ὁ Σεβαστὸς ὕστερον πολλάκις ἐμέμνητο, οὐκ ὢν εὐχερὴς οὐδ' οὗτος ἐς μάχας μᾶλλον τόλμῃ ἢ τέχνῃ χρῆσθαι. Augustus' praise of Fabius as "the most cautious commander" (*dux cautissimus*) in the Forum Augustum *elogium* (as below, n. 95) is proof that he deployed Fabius as an *exemplum* of military caution, establishing Fabius as an imitable model for himself and others.

applied to him: "one person, by being watchful, restored the commonwealth for us."[94] The twist is that Augustus has substituted "watchfulness" (expressed in the telltale ablative gerund) for "delay" as Tiberius' means of preserving the commonwealth. Finally, Augustus included Fabius in the gallery of "outstanding men" (*principes* or *summi viri*) who were honored with statues and short inscriptions (*elogia*) in the Forum Augustum. While only a fragment of Fabius' *elogium* from the Forum Augustum survives, its complete text is preserved in a copy found in Arretium.[95] Scholars generally agree that Augustus was presenting these "outstanding men" to other aristocrats as models for emulation and standards for evaluation, while implicitly claiming to have surpassed their achievements himself. In particular, Fabius' *elogium* says that he was chosen *princeps senatus* for two five-year terms (quoted above, n. 79; Fabius died before the second term ended). Meanwhile Augustus reports, in *Res Gestae* 7, that he himself was *princeps senatus* for forty years. Even as he honors Fabius' achievement in the *elogium*, then, Augustus permits attentive viewers to recognize how far he himself surpassed Fabius' standard.[96]

Three hundred and fifty years later, Fabius is adduced in Ammianus' history as an *exemplum* for the Roman general Theodosius. On campaign against some Mauretanian tribes, Theodosius kept his small force in the town of Tipasa for an extended period, "like the Cunctator of old," seeking to overthrow a more numerous enemy through stratagem and diplomacy rather than risking set battle.[97] Here Fabius seems to exemplify the idea of waiting, not rushing into battle, and looking for alternative ways to victory. After a (probably short) lacuna, Ammianus further compares Theodosius' strategy to that which Pompey employed against Mithridates, thus adducing another *exemplum* of craftiness. To articulate this latter comparison, however, Ammianus uses Fabian language, saying that Theodosius (apparently: the name is lost in the lacuna) proceeded "via trickery and delay (*mora*), in hopes of defeating an enemy who kept foiling (*frangentem*) his attacks."[98] Presumably this vocabulary occurred to Ammianus here

---

[94] Suet. *Tib.* 21.5: *ordinem aestivorum tuorum ego vero <...>, mi Tiberi, et inter tot rerum difficultates* καὶ σαύτην ἀποθυμίαν τῶν στρατευομένων *non potuisse quemquam prudentius gerere se quam tu gesseris, existimo. ii quoque qui tecum fuerunt omnes confitentur, versum illum in te posse dici: unus homo nobis vigilando restituit rem.*
[95] *CIL* vi 40953 (Rome fragment), 11.1828 = *ILS* 56 (Arretium copy).
[96] For the function of the gallery of *principes viri*, see e.g. Spannagel 1999, 326–44 and Frisch 1980 (p. 96 on Augustus and Fabius).
[97] Amm. Marc. 29.5.32: *ubi* [sc. *Tipasae*] *diutius agens, ut antiquus ille Cunctator, pro negotio consultabat, commentis potius et prudentia quam periculosis congressibus hostem... oppressurus.*
[98] Amm. Marc. 29.5.33: <...> *ulterius per ambages et moras hostem frangentem suos impetus oppressurus, ut quondam Pompeius Mithridatem.* The syntax is not Fabian, however, as *mora* and *frangere* are not construed together.

because he still had the *cunctator* legend in mind, which he invoked shortly before.

In the passages just discussed, Fabius is constituted and invoked as an *exemplum* – whether a direct model for action, or a moral canon by which actions can be evaluated – because he is "good to think with." Any military commander, and anyone else whose social persona could be conceptualized in military terms or articulated by a military metaphor, might someday need to deliberate whether to "join battle" now – i.e. undertake the social performance normally expected of one in this situation – or to pursue a larger end through different means, thus withholding the expected social performance. Such a deliberation necessarily brings alternative sets of values into competition, one set more familiar and accepted, and the other less so; it also, inevitably, implicates one's personal reputation. The value of the Fabian *exemplum* lies precisely in its modeling of how to weigh such alternatives, and of what consequences may follow from choosing the one or the other. Fabius is "good to think with" because any Roman aristocrat may, in the fullness of time, confront the Fabian predicament for himself.

CONCLUSION: TRACES OF A DIFFERENT FABIUS

Hans Beck has recently remarked that the ancient biographical tradition as instantiated in Plutarch's *Fabius* – from his "slowness" as a child to his criticism, in old age, of Scipio's confrontational strategy[99] – attempts to bring the entire narrative of Fabius' life into focus around the characteristic of *cunctatio*.[100] In so doing, Plutarch merely carries certain tendencies of the Fabian tradition, as analyzed above, to their logical endpoint. Yet traces remain of a different, even discordant, Fabius. In his first consulship, in 233 BC, Fabius defeated the Ligurians, received a triumph, and dedicated a temple to Virtus. Beyond this bare mention, nothing about the circumstances of this dedication is related in surviving texts. Yet it is attractive to conjecture that, at a crisis during a climactic battle, the consul restored Roman fortunes by loudly vowing a temple to the divine manifestation of the military quality that was most needed at that very moment, and so inspired his soldiers to carry the day. At any rate, the victory, triumph and temple dedication (to the most martial of goddesses) makes Fabius look like a "normal" mid-republican *nobilis* who seeks to fuse personal aggrandizement with service to the commonwealth precisely

---

[99] Plut. *Fab.* 1.5; 25–27. [100] Beck 2000, 90; Beck 2005, 269–70, 301.

by leading troops to victory in battle – the very fusion of means and end that the *Cunctator* of legend explicitly rejects.[101] If we accept the *cunctator* tradition as historical, we might posit a development in this figure from the relatively young first-time consul, pursuing *gloria* in traditional ways, to the mature senior statesman-general who realizes that circumstances in the Hannibalic War are different.[102] Yet in his fifth consulship, in 209 BC, Fabius recaptured Tarentum and received his second triumph. He also removed from that city a colossal statue of Hercules, which he dedicated on the Capitol in Rome along with a bronze equestrian statue of himself. The pious dedication of war booty, accompanied by explicit monumentalization of the victor/dedicator, is another familiar, even banal, mode of self-advertisement among Roman *nobiles* of the middle republic.[103] The tradition about the recapture of Tarentum holds, moreover, that Bruttian soldiers betrayed the city to the Romans, and that Fabius subsequently ordered or countenanced the slaughter of all Bruttians in the city, seeking to efface the story of treachery and cause the city to appear to have been taken by force. But why should the *Cunctator* of legend be ashamed to take Tarentum by craft? Perhaps we posit that Fabius' "delayer" phase had only to do with the crisis of 217–216,[104] after which he reverted to pursuing traditional forms of military glory in traditional ways (including the preference for *virtus* over stratagem).[105] Yet the "delayer" tradition still represents Fabius as urging this strategy upon Livius Salinator, the consul of 207, and also – as we have already seen – upon the senate in 204 when arguing against Scipio's proposal to invade Africa.[106]

---

[101] Ligurian victory: Plut. *Fab.* 2.1; Forum Augustum *elogium* (as above, n. 95). Cic. *Nat. D.* 2.61 connects this victory with the temple of Virtus. On this temple, and M. Claudius Marcellus' later encroachments upon it, see Ziolkowski 1992, 58–60; Palombi 1993; Beck 2005, 276–7; McDonnell 2006a, 212–28.

[102] Fabius is commonly taken to be about forty in 233, the usual age for first consulships among nobles of this era (e.g. Beck 2003, 272–4). But Feig Vishnia 2007 proposes backdating Fabius' birth by fifteen to twenty years, making his first consulship very late and making him quite old – perhaps in his seventies – during his years of great eminence (*c.* 217–209 BC).

[103] On Fabius' dedications see Strabo 6.3.1; Plin. *HN* 34.40; Plut. *Fab.* 22.8; *De vir. ill.* 43.6; cf. Livy 27.16.8. Discussion by Sehlmeyer 1999, 125–9 with further bibliography.

[104] Or perhaps down to 214, when the "Fabius as shield/Marcellus as sword" metaphor still presupposes Fabius the *cunctator*. Yet some texts credit Fabius with "traditional," personal military valor even during his dictatorship in 217, when he rescues Minucius from Hannibal's trap: Plut. *Fab.* 12.3–4; Sil. 7.598–616 (an epic *aristeia* naming about a dozen Africans who fall to Fabius' own weapons).

[105] On the fall of Tarentum see Livy 27.16.6 (concealment of the treachery is mooted as the motive for the slaughter, though Fabius is not expressly implicated), and Plut. *Fab.* 22.5 (asserting that desire for concealment is the only possible explanation for the slaughter, which implies that Fabius was overcome by lust for traditional glory). On the *gloria* he gained from taking Tarentum, see Livy 27.40.9.

[106] Livy 27.40.8–9.

There is no easy way to untangle these strands. But one simple point does emerge from their intertwining: namely, that the "delayer" tradition does not quite manage to efface a more complex historical actuality, some of whose traces are visible but not enough of which survives to allow a compelling, all-inclusive narrative of Fabius and his political and ethical commitments to be written.[107] The commitments and concerns of the "delayer" tradition are available, however, and can be described. This tradition represents Fabius as advocating a distinctive approach to confronting Hannibal – an approach based on a particular interpretation of the fundamental values that underwrite Roman aristocratic action. His views, at first reviled, in time are accepted as valid: they carry the day, confer greater *gloria* upon him, and play a central role in preserving the *res publica* amidst a grave military crisis. As a result, Fabius is elevated to exemplary status for future generations. This, the *cunctator* legend, is what mattered most about Fabius to later generations.

---

[107] Beck 2005, 269–301 takes steps in this direction, yet observes that the gap between the exemplary "delayer" of legend and the historical person is vast (301).

CHAPTER 10

The rise of the consular as a social type in the third and second centuries BC

Martin Jehne

Striving hard for decades to win the consulship was the way of life most acceptable for members of the Roman elite. This seems to be one of the very few facts which is not contested in modern research on Roman politics in the middle and late republic.[1] But what happened when these men succeeded? The term in office, often prolonged for fulfilling some additional tasks as proconsuls at some distance from Rome, kept the proud magistrates busy. But what came afterwards when they returned to the city? Traditionally, we tend to see the *consulares* in the centre of Roman politics as embodying the common good in contrast to the incumbent consuls, dominated by personal ambition. But we must ask when this habit came into existence and how the consular role changed over time. What I want to present here are only some reflections on the origins and the rise to eminence of the consular as a social type in the third and second centuries.

Evidently, we should not expect the perspectives of magistrates to be the same from the beginning of the republic to its end or even further. The significance of office for personal rank should not be estimated too highly for the patrician state, when the *primores*[2] were probably the leading members of patrician families, perhaps with some prerogatives for the *gentes maiores* in relation to the *gentes minores*.[3] They were well known and

---

Project "Consuls, consulars and the government of the Roman republic" (HUM2004–02449 and HUM2007–60776/HIST) funded by Ministerio Educación y Ciencia, Gobierno de España.

[1] This does not imply that everybody really competed and even less that everybody succeeded. In fact, there must have been many losers who dropped out at different steps on the ladder to the top. Unfortunately, there is no way to calculate their numbers, even in range and scale. We would be able to understand better what being a Roman noble meant for the individual if we had more information on the losers. For some reflections on the problem and some examples from imperial Rome, cf. Heil 2005.

[2] As Livy likes to call the leaders of the *res publica*; cf. e.g. Livy 3.63.6; 3.69.3; 3.72.1.

[3] On this distinction cf. Smith 2006b, 254f. According to Cic. *Rep.* 2.35, members of *gentes maiores* were allowed to speak before members of *gentes minores* – a late construction, no doubt. For the lasting success of the *gentes maiores* in striving for office during the third and early second centuries, cf. Beck 2005, 121f., 126f., 130, 134, 138f., 144, 147 (tables on pp. 150 and 152).

resourceful, whether they served as magistrates or not. Some impression of how the life of a Roman aristocrat could have unfolded in archaic Rome may be extracted from the anecdote of Cincinnatus. According to Livy, Cincinnatus was busy ploughing his fields when some prominent Romans arrived to announce his appointment as dictator.[4] Whether this actually happened is not my concern here, nor am I interested in the highly moralistic colouring of the episode in later reports, praising the simple life of the ancestors.[5] In this context, it is only relevant that later Romans saw the lives of their forefathers as oscillating between public obligations and private activities outside Rome.[6] This could have been the normal pattern of life for the leading men until at least the third century BC. Between offices a successful *nobilis* took care of his economic interests and lived the social life of the landed gentry. Temporary retirement from the business of the *res publica* was certainly not unusual or a reason for criticism. Senators stayed in their *villae* outside Rome and were called to senate meetings by *viatores*. Cicero and the rest of the later tradition explicitly characterized this way of life as a peculiar habit of the past.[7] The elder Cato still praised hard work with his own hands as an honourable deed even for wealthy landowners, but in his lifetime this was already rather old-fashioned.[8] In

---

[4] Livy 3.26.6–11.

[5] Livy 3.26.7: *Operae pretium est audire qui omnia prae divitiis humana spernunt neque honori magno locum neque virtuti putant esse, nisi ubi effuse affluent opes*. The recent monograph of Hillyard 2001 is interesting in examining the myth of Cincinnatus in the USA, but unprofessional and derivative in its analysis of the Roman figure and early Rome. For a lot of erudite combinations and speculations on the Cincinnatus story, cf. now Liou-Gille 2007.

[6] According to Livy 3.26.8, the piece of land that Cincinnatus was ploughing was situated on the other bank of the Tiber at a place which was still called *prata Quinctia* (cf. Paul. Fest. 307 L. s.v. *Quinctia prata*; Dion. Hal. 10.8.4). Plin. *HN* 18.20 locates this place *in Vaticano*. This would mean that the senators did not have to walk a long way to meet Cincinnatus while the new dictator could quickly arrive to perform his duties in the centre. For Livy (and Dionysius), the miserable economic situation of Cincinnatus is a consequence of the trial of his oldest son Kaeso. The father gave bail for the son, and when the son went into exile, most of the father's property fell to his creditors (Livy 3.13.6–10; Dion. Hal. 10.8.4). Perhaps Livy's Cincinnatus still owned a house in the city to return to when he became dictator; cf. Livy 3.26.11: *Ea frequentia stipatus antecedentibus lictoribus deductus est domum* (in fact, we cannot be sure if Livy meant for him only to be led 'home', thus meaning the city in a general way, or 'into his home'; Liou-Gille 2007, 323 n. 160 suspects that the house was the property of a relative or a client).

[7] Cic. *Sen.* 56: *a villa in senatum arcessebantur et Curius et ceteri senes, ex quo, qui eos arcessebant, viatores nominati sunt*. Cf. Columella, *Rust.* praef. 18: *Illis enim temporibus…procures civitatis in agris morabantur et, cum consilium publicum desiderabatur, a villis arcessebantur in senatum; ex quo, qui eos evocabant, viatores nominati sunt*; Plin. *HN* 18.21; Dion. Hal. 11.4.3.

[8] Cato, *Or.* fr. 93 (from the speech *de suis virtutibus contra Thermum*, Sblendorio Cugusi 1982, 88 with commentary 278–82; cf. *ORF* 7 fr. 69); Plut. *Cat. Mai.* 21.3; Cic. *Sen.* 24; 55f. There is no good reason to assume that Cato's family business was in need of the manual labour of the young Cato himself (although Cato is called *pauper* in Livy, *Per.* 48 even when he was an old man); cf., for the economic background of the young Cato, Astin 1978, 2f. So working with his own hands was clearly a symbolic act for Cato and other great landowners, emphasizing plain living and the ability to cope with physical stress as the ideal of the Roman upper class.

the early republic, however, the Roman patrician did his public service as a magistrate and a senator just as the Roman small farmer made his contribution as a soldier: regularly, but not continuously.

Cicero's life was very different. He too had to take care of his financial interests[9] and, of course, he spent a part of the year on his estates communicating with the local upper classes. But for most of the year, he lived in Rome and went to senate meetings, to the forum for judicial cases and popular assemblies, to his fellow peers for *convivia* to show off his erudition and to do politics in an informal way. Days, months and years went by with politics, and even if Cicero was a special addict – which he was, no doubt – he was not alone. Roman senators of the late republic could be expected to consider politics as a lifelong, full-time job.

The picture I paint of my protagonists Cincinnatus and Cicero and their times is without a doubt radically simplistic: modelling extremes, not allowing for exceptions and different methods of seeking fulfilment in life. Nevertheless, I think that the poles are well marked by my examples, and evidently, the movement over the course of time went from the side of the Cincinnatus pole in the direction of the Cicero pole. The change is above all a consequence of two well-known facts: the fierce competition for office and, closely related, the growing importance of the senate. Both factors combined to generate the *consularis* as a social type in the political culture of the republic.

The point at which competition for office grew to be more intense and had to be regulated by rules and laws is not easy to determine. The Licinian-Sextian laws of 367/6 BC were certainly a starting point, probably introducing the collegial consulship for the first time, certainly admitting plebeians to the posts, thereby adding to the number of ambitious, leisure-class Romans who could aspire to become consuls.[10] As Alexander Bergk mentions in his paper in this volume, the Roman wars in southern Italy and Etruria at the end of the fourth and at the beginning of the third century produced a vast amount of booty. From that point on, the consulship became economically appealing, because a successful commander could now invest a large share of booty for public purposes, but in his own name.[11] With the rise of Roman rule over Italy, then Sicily and Sardinia

---

[9] Cf., for instance, Früchtl 1912, esp. 68–89; Boren 1961–2.
[10] Cf., for sources and a short commentary, Flach 1994, 294–7.
[11] In fact, the usual opinion that generals owned all or part of the war booty was attacked by Churchill 1999 – successfully, or so I think. But even if booty was considered the property of the community, commanders could spend a lot of it on public buildings or donations to the city's populace. Those investments were connected to the name of the victorious and generous commander, who thus profited from popular favour (cf., for instance, Livy 37.57.11 on M'. Acilius Glabrio, cos. 191; see Churchill 1999, 101–5).

and Corsica, the renown and acknowledgement that would be expected by a Roman landowner dominating the social system around his estates could no longer compete with the lure of military command and the chance to influence politics in the capital. I think this helped create an attitude that a noble had to keep to public service in order to remain a leading personality in the *res publica*. A Cincinnatus, retired from office and eager to mind his own business, could not hope for a call from the senate any more. He had to be aware of the possibility that he was out forever.[12]

A telling anecdote of Cato the Elder may help us to grasp something of the period of transition. As Cicero and Plutarch write, Cato used to pay a visit to the small hamlet of M'. Curius Dentatus in the Sabine countries every now and then, reflecting on ancient times when Rome's great commanders still cultivated their fields personally.[13] Similar stories of frugality are told about Fabricius Luscinus.[14] The reports concerning the economic background of these heroes of the Pyrrhic War imply that they could only function as army leaders because warfare was a seasonal affair, as was agriculture. These commanders were thus in need of some time in which to take care of their farms in the same manner as their soldiers. But even if we should be sceptical about this construction of the good and simple life of former times, we are dealing with an epoch for which it can be plausibly argued that active members of the office-holding group still spent much of their time between holding offices outside of Rome, on their estates.[15]

During the First Punic War, opportunities to win honour and booty multiplied. As Bruno Bleckmann showed in his splendid monograph, Roman commanders more or less made their own wars.[16] They operated independently of senatorial directives and tried to end fighting before the end of their terms, not to avoid further bloodshed but to be able to qualify for a triumph as the prime reward for final victory. Tim Cornell has argued for a similar attitude among generals in an even earlier period, during the so-called Samnite Wars.[17] But in any case, in the First Punic War

---

[12] Livy assigns another dictatorship to Cincinnatus in 439 BC (Livy 4.19.12–14). An example of a man who seemed to be out of politics permanently but was called back even from exile for another consulship is M. Livius Salinator, cos. II 207. But this happened in the emergency of the Second Punic War in 208 'when there was an acute shortage of experienced generals' (Patterson 1942, 331).

[13] Cic. *Rep.* 3.40 (cf. *Sen.* 55); Plut. *Cat. Mai.* 2.1–3. Cf. Beck 2005, 189.

[14] Sen. *Prov.* 3.6: *Fabricius quod rus suum quantum a re publica vacavit, fodit*; cf. Beck 2005, 204f.

[15] Cf. the passages cited above, n. 7.   [16] Cf. Bleckmann 2002, 111, 139–144, 202f. etc.

[17] Cf. Cornell 2004, 125f., 129. Fronda 2006, 407–9 accepts Cornell's criticism of the tendency to see in the Samnite Wars a coherent string of campaigns over many years, but rightly argues for a conscious Roman strategy of exploiting local conflicts to improve the Roman position against the Samnites.

triumphs were numerous,[18] iterations of the consulate were scarce, family members of successful commanders won elections, praetors still got military commands as a matter of course and prorogations occurred only rarely.[19] These developments are best explained by fierce aristocratic competition for attractive positions of command, by the insistence on access to command for more than a happy few as a life principle of oligarchy, by the absence of any clear-cut hierarchy of high office, and by the limited influence of the senate as a body on the organization of warfare and on the results of elections.[20] If we accept this, we must conclude that this was not a period in which being a senior member of the senate with a splendid career record but no chance to get further commands promised a position of power. While it became more and more attractive for aristocrats to be successful generals, the fact that they were did not automatically imply that former commanders were able and willing to control politics via the senate.

So let us have a look at another development which triggered the rise of the full-time politician that can be detected in the role of *consulares*: the growth of senatorial business and the increasing significance of the senate. The fundamental principle of the Roman republic was the ever-changing state of the members of the political class who went from being *magistratus* to *privatus*. Even before the *cursus* was established and rules became stricter, it was a matter of course that nobody could serve continuously as a magistrate. For an outstanding political career we may look once more at the plebeian hero Curius Dentatus: as far as we know, he was active in political life for *c.* twenty years, being elected three times consul (290, 275, 274), once *censor* (272), once *praetor suffectus* (283), once tribune of the plebs (291?) and *duumvir aquae perducendae* (270). He was even consul in two successive years (275, 274).[21] So he spent about one third of this period in office, but not more. In the meantime, he could have attended the senate, which provided the opportunity to influence the fate of the *res publica* – if he was not too busy to live an exemplary life on his estate for Cato to admire. For a member of Rome's political class, holding office was not at all an every-year event: once the censors wrote him down on the senate roll and he behaved acceptably, he was just a senator for the rest of his life.

---

[18] Itgenshorst 2005, 266 lists seventeen triumphs for the twenty-five years of the First Punic War, which is quite a lot.
[19] Cf. Bleckmann 2002, 232–5; Beck 2005, 106–8, 127–30.   [20] Cf. Bleckmann 2002, 234–41.
[21] Details of Dentatus' career are uncertain and the subject of scholarly controversies, but not important in this context: I follow the results of Beck 2005, 189–202 (with discussion of problems and earlier reconstructions). In the third century, before the Second Punic War, Dentatus was the only one who got a third consulship; cf. Beck 2005, 97–9.

Unfortunately, we do not really know how often Roman senators went to the meetings or how frequently these meetings were held before we get to the Ciceronian age. For Dionysius of Halicarnassus and for Livy in his first decade, senators are always available to deliberate on public business, to go to the forum and calm the people down, to talk to foreign ambassadors, and so on. There is an interesting passage in Valerius Maximus' chapter on ancient institutions reinforcing this impression of the permanent presence of senators in Rome:

> But to pass from manners corrupted by luxury to the austere institutions of our ancestors, the senate in former times kept regular station in the place which even today is called the *senaculum*. They did not wait to be assembled by proclamation but would proceed thence to the senate house immediately when summoned. For to their thinking a citizen who discharged offices due to the commonwealth not of his own volition but in compliance with an order deserved but questionable commendation, since any service forced by authority redounds to the credit of him who requires it rather than of him who renders it.[22]

If we leave aside the moralistic interpretation by Valerius at the end, which is not at all convincing, we can observe here the senators' habit of being ready for meetings as part of a daily routine. As we know, several *senacula* existed at Rome near meeting places of the senate,[23] with the most important being the place in the Forum beneath the *curia Hostilia* and the so-called *Graecostasis* where foreign envoys were expected to stay and wait for their turn.[24] It is impossible to say which period Valerius Maximus had in mind when he mentioned this ancient institution 'which even today is called the *senaculum*'. Usually scholars think of the early and middle republic.[25] Mommsen's guess that waiting in the *senaculum* was the habit of older people no longer strong enough for military command or work at home[26] corresponds with the use of *seniores* in contrast to *senatores* in Varro's notice on *senaculum*.[27] When the senate was still an association of

---

[22] Val. Max. 2.2.6: *Sed ut a luxu perditis moribus ad severissima maiorum instituta transgrediar, antea senatus adsiduam stationem eo loci peragebat qui hodieque senaculum appellatur; nec exspectabat ut edicto contraheretur, sed inde citatus protinus in curiam veniebat, ambiguae laudis civem existimans qui debitis rei publicae officiis non sua sponte sed iussus fungeretur, quia quidquid imperio cogitur exigenti magis quam praestanti acceptum refertur.* (Translation by D.R. Shackleton Bailey, Loeb edition).

[23] Fest. 470 L. s.v. *Senacula*. Cf., for the different *senacula*, Mommsen 1887–8, III 2, 914; Mason 1987, 39–50.

[24] Varro, *Ling*. 5.156: *Senaculum supra Graecostasim, ubi Aedis Concordiae et Basilica Opimia.*

[25] Cf. Mommsen 1887–8, III 2, 914f.; Mason 1987, 43f., 50 (who emphasizes that we have a dated reference to *senaculum* as some space in the Forum area in Livy's report on the activities of censors in 174 BC, 41.27.7).

[26] Mommsen 1887–8, III 2, 914f.

[27] Varro, *Ling*. 5, 156 (continuing the text quoted above, n. 25): *senaculum vocatum, ubi senatus aut ubi seniores consisterent, dictum ut gerousia apud Graecos.* Cf. Fest. 470 L. s.v. *Senacula* (see below, n. 28), and see Mason 1987, 41f.

seniors, they possibly assembled regularly in the *senaculum* in the Forum,[28] talking to each other and making deals, demonstrating their important status in society by placing themselves in an elevated place, willing to help simple citizens when approached deferentially, and walking into the senate house when the magistrate called. But when the city grew along with the senate, the *senaculum* was perhaps reduced to a place where the members gathered in cases of crisis when they needed to be readily at hand for the magistrates to consult,[29] and where they could enjoy a privileged view of the games which took place in the Forum.[30] So we should not conclude that the majority of the senators walked daily to the *senaculum* in the third century, or that they were frequently called into the senate by a magistrate.

Possibly, a Roman ex-commander was not even asked to visit the senate every year. In the only surviving text giving us information on the famous *lex Ovinia*, a lemma of Festus on *praeteriti senatores*, the situation in existence prior to Ovinius' initiative is characterized in a rather unexpected way. I quote Festus' note:

Passed-over senators in former times were not in disgrace, because, just as the kings used to choose for themselves, and to choose as replacements, those whom they would have in public council, so after the kings were expelled the consuls also, and the military tribunes with consular power, used to choose for themselves all their closest friends from the patricians and then from the plebeians; until the tribunician Ovinian law intervened, by which it was laid down that the censors should <be bound by oath to> enrol in the Senate all the best men from every rank. Thus it came about that those who were passed over and removed from their seats were considered dishonoured.[31]

---

[28] That only this *senaculum* was considered as a gathering place for elders is implied in Fest. 470 L. s.v. *Senacula*: *Senacula tria fuisse Romae, ... Unum, ubi nunc est aedis Concordiae inter Capitolium et Forum, in quo solebant magistratus dumtaxat cum senioribus deliberare, alterum ...*

[29] So perhaps in the emergency situation of 211 BC when Hannibal marched on Rome; cf. Livy 26.9.9; 26.10.2.

[30] Mommsen 1887–8, III 2, 893 convincingly argues that senators could view the games in the Forum from the *senaculum*. With the *senaculum* overtopping the *Graecostasis*, the gathering place of the foreign envoys (Varro, *Ling*. 5.155–6), we are in the fourth century: for the name *Graecostasis* to be justified we need to have Greek legates coming to Rome more often, as occurred in the fourth century. Moreover, we have the note in Just. *Epit*. 43.5.10 indicating that Massilia was honoured for helping Rome with the distress caused by the Gallic sack by providing a place for its ambassadors among the senators at the games. This can be explained as a promotion from the *Graecostasis* to the *senaculum* (cf. for this Jehne 2009, 160f.).

[31] Fest. 290 L.: *Praeteriti senatores quondam in opprobrio non erant, quod, ut reges sibi legebant sublegebantque quos in publico consilio haberent, ita post exactos eos consules quoque et tribuni militum consulari potestate coniunctissimos sibi quosque patriciorum, et deinde plebeiorum, legebant; donec Ovinia tribunicia intervenit, qua sanctum est, ut censores ex omni ordine optimum quemque curiati<m> in senatu<m> legerent. Quo factum est ut praeteriti essent et loco moti haberentur ignominiosi*. (Translation from Cornell 2000, 73. I put the translation of his conjecture <*iur*>*ati* for the *curiati* in the MS at the end into brackets; cf. for discussion below, n. 37.)

Few scholars have accepted Festus' exposition, but since Cornell made the case that we have little reason to ignore such an explicit statement,[32] we have to reckon with a senate which was appointed every year anew by the consuls.[33] A former magistrate who had no friend in office could be ignored for the senate of the year, and since being passed over was no problem of status – or that is what Festus suggests – this man was free to live happily in the countryside. Even if we reduce the freedom of magistrates to promote the group which they consulted to active service in the senate[34] and assume some sort of sleeping membership for senators now passed over,[35] we still have a situation in which there are gaps in the senatorial occupation as a normal career pattern.

It is not altogether clear what changes were introduced by the *lex Ovinia*, which is probably to be dated to 312 BC or shortly before.[36] Now censors were responsible for the *lectio senatus*. If they had to select *curiatim*, as Frank Ryan argued following a popular conjecture for *curiati* preserved in Festus' text,[37] we would have to conclude that the *curiae* were still the dominant form of organization for Roman citizens in the late fourth and

---

[32] Cornell 2000, 73–5; cf. Cornell 1995, 248; Bleckmann 2002, 142; cf. earlier Ryan 1998, 140.

[33] If the senate really came into being as the advisory board of the king it would not be surprising if this council continued to be the advisory board of the high magistrates of the early republic, changing together with them (or him). Cf. Cornell 1995, 247f.

[34] Perhaps these were the people frequenting *senacula*, available for a call into the senate on short notice (cf. above, n. 22), while others had to be called in from the countryside (cf. above, n. 7).

[35] This seems to be the view of Mommsen 1887–8, II 1, 420f.

[36] Cf. Giangrieco Pessi 2000, 332–7; Elster 2003, 84–7; Humm 2005, 194f.; earlier, Rotondi 1912 (1966), 233f. The alternative datings discussed by Cornell 2000, 75–9, who himself decides for the period between 339 and 334 BC (cf. Cornell 1995, 369: 339–332 BC), are criticized by Humm 2005, 190–4.

[37] Cornell 2000, 83f. (cf. Cornell 1995, 468 n. 3) reanimated the old emendation *iurati* which was already supported by Hofmann 1847 (1972), 5–7 and Willems 1968 (1878–85), I, 169–71; cf. also Giangrieco Pessi 2000, 328f. Cornell's argument for the obligation of censors to undertake the *lectio* under oath draws upon some evidence for praetors swearing to select jurors from the best men (cf. Cic. *Clu.* 121; *lex repetundarum*, Crawford 1996b, I, p. 66f.) and the case of Augustus in 18 BC (Cass. Dio 54, 13, 2). But Ryan 1998, 150f. objected that the analogy between praetors and censors is weak and that Augustus' *lectio* in 18 BC was a special case. Moreover, Ryan 2001, 83–9 tried to show that in his speech for Cluentius, Cicero even contrasts magistrates acting under oath with the censors who did not (*Clu.* 121; 126; 127). So Ryan pleads for *curiati<m>*, a solution which is paleographically very simple (cf. – in addition to Ryan – Humm 2005, 199–201; Urso 2005, 152). Nevertheless, Ryan 1998, 151 all too easily dismisses the claim of Zonar. 7, 19 that censors swore to do their job without any feelings of favour or enmity, but to the best of their knowledge for the advantage of the community. That this is only a general oath and not a special one for *lectiones* is not a good argument against the possibility that *curiati* in the preserved text of Festus is a corruption of *iurati*. The notice of Zonaras is excerpted from book 6 of Cassius Dio's *Roman History*, which is not to be neglected, as some recent research has made clear: Bleckmann 2002, 35–6 established the high value of the tradition preserved in Dio's fragments on the middle republic, and Urso 2005, 163–93 made his case for a well-informed *liber de magistratibus* from the very end of the republic as the source of Dio's remarks on magistracies in his early books. So we must take this remark from Zonaras seriously.

early third centuries.[38] This reconstruction would have some important consequences: a former consul or praetor would not get into the senate more or less automatically because it could happen that the seats of his *curia* were already filled, so the senate would not have been a body of ex-magistrates in the same way as it certainly was in the second century;[39] furthermore, the *lex Ovinia* must have been repealed at some moment unknown to us, because the rules of the famous *lectio* of Fabius Buteo in 216 BC show nothing of a connection to *curiae*.[40] But Ryan's view rests on presuppositions which are highly hypothetical,[41] so we cannot build on this. Nevertheless, it seems to be safe to accept that a larger body of lifetime senators only came into being at the end of the fourth century.

If we look at the careers of Roman nobles in the third century, we may observe that successful men spent more time in high office than their successors in the second and first centuries. But we should not suppose too quickly that it was attractive for these men to live in the city as busy senators while not in office – something which Cicero and his colleagues certainly did. The war heroes of the third century were willing to march out for another campaign, but without office, private affairs and perhaps also a life of leisure on the estates should still have been at least as important as working in the senate.

Hard evidence on lifestyle is lacking, so we have to resort to structural construction for some impression of the senate's influence. Evidently, a senator's importance depended on what the senate had to do. I suspect that regular business did not involve very much before the later third century: deciding on levies and taxes and providing necessary funds, finding

---

[38] Already Ryan 1998, 155f. combines the selection from the thirty *curiae* with the general view that the senate was later a body of 300 men, so the reform meant that censors had to choose ten members of each of the thirty *curiae*. Ryan 2001, 90f. even goes one step further and emends <de>curiati<m>, making more explicit the censors' choice of ten men from every *curia* which he sees behind the enigmatic *ex omni ordine*. There are some hints of *decuriae* of senators; cf. Mommsen 1887–8, III 2, 851f. If Ryan is correct, this way of recruiting senators prescribed by the *lex Ovinia* possibly produced the senate's *decuriae*, which clearly became unimportant in later times. But the supposed connection of *curiae* and senate is weak: the careful investigation of all the evidence on *curiae* by Smith 2006b, 184–234 found no hint at all of that (cf. p. 254 n. 11: 'it is impossible successfully to relate the *curiae* to senate membership').

[39] Cf. also Ryan 1998, 156.   [40] Ryan 1998, 153, 155, 158, 161.

[41] Cf. above, n. 37f. Furthermore, the assumption that the senate of the third century included precisely 300 members is only a guess: there is some information suggesting 300 senators at the beginning of the republic (Fest. 304 L. s.v. *Qui patres*; Livy 2.1.10), which is nothing to build upon; and there is the fact that Fabius Buteo recruited 177 new senators in 216 BC (Livy 23.23.7), which is interpreted by many scholars as an indication that he had to supplement the senate up to a *numerus clausus* (cf. also Humm 2005, 204–8), but cf. against this below, n. 53. Moreover, since it is perfectly possible that the *lex Ovinia* was abrogated or modified before the Second Punic War, the establishment of a *numerus clausus*, if it ever existed, could have been part of the changes.

ways to cope with prodigies, accepting new cults, listening to foreign envoys, discussing politics, which involved recommending war or peace and dealing with internal discontent expressed by the tribunes of the plebs. For laws and elections, the senate had to produce the *auctoritas patrum*.[42] All in all, this agenda was important, but did not require senators to be available at all times. Consuls were elected in the *comitia centuriata* in the third century, no doubt, but unfortunately we do not know if or how often competing candidates engaged in public election campaigns. The alternative would have been the recommendation of candidates by the senate with the consequence that ambitious men eager to win would have had to court the senate more than the people. But even for that, a fairly short period before the election date should have been sufficient. At the end and at the beginning of the magisterial year in March, senators needed to be present for the elections and to prepare for campaigns which required *senatus consulta*. Then there were *ludi* where senators would be present, and without a doubt many of them were on the spot during times of internal conflict. But since the magistrates with *imperium* often spent most of their time in office commanding troops in the field, away from the city, and would have had to come back to Rome to summon the senate for a meeting, the senators themselves would only have needed to travel to Rome on those occasions when there was urgent business to conduct. And the senate always functioned properly, even when many members were absent. As Frank Ryan made clear for later periods, the presence of one third of the members made a *frequens senatus* required for some topics.[43] If there were really 300 senators in the third century, it would mean that the attendance of 100 was sufficient to conduct business, and that a smaller number would often have been present.[44]

One of the major fields of senatorial activity was diplomacy. Envoys from a foreign community could expect to get a hearing in the senate and a decision on their problem. Vice versa, when Rome felt the need to send legates to other states, the decision was discussed and resolved in the senate. Of course, these envoys were recruited from the body of senators. But there is no reason to assume that the arrival of external envoys and the sending of legates happened frequently in the fourth and early third

---

[42] After legislation had been passed until the later fourth century, then prior to the adoption of legislation in subsequent years. For a discussion of the *lex Publilia de auctoritate patrum* of 339 BC and of the *lex Maenia de auctoritate patrum*, perhaps of 279 BC, cf. Graeber 2001, 25–8, 150–6.

[43] Ryan 1998, 27–36, esp. 28.

[44] Cf. the explicit mention of a quorum of 100 in the *senatus consultum de Bacchanalibus* of 186 BC, *ILLRP* 511, lines 6; 8 f.; 17f.

centuries.⁴⁵ At most, the coming of large numbers of ambassadors to Rome was a phenomenon of the late third and even more of the second century when Roman contact with the Greek world was as well established as Roman power. It seems to be true that the Greeks were especially fond of sending and accepting embassies with great frequency in order to deal with nearly every matter imaginable.⁴⁶ We should not assume too quickly that Italian communities acted in the same way. That most of the embassies to Rome on record come from Greece is not a picture painted only by the hazards of evidence.⁴⁷ So the burden placed upon the Roman senate grew considerably with the increasing number of embassies, and this seems to have happened only in the early second century.⁴⁸ At this time, most Greek *poleis* started to send envoys to Rome to ask for favours and decisions in competition with their neighbours, which meant endless hearings in the senate. The senate had to meet again and again, and the job of a senator

---

⁴⁵ The lists of embassies from the times of the kings and the early republic which Canali de Rossi 2000, 2005 and Auliard 2006, 281–304 have collected from the literary sources are impressive, but not inconsistent with my assessment. Apart from the obvious need for source criticism – the reports in Livy and Dionysius tell us more about late-republican assumptions about the workings of interstate contact than about what happened in the regal period – most of the embassies have to do with declaring war and organizing peace. So we have two to four embassies at the beginning and at the end of the campaigning season. This does not add up to a senate frequently handling foreign envoys and their requests.

⁴⁶ Strabo 9.2.2 (401 C) writes, following Ephoros, that the Greeks emphasized education and communication while barbarians only practised bravery; the Romans began to improve in education when they came into contact with more erudite communities, thereby establishing their rule over all of them. That this reasoning implies that Romans learned diplomacy from the Greeks is a bold assumption of Dench 2005, 88 n. 164.

⁴⁷ Cf. the collection of Canali de Rossi 1997, who assembled a list of 780 Greek embassies to Rome during the republican era. Since the information often comes from inscriptions, and given that the tendency of Greek cities to set up inscriptions was more developed than that of the ancient Italian peoples, there is undoubtedly some bias in the evidence. But this is not the whole story.

⁴⁸ In the lists of Canali de Rossi 1997 we can easily check the distribution of Greek embassies to Rome over time. We find 58 embassies in the third century BC, 304 in the first half of the second century BC, 113 in the second half of the second century, 233 in the first half of the first century, and 64 from the years 49–30 BC. These figures do not tell us exactly what really happened because we have to consider that the text of Livy, who noted the arrival of several Greek embassies, breaks off in 167 BC. But I think that the picture is not completely distorted in this respect. We should accept a new dimension in the number of embassies from the moment when Rome became regularly involved in the Greek east; cf. Coudry 2004, 561; Ferrary 2007, 116. In 67 BC, a *lex Gabinia* tried to cope with the huge number of embassies by restricting their admission to senate hearings in the month of February (cf. for this law Bonnefond-Coudry 1984). In fact, there can be no doubt that the magistrates and the senate felt free to deal with embassies during other months of the year if the situation demanded immediate action; cf. Bonnefond-Coudry 1989, 329; Jehne 2009, 157f. The list of Bonnefond-Coudry 1982, 67f. with epigraphically attested dates of senate meetings with foreign envoys shows a distribution throughout the year, which is significant even if the quantity of evidence is not abundant.

required more and more time.⁴⁹ Now a Roman consular could be busy working for the *res publica* throughout the year.

Former consuls had been in existence since the consulate had been created, of course, but the formal rank of *consularis* was connected to a hierarchy in the senate. A consulship was not only a chance to command and to win renown and riches in the process, but also a ticket into a permanent status group. Being *consularis* could be felt in everyday senatorial business, when former consuls were asked regularly to speak in preference to many other senators. However, we do not know exactly when the order of *sententiae* was formalized according to rank. Livy supposes that this procedure was already established at the time of the decemvirate,⁵⁰ but this is evidently a projection of later practice onto early Rome.⁵¹ It seems reasonable to assume that the prerogative of the former consul did not develop before the praetorship was downgraded. If we accept this, we get into the period after the First Punic War, perhaps into the later part of the third century.⁵² When Fabius Buteo refilled the senate after Cannae in 216, his choices were not personal, but he followed formalized criteria.⁵³

---

⁴⁹ Cf. Bonnefond-Coudry 1989, 329–33, who resumes her investigation into the distribution of senate meetings over the year and their agendas by stating that most senatorial activities were not bound to fixed dates or periods: 'il apparaît que c'est en réalité la majeure partie des activités du Sénat qui échappe à toute périodicité, c'est-à-dire se développe tout au long de l'année' (329). But this is probably only the outcome of a longer development.

⁵⁰ Livy 3.40.8.

⁵¹ The same holds true for Dion. Hal. 6.68.1; 6.69.1; 7.21.4; 7.47.1; 10.50.4; 11.4.4 f.; 11.6.2; cf. Mommsen 1887–8, III 2, 965f., who nevertheless believes in the early prerogatives of *gentes maiores*. Furthermore, he accepts the presence of an early republican list establishing the order of precedence of the speakers participating in senatorial deliberations.

⁵² Cf. Beck 2005, 63–70; see also Bergk in this volume, pp. 61–74. A special problem is the *princeps senatus*, whose existence is perhaps connected to the development of a senate in which members were ranked in a list according to the offices which they had previously held (cf. Ryan 1998, 137 with n. 2). Ryan 1998, 137–224 analyses the whole problem and criticizes the tradition for early *principes* (like Valerius Maximus, dict. 494), but still accepts the existence of *principes* in the earlier third century (cf. also his revised list: Ryan 2003, 113). In fact, the only serious evidence for *principes* in the first half of the third century or even earlier is Plin. *HN* 7, 133, which refers to three Fabian *principes senatus* in successive order. But Ryan 1998, 173–5 argues convincingly against the *principatus* of the first one, Fabius Ambustus (cos. I 360). Thus the whole testimony is suspect, even if Ryan tries to save the rest.

⁵³ Livy 23.23.5f. This explicit emphasis on formal criteria gives us some – widely neglected – arguments concerning the old controversy over whether the senate had a *numerus clausus* or not. Since Fabius Buteo added 177 new senators to the existing ones (Livy 23.23.7) and said that he did not want to prefer thereby one man to the other (Livy 23.23.4), it would have been in contradiction to this method of choosing if he had accepted some people with the *corona civica* and consciously ignored others who had been decorated in the same way. So we can safely assume that Fabius' *lectio* did not aim at bringing the senate to a fixed number. On the contrary, the members of all the groups added up to 177 men – but we should recognize the possibility that some simple farmers who had once won the *corona civica*, but who now lived far away from Rome, were not known to the dictator. To be sure, my pleading against a *numerus clausus* does not mean that no notion of the proper size of the senate was in existence, but I do not believe in a fixed number of senators. Now Stein

He promoted at first all of the former curule magistrates who had served since the last *lectio*, then the former plebeian magistrates, and last, because he needed additional senators, soldiers with a visible record of bravery in form of spoils or the *corona civica*.[54] If Livy's report about this *lectio senatus* is reliable, we have here a clear indication of Roman consciousness that membership in the senate should be related to successful service for the community, privileging above all success in elections and constructing a formal hierarchy.[55] At this moment, the *cursus honorum* seems to have been established,[56] and it is at least probable that formalized criteria of rank were a principle not only for the recruitment of senators, but also for the internal speaking order.[57] That Fabius Buteo did not invent the recruitment of ex-magistrates is clear from Livy, who explicitly mentions that Fabius admitted men into the senate who had been curule magistrates since the last censorship.[58] From this we can safely conclude that all the previous holders of curule office had already entered the senate as a matter of course.[59] As we know, there existed a list of senators which the censors had to make anew every five years – a procedure during which they could not avoid writing down the senators in some order. In combination with the fact that a fixed career pattern had evolved at this time, it was not a big step to arrange the list according to rank. These innovative censors of the 230s or 220s created the hierarchical list which enabled the chairman of the senate meeting to call on the senators in a clear-cut order. When this practice was established, the consular was born.

2007, 142–58 has analysed the *lectio* of Buteo in a new way. He argues that there was no need for a *lectio extra ordinem* even after the many losses in the first years of the war because even a small senate worked well enough (144f.). For Stein (151), who relies on Livy's report (Livy 23.22.1–11), this unusual action is motivated by the desire to re-establish solidarity in a way other than through the incorporation of Latin notables as Sp. Carvilius Maximus had recommended; the exceptional form – the appointment of a second dictator without *magister equitum*, as well as the recall of the consul from the front line only for the nomination – was chosen to eliminate popular intervention. Stein sees Q. Fabius Maximus as the instigator of the whole operation (146f.).

[54] Livy 23.23.5f. Stein 2007, 152–6 convincingly demonstrates that most of the new senators were probably already *equites* or at any rate well off, otherwise they would not have had houses in which to expose spoils for the people to admire. But as Stein emphasizes, the criteria for selection were heavily meritocratic.

[55] Cf. Ryan 1998, 156f.; Stein 2007, 152f., 156–8, who even assumes that the censors of 214, 209, 204 and 199 continued to apply Buteo's criteria for the recruitments of new senators.

[56] But one has to admit that in Livy 23.25.5 the former magistrates are united under the heading *magistratus curules*, so unfortunately this is no clear proof of the hierarchical ranking of consulars and praetors.

[57] Cf. Ryan 1998, 155–68 for testimonies on the *locus sententiam dicendi*; cf. *ibid.* 125 n. 195.

[58] Livy 23.23.5.

[59] Cf. Ryan 1998, 160. His additional argument that Fabius Buteo could not be the father of a new regulation because he was so focused on the perfect rules of the forefathers that he would never change anything (*ibid.* 161) is probably only a joke.

That *consulares* came into being in the later third century does not necessarily imply that they mattered. Roman *consulares* never got any formal privileges other than being asked to speak in the senate before the non-consulars. When the law of 194 BC reserved special seats for senators in the theatre[60] the whole order profited from the new regulation, and there was no additional prescription that *consulares* had seats in front of their fellow senators. Thanks to the dress code, every citizen could probably identify a senator when he met one on the streets of Rome,[61] but it was impossible to say from appearance only if this senator was a consular.[62] Needless to say, this does not mean that the other senators did not respect the priority of *consulares* in contexts where there were no formalized rules, but it is important to note that only in the senate's order of *sententiae* was the prerogative of consulars clear cut. So if a consular abstained from going into the senate there was no way to manifest his special status above the other senators, or at least he could not do so before he was dead and his son also had died, so that the family could honour him with a *pompa funebris*. Then the consular father was represented by an actor wearing his death mask and the official dress of curule office and following the twelve lictors. This was the only effective way to symbolize the consulship in contrast to other curule magistracies.[63]

---

[60] For this law, see e.g. Ungern-Sternberg 1975.

[61] The *toga praetexta* and the golden ring were not the exclusive privileges of senators; cf. Scholz 2005, 417–20. In the city of Rome, the *latus clavus* was significant if it was wide enough and could not be mistaken for the *angustus clavus* of an *eques*. That we get no clear standard for the width of the *latus clavus* from the representations in sculpture should be a warning against overestimating the message sent by dress code (so rightly Bergemann 1990, 23f.; cf. also Boschung 2005, 98). Even the distinction of senatorial and patrician shoes (cf. Goette 1988, 449–64) could be misleading because it was not always applied, even in statues of the emperor (cf. again Bergemann 1990, 23f.; Boschung 2005, 98). Moreover, since these shoes were similar it was difficult to recognize a patrician senator when meeting one on the street and even impossible if the toga hid the essential laces (cf. Goette 1988, 451). However, when followed by a large retinue, a senator should have been recognized as such even if some *equites* used fairly wide *clavi*, at least if he moved around in the city and not in a municipal context where the use of senatorial insignia by the members of the local elite was widespread. But in order to be identified as a consular a senator needed to be known to some of the people in the area.

[62] In the depictions of groups of senators in visual art, there is no clue to distinguish *consulares* from other senators; the only indication of difference between the senators themselves is patrician shoes, but this is a difference of status not related to senatorial rank. Cf. Boschung 2005 (that his examples are from the early empire is no reason to doubt the relevance of his observations for the republican period).

[63] To be sure, the father was represented as a past consul, not in the context of his later activity as a leading member of the senate. Cf., for the choreography of the *pompa funebris*, Flower 1996, 97–106, who also discusses the question of whether the deceased was represented himself at his own funeral by an actor (p. 104f.). She comes to the conclusion that two pieces of evidence (Suet. Vesp. 19.2; Diod. Sic. 31.25.2) prove this to be correct. I agree, but this representation is part of

In Roman banquets, there existed the *locus consularis* as the place of the most distinguished guest at the dinner table.[64] The evidence is late[65] and tells us nothing about the starting point of this expression, but it could not have come into being before the senatorial hierarchy was firmly established, placing it in the late third or second century at the earliest. The term was not an official one, and *consularis* is more probably an adjective meaning 'the consul's place' and not a noun in the genitive meaning 'the place of the consular'.[66] Anyway, we have to admit that the individual occupying this seat was not necessarily a consular, but only the most renowned participant within the group – according to the host.

Now, what did these *consulares* do, after all? In the long run, people can only feel important when there are others who accept that they are important. Since the particular role of *consulares* was bound to the senate, this should be the place to look for consular activity of some significance. We are used to seeing the senate as the centre of Roman politics at least

---

the buffoon activity which is a strange element in the funeral ceremonies; cf. for this especially Sumi 2002. Accordingly, I do not believe that the deceased was represented in the same way as his ancestors, namely as a walking magistrate. Rather the actor emphasized the individual character of the dead person. In contrast, the opinion of Sumi (569) that actors represented five Caesars in triumphal robes at the dictator's funeral because of his five triumphs seems to suggest that the deceased was impersonated like his forefathers in the garment of his highest political honour, but Sumi's reconstruction is not convincing. He relies on Suet. *Iul.* 84.4: *deinde tibicines et scaenici artifices vestem, quam ex triumphorum instrumento ad praesentem usum induerant, detractam sibi atque discissam iniecere flammae*. From this Sumi concludes that the clothing from the triumphal equipment has to be the golden toga of the triumphator, and since there are several actors there must have been several fake triumphators. But what shall we make of the *tibicines* in this picture? It seems to be impossible that the dead Caesar was staged as a triumphator with a trumpet. It seems to be far easier to assume that they all wear things customary at a triumph – the well-known wreath included – but not the triumphator's robe, and that they were part of a theatrical performance to which Suetonius alludes (*Iul.* 84.2; Sumi 2002, 568 argued against a tragic performance at the funeral). Moreover, one of the privileges of Caesar was the right to wear the triumphal garb always and everywhere (Cass. Dio 44.4.2; App. *B Civ.* 2.106 [442]). So it is even possible that an actor who had to impersonate the deceased Caesar in his individual habitus wore this special dress as a marker of the dictator recognizable to all. Altogether, the actor playing the role of the dead did not walk in the succession of family members and did not have to follow some lictors (cf. also Mommsen 1887–8, 1, 440). The place of the deceased in the procession was in the middle, where he was carried along as a real body following his successful ancestors and preceding his surviving family members.

[64] Plut. *Mor.* 619 B; cf. Teodorsson 1989, 87f. For the arrangements at Roman dinner tables, see Stein-Hölkeskamp 2005, 101–11; Schnurbusch 2005.

[65] An additional problem is Petron. *Sat.* 65.7, where the comparable place is called *locus praetorius*. Perhaps the reason is the municipal setting of the dinner of Trimalchio. In the cities outside of Rome, an office-holder called *consul* did not exist, but *praetor* could always be used as a generic term for officials in command.

[66] Plut. *Mor.* 283A (*Quaest. Rom.* 80) gives proof of the priority of consuls at banquets. According to Plutarch, triumphators used to invite the consuls officially to their triumphal feasts and uninvited them unofficially, for a consul, if he turned up, had to get the place of honour at the table, which would normally be reserved for the triumphator on his great day.

from the middle republic onwards and the *consulares* as the leading group of the senate, not always united, of course, but determining the various collective decisions by fighting it out amongst themselves without having to be afraid of the majority of minor senators.[67] The problems of the late republic for which we have more information for everyday business are attributed at least in part to the fading influence of the senate. But if we concede that the hierarchy of offices is a relatively late development, and that the connected splitting of the senate into ranks only evolved in the 230s or even some years later, we may conclude that the status of the *consulares* as the leading group in the senate did not exist before this date. Combining this with the new analysis of Roman warfare by Bleckmann and Cornell[68] and with our estimation of senate activities until the middle of the third century, we should perhaps reduce our vision of the senate directing Roman politics to some occasional initiatives. Furthermore, we should identify the big men in this system as the peers with personal authority, which could be increased by office-holding and military success, but which was still based in familial tradition, socio-economic power and personal quality. The rise of the *consulares* as a group of leaders only happened when the senate worked almost continuously and the agenda included important decisions with great frequency.

The crisis of the Second Punic War brought some important progress for the power of the *consulares*. This seems to be a surprising development in the light of the suspension of the new rules for office-holding and the multiple consulships of some great commanders.[69] But in the new senate that Fabius Buteo had to form as a consequence of the many losses at Cannae, only a small group of experienced men were left. Many of them were absent on active duty, while only some were present in Rome. Since this senate of newcomers needed leadership as never before, it should have been a natural reaction to seek guidance from the people speaking first. Moreover, the military situation did not allow for long delays in decision-making and called for some central coordination in a new way. Last but not least, the senate had reacted in an exemplary way after Cannae, with the consequence that Rome had avoided the loss of solidarity which so often comes with defeat. Instead, the Romans recovered quickly and held

---

[67] For the status group of the *consulares* in the Ciceronian era, cf. now Whitehead 2005 (with some examples showing their influence).
[68] Cf. Bleckmann 2002; Cornell 2004.
[69] Cf., for iteration of the consulship and especially the exceptional situation of the Second Punic War, Beck 2005, 96–105. For the *lex* of 217 suspending restrictions on iteration and continuation of office, cf. Beck 2005, 49–51; Elster 2003, 197f.

Hannibal at bay.⁷⁰ So it seems to be a logical consequence that the senate was held in high esteem after managing this crisis, and that the many junior senators stuck with the *consulares*.

After the Second Punic War we have a new situation for *consulares*. While, during the war, losses had created fairly good career prospects for new men to rise to the praetorship, the dramatic increase in competition for office after the war⁷¹ produced and reinforced some rules for the *cursus honorum*. The losers were the most promising and successful members of the political class. We have only to look at Scipio Africanus and Flamininus. Age prescriptions for office, fixed for a long time in the *lex Villia annalis* of 180, but begun earlier, forced younger stars to wait, and barriers to repetitions of the consulate, leading to a total prohibition probably in 151, generated new strategies among the former consuls. The years in high office of even the most successful *nobiles* started to drop in the second century, averaging at about four years in the first century.⁷² Of the 102 consuls between 200 and 151 BC,⁷³ ten served a second term, one a third. This means that the figures for consuls who iterated the high office in the second century were roughly equal to those in the third century, that is, *c.* 10 per cent of all office-holders (the great wars against Pyrrhus and Carthage notwithstanding).⁷⁴ The interesting point is that in the first half of the second century, there was no resort to the iteration of successful commanders during great wars any more, and for the biggest cluster of iterations in the 150s we find no close relation to military crisis.⁷⁵ Prorogation was a suitable enough method of

---

⁷⁰ The reactions of the senate immediately after getting the first news from the disaster: Livy 22.55.1–8; Polyb. 3.118.7–9; the demonstration of solidarity when the surviving consul C. Terentius Varro came home: Livy 22.61.14f.; Plut. *Fab.* 18, 4f. Cf. Seibert 1993, 205–11.

⁷¹ For competition in elections, see the impressive lists of candidates in Evans 1991.

⁷² I calculate one year as a *praetor* with one year of prorogation as a provincial commander and one year as consul and another year in the provinces. There could, of course, be longer prorogations, and occasionally someone succeeded in becoming consul more than once. But my reckoning should provide a good average. Compare with this figures for the years in office of Curius Dentatus above. To be sure, career prospects in the second century were different from those in the third, not so much for mediocre but for outstanding consulars.

⁷³ We have two more because in 162 the consuls had to abdicate, but nevertheless the term was counted when they won the consulship for the second time (cf. below, n. 75).

⁷⁴ Cf. the calculations of Beck 2005, 96–105.

⁷⁵ We have second consulships for C. Popillius Laenas in 158, C. Marcius Figulus in 156, P. Cornelius Scipio Nasica Corculum and M. Claudius Marcellus in 155, and a third consulship for the same Marcellus in 152. Since Marcius Figulus and Scipio Nasica both had to abdicate from their first consulships in 162 because of some fault with the auspices, their second consulships are more or less compensations for the disappointing firsts. So there remains a real second term only for the great Popillius Laenas, where we find no connection with war, and three consulships for M. Marcellus, who indeed went to war: in 155, he won a triumph over the Ligurians; in 152 he had to cope with the crisis in Spain, but was not equally successful. All in all, the need for experienced military commanders is no tight-fitting explanation for iterations after the Second Punic War.

ensuring that an experienced commander could bring a war to an end, but it was no remedy against the hazards of command when new wars broke out.

In the same period, senatorial business grew dramatically. I have already mentioned the proliferation of foreign embassies from Greece, which reached a peak in the first half of the second century. The Roman strategy of not establishing direct rule in the Greek east in spite of military victories seems to have given a special push to the rise of senatorial power. For this political structure of incertitude resulted in a plethora of embassies to the city.[76] The only governing body suited for dealing with the requests of these delegations was the senate,[77] which as a result was able to develop new means of further influencing and controlling foreign policy. An important consequence was that meetings had to be summoned more frequently to cope with these additional tasks. The envoys wanted to enhance their opportunity of obtaining a favourable decision, so they courted senators for support. By this reciprocal service, relations of patronage were established and deepened, and senators felt more important than before, no doubt enjoying the sweet tongues of Greek petitioners. And since no embassy could try to win hundreds of senators over to their case in private interviews, envoys had to go for the men with clout. The speaking order within the senate was the obvious line of orientation for outsiders not so well informed about the details of personal power in Rome, so busy envoys would try to get a hearing with *consulares*. Thus, the morning salutations of Roman senators got more crowded, but it was especially the *consulares* who could count not only on the regular attendance of their own clients, but also on that of foreign envoys, perhaps accompanied by their Roman patrons, looking to court the big men.[78]

Foreign embassies and foreign policy were not the only business which demanded the attention of the senate, although it was an important area and probably the most renowned sphere of senatorial activity. The supposed dictum of Pyrrhus' envoy Cineas that the senate seemed to be an assembly of many kings to him[79] was perhaps an estimation even better

---

[76] Cf., for the sophisticated Roman procedure of welcoming foreign ambassadors which seems to have been established in this time, Coudry 2004. Those detailed prescriptions for single steps in a fixed order only make sense when there were a lot of embassies arriving in Rome.

[77] The Greek alternative would have been to bring all these embassies before the people. That Rome dealt with all diplomatic business in the senate is clearly an aristocratic element of the Roman constitution, as Polybius observed (6.13.7–9; cf. Ferrary 2007, 114).

[78] An impressive example of the regular attendance at the morning *salutationes* in Rome is provided by an inscription for two ambassadors from Teos who acted on behalf of the Tean foundation Abdera; cf. for the text Eilers 2002, C 101 (238f.), ll. 21–6. Cf. also Livy 45.20.10.

[79] Plut. *Pyrrh.* 19.6; cf. Flor. 1, 13, 20. Cf. Ferrary 2007, 116.

suited to the second century.⁸⁰ Now it became customary for senatorial embassies to go out to assist – and control – the commander in organizing territories overseas after victorious wars.⁸¹ Senatorial legates were dispersed all over the Mediterranean world to inspect, regulate, and deliver letters and orders of the senate.⁸² To the eyes of foreign communities, the Roman senate ruled the world. Because of the right to decide on prorogations of command which the senate had safely in hand,⁸³ consuls and proconsuls were constantly reminded not to forget the senate at home. And in the senate, the order of speakers was established according to rank, so that *consulares* had the opportunity to form opinions and to sketch lines of compromise which left little to say and to do for the lower ranks.⁸⁴

It is time to summarize. In order to get into a position of leadership, the *consulares* had to climb to the top of the senate, and the senate needed some interesting and important tasks to discuss and to decide upon to make regular attendance worthwhile to its members. Fortunately, we have some tools with which to date the splitting of the senate into ranks by analysing the development of careers in Rome and the formation of a fixed order of magistracies. As I have tried to make clear, walking in the footsteps of Hans Beck and Alexander Bergk, the formal rank of *consulares* at the top of the senate seems to have been established in the late third century.

From the second century on, the military career of a Roman senator usually ended after the consulship (men like Marius being extreme exceptions). This group of healthy, successful men, not able to prove their military capacities any more, came into being at about the same time as the senate became more significant and it ceased to be acceptable for Roman nobles to live on their estates and allow others to conduct public business. So the transfer of energy to the field of senatorial politics was an interesting alternative for *consulares* – *faute de mieux*. The influence of

---

⁸⁰ Cf. also 1 Macc. 8.14–16 for the praise of the senate as the governing body of Rome.
⁸¹ We hear of this institution, the sending of senatorial *decem legati* for reorganization after war, for the first time in 241 BC (when it was perhaps all new; cf. Schleussner 1978, 9 n. 2), then again after the Second Punic War in 202. It became standard in the second century. Cf. for these embassies Canali de Rossi 2000, nos. 37 (241 BC), 57 (202 BC), 62 (196 BC), 72 (188 BC), 115 (167 BC), 134 (154 BC), 148 (146 BC), 149 (146 BC). There are others in the late republic.
⁸² Of the 166 Roman embassies which Canali de Rossi 2000 collected from the time of the kings to 60 BC, 82 are dated to the period from 200 to 151 BC (nos. 58–140).
⁸³ As the term makes perfectly clear, *prorogationes* were originally granted by the popular assemblies; cf. Kloft 1977, II, 47–56, who argues that prorogations by the senate alone, without any popular participation, became standard procedure only in the second century. As the documentation of Beck 2005, 106–12 points out, prorogations were rare till the Second Punic War.
⁸⁴ Ryan 1998, 126–33 showed that even *tribunicii* and *quaestorii* spoke in the senate now and then, which is interesting enough. But I am still convinced that it was, usually, the *consulares* who more or less shaped opinion.

consulares depended on the influence of the senate as an institution and on the regular opportunity to decide not only on petty problems. The senate's right to handle important questions grew out of the great wars, in which there were several theatres of war where different Roman commanders and armies had to operate. To solve the problem of determining whom to send where, the senate became the centre for overall, strategic decision-making, even if *provinciae* of magistrates of equal rank were sorted out by lot.[85] With the regular use of prorogation in the late third and second centuries, senatorial support became more important for consuls who wanted to stay in command.[86] In addition to that, the mass of embassies from foreign communities increased dramatically in the second century when Rome expanded into the Greek east, where this form of diplomacy was well established. So in this period it was more and more interesting and important for a Roman aristocrat to be a leading member of the senate and to pose regularly as a powerful man who could – to cite Cicero's characterization of the *princeps senatus* Aemilius Scaurus at the end of the century – nearly rule the world by a nod.[87] The *consulares* of the second century found in this form of senatorial activity a form of compensation for their lost position as army leaders.

Since many of these *consulares* now focused on influencing Roman politics via senatorial decrees, the city of Rome became even more important for Roman political life than it had been before. The *consulares* were so successful in making the senate (and the law courts and the assemblies!) the centre of politics that it became a risk to be absent from Rome, even if the reason for absence was military service. At the same time, because the plebs of Rome did not serve in the legions any more, good rhetorical entertainment in the city began to rival scars from the battlefield as a method of obtaining political recognition. As a consequence, from the end of the second century on, younger Romans tended to stay in Rome to further their careers by lobbying there instead of losing time in military service abroad under the command of a consul or proconsul.[88] The result of this

---

[85] Cf., for the origin of the practice of distributing *provinciae* by lot, Bunse 2002a.

[86] Cf. the example of T. Quinctius Flamininus in 197, who activated his relatives and friends to squeeze a prorogation out of the senate (Polyb. 18.10.7; 18.11.2; Livy 32.32.7; Plut. *Flam.* 7.3); cf. Pfeilschifter 2005, 327–31.

[87] Cic. *Font.* 24: *M. Aemilio Scauro... cuius... nutu prope terrarum orbis regebatur.* Cf., for this powerful figure, Bates 1986.

[88] Cf. the fate of Ti. Gracchus, who lost ground in his competition with Sp. Postumius because Postumius remained in Rome and practised in the law courts while Gracchus embarked on his military service; Plut. *Ti. Gracch.* 8.6.

victory of the *consulares* over the *consules* was a decreasing world of Roman politics as the other side of an increasing Roman empire.

Thus, the question of how the highly competitive Romans succeeded in forming something like a common foreign policy without depending too much on the ambitions of various governors looking for spectacular military action may be answered by looking at the role of *consulares*. The former consuls usually could not increase their rank much more, even within their own family trees, so they were free to look after the interests of the *res publica*.

CHAPTER 11

Privata hospitia, beneficia publica? *Consul(ar)s, local elite and Roman rule in Italy*

Michael P. Fronda

Livy 42.1 preserves an anecdote that says a great deal about the interaction between Roman consuls (and consulars) and local Italian aristocrats. In 173,[1] the consul Lucius Postumius Albinus departed for Campania to resolve a dispute over the boundaries between public and private lands, and along the way he stayed over at Praeneste. Before arriving, he had sent word ahead demanding that the local magistrates come out to greet him. He stipulated that he should be housed and entertained at public expense, and he further ordered the Praenestines to prepare pack animals for his trip to Campania. Livy claims that Postumius made these high-handed demands because he was angry at the Praenestines for failing to show him appropriate respect when previously, as a private citizen, he had gone to sacrifice at the temple of Fortuna. Livy condemns Postumius for abusing his consular authority and he concludes that the locals, who appear to have accepted Postumius' demands without incident, must have acquiesced out of modesty or fear; Livy's assessment is not implausible.

This episode highlights the tensions and the ambiguities inherent in the relationship between Rome and the allied communities in Italy during the republican period. On the one hand, the Italian allies were subject to Roman hegemony, and many had been forced into alliance with Rome as the result of military defeat. The occasional arrival of a Roman consul or any other high magistrate, especially one possessing *imperium*, demanding preferential treatment and public or private gestures of deference, must have reinforced this reality. Indeed, Postumius' anger at his earlier treatment at Praeneste suggests that Roman aristocrats had grown to expect deferential treatment when they visited Italian communities even when not holding public office. On the other hand, Roman and local aristocratic families often shared close personal and familial bonds. In fact, in the same passage in which he describes the Postumius affair, Livy comments on how

[1] All dates are BC unless otherwise noted.

Roman senators and local aristocrats commonly enjoyed mutual hospitality (*hospitium*), with senators opening their homes to guests (members of the Italian elite) in whose houses they would in turn stay when outside of Rome. Moreover, this example demonstrates that it made good practical sense for local elites to forge strong personal bonds with members of the Roman elite and continue to reaffirm those bonds, since, as Postumius' abusive behavior shows, failing to do so could have serious consequences.

This paper will examine the nature and consequences of the personal and familial bonds between Roman and local (that is, Italian) elites. We will not focus, however, on whether or not local elites were motivated to forge ties with their Roman counterparts in order to earn Roman citizenship and thus be incorporated into the Roman political hierarchy. Rather, the topic will be approached from a different perspective, which will reveal how local elites used their associations with the great Roman noble houses and with individual Roman magistrates, especially with those wielding *imperium*, to advance their own political standing at the local level. Roman consuls and consulars, the individuals most typically associated with the power of *imperium* and frequently the most prestigious Roman aristocrats, were key players in this dynamic. Public favors bestowed by Roman consuls and consulars upon their friends (local elite individuals and families) strengthened the political power of the latter, thus altering the local political landscape. Exploring this dynamic from the Italian perspective will shed new light on the nature of Roman–Italian relations and, ultimately, Roman hegemony in Italy.

Roman magistrates with *imperium*, primarily consuls and dictators, but also praetors and promagistrates, possessed truly awesome power vis-à-vis the Italian elite. Consuls in particular had almost unlimited military and administrative authority, including the power of life and death, within their provinces.[2] Although the senate reserved the right to declare war or peace and to ratify treaties, in practical terms the senate would often have relied on input from the general in the field when deliberating, and any decisions that the commander made in the field would have greatly shaped the final post-war settlement imposed upon defeated Italian communities.[3] In times of crisis, such as when an Italian city was first conquered by the Romans, or if it revolted, or underwent some sort of political disruption that attracted the attention of the Romans, this magistrate held the fate of

---

[2] Polyb. 6.12.5–8.
[3] Eckstein 1987, xi–xxii, 319–24. Eckstein argues that the senate exercised greater control over magistrates and foreign affairs in provinces closer to Rome, but even in northern Italy "there was room for important individual initiative" (p. xii).

a local community in his hands, and his decisions could have grave consequences: he could execute members of the local aristocracy, redistribute property, enslave the local population, and he was often granted broad discretion to act as he saw fit while on the spot. For example, the senate sent both consuls of 303, Lucius Genucius Aventinensis and Servius Cornelius Lentulus, to investigate the Frusinates, who were implicated in a revolt by the Hernici. The result of their investigation, Livy tells us unapologetically: the Frusinates were mulcted of one third of their territory, and the alleged ringleaders of the conspiracy were scourged and beheaded.[4] Similarly, in 265 a consular army under the command of Quintus Fabius Maximus Gurges was sent to suppress some sort of political disturbance in Volsinii, where members of the freedman class had gotten a hold of all the land and taken control of all magistracies.[5] Volsinii was besieged; the men who had seized the magistracies were executed, the city was razed, and the surviving Volsinian citizens were resettled at a new site. Zonaras states explicitly that the consul oversaw the executions and destruction of the city.[6] It must be stressed that a Roman general wielding *imperium* was likely the most powerful figure with whom an Italian community would come into contact, for his decisions and actions could literally remake a conquered city.

Any holder of *imperium* would have been a fearsome figure for a local ruling class to deal with. When Italy was the main theater of Roman warfare and conquest, however, it was mainly the consuls, as Rome's primary war leaders, and occasionally former consuls (proconsuls and dictators), who brought this power to bear against Italian communities during times of conflict. In fact the *imperium* of the dictator, to which even the consuls were subject, was limited to Italy.[7] Therefore, this most powerful of offices was conceived of, or at least came to be defined as, one dealing exclusively with Italian affairs, chief among which was conducting war against dangerous enemies in Italy. It was also regularly stipulated that dictators be former

---

[4] Livy 10.1.3.
[5] Zonar. 8.7; Livy, *Per.* 16; Val. Max. 8.1. ext. 2; Flor. 1.16; Oros. 4.53; *De vir. ill.* 36.1–2; John of Antioch fr. 50 (= *FHG* 4.557).
[6] According to Zonaras (8.7), Q. Fabius Maximus Gurges was mortally wounded during the siege, but he later states that the consul, unnamed, scourged to death the freedmen and destroyed the city. The anonymous *De viris illustribus* (36.2) says that Decius Mus was the consul sent to suppress the disturbance. Mus was probably sent as suffect consul and it is he, therefore, who oversaw the punishment of the Volsinians. See Broughton 1951–86, 1, 201–2.
[7] The office was apparently so powerful that it was more limited with regard to length of office and geographic scope than the consulship. In only one case before the age of Sulla was a dictator assigned outside of Italy, when Aelius Atilius Calatinus was sent to Sicily in 249. Cass. Dio 36.34.2–3; Livy, *Per.* 19; Zonar. 8.15; *Fast. Cap.*; see also Flor. 1.18.12; Broughton 1951–86, 1, 215.

consuls themselves,[8] though there were cases in which this rule was ignored. Indeed, of the sixty-five triumphs awarded between 361 and 264, fifty-five were celebrated by consuls, four by proconsuls, and six by dictators, all of whom were former consuls. In other words, all of these triumphs were celebrated by consuls or consulars, underscoring the centrality of the consulship with regard to Roman–Italian relations in the fourth and third centuries. During this period of conquest, consuls and consulars would have served as an important link or point of contact between the Roman senate and the Italian elite. Indeed, one can imagine that in some cases "first contact" was the arrival of a consul at the head of a Roman army, met by a delegation of local aristocrats.

Between 264 and 218 most of Rome's fighting took place outside of the Italian peninsula. Hannibal's invasion and the subsequent revolts of many of Rome's subject allies turned Italy once more into a militarized zone, but for more than a century after the Second Punic War the peninsula, with the exception of Liguria and Cisalpine Gaul, ceased to be a theater of war. Yet even as Rome extended its hegemony overseas, Italian communities still found themselves subject to the *imperium* of Roman magistrates, and consuls and consulars continued to be sent to deal with problems throughout Italy. For example, in 175 the senate sent the consul M. Aemilius Lepidus to suppress some sort of political disturbance in Patavium.[9] During the famous, though nebulous, suppression of the Bacchanalia in 186, the consuls Spurius Postumius Albinus and Quintus Marcius Philippus spent much of their terms investigating the cult.[10] According to Livy's admittedly problematic account, the consuls conducted investigations and held trials not only in Rome but also throughout Italy.[11] As mentioned at the beginning of this paper, the consul Lucius Postumius Albinus (173) was on his way to Campania to settle a land dispute when he stopped at Praeneste and ordered the local population to supply him with lodging, entertainment and pack animals.[12] Livy concludes the episode by claiming that the consul's actions set an unfortunate precedent for subsequent magistrates, who placed ever more burdensome demands on the Italians.[13] Livy implies, therefore, that Roman magistrates frequently imposed themselves on Italian communities, which in turn were too frightened of their power to deny them. Indeed, in the same year that Postumius cowed the Praenestines, the censor Quintus Fulvius Flaccus (cos. 179) stripped the roof tiles from the temple of Juno Lacinia, near Croton, in order to use them in

---

[8] Livy 2.18.5.　[9] Livy 41.27.3–4.　[10] Livy 39.8–20; Val. Max. 6.3.7; *CIL* I² 581.
[11] Livy 39.18.1–3, 7; 39.19.1; 39.20.1; 39.23.3.　[12] Livy 42.1.6–7.　[13] Livy 42.1.12.

the construction of the temple of Fortuna Equestris. The local population was too frightened to stop him because of his power as censor (*auctoritate censoria*).[14]

Still, consuls in the second century remained primarily war leaders who tended to exercise *imperium* away from Rome's subject allies in Italy. To be sure, in the first half of the second century the peninsula north of the Po River was a militarized zone, and Liguria and Cisalpine Gaul were frequently consular or proconsular *provinciae*.[15] However, consuls less frequently dealt with problems south of the Po, except in highly unusual circumstances. Livy's introduction to the Bacchanalia affair underscores this: the events of 186 "diverted the consuls from the army and the administration of wars and provinces to the suppression of internal conspiracy."[16] Such a perceived serious crisis warranted the attention of the consuls, but their normal realm was foreign affairs and especially war. In their place, lesser magistrates *cum imperio* played a more prominent role in Italian affairs. In 190, for example, the praetor P. Iunius Brutus was ordered to raise an army to serve against the Etruscans (*in Tuscos*), while his colleague M. Tuccius was given a large force to hold Apulia and Bruttium (*ad Apuliam Bruttiosque obtinendos*); both were prorogued in 189.[17] Praetors or propraetors also held *provinciae* south of the Po in 187, 185, 184, 181, 180 and 172.[18] L. Licinius Lucullus (pr. 104) was given command against a slave revolt in Italy.[19] Praetors took over the investigations into the Bacchanalia, which, as we have seen, were initially assigned to the consuls.[20] Perhaps most tellingly: when Fregellae revolted (*c.* 125), it was destroyed by the praetor L. Opimius.[21] This is in sharp contrast to the revolt of Falerii in 241, which was suppressed by both of the consuls for that year, and for which both celebrated triumphs.[22] This highlights the degree to which Italy

---

[14] Livy 42.3.1–5.
[15] Consuls/proconsuls were assigned Gaul and/or Liguria in 197, 196, 195, 194, 193, 192, 191, 190, 188, 187, 186, 185, 184, 183, 182, 181, 180, 179, 178, 177, 176, 175, 173, 172, 171, 170, 169, 167, 166, 159 and 158.
[16] Livy 39.8.1: *consules ab exercitu bellorumque et provinciarum cura ad intestinae coniurationis vindictam avertit*.
[17] Livy 37.2.1, 6, 9; 37.50.13; 38.36.1. The reason an army was raised against the Etruscans is never explained. The previous year troops had been stationed in Bruttium and in the vicinity of Tarentum and Brundisium to guard the coast (Livy 36.2.7), which may explain M. Tuccius' mission. See Broughton 1951–86, I, 356, 362–3.
[18] All of these *provinciae* were in southern Italy: Apulia, Bruttium or the vicinity of Tarentum.
[19] Diod. Sic. 36.2; the revolt probably took place in Capua, but the text is not explicit.
[20] Livy 39.41.6; 40.19.9–11.
[21] Livy, *Per.* 60; Vell. Pat. 2.6.4; Val. Max. 2.8.4; for further references see Broughton 1951–86, I, 510.
[22] Zonar. 8.18; *Act. Tr.* (recording the two triumphs *de Falisceis*); Livy, *Per.* 20; Val. Max. 6.5.1; Eutr. 2.28; Oros. 4.11.5–10.

moved from being a consular prerogative to an area of administration that could be dealt with by an *imperium*-holder of lesser rank, even in times of war. The ramifications of this transformation will be discussed at the end of this paper, but for now it is enough simply to take note of it.

Thus far we have focused on conflictual interaction between Italians and Roman aristocrats, especially magistrates *cum imperio*. Yet not all dealings between Roman and local aristocrats were hostile. Rather, a wide range of personal relationships and connections bound members of the Roman and Italian ruling classes. Formal guest-friendship (*hospitium, xenia, proxenia*) between Roman and Italian elite families was a long-standing and widespread practice.[23] Looking again at the Postumius-Praeneste affair, Livy claims that *hospitium* between Roman and Italian elite families was common.[24] In a later passage, he talks about a certain Lucius Rammius of Brundisium, who in 172 was allegedly approached by Perseus of Macedon to poison a number of prominent Romans.[25] Rammius was chosen for this plot because "[he] was a leading citizen (*princeps*) of Brundisium, and he entertained in *hospitium* all Roman generals and ambassadors, as well as distinguished individuals from foreign lands, especially royalty."[26] The brother of Q. Fabius Maximus Rullianus (cos. 310) had been educated in the house of family friends (*apud hospites*) in Caere,[27] while Cicero mentions that the father of one of his clients, Sextus Roscius, a leading citizen of Ameria in Umbria, maintained "not only *hospitium* but also private relations and intimacy with the Metelli, Servilii and Scipiones."[28] Ti. Sempronius Gracchus (cos. 215, 213) shared *hospitium* with a certain high-ranking Lucanian named Flavus.[29] On two identical inscriptions from Interamna, local aristocrats Quintus and Caius Poppeius take credit for

---

[23] Guest-friendship between elite individuals, *hospitium privatum*, involved the mutual obligation to provide hospitality, accommodation and other forms of assistance. Depending on the social status of the two partners, *hospitium* could take on aspects of a patron–client relationship. The bond of *hospitium* was hereditary, shared by the descendants of the original *hospites*, and the relationship could only be dissolved by a formal declaration. See Patterson 2006, 140–3; Wagner-Hasel 1998.
[24] Livy 42.1.10–11.
[25] Livy 42.17. He is called Erennios (Ἐρέννιος) in the parallel account of Appian (*Mac.* 11.7–8), and appears to be the same individual as Gaios Dazoupos Rennios of Brundisium (Γαῖος Δάζουπος Ῥέννιος Βρεντεσινὸς) mentioned in an inscription found at Dodona (Cauer² no. 247); see Roberts 1881, 113–15; Giles 1887, 170.
[26] Livy 42.17.3: *Princeps Brundisi Rammius fuit; hospitioque et duces Romanos omnes et legatos, exterarum quoque gentium insignes, praecipue regios, accipiebat.*
[27] Livy 9.36.2–3. Livy's sources record different names for the consul's brother: Marcus, Caeso or Gaius.
[28] Cic. *Rosc. Am.* 15: *Nam cum Metellis, Serviliis, Scipionibus erat ei non modo hospitium verum etiam domesticus usus et consuetudo.*
[29] Livy 25.16.5–6.

building a local bath-house meant to serve townsmen, colonists and *hospitibus adventoribus*.³⁰ As a final example, there is the famous bronze *tessera hospitalis* from Trasacco, in the territory of the Marsi. It is in the shape of a ram's head cut in half lengthwise, and inscribed with the word HOSPES and two names: T. Staiodus N. f. and Titus Manlius M. f. The former is a local aristocrat, the latter possibly Titus Manlius Torquatus (cos. 235, 224).³¹ If so, the *tessera* attests to a formal bond of *hospitium* between a Roman consular and a local elite household.

Sometimes the bond between Roman and local elite could be further strengthened by intermarriage, at least when members of the local community possessed *conubium*. The most famous example of this comes from Capua, where the highest magistracy, the office of *meddix tuticus*, was held in 216 by Pacuvius Calavius, who was related by marriage to the Claudii and Livii.³² This does not appear to have been an unusual occurrence, as Livy states that marriage had "mixed together a great many distinguished and powerful [Campanian] families with the Roman,"³³ suggesting that the practice was widespread among the Campanian aristocracy. Indeed, Livy (26.33.3) mentions that there were many Capuans and Romans who were linked by marriage (*adfinitatibus*) and by blood relations (*propinquis cognationibus*) that resulted from their possession of *conubium*. He later notes (26.34.3) that when a number of Capuan aristocratic families were sold into slavery, the Romans exempted daughters who had married outside of their paternal household (*enupsissent*), either into loyalist Capuan families or into families from other communities, including presumably Rome. There is no reason to believe that Livy exaggerates the extent of Roman–Capuan intermarriage; a century of *conubium* must have produced more than a handful of marriages.³⁴ Moreover, other *cives sine suffragio* and the citizens of Latin colonies had the right to contract marriage with Roman citizens.

---

³⁰ *CIL* I² 1903: *Q. C. Poppaeei Q. f. patron.* | *municipi et coloniai* | *municipibus coloneis incoleis* | *hospitibus adventoribus* | *lavationem in perpetuom de* | *sua pecunia dant.* ("Quintus Poppaeus and Gaius Poppaeus, sons of Quintus, patrons of the *municipium* and *colonia*, gave out of their own money a permanent bathing-room to the townsmen, colonists, residents, *hospites* and visitors").

³¹ *CIL* I² 1764 = *ILLRP* 1066; see Barnabei 1895; Letta & D'Amato 1975, 216–17; Patterson 2006: 141.

³² Livy 23.2.5–6.

³³ Livy 23.4.7: *multas familias claras ac potentis Romanis miscuerat*. Pacuvius Calavius may have been related to Appius Claudius Pulcher (cos. 212) and Marcus Livius Salinator (cos. 219): Lazenby 1978, 89; Frederiksen 1984, 232.

³⁴ Livy's references in 26.33–4 to Capuan–Roman intermarriage are located in his discussion of the senatorial debate and acts concerning the fate of Capua after its recapture during the Second Punic War. Livy claims that punishment was meted out on a family-by-family basis, with too many decrees for it to be worth mentioning all of them (26.34.2), implying again that there were many more specific cases than those highlighted in his narrative. These acts may have been available in Cicero's day: see Cic. *Leg. agr.* 2.88; Fronda 2007, 97 n. 39.

It is safe to conclude that Roman aristocrats were bound by marriage ties to local elites in many other communities throughout Italy.[35]

At other times the ties between Roman and Italian elites were less formal than *hospitium* or marriage. Thus, for example, in 277 a group of aristocrats from Croton planned to hand their city over to the Roman consul P. Cornelius Rufinus; Zonaras (8.6.2) refers to the aristocrats from Croton as "friends" (ἐπιτήδειοι) of the consul. During the Second Punic War, the Roman garrison commander in Tarentum, Gaius Livius, was caught off guard by a plot by some Tarentine aristocrats to betray the city to Hannibal because he had grown friendly with some of the conspirators and frequently banqueted "with his intimates" (μετὰ τῶν συνήθων), presumably including local aristocrats.[36] Such friendships and amicable interactions must have become more numerous over time. Sallust speaks of Roman nobles of the second century who were influential among the allies (*potentes apud socios*) or who had friends (*amicos*) among the Latins and Italian allies.[37] Finally, according to Appian, on the eve of the Social War the senate dispatched individual Roman aristocrats to specific Italian cities with which each man was μάλιστα ἐπιτηδείους, in order to determine the causes and the nature of the unrest.[38] The words μάλιστα ἐπιτηδείους are probably best rendered as "most suitable," but could also mean "very friendly," as it is clear that the senate chose men because they had first-hand knowledge of and/or friends or other personal connections in the Italian cities to which they were sent. The context also implies that such connections were prevalent.[39]

Between the fourth and first centuries there was an array of both formal and informal friendly bonds between Roman and Italian aristocrats, which appear to have become more numerous over time. Consuls did not have a monopoly on these relationships. However, as the examples cited above indicate, consuls and consular families feature prominently in Roman–Italian aristocratic intermarriage, informal friendships and formal *hospitium*. This makes sense given the role of the consuls in foreign policy

---

[35] According to Diodorus Siculus (37.15.2), when the Roman army under Marius faced a Marsic army in 90, the soldiers on both sides recognized many friends and relatives by intermarriage. The anecdote is mentioned only by Diodorus, but if it is accurate, it is evidence for the extent of Roman–Italian intermarriage by the time of the Social War.

[36] Polyb. 8.24.4–30.12, esp. 8.25.5–7, 8.27.1–7. Polybius' entire account of the plot to betray Tarentum assumes a good deal of friendly interaction between the Roman garrison commander and his officers and members of the Tarentine aristocracy.

[37] Sall. *Iug.* 8.1; 40.2.

[38] App. *B Civ.* 1.38: ὡς δ'ἐπύθοντο, περιέπεμπον ἐς τὰς πόλεις ἀπὸ σφῶν τοὺς ἑκάστοις μάλιστα ἐπιτηδείους, ἀφανῶς τὰ γιγνόμενα ἐξετάζειν.

[39] See also Diod. Sic. 37.15.2.

and war-making: during the period of the conquest of Italy the consuls would have been in the best position to forge relationships with members of local ruling classes. By the late republic some of the links between certain Roman consular and Italian families would have been among the oldest and perhaps strongest of the many Roman–Italian aristocratic associations.

Up to this point we have discussed two contradictory modes of Roman–Italian aristocratic interaction, and how these two modes were embodied by Roman magistrates *cum imperio* (especially consuls) who both inflicted savage punishments on and formed close personal bonds with Italian aristocrats even within the same communities. We will now look more closely at the intersection of Roman foreign policy, magisterial power and Roman–Italian aristocratic relations, and its consequences for local politics.

The degree to which Roman foreign policy was highly personal and individualized cannot be stressed enough. Roman diplomacy under the republic remained relatively primitive and amateur: there were no professional diplomatic corps or permanent embassies in foreign states, communications were limited, and the intelligence on which to base policy decisions was limited and often not up-to-date.[40] Frequently the Roman senate had little idea what was going on in other states, even those close to home and within Italy.[41] Given these constraints, the senate had to rely on the advice and expertise of individuals who supposedly had particular knowledge of given Italian communities. Roman *nobiles* with personal connections to local communities were liable, therefore, to be sought as ambassadors or information gatherers.[42] In other cases, the senate relied on the magistrate in the field to "make the call" regarding local communities, generally accepting their firsthand knowledge and recommendations regarding the situation. Interstate relations and foreign policy functioned, therefore, through individuals; it was highly personal and highly individual. And, as we have seen, the perceptions and decisions of individual Roman aristocrats, especially those wielding *imperium*, could have devastating results for a local community.

It clearly behooved the Italians to seek the favor of those individual Roman aristocrats who potentially controlled their destiny. As such, we

---

[40] For the primitive nature of Roman diplomacy, see Eckstein 1987, xviii–xix; Eckstein 2007, 121.

[41] For example, when Sp. Postumius Albinus (cos. 186) returned to Rome after investigating the Bacchanalia, he reported that he found the colonies of Buxentum and Sipontum to be abandoned (Livy 39.23.3–4). The senate was apparently unaware of the situation otherwise.

[42] See Caes. *B Gall.* 1.47; Marcus Mettius was selected as an ambassador to Ariovistus because he enjoyed guest-friendship (*hospitio utebatur*) with the German king. Personal connection to a foreign state or region was a criterion for diplomatic and military appointments in both classical Athens and Sparta: Mitchell 1997, 73–110.

would thus expect to find examples of local aristocrats – individuals, families or other groups – approaching the Roman senate or even specific magistrates in order to win them over and thus gain protection for themselves and/or their communities. Indeed, the sources are replete with examples of such appeals.

Thus, in 319 the consul Lucius Papirius Cursor was about to invest the city of Satricum, when "two factions" (*duae factiones*) of local aristocrats, the one that had been in favor of defection and the other that had been steadfastly loyal, both attempted to win over the consul by offering him their services.[43] In 318 the Samnites sent a delegation to Rome to renew a truce; when the senate rejected their initial request, the envoys went around and appealed directly to individual Roman aristocrats, and thereby gained a two-year renewal.[44] Even if the Livian accounts of these two fourth-century events contain a good bit of literary embellishment, both assume that personal appeals between aristocrats were a part of interstate relations. One final fourth-century example shows an appeal by a local elite family: in 302 the Romans responded to the Cilnii, a powerful family (*genus praepotens*) in Arretium, who were threatened by some sort of local disturbance. In response the Romans sent the dictator M. Valerius Maximus Corvus, who according to Livy celebrated a triumph over the Arretines.[45] But Livy also reports that some of his sources say that the dictator reconciled the Cilnian family with the "plebs." The context of the passage suggests that the Cilnii remained in power. Whatever the exact nature of the affair, it appears that the family called on the Romans for military assistance and benefited from the final settlement. When P. Cornelius Rufinus' ἐπιτήδειοι from Croton approached him in 277, they surely invoked their friendship. In 265 it was an appeal by the citizens of Volsinii (surely leading citizens) that convinced the Roman senate to send a consular army to suppress a local political disturbance.[46] During the Second Punic War, a certain Nicias of Engyion in Sicily made a personal appeal to M. Claudius Marcellus and saved the lives of his fellow townsmen; Marcellus also rewarded Nicias with an estate and gifts.[47] Although this took place in Sicily, similar appeals must

---

[43] Livy 9.16.2–10.
[44] Livy 9.20.1–3. Livy claims that the Samnites sought to renew a treaty (*foedere renovando*) but gained only a two-year truce (*indutiae biennii*). The Samnites probably sought a renewal of the truce made after the Caudine Forks, and thus Livy's reference to a *foedus* is an error: Forsythe 2005, 300–1; Fronda 2006, 398–9 n. 4 *contra* Salmon 1929, 13; Crawford 1973, 2 n. 10; Oakley 1997–2005, III, 263–4 n. 2.
[45] Livy 10.3.1–2, 6; 10.5.12–14; the *Fasti Triumphales* record that Corvus celebrated a triumph over the Etruscans and Marsi.
[46] See above, n. 5.   [47] Plut. *Marc.* 20.7.

have been common in Italy during the Second Punic War. In fact, in 210, the Capuans sent an embassy to Rome to appeal the senate's decision to confiscate all Capuan territory and abolish the city as a civic entity, citing the widespread intermarriage between Romans and Capuans as reason for showing clemency.[48] Finally, Italian appeals are documented in the second century: in 175 ambassadors from Patavium requested help from the senate to put down a civil disorder, which was suppressed when one of the consuls arrived on the scene.[49]

A certain pattern emerges from these examples. Although the sources often speak of the Romans dealing with the people of one or another Italian town as a corporate entity, more detailed episodes show that the Roman ruling class, whether acting together in the senate or (especially) through individual magistrates with *imperium*, rarely treated all members of a local aristocracy equally. Rather, their actions and decisions, and the political settlements they imposed, tended to favor individuals, families or groups within a local aristocracy, presumably at the expense of other local groups. At the same time, various points of contact such as friendship, *hospitium* and marriage between members of the local aristocracy and the responsible Roman magistrates must have resulted in special treatment or political advantages during such times of crisis or dispute. A Roman magistrate could exercise a great deal of personal discretion when deciding the fate of a city. The interests of the groups or individuals he favored, whose innocence he believed in or whom he felt that he could trust would have been important factors in his decision-making. Thus, whenever possible, local aristocrats appealing directly to the consul or to some other influential Roman aristocrat would have invoked pre-existing bonds (marriage ties, friendship, *hospitium* or other links), or at least would have attempted to forge new personal ties that would prove their trustworthiness and thereby give them an advantage in negotiations. In a diplomatic environment where personal connections had real political consequences, it had to be the case that those local elites who were the friends of a Roman magistrate or who in some way had influence with him would anticipate that they would come out ahead in any settlement.

What could a local Italian notable expect to receive? A Roman magistrate might simply reward a local aristocrat with money or land, with which, since wealth and political power were inextricably linked, his local political position could be reinforced. Or the Roman magistrate could make a more symbolic act, such as the exchange of prestige gifts or the awarding of

---

[48] Livy 26.33.3. [49] Livy 41.27.3–4.

public honors. Correspondingly, some individuals or groups of local aristocrats lost out. In more extreme circumstances they would have faced execution or exile, or their property would have been confiscated and/or handed over to local political rivals, thereby undermining their own wealth and status. In other cases, they might simply have lost ground relative to those aristocrats who accumulated greater symbolic capital through gifts and other rewards handed out by the Roman magistrate in charge. M. Claudius Marcellus' treatment of local aristocrats during the Second Punic War exemplifies this punishment–reward pattern. According to Plutarch, his generous benefaction both to cities and to "private individuals" (ἰδιώτας) in Sicily was noteworthy,[50] and we have already mentioned how he gave Nicias of Engyion a variety of gifts, including land. Livy supplies a more fulsome example: in 216 and 215 Marcellus commanded a Roman army near Nola, in Campania, where he conducted investigations in response to rumors that some Nolans were planning to defect. He ordered the execution of a number of local senators on suspicion of disloyalty, but he also rewarded specific aristocrats, including a young man named Lucius Bantius. Marcellus heaped praises on the young man in public and gave him gifts: five hundred denarii and a "fine horse" (*equum eximium*). He also ordered his lictors to allow Bantius free access to himself.[51] Marcellus thus invested Bantius with signs of aristocratic status and privilege, and he made a public gesture of friendship by granting him free personal access. Personal access was also a valuable resource, since it allowed Bantius to have the ear of the magistrate and therefore influence his decisions. We may also recall that the Samnite ambassadors in 318 succeeded because they had similar physical access to Roman aristocrats. Overall, by doling out punishments and rewards, and through selective political and military assistance, a Roman magistrate could radically alter the local political landscape, essentially placing certain groups in power, or at least greatly reinforcing their position.

Numerous examples provide additional support for this conclusion. Thus, the Cilnii relied on Roman military support in order to suppress political opposition and thus preserve their authority. When the Romans sent a consular army to help the Volsinians in 265, the city was destroyed and resettled at a new location twelve miles from its original site.[52] According to Zonaras, the freedman class had seized political power, but many details

---

[50] Plut. *Marc.* 20.2.   [51] Livy 23.15.7–15.
[52] For the relocation of Volsinii, see Zonar. 8.7; Harris 1965, 113–14; Staccioli 1972; Barker & Rasmussen 2000, 100, 266; *contra* Scullard 1967, 126–32. For complete references, see above, n. 5.

of the account are suspect.⁵³ It is more likely that the Volsinii defected, or that some of the ruling elite planned to revolt. If so, then the consul on the spot surely rewarded those aristocrats deemed loyal. Obviously, loyalists will not have been executed, and when Volsinii was refounded, the Romans would have influenced how land was distributed. We can imagine trusted local aristocrats came to possess significant property. One suspects that this same general pattern played out in the Patavium affair in 175. According to Livy (41.27.3): "The senate gave [the consul] Marcus Aemilius the task of suppressing a sedition (*seditionem*) of the Patavians in the Veneto, whom their own ambassadors reported had become enflamed to internal war because of a struggle between factions (*certamine factionum*)." The ambassadors reported that the "madness of the people" (*rabiem gentis*) could not be controlled, but the consul's arrival quickly put an end to the disturbance.⁵⁴ Livy's language implies some sort of class conflict whereby a "people's party" was attempting to overthrow the ruling aristocracy. The political situation was probably more complex, however, with the local ruling elite deeply divided along personal or family lines, and Roman intervention probably took the form of arbitration between these rival factions. Indeed, the ambassadors from Patavium may have represented only one party who sought Roman aid to secure their own power vis-à-vis their aristocratic rivals. The arrival of the Roman consul, therefore, would have restored political order, as he could have been expected to favor one group of aristocrats over their rivals, or to reaffirm the political dominance of one or more aristocratic factions.

Finally, there is a particularly remarkable case from the Second Punic War. An aristocrat named Statius Trebius from the Samnite town of Compsa contacted Hannibal after the battle of Cannae and promised to turn over his city should Hannibal bring his army near. Trebius was a leading aristocrat (*nobilis*) who had been opposed by an aristocratic faction composed of the Mopsii, a family who held power because of the favor or friendship of the Romans (*factio Mopsiorum familiae per gratiam Romanorum potentis*).⁵⁵ Compsa had been conquered c. 290 and perhaps again c. 270. Thus, for more than fifty years, two generations after Roman conquest, an aristocratic family's political power continued to be strongly linked to their association with Rome.⁵⁶ This suggests that the Romans had actively installed the Mopsii as the dominant family, or perhaps that

---

⁵³ See Capozza 1997.   ⁵⁴ Livy 41.27.4.   ⁵⁵ Livy 23.1.1–3.
⁵⁶ Compsa was a principal town of the Hirpini, who were defeated near the end of the Third Samnite War and again after siding with Pyrrhus. Compsa presumably fell sometime in this period. See Salmon 1967, 275–6, 285–90; Uggeri 1998.

Privata hospitia, beneficia publica? 245

the Roman settlement in 290 created conditions favorable to the Mopsii, allowing them to consolidate their power for two generations. Or, it is possible that the Romans provided ongoing or at least more recent support for the Mopsii, thus guaranteeing their political ascendancy. In any case, Livy's passing reference to the Mopsii is a strong reminder of how Roman political favoritism played out at the local level.

In addition, we should not see this friendship–politics dynamic as functioning on exclusively unilateral terms. That is, it was not always the case that the Roman consul showed up on the scene and imposed a settlement, which in turn happened to favor his local friends. Rather, local aristocrats themselves were not infrequently active players, seeking out powerful Romans and attempting to leverage their friendships for personal advantage. Such activity was not, therefore, simply reactive (e.g. appealing for mercy), but often entailed proactive manipulation on the part of Italian aristocrats in order to better their own political fortunes and even to undermine the standing of their local political enemies.

A powerful example from the Second Punic War brilliantly illuminates this dynamic and neatly ties together the various threads of the argument in this section: Scipio's settlement after the recapture of Locri in 205.[57] Locrian elite support for Hannibal or Rome seems to have split along local factional lines, as some leading Locrian citizens had taken refuge in nearby Rhegium after they were driven out by the opposing faction that handed over the city to Hannibal.[58] Livy tries to oversimplify the picture, painting the "leading men" as loyal to Rome and the "plebs" as in favor of Hannibal, but clearly there were aristocrats on both sides of the fence. In fact, we later hear that these exiled leading men were motivated to act not only because they missed their homeland, but also because they wished to exact revenge against their enemies.[59] They approached Scipio in Sicily, therefore, with a plan to win back Locri; presumably they expected not only to liberate their hometown, but also to (re-)establish their own political dominance while punishing rival factions. Livy adds an intriguing detail: when the Locrians appealed to Scipio, some exiles were already there with him in Sicily; the context implies that the exiles with Scipio acted as intermediaries or somehow made the Locrian appeal more attractive to him.[60] Thus, physical access to the magistrate yielded practical benefits. The plot worked to perfection and the Locrian exiles

---

[57] Livy 29.6–8.
[58] Livy 29.6.5: *Locrensium principibus qui pulsi ab adversa factione quae Hannibali Locros traditerat.*
[59] Livy 29.6.7: *simul cupiditate inimicos ulscendi arderent.*   [60] Livy 29.6.8.

re-took the city with Roman military support. Scipio then assembled all the Locrians and publicly chastised them for siding with Hannibal. He punished the leaders of the revolt (*de auctoribus supplicium sumpsit*) and gave their property to the "leaders of the other faction" (*alterius factionis principibus*) on account of their remarkable loyalty to Rome.[61] We must assume that the anti-Roman faction whom Scipio punished as the leaders of the revolt had been in a position of political dominance early in the war, since Locri had in fact defected. Scipio's settlement in 205 fundamentally altered the political scene at Locri; he eliminated or at least weakened what had been the dominant party, while strengthening their aristocratic rivals. In effect, he created a new ruling elite who owed their position to Rome, or at least to Scipio. Moreover, the personal ties between Scipio and his friends obviously played into the consul's decision to attack the city and the nature of the punishment meted out. Indeed, it was a faction of local aristocrats who were the main movers behind the events.

Thus far I have argued that there were clear advantages for local aristocrats who forged strong ties with Roman aristocrats; this is perhaps obvious. Additionally, the Roman aristocracy, or more precisely, individual Roman aristocrats, tended to deal with sub-groups of a local aristocracy (individuals, families or "factions"). This too is perhaps unsurprising, given the highly personal nature of politics and interstate relations. Nor is it surprising that Roman–Italian aristocratic interaction would have been particularly intense in times of crisis, such as war, when the opportunities for Italian aristocrats to display loyalty to Rome and in turn receive patronage, or fail to do so and suffer the consequences, were amplified. But what about periods when there was no crisis? Did Italian aristocrats profit politically, at the local level, from their personal connections to members of the Roman elite? I wish to focus on the "long second century," after the Romans' victory in the Second Punic War left them unchallenged masters of Italy, but before all Italians were politically incorporated through the *lex Julia* and *lex Plautia Papiria*.

Before proceeding it must be stressed that I am not concerned with whether Italian elites during the second century sought greater inclusion in the Roman political system, including the right to vote in Roman elections, to hold Roman magistracies and to be enrolled in the Roman senate.[62] Such aspirations may have existed, and indeed the second century

---

[61] Livy 29.8.1–2; whether the rebel leaders were killed is unclear, though execution is implied in Livy's use of the idiom *supplicium sumpsit*.
[62] Salmon 1962, 113–14; Brunt 1965, 101–6; Sherwin-White 1973, 134–9 (arguing that the Italians sought "equality" first and foremost, regardless of citizenship status); Gabba 1976, 70–130; Gabba 1989, 207–12, 225–37; David 1996, 135–9; Keaveney 2005b, 3–18.

saw both individual Italians and whole communities more fully integrated into the Roman political system.[63] But framing the question in this way is fundamentally Romano-centric. It assumes that greater political integration was an important if not overriding ambition of Italian aristocrats, and fits neatly into a narrative wherein the Social War arose from Italian frustration at failing to achieve these alleged goals. These assumptions have been rightly challenged in recent years.[64] Instead, I want to consider the question from the local, Italian perspective. The evidence for Italian politics at the local level, the domestic affairs and internal political dynamics of individual Italian communities, is unfortunately slender, and the second century is particularly poorly documented. Still, there are enough hints in the sources to show that the friendships, marriage ties and other personal links that an Italian aristocrat maintained with Roman aristocratic families brought prestige and yielded political advantages at the local level.

We can flesh out the picture of local politics with some later, comparative evidence. The famous election notices from Pompeii, although dating mostly to the last few years before the destruction of the city in AD 79, reveal a wealth of information about campaigns for local political office, which may shed light on an earlier period. One set of notices in particular is worth focusing on: those concerning local aristocrat Marcus Epidius Sabinus' candidacy for the office of *duumvir*. Several of these notices advertise the endorsement of Titus Suedius Clemens, such as the following: "I pray that you elect Marcus Epidius Sabinus *duumvir* with judicial power, in accordance with the opinion of Suedius Clemens."[65] Titus Suedius Clemens was sent by Vespasian to investigate the usurpation of public lands by private individuals in Campania and subsequently restored some state lands to Pompeii.[66] That an imperial official endorsed a candidate for a local political office is intriguing. It does not matter whether Suedius Clemens took an active interest in an election at Pompeii. Rather, the election notices suggest that the local aristocrat Epidius Sabinus, or his supporters, believed that his candidacy could be helped by association with such a powerful patron. In other words, Epidius Sabinus appears to have believed that mentioning the support of an imperial official would win him votes. The Pompeian election notices are notoriously formulaic,

---

[63] For example, Fundi, Formiae and Arpinum were "upgraded" to full citizenship in 188 (Livy 38.36.5–7). See Wiseman 1971, 13–32 for a summary of patterns of entry into the senate by municipal elites.
[64] Mouritsen 1998, 87–108; Pobjoy 2000.
[65] *CIL* IV 791 = *ILS* 6438b: *M. Epidium Sabinum | ex sententia Suedi Clementis D. V. I. D. O. V. F.* For similar endorsements, see *ILS* 6438c, 6438d (= *CIL* IV 768, 1059).
[66] *CIL* X 1018 = *ILS* 4942; see Comparette 1906, 180.

often commending a candidate's moral qualities or good family.[67] Given the lack of political parties with identifiable platforms and/or ideologies, it seems that campaigns appear rarely to have focused on specific issues, and there was a high degree of similarity between candidates in terms of birth, experience and electoral rhetoric; the ability of a candidate to convince the voters that he had more powerful friends in Rome may have been one of the few ways in which he could distinguish himself from his political rivals.[68] This makes a certain amount of intuitive sense, for a man who had the ear of powerful friends and who could offer the community favors and *beneficia* would have been an attractive candidate.

Cicero is an example from the republican period of just this sort of potentially powerful patron. In 46, the former consul wrote a letter to Brutus (*Fam.* 278) requesting a favor for the people of Arpinum, his hometown. Cicero informs Brutus that representatives from Arpinum had been sent to inspect property and to collect rent from public lands in Cisalpine Gaul, the income from which was used for the upkeep of temples and public buildings in Arpinum. Cicero then asks Brutus to look after the representatives and expedite their business.[69] This is a clear instance of a Roman aristocrat of the late republic, in this case a consular, acting as the patron of an Italian city where he had personal connections. Cicero also gives the impression that this is not a singular act of patronage, but rather that he regularly did favors for his hometown.[70] But there is more, for Cicero explains to Brutus why he is particularly keen to have the matter taken care of: "For while I am in the habit of taking care of my fellow townsmen, this year especially concerns my attention and obligation. For I wanted my son, my brother's son, and a very close associate of mine [*maxime necessarium*], M. Caesius, to be elected *aediles* this year to manage the town."[71] Thus, Cicero appears to believe that his *benficia* will cast his local clients in a good light and aid their campaign for local high office. Even if Cicero's explanation is disingenuous, he clearly expects Brutus to accept the rationale, suggesting that a Roman aristocrat would have found the situation plausible. Moreover, for Cicero's favor to help his friend's and relatives' campaign, his patronage must have been advertised in some

---

[67] Franklin 1980, 18–21; Cooley & Cooley 2004, 112.
[68] Yakobson 1992, 45–6; Flower 1996, 60–70; Lintott 1999b, 173–6; Farney 2007, 19–26.
[69] Cic. *Fam.* 278.1–2.
[70] Cic. *Fam.* 278.1: *non dubito quin scias non solum cuius municipi sim sed etiam quam diligenter soleam meos municipes Arpinatis tueri.*
[71] Cic. *Fam.* 278.3: *quod quum semper tueri municipes meos consuevi, tum hic annus praecipue ad meam curam officiumque pertinet: nam constituendi municipii causa hoc anno aedilem filium meum fieri volui et fratris filium et M. Caesium, hominem mihi maxime necessarium.*

way, and perhaps more importantly, efforts must have been made to associate Cicero's municipal clients with his *benficia*. Thus, we can imagine electoral notices, probably similar to the examples from Pompeii, and the candidates themselves calling attention to their connections to Cicero and perhaps even other powerful Roman elite. This letter is direct evidence of the tangible local political advantages that could be gained by having family or friendship ties with a Roman *nobilis*, especially a *consularis*.

It is reasonable to conclude that Roman aristocrats acted as patrons for Italian elites in the period after the Social War, when the *municipes* could return the favor through their political support. Can we see this dynamic at work in the previous century? The evidence is less explicit, but it is likely that Italian aristocrats benefited from their personal associations with Roman *nobiles*.

First, there is no doubt that individual Roman *nobiles* acted as benefactors for Italian cities in the second century. Many of the communities receiving patronage were Roman colonies or *municipia*. For example, in 179 the censor M. Aemilius Lepidus (cos. 187, 175) built a mole at Tarracina, where he also owned property. In fact, Aemilius was censured because he allegedly charged private expenses to the public contract.[72] There is little doubt that Aemilius' decision to invest public money in this project was related to his personal connections to the town. Similarly, in 170 the praetor C. Lucretius Gallus used spoils to build an aqueduct and decorate a temple in Antium, where he owned an estate. In 174 the censors Q. Fulvius Flaccus (cos. 179) and A. Postumius Albinus (cos. 180) sponsored a wide range of public works at Potentia, Fundi, Pisaurum and Sinuessa.[73] Yet there are also records of *beneficia* to communities that did not possess Roman citizenship. Thus, L. Mummius took paintings and statues from the sack of Corinth and distributed them in towns throughout Italy, including the Latin colony Fregellae and the allied city of Pompeii.[74] Patronage of local communities took other forms besides sponsoring public building and munificence. For example, in 117 the brothers Quintus and Marcus Minucius Rufus acted as arbiters in a land dispute between the people of Genua and their neighbors, the Langenses Viturii. The Minucii had a personal connection to Genua,[75] so it is not coincidental that their decision, commemorated in a long inscription, seems to favor the Genuans.[76] This last example recalls

---

[72] Livy 40.51.2.   [73] Livy 40.27.5–13.   [74] Patterson 2006, 146.   [75] Patterson 2006, 144.
[76] *CIL* I² 584 = *ILS* 5946. The inscription identifies state land supposedly owned by Genua but in the possession of the Viturii (13–23), and it fixes various rents that the Viturii must pay to the Genuan treasury (25–7, 35–6). Any Viturii who were imprisoned because of the land dispute were set free (43–4), but the ruling assumes that the Viturii had been justly condemned for wrongs (*ob iniourias*).

Cicero's dealings with Arpinum, and one can imagine that local Genuan aristocrats called on their Roman patrons to settle the affair quickly and profitably.

Second, if Roman aristocrats acted as patrons for Italian communities to which they had personal ties, then we would expect to see their local contacts (friends, *hospites*, clients, etc.) trying to leverage their connection to Rome for political gain. They may have called attention to munificence paid for by their patrons and thereby associated themselves with the *benficia*, or they may have advertised their own role in obtaining favors for their hometown through Roman patron-friends, or they may have simply cultivated friendships with Roman aristocrats in the hope of receiving gifts or money that would enhance their prestige and better their political prospects. In fact, Livy preserves a specific example of this behavior in the second century by Rammius of Brundisium. According to Livy, Rammius maintained *hospitium* with both Roman and foreign aristocratic households,[77] and indeed an inscription found at Dodona names Rammius as the recipient of *proxenia* from the people of Epirus, for the "continued goodwill" that he showed them.[78] Further, Livy claims that he was interested in cultivating a more intimate friendship (*amicitiae interioris*) with Perseus of Macedon in order to obtain a great fortune (*magnae fortunae*).[79] *Fortuna* might refer to anything from wealth to rank or status, but the distinction does not matter since politics and wealth were closely intertwined, and increased wealth would presumably be used to improve political standing.

But political status was not derived from wealth alone, although it was a prerequisite for elite standing, enabling an aristocrat to behave in accordance with his rank and to satisfy the expectations of his community. Public gifts, awards and honors could also enhance an aristocrat's status. In addition, he could increase his symbolic capital through an array of gestures and actions, including the reception of other aristocrats as guests or clients into his house. The more powerful friends, clients and relatives an Italian aristocrat had, the greater his prestige, but only if these associations were made known. To this end, various public displays of friendship called attention to an aristocrat's connections and performed a clear political function. Thus, the ringleaders of the revolt of Tarentum convinced the Roman garrison commander of their friendship by attending public events with him.[80] Similarly, the leading figures in Capua's defection invited Hannibal to the city, where they arranged for the whole town to greet him at the gates; he then dined at one of their houses with other local aristocrats

---

[77] Livy 42.17.3.   [78] See above, n. 25.   [79] Livy 42.17.4.   [80] Polyb. 8.25.7–11; 8.27.1–6.

Privata hospitia, beneficia publica? 251

in attendance.⁸¹ Both episodes show aristocratic friendship publicized for political gain.

I suspect that *tesserae hospitales* were another medium for advertising. These *tesserae* were made in matching pairs, in the form of animals, clasped hands or other symbols "cut in half," with each "half" containing similar inscriptions identifying the two parties sharing *hospitium*.⁸² Their original function was, therefore, identification: when the two *hospites* or their descendants met, the corresponding tokens could be matched up, proving the identity of each party and verifying their mutual obligations.⁸³ Yet many of the surviving *tesserae* are of high quality. The *tessera hospitalis* from Trasacco, for example, is made of finely crafted bronze. The "neck" of the ram's head appears to be broken; it could have formed part of a handle, perhaps a tang that was inserted into a staff. The quality of the item suggests that the *tessera* was not only functional but also a prestige item, and as such may have been put on display. It is well known that the *atrium* of the Roman *domus* was filled with items on display, including spoils from battle, cult objects, an elaborate strongbox (*arca*), and cupboards containing the *imagines*. The *tablinum*, on the central axis of the *atrium*, was also furnished with cupboards and housed objects and documents related to magisterial office.⁸⁴ One imagines that *tesserae hospitales* were kept in a cupboard or display case in the *atrium* or in a corresponding room of an aristocratic house elsewhere in Italy. Indeed, some *tesserae* have holes for a cord to be strung through them, perhaps so that they could be hung in a display case.⁸⁵ *Tesserae* attesting *hospitium privatum* tended to be rather small,⁸⁶ however, and for tokens of this size to be effective display items, they would have

---

⁸¹ Livy 23.7.8
⁸² See Nicols 1980, 555; Patterson 2006, 141. DeGrassi identifies six *tesserae hospitales* from the republican period (*ILLRP* 1064–9).
⁸³ Plaut. *Poen.* 1047–52. ⁸⁴ Flower 1996, 186–209; Welch 2006, 114–15.
⁸⁵ For two such examples from Spain, see MLH IV, K.18.1 and K.23.2. Both are in the shape of a pig or boar, cut lengthwise and inscribed, with two holes punched through. For the display of *tesserae*, see also Patterson 2006, 151.
⁸⁶ The ram's head on the Trasacco *tessera hospitalis* is only about six centimeters long. Compare the *tesserae hospitales* with the later *tabulae hospitales* (or *tabulae patronatus*) recording *hospitium publicum* between an individual or family and an entire tribe or city. These bronze plaques are much larger than a *tessera hospitalis*, typically of the order of thirty centimeters on a side (for a particularly fine example, see *AE* 1961, 96 = Nicols 1980, no. 22, which records the establishment of *hospitium* between Castellum Toletum and a prominent local in AD 28). The *tabulae* probably derived from *tesserae hospitales*, for already during the second century BC the *tesserae* carried more elaborate inscriptions requiring a larger format, and one first-century BC *tessera hospitalis* (*ILLRP* 1069) is in the form of a *tabula*. Since the later *tabulae* were designed to be hung on display in the patron's house, we can project this function back onto the earlier *tessera* format. Indeed, it is likely that form and function developed in pace, with *tesserae* increasing in size and elaboration from the second century to satisfy growing elite demand to display them as prestige items and advertise their aristocratic associations. See Nicols 1980.

had to be collected and shown in large numbers. It is likely, therefore, that aristocrats strove to build imposing sets of *tesserae hospitales* with which to impress their guests. The more *hospites* an aristocrat had, the more *tesserae* he could collect and show off, thereby increasing his reputation.[87]

Having prestigious associates, whether they were friends, clients, *hospites*, family members or dependents, was itself a source of prestige and a marker of elite status for an Italian aristocrat, regardless of where such friends came from: his own community, Rome, a neighboring city or a far-off land. It is worth underscoring this point. Local aristocrats must have entered into friendships and forged bonds of *hospitium*, and both sought favors from and granted favors to aristocrats from other cities besides Rome. We must therefore envision multilateral connections between and among aristocracies throughout Italy. Cicero illustrates this complex network of aristocratic connections and interrelations in his defense of Aulus Cluentius Habitus. His client was from Larinum in Apulia, the son of a prominent local citizen of the same name. The younger Cluentius was accused of poisoning his stepfather, Oppianicus the Elder. The charges were brought by his stepbrother, Oppianicus the Younger, who was married to a woman named Papia from Teanum, a town about twenty miles from Larinum. Oppianicus had two close friends, the brothers Caius and Lucius Fabricius (*Fabriciis semper est usus Oppianicus familiarissime*), who came from Aletrium, situated only forty-five miles away from Rome. Cicero owned property in Aletrium, and the two brothers had previously come to Cicero's house in Rome and appealed to him in person as a neighbor. Moreover, Cicero once defended the freedman client of the Fabricii brothers, a fact that caused him some embarrassment. We also learn that the elder Cluentius had secured the patronage of a Roman senator, Marius Babrius. Whatever one thinks about the merits of this famously convoluted case, it is clear that the local aristocrats not only had friendships and patron–client relationships with powerful Romans (such as Cicero), but contracted marriages and friendships with other Italian communities, both nearby and distant. The events described in the *Pro Cluentio* took place after the Social War, but this is a relatively early speech (*c.* 66), and it is unlikely that such relationships appeared only after the war. Indeed, we may recall that Rammius of

---

[87] Nybakken 1946 argues that *tesserae hospitales* were not widely used because having tokens to guarantee *hospitium* violated the Roman custom of *fides*. This overlooks the possibility that *tesserae* were used primarily as prestige display items rather than forms of identification or to prove *hospitium* existed to a less mindful *hospes*. Indeed, I suspect that a *tessera* rarely left its owner's house, where it was displayed to visitors.

Brundisium cultivated personal relations with aristocrats from Rome, cities in the Greek east and presumably other Italian states for political gain.

It remains to consider briefly the implications of the foregoing discussion. The main thrust of this discussion has been that Italian elites used their connections to the Roman aristocracy to further their political standing within their own local milieus. Long ago Münzer discussed how wealthy families from Etruria, Samnium, Campania and other places moved to Rome in the early and middle republic and bound themselves to the great patrician clans through marriage and other alliances, and for much of the last century scholars have tended to see this as part of a broader strategy by the Italian aristocrats to obtain Roman citizenship, thereby enjoying the benefits it allegedly provided or even seeking integration into Rome's ruling class.[88] In recent years, scholars have begun to question this picture as teleological and anachronistic.[89] Yet it pushes the point too far to argue that the Italian elite would not have recognized the political advantages of forging strong ties with Roman aristocrats. Rather, in the competitive political environment of republican Italy, a local aristocrat would have tried to accumulate symbolic capital through such associations, friendships, marriage ties, exchanges of gifts, public gestures and so forth. In certain cases, including several discussed earlier in this paper, Italian elite families would have leaned heavily on Roman aristocratic support, whether this took the form of occasional Roman military intervention in local affairs, the granting of favorable terms in settlements, financial or political backing, or even benefaction, which might shed favorable light on the local aristocratic friends of the great Roman patron – a sort of "trickle-down effect" of symbolic capital. And, as we have seen, Italian elites continued to receive this support throughout the republican period.[90] Private bonds yielded political advantages.

There is a tendency, however, to focus too much on the relationship between Romans and Italians. Rome was after all the dominant state, and eventually there would be a political, cultural and conceptual synthesis of the two: in the end, the Italians did become Romans. We are also dependent on literary sources that place Rome at the center of events and thereby obscure events at the local level. Still, we can conclude that Italian aristocrats forged personal ties with their counterparts in other Italian communities. These elite-level marriages, alliances, *hospitia* and friendships had political overtones. Indeed, we must imagine that powerful local figures would have hoped to make as many political alliances as possible, with

---

[88] For examples, see above, n. 62. [89] See above, n. 64. [90] *Contra* Mouritsen 1998, 71–2.

both Romans and non-Romans (even with "foreign" elites, as we saw in the case of Rammius of Brundisium). Italian aristocrats did not make these connections necessarily in order to "become Roman," any more than to become Capuan or Brundisian or Tarentine. Rather, having and advertising connections with high-ranking people was a typical aristocratic behavior. Having a great many powerful friends, *hospites* and relatives brought many benefits, both tangible and symbolic, which might allow a local aristocrat to stand out among his rivals in his own political setting. In this view, the Roman ruling class was but one of many potential sources of potential personal-political associations.

Thus far I have taken a more or less structural approach, but the dynamic of Roman–Italian aristocratic interconnections cannot have been static, completely immune to broader historical developments. It has been pointed out, however, that after the Second Punic War Rome will have "bulked larger on the horizons" of the Italian allied communities.[91] Roman hegemony expanded and Rome grew from a powerful city-state to the capital of a world empire. As the city's power grew, so too did its population and the extent of its territory. The spread of the *ager Romanus*, increasing numbers of Roman *cives* living abroad, Roman citizen colonies and even Latin colonies (which contained Roman citizens, at least after the right to obtain citizenship *per magistratum* was granted to those possessing Latin status[92]): all of these increased the chances of and/or encouraged communication and interaction between Romans and non-Romans in Italy. To be sure, having powerful and important friends continued to have political value, but Rome was increasingly the locus for the most powerful men in Italy. Over time, competition to secure the most powerful alliances will have become, effectively, competition to befriend, marry into or otherwise insinuate oneself into the great Roman noble houses. The growing number of aristocratic interconnections might be considered a form of Romanization, and perhaps it is on this personal level that Roman imperial success is to be located.

At the same time, I suggest that there was a corresponding countercurrent. This brings us back to our initial discussion of Roman magistrates *cum imperio*, especially the consuls. During the second century, if not earlier, Italy appears to have become less important, for except in unusual

---

[91] Keaveney 2005b, 22.
[92] Various dates for the grant of *civitas per magistratum* have been proposed: *c.* 124 after the revolt of Fregellae (Tibiletti 1953; Piper 1988; Keaveney 2005b, 84); immediately before the Social War (Sherwin-White 1973, 111–12); after the Social War, possibly not before the imperial period (Bradeen 1959).

circumstances Rome's highest magistrates were sent elsewhere to carry out their primary function, making war, while problems in Italy were dealt with instead by lesser magistrates. There were fewer opportunities for Italian (south of the Po) elites to come into contact with the consuls and thereby forge new personal relations with them or to reinforce old ties. This mirrors a harsh political and to some degree social reality. While Italian aristocrats competed to secure valuable political alliances, especially with Roman *nobiles*, they could offer less and less to their Roman friends in return. After the Social War the Italians could offer tangible political support in the form of votes. There is also little doubt that Roman *nobiles* valued having many aristocratic connections for, as we have seen in our earlier discussion of the Italian elites, having prominent friends and relatives was in itself a source of prestige and a marker of status. Yet the growing difference in power between Roman and Italian aristocrats before the Social War cannot be ignored. Although in theory they had the same social rank as Roman aristocrats, most Italian aristocrats found themselves in an increasingly subordinate position, and by the end of the second century many members of the Italian elite were essentially clients of the great Roman noble houses, whatever their formal or legal relationship (including *hospitium*).[93] These circumstances surely increased the chances that mutual expectations would not be satisfied, leading to heightened tensions and conflict. Indeed, Postumius' clash with the Praenestines may be an early and unfortunate example. It is in this context of growing frustration, resentment and perceptions of unfulfilled obligations that the coming of the Social War can be understood.

---

[93] For the absorption of *hospitium* into *clientela*, see Badian 1958, 11–12, 154; Wiseman 1971, 34–7; Nicols 1980, 549.

PART IV

Ideology, confrontation and the end of the republican consulship

CHAPTER 12

Consular appeals to the army in 88 and 87: the locus of legitimacy in late-republican Rome

Robert Morstein-Marx

In mid-March of 49, Cicero was in anguish over what to do now that Pompey had crossed to Greece and Caesar was pressing him for support or at least neutrality. His personal obligation to Pompey weighed heavily with him, he writes, but on the other hand he represents joining Pompey as committing himself to fight a civil war with Sullan vindictiveness and ferocity. From Formiae he writes to Atticus on March 18 that he was deterred from joining Pompey above all by "the kind of war intended, savage and vast beyond what men yet see."[1] It is interesting that for Cicero at this point it is *Pompey*, not Caesar, who is the Sullan counterpart: *Sulla potuit, ego non potero?*[2] Cicero then runs through some historical precedents, which he ultimately rejects – those of Tarquin, Coriolanus and the Athenian Hippias – and one that he embraces: that of Themistocles, according to the tradition that made him commit suicide in order not to join the Great King's war against his country. He proceeds: "But you may object that Sulla, or Marius, or Cinna acted rightly. Yes, justifiably, perhaps (*immo iure fortasse*); but once victorious, they were unequalled in cruelty and slaughter."[3] Cicero goes on to reject this kind of war quite forcefully, especially since Pompey and his friends were preparing (he claims) to surpass even those bloody precedents in savagery.

Cicero's imaginary interlocutor's objection – that "Sulla, or Marius, or Cinna acted rightly" – and his response – "yes, justifiably, perhaps," while drawing an implied distinction between their behavior *before* and *in* victory[4] – should pique our interest. Evidently he did not put Sulla, Marius and Cinna in quite the same category as Coriolanus, Tarquin or Hippias. He concedes that they may be seen as having had justice on their side,

---

[1] Cic. *Att.* 9.10.2; in Shackleton Bailey's translation. See also 9.7.4; 9.9.2.
[2] Cic. *Att.* 9.10.2. Cf. Cic. *Att.* 9.6.7: *bellum crudele et exitiosum suscipi a Pompeio intellegebam*; 9.4.2: εἰ πόλεμον ἐπακτέον τῇ χώρᾳ καὶ πολιορκητέον αὐτὴν τυραννουμένην. (Exactly Sulla's justification!)
[3] Cic. *Att.* 9.10.3; with Shackleton Bailey's note. [4] See below, n. 16.

although their actions were deeply tainted by the use they made of victory. But this nuanced point of view is a far cry from the nearly unanimous chorus of disapproval raised in modern scholarship against these men's decisions to take up arms against what is frequently, but tendentiously, referred to as "the state."[5] In this usage, however, "the state" is not a neutral description of a particular locus of governmental authority, but a normative one that presupposes *legitimacy* – and that is precisely what was contested by Sulla in 88 (and 83–82), by Marius and Cinna in 87 (as well as Caesar in 49).

We should avoid adopting language that presupposes a given conclusion. In distant hindsight, of course, Sulla's choice to take up arms may be seen (and usually is seen) as perhaps *the* fateful step toward the ultimate collapse of the republic in a series of civil wars.[6] A very common view (which frequently presupposes that Sulla's action was more or less treasonous or mutinous) is that the event is a landmark moment in the development of a "professional" or "client" army without a thought for the republic or its traditions – the natural and inevitable result, so we are frequently told, of Marius' recruitment of men without property (the so-called *capite censi*) with which to cross into Numidia in 107.[7] Grave doubts have now been registered about that venerable theory, even at its most basic level: we have no idea, in fact, just what proportion of the army besieging Nola in 88 consisted of men without property. But since many of the premises of our understanding of agrarian, demographic and military transformations in the second to first centuries are currently in flux, they can hardly be employed to frame our interpretation of this event anyway.[8] A hint has often been found in Appian's ascription of "mercenary" motives to Sulla's

---

[5] Cf. Gabba 1976, 27: Sulla "persuade[d] the legions to challenge, for the first time in Roman history, *the state's* authority" (my emphasis); Dahlheim 1993, 97: "unschwer als Staatsstreich zu identifizieren" (100: "Hochverrat"). Even Keaveney, in his rather sympathetic portrayal of Sulla, takes the majority perspective in describing Sulla's march as "turn[ing] his arms against *the state*" (Keaveney 2005a, 50 – my emphasis; but note the subtle change of phrasing from that of the original edition, which evidently attributed too much treasonous intention to the *army*: Keaveney 1982, 62). But Meier 1966 (1980), 222–8 is admirably nuanced, and at 237 acknowledges that "die Soldaten glauben konnten, im Sinne des senates und der rechtlichen Ordnung zu handeln."

[6] E.g., recently, Mackay 2004, 125 and (attributing even more, and more immediate, significance to Sulla's decision) Flower 2010, 92.

[7] Keaveney 2007 now offers a valuable corrective. Yet he may not go far enough: that Sulla "created" the "revolutionary army" is surely overstating the case; nor can "politicizing" the (citizen) army really have been so very revolutionary (see below, n. 79).

[8] Challenging the former consensus established by (esp.) Gabba 1976, 1–69 and Brunt 1988, see (esp.) Morstein-Marx & Rosenstein 2006, 630–2; Keaveney 2007. For the recent debate on the broader issues of agrarian and demographic history, see (esp.) Lo Cascio 1994; Morley 2001; Rosenstein 2004 (the objections of Keaveney 2007, 16–23 seem indecisive); Scheidel 2004; de Ligt 2007; and the conference papers in de Ligt & Northwood 2008.

troops: famously, they "were eager for the campaign against Mithridates since they thought it would be profitable and also believed that Marius would enroll other troops in place of themselves."[9] Yet it has been noted that this hardly suggests that the army was impoverished or any more disaffected from the republic than had been many others in past Roman history: "the Roman soldier, irrespective of his other motives, expected, when he went on campaign, to profit thereby from loot and plunder."[10]

If, then, we set aside some traditional but questionable assumptions about the disaffection, disloyalty or degeneration of the post-Marian army, we might be in a position to appreciate more precisely the issues of political legitimacy that had arisen in 88 and 87. Sulla's march can hardly have been generally viewed as a sort of coup against "the state," if Cicero was prepared to concede that he (along with Marius and Cinna the next year) may have had justice on his side. True, it is at least possible that in March of 49 Cicero was thinking in the first instance of Sulla's return from the east in 83, to which the prospective return of Pompey was obviously analogous, rather than the crisis of 88. Yet the order of names ("Sulla, or Marius, or Cinna") suggests that the march on Rome in 88 was indeed (also?) in mind, and in any case it is hard to see how Cicero would have discriminated sharply between the two acts of civil war, or if he did, how he could leave unspoken such an important caveat. Thomas Mitchell rightly comments that Cicero's numerous other "remarks on the death of Sulpicius and on the events surrounding it fit the pattern of his thinking in all the internal crises of his career and leave little reason to doubt that, whatever his misgivings about Sulla's cruelty in victory, he approved his drastic resort to military force to free the state from the domination of a turbulent tribune."[11] This is a man, after all, who had only the highest praise for L. Opimius and Scipio Nasica, the men most conspicuously responsible for the killings of the Gracchi brothers, and at the end of his life thought civil war was worth inciting in order to destroy the likes of Mark Antony.[12] Yet Cicero was no extremist, as his discussion of the tribunate in the *De Legibus* shows.[13] As it happens, other sources too take a positive view of Sulla's cause in deciding

---

[9] App. *B Civ.* 1.57/250 (cf. 252). I return to this matter below, at n. 71ff.
[10] Keaveney 2007, 37. See Morstein-Marx & Rosenstein 2006, 632. For the legionary's traditional "profit motive," see Harris 1979, 101–4 and (e.g.) Polyb. 1.11.2 (First Punic War); Livy 42.32.6 (war with King Perseus); Sall. *Iug.* 84.4 (Marius' Numidian campaign); cf. App. *Pun.* 75 (Third Punic War, with Harris 1979, 102).
[11] Mitchell 1979, 67; full discussion at 64–76.
[12] For Opimius, see e.g. Cic. *Sest.* 140. For Scipio, see the unqualified praise at Cic. *Dom.* 91; *Planc.* 88; *Off.* 1.76; *Brut.* 212; and see *Rep.* 6.12 Powell (with Macrobius' résumé: ad loc.).
[13] Cic. *Leg.* 3.19–26.

to take up arms against Sulpicius' violence; for example, the disinterested and relatively dispassionate Asconius writes simply that because Sulpicius had seized control of the state by force, "his armed suppression by the consuls *was thought to have been just*"[14] (emphasis added), while in Cicero's *De legibus* Quintus is made to refer to the armed defeat of Sulpicius as an act of self-defense by nothing less than the *res publica* ("the state!").[15] Scholars have not always been very attentive to the fact that such criticism of Sulla's actions in 88 as appears in our sources – which is relatively muted anyway in comparison to that of his final victory in 82 – appears to focus not on the decision to strike back against Sulpicius and Marius but on the savagery with which he ultimately conducted his assault on the city and persecuted his enemies without regard for the tribunician office or the past services of Rome's "Third Founder."[16]

Why does this matter? Because in recovering the issues that were raised in such conflicts over legitimacy we can expose central strands of republican political culture that have been lost in the "frozen wastes" of much of twentieth-century republican historiography. In so doing we lay the groundwork for a fresh look at the "transformation of the Roman republic" that gives proper weight to fundamental contests over political legitimacy against the background of a distinctive political culture.[17] I will contend that in the cases both of Sulla in 88 and of Cinna in 87 the character and role of the consulship were a central issue in the civil conflicts of those years, especially for the legions who followed them, and that attention to the claims of legitimacy that these men and their followers staked will

---

[14] Asc. 65C: *cum per vim rem p. possidisset et ab initiis bonarum actionum ad perditas progressus est [sc. P. Sulpicius]; quod et initium bellorum civilium fuit, et propter quod ipse Sulpicius consulum armis iure oppressus esse visus est*. Note that Asconius does not claim to be offering his own opinion but a general one. Although Plutarch's anti-Sulpician account might be dismissed as likely to be tainted by its ultimate source (Sulla's memoirs), note how Livy, *Per.* 77 and Vell. Pat. 2.18.5–19.1 both lay emphasis on the illegitimacy of Sulpicius' prior actions, as does even Appian's relatively neutral version, which even refers to alleged plans and threats of the tribune to kill the consuls if they did not yield: *B Civ.* 1.56/245, 56/247.

[15] Cic. *Leg.* 3.20: *de Saturnino, Sulpicio, reliquis dicam, quos ne depellere quidem a se sine ferro potuit* res publica.

[16] Levick, however, hits the mark (1982, 508): "Sulla's victory was justifiable; the way he used it unforgivably vindictive"; cf. Mitchell 1979, 71. Cf. esp. Plut. *Sull.* 9.6–10.2; Val. Max. 3.8.5; Cic. *Att.* 8.3.6; note Appian's heightened tone of criticism from *B Civ.* 1.58/257 on (though even now not without positive comment, e.g. 1.59/264, 63/281). Yet Velleius appears to remain largely exculpatory (2.18.6–19.4; cf. 20.1: *Non erat Mario Sulpicioque Cinna temperatior*). On the desertion of nearly all of Sulla's officers – only mentioned by Appian – see below. Sulla's moral downfall in victory seems to have been a fixed element in the tradition (cf. Sallust's interesting verdict on Sulla at *Iug.* 95.4); it evidently reappears in the Cicero text with which this paper began.

[17] See Morstein-Marx & Rosenstein 2006, 629–35, and for the Caesarian parallel, Morstein-Marx 2009.

cast some light on contemporary understanding of the meaning of the consulship in republican political culture.

Let us recall the immediate antecedents to Sulla's decision, and his army's, in 88. The tribune Publius Sulpicius[18] had taken up the cause of the so-called "new citizens" who, recently enfranchised under the *lex Iulia*, had been restricted to ten (or eight) new tribes where their votes would be greatly outweighed by the thirty-five tribes of "old citizens."[19] Sulpicius had employed street violence to sweep aside the unified resistance of the consuls to his controversial legislation on behalf of the newly enfranchised Italians; the consul Pompeius' son was killed in the melée, and in practice Sulpicius' violence drove them both from the City.[20] He may even have deprived Pompeius of his consulship as Plutarch (*Sull*. 8.4) claims, though doubts might be entertained on that point.[21] He then compounded the offense by depriving one consul, Sulla, of his province (the major campaign that was being prepared against Mithridates) and putting it in the hands of Gaius Marius, despite the fact that the old general held no public office – a procedure for which there was no precedent at the time and that was arguably illegal, as Diodorus happens to call it.[22] Scholars sometimes cite as a precedent the transfer of the Numidian command to Marius in 107,[23] but this is a false analogy that misses the central point. By the *lex Manlia* of 107 a sitting consul had been *given* command of the most important war then underway at the expense of a proconsul, thus from a traditional perspective receiving exactly his due; in 88, however, a sitting consul was *deprived* of the major command already entrusted to him to the advantage of a *privatus* who held no official position whatsoever. Sulpicius' plebiscite can therefore be seen, and surely was in fact seen by Sulla and many in his army, as a direct offense against the traditional prerogative of the consulship and its war-making role, which the *lex Manlia* had actually reaffirmed.

[18] I remain doubtful that Sulpicius carried the normally patrician cognomen "Rufus," attested only by Val. Max. 6.5.7; Mattingly 1975.
[19] The controversy over the number of new tribes is irrelevant for our purposes: see Gabba 1967, 147–8 for what seems to me to be the most probable view, but cf. Lewis 1968; Nicolet 1976a, 233–4; Keaveney 1987, 170; and now Bispham 2007: 189–99.
[20] On the gravity of Sulpicius' violations of constitutional tradition, see esp. Meier 1966 (1980), 221, 223, who acknowledges the force of Sulla's claim that Sulpicius' laws were *perniciosae leges* (Cic. *Phil*. 8.7; cf. Caes *B Civ*. 1.7.5 for *perniciosae leges* as a justifiable basis for resorting to the *senatus consultum ultimum*); also 227–8. Dahlheim 1993, 108–10 rightly notes that scholars' propensity to sympathize with the grievances of the Italians induces us to overlook Sulpicius' actions and methods.
[21] Keaveney 1983, 60–1. But note that Hinard 1985, 64 and Seager 1994, 169 accept Plutarch.
[22] Diod. Sic. 37.29.2 παρανόμως; cf. Meier 1966 (1980), 140, n. 471; Dahlheim 1993, 101–2.
[23] Badian 1970, 46.

This is an impressive charge sheet, and it helps us to see more clearly the dimensions and nature of the offense that Sulla was to claim Sulpicius and Marius perpetrated. While it is true that in the very sketchy account Appian gives of Sulla's speech to his troops he gives the impression that the consul spoke only of a *personal* offense against himself (τὴν δ᾽ ὕβριν [probably *iniuria* in his source] ... τὴν ἐς αὐτόν),[24] I argue that – as would be the case with Caesar in 49 – the "personal" was fully wrapped up in a larger context of Roman political values.[25] I think it virtually certain that Sulla's soldiers understood him to have recounted not a merely personal affront to their commander's honor but a gross violation of republican norms: an assault on the *dignitas* of the consuls – and thus, indirectly, of themselves, the Roman people who had elected them.

This leap from the *dignitas* of the consuls to the *dignitas* or *maiestas* of the Roman people might at first seem quite a stretch, so let me now support my suggestion with a look at the second of my instances, the consul Cinna's appeal to the army in the very next year. This is a less well-known story, and a little more background needs to be sketched in to make it fully comprehensible.

The immediate prelude can be told fairly briefly. In early 87, after Sulla's departure to take up the war against Mithridates, the consul Gaius Cornelius Cinna revived Sulpicius' proposal to distribute the "new" Italian citizens among all the tribes; Sulpicius' law had been annulled the previous year by Sulla after he had fought his way back to the city, but the restriction of the "new citizens" to a small minority of tribes who voted last remained a brewing source of strife after Sulla's departure. Cinna championed the "new citizens," his colleague Gnaeus Octavius the "old," and once again partisans of the two sides were at daggers drawn (or rather roving the streets with concealed daggers, according to Appian).[26]

A number of tribunes sought to veto Cinna's proposal,[27] but they were allegedly attacked by armed henchmen of the "new citizens" on the very

[24] App. *B Civ.* 1.57/251. For *iniuria*, cf. Flor. 2.9.6 and the parallel case of Cinna below. See Behr 1993, 69–76 for Sulla's "public" or "civic" apologia. I differ chiefly in regarding the "personal" and "public" justifications as deeply intertwined, indeed fundamentally as indistinguishable (see below, n. 25). This is a society, let us recall, in which the soldier's oath of obedience was to his *commander*, not to the *res publica* – not because military allegiance was in fact merely personal but because the latter was "incorporated" in the person of the consul or other commander. (On the *sacramentum*, see below, n. 41.)

[25] See Morstein-Marx 2009.

[26] App. *B Civ.* 1.64/289–90. For a recent narrative of the events described here and further bibliography, see Lovano 2002, 32–8.

[27] App. *B Civ.* 1.64/290 says a majority (τοὺς πλέονας δημάρχους). This evidence is supposed to conflict with that of Livy, *Per.* 79 (*pulsus urbe a Cn. Octavio collega cum sex tribunis plebis*, which, however, in such a compressed notice could be taken to mean that six tribunes joined Octavius in the attack on Cinna) and Gran. Lic. 35.2 (*Cinna se<xque> tribunis patria pulsis*, which is, however,

rostra, at which point Octavius swept into the Forum with a dense crowd of armed men, separated the rioters, and drove Cinna from the temple of Castor, where evidently the voting was being conducted.[28] Octavius' followers killed many men among the "new citizens" and drove others to the gates of the city, including his colleague. In his flight from the city, Appian claims, Cinna called upon the slaves to rise up and assert their freedom; when this failed to elicit the desired response (according to Appian) he fled to the towns of the "new citizens," from Tibur and Praeneste all the way to Campania, calling upon them to rebel and exacting financial contributions. While he was joined by some low-ranking senators such as Q. Sertorius and C. Marius Gratidianus,[29] the senate as a body took a truly remarkable step by abrogating Cinna's consulship along with his citizenship on the grounds that he had "abandoned the city in danger" (!) and offered freedom to the slaves.[30] The senate seems to have discovered dubious justification of the extraordinary measure in the Sybilline Books – although our source (Granius Licinianus) indicates in a vexed passage that traditional religious procedure was violated in some way in the process.[31] The religious machinations seem clearly designed to compensate for the highly questionable legality of the move (cf. Velleius' word *iniuria*: 2.20.3), for the consulship was in the gift of the people, not of the senate.[32] And

---

Mommsen's attractive, but uncertain, emendation of the text). For the problem, which matters little for our purposes, see Bennett 1923, 8 n. 36 and Katz 1976, 499–501.

[28] On the site, see Morstein-Marx 2004, 58–9.

[29] App. *B Civ.* 1.65/295; Plut. *Sert.* 4.4–5; with Bennett 1923, 9–10; Katz 1976, 498–518; and, on Sertorius, Konrad 1994, 59–65. Quite possibly all three men mentioned by Appian here (including C. Milonius: on the name, cf. Gran. Lic. 35.11, 19) were among the tribunes expelled with Cinna (see above, n. 27; but cf. *contra* Katz 1976).

[30] App. *B Civ.* 1.65/296; Katz 1976, 501–2 and recently Lovano 2002, 35–6. Regarding the precise import of the decrees, Gabba 1967, 184 inferred from Velleius' wording (*ex auctoritate senatus consulatus ei abrogatus est*: 2.30.3) that the *comitia centuriata* followed up a *senatus consultum ultimum* with a popular vote of abrogation, which would at least formally have given the *populus Romanus* its due place. Appian, however, mentions only the senatorial decision at 1.65/296 and makes Cinna explicitly declare that the people were not consulted (1.65/298 χωρὶς ὑμῶν); note also that later the senate alone is forced to retract the decision (1.69–70/317–19). Velleius' wording anyway hardly necessitates the conclusion that some body other than the senate acted formally to abrogate Cinna's consulship. Most scholars have therefore followed Mommsen 1887–8, I, 630 n. 4 in concluding that the senate had acted alone, perhaps using the device of folding Cinna's deposition into a *hostis*-declaration (which could be the import of the vote μήτε ὕπατον μήτε πολίτην ἔτι εἶναι): see Meier 1966 (1980), 228; Bauman 1973b, 285–8; Seager 1994, 174; Kunkel & Wittmann 1995, 257.

[31] Gran. Lic. 35.1–2; cf. Bennett 1923, 8–9; Katz 1976, 503–4. It remains unclear whether the violation consisted in sidestepping the *decemviri sacris faciundis* altogether, or in quoting the books *palam*, i.e. perhaps in a *contio* (cf. the incident of 56: Cass. Dio 39.15.4 with Morstein-Marx 2004, 167). The latter course would suggest a special public relations effort, perhaps (despite Cinna's unpopularity in the city) an attempt to assuage any disquiet over the apparent violation of *mos maiorum* and the constitutional rights of the people.

[32] This point needs no special demonstration, but for its resonance in this controversy note Velleius' comment (2.20.3: *iniuria homine quam exemplo dignior*), which suggests institutional over-reaching

certainly the sequel proved that it was rather unconvincing to claim that a consul, elected by the votes of the Roman people and surrounded by the lictors and *fasces* that symbolized *imperium*, was in fact their enemy and deprived even of the rights due a Roman citizen without any recourse to the people or a popularly authorized court. The senate may even have gone so far as to "elect" as suffect consul Lucius Cornelius Merula, the *flamen Dialis*, without a popular vote at all, an act by which it would have lapsed into blatant illegality.[33]

This rather cavalier disregard for the traditional rights of the Roman people sets the stage for Cinna's next move, which is described in very interesting detail by Appian and deserves closer attention than it has thus far received.[34] We are told that Cinna came to Capua in order to try to win over the army of Appius Claudius, which was still pursuing the siege of Nola.[35] (Presumably these were not the same legions to whom Sulla had appealed the year before – or else they had been severely disappointed.[36]) At first apparently maintaining his claim to consular authority, he came before an assembly of the army[37] in full consular regalia but then had his lictors lay down his *fasces* as if he were a mere private citizen (παρελθὼν

and a weak formal justification, as do also Cinna's speech to his troops (below), his bullying of the senate at App. *B Civ.* 1.69–70/317–19, and Cicero's acknowledgement of the strength of Cinna's legal argument at *Att.* 9.10.3.

[33] Scholars usually assume that in some formal sense the people did vote on Merula, but only Katz 1979, 163, n. 3 actually defends the assumption. Yet both App. *B Civ.* 1.65/296 and Vell. 2.20.3 place the selection of Merula in such close association with the deposition of Cinna as to arouse suspicion that here too the senate acted alone. (Diod. Sic. 38/39.3 is unspecific.) If Merula had been elected by the people, this would presumably have made the later negotiations between the senate and Cinna much stickier; as a matter of fact, Merula appears to have been deposed again by a senatorial decision alone (App. *B Civ.* 1.69/316–70/319) – at the request of *Cinna*, be it noted! – which seems to imply that the senate was in a position to undo alone what had been done. Katz himself had earlier argued that Marius' demand for a new *law* annulling his outlawry implied that the original senatorial *hostis*-declaration was formally ratified by a law of the people (Katz 1975, 102–4); the absence of such a demand in Merula's case looks significant.

[34] See, however, now Keaveney 2007, 38–9; cf. 73.

[35] Claudius: Livy, *Per.* 79; Nola: Vell. Pat. 2.20.4. See Gabba 1967, 185 with 165.

[36] Meier 1966 (1980), 237–8, who thinks that this is why the troops were ready to throw in their lot with Cinna. Badian 1970, 50 sees their decision in a solely mercenary way – but did *these* soldiers have any expectation of rich booty? (Cinna was not proposing to take them to Asia.) Velleius claims that the soldiers hoped for a reward (*corruptis . . . spe largitionis militibus*); but as Keaveney notes (2007, 39), this was a normal motive for Roman soldiers and does not contradict an overlapping "political" motivation.

[37] This should be added to the list of military *contiones* in Pina Polo 1989. How Cinna gained access to the army is an intriguing question, since the proconsul Ap. Claudius is usually thought to have adhered to the senate: he is conspicuously absent through the whole scene, and was soon charged and deprived of his *imperium* by a Cinnan tribune (Cic. *Dom.* 83, with Bennett 1923, 10, n. 47; Weinrib 1968, 41–3). By contrast, both Appian and Velleius make a point of noting how Cinna "cultivated" (ἐθεράπευε) or "seduced" (*corruptis*) the officers of the legion, who explicitly in Appian's account and implicitly in Velleius' orchestrate Cinna's acceptance by the soldiers (App. *B Civ.* 1.65/298, 66/301;

ὡς ὕπατος ἐς μέσους τάς τε ῥάβδους καθεῖλεν οἷα ἰδιώτης) and, bursting into tears,[38] addressed the soldiers with the following speech:

παρὰ μὲν ὑμῶν, ὦ πολῖται, τὴν ἀρχὴν τήνδε ἔλαβον· ὁ γὰρ δῆμος ἐχειροτόνησεν· ἡ βουλὴ δ' ἀφείλετό με χωρὶς ὑμῶν. καὶ τάδε παθὼν ἐν οἰκείοις κακοῖς ὑπὲρ ὑμῶν ὅμως ἀγανακτῶ· τί γὰρ ἔτι τὰς φυλὰς ἐν ταῖς χειροτονίαις θεραπεύομεν; τί δὲ ὑμῶν δεόμεθα; ποῦ δὲ ἔσεσθε τῶν ἐκκλησιῶν ἢ χειροτονιῶν ἢ τῶν ὑπατειῶν ἔτι κύριοι, εἰ μὴ βεβαιώσετε μέν, ἃ δίδοτε, ἀφειρήσεσθε δ', ὅταν αὐτοὶ δοκιμάσητε; (App. B Civ. 1.65/298–9)

From you, citizens, I received this office, for so the people voted; but the senate took it away without any referral to you. And though after suffering these things I am beset by my own woes, still I am outraged on your behalf. For why would we cultivate the tribes in elections any longer? Why would we need you any longer? How after this will you be masters of the assemblies or elections or the consulships,[39] if you do not confirm what you have given, and what you have decided is stripped away from you?[40]

He gave this speech to incite the soldiers (ἐς ἐρέθισμα) and aroused great pity for his plight by tearing his clothing (apparently his *toga praetexta*) and, after leaping down from the podium into their midst, lying prostrate on the ground. Appian says that the men were moved to pity, lifted him up, seated him on his *sella curulis* and raised the *fasces*, calling upon him to revive his spirits since he was consul and to lead them wherever he wished. The officers then seized the opportunity to administer the military oath to obey Cinna,[41] who proceeded to raise money and troops among the allied

---

Vell. Pat. 2.20.4). Given Velleius' *spe largitionis*, we are probably to understand this as bribery, at least in part. (Maurenbrecher referred a fragment of Sallust's *Histories* to this moment [1.27 M], but McGushin 1994, 218 banishes it to those of uncertain reference and points out the lack of any good reason to prefer this incident to others.) As to the question of the identity of these officers, it would be pressing syntax too far to assume that at 1.65/298 Appian means to mark *archontes* and senators as mutually exclusive rather than slightly overlapping categories: *some* tribunes will still have been senatorial at this time (see de Blois 2000, 15–16, 29, with bibliography: note the example of Julius Caesar in 81). This instance is often used to try to determine the nature of the *archontes* who famously refused to follow Sulla in his march on Rome (App. B Civ. 1.57/253): see below, at n. 64ff.

[38] On the motif of weeping generals, see MacMullen 1980 and Flaig 2003, 110–15.
[39] One senses a possible hendiadys here ("consular elections"), but I translate literally because this brings out the important emphasis on the subjection of the consulship to popular control.
[40] A complicated sentence: John Carter (Penguin edition) translates "and if your decisions are annulled because the senate withholds approval," while Horace White (in the Loeb edition) renders it "and whenever you give your decision fail to secure it."
[41] The oath, described by Appian as τὸν ὅρκον τὸν στρατιωτικόν, is evidently the traditional *sacramentum*: cf. Appian's wording here (σφᾶς ἄγειν ἐφ' ὅ τι χρῄζοι) with Dion. Hal. 10.18, 11.43. See now Keaveney 2007, 71–7 against Gabba 1967, 185 and Campbell 1984, 20, who argues, despite Appian's explicit statement, that this was an oath of personal loyalty. Keeping in mind that the soldiers had by their actions accepted Cinna's status as consul, nothing in fact could be more

cities. "Many," even of the aristocracy in Rome, joined him (πολλοὶ καὶ
τῶν ἐν Ῥώμῃ δυνατῶν ἕτεροι), being displeased with political stability
according to Appian (*B Civ.* 1.66/302), but possibly because they actually
supported his cause.

I would like particularly to note here how, in this section of his text,
Appian constructs the army at Capua as Roman citizens whose feelings can
be aroused by an appeal to republican, civic values.[42] This is important
because until recently there has been a pervasive tendency among historians
to treat the armies of the late republic as if they were distinct and separable
from the rest of the citizen population: a dispossessed, rural proletariat that
had lost all loyalty to the *res publica* and looked only to the material benefits
they could obtain through their own strong right arm and the open hand of
their commander.[43] More recently this widely held view, which has fitted
so attractively into prevailing grand theories of republican "decline and
fall," has been contested by myself and others,[44] and in that connection

---

"traditional" than to swear to follow their consul's orders (Harmand 1967, 301–2): note also Livy 3.20.3; 22.38.3: *iussu consulis (-um)*; and Ser. *Aen.* 7.164: *nisi praecepto consulis*; with Smith 1958, 29; Harmand 1967, 300. The exact phrasing of the *sacramentum* does not seem to be preserved. On the oath, see conveniently Smith 1958, 29–33; Brand 1968, 91–3; Nicolet 1976a, 102–5; Eder 2001; on its nature, esp. Rüpke 1990, 76–94. The oath was often repeated to a new commander, which explains its appearance here: the ritual signified above all that, by whatever means, Ap. Claudius was being replaced (see above, n. 37).

[42] This has not gone entirely unnoticed: see Lovano 2002, 36 and now esp. Keaveney 2007, 38–9. I would build more on this observation.

[43] E.g. Badian 1970, 48: "The new class of the dispossessed in arms, mercenaries in their own country, now inured by the Social War to the devastation of Italy, had nothing to hope for but booty, and no one from whom to expect it but their leader. These men had no stake in the *res publica*." Cf. Syme 1939, 352: "Excited by the ambition of military demagogues, the claims of the armed proletariat of Italy menaced and shattered the Roman republic." Brunt 1988, 257–9 acknowledges a series of notable occasions (including Cinna's appeal) on which commanders in the civil wars used political arguments to win or maintain the loyalty of their soldiery, but ultimately judged that "the soldiers... were surely more decisively influenced by personal considerations" (259), especially material ones (cf. 77). See further on this large topic the very selective bibliography given above, n. 8; see also the special study by Erdmann 1972 (very much in the traditional vein). De Blois 2000 reasonably qualifies older views of the "professionalism" of the late-republican military, claiming that the soldiery formed a distinctive sociological group, united by habituation, interaction and material interest, but also that they remained "citizens under arms" and "not completely estranged from Roman republican political culture" (21). He locates a destabilizing element not in any changed constitution of the lower ranks of the soldiery over the first century BC but in that of the mid-rank officer class, decreasingly senatorial and increasingly Italian (esp. 15–16, 29, 30); yet he too, in my view, exaggerates the alienation of first-century Roman armies from the traditional political system, since Sulla, Cinna and Caesar (e.g.) could all be seen as justified with reference to republican political values in their response to "illegitimate" political action (cf. 22). See also below, n. 65.

[44] Morstein-Marx & Rosenstein 2006, esp. 630–3; Morstein-Marx 2009; and now also Keaveney 2007, esp. 23–34 (on the "politicization" of the army that Keaveney diagnoses, see below). Particularly important is the lack of evidence that Marius' precedent in 107 was regularly followed, or remained exceptional, as suggested by Gell. 16.10.11; cf. Lo Cascio 2001, 126, with nn. 53 and 54; also Evans 1994, 74–6.

it is worth noting that in the scene Appian sketches of Cinna's appeal to his army the soldiers are portrayed as motivated not by personal loyalty or material gain but by the symbolic power of Cinna's approach to them and by his words,[45] which are remarkably reminiscent of public political speeches in Rome (*contiones*). I propose therefore to interpret the speech Appian gives to Cinna in the way I have in the past looked at *contiones* in Rome itself, that is, as the sort of appeal considered rhetorically effective before its audience – an audience that is, in this case, an assembly of Roman soldiers.[46] And what is especially notable from this standpoint is that the form and ideological content of the speech are virtually identical to those that characterize the urban *contio*.[47]

Immediately striking is Cinna's form of address to the soldiers: πολῖται, that is, "citizens" rather than "soldiers."[48] One thinks immediately of the famous anecdote according to which when Julius Caesar addressed the mutineers of 47 as *Quirites*, the traditional form of address for the Roman people in the civic sphere, implying thereby that they were in fact soldiers no longer, this was almost enough to end a dangerous rebellion involving several veteran legions.[49] Obviously, that is not what Cinna is trying to do here. Rather, by addressing the soldiers before him as "citizens,"[50] Cinna appeals to them specifically in their capacity as members of the civic community – in fact, as his subsequent words make clear, as *voters* in the *comitia centuriata* who had elected him (and who are therefore now uniquely entitled to restore their gift). From a rhetorical point of view, the force of Cinna's argument rests upon his soldierly audience actually accepting his characterization of them as voters in consular elections. The *populus* who had voted to make him consul is construed as identical to the audience before him ("from you . . . I received this office"); it was in

---

[45] Vell. Pat. 2.20.4, it is true, implies that the lower officers were bribed, but does not make this claim about the *gregarii* (see above, n. 37, and below, n. 46).
[46] Tribunes and centurions presumably played the most important role in such assemblies as auditors and conduits of information (see de Blois 2000, 23–4). Here they appear to be the orchestrators of a drama put on for others, i.e. the common soldiers.
[47] Seager 1994, 175: "[he] addressed the men in true *popularis* fashion."
[48] For the significance of this choice between *cives/Quirites* and *milites* (a *topos*), cf. Livy 28.27.4 and 45.37.14, Tac. *Ann.* 1.42.2, and the Caesar anecdote. Such a distinction does not seem to be implied in πολῖται at Dion. Hal. 6.9.1 (A. Postumius at Lake Regillus).
[49] App. *B Civ.* 2.93 (NB: πολῖται); Cass. Dio 42.53.3; Plut. *Caes.* 51; Suet. *Iul.* 70; Tac. *Ann.* 1.42.2. Chrissanthos 2001, esp. 73–4 nicely shows how much the famous anecdote leaves unsaid about Caesar's appeasement of the mutineers.
[50] It seems unlikely that in this scenario Cinna could possibly have used the formal title *Quirites*, which was ordinarily reserved for citizens in the urban, civic sphere, and judging from the Caesarian anecdote, would be dangerously close to telling his audience that they were no longer soldiers at all. *Cives* (cf. Livy 28.27.4 and Tac. *Ann.* 1.42.2) seems a more likely alternative here.

their capacity as voters, not as soldiers as such, that *they* (χωρὶς ὑμῶν) had been insulted when the senate had neglected to consult or even to consider them when it removed Cinna from office. The consequences of allowing the senate's action to stand thus will fall upon *them*: senators will no longer have to flatter and supplicate them in their tribes during votes ("why would we cultivate the tribes in elections any longer?"). If they do not defend and maintain what *they as voters* have determined, they will no longer "be masters of the assemblies or elections or the consulships." Throughout this brief passage references to voting are densely clustered and emphatic, with repetition of the word itself (ἐχειροτόνησεν/χειροτονίας/χειροτονιῶν) and a variety of paraphrases or clear allusions to voting and canvassing.

As I noted, in this speech Cinna is made to employ some central themes of the oratory of urban *contiones*. The reference to the Roman people's prerogative of receiving supplication by its leaders in the electoral season is one familiar from the *rostra*;[51] indeed the idea that the vote is more than simply a crucial buttress of freedom but actually secures the dedication of the political elite to the popular interest is formulated even more crisply here than in surviving specimens of contional oratory, though it clearly belongs to the same current of public discourse. We should recall L. Crassus' famous (or notorious) plea, "do not permit us to be in servitude to anyone but all of you together,"[52] a particularly notable statement of the obligation that the *beneficium* of popular election placed upon its recipient: to reciprocate by devoting selfless attention to the interests of the Roman people as an undivided whole.[53] And Cinna's emphasis upon the vote makes an unusually clear statement of what otherwise tends to be hinted at in contional oratory: that *suffragia* are the means by which the people enjoy influence (*gratia*) over their leaders and a way of indirectly pursuing their own interests.[54] Cinna here raises the specter of an aristocracy cut from its popular moorings, not so much "cheating on its debt" to the electorate, as some contional orators cried, but pre-emptively abolishing the

---

[51] See Cic. *Leg. agr.* 2.71 with Morstein-Marx 2004, 222, n. 82.
[52] *ORF* no. 66, fr. 22–6, pp. 243–5: *Nolite sinere nos cuiquam servire, nisi vobis universis.*
[53] See Morstein-Marx 2004, 235–6, with 262, and for the broader ideological construction of public office as a "gift" of the people calling for selfless dedication to the popular interest in repayment of the debt, see 258–66.
[54] See Cic. *Leg. agr.* 2.17: *unus quisque studio et suffragio suo viam sibi ad beneficium impetrandum munire possit*, or the way in which the orator links *suffragia* with *gratia* and *libertas* at *ibid.*, 2.71. Cf. the celebration of the *lex Cassia tabellaria* (which instituted the secret ballot in most trials) on coins of 126 BC and 55 BC, with Cic. *Sest.* 103 characterizing the popular view of the law as a key protection of the people's *libertas* (Morstein-Marx 2004, 84–5). We have been so dismissive of this element of Roman popular ideology that Ritter was prepared to reject the apparent association between *suffragium* and *libertas* made on the coins (1998, 608–14).

debt altogether.⁵⁵ Either way, the result would be the same. Cinna points down the road to the situation described by Sallust's demagogic tribune Licinius Macer: when unworthy men forget their debt to the people after their election, everyone falls "under the tyranny of a few men."⁵⁶

Unfortunately, we cannot be absolutely sure that Cinna actually expressed himself with precisely the words Appian gives him. Given the license with which ancient historians worked up speeches to complement their narrative, and the perennial question of Appian's source(s) – Livy, using Sisenna? or perhaps Sisenna directly?⁵⁷ – a shadow of doubt must remain over any attempt to identify the actual arguments made by Cinna at Capua in 87. Yet deep *a priori* skepticism seems unwarranted, since it is doubtful that Appian on his own could have fabricated a speech that is so neatly consistent with distinctive themes of late-republican contional oratory. We should be prepared to concede at least that Appian was following a very good source here, and that that source thought this kind of argument was the appropriate one for Cinna to make; and that is enough to make the speech worthy of notice. I would like to suggest that it fits into a pattern of essentially civic persuasion directed toward the soldiery, characterized thereby as citizens rather than as the quasi-mercenary client-soldiers who spook about in many modern accounts. So let us step back a bit. In only the previous year, a consul had come before an army to complain about his treatment at the hands of certain home authorities. Let us return now to Sulla, haranguing the legions at Capua after news came of his dismissal from the Mithridatic command.

After his more or less forced departure from the city, Sulla joined the legions surrounding the rebel stronghold at Nola. While there, Sulla learned of the passage of the Sulpician law depriving him of the command and immediately came before an assembly of the army. Appian tells us that the consul spoke to the soldiers of the "outrage" (τὴν δ᾽ ὕβριν) inflicted upon him by Sulpicius and Marius and only urged them to be prepared to follow his orders, saying nothing of any further plans; the troops divined his meaning and responded that Sulla should lead them to Rome.⁵⁸ But as

---

⁵⁵ See esp. Sallust's Macer, *Hist.* 3.48.5–6, and Marius, *Iug.* 85.8, with Morstein-Marx 2004, 232, 266.
⁵⁶ *Omnes concessere iam in paucorum dominationem:* Sall. *Hist.* 3.48.6.
⁵⁷ See Gabba 1956, 13–88, who argues that with the Social War Appian changes sources (to Livy) and later changes back (to Asinius Pollio). If, however, Appian used Pollio after 59 instead of relying on the Livian annals (and, as Gabba argues, some other non-Livian source before the Social War), then it seems quite possible that for the 80s he had likewise gone back to Sisenna, "the standard history of the period" (Badian 1964, 212–14) and, despite Sall. *Iug.* 95.2, not outright pro-Sullan (Rawson 1979). Of course, Livy was necessarily dependent on Sisenna, so it would be an empty exercise to try to distinguish very sharply between these strands in our accounts.
⁵⁸ App. *B Civ.* 1.57/251–2.

Christian Meier has pointed out, we should keep in mind that what was immediately in prospect was not a civil war, but a police action led by the duly elected consul against a seditious tribune in the style of Saturninus.[59] Retrospective judgment must avoid the fallacy of imputing hindsight to historical agents.

There is some memorable editorializing by Appian here in which he purports to tell us what the soldiers were really thinking and why they were the first to bring up this course of action openly.[60] But let us set this aside for the moment, reminding ourselves that what is in the agents' minds can only be inferred circumstantially, and for this very reason conjectures – often very tendentious – about these mental phenomena are conveniently easy to make and virtually impossible to refute. In such matters, Appian's conjectures (or those of his source) may not always be better than those we ourselves might reach on the basis of the available evidence. So we might turn Appian's assumptions on their head, and ponder whether it is not rather likely that the average centurion and the men under his command could have convinced themselves that Sulla's cause was in fact the legitimate one. Before them stood their duly and deservedly elected consul, the highest magistrate of the Roman people, a military hero of the final phase of the Italian revolt under whom they had themselves served and whom indeed they had honored with the "grass crown" for saving the army – *this* army, in fact.[61] Quite apart from the personal ties of loyalty between a commander and his men, these were powerful markers of legitimacy that must have predisposed his men in his favor. Then there was what he told them: the outrages done to him – and surely the *whole* story from the violence of the "tyrannical" tribune with whom he had contended at the outset, through the murder of his colleague's son in the violence that had intimidated the whole city and deprived even the senate of its freedom, his own expulsion along with the other consul, followed finally by the last straw, the "illegal" vote depriving a consul of the Roman people of his duly assigned province.[62] It does not actually seem surprising that Marius'

---

[59] Meier 1966 (1980), 224: "Er unternahm vielmehr zunächst nur eine Polizeiaktion gegen den *seditiosus tribunus* und dessen *factio* und bewirkte mit seiner Armee und ohne Senatsbeschluß, was früher auf Grund des *senatus consultum ultimum* auf nicht weniger gewaltsame und viel blutigere Weise ins Werk gesetzt worden war."

[60] See above, nn. 9, 10.

[61] The *corona graminea/obsidionalis*: Plin. *HN* 22.12: see Behr 1993, 53–4. On the military operations of 89, see Keaveney 2005a, 43–4.

[62] See above, n. 22. Incidentally, although Badian 1970, 47 and Seager 1994, 170 plausibly suppose that Sulla himself aroused the fear in his soldiers that Marius might replace them, Appian has him refer only to Marius' *hubris*. Dahlheim 1993, 100, n. 4 rightly notes that this concern was hardly Sullan

military tribunes were stoned when they arrived to take the army away from the consul.[63]

The common interpretation of Sulla's army as essentially treasonous or disaffected from the traditions of the republic has no doubt drawn some of its plausibility from Appian's comment that when the legions moved out for Rome, "the officers of the army (οἱ μὲν ἄρχοντες τοῦ στρατοῦ) except for one quaestor deserted him and ran off to Rome, since they could not bring themselves to lead an army against their country."[64] Since this intriguing episode has often been seen as a precious clue to the real attitude of the senate or nobility in this crisis, there has been much discussion as to whether by *archontes tou stratou* Appian chiefly meant senatorial senior officers, who are presumed to reflect the attitudes of the senatorial order as a whole, or *equites*, who were by this time making inroads into the military tribunate, and even sub-equestrian centurions.[65] The fact that Appian notes the exception of a single *quaestor*[66] seems to point toward the former interpretation, but in the important parallel case of Cinna, Appian's wording suggests rather the contrary.[67] The apparent contradiction is overcome if we regard *archontes* as convenient shorthand, flexible and quite general ("officers"), including legates, quaestors, tribunes and centurions. In that case, however, the assertion is obviously either extremely inexact or grossly exaggerated, since it is virtually inconceivable that Sulla marched four (or six) legions to Rome in good order after having lost his entire officer corps – especially the "middle cadre" (de Blois) of tribunes and centurions who were crucial not only for daily operations

---

propaganda but a natural concern. The precedent of Marius' recruitment in 107 of a new army *per ambitionem* (Sall. *Iug.* 86.3) to carry on the war in Numidia will have been recalled.

[63] Plut. *Sull.* 8.4–9.1. Note ὡς ἐπύθοντο ταῦτα, which (for what it is worth) implies that the soldiers were motivated by outrage rather than material self-interest. Keaveney 2005a, 52–3 rightly stresses Sulla's claims to legitimacy and his troops' "clear political awareness" in accepting those claims. Cf. Meier 1966 (1980), 223, and 237 ("die Soldaten glauben konnten, im Sinne des senates und der rechtlichen Ordnung zu handeln," although he still accepts the primacy of Appian's fear-motive).

[64] App. *B Civ.* 1.57/253.

[65] See Mitchell 1979, 69–70; Levick 1982 (senatorial officers not singled out); *contra*, Keaveney 1983, 63–4; Keaveney 2007, 38; and apparently de Blois 2000, 22, 29, who infers that senatorial higher officers and the "middle cadre" reacted differently to Sulla's appeal in 88, although this is not actually stated in the evidence. The episode is read with varying degrees of emphasis as a senatorial verdict on Sulla's cause by (e.g.) Meier 1966 (1980), 224 (though cf. 223); Gabba 1976, 27; de Blois 1987, 87–8; and esp. Keaveney 1983, 63–8 (cf. 2005a, 53); Mitchell and Levick complicate the picture.

[66] Generally identified as L. Licinius Lucullus (Badian 1964, 220). Rawson awkwardly notes that Hortensius and Sisenna may also have been on Sulla's staff – if so, did *they* desert him (1979, 334)?

[67] App. *B Civ.* 1.65/298 τούς τε ἄρχοντας αὐτοῦ καὶ ὅσοι ἀπὸ τῆς βουλῆς ἐπεδήμουν. See above, n. 37.

but even for maintaining the army's obedience.⁶⁸ And if Appian's claim is grossly exaggerated, then it is hard to say just what, if any, historical reality we can extract from it.

Perhaps some conspicuous, high-ranking officers did in fact refuse to take part in the undertaking, citing precisely the grounds Appian mentions. If we allow Appian's claim this much credibility, then let us also look equally closely at the wording of the explanation he gives: "since they could not bring themselves to lead an army against their country." That is far from saying that they actually favored Sulpicius' and Marius' cause over Sulla's in this mess – any more than in 49 Cicero, in the passage with which this paper began, favored Caesar over Pompey. Indeed, the *archontes*' rationale seems identical to that expressed by Q. Mucius Scaevola Pontifex in defense of his decision to remain in Rome during the *Cinnanum tempus*, despite his revulsion for the regime: he saw how badly it would turn out, yet he preferred even this to marching upon Rome in arms.⁶⁹ This too Cicero approves in February 49, though without suggesting an ounce of sympathy for Caesar's cause or any betrayal of Pompey's. These officers' restraint and scruples may well have been greater than their soldiers' but their views on the injury done to the consuls by Sulpicius and Marius may have been no less severe. Therefore, given the moral and legal complexities involved in this fateful decision and our uncertainty about crucial details, including just who these *archontes* were, it seems rash to draw out of this murky episode the considered verdict of the senatorial order upon Sulla's cause in general.⁷⁰

Most modern historians tend to follow Appian without demur when he makes mention only of mercenary motives for the readiness of the Capuan

---

⁶⁸ Legions: cf. Oros. 5.19.4 with App. *B Civ.* 1.57/253; Plut. *Sull.* 9.5; Gabba 1967, 166; Erdmann 1972, 88. On the influence of the "middle cadre," see above, n. 46.

⁶⁹ Cic. *Att.* 8.3.6. On Scaevola, see Mitchell 1979, 88–90; on Cicero's application of Scaevola's example to his own case, Mitchell 1991, 245.

⁷⁰ Similarly, the embassies sent to Sulla by the senate (App. *B Civ.* 1.57/253–6; Plut. *Sull.* 9.5) in a Rome dominated by Marius and Sulpicius are also sometimes rather naively interpreted as authentic expressions of the will of the nobility or senatorial order. Appian clearly notes that the last embassy at least was sent at Marius' and Sulpicius' behest, while Plutarch explicitly says that "the senate was not a free agent but was governed by the commands of Marius and Sulpicius." True, Plutarch used Sulla's memoirs; but Appian's account is not slavishly pro-Sullan. It stands to reason that some senators will indeed have sympathized with Marius and Sulpicius, while others who favored Sulla's original cause will have been shocked and terrified by the possible consequences that were now suddenly looming. But to take these embassies as evidence of the authentic will of the senatorial order at this moment is to overlook the fact that opposition to Sulpicius and Marius was paralyzed by the rout of both consuls in the first phase of the conflict. On interpretation of the embassies, see Mitchell 1979, 71, n. 35; and *contra*, Keaveney 1983, 65–8.

legions to follow their consul.⁷¹ And yet if we consider the question of legitimacy from the legionary perspective we might see their actions not as a sign of alienation or disaffection from the republic but perhaps indeed the reverse.⁷² For what it is worth, Appian may well be right (*B Civ.* 1.57/250–2) that the legions feared that Marius would enroll a different army in place of themselves, and therefore that they would be deprived of the easy pickings of an eastern campaign. But historians are familiar with "double determination" in human motivation: human beings are frequently conscious of having more than one motive for a given action, and these motives often work on different planes ("expediency" and "justice," for example) whose relative weight is inherently problematic to assess from the outside and frequently controversial. Motivation is far from a "zero-sum game," and the attested and quite plausible material interest that the legions besieging Nola had in defending their consul against the *hubris* of Marius and Sulpicius in no way excludes the hypothesis that they saw themselves as acting in defense of the republic's traditions rather than against them. If at a deeper level these kinds of patriotic self-justifications coincided with hopes for material benefit, in principle (as we have seen) this is no different from the way in which the "profit motive" influenced Roman soldiers reaching back to 264 and no doubt beyond.⁷³

Too rarely, if ever, does Sulla's consular status receive appropriate emphasis as a *prima facie* mark of legitimacy for the soldiers who followed him from Capua to Rome – presumably because Appian says nothing explicitly about it, while he does say something about the troops' more "mercenary" motives. Yet much is lost when the historian, in an excess of

---

[71] Keaveney 2005a, 51–2 is a notable exception, in a paragraph substantially rewritten since the original edition of 1982. The changes seem to reflect Keaveney's recent work on the "revolutionary" Roman army, in which he refers often to this episode in passages that clarify his most recent position (Keaveney 2007, 25–6, 37–8, 94–5).

[72] Morstein-Marx & Rosenstein 2006, 633. "Legality" and "legitimacy" are often conflated (see below); but even the question of legality was thoroughly confused, given the doubtful status of Sulpicius' laws and the entirely reasonable doubt whether, after Sulla and his colleague were effectively driven from Rome through the use of violence, the senate could be thought to enjoy autonomous agency. Under such circumstances the "Rechtsargument" (on which Dahlheim 1993, 100–4 puts misplaced stress) becomes hopelessly tangled. The sterility of the legalistic approach becomes evident when Dahlheim finds a crippling weakness of Sulla's case in the lack of a *senatus consultum ultimum* (SCU) authorizing armed suppression of Sulpicius, while on the very next page acknowledging that even the introduction of the SCU itself was "ein Akt der Usurpation." The SCU was itself a "political" instrument whose justification could be found not in strict law but in larger norms and values: cf. Drummond 1995, 79–113; Lintott 1999a, 89–93. And did not the senate itself soon decide (now under Sulla's supervision) that Sulpicius' laws were themselves "illegal"?

[73] See above, n. 10.

evidentiary scrupulousness, declines to unpack the unspoken implications of our sources simply because something is not explicitly said. After looking closely at the example of Cinna, which lies only just around the historical corner, I hope it will seem less bold than it might otherwise seem to presume a higher level of Roman civic consciousness among the late-republican soldiery than is normally conjectured, and thus to suggest that when Sulla denounced the *hubris* done him by Sulpicius and Marius, he was actually invoking republican civic values, which included the highest respect for the consuls, whom the Roman people had elected.[74]

Elsewhere, while advocating a more nuanced assessment of Julius Caesar's public justification of his march into Italy, I have argued in favor of the sociological, Weberian concept of "legitimacy" rather than the juristic notion of "legality" that tends to dominate our field[75] – chiefly, I suspect, because the towering figure of Mommsen set the terms of that debate in the middle of the nineteenth century, but no doubt also because it reflects the long-standing modern project of imposing a highly juristic structure upon the political use of violence. For the analysis of civil war, however, the concept of "legitimacy" is more useful than "legality," both because the latter idea biases the debate in favor of those who happen at the time to be in control of institutions (who, to varying degrees, are in a position to make the law what they want it to be), and because the arbiters of "legitimacy" are ultimately the citizenry in general rather than the legal experts. For the purposes of a historian who is empirically investigating social and political movements, citizens, not lawyers, are the ones who really matter, since citizens determine political legitimacy by their active or passive support for a regime (or the reverse), whatever the lawyers have to say on the matters referred to their jurisdiction.

Political legitimacy, as Weber and those in the Weberian tradition have seen it, is what produces the interesting, and anarchists might say oxymoronic, phenomenon of "willing obedience" in political subjects. Weber was interested in the different ways in which "willing obedience" was engendered in political subjects, and how this could be used to establish an abstract typology of societies in terms of their organization of domination (the famous triad of traditional, rational-legal and charismatic); the contemporary theorist David Beetham focuses instead on the different elements that constitute the judgments that create "willing obedience" in political subjects in any given society, past as well as present – namely (in his view), *legality* (adherence to the established law or custom), *normative*

---

[74] See above, nn. 24, 25. [75] Cf. above, n. 72.

justifiability (adherence to central political values and beliefs) and what he calls in a quasi-technical sense *legitimation* (that is, confirmation and affirmation by public acts of consent, such as elections).[76] Yet however we slice the cake, in the Weberian tradition, which is a much more fruitful approach for historians than the juristic one, the "focalization" of legitimacy (to borrow a useful term from narratology) is oriented through the eyes of the mass of citizens whose remarkable and sometimes quite paradoxical obedience is counted on by regimes of all kinds day in, day out.

Now if we look at the Roman republic in these terms, we could ask ourselves when, if ever, the "willing obedience" of its citizens to the republican political system was withdrawn. The outbreak of civil wars in 88 and 49, on a traditional view, might seem to mark such a moment. Yet we must be careful here: the republican political system, or the political traditions of the republic – in a phrase, the *mos maiorum* – cannot simply be identified with the senate at any particular moment. On the contrary, a particular senate – say, one that could go so far as to vote a consul out of office and possibly even replace him with another on its own authority, to take Cinna's case – might behave starkly at variance with deeply traditional standards of legality and normative justifiability. The senate was not, in short, *the* locus of legitimacy, plain and simple. We have been too ready to treat it as such, however, so that in moments of crisis, which are in part *crises of legitimacy*, whichever party happens to be opposed by the majority vote of the senate (no matter how legitimately or illegitimately that majority is constituted or conducts itself) tends to be regarded by modern scholars as rebelling against legitimate authority, "the state," the republic and its political traditions. I have argued above that if we consider the matter carefully from the perspective of the soldiers to whom Sulla and Cinna addressed their appeals in 88 and 87, that is not what we see.

On the other hand, in both cases I think we can observe the reverence of Roman citizens, and perhaps especially soldiers, for the consul and the consulship. Especially noteworthy, however, is the rationale for this reverence suggested in the speech Appian provides for Cinna, where the respect the office inspires is rooted explicitly and emphatically in its nature as a gift of the Roman people, which they confer by means of their *votes*, demanding in return deference and thereby exercising some control over their political elite. From this perspective, the consulship is a symbol of legitimacy whose potency derives from its nature as the embodiment of a *decision of the people*. This gives special point to those occasional spectacular acts

---

[76] Weber 1968, 212–13; Beetham 1991, 15–24; cf. Morstein-Marx 2009, 33–40.

of popular "delegitimation" when the *fasces* were ritualistically destroyed by angry crowds: what this ritual seems to represent is the withdrawal by the *populus Romanus* of the gift it had bestowed.[77] On the other hand, derogation of the consulship by other magistrates or the senate could also be seen from this same perspective as an offense against the majesty of the citizenry who had elected the consul: thus in Cinna's speech the deposition of the consul is represented as thrusting the Roman people out of their proper role as electors, as arbiters of *honos* in the community – *the* principal mechanism by means of which they force their political leaders to orient themselves toward the people and their interests. When Cinna says "Why would we cultivate the tribes in elections any longer? Why would we need you any longer?" he is pointing to the danger of a complete breakdown of a central feature of the republican system – the sabotaging of the meritocratic principle so that *honores* would be distributed by and for the few without regard for the *commoda* and *dignitas* of the Roman people.[78] These were civic arguments, and it is of considerable interest that in these appeals the "popular perspective" so redolent of the Forum and *rostra* is shown to have been shared as well by soldiers, who are usually seen more in the character of virtual clients or quasi-mercenaries than as the "citizens" that Cinna (or Appian's Cinna) calls them.[79]

---

[77] See Goltz 2000. Famously, following the precedent of Valerius Publicola the *fasces* were also lowered before the people in *contiones*: Livy 2.7; Plut. *Publ.* 10.7; Cic. *Rep.* 2.53; Val. Max. 4.1.1. Our sources interpret this as a way of demonstrating the subordination of consular *imperium* to the *maiestas* of the people, but this does not actually stand in contradiction with the idea that the consul gains his authority precisely by embodying the people's will.

[78] Cf. Morstein-Marx 2009, esp. 5–12.

[79] In his more recent work, Arthur Keaveney has begun (quite rightly) to emphasize the "political awareness" (2005a, 52 – not in the 1982 edn) of the late-republican Roman army, in opposition to those who have seen it as a "professional," almost mercenary force; this is in fact now the leitmotif of his recent book on the army in the "Roman revolution" (Keaveney 2007). Somewhat paradoxically, however, the "political awareness" of the army turns out to play much the same role in Keaveney's interpretation of the downfall of the Roman republic as did the "professional"/client army in the traditional interpretation: he deplores "the indisputably ruinous precedent" whereby Sulla "politicised the Roman army" and asserts that "he introduced into the military gathering issues and concerns which had no business there but properly belonged in its civil counterpart in the city" (Keaveney 2007, 95). In my view, this presupposes an anachronistic distinction between soldier and citizen that is found in many modern states but is quite alien to ancient republics and democracies. Romans remembered that their state had been liberated more than once by their citizen-soldiers when its proper functioning had been suspended by "tyrants" (cf. the expulsion of the Tarquins and the first two Secessions of the Plebs). This is a state in which the assembly of the *populus* was originally an assembly of the army, and whose generals, whom the soldiers swore to obey, were magistrates of the Roman people. The army of the Roman republic was *always* politicized.

CHAPTER 13

Consules populares
Antonio Duplá

THE *POPULARES* AND THE CRISIS OF THE REPUBLIC

The *optimates–populares* conflict is one of the distinctive events of the last century of republican Rome.[1] From the mid-second century until the civil wars of the 40s, the ancient authors describe a series of critical episodes that allow a degree of continuity to be established.[2]

At relatively regular intervals, we witness popular movements led by the plebeian tribunes, socio-economic demands (whether to do with agrarian reform, the corn supply or the founding of colonies), disputes between the senate and the assemblies about their respective powers, an abundance of laws and proposals[3] as well as of assemblies (especially *contiones*), and even repressive mechanisms of doubtful "constitutionality," such as the so-called *senatus consultum ultimum*. In this sense, the harmony (*concordia*), real or imaginary, that the ancient authors attribute to other republican periods appears to have been lost: the citizens and the ruling classes frequently appear divided and the mechanisms of consensus and social cohesion function less effectively.[4]

I thank Francisco Pina Polo and Martin Jehne for comments that have greatly improved the text, and David Peterson for the translation. All the dates are BC. This work was supported by the M.E.C. (Spain. Research project "Cónsules, consulares y el gobierno de la República romana" / HUM 2004–02449 and HUM2007–60776/HIST).

[1] On *optimates* and *populares*: Strassburger 1939; Hellegouarc'h 1963; Martin 1965; Meier 1965; Serrao 1970; Seager 1972; Perelli 1982; Vanderbroek 1987; Burckhardt 1988; Mackie 1992; Wiseman 1994; Ferrary 1997.
[2] This continuity seemed evident to the ancient authors (Cicero, Sallust, Velleius Paterculus, Appian, Cassius Dio, etc.): *assidua senatus adversus plebem certamina* (Tac. *Dial.* 36.3).
[3] *Corruptissima re publica, plurimae leges* (Tac. *Ann.* 3.27); Cic. *Vat.* 16; Millar 1986, 1995, 1998; Ducos 1984, 154–70.
[4] "There is 'consensus' in a society when we can observe among its members a fairly general agreement on the form of government regarded as legitimate." (M. Duverger, *The Study of Politics*, 103; cited in Mackie 1992, 52, n. 10). But, from then on, "Selbstverständliches war nicht mehr selbstverständlich" (Burckhardt 1988, 16).

The term *popularis* is a concept vital to the analysis of the late-republican crisis. However, the polisemicity of the term often complicates that analysis. It is in this context that it becomes both necessary and worthwhile to attempt to understand the meaning of the term *popularis*.[5] Drawing on the evidence of our sources, *popularis-populares* can refer to:

a) an individual favorable, in one way or another, to the *populus* or who seeks its approval;
b) a political stance or attitude opposed to the senatorial majority, from different possible perspectives;
c) a political strategy, based on the tribunate, the assemblies, especially the *contiones*, and the *eloquentia popularis*;
d) a social tendency and a political tradition, during the last century of the republic, that appeal to a series of ideas and proposals, episodes, leaders and martyrs all related to the defense of the political rights of the *populus* and the improvement of its living conditions, generally in opposition to the senatorial oligarchy (*optimates*).[6]

It is thus wrong to regard the *populariter agere* as merely a more or less opportunist option in the political career of a *nobilis*. That could, of course, be the case – hence Sallust's criticism of the *mos partium et factionum* and of the ambitious young aristocrats who used the popular cause for their own interests.[7] However, Sallust himself recognizes the justice behind the *populares*' demands and the *superbia* of the senatorial oligarchy.[8]

The term *popularis* usually appears in the sources associated with the plebeian tribunes. However, it is also applied on occasion to certain consuls who enjoy great popularity (like Pompey), who promote policies traditionally considered *populares*, or who display a *popularis* anti-noble attitude and join forces with recognized *popularis* leaders (like Marius), or even to those who follow a *popularis* trajectory over the length of their political careers (like Caesar). On the other hand, we have the case of Cicero, self-proclaimed *consul re, non oratione popularis*. Before we begin to analyze the different examples of consuls *populares*, it is important to establish several general points.

---

[5] The labels *optimates* and *populares* might mean different things at different times (Martin 1965, 224; Yakobson 1999, 174).
[6] Something acknowledged early by Strassburger 1939, 794.
[7] Sall. *Iug.* 41.1; *Cat.* 38. It is possible that Sallust was thinking of events in the 60s, when several of the best-known *populares* tribunes were prosecuted and condemned. See Wiseman 1994, 398: "The very successes of the *populares* had compromised their integrity."
[8] Sall. *Iug.* 5.1 (*superbia*). Basic texts for the demands and beliefs of the *populares*: *Cat.* 20 (Catiline's speech); *Cat.* 33 (Manlius' letter); *Iug.* 31 (Memmius' speech); *Iug.* 85 (Marius' speech); *Hist.* 1.55 (*Or. Lep.*); *Hist.* 3.48 (*Or. Macr.*); *Iug.* 41–3; cf. Cic. *Sest.* 96ff.

First, we should not forget that our single most important source is Cicero, who brings with him the well-known complications that the analysis of his writings entails. In this case, the task is complicated even more by the fact that Cicero describes himself in 63 BC as a genuine *consul popularis*, something that fits uneasily with his later career. Given his political and forensic protagonism, his use of the term is almost always charged with rhetorical or political meaning. On the other hand, the relatively late coinage of the term by Cicero does not mean that there had not previously been political and social conflicts analyzable from the *optimates* vs. *populares* perspective.[9]

As regards his own political stance, we accept that from the process against Verres (70) onwards through the 60s, Cicero, a *homo novus*, did not vacillate about aligning himself clearly with Pompey and in opposition to well-known *optimates*, thus gaining in popularity and steadily advancing in his *cursus honorum*. It ought, however, to be pointed out that his *popularis* stance was always a moderate one, and that the conflict with the senatorial leaders was carefully tempered and generally non-polemical.[10] From mid-63 onwards, and particularly after the formation of the so-called First Triumvirate, he distanced himself from potential *populares* stances, and he progressively moved toward the *optimates*, although always attempting to preserve his own autonomy. This evolution affects the sense, more positive or negative, afforded to the term *popularis* in his writings.[11]

Second, we know that at given moments the *optimates* would adopt measures traditionally regarded as *populares*. Normally these would be *leges frumentariae*, introduced in response to periods of social tension and to crises in the grain supply to Rome. The intention was to dilute social protest and prevent the *populares* from making political capital out of such protest. While the *optimates*' rejection of the agrarian laws was generally firm, we can cite various *frumentariae* initiatives, such as the Terentia-Cassia in 73 or the *senatus consultum* proposed by Cato in 62.[12] Although such initiatives might appear to confuse the issue, it seems reasonable to suppose that given the different political perspective, as well as the support of both the senatorial majority and individuals unmistakably *optimates*, the plebs would not have been fooled. This brings us to the distinction between true

---

[9] Martin 1965, 5 begins his study in the post-Sullan period, although he also then analyzes the earlier period. Cicero himself uses the term in reference to earlier periods. We will also find numerous references in the *Rhetorica ad Herennium*, probably from the 80s (Pina Polo 1996, 93–5), and in the surviving fragments of the speeches of the Gracchi and others.
[10] As can be seen in his attitude toward Hortensius and Catullus in *de imperio Cn. Pompei*.
[11] Seager 1972; Ferrary 1982; Perelli 1982, 23–38. [12] Burckhardt 1988, 239–67.

and false *populares*, with their attitude toward conflict with the senate, or rather the *factio paucorum*, possibly being important. For example, Sulla, despite proposing and carrying through both agrarian and colonial laws, was never considered a *popularis*, but rather quite the opposite.[13] On the other hand, some proposals, such as the re-establishment of the tribunician powers in the 70s, are the result not just of *populares* demands, but also of a broader senatorial support based on pragmatism and the political opportunism of certain *nobiles*.[14]

Third, given that our focus is historical rather than philological, we analyze not only those consuls characterized expressly as *populares* in the sources (Pompey, Crassus, Caesar and Cicero), but also those other consuls related in one way or another to the *popularis* movement. The connection might be their political deeds, their proposals, their alliances or even the way they are portrayed in our sources, without the explicit label of *popularis*. In this way we can better appreciate their importance as a symptom of the republican political crisis, and specifically of the political division of the Roman ruling class.

The list of *consules populares* is not a long one. We ought not forget that a significant number of popular leaders were murdered during their tribunates (such as Tiberius and Caius Gracchus, Saturninus, Sulpicius Rufus) and we cannot be certain how far they would have reached along their *cursus*. We also know of a more limited group of possible candidates who, for one reason or another, such as violence, never achieved the consulship; for example, Clodius, C. Memmius and C. Servilius Glaucia, candidates in 99[15] and both assassinated, or M. Lollius Palicanus, candidate in 66.[16]

---

[13] Cic. *Clu.* 151: *homo a populi causa remotissimus*. According to Cicero (*Sest.* 140), the true *populares* were those *qui senatus consilium, qui auctoritatem bonorum, qui instituta maiorum neglexerunt et imperitae aut concitatae multitudini iucundi esse voluerunt*. For Mackie, this is a distinction assumed by the Romans, and he insists on the defense of the powers and rights of the *populus* against the senate as being the defining characteristics: "The key to the political role of *populares*, and what also gave substance to the notion of 'true' versus 'false' *populares*, is public commitment (from whatever hidden motives) to an ideological theme of popular rights and powers. In the absence of a coherent *popularis* group or 'party', it was public commitment to this abstract theme that gave the *popularis* politician his identity" (1992, 71). For Yavetz (1988, 38–57), the key element is the willingness to openly confront the oligarchy, rather than concrete proposals. There would lie the fundamental difference between Pompey or Cicero and Caesar. Yakobson 2006a, 391.

[14] From a pragmatic point of view Cicero judged Pompey's rehabilitation of the full tribunician *potestas* favorably (*Leg.* 3.26).

[15] Memmius: Livy, *Per.* 69; Oros. 5.17.5. Glaucia: his electoral possibilities were emphasized by Cicero (*Brut.* 224). Badian, 1962, 207ff.; Yakobson 1999, 160.

[16] On Palicanus, Val. Max. 3.8.3; Yakobson 1999, 162f.

CONSULES POPULARES

The earliest individuals characterized as *populares* date from the early republic. This is the case with the consuls of 449, Lucius Valerius Potitus and Marcus Horatius Barbatus, of whom Cicero would say: "*Lucique Valeri Potiti et M. Horati Barbati hominum concordiae causa sapienter popularium consularis lex sanxit ne qui magistratus sine prouocatione crearetur.*" Irrespective of the historical value of this episode, it is both interesting and demonstrative of the connection established by Cicero between the consuls, the *popularitas* and the *provocatio ad populum*.[17]

Additionally there is a passage in Cicero, in which he refers to a series of earlier consular figures that would later be championed by the *populares*, characterizing the latter as *seditiosi cives*.[18] Among these figures we find some consuls, like Publius Valerius, supposed author of the first *de provocatione* law in the early years of the republic, C. Flaminius, Q. Pompeius, P. Cornelius Scipio Africanus, P. Licinius Crassus and P. Mucius Scaevola. It is worth noting that, in the better-documented cases, these seem to have been political figures who either, with plebeian support, came into conflict with the senatorial majority (C. Flaminius, tr. pl. 232, cos. 223, 217;[19] P. Scipio, cos. 147, 134[20]), or supported *popularis*-style reforms (like P. Licinius Crassus and P. Mucius Scaevola with respect to T. Gracchus).[21] Regarding Q. Pompeius (cos. 141), the career of this *homo novus* is frequently portrayed as a triumph over the traditional *nobilitas*;[22] and this reading would similarly be applicable to C. Marius. While it is true that these examples are often radically different, with some of them being of doubtful historicity and

---

[17] "And a law proposed by the consuls Lucius Valerius Potitus and Marcus Horatius Barbatus, men who wisely favored popular measures to preserve peace, provides that no magistrat not subject to appeal shall be elected" (Cic. *Rep.* 2.31.54). On the importance of 449 in the Roman historical tradition, Martin 1965, 217 n. 2; Ferrary 1984, 88–90; Powell 2001; cf. Livy 3.55.1–5.

[18] Cic. *Luc.* 13. The *Lucullus*, also known as *Acad. Pr.* [II], is dated to the year 45 (Powell 1995a, xiv).

[19] Polyb. 2.21.8; Livy 21.63. He was elected consul twice, despite his continuous conflict with the senatorial majority. Yakobson 1999, 158.

[20] The case of Scipio Aemilianus shows the role of the plebs as protagonists and the importance of popular support beyond the will of the senatorial majority (Plut. *Aem.* 38.3; Meier 1965, 582; Astin 1971, 26–34, 182ff.; Gruen 1974; Gargola 2006, 164). His support for the tribunes and the *lex Cassia tabellaria* was just as pragmatic as Cicero's acceptance of the tribunate in *de legibus* (Yakobson 2006b, 393). Indeed, Meier (1965, 583) does not include Scipio in the subsequent *popularis* tradition.

[21] P. Mucius Scaevola, cos. 133, opposed the violent repression of T. Gracchus led by Scipio Nasica (Cic. *Dom.* 91; *Planc.* 88; *De or.* 2.285; *Tusc.* 4.51; Val. Max. 3.2.17; [Aur. Vict.] *De vir. ill.* 64.7). P. Licinius Crassus, cos. 131, would be a member of the agrarian commission after the death of Tiberius Gracchus (Plut. *Ti. Gr.* 21.1).

[22] Cic. *Font.* 23; *Mur.* 16; Meier 1965, 580; Yakobson 1999, 13ff. For the idea of the *homines novi* as a victory over the nobilitas: *Rhet. Her.* 1.8; Sall. *Iug.* 65.5; 73; 85.4; Cic. *Leg. agr.* 2.3.7.

others seeming never to have exercised a genuinely *popularis* leadership, the important point is that they were regarded as precedents by the *populares*. If the passage is an echo of a contemporary opinion, it records what seems to be a historical *popularis* tradition, with its heroes and deeds. In any case, it is clear that the conflict between the *populus* and the senatorial majority predates the Gracchi.

M. Fulvius Flaccus

In 125, between the tribunates of Tiberius and Caius Gracchus, after the assassination of the former and his followers, and in the context of the activity of the agrarian commission and the growing unrest amongst the Italian *socii*, M. Fulvius Flaccus, a member of the agrarian commission, became consul. During his consulship he proposed two *rogationes* that would offer the Italians either citizenship or the *provocatio*, in the latter case as a defensive mechanism against the excesses of the Roman magistrates.[23] But, as he was sent to aid Massalia against Salluvian and Vocontian Gauls, neither proposal prospered. His *cursus honorum* is quite exceptional since after his consulship he would become a plebeian tribune in 122, along with C. Gracchus, as well as a member of the commission derived from the *lex Sempronia agraria*. He would also meet the same fate as Gracchus: being murdered and beheaded, with his body thrown into the Tiber and his possessions sold off.

C. Marius

Toward the end of the second century, the case of Caius Marius is noteworthy for various reasons, besides his oft-debated political beliefs. Some years after a tribunate that saw some *popularis* initiatives (*lex Maria tabellaria*), he became consul in an atmosphere of anti-noble tribunician agitation and strong popular support.[24]

His first speech as consul was a diatribe against the traditional *nobilitas* and in support of a *nova nobilitas* (Sall. *Iug.* 85). We cannot be sure what portion of the speech stems from Marius' own ideas rather than from Sallust's later reconstruction (perhaps based on ideas taken from Cicero

---

[23] *Rogatio Fulvia de civitate sociis danda* (Val. Max. 9.5.1; App. *B Civ.* 1.21); *rogatio Fulvia de provocatione* (Val. Max. 9.5.1); Münzer 1910; Lintott 1994, 75–6. Plutarch insists on his strong and aggressive manner, in contrast to the more peaceful Gracchus (*C. Gracch.* 14–16). Broughton 1951–86, I, 510.

[24] *Seditiosi magistratus volgum exagitare* (Sall. *Iug.* 73.5); supported by *opifices agrestesque omnes* (*Iug.* 73.6), *equites* (*Iug.* 65.4). Yakobson 1999, 158ff.

himself), but it seems reasonable to suppose there is at least some original input from Marius. Several aspects of Marius' consular period are of interest to us: first of all, the fact that he was a *homo novus*; his open hostility toward Metellus, the prominent *nobilis*; then his award of the command of the African war by popular insistence, overriding a senatorial decision (Sall. *Iug.* 73.7); later, his alliance with the *popularis* tribune L. Appuleius Saturninus and, in particular, the granting of land to veterans, thus introducing a new type of agrarian distribution and a new model for relations between a commander and his legionaries. Developments of this kind had been seen before, but not on the same scale. The use of his veterans as shock-troops in the political arena was also new.

From a political perspective, his support of the so-called *de provinciis praetoriis* law is assumed, and this implies a significant degree of participation by the assemblies in areas previously controlled by the senate, a policy generally regarded as being *popularis*-inspired.[25] He also seems to have been responsible for the founding of a colony on Corsica, in accordance with Saturninus' policy for the foundation of colonies, a measure generally favored by the *populares* leaders. We also know that, in relation to Saturninus' policy, Marius is regarded as having favored the granting of the citizenship to three individuals in each colony as a way of rewarding the Italian allies. For these and other reasons, it seems clear that Marius was in favor of the concession of Roman citizenship, if only on a selective basis.[26]

Marius' role in the suppression of Saturninus and Glaucia in 100, and his later excesses in the 80s, do not seem to have affected his popularity.[27] This is the only context that explains Cicero's insistent references to Marius toward the end of his speech *pro Rabirio perduellionis reo*, in which he attempts to legitimize the *senatus consultum ultimum* against the plebs and to justify the murder of Saturninus and his followers.[28] The presence of a consul among the anti-noble ranks, with all that his presence would have entailed (his *imperium*, popularity, his *dignitas* and his veterans) opens up a new dimension in Roman political conflict, until then restricted largely to tribunician activity.[29]

---

[25] Crawford 1996b, 1, 237.   [26] Cic. *Balb.* 46, 48; Val. Max. 5.2.8; Plin. *HN* 3.80.
[27] Although he would have to renounce the censorship and make do with an augurate in 97 (Plut. *Mar.* 30.4, Yakobson 1999, 161, n. 32; Broughton 1951–86, II, 8). In fact, during the backlash against Saturninus and Glaucia, Marius stood out by accepting their surrender, although he could not avoid their being lynched by the mob (App. *B Civ.* 1.32; Plut. *Mar.* 30; Vell. Pat. 2.12.6).
[28] Cic. *Rab. perd.* 20ff.; but cf. *Off.* 3.20.79. His portrayal is very negative in Cassius Dio (26.89; 31.102); Plut. *Mar.* 31–2; Vell. Pat. 2.23.1; Perelli 1982, 56.
[29] Weynand 1935, 1397.

CINNANUM TEMPUS

During the turbulent decade of the 80s we meet L. Cornelius Cinna (cos. 87–84), never termed *popularis* as such, and heavily criticized in the sources to the extent that his consulships are represented as an authentic *dominatio*, a period of tyranny. For some, following Asconius, his policy was centered on the defense of the interests of the *equites*.[30] However, his conflict with Cn. Octavius is described by Appian in terms of the full or partial integration of the new Italian citizens, a theme central to the *optimates* vs. *populares* conflicts.[31] Indeed, the repeal of the Sullan laws and the restoration of those proposed by Sulpicius Rufus, in particular those that dealt with the inscription of new citizens, Italians and freedmen, should clearly be regarded in these terms. Other episodes have also been interpreted in terms of the *popularis* tendency, particularly when, declared *hostis publicus* by the senate, he appeared in Nola in front of the troops in an attempt to win their support and recover his position.[32] Recently, Cinna has been vindicated as an advocate of counting on the new Italian citizens as political and military allies. To a certain degree, then, Cinna would have been a pioneer in leading a political project supported by the new Romano-Italic civic community and based on a broad social consensus.[33]

The consul *suffectus* in 86, after Marius' death, L. Valerius Flaccus, proposed a law regulating debts, but it is difficult to know how far-reaching the law was and who its real beneficiaries would have been, as the consequences of the *bellum sociale* and the war in Asia would probably have affected the rural Italian plebs as much as any particular group of *publicani*.[34] As for the consuls from the years 84 to 82 (Cn. Papirius Carbo, L. Cornelius Scipio Asiaticus, C. Norbanus and C. Marius), we know about their understandably anti-Sullan tendencies and their military actions, but little or nothing about political measures.[35]

---

[30] Asc. *Tog. cand.* 89; Cic. *Phil.* 1.34; 2.108; *Brut.* 227; Sall. *Hist.* 1.64M; Val. Max. 6.9.6; Vell. Pat. 2.23.3; Plut. *Caes.* 1.1; *Sull.* 10, 22.1; Tac. *Ann.* 1.1; [Aur. Vict.] *De vir. ill.* 67.6.

[31] App. *B Civ.* 1.64; Plut. *Sull.* 10: Cinna, "a man of the opposite party."

[32] App. *B Civ* 1.65–6. Cinna intervenes there "in a true *popularis* fashion" (Seager 1994, 175). For a detailed analysis of this episode, cf. Morstein-Marx in this volume.

[33] Lovano 2002, 51, 77. Lovano analyzes the sources for Cinna, and concludes that the image we have of the *dominatio cinnana* has largely been conditioned by the Sullan tradition (*ibid.*, 141–59; cf. Cic. *Brut.* 308: *triennium sine armis*). Previously, Gelzer (1968, 17–20) had characterized Cinna as *popularis*, pointing out his possible influence on Caesar's subsequent policy. On the difficulty of knowing exactly what happened during the *dominatio cinnana*, Seager 1994, 180ff.

[34] *Lex Valeria de ere alieno* (Vell. Pat. 2.23.2: *turpissima*; Cic. *Font.*1.1; *Quinct.* 17). Seager (1994, 180), points out that it was criticized by the more conservative sources; but cf. Sall. *Cat.* 33.2: *volentibus omnibus bonis* ("with all the good citizens desiring it"); Lovano 2002, 72ff.

[35] Sources in Broughton 1951–86, II, 60ff.; cf. *Fam.* 1.9.11. See Münzer (1900, 1930, 1936) and Kroll (1910) on the four consuls. On Cornelius, Cic. *Sest.* 7: *optimus vir*, and *calamitosissimus*. On Cn. Papirius Carbo: *malus civis, improbus consul, seditiosus homo* (Cic. *Verr.* 2.1.37; Sall. *Hist.* 1.38.1).

M. Aemilius Lepidus

Another example of the depth of the divisions in the heart of the ruling classes when the consuls themselves became involved is offered by Marcus Aemilius Lepidus, consul in 78.[36] After Sulla's retirement from politics, conflict immediately developed amongst the *nobilitas* between those wishing to repeal his measures and their opponents. Lepidus, despite his Sullan background, seems to have been chosen against the wishes of Sulla and with the support of Pompey, to propose the revision of the *acta Sullae*.[37] This meant the return of exiles, the restoration of the civic and political rights of the condemned, and the return to the previous owners of the properties and lands that had been confiscated and assigned to Sullan veterans. This series of measures was bound to upset the political, social and economic order in Rome given the wide range of groups and interests affected. There are also references to a *lex Aemilia frumentaria*, little known, but plausibly a response to the Sullan restrictions on grain distributions.[38] Senatorial opposition and his own radicalization would bring him close to a *popularis* stance, as can be seen in the speech recorded by Sallust (*Hist.* 1.55) in which Lepidus rejects both the Sullan tyranny and the *otium cum seruitio*, denounces the situation of the rural plebs and of Sulla's veterans, and calls on the *populus ad recipiundam libertatem*.

The revolt in Etruria seems to confirm Lepidus' diagnosis of the situation in the countryside. However, his social and political support would prove inadequate and when, in addition to the program outlined above, he ran for re-election to the consulship and the re-establishment of the tribunal powers, the senatorial response was the *senatus consultum ultimum* and his being declared *hostis publicus*.[39]

C. Aurelius Cotta

In this same context of the dismantling of Sulla's policies, particularly those related to the tribunate, and the divisions within the ruling class, we can place the consulship of C. Aurelius Cotta (cos. 75), author of a law that allowed the tribunes access to other magistracies.[40] However, once

---

[36] Sources on his consulship in Broughton 1951–86, II, 85; Labruna 1975; Perelli 1982, 151–6.
[37] Plut. *Sull.* 34.4–5; *Pomp.* 15.1–2 (Sulla compared Lepidus, "one of the worst," with Catullus, "one of the best"). Yakobson 1999, 161.
[38] Gran. Lic. 36.35; Sall. *Hist.* 1.55.11; 1.77.6; Burckhardt 1988, 251.
[39] See the *princeps senatus* L. Marcius Philippus' speech against Lepidus (Sall. *Hist.* 1.77); App. *B Civ.* 1.105, 107; Plut. *Pomp.* 16.3; Livy, *Per.* 90; Flor. 2.11.7.
[40] *Lex Aurelia de tribunicia potestate*: allowed the tribunes access to other magistracies (Cic. *Corn.* in Asc. 66, 78C; Ps. Asc., p. 200 St; Sall. *Hist.* 3.48.8).

again, alongside the expected popular support, there appear to have been important senators in favor of the measure, and of the dismantling of the more radical aspects of the Sullan reforms in general.[41]

Cn. Pompeius (Pompey)

The full restoration of the tribunician *potestas* was the work of the consuls for the year 70, Cn. Pompeius (Pompey) and M. Licinius Crassus, and it earned them great popularity.[42] Pompey had already promised to do this in his first speech as *consul designatus*, and it would be practically the only example of co-operation between the two consuls. During his consulship it seems probable that he supported the proposals of the tribune Plautius for an amnesty in favor of the supporters of Lepidus, including those who had fled to Hispania with Sertorius. According to Seager, such support would be another example of the conciliatory spirit displayed by Pompey in Hispania and Sicilia. However, he seems to have failed to win land distributions for his veterans since a possible *lex Plautia agraria* does not seem to have been implemented.[43] Later on, during the 60s, Pompey would feel the need to turn to the plebeian tribunes and popular support in general in order to consolidate his political position against the *optimates* increasingly jealous of his power. Thus he received a series of constitutionally novel military commands (*imperia extra ordinem*) much to the delight of the plebs, but frowned upon by the senatorial oligarchy.[44]

The identification of Pompey as a *popularis* figure does not necessarily presume his adoption of a radical position at any time. The divisions among the *nobilitas* over the Sullan reforms, the popularity derived from the tribunician restoration and his military *curriculum*, his immense wealth and his veterans all translated into a huge amount of popular support. In addition to these factors, the inflexibility of his *optimates* adversaries, wary

---

[41] But see Asc. 67C: *invita nobilitate magno populi studio*. The tribune Licinius Macer's speech (Sall. *Hist.* 3.48) summarizes synthetically the criticism of the situation and the arguments in favor of the full tribunician restoration.

[42] Plut. *Pomp.* 21; Cic. *Leg.* 3.26. In Cicero's *De legibus* (3.19–26), it is interesting to see the debate between the more extreme vision of his brother Quintus and his own more pragmatic stance toward both the tribunate and the *leges tabellariae*, which Cicero would have liked to reform. In a different context, in his defence of Cornelius, Cicero had vindicated the glorious history of the tribunate (Asc. *Corn.* 76–8C). According to Yakobson (2006b, 396ff.), Cicero accepts the importance and inevitability of the popular element in the "Roman constitution."

[43] On the tribune Plautius, Broughton 1951–86, II, 128; Seager 1994, 227.

[44] The *lex Gabinia de bello piratico*, in the year 67, and the *lex Manilia de imperio Cn. Pompei*, in 66 (Broughton 1951–86, II, 144, 153). For Perelli (1982, 161) both laws, *Gabinia* and *Manilia*, are undoubtedly *causae populares*.

of his excessive power, pushed him toward the role that he would eventually play in Roman politics. These circumstances allow us to analyze his alliance with Caesar and Crassus, up until the second half of the 50s, in the context of the conflict between *optimates* and *populares*.[45]

In general, Pompey displayed a coherent and conciliatory attitude as well as being very efficient in his undertakings. When compared to the corrupt and incompetent *optimates*, this only increased his unquestionable leadership among the plebs. However, despite his undoubted popularity and prestige, at no time can he be regarded as an authentic *popularis* leader, and from the 60s onwards he would always be below Caesar in the plebs' affections.[46]

M. Licinius Crassus

M. Licinius Crassus, colleague of Pompey in the consulships of 70 and 55, and the third member of the so-called First Triumvirate, is associated with the *populares* for the measures taken in 70 and for his support for Caesar in 59, but at no point does he stand out as a genuine *popularis* leader.[47]

C. Iulius Caesar

In C. Iulius Caesar we have, for the first time, it has been said, a genuine lifelong *popularis*. His whole career, from Sulla's famous comment to the justification of civil war,[48] is related to the support of the plebs and the defense of their rights, in particular those of the tribunate, to the quest for popular precedents and a political opposition to the senatorial majority, particularly its most intransigent core, the *factio paucorum*.

He is present in all of the significant political episodes from the 70s onwards: the tribunician restoration, the *imperia extra ordinem*, the trial of Rabirius, the Catilinarian conspiracy, etc. From his earliest days in public office, for example as *quaestor viae Appiae* or during his aedileship in 65, he

---

[45] The consular elections in 55 were characterized by the *optimates*' complete opposition to Pompey and Crassus, with the *libertas rei publicae* supposedly at stake, according to Cato (Suet. *Iul* 24; Cic. *Att*. 4.8.2; *Q Fr*. 2.4.6; Cass. Dio 39.27–31; Plut. *Pomp*. 51–2; *Crass*. 14–15; *Cat. Min*. 41.2; *Caes*. 21; *Comp. Nic. et Crass*. 2.1; Val. Max. 6.2.6; Livy, *Per*. 105; App. *B Civ*. 2.17–18; Vell. Pat. 2.46.1; Millar 1998, 162–6; Yakobson 1999, 169f.).

[46] Cic. *Att*. 1.14.1–2, on his return from the east. Supposedly, his pact with Sulla at the beginning of his career would always count against him (Yavetz 1988, 49ff.); later on, his support for Milo would also damage his popularity (Cic. *Q Fr*. 2.4.5; 2.3.2); Cass. Dio. 40.50.5; App. *B Civ*. 2.27; Plut. *Pomp*. 58.4; Cic. *Fam*. 8.14.3; *Att*. 2.19.2–3; 2.20.3; 7.3.4; Sall. [*Ad Caes. sen*.] 2.3.1).

[47] References are sometimes implicit: Cic. *Att*. 2.9.1, 19.2, 20.4; 12.21.1; Cass. Dio 38.4.4, 5.5.

[48] *Nam Caesari multos Marios inesse* ("for in Caesar there are many Marii") Suet. *Iul*. 1.1; Plut. *Caes*. 1.

displayed a clear tendency to win the support of the plebs, thus irritating the *optimates*. This much is evident from the annoyed response of Q. Lutatius Catulus to his restoration of Marius' trophies during the aedileship of 65.[49]

During his consulship Caesar proposed a series of laws in accordance with the *popularis* tradition, to the extent that Plutarch would remark that he seemed more like a tribune. In this category we can include the publishing of the senate's and the assemblies' minutes, the agrarian laws, and even the *de repetundis* legislation, which brings us to the question of the relationship between the *populares* and imperialism.[50]

Cicero always placed him firmly among the *populares*, and would refer in similar terms to the members of the First Triumvirate. In his intervention in favor of the extending of Caesar's proconsular *imperium*, Cicero would once more refer to his being *popularis*.[51] Caesar's justification for the crossing of the Rubicon and the resulting inevitability of armed conflict was also based on the *popularis* tradition, specifically the defense of the *dignitas* of the plebeian tribunes.[52]

In fact, his consulship proved to be a paradigm of the conflict between the impotence of the traditional senatorial authority and the impetus of a consul who knew what he wanted and was backed not only by his own popularity and resources, but also by supporters as important as Pompey and Crassus.[53] With such forces at work and with the legitimacy bestowed by the comitial decisions, the transformation of the nature of Roman political power is evident.

Marcus Tullius Cicero, consul popularis

The case of Cicero merits special attention. In several of his speeches, especially in those directed against the *rogatio Servilia agraria* in the early stages of his consulship (also in the *pro Rabirio perduellionis reo* and in the *Philippicae*), Cicero presents himself as the champion of the plebs, as a genuine *consul popularis*.[54] Previously his political trajectory had been fairly

---

[49] Suet. *Iul*. 11; Plut. *Caes*. 6.1–4; Vell. Pat. 2.43.4.
[50] Plut. *Caes*. 14.2; *Pomp*. 47–8; *Cat. Min*. 31.4–32; Suet. *Iul*. 20; *Aug*. 36.1; Cass. Dio 38.1–13; App. *B Civ*. 2.9–14; Cic. *Att*. 2.9.1–2, on his *popularitas*; *Phil*. 2.116; 5.49; *Att*. 2.3.4; 2.19; 2.20.4. On the division of roles with the tribune Vatinius, Cic. *Vat*. 15; Meier 1965, 574; after Caesar's death, Cicero's criticism of him is unbridled (*Off*. 2.84).
[51] Cic. *Cat*. 4.4.9; *Att*. 2.19.2; *Prov. cons*. 38; cf. Cass. Dio 37.22.1.   [52] App. *B Civ*. 1.22.5.
[53] All *optimates* swear the clause, imposed by Caesar, making the *lex agraria* obligatory (Plut. *Cat. Min*. 32.3–6; Cass. Dio 38.7.1–2). On *optimates* and their weak opposition in the face of Caesar's agrarian laws, see Bellemore 2005; a weakness confirmed by Cicero in the *pro Sestio* and the correspondence for that year (*Att*. 2.13.2; 2.15.2; 2.18.1–2; 2.19.3; 2.20.3).
[54] *Leg agr*. 1.23: *consulem veritate, non ostentatione popularem*; *Leg. agr*. 2.6, 7, 15; *Phil*. 7.4; *Fam*. 12.4.1.

moderate. It is true that he supported Pompey, intervening openly in his favor in support of the *lex Manilia*, and that he presented himself publicly as *popularis*,[55] but he always measured his ground and never radically opposed the senatorial class. It appears that his status of *homo novus* put him in a special position that allowed him a more autonomous stance once the consulship had been attained.

Even so, Cicero's intervention proves somewhat surprising when he confronted a project that had important supporters and undoubted popular approval.[56] Cicero's line of argument is clear: the need to distinguish between the true and the false *populares*. While he is the genuine *consul popularis*, the *rogatio* masks the tyrannical aspirations of the tribune Servilius Rullus, and poses a real threat to the state. Rullus has little in common with the decent *populares* of the past, and is instead a demagogue motivated purely by his own interests and not by those of the *res publica*.[57]

What is interesting is the effort made by Cicero to define a *popularis* context far removed from radicalism, and more concerned with *concordia* and with the *fides* between the Forum and the *Curia*.[58] As opposed to the *regnum* and *dominatio* of the decemvirs[59] and their plundering of the state's most prized possession, Cicero defends the genuine *populares* values: *pax, libertas, otium*.[60]

Since the matter at hand was a *rogatio agraria*, however, Cicero felt he should pick apart its contents and reject the land redistributions, especially those that affected the *ager Campanus* and the economic interests of its owners. In this way, he confronted specific socio-economic proposals and measures, showing that the *popularis* label was not restricted to a general political stance, but was also applicable to specific issues.

---

[55] Cic. *Comment. pet.* 51, 53: but cf. 5: *nos semper cum optimatibus de re publica sensisse, minime popularis fuisse*. On Cicero's careful arguments in support of the *lex Manilia*, Linttott 2008, 427–30.

[56] Marinone 2004, 85. Cicero's second speech, delivered in a *contio* in early January, after an earlier intervention in the senate, would be his first important display of political eloquence (Boulanger 1960, 26). Cf. Quint. *Inst.* 2.16.7: *Aut non diuina M. Tulli eloquentia et contra leges agrarias popularis fuit?*

[57] *Gracchorum benignitas*: *Leg. agr.* 2.81. On the distinction between true and false *populares*: *Leg. agr.* 2.7, 10, 15, 27, 43, 63, 84, 102; cf. *Cat.* 4.4.9. See above, n. 13.

[58] Cic. *Leg. agr.* 3.4. This is part of the image of his consulship that Cicero sought to present by publishing together a selection of his consular speeches (Cape 2002). According to Cape, after Cicero's consulship he would offer examples of practical political negotiation, establishing different responsibilities and rules of conduct for the consul, the senate and the people.

[59] Throughout the speech, Cicero continually identifies Rullus and the decemviral commission that he proposes with tyranny: *dominatio* (2.25), *reges constituuntur, non viri* (2.29), *potestatem verbo praetoriam, re uera regiam* (2.32); 2.33, 35, 43, 57. Demagoguery and manipulation are constants in the choice of terms, with Rullus eventually being termed a *repentinus Sulla* (*Leg. agr.* 3.10).

[60] *Leg. agr.* 2.9; cf. *pax, concordia, otium* (1.23, at the senate); 2.6; 2.102.

In his defense of Rabirius, accused of participating in the murder of Saturninus in the year 100, Cicero once again resorts to the comparison of the tribune Labienus, the accuser, with previous *populares*, particularly C. Gracchus. Once more he is portraying himself as a true *popularis*, defender of the *iura populi* against the cruelty of Labienus, who, by resorting to the archaic *duoviri perduellionis* procedure and demanding the death penalty for a citizen, was circumventing the Porcia and Sempronia laws *de provocatione*. In reality, Cicero portrays himself as the true heir to the spirit of C. Gracchus.

Cicero's treatment in the two *orationes* of important popular leaders from the past, such as Tiberius and Caius Gracchus, Saturninus and even C. Marius, and the reaction to it by the plebs, is also significant. In the case of the Gracchus brothers, what stands out is the positive image presented, in contrast to both Cicero's earlier speech in the senate and later evaluations.[61] In the *pro Rabirio* and on the subject of the murder of Saturninus, the plebs noisily protest the consul's justification of the murder and his characterization of Saturninus as a *hostis publicus*; Cicero also refers to the way that Labienus carried a portrait (*imago*) of Saturninus to the *rostra*.[62] Cicero needed to tailor his evaluations and descriptions according to the audience, while the plebs, or part of it, at least, liked to remember its leaders and martyrs, and would react if they were criticized and their memories defiled. Cicero's self-proclamation as *popularis* is all the more surprising when compared to his subsequent, very critical opinions on the *populares*; for example, those contained in *pro Sestio* or in *de officiis*, and the countless political attacks he would direct toward them in later years.[63]

In summary, we can identify various distinctive characteristics of Cicero's *popularis* stance.[64] When he vindicates other *populares* leaders, he refers almost exclusively to the Gracchi, but only does so in speeches to the people. As has already been said, he attempts to distinguish between true and false *populares*, and between radicals and moderates,[65] and always stresses the need for collaboration between the senate and the people.[66] His

---

[61] *Leg. agr.* 2.10: *duos clarissimos, ingeniosissimos, amantissimos plebei Romanae viros, Ti. et C. Gracchos*; cf. *Leg. agr.* 1.21; 2.81; *Rab. perd.* 14–15; but later, in *Off.* 2.43, he would justify their murder. These consular speeches to the *populus* are interesting documents for exploring the plebs' collective memory (Martin 2000).

[62] Cic. *Rab. perd.* 18; 25.   [63] Cic. *Sest.* 96–143; *Off.* 2.72–85; *Amic.* 95.

[64] From a number of different sources we get the impression that the plebs, despite showing him support on a number of occasions, never considered him one of their leaders.

[65] This is obvious as regards Pompey, but even in 63, Cicero distinguishes between Caesar and the *levitas concionatorum* (*Cat.* 4.4.9).

[66] His theoretical defense of the *leges de provocatione* is in contradiction of his arguments in defense of Rabirius or on the execution of the Catilinarian conspirators.

opposition to the *optimates*, at least after the process against Verres, is linked directly with his support for Pompey, and the intention is always to avoid open hostility. His popularity inevitably suffered with the execution of the Catilinarian conspirators, and in political terms the turning point would be the formation of the First Triumvirate.[67] From then onward his distancing of himself from the plebs and his movement toward a *rapprochement* with the *optimates* would become increasingly pronounced.

It is not easy to interpret this *popularis* stance. It could simply be a product of Cicero's own vanity, a *novus homo* attempting to overcome the traditional senate–people hostility;[68] or it could be a genuine stance during the first months of the consulship, and only later, both during the same consulship and in subsequent years, would he be pushed toward the *optimates*. It could also have been pure demagoguery and political opportunism,[69] especially with regard to Pompey; or it could simply confirm the existence of a contional oratorical style that, in that specific context, regardless of who the speaker was and what his political outlook was, was necessarily *popularis* in tone.[70]

SOME OBSERVATIONS ON THE *POPULARES* CONSULS

From such a brief review of those consuls who can be identified in one way or another with *popularis* activity in the late Roman republic it would be dangerous to draw too many conclusions. Aside from the issue of hypothetical personal motives whose influence it is impossible to gauge accurately, most of these consuls can be regarded as promoting measures favorable to the plebs, whether in agrarian laws, laws concerning new colonies, or the full restoration of the tribunician *potestas*. Additionally, in almost all these cases, they are seen to intervene in the *contiones*.[71] As would seem logical, their arguments, as far as we know what they were, were centered on the defense of the supposed true interests of the plebs, even when this involved opposition to proposals that could be regarded as typically *populares*, as in the case of Cicero against Rullus.

---

[67] Cic. *Att.* 2.3.4 (December 60); his distancing from Pompey was apparent even earlier (*Att.* 1.20.2, May 60; 2.1.6, June). See Lintott 2008, 169f.
[68] Meier 1965, 570.
[69] His attitude toward the agrarian legislation is opportunistic. When facing the people he would defend the utility of the agrarian laws (*Leg. agr.* 2.10), but in practice opposed all of the proposals; on the other hand, in his correspondence, he was capable of recognizing the usefulness of a measure such as the *rogatio Flavia agraria* for clearing out the city's bilge-water and repopulating the deserted regions of Italy (*Att.* 1.19.4; previously he had talked of the rich landowners as his army; cf. *Leg. agr.* 2.70).
[70] Morstein-Marx 2004, 204ff.   [71] Pina Polo 1989, 281–308.

From a more general political viewpoint, the presence of consuls who can be related more or less directly with the *populares* alongside the usual plebeian tribunes represents a qualitative widening of the divisions within the ruling class. The existence of a direct link between the expression of the popular will, which, as well as other forms, assumes that of the *optimates–populares* conflict, and the division of the Roman ruling class has already been noted.[72] Going no further than the fact that all the popular leaders were members of that ruling class, the *nobilitas*, the connection seems self-evident, but I think that the involvement of consuls on the *popularis* side widens enormously the scale of the division and the conflict.

The terms of this conflict had changed significantly since the last third of the second century, particularly regarding the meaning of *populares*. Now the term was used not just in reference to tribunes in conflict with the senatorial leaders, and who proposed measures favorable to the plebs and that threatened traditional order, but also in reference to powerful and prestigious individuals of the consular class whose actions could affect foreign policy and the running of the empire. It was no longer merely a question of individual young men, in the early years of their political careers, seeking the support of the plebs and using their popularity to make headway in the *cursus honorum* and thus to consolidate their political positions. The consuls had already reached the summit of the *cursus*, and their *popularis* alignment reflects the breakdown of political consensus that was affecting the very heart of the senatorial elite. In any case, this shift in alliance is another sign of a profoundly divided ruling class. The complexity of political relationships in this period is reflected in the thoughts and commentaries of Cicero on the theme of *optimates* and *populares*, and in his efforts to single out Pompey as a moderate *popularis*, in contrast to the radicals.[73]

It is possible that Cicero was aware of the danger represented by such polarization and by the possible identification of the senate as being a partisan body, controlled by the *optimates* and set against all proposals for reform. In a political system in which, as Yakobson has pointed out, the ruling class is not omnipotent and the popular element is a key part of the system, the *populares* posed a real threat to the cohesion of the traditional senatorial leadership of Roman society.[74]

---

[72] North 1990a.
[73] Cic. *Att.* 1.14.1; *Leg.* 3.26. The speech *de imperio Cn. Pompei* in support of the *lex Manilia* is a good example of this policy. However, cf. *Att.* 2.9.1 (April 59), for harsh private criticism of Pompey after his support for Clodius' plebeian *adoptio*.
[74] Yakobson 1999, 231ff.; cf. Hölkeskamp 1997a, 234ff.

As regards the nature of that conflict, it is clear that at no stage was a global alternative to the established system ever considered. The proposals of the *populares* were never more than reforms, though some of them were important, admittedly, to the traditional republican regime. No one questions the central elements of the *res publica* in Ciceronian theory; the senate, the magistracies, the assemblies – it is the relative division of powers between them that is questioned.[75] The target of the proposed reforms was an intransigent minority, the senatorial oligarchy, the *factio paucorum*. Even so, the proposals were very wide-ranging, affecting both the traditional balance of power, such as the range of powers of the senate and the assemblies, and socio-economic interests, plebeian as well as aristocratic.[76] As such, the supposed "ideological vacuum" as which some modern historiography has characterized late-republican Rome, as recently denounced by T.P. Wiseman, in my opinion simply does not exist.[77] The analysis of two speeches from Cicero's consulship serves to illustrate this thesis. In both cases, in his opposition to the *rogatio Servilia* and in his defense of Rabirius, we are dealing with controversial matters that go beyond mere political tactics or opposed moral values. They affect specific material interests, both those of the plebs and those of the rich landowners, as well as particular civic powers and rights, the *senatus consultum ultimum* and the *provocatio*. In this sense, I feel that to talk in terms of there being an "ideological monotony" in these contional debates does not do justice to the scale of the disputes.[78] In order to do otherwise, we would need to revise the idea of what we understand by "ideology."[79]

---

[75] The balance between *iura*, *officia* and *munera*, based on the *potestas magistratuum*, the *auctoritas senatus* and the *libertas populi* (Cic. *Rep.* 2.57); Hillard 2005. See Cicero's criticism on democracy and the Athenian assemblies (*Rep.* 1.27.43, 3.33.45; *Flac.* 16, 18); Ferrary 1997, 229.

[76] In contrast to the idea of a broad social consensus in favor of senatorial leadership (Morstein-Marx 2004, 234), from C. Gracchus onward a new political balance of power becomes clear, essentially an increase in the control of the senate by the assemblies and their leaders (Seager 1994, 86).

[77] Wiseman 2002; Yakobson 2004, 210.

[78] Following Morstein-Marx (2004, 204ff.), since in the *contiones* everyone is *popularis*, or at least portrays themselves as such (like Cicero), in the sense that they portray themselves as defenders of the *populus*, there is no "ideological competition" there (on this "ideological monotony," *ibid.*, 230ff.).

[79] Ideology: "an action-oriented, more or less coherent set of ideas about society held, more or less firmly and more or less articulately, by some large group of people" (Drucker 1974, cited in Mackie 1992, 51 n. 9). On the ideological aspect of the *optimates–populares* conflict, Perelli 1982; Mackie 1992; Ferrary 1997. Cf. Mackie 1992, 66: "in order to challenge the status quo, it was appropriate, and essential, to challenge the ideology on which the status quo depended. This *populares* did, so efficiently." Finley 1983, 141: "The ideology of a ruling class is of little use unless it is accepted by those who are being ruled, and so it was to an extraordinary degree in Rome. Then, when the ideology began to disintegrate within the elite itself, the consequence was not to broaden the political liberty among the citizenry but, on the contrary, to destroy it for everyone."

As for the mechanisms of cohesion, it is true that they survived, although in co-existence with other initiatives and tendencies, some politically directed and others spontaneous, which suggest a new situation. The mechanisms that traditionally ensured political and social cohesion seem to have no longer been sufficient: alongside the *mos maiorum*, coined principally by the *nobilitas*, comitial law would now also be cited as a source of authority.[80] Refuge in the law, which implies a degree of belief in the efficacy of the legislative procedures and in the political will that they express as well as in the source of power from which they originate (the *comitia*), is a sign of the times. Moreover, it is an important component of the *libertas popularis*, a *libertas* associated with *rostra, contiones, tribuni* and *leges*,[81] and different from the *libertas* of the *optimates*, more closely linked with *concordia*.[82]

To summarize: as recently has been argued, during the crisis or transformation that the republic went through, itself a lengthy historical process related to the Roman conquest of and expansion in the Mediterranean, and without one exclusive explanation, a fragmentation of legitimacy took place.[83] From 133 onwards, the crisis was clearly visible to the Romans themselves and the appearance of terminology such as *optimates–populares* is in itself symptomatic of political division and of the disputes over the legitimacy of different sources of political power: the senate and the people.[84]

In this context, the so-called *populares consules* represent an important development. These individuals, for various reasons (as *homines novi*, or as individuals excluded from the *optimates*, or because of the mistrust of other groups among the *nobilitas*, or because of an ambition with no limits),[85] did not feel bound by group loyalty to their equals among the *nobilitas*. All the advantages and possibilities offered by a *nobilis* origin

---

[80] Lintott 1999b, 6. Cic. *Leg. agr.* 2.102: *libertas consistit in legibus* (though in a *contio*); *Clu.* 146; Sall. *Hist.* 1.55.4 (*Orat. Lep.*); Malcovati, *ORF*, 1, p. 158 = Val. Max. 3.2.17, on T. Gracchus). See above, n. 3. However, for Gruen (1974, 507) the numerous laws serve only to confirm the *mos*.

[81] On *libertas popularis*, Venturini 1973; on *libertas*, Wirszubski 1968; Brunt 1988, 320–50. See Morstein-Marx (2004, 51) on a denarius from one Lollius Palicanus and the *libertas populi*.

[82] On Opimius, cos. 121, the plebs and the temple of Concordia, see Morstein-Marx (2004, 102); Vell. Pat. 2.7.3; Cic. *Sest.* 140.

[83] Morstein-Marx & Rosenstein 2006, 625ff. These themes are central to the current debate about the character of the Roman political system, stimulated by F. Millar: Jehne 1995, 2006; Bruhns, David and Nippel 1997; Millar 1998, 2002; Yakobson 1999, 2006b; Hölkeskamp 2000, 2004b, 2006a; Morstein-Marx 2000, 2004; Mouritsen 2001; David 2006; Morstein-Marx and Rosenstein 2006; Zecchini 2006; Duplá 2007.

[84] Mackie 1992, 60ff; Yakobson 1999, 179: "the very appearance of the 'party' divisions testifies to the weakening of the ruling class and to the collapse of its unity."

[85] Cf. Cicero's remarks on why politicians became populares (*Prov. cons.* 38); *Har. resp.* 43–4 (the motives, always personal, of the different *populares* leaders); *Phil.* 5.49.

(or a recently acquired *nobilitas*) tied to political radicalism caused an enormous subversive potential,[86] which became a reality when the social and political pressure resulting from popular discontent was channeled by certain members of the ruling class.

We should add in one other dangerous element: these powerful leaders, with their *imperium* and, in most cases, military resources as well, could at any given time satisfy social demands in ways that went beyond the traditional mechanisms of the republic. Their freedom of movement, interest in their personal careers or political and ideological horizons went beyond the established legal and political limits, and thus the internal cohesion of the *nobilitas*, the bedrock of its hegemony and of the basic republican consensus, was threatened.[87]

This evolution is not unrelated to the history of the *popularis* movement and the first reformist tribunes. One reading of the tragic fate of the Gracchi is that in order to implement their programs the *populares* needed the active support of magistrates *cum imperio*.[88] This represents a true turning point, with the balance of power shifting and the senate finding itself powerless against a determined consul *popularis*, as Caesar would show in 59.

These new circumstances allow us to observe, from the end of the second century onward, behavioral patterns that in some ways anticipate later autocratic models. In this, the *consules populares* that we have discussed play an important part, as do the plebs. However, it would perhaps be wrong to analyze the phenomenon in the context of modern and thus possibly anachronistic, democratic criteria.

In my opinion, we should not discuss Roman politics in modern democratic terms, and certainly not in the sense of deliberative democracy, with its open and public debate of alternative proposals, but rather in the etymological sense, that is, of the power, visibility and autonomy of the people, even though inevitably with aristocratic leaders. What we are witnessing is not the intensification of democracy, but rather the assertion of personal leadership backed by unquestionable popularity and huge political, economic and military resources.[89] In this sense it is a crisis without a solution

---

[86] Yakobson 1999, 207ff.
[87] The essence of the republican system is well synthesized by Crawford (1992, 23): "the collective rule of an aristocracy, in principle and to a varying extent in practice dependent on the will of a popular assembly."
[88] Seager 1994, 85.
[89] Martin 1965, 225: "Ein wichtiger Teil der Geschichte popularer Politik gehört zur Vorgeschichte der Monarchie in Rom" ("A significant section of the history of popular politics belongs to the early history of monarchy at Rome"). Yavetz 1988, 54ff.; Martin 2000, 40.

within the traditional parameters of the republican aristocracy,⁹⁰ but that will find one in a closer relationship between the individual leaders and the *populus*.⁹¹

---

⁹⁰ See Meier (1966) and the "Krise ohne Alternative," Brunt's (1968) critique and Meier's new Introduction to the second edition (1980, xiv–lvii); Hölkeskamp 2004b; Morstein-Marx and Rosenstein 2006.
⁹¹ Noè 1988.

CHAPTER 14

The consulship of 78 BC. Catulus versus Lepidus: an optimates versus populares affair

Valentina Arena

INTRODUCTION

It has long been known, if not always plainly stated, that the Roman elite commonly described in our sources as *optimates* acted in support and defense of the Sullan constitution, interpreted as the traditional republican settlements centered on the senate. However, what scholars have failed to see is that such support for the Sullan arrangements could be justified in the political conflicts of the first century BC by recourse to Stoic language, which in this period was widely familiar to the educated elite and informed Roman political discourse. The aim of this paper is to show that Stoicism provided the basis for many of the conventional ethical assumptions held by the Roman *optimates* and constituted an important part of their ideological tradition, which could indeed be mobilized to support and defend the Sullan constitutional settlements. To demonstrate this, I shall attempt to reconstruct and articulate the ideological premises of the language that politicians such as Catulus employed in their political careers.[1]

Throughout his career, Catulus sought to preserve the Sullan political order against those forces that threatened its existence. In his consulship in 78 BC, he opposed his colleague Lepidus, who, after initial hesitation, dedicated the rest of his year in office to opposing and dismantling the Sullan constitutional arrangements.

After a brief account of the events of the year, I shall explore the language used by our philo-Sullan sources to characterize the two consuls and highlight its distinctive moral nature. In order to understand its meaning, I shall turn to the analysis of emotions in the third book of Cicero's

---

I would like to thank Angus Gowland and Jonathan Prag for their comments on an earlier draft of this paper.

[1] On the role played by philosophy in the Roman political conflicts see Schofield 2000, 453–6, with bibliography. Griffin 1989 is perhaps the best treatment of the topic. For the ideological distinction between *optimates* and *populares* see most recently the excellent treatment by Morstein-Marx 2004, 204–40, esp. 204–7.

Tusculanae Disputationes, where, in a context very much rooted in Roman contemporary politics, Cicero presents a Stoic interpretation of this moral-political vocabulary, which we can assume was plausible to his readers. Following this interpretation, I shall then analyze the political principles advocated by Catulus and his associate Philippus in their fight against Lepidus and Pompey. These political ideas appear to be consistent with a model of Stoic philosophy and reveal a conception of the commonwealth very much compatible with the views of Polybius and Panaetius. They also provided Catulus and Philippus with the conceptual arguments to combat the attacks against the Sullan constitutional arrangements and defend their prominent senatorial position within the commonwealth.

THE CONSULSHIP OF 78

M. Aemilius Lepidus and Q. Lutatius Catulus were the successful candidates in the consular elections for 78 BC. Despite the fact that both belonged to the same very traditional and noblest echelon of the senatorial elite, their careers and political behavior while in office distinguished them so radically that they have come to represent, in ancient as well as in modern scholarship, the epitome of the opposition between *optimates* and *populares*.[2]

M. Aemilius Lepidus was a patrician, whose candidacy was supported not only by Pompey and his veterans, but also by some of the most eminent figures at the time in Rome, such as the Caecilii Metelli, the Aemilii Lepidi and perhaps also the consuls of 79, Appius Claudius Pulcher and P. Servilius Vatia.[3]

Q. Lutatius Catulus was of a similarly distinguished background. He was the son of the consul of 102, who, victorious over the Cimbri in 100, had eventually become a victim of the *Cinnana dominatio*. Catulus was related through maternal ties to the Domitii Ahenobarbii and, through his stepmother Servilia, to Quintus Servilius Caepio, the consul of 140 BC. In the consular election for 78 BC he was essentially the Sullan candidate, supported by the minority Sullan aristocracy, the veterans of Sulla and the

---

[2] On the consulship of 78 see Criniti 1969; Hayne 1972; Labruna 1975; and most recently, Weigel 1992, 14–19.
  On the interpretation of these events as a political battle between *optimates* and *populares* see Sall. *Hist.* 1.55M and 1.77M. Among modern historians, see for example Mommsen 1902, III, 3–39; Labruna 1975, 17–19.

[3] On M. Aemilius Lepidus see, in addition to the works in n. 1, also Klebs 1893, 554–6; Gundel 1969, 577.

dictator himself, to whom, incidentally, he was also related through his fifth wife Valeria.[4] However, thanks perhaps precisely to this kind of support, Catulus was victorious in the election, but placed second behind Lepidus, who had been backed by Pompey and his men.

As soon as they entered office, the consuls began to oppose one another, as Appian himself reports, on almost every issue.[5] On the first day of their consulship, they argued about the date on which the *Feriae Latinae* should be celebrated and over the appointment of the *praefectus urbis*, who was to be left in charge of the city during the consuls' absence for the festival's celebration.[6] The matter in itself did not seem to be of great significance, but the two consuls fought about it "as if it was a matter of winning control of the commonwealth" (Sall. *Hist.* 1.54M).

The senate, after the *sortitio* had assigned the consular provinces, in the hope of distracting the feuding consuls from their rivalry, assigned the restoration of the ancestral Basilica Aemilia to Lepidus and the repair of the Capitolium, damaged by the fire of 83, and the construction of the Tabularium to Catulus.[7] However, the senate's attempt failed and Lepidus resumed his opposition to Catulus. After an initial moment of hesitation in which he rejected the proposal to restore the full powers of the tribunate of the plebs, Lepidus began his fight against the most conservative aspects of the Sullan settlements, which were in turn supported vigorously by Catulus.[8] In January–February of 78, he launched a direct and violent attack against Sulla, his institutional arrangements and his satellites in his *Oratio ad Quirites*, preserved by Sallust in the *Historiae*. During February and March of the same year, he maintained a high level of attack against the current state of affairs. He made several generic proposals of clear popular appeal, which were aimed at gaining the sympathies of specific interest groups, such as the ex-Marians, the ex-Cinnans, the *Italici* and the Etruscan farmers. He proposed, on the one hand, the rehabilitation of the political exiles and, on the other, the restoration of land to the farmers and

---

[4] On Quintus Lutatius Catulus (cos. 78) see Münzer 1927. On the relationship with other eminent political figures of the time see Syme 1939, 21–4. See also Broughton 1951–86, 3, 85 and Labruna 1975, 13–24.
[5] App. *B Civ.* 1.105.491.
[6] Sall. *Hist.* 1.54; see also Mommsen 1887–8, 1, 669 n. 1 and Wissowa 1912, 125 and n. 4.
[7] On Lepidus' restoration of the Basilica Aemilia see Plin. *HN* 35.13. It appears, however, that Lepidus' intervention must have been more extensive than Pliny's passage suggests, if Aemilius Lepidus (the future triumvir) could celebrate in 61 on a coin the *Aimilia ref(ecta)* (Crawford 1974, 419/3a–b). Alley 2004, 27 suggests that Lepidus carried out this restoration in 80. For the evidence on Catulus' intervention on the Capitolium and Tabularium see Münzer 1927, 2087.
[8] On the refusal to restore the tribunate of the plebs' powers see Gran. Lic. p. 34, 1, Flemish and *ORF*³ 332; on his fight against the Sullan constitution at such an early stage in office see Flor. 2.11.2.

Italic citizens. According to Florus' own words, his aim was *res gestas acta rescindere*, that is, to turn upside down the actual political status quo and, as such, to suppress the Sullan constitutional arrangements.[9]

In any case, this line of attack came to a momentary halt because of Sulla's death in March. The death of the dictator and the organization of his funeral became, once again, the focus of a renewed and dramatic opposition between the consuls, an opposition loaded with political significance. Catulus, supported by the majority of the Roman senators (presented in our sources as *optimates*), proposed exceptional honors and a public funeral, the first of its kind, while Lepidus, abandoned now by Pompey (who saw in him a potential Sertorius), appealed to his followers and strongly opposed it. Behind the logistical matter of the dictator's funeral lay an important political issue on which both sides made a clear statement regarding the inviolable nature of the Sullan constitution. The city and its political leaders were divided into two groups.[10] After a violent discussion in the senate and the specter of a *stasis*,[11] a *iustitium* was proclaimed until magnificent and solemn funeral rites and the burial of Sulla were held. This was a victory for Catulus and his group. However, as Appian reports, while leaving the funeral, the two consuls began to quarrel immediately over the validity of the *acta Sullae* (Flor. 2.11.1) and the city favored one side or the other.[12] Somehow the political panorama was now changing. On the one hand, thanks to Catulus' political activity, the Sullan aristocracy now found itself revitalized, and aristocrats such as Marcius Philippus, Licinius Lucullus and Sisenna openly allied with him. On the other hand, Lepidus had gathered around himself figures such as M. Iunius Brutus, Mam. Aemilius Lepidus Livianus, Cinna Minor and perhaps Crassus. Aemilius Lepidus Livianus had sought, unsuccessfully, to convince Caesar to align himself with Lepidus, while Pompey and his veterans, however alert, did not seem to wish to be directly involved or to participate openly.

The last united political action of the two consuls was the refusal, on the senate's advice, to receive the embassy of Mithridates VI Eupator, which aimed to define the consequences of the second Mithridatic war. From that point forward, subsequent political acts were mainly Catulus' doings, as also indicated by the inversion of the consular names in our records.[13] It

---

[9] Livy, *Per.* 90; Flor. 1–2; Gran. Lic. p. 34, 1, Flemish.
[10] App. *B Civ.* 1.105.491; Plut. *Sull.* 18; *Pomp.* 15.4.
[11] App. *B Civ.* 1.105.493.   [12] App. *B Civ.* 1.105.491.
[13] For the Mithridatic embassy see App. *Mithr.* 67.284. The main political actions of Catulus were the renewal of the *foedus Gaditanum* and the *s.c. de Asclepiade Clazomenio sociisque*, usually known as *de tribus navarchiis*. For the inversion in the order of the names see Taylor & Broughton 1949, 1968. For the documents where Lepidus is mentioned before Catulus see Münzer 1927, 2083.

is at this stage that Lepidus is reported in our sources to have accentuated further his seditious behavior by allying himself with the dispossessed and the Italici. When in May–June a revolt broke out in Etruria against the Sullan settlements, the senate sent the two consuls to subdue it, forcing them, however, to take an oath not to resolve their differences by the use of violence before the end of their consulship. However, once the revolt was suppressed, the senate's attempt to contain the consuls' enmity was proved to be in vain. Under the watchful eye of Catulus, who had been observing with suspicion his rival's movements, Lepidus sent the senate his *mandata*, his conditions. He requested the restoration of the full powers of the tribunate, the enactment of the *frumentationes* previously proposed by him, the recall of the proscribed, and a second consulship for himself.[14] This unacceptable demand, which well recalled to the senators' minds the behavior of the most seditious of Roman senators, combined with the threat of a military march on Rome and increased by the force of Philippus' oratory, propelled the senate to proclaim the *senatus consultum ultimum* and Lepidus *hostis*. The task of defending the *res publica* (or more precisely, in Philippus' words, the *senatus auctoritas*) against Lepidus was assigned to the interrex Appius Claudius Pulcher, to the proconsul Catulus and to all the other magistrates *cum imperio*, while an *imperium extraordinarium* was granted to Pompey to fight as pro-praetor alongside Catulus. Lepidus was doomed to be defeated. Catulus was victorious in battle first near the Campus Martius and eventually at Cosa, while Lepidus died in Sardinia in the summer of 77, perhaps of consumption and grief at the news of his wife's divorce.[15]

CATULUS THE *OPTIMAS* AND LEPIDUS THE *POPULARIS*

This is, in brief, an account of the events surrounding the consulship of 78. Following the ancient evidence, it is possible to summarize and present this consulship, as modern scholarship has long done, as the history of the contest over the constitution of Sulla, strongly supported by the Sullan Catulus and attacked initially with caution, then with outright violence, by the Marian Lepidus.[16]

---

[14] On the reintegration of the tribunate's powers see Sall. *Hist.* 1.73; 1.77. 14M; on the preservation of the *frumentationes* see Sall. *Hist.* 1.77. 6M; Ex(s)up. 6.7; on the recall of the proscribed see Sall. *Hist.* 1.77.6M; Ex(s)up. 6.3; Flor. 2.11.3; on the request of a second consulship see Sall. *Hist.* 1.77.15M; Plut. *Pomp.* 16.4.

[15] On Lepidus' divorce see Plin. *HN* 7.12 and 186; Plut. *Pomp.* 16.9.

[16] This popular view of the consulship of 78 induces the ancient authors to overlook the senators' not immediate aversion toward Lepidus as well as the temporary consul's willingness to co-operate with them. For the ancient evidence on Catulus see App. *B Civ.* 1.105.491; 494; Ps. Asc. 255 St.;

This dichotomy, which becomes apparent when Catulus is obliged to confront Lepidus' actions, manifests itself, amongst other aspects, in the use of a very distinctive vocabulary adopted by our extant (and, for the most part, pro-Sullan) sources, to describe the contenders and their political behavior.[17] The contemporary Cicero (*post quem* date for Catulus' death is 61 BC)[18] presents him as "leader of his order and a guiding voice in state policy,"[19] the ideal companion for the *optimate* path,[20] the *sapientissimus optimus civis et vir*,[21] the *vir clarissimus amantissimus rei publicae*,[22] the *pro Sestio*'s ultimate example of an *optimas* "who could never be moved from his chosen course by fear of danger's tempest or hope of honor's gentle air" and always "accustomed freely to censure and indict the people for rashness or the senate for error."[23] Again, he is portrayed as a *clarissimus* and *fortissimus vir* in the third Catilinarian (3.24) and as *moderatum prae se ferens gaudium* in Valerius Maximus (2.8.7). His *clementia* is mentioned by Orosius (5.22.18) and his *verecundia* by Velleius Paterculus (2.32.1). In the *pro Lege Manilia* (59) Cicero describes him as that kind of man for whom there is no enterprise that he cannot "*consilio regere et integritate tueri et virtute conficere.*"[24] It was thanks to his *virtus* that he, despite his juvenile indulgences, quelled the flames of the civil war (Val. Max. 2.8.7). The role played by wisdom and justice in Catulus' character is praised by Plutarch, who also reports the great influence Catulus exerted in the senate (Plut. *Caes.* 7).[25] According to Dio, "Catulus... was a man who always, more conspicuously than anyone who ever lived, preferred the common weal to

---

Flor. 2.11.5; Oros. 5.22.16; on Lepidus see Sall. *Hist.* 1.77.6–7M and 17; App. *B Civ.* 1.105.491; Oros. 5.22.16; Ex(s)up. 6.3ff. Plut. *Pomp.* 16.1ff. As for modern scholarship see, for example, Münzer 1927, 2083; Criniti 1969, 416 n. 279; Labruna 1975, 38–9.

[17] On the nature of the available sources for this period see Lana 1961, 81–7.
[18] See Cass. Dio 37.46.3.
[19] Cic. *Pis.* 6: *Catulus, princeps huius ordinis et auctor publici consilii*. Cf. Vell. Pat. 2.43.3: *Catulus omnium confessione senatus princeps*. Mommsen 1887–8, III, 969–71 shows that appellative *princeps senatus* is not used in its technical sense, but simply as "the foremost man in the senate." Cf. Cic. *Verr.* 3.210, where he is named amongst the *principes civitatis*. See also Cass. Dio 36.30.4.
[20] Cic. *Att.* 1.20.3 (SB 20).
[21] Cic. *Red. sen.* 9. See also Cic. *Verr.* 1.44: *hominem sapientissimum atque amplissimum*; and Corn. II 5 Cr.: *sapientissimus vir atque humanissimus*. He is also described as *summus vir* in Cic. *Leg. Man.* 66 and *Balb.* 35.
[22] Cic. *Leg. Man.* 51. See also Cic. *Brut.* 222: *praesidia rei publicae*.
[23] Cic. *Sest.* 101, 122. Cicero had also personal motives for supporting Catulus: not only did the *consularis* share the same political view, but he also approved of Cicero's political behavior during the Catilinarian conspiracy (Cic. *Red. sen.* 9; *Dom.* 113), and first attributed to him the title of "father of the country" (*Pis.* 6; *Sest.* 121; *Phil.* 2.12). The poet Archias, defended by Cicero and engaged to write a poem in glorification of Cicero's consulship, lived in the house of the two Catuli (*Arch.* 6).
[24] Cf. *Brut.* 133: *in sententia dicenda cum prudentia, tum elegans quoddam et eruditum orationis genus.*
[25] Cf. Plut. *Pomp.* 16 and Plut. *Cat. Min.* 16. Cf. also Plut. *Galb.* 3.1.

everything else" (37.46.3). And despite his eminent position in the senate, the people trusted him, since they regarded him as one who at all times spoke and acted for their advantage (Cass. Dio 36.30.5). In reporting Sulla's words to Pompey after the consular elections for 78, Catulus is presented as the *aristos*, who had to concede to Lepidus, the *kakistos*. Sulla said: "I see, young man [Pompey], that you are really pleased with your victory and surely it was a beautiful and noble thing for Lepidus, the worst of all men, to come first in the consular election before Catulus, the best of all men, thanks to your influence on the people" (Plut. *Pomp*. 15.2).[26]

Thus, if Catulus is represented as the most virtuous, endowed with the gifts of *clementia*, *verecundia*, *moderatio* and *prudentia*, as the *princeps senatus*, who always keeps firmly in mind the commonwealth, if Catulus is the best man, Lepidus is, according to our sources, the worst. And he stands for everything that Catulus does not. He is the "worst and most shameless of all men... traitor to us," inveighs Marcius Philippus, close ally of Catulus, in his speech to the senate reported by Sallust, "unfaithful to your group, the enemy of all good men" (Sall. *Hist*. 1.77.15). Lepidus is "a brigand at the head of some camp-followers and a few cutthroats" (Sall. *Hist*. 1.77.7); the "lowest of all criminals – it is difficult to say whether he is more vicious or more cowardly – [he who] has an army for the purpose of overthrowing our liberty" (Sall. *Hist*. 1.77.3). Only through acts of sedition did he obtain a command and an army (Sall. *Hist*. 1.77.4). He is described by Plutarch and Florus as insolent, impulsive and acting in rages of *furor*.[27] As Granius Licinianus famously wrote, "*nam erat natura turbulentus et inquietus*."[28] *Turbulentus* is often used in its passive sense of "agitated"; however, in hendiadys with *inquietus* it assumes the active meaning of "provocateur of disturbances," which is usually accepted in both ancient and modern literature.[29] These are the traits frequently adopted to characterize the *populares*, the *homines turbulenti atque novarum cupidi*,

---

[26] See also Cic. *Phil*. 2.12; *Verr*. 2.3.210; Oros. 5.23. Cf. also Plut. *Sull*. 34.28, where Lepidus is described as *emplēktaton*, the most unstable.

[27] On the association of Lepidus and *furor* see Oros. 5.22.16. See also the description of Lepidus as *rei publicae pestem* at Sall. *Hist*. 1.74M. Cf. Sall. *Hist*. 1.77.1M. Lepidus is described as *thrasus* in Plut. *Sull*. 34.21 and as *emplēktaton* at 34.28. *Thrasus* in its superlative form is also deployed to describe Catilina in Dio (44.4.4) and Clodius in Plutarch (*Cat. Min*. 31.2; *Ant*. 2.6) and in Appian (*B Civ*. 2.22.81). Milo is reported as talking in these terms about Clodius and Caesar (App. *B Civ*. 2.14.50).

[28] Gran. Lic. p. 35, 10, Flemish.

[29] On the passive use of *turbulentus* see Cic. *Brut*. 103 (on Ti. Gracchus). Labruna 1975, 76 and Scardigli 1989, ad loc. interpret *turbulentus et inquietus* as "subversive," that is, "opponent of the status quo and in favor of profound changes." *Contra* Jal 1963, esp. 348 n. 5, who interprets these adjectives as indicating the fickle nature of Lepidus: after having been supported by the vast majority of Roman aristocracy, Lepidus moved against them, allying himself with the *populares*.

as Cicero calls them (*Rab. Post.* 33), and therefore with whom Lepidus, also described as *cupidus rerum novarum* by Florus (2.11.1), is implicitly associated.[30]

THE MORAL LANGUAGE OF PSYCHOLOGY

Thus, it is apparent that the descriptions of the two consuls of 78 have a clear moral subtext. Catulus is *bonus*, or even better, *optimas*, *sapiens* (or *sophos* according to our source), *fortis*; *dikaios*, he has *clementia*, *verecundia* and *moderatio*; Lepidus, on the other hand, is *turbulentus*, *inquietus*, *audax*, *thrasus* and *emplēktaton*.

Previous scholarship has pointed out the unambiguous rhetorical nature of this language, which, according to these scholars, belongs to the realm of invective or, its opposite, encomium. Thus, scholars have emphasized that the Roman orators in the political battles of the first century BC needed to show that their opponents were malicious by nature and that their destructive actions were not the result of an unfortunate concatenation of external circumstances, but rather intrinsically ingrained in the bad nature of the perpetrators.[31] Essentially, the aim of such rhetorical language was moral praise or condemnation. Even the more historically focused studies, which have pointed out the political use of this language, have agreed that all these terms fall short of a "technical meaning" and possess more value for their colorful expressions, rather than their conceptual significance. Thus, they all agree that the *boni*, the *optimates*, who are wise and temperate, correspond to the supporters of the status quo, while the *audaces*, *turbulenti* and *mali* are the subverters of the contemporary regime.[32]

In order to make sense of the use of such language in the political sphere, it may be helpful to turn to a work of the time, Cicero's *Tusculanae Disputationes*, which, composed in 45 BC, deals with psychological language as understood in the first century BC. In his treatment of emotions in Book III of the *Tusculanae*, Cicero, in an attempt to show that all emotions

---

[30] See Hellegouarc'h 1963, 518–34 on the vocabulary adopted to describe the *populares*. Cf. also Flor. 2.11.5: *cum turbidis contionibus velut classico civitatem terruisset*.

[31] Hellegouarc'h 1963, 526–34; Achard 1981, 239–60. An exception to this trend is represented by Michel 2003, esp. 549, who, however, does not develop the connection between this philosophical inspiration and the existence of ideological trends within Roman political discourse.

[32] Wirszubzki 1961, 13–14; Hellegouarc'h 1963, 521; Jal 1963, 348 and n. 5; Weische 1966, 23–33; David 1980; Pina Polo 1991, 131–50; Taldone 1993. Often scholars refer to the moralizing character of the terms adopted by ancient authors without investigating it further. See, for example, Criniti 1969 at 373, n. 149. The same observation can be applied to Catulus' positive labeling, usually recognized as a general expression of consensus on the part of the conservative historiography. Of this view are Labruna 1975, 133; Hellegouarc'h 1963, 227–33.

derive from mental unsoundness rather than being normal and natural experiences, laments the inadequacy of Greek to discuss the topic.[33] What the Greeks term *pathē* in normal Latin usage, Cicero claims, is equivalent to *perturbationes animi*, "emotions," which are movements of the mind not obedient to reason (3.7). When the mind is not governed by natural *ratio*, it falls into a state of ill-health. This is a condition opposed to wisdom, which coincides with the *sanitas* of the mind and consists of a serene and steady temper (3.8–9). Thus, "since it is necessary that those whose minds are not disturbed by any movement or, as it were, sickness, are called 'sane,' those who are in the opposite condition must be termed 'insane'" (3.11). The state into which men fall when they are not under the control of intelligence, appointed by nature to rule over their mind, is called very inadequately, in Cicero's opinion, *mania* (madness) in Greek, in Latin either *insania* (insanity) or *furor* (frenzy). *Insania*, Cicero explains, is a condition of the mind where the person affected is rather foolish and lacks in consistency, that is, in health, while *furor* is a more serious state since it consists of a total darkening of the mind. Although *furor*, which the Greeks call *melancholia* as if it were caused by black biles, rather than being a more serious form of anger, fear or grief, may appear a worse condition, in reality it "is the sort of thing that can come upon a wise person, while *insania* cannot" (3.11).

Thus, those who are affected by *furor*, one of the descriptions attributed to Lepidus and the *populares*, could also be wise individuals who experience a temporary suspension of *recta ratio*. Cicero carries out this analysis at the beginning of Book III, the preface of which clearly contextualizes the theoretical discussion of emotions within the historical scenario of the republican battle against the domination of the tyrant Caesar.[34] In this preface, Cicero admonishes the *optimus quisque* not to follow "those who judged that public office, military commands, and the popular glory are the greatest goals [to which] a person can aspire" (3.3). In doing so, they would end up pursuing "not a solid figure of virtue but only a shadow-shape of glory" (3.3). While real glory is the unanimous praise of good persons, a legitimate and worthy pursuit, popular glory offers only a perverted

---

[33] On Cicero's translation from Greek and his pride in the higher ability of Latin language to render philosophical concepts see Powell 1995b, esp. 283–4. On the Stoic treatment on emotions and Cicero's analysis of the third book of the *Tusculanae Disputationes* see Graver 2007, esp. 120–2.

[34] See Gildenhard 2007, 167–81, who underlines the Roman emphasis of the preface. The fact that Cicero has also clearly in mind the contingent concrete world of Roman politics is betrayed by the references he makes both to Scipio Nasica and his Stoic-like behavior in his opposition to Tiberius Gracchus, and to his own consulship (4.52). On the *proemium* of Book III see also Koch 2006, 69–72.

caricature of the virtue that belongs to true distinction. This false glory blinds the people to the point that, in the search for it, "some have overthrown their governments, and others have ruined even themselves" (3.4). Thus, the members of the Roman elite, whom Cicero addresses here, should always act under the control of their *ratio*, and should never be deceived by the meanderings of the path or the lure of pleasures and money.[35] If they were to let themselves be troubled by such emotions, they would not be far from insanity and no longer, at least temporarily, wise (3.4). Under these conditions, Roman politicians would be subject to emotions such as anger, fear, grief, and could, in a word, be labeled, as Lepidus was, *furiosi* and *turbulenti*, and ultimately unwise. Men, therefore, are not unwise by nature, since all men participate in the universal *ratio* and as such possess a spark of *virtus*. If led astray, however, these *optimi viri* could become, as a matter of fact, *furiosi* and bring down destruction upon themselves and the republic.[36]

The wise, however, "will always be free of disturbance of the mind" (3.15) and will be described in Greek as *sōphrōn*. Once again, claiming that Latin is better equipped than Greek to discuss these issues, Cicero renders *sōphrosunē* ("self-control") sometimes as *temperantia*, sometimes as *moderatio* or even *modestia* (3.16). "It may be possible, however," he continues, "that the best term for it is 'frugality.' The Greeks adopt a corresponding term [*chrēsimoi*] that is too narrow in its application ... but *frugalitas* is a broader term, carrying with it not only *abstinentia* (restraint) and *innocentia* (harmlessness) ... but all the other virtues as well ... hence 'frugality' implies the three virtues of courage, justice, and prudence (*fortitudo, iustitia, prudentia*)" (3.16–17). These are, therefore, the qualities of the wise man who possesses the knowledge of things divine and human (4.57), and whose *virtus* is *ratio* at work. He is *fortis, moderatus, temperans* and *sōphrōn*, and is thus endowed with all those virtues that in our pro-Sullan sources characterize Catulus.

This understanding of emotions as mental disturbances that affect a serene mind and create a condition of general mental unsoundness is, as Cicero claims, omitting its Platonic roots, Stoic in origin. In the third and fourth books of the *Tusculanae Disputationes* Cicero is very keen to

---

[35] Cf. also Cic. *Tusc.* 4.23–4, where the desire for glory and money as well as hatred of women are presented as a sickness of the mind caused by the lack of reason's application.

[36] According to Gildenhard 2007, 176, *optimus quisque* refers to the most outstanding members of Rome's civic community, i.e. the Caesars and the Pompeys. Cf. Graver 2002, 75 who sees an element of "class-consciousness" behind Cicero's choice. See also Gildenhard 2007 at 74 and 175 on the role played by cultural educational influences in leading men away from right reason.

show that the Stoic discourse on emotions is not only congruent with ordinary ethical notions held by the Romans, but also already ingrained in their ancient traditions.[37] The Twelve Tables, perceived by the Romans themselves as the foundation of their judicial system, prohibited a person in a condition of frenzy from managing his own affairs. "Hence the law read not 'if he be insane' (*si insanus*) but 'if he be frenzied' (*si furiosus escit*). For they judged that a person who is foolish, lacking in consistency, who is in health, was still capable of handling ordinary responsibilities and of managing his life in the usual and customary way, but frenzy, they thought, was a complete darkening of the mind" (3.11).[38] Thus, in his attempt to show that early Latin speakers adopted a language and a norm on mental derangement that were in tune with later Stoic thinking, Cicero, one may suggest, appears to be engaged in an important cultural operation.[39] He seems to provide the members of the political elite, not so versed in philosophy,[40] with a compendium of philosophical systems that lie at the foundations of their political language and, as such, remind them of the role that the study of philosophy should play in the political conflicts of the time.[41] This interpretation of Cicero's intentions may prove ill-founded, or rather generated by an unduly forceful strain placed on the Latin language by Cicero himself. However, it remains the case that, in proposing this association between Stoic philosophy and the ethical language of the political arena, Cicero ought to have acted in a plausible way, making claims that his readers should have regarded as legitimate. Cicero therefore provides us with a window on how this moral language could have been interpreted in the first century BC, offering a theorized view of commonly held notions encapsulated, at times even unconsciously on the part of the speakers, in everyday political discourse.

---

[37] See Cic. *Tusc.* 3.8–9. Cf. Cic. *Tusc.* 4.53 regarding the consistency of Stoic definitions of moral qualities with the notions possessed by all speakers. On this point see Graver 2002, ad loc.
[38] On *furor* in Roman law see Diliberto 1996. See also Graver 2002, ad loc.
[39] Cf. the fourth of the *Paradoxa Stoicorum* (*omnes stultos insanire*), which likewise deals with insanity.
[40] Writing to Atticus regarding the need to modify the protagonists of his *Academica*, Cicero admits that Catulus, Lucullus and Hortensius were considerably less learned in philosophy than he made out in the dialogue, "prominent men, of course, but not at all literati" of the sort represented (*Att.* 13.12.3 = SB 320). They were characterized "not indeed by lack of education but by a recognized unfamiliarity with those subjects" (*Att.* 13.16.1 = SB 323) and, as such, "the arguments [in the first edition] were more philosophical than anything anyone would think they could ever even have dreamed of" (*Att.* 13.19.3 = SB 326). It is not surprising, therefore, that Cicero emphasizes that Catulus' arguments in the *Academica* are derived from his father, whose view he simply reports (*Acad. post.* 2.11–12; 2.148; cf. *Off.* 1.133; *Brut.* 133; 134). On Catulus the Elder's cultural milieu see Reid 1885, 41–3; Alfonsi 1960, 61–70; Garbarino 1973, 481–3.
[41] For a reading of the *Tusculanae Disputationes* as a protreptic to the study of philosophy in relation to contemporary politics see Gildenhard 2007.

OPTIMATES' IDEAS AT WORK

Thus, Cicero's treatment of emotions offers us a key to a full understanding of the descriptions of Catulus and Lepidus. It allows us to interpret, within their wider philosophical context, the political arguments put forward by the *optimates* in their opposition to Lepidus in 77 and to Pompey in 67 and 66. The political principles to which they adhered are reported by Sallust, in his *Historiae*, in Philippus' speech pronounced in 78 in support of the *senatus consultum ultimum* as well as by Dio and Plutarch in the orations delivered by Catulus in 67 and 66 against the granting of extraordinary powers to Pompey.[42] As far as the authenticity of these speeches is concerned, it is impossible to assert beyond any reasonable doubt whether they are a complete fabrication of the ancient authors or rather contain, if not the exact words pronounced by the Roman politicians, at least concepts homogeneous with those they adopted in the political arena of the time.

In Sallust's *Historiae* Philippus, a keen supporter of Sulla, openly avowed his support for Catulus' policy in 78.[43] However, his speech may call to mind the speech delivered by Cato against the Catilinarians in Sallust's *de Catilinae coniuratione*, as well as the orations pronounced by Cicero against Antonius in the *Philippicae*.[44] While the similarities with Cicero's *Philippicae* depend on the circumstances in which the two orators find themselves (so that Cicero, like Philippus, criticizes the inertia of the senators, invokes against his enemy the ultimate decree, and tries to justify on the part of his youthful ally the use of a private army), Philippus' resemblance to the Sallustian Cato finds its origins in the close association of Lepidus with the revolutionary Catiline. Despite the fact that Philippus' speech does not have the same paradigmatic ethical value as Cato's oration and appears much more bound to the contingent situation of the time, the two politicians are linked by their victory over a subversive movement

---

[42] Philippus' speech: Sall. *Hist.* 1. 77M; for Catulus' oration against the *lex Gabinia* in 67 see Cass. Dio 36.31–6; against the *lex Manilia* in 66 see Plut. *Pomp.* 30 and Cic. *Leg. Man.* 59.

[43] Consul in 91 and censor in 86, Philippus in 82 returned as legate in Sardinia for Sulla and most probably pronounced the funeral oration of the dictator. Livy, *Per.* 86; App. *B Civ.* 1.105; Sall. *Hist.* 1.77.6M. On Philippus' support for Catulus see Sall. *Hist.* 1.77.6M.

[44] Sall. *Cat.* 52. For the parallels with the Sallustian Cato see La Penna 1968, 258. As for the echoes of Cicero's *Philippicae* in Philippus' speech, see Syme 1964, 220–2. Gagé 1952, 66–8 claims that Cicero's *Philippicae* derive their name not from Demosthenes' work, as usually thought, but from the speeches of Philippus against Lepidus. See Pasoli 1967, 70–1 on the similarities between the civil wars in 77 and 44. See also McGushin 1994, 146–7.

and by their success in guaranteeing the safety of the property-owning groups of Rome and Italy.⁴⁵ Thus, scholars have interpreted the speech of Marcius Philippus as the counterpart of the speech of Lepidus, composed according to the Thucydidean practice of exemplifying the alternatives of a given situation by a pair of speeches, and thus a product of Sallust's rhetorical elaboration.⁴⁶ However, it appears that Sallust has made an effort to reproduce not only Philippus' rhetorical style, at least as described by Cicero, but also his political language.⁴⁷ As Paananen asserts in his study of Sallust's political vocabulary, "the content of the word [*boni*] is meaningful from the viewpoint of the speaker, Marcius Philippus, not from that of Sallust."⁴⁸ Thus, it is also possible to deduce that Sallust, who in *Bellum Iugurthinum* claims to write out in full Memmius' speech (*orationem eius perscribere*),⁴⁹ may have had access to the senate's archive and read the original speech by Philippus. Although, according to the criteria of ancient historiography, he would have been expected to insert a speech that was both rhetorically ornate and well suited to the narrative context, Sallust may have resorted in his composition of Philippus' speech to the *topoi* that he perceived to be part of the *optimates*' ideological tradition.⁵⁰ As such, what we have in the extant speech, if not Philippus' exact words, is Sallust's perception of the ideological tradition of Philippus and his associate Catulus, both active just twenty years or so before Sallust's composition of the *Historiae*.

Catulus' political arguments are also found in Dio, who reports in direct speech Catulus' oration delivered in 67 against the granting of extraordinary powers to Pompey, and in Plutarch, who refers to Catulus' attempt to rouse the senators against the *lex Manilia* in 66.⁵¹ To identify Dio's sources is not a problem with a simple or easy solution. A fragment in Sallust's *Historiae* reports in *oratio obliqua* an argument that Dio attributes to Catulus in

---

⁴⁵ La Penna 1968, 262–3.
⁴⁶ McGushin 1994, 113, 132. On the speeches in Sallust's *Historiae* see Ullmann 1927, 24–48; Büchner 1982, 160–243. On Sallust and Thucydides see Perrochat 1949; more recently, Nicols 1999, 329–44.
⁴⁷ For Philippus' rhetoric see Cic. *De or.* 2.316; *Brut.* 173; 186. Along these lines, see Ullmann, 1927, 42; Syme 1964, 199. *Contra* Büchner 1982, 241; Sklénar 1998.
⁴⁸ Paananen 1972, 62.   ⁴⁹ Sall. *Iug.* 30.
⁵⁰ On the historicity of Sallust's speeches see Büchner 1982, 204–38, esp. 241: "behind all speeches and letters stand historical speeches and letters." On the role of the *topoi* as conveyor of authorial voice see Nicolai 2002, esp. 50–1.
⁵¹ Catulus took a similar stance in 66 against the *lex Manilia*, which granted extraordinary powers to Pompey to fight against Mithridates. Lintott 1997, Appendix A, 2521 postulates the possibility that the speech in Dio had been delivered in 66 (Cic. *Leg. Man.* 52). However, Plut. *Pomp.* 30 seems to support the opposite view.

his speech. This may be an indication that Dio, who in his work refers to Sallust in passing (40.63.4), had read all the works of the Roman historian, and adjusted them to his aims.[52] However, regardless of the identification of his source for the composition of Catulus' speech, it is possible to argue with a certain degree of plausibility that Dio must have consulted, if not Catulus' original speech, a source very close to his time. Dio, in fact, despite his rhetorical re-elaboration of the speech, makes explicit references to the republican political concepts usually adopted by the Roman elite, which were completely alien not only to his world but also to his personal political interests, generally focused as they were on the relation of the *basileus* with the *tyrannos*.[53] Thus, these texts, together with the Plutarchan reference to Catulus' incitement to defend liberty by enacting a secession,[54] show the political concepts that *optimates*, such as Catulus and Philippus, adopted in the political conflicts of the time, or at least those that sources close to their time perceived as consistent and plausible with their ideological tradition.

In these texts, the *optimates*' opponents are presented as tormented in their minds by emotions such as ambition and fear (Sall. *Hist.* 1.77.11M), as the worst and most foolish men who force the wise and the good to follow their lead (Sall. *Hist.* 1.77.1M), as men who attempt to infect them with their madness (Sall. *Hist.* 1.77.9M). By their actions, they overthrow the highest principle of *concordia* (Sall. *Hist.* 1.77.13–4M), the supreme dominion of laws and liberty (Sall. *Hist.* 1.77.11M), and disrupt the preeminence of the *senatus auctoritas* (Sall. *Hist.* 1.77.1M; 22M). Again, by conferring extraordinary powers on one man alone they defy the supremacy of laws and of the *mos mairoum* (Cass. Dio 36.32, 34, 36), disregard the sovereignty of the people (Cass. Dio 36.33, 36), and destroy the principle of geometric equality, the essential concept at the foundation of the *res publica* (Cass. Dio 36.32). In a word, their enemies are fools, subject to the most abject passions, and, acting against the principles of justice and wisdom, destroy any opportunity to live in harmony.

This language, adopted in the political arena to defeat Lepidus in 77 and oppose the *lex Gabinia* in 67, is clearly reminiscent of philosophical

---

[52] Sall. *Hist.* fr. 5.24 M: *nam si in Pompeio quid humani evenisset*; Dio 36.36a Xiphilinus. The argument runs as follows: it would be dangerous and, in a sense, irresponsible to concentrate so much power in the hands of one individual, since he could perish and the future would be left uncertain. Cf. Val. Max. 8.15.9; Vell. Pat. 2.32.1–2. Büchner 1982, 205–7 and Syme 1964, 198 postulate that Sallust's *Historiae* also contained an oration of Gabinius.

[53] On Dio's speeches see Millar 1964, 34; Millar 1961, esp. 14–15. On Dio and the theme of political ideas see Lintott 1997, 2517 and 2520. For the passages on sovereign and tyrant see Millar 1964, 78.

[54] Plut. *Pomp.* 30.

concepts that themselves inform the political arguments of politicians such as Catulus and Philippus. In an attempt to analyze these concepts further, it appears, at first sight, that these ideas pervade all Greek political thinking and it is therefore hard to ascribe them to any specific philosophical school with a distinctive way of thinking about politics. The notions of concord and wisdom are present as ideals since the time of Homer (*Od.* 19.109–14) and Hesiod (*Op.* 225–37), and the idea of friendship as an essential factor for the lasting happiness of a community is a commonplace in Plato (e.g. *Leg.* 628) and Aristotle (e.g. *Eth. Nic.* 8. 1155a22).[55] However, Cicero in the *Tusculanae Disputationes*, as discussed above, shows how this markedly psychological language could be read in the Roman political context in a Stoic mode and was understood as such by his contemporaries, or at least so he could plausibly claim. Thus, following this line of inquiry, it is possible to reconstruct and understand in full the political ideals of the *optimates* tradition adopted by Catulus and his associates in advocating their line of policy. As shown above, they claim to be standing for the primacy of laws that should not be defied either by the use of violence against the *res publica* or by the assignment of special commands to a single individual.

This idea is of Stoic origin and is well attested in a fragment of Chrysippus. It is also reported in the words of the Stoic Laelius in Cicero's *De republica*.[56] The supremacy of true law, sovereign reason intrinsic to nature, is also the subject of Cicero's *De legibus*, in which he claims that positive laws have no value unless they conform to this true law, which is divine, eternal and consistent. If Ferrary is correct in identifying the good laws of the *De legibus* with the *mos maiorum* of old,[57] it appears clear how Cicero, at least, could interpret and adopt Stoicism to support the traditional *res publica*. One of the essential characteristics of this political system was the proportional distribution of honors and duties, as embodied in the *comitia centuriata*, which assigned more political weight to those who had to carry the majority of the military and economic burden. This concept, as Nicolet has demonstrated, corresponds to the idea of geometric equality and is explicitly advocated by Catulus in his opposition to the concentration of excessive powers in the hands of Pompey.[58] Catulus claims that "if the command brings honor to those deemed worthy of it, all whom it concerns

---

[55] Baldry 1959, 14.
[56] For Chrysippus see *SVF* 3.314 = Long and Sedley 67, R: "Law is king of all things human and divine. Law must preside over what is honorable and base, as ruler and as guide, and thus be the standard of right and wrong, prescribing to animals whose nature is political what they should do, and prohibiting them from what they should not do." As for Laelius, see Cic. *Rep.* 3.33 = *SVF* 3.325.
[57] Ferrary 1995.   [58] Nicolet 1976b.

ought to obtain that honor – and this is democracy – and if it brings labor, all ought to share that labor proportionally – this is equality" (Cass. Dio 36.32).[59]

This idea is also present in the Stoic doctrine of justice, which is conceived as "refraining from harming anyone" (Cic. *Off.* 3.28) and "assigning each his own due" (Cic. *Off.* 1.11–20).[60] This concept stems from the distinctive Stoic notion of *oikeiōsis*, that is, natural sociability. According to this notion, men are provided with a natural disposition to identify with other human beings and their interests.[61] As such, they are naturally inclined to behave altruistically, since they perceive other human beings as related to themselves. Thus, depending on the circumstances in which they find themselves, the wise men are prepared to engage in politics with the aim of promoting virtue and restraining vice.[62] They prefer to be active in a state that is "making progress towards the ideal society" (Stob. *Ecl.* 2.94.8–11, *SVF* 3.611), an ideal that for Panaetius was, with all probability, the mixed constitution.[63] As Cicero reports in the *De republica*, "[Laelius] remembered that you [Scipio] were in the habit of discussing politics very frequently with Panaetius when Polybius was present, the two Greeks perhaps most accomplished in the subject, and that you produced many arguments to show that by far the best form of government is the one bequeathed to us by our ancestors" (1.34 = Panaetius fr. 119 = Long and Sedley 67. I).

It has long been thought that Panaetius' conception of the ideal constitution had deeply influenced the work of his pupil Polybius, who interpreted the Roman political system of his time as a mixed constitution with an aristocratic predominance (23.14.1), centered on the senate (51).[64] A passage in Cicero's *De legibus* (3.13–15) confirms the Panaetian authenticity of these political principles. In this passage, Cicero claims that Diogenes and Panaetius, amongst others, discussed the role of magistrates, and seems to imply that they upheld the principle that there should not be "a single magistrate in the commonwealth whom the rest should obey" (3.15), since this would be tantamount to preserving the title of king, which the

---

[59] On Dio's political vocabulary see Freyburger-Galland 1997, esp. 116–22.
[60] Schofield 1995. Cf. Cic. *Off.* 3.27; *Fin.* 3.62–3; *Leg.* 1.33.
[61] See Cic. *Fin.* 3, 62–3; *Off.* 1.11–12. For a modern discussion of *oikeiōsis* see Pembroke 1971.
[62] See Brunt 1975, 16–17; Vander Waerdt 1991, 200–7.
[63] D.L. 7.131, *SVF* 3.700. See also Long and Sedley 1987, ad loc., according to whom the fragment most likely refers to Panaetius' political ideas rather than those of Zeno or Chrysippus.
[64] Arnold 1911, 280–1; Long and Sedley 1987, ad loc. *Contra* Brunt 1975, 17–18. On the difficulty of detecting Paentius' political thought from Cicero's *De republica*, see Ferrary 1988, 363–81. For a democratic preference in the thought of the early Stoa see Erskine 1990.

ancestors had abolished. It is interesting to observe that this is the argument adopted by Catulus not only in his opposition to the *lex Gabinia*, which assigned almost unlimited powers to Pompey, but also, according to Cicero, during the Arpinate's consulship in 63.[65] In opposing the accumulation of great powers in the hands of one man, Catulus returns to a fundamental principle of the mixed constitution, namely the sovereignty of the people.

The appointment of Pompey would in fact defy the people's voting power, since the magistrates they had elected would not then be taken into account, and, although appointed in conformity to law, they would not have any specific task to carry out and therefore would be left only to walk around in their purple togas without any real responsibility. However, when it became clear that Catulus would not have been able to win his battle, he decided to return, once again, to the principle of popular sovereignty. In his strenuous opposition to this law, he proposed a modification to the law, so that the people could hold for themselves the power to elect Pompey's *legati* and divest him of this faculty. In this way, if his proposal were approved, these *legati* would not be bound to the general, but would act independently in the interest of the people (Dio 36.33, 36). The idea of the people's sovereignty that Catulus supports assigns them the role of electing the magistrates, who, in turn, are endowed with the duty of enacting the policies that they regard as in the best interests of the people, although potentially contrary to their will.[66] As such, although the magistrates receive their *potestas* from the people, they are bound to obey the authority of the senate and to conform to its *consulta*. In accordance with this principle, Catulus' political associate Philippus in his opposition to Lepidus stresses the centrality of the *auctoritas senatus*, which, in his opinion, is jeopardized not only by the violent acts of Lepidus, but also by the reluctance of some senators to act against him. The *publicum consilium*, the decisions of the senate and its authority are at the center of the working of the commonwealth and represent the focus of the mixed constitution as also conceived by later Stoics. In the *De legibus* (3.27–8), a work deeply indebted to Stoicism, Cicero approves of the idea that the senate should be composed of ex-magistrates without the recourse to censorial designation because this measure would ultimately reinforce the role of the people. However, in order to enhance the authority of the senate, he proposes that the senate's decrees should be duly ratified, so that

---

[65] Cic. *Red. sen.* 9.
[66] For a different concept of popular sovereignty active in Roman politics, see Hadot 1970.

in the actual business of governing, the senate with its authority and the people with its power could maintain a moderate and harmonious order of the commonwealth.

These ideas not only informed the political arguments put forward by Catulus and Philippus in the fight against Lepidus and Pompey, but also may be found articulated in the first *lex de vi* allegedly proposed by Catulus in 78. According to Cicero's testimony (*Cael.* 70), Catulus proposed a "law on violence [that] has to do with the *imperium*, *maiestas* and the condition of the fatherland and with the safety of all." This law, passed during desperate times for the state, as Cicero specifies, was directed against the "seditious and wicked citizens who have made armed onslaught against the senate, have laid violent hands on magistrates, and have attacked the commonwealth."[67] Although the extensive speculation about the exact nature of this law and its relation to the *lex Plautia de vi* does not allow us to dwell too much on it, it is interesting to note in accordance with Labruna that the phrasing of this law, or at least its inspiring principles, appears to be consistent with the ideology expressed by Philippus in his speech against Lepidus.[68] In Labruna's opinion, the two objects in the phrasing of the law, the senate and the magistrates, are encapsulated and unified by the third element, the *res publica*, in which, therefore, the senate appears to play the most important role, as it is ultimately composed of ex-magistrates. Once again, as in Philippus' speech, the *auctoritas senatus* is the principle to which Catulus and his associates conform. This principle, attributed to Philippus' speech in 77, occurs again in the *Rhetorica ad Herennium*, whose composition is dated between 86 and 82:[69] "The senate's function is to assist the state with counsel; the magistracy's is to execute, by diligent activity, the senate's will; the people's is to choose and support by its votes the best measures and the most suitable men." Thus, once again, the role of leading the government of the community is ultimately recognized as belonging to the senate.

This is not in itself surprising. Sulla's reforms had the aim of strengthening the role of the senate and institutionalizing and reinforcing the senate's control over the magistrates and the assembly.[70] The reinstatement of the prerequisite *senatus consultum* on any law proposal, the assignation of the

---

[67] Cic. *Cael.* 1: *Seditiosis consceleratisque civibus qui armati senatum obsiderint, magistratibus vim attulerint, rem publicam oppugnarint.*

[68] For a general overview on this law see Lintott 1999a, 107–24. The most recent contribution on this topic is Kelly 2005, according to whom the law was proposed by Catulus (cos. 102). For Labruna's interpretation see Labruna 1975, 82–114, who, however, dates the law to 77.

[69] Calboli 1969, 17.   [70] Laffi 1967.

juries to the senate, the limitations on the tribunician *potestas* that could no longer be used against the senate's *consulta*, and ultimately the increased number of magistrates could all be read as aiming at realizing that mixed constitution with an aristocratic preponderance that had been the ideal for Polybius and, most likely, Panaetius.

It comes, therefore, as no surprise that the consulship of 78 could be described as a fight over the Sullan constitution and that, as shown above, it could be defended by Catulus and his associates in Stoicizing terms. Ultimately, even Cicero, who had long lamented the atrocities perpetrated by Sulla, in practice opposed the restitution of the *ius honorum* to the sons of the Sullan proscribed. Sullan reforms pleased a certain section of the community in 63 (Plut. *Cic.* 10.2) and, as Quintilian would later say, "the commonwealth was so essentially dependent on the Sullan laws, that their repeal would have inevitably involved its destruction" (*Inst.* 11.85).[71]

CONCLUSION

It has been long recognized that in the late republic a philosophical meaning, mainly expressed in theoretical treatises, was attached to the term *optimates*, originally used to identify a group of people of high social status and considerable means.[72] However, what I have shown is that such a philosophical dimension was also actively present in the real political conflicts of the time. Both Catulus and his close associate Philippus employed philosophical concepts of Stoic origins to justify their course of actions. Such a rhetorical mode does not necessarily imply that they were Stoics, in the sense of being adherents of a school whose tenets should dictate their conduct, but it indicates that they had at their disposal a political language with a philosophical substrate.[73]

The two consuls' actual political behavior may have been determined by family relations, personal enmity, political friendship or personal and group interests, just to mention a few of the possible explanations. However, the

---

[71] On Cicero's behavior see Cic. *Rosc. Am.* 153–4; *Pis.* 4. For the only fragment from Cicero's *rogatio de restituendis proscriptorum liberis*, see Crawford 1994, 201–7.

[72] Cf. also the *elogium* of Scipio in *CIL* I² 9. For this view see Ferrary 1982, 736–7; *contra* Hellegouarc'h 1963, 500–5, according to whom the terms *optimi* and *boni*, but not *optimates*, were provided with a moral nuance. On the etymology of the term see Ernout & Millet 1951: *optimus<ops*; de Witt 1937, 703: *optimus<ob* as "from above."

[73] Along the same lines, see Brunt 1975, 7: "Stoicisms permeated the writings of authors like Virgil and Horace who professed no formal allegiance to the sect, and became part of the culture that men absorbed in the early education. One might think it exercised an influence comparable in some degree with that which Christianity has often had on men ignorant or careless of the nicer points of systematic theology."

language that they adopted to justify their actions, learnt in their training in the Forum as well as in Greece, had a predominantly, if not exclusively, Stoic character. Even if Catulus and his associates were not fully aware of the deepest philosophical dimensions of the arguments they adopted, they would clearly recognize their affiliation with this ideological tradition as something that set them apart from their rivals. Sulla's constitutional arrangements did reinforce the authority of the senate as superior to that of the magistrates and the assembly and so strengthened the political power of the Roman elite. But by turning to this set of ideas, Catulus and his associates could plausibly defend these constitutional reforms without necessarily exposing the cynical protection of their own interests, which were then at stake.

CHAPTER 15

Consulship and consuls under Augustus

Frédéric Hurlet

It seems paradoxical to devote time to a study of consuls and the consulship under Augustus in a monograph dealing with the constitution of the Roman republic. Yet such a choice is perfectly justified when we remember that Augustus' great skill was in situating the new regime and its *modus operandi* within a context of historical continuity. The significant consequence of this axiom is that the consulship under Augustus can be analyzed not only for its own sake and for its many evolving aspects, but also for what it teaches us about late-republican practices, many of which Augustus revived. The continuity between the Roman republic and the regime founded by Augustus appears to be more or less pronounced depending on whether we look at the consulship from a purely formal point of view or whether we look at the consuls and the position that the *princeps* allotted to them. The guiding line of the following demonstration will be to stress that if the office of the consulship was never the object of legal reforms aimed at weakening its powers, the holders of this magistracy would have had no other choice but to make do with the new political environment resulting from the seizure by a single man and his family of the *res publica*, from Actium onward. For Augustus and the consuls, the crux of the problem lay in finding a relationship that would prevent the latter from contesting the former's superiority without infringing on the very foundations of consular power and prestige.

PRELIMINARY REMARKS AND HISTORIOGRAPHICAL CLARIFICATIONS

The study of the consulship under Augustus has normally been dissociated from the study of the place occupied by those who held this magistracy, even though they are two complementary aspects of the same question. Purely institutional elements drew the attention of specialists at first, as of

Translation by Kevin Streety.

the nineteenth century. We must go back to Mommsen to find a method of analysis that can be applied to the central theme of the book and whose influence was felt throughout the twentieth century.[1] In his *Römisches Staatsrecht*, he studied the consulship in volume II, entirely devoted to the magistracies, in accordance with the spirit of a textbook viewing public law as a system and, to this end, endeavoring to provide a legal definition of the Roman *res publica*.[2] The characteristic absence of any diachronic perspective distinguishes this original project from the multiple surveys dealing with the history of the institutions as they evolved,[3] but this does not mean that Mommsen's *Public Law* is of no use in defining the place occupied by the consulship in the new regime. Indeed, references to the consulship under the empire are numerous in the chapter in question, reflecting the state of the sources, and several of these general remarks can be noted for their pertinence to the subject under study here.

First, Mommsen underlined an undeniable element of continuity, stating that "*überhaupt erscheint das Consulat in der Kaiserzeit noch entschiedener als unter der Republik als die erste der damals noch vorhandenen wirklichen ordentlichen Magistraturen, da ja die Dictatur aufgehört hatte und auch die Censur bald verschwand.*"[4] He also noted the split brought about in this area by the creation of the imperial regime in a sentence that attests to his lucidity and to his great merit as a historian: "*Auch in der Kaiserzeit änderte sich wohl die Macht-, aber nicht die Rechtsstellung des Amtes, wie auch sein äusserer Prunk nicht ab-, sondern zunahm.*"[5] In this excerpt, the opposition between "*Macht*" and "*Rechtsstellung*" expresses the idea, later acknowledged, that the consulship evolved under Augustus less through institutional reforms than through the new political situation arising from the extraordinary position occupied by Augustus at the head of the state. However, Mommsen neither continued nor refined this fundamentally correct judgment, imprisoned as he was by a system that forced him to give a solely legal definition for each form of power, thereby either excluding more historical analyses or else confining them to a single or partial

---

[1] Hölkeskamp 1997b, 93–111.   [2] Mommsen 1887–8.

[3] For example, Mommsen's *Staatsrecht* conflicts in many respects with the textbooks of Siber 1952 and de Martino 1972–5, IV, 619–21 (for the consulship under Augustus), which were intended to study the development of the institutions by showing their historical transformations. The two academic traditions exist – the *Staatsrecht* itself and the *Verfassungsgeschichte* – and are fundamentally different.

[4] Mommsen 1887–8, II, 88: "the imperial consulship even more than in republican times appeared as the highest of all remaining magistracies, since the dictatorship and also the censorship soon ceased to exist."

[5] Mommsen 1887–8, II, 87: "In the imperial age, the inherent powers of the consulate changed, although its legal status did not, just as its surrounding glamour did not decrease, but increase."

sentence. Another drawback to Mommsen's method – in keeping with the spirit of the textbook, which minimized the importance of periodization – is that he extends the study up to the imperial era, when the documentation existed, while at the same time failing to discuss the evolution of the consulship at a time as decisive as that of the passage from republic to empire. Mommsen's followers have been numerous throughout the twentieth century and up until the present day.[6] Among those who continue to follow this method, placing at the center of political life the functioning of institutions, we should name Girardet and Ferrary, who were both interested in the evolution of the consulship under Augustus, each arriving at different solutions, as we shall see later. The time seems to have thus come for a survey of the question, taking care to no longer focus attention solely on the institutional machinery of this magistracy at a given time. Indeed, historiographical research in the twentieth century has shown that far from their being inseparable, the relationship between society and the Roman state was one of such close interaction that the transformations of one had an influence on the structures of the second and vice versa.[7] Given this, the most credible option with which we are left is to study the legal aspects of all forms of power and their evolution in direct relation to the transformations of the political and social context.

The abundant scholarly output of Syme reminds us to this end that Augustus and the new regime can be analyzed, with some success, by a method different from that of an exclusively institutional approach. For the subject that interests us, the English scholar did more than anyone to contribute to the reversal of the Mommsenian schema that had become the traditional approach employed to provide an account of the nature of the Augustan principate, through a study of the consuls of the Augustan period more than a study of the consulship *per se*. Indeed, the prosopographical perspective taken up by Syme (and of which he was one of the most brilliant representatives) led him to take an interest in men (in particular their origins, their careers and their relations with the *princeps*) more than in institutions. In *The Roman Revolution*, we find portraits of consuls (some rather colorful) during the Augustan period (there were 119 between 31 BC and AD 14), but also an analysis of the place occupied by these consuls in

---

[6] Cf. the recent textbook of Roman public law in the spirit of Mommsen by Rainer 2006, which devotes only one page to the consulship during the imperial era and without distinguishing Augustus' principate from that of his successors (247). On the methodological and epistemological problems raised by Rainer's essay, cf. my critical remarks in a review in *Latomus* 67 (2008, 1090–3). Scheid's synthetic notes should also be consulted in Jacques & Scheid 1990, 58–9.
[7] Cf. Hölkeskamp 2004b, 19–29.

the process that led to the progressive disappearance of the old Roman aristocracy and the promotion of a new nobility extending throughout the whole of Italy.[8] Evolution in the choice of consuls has also been the subject of Syme's attention. It has been shown that after an initial period during which, besides Augustus, several new men close to him (and considered as *viri militares*) were elected to the consulship (28–19 BC), the members of the old republican nobility once again monopolized this magistracy from 18 BC to the end of the last decade before our era. As of that time and until AD 14, the opening of the consulship to the elites of Italy became continually more pronounced.[9]

Within the scope of this overview, our point is not to favor one approach over the other. Indeed, the methodology of Mommsen and that of Syme are not as antithetical as has been previously imagined, since their analyses, far from being mutually exclusive, bring to light two aspects of Augustus' power that are *in fact* complementary: in the case in point, his shaping of institutions and the more pragmatic realities arising from his need to enjoy the support of a senatorial aristocracy recomposed by the new regime for its own benefit. It is my intention to take a different and more specific path by reconciling the viewpoint of the jurist with the renewed vision of the historian of political life by studying the interactions between the establishment of the new regime and the consulship's adaptation to this new reality. An examination of the articulation between the continuities and the novelties is the best angle from which to start a study of the consulship and the place occupied by consuls under Augustus. The following section will have it as its object to determine to what extent and under what terms the consulship of the Augustan age continued in the line of republican institutional practices, while the section after that will deal with the various modifications to this magistracy during the period. From this appraisal, we can already presume that if there were changes, the most important was not purely institutional. Rather, it is to be found in the necessary subordination of the consuls to the *princeps* and the consequences following from this *de facto* situation (which will be examined in the final section): for example, the redefinition of the functions of the consul and the necessarily new way in which Augustus and the senatorial aristocracy perceived the consulship.

---

[8] Syme 1939, vii: "Emphasis is laid, however, not upon the personality and acts of Augustus, but upon his adherents and partisans."

[9] On the evolution of the consuls' familial origins (*homines novi* or members of the nobility), cf. Syme 1939, 372–3, 434–5.

CONTINUITY OF THE REPUBLIC

Such continuity is obvious from an institutional point of view if we take the formal powers of Augustan consuls into greater account than the necessarily novel place that they were granted in the new regime. Despite the conclusions reached by Giovannini and Girardet, to which I shall return later, to this day there exists no decisive argument that would lead us to assume the existence of one or more fundamental institutional modifications of the consulship under Augustus. We can imagine that the new regime had more reason to be wary of the potential power of the consuls in military affairs than of their capacities with regard to civil matters. Even so, should the regime have legislated in order to reserve for the *princeps* what had been one of the foundations of consular authority in the Rome of the republic and the empire, to wit, the opportunity offered each year to two persons to hold concurrently the office with the greatest civil and military powers in the *res publica*? At this stage of our investigation, it behooves us to focus briefly on the institutional aspects if we wish to appreciate fully the stakes involved in determining the existence or non-existence of a reform of the consulship. Under the republic, the consul was as such invested with an *imperium* that took a specific form according to whether he was inside the *pomerium* of Rome (i.e. the *imperium domi*) or outside the *pomerium* (i.e. the *imperium militiae*). Otherwise a civil magistrate would become a general-in-chief as soon as he crossed the religious boundary during the year of his mandate, making sure to put on the military uniform (the *paludamentum*) and to add the axes to the twelve *fasces* carried by as many lictors. This practice is evidenced by the sources, but it is well known that it finally disappeared during the middle of the first century BC as the consuls came to settle more and more in the *Urbs*, given the tendency for the government of provinces to be given over to former consuls (and also former praetors) with the title of proconsul. The main question to be asked in the scope of this chapter is whether Augustus was responsible in one way or another for such an evolution, and if so, how.

The existence of a rule forbidding higher magistrates, or in any case consuls, from occupying a military command in a province during the term of their office has been unanimously accepted for some time, which is all the more surprising considering that no source exists directly referring to such a rule. A tradition beginning in the sixteenth century with the jurist Hotman would have Theodor Mommsen attributing authorship of this law, which he named the *lex Cornelia de provinciis ordinandis*, to

Sulla.[10] It is to Giovannini's credit to have shown that such a regulation would have been contrary to the political practice in force from the years 80 to 50 BC and quite simply did not exist at the time.[11] He continued, however, to be a prisoner of Mommsen's system, at least up to a certain point, in that he refused to relinquish the idea that an institutional measure had been voted in due form that would have taken away the military component of the consul's *imperium*. Unlike Mommsen, he dates such a decision from the year 27 BC,[12] when Augustus instituted an interval of five years between the exercise of the office of consulship and proconsulship. This proposal was accepted by Nicolet and at first by Roddaz,[13] being nuanced only from a chronological point of view by Girardet, who preferred to date this law, which he named the "*Entmachtungsgesetz des Konsulates*," to the year 19 or 18.[14] Recently, however, a study by Ferrary has questioned this new (and fragile) consensus by advocating the idea that a law depriving the consulship of the military component of its *imperium* was never voted under Augustus – no more in 19/18 than in 27.[15] The arguments that he puts forth are numerous and convincing. Such an overall reform of the highest of the magistracies is attested to in none of the sources – this being an argument *e silentio* that we should make with caution, but that is not valueless when we consider the considerable political implications that such a law would have had; besides, it would have been counterproductive, since it would have run the risk of putting an official end to one of the centuries-old institutional foundations of the consulship in a Roman society disinclined toward any brutal change. Finally, it would have been useless, as Augustus was in a position to bring about an identical result in practice, that is, the non-practice of the *imperium militiae* by the consuls using indirect means, as we shall see below. After all is said and done, the most credible hypothesis given the current state of our knowledge is the simplest, which concludes that no law depriving the consulship of its military powers ever existed.

The exercise of the consulship during the Augustan period is part and parcel of the practice of institutional continuity, with the official program of the *res publica* providing a legal framework. This process of restoration of the state, officially begun January 1, 28 for the consulship, as evidenced by the publication of a new *aureus* of that year,[16] was presented the same year

---

[10] Mommsen 1887–8, I, 57–9; II, 94, 214–15; III, 1086–7, 1102–3.   [11] Giovannini 1983.
[12] Giovannini 1983, 118–19, 151.   [13] Nicolet 1992, 163–6; Roddaz 1992, 189–211.
[14] Girardet 1990, 89–126 = Girardet 2007, 385–423. Cf. also Giovannini 1999, 95.
[15] Ferrary 2001, 101–54. Cf., in the same vein as Ferrary, Roddaz 2003, 412–14; Hurlet 2006, 28–30.
[16] Rich & Williams 1999, 169–213.

and in subsequent years as a return to traditional practices, namely those of the late-republican era. The point was to close the interlude opened by the era of the civil wars characterized by institutional disturbance (*non mos, non ius*, to quote Tacitus).[17] The testimony of Cassius Dio presents an atmosphere of restoration following the return of Augustus to Rome after his victories over Antony and Cleopatra, stating at the beginning of his account of the year 28 that "Caesar (Octavian) conformed in all other respects to the usages handed down from the earliest times."[18] The context of the year in question lent itself to the restoration of certain institutional practices unique to the republican consulship, some of which are quite well known.

First, through an examination of the consular *fasti*, we can establish that Octavian, wishing to return to strict republican principles, put an end to the practice, started by Julius Caesar and common during the Triumvirate, of making use of one or several couples of suffect consuls. Indeed, after AD 28, we see only ordinary consuls, at the rate of two per year, unless one of these died and was replaced by a suffect consul in accordance with the traditional rule.[19] This practice lasted until 5 BC, at which date the suffect consuls once again increased in numbers (I shall come back to this later). Cassius Dio's account provides further details when he states, after (and in relationship to) his preliminary remarks on the return of traditional practices in 28, that "Caesar delivered to Agrippa, his colleague, the *fasces* as it was incumbent upon him to do, while he himself used the other set."[20] We are to understand that the traditional alternation of the *fasces* had been suspended during the Triumvirate, quite certainly because they had been monopolized by the triumvirs. After January 1, 28, Octavian returned to the pre-Triumvirate era custom in that there were two series (or sets) of twelve *fasces* used in turn by Octavian and Agrippa depending on the month: the former using them during odd-numbered months, the most important since important matters of state were dealt with in January and July (for example, elections for the following year), while the latter used them during even-numbered months. Thus the fundamental principle of consular collegiality was restored in the most traditional forms of its application.[21]

---

[17] Tac. *Ann.* 3.28.1.   [18] Cass. Dio 53.1.1.   [19] Bleicken 1998, 322.   [20] Cass. Dio 53.1.1.
[21] Cf. as well Cass. Dio 53.1.2, who lists amongst the number of ways that collegiality was restored the fact that Octavian "provided [Agrippa] with a tent similar to his own whenever they were campaigning together, and the watchword was given out by both of them" (on the meaning of this passage, cf. Hurlet 2009, 79–80).

It is telling that this passage from Cassius Dio has been used by historians not only to understand the events of 28, but also as a fundamental account of a purely republican rule, that is, the alternation of the consular *fasces*, which had lasted without interruption until the foundation of the Triumvirate in 43.[22] Cassius Dio continues his description of the measures taken in 28 by pointing out that, amongst the other ancestral practices that Octavian restored, "on completing his term of office he took the oath according to ancestral custom."[23] This is another piece of precious information pertaining to an otherwise scarcely attested republican practice. Each of these examples is a witness to a certain form of continuity between the republic and the empire with regards to the consulship.

DEVELOPMENTS WITH REGARD TO THE REPUBLIC

Despite all this, it would be wrong to pretend that Augustus' principate did not accelerate a certain number of developments first seen at the end of the republican era and that affected the consulship, in their turn. It is undeniable that the superior magistracy of the republican *cursus honorum* experienced a depreciation from the 40s onwards, given the competition embodied in the dictatorship of Caesar (every ten years at first and then perpetual) and then later in the Triumvirate. The suppression of the powers of the Triumvirate and the program of restoration of the damaged *res publica* returned the consulship to its place at the head of the state as of January 1, 28, but only temporarily.[24] In the context of the 20s, the restoration of institutional order in this form was viable only so long as Augustus continued to perform the functions of consul. This form of principate, which we could describe as consular, lasted in this way until 23, at which date the *princeps* abdicated the consulship that he had held continuously since 31, to take up the tribunician power.

The events of the summer of 23 in this respect consecrated a split: the consulship was, once and for all, no longer a part of the sum of imperial powers and from that point would only be employed by Augustus in a one-off manner (in 5 and 2 BC for several months and in connection with the early public careers of his adopted sons, Caius and Lucius). This situation was exceptional and must have been seen as such at the time, as the consuls now relinquished the first place in the *Urbs* to the holder of a tribunician power that originally was not meant to be bestowed upon

---

[22] For a more detailed analysis and a use of Cassius Dio in the framework of a work studying the institutional aspects of power during the republican era, cf. Vervaet forthcoming.
[23] Cass. Dio 53.1.1. [24] As noted by Roddaz 2003, 401.

the executive ruler. Giving up the consulship must not have been an easy decision for Augustus to make, as we see clearly in the remark by Suetonius that Augustus "also demanded that whenever the consulship was conferred on him, he should have two colleagues instead of one."[25] This proposal for an increased number of consuls, which cannot be dated with any certainty (either before 23 or in 19,[26] in connection with the measures taken that year that we shall examine later), was intended to permit a greater number of former praetors to take up the supreme magistracy – and thus accede to consular functions – without taking away any of the considerable powers that Augustus held by right of his position as consul.

The proposal was eventually dismissed. Suetonius reports the reaction of senators, saying that "all cried out that it was a sufficient offense to his supreme dignity that he held the office with another and not alone." Beyond this stated (and reassuring) reason, in line with conventions inherent to political communication in the senate, the principal reason for this failure was opposition by the majority of senators to such a profound alteration in republican tradition. Augustus was thus left with no other possibility than to continue to base a portion of his powers on his consulship or else to permanently renounce this magistracy and find another instrument allowing him to take part in the formal government of the *Urbs*. In the end, he chose the second solution.

The measures taken in 19 were the last in the process of defining the necessarily complex relations between the two annual consuls and Augustus. We must remember that electoral disturbances broke out as of 22–21, and once again more seriously in 19 partly because Augustus refused to be a candidate for the consulship and did not accept being strong-armed by the centuriate assemblies, who had nonetheless elected him against his will. It was thus necessary to find another consul, and one was accordingly found, albeit with difficulty and under conditions that I will later have reason to come back to. In addition, in 22, the Roman people had once again lamented and criticized the abdication of the consulship, to which they directly ascribed several natural catastrophes, such as a flooding of the Tiber, plague or lightning that struck numerous objects, including statues in the Pantheon.[27] These were literally prodigies,[28] which some Romans

---

[25] Suet. *Aug.* 37: *Exegit etiam ut quotiens consulatus sibi daretur, binos pro singulis collegas haberet*. Cf. Kienast 1999, 106.
[26] Concerning this proposal and its dating, cf. Dettenhofer 2000, 103 n. 84.
[27] Cass. Dio 54.1.1–3 states that "the Romans . . . believed that these woes had come upon them for no other reason than that they did not have Augustus for consul at this time also."
[28] Cf. Becher 1985, 471–9; Rosenberger 1998, 238.

were able to interpret as a consequence of the preceding summer's reform. These events bear witness to the idea that the consular principate continued to enjoy support, especially among the people, after and despite the measures taken in 23.

On his return from the orient in 19, Augustus had a certain number of important measures adopted that have recently led many to re-evaluate the importance of this year in the evolution and the shaping of the new regime. Among the decisions concerning the consulship, Cassius Dio states in a well-known passage that Augustus "took the authority of consul for life, and in consequence had the right to use the twelve *fasces* always and everywhere and to sit in the curule chair between the two men who were at the time consuls."[29] This passage has been much commented upon, and we would do well to remember Ferrary's interpretation: Augustus was given on this occasion the *insignia* of the consulship for life, indissociable from a certain capacity to exercise the consular *imperium* in specific areas that were not covered by the tribunician power (in particular, the *census* and jurisdiction).[30] The mere fact of sitting between the two consuls and having the right to use the twelve *fasces* always and everywhere (even in Rome) made of Augustus a dignitary with all the external appearances of a consul but without the title. This was the result of a compromise between the consular principate as it had been imagined from the start (28–23) and the proposal for an increased number of annual consuls.

The consulship suffered from a comparison with the sum of extended powers granted to Augustus, but the consuls continued to exercise the functions that had been assigned to the consulship under the republic, even after (and despite) the measures of 19. They still dispensed justice; one of them continued to preside over consular and praetorian elections each year without Augustus encroaching on such prerogatives except in times of disturbance (for example, in AD 7, when he was brought to intervene in an authoritative manner);[31] as before, they caused several important *senatus consulta* and laws to be voted upon – with Augustus' approval, we should add (for example, the consuls' *lex Fufia Caninia* of 2 BC, the *lex Aelia Sentia*

---

[29] Cass. Dio 54.10.5.
[30] Ferrary 2001, 121–30, which contains the principal bibliographical references on the reforms of 19. Concerning the reforms, Ferrary acknowledges the use that he made of the then unpublished article by Cotton & Yakobson 2002, coming to the same conclusions on several essential points (the unique and temporary quality of Augustus' *imperium*), but differing from them on several other important points.
[31] Nothing in the sources tells us that Augustus presided over the electoral *comilia centuriata* or that he legally used his power to control candidacies (making do with the republican practices of *commendatio* and *suffragatio*); cf. on this subject Ferrary 2001, 128.

of AD 4, the *lex Valeria Cornelia* of AD 5 or the *lex Papia Poppaea* of AD 9). The measures of 19 clarified these relationships in terms of the practice of power in Rome: civil matters were to be managed by Augustus primarily by means of the tribunician power, whereas the consuls kept all of the competencies attached to their *consulare imperium domi* and continued to make use of them in a spirit of perfect collaboration with the *princeps*.

The consulship was affected by various isolated reforms under the principate of Augustus. Among these, the *lex Iulia de maritandis ordinibus* dated to 18 BC (which may possibly have been preceded in 28–27 by an initial series of measures serving the same purpose)[32] granted privileges linked to marriage and paternity and, as such, directly concerned the consulship. It is in this way that we know that, in accordance with this law, the *fasces* were given first, as a matter of priority, not to the elder of the consuls, but to him "who either has more children under his control than his colleague, or has lost them in war. But if both have an equal number of children, the one who has a wife, or is eligible for marriage, is preferred. If, however, both are married and are fathers of the same number of children, the standard of honors of early times is restored and the elder is first to assume the *fasces*. But when both consuls are without wives and have the same number of sons, or are husbands but have no children, there is no provision in that law as to the age."[33] We should note that the law of 18, far from weakening the power of the consuls, intended rather to redefine their position in line with Augustus' natalist policy directed at the senatorial aristocracy. This general conclusion holds for the *lex Valeria Cornelia* of AD 5, which created ten "destining" centuries named after the recently dead princes and redefined the sole terms of election to the consulship.

It should be remembered that no measure took away from the consuls their capacities in any area whatsoever, be it civil or military. This is hardly surprising in light of Augustus' policy of situating his actions within a strategy of continuity with the institutions of the Roman republic (see above). Only one step can be said to have substantially altered the powers and competences of the consulship, albeit indirectly. This was the reform of the proconsulship, most likely dating to January of 27, which (re-)established a period of five years between the exercise of the consulship and the right to draw lots for a consular proconsulship position (Africa and Asia). The consequence of this was that, except for Augustus, who was

---

[32] For the technical questions, I would suggest Moreau 2003, 461–77, who is in agreement on this point.
[33] Gell. 2.15.4–7.

given in 27, on an extraordinary basis, a series of provinces under military control to govern, all concrete possibility of making use of the consuls' *imperium militiae* was taken from them, since they were no longer permitted to govern a province during the same year as or at the end of their magistracy in an independent manner – that is, as proconsuls.[34] The stakes were considerable, since this law made Augustus the only dignitary with the power to concurrently hold civil and military power; moreover, from 23 onward, this power was granted for life, when he was given permission to cross the *pomerium* as often as he wanted without the need to renew his *imperium* each time. The skill with which he effectively put an end to the consuls' military activities without effecting such a brutal split in the framework of the law should be noted, even while he took as his precedent Pompey, who had caused the principle of a five-year interval between consulship and proconsulship to be voted in 52.

AUGUSTUS' AND THE ARISTOCRACY'S VIEW OF THE CONSULSHIP

It is time to go beyond a strictly institutional point of view in order to consider the way in which the consulship was perceived by Augustus and under Augustus' reign. By this, we mean a study of the consulship less as a static institution and more as a lived reality. The depreciation of the consulship when compared with the sum of the powers granted to Augustus, although undeniable, must nonetheless be nuanced. It in no way means that this magistracy had lost all political meaning. In this last section, the guiding question will be what value should be attributed to the practice of the consulship under Augustus. If it is patently obvious that the consulship was no longer one of the centers of power, its attribution continued to be the subject of forceful demands on the part of an aristocracy in search of new fields of competition once the supremacy of Augustus and his family was no longer seriously questioned. Augustus favored competition within the senatorial aristocracy as long as it was confined to the magistracies demoted to secondary status.[35]

Senatorial competition for the post of consul in the 20s and 30s BC went through several stages in relation to the process of defining imperial powers before coming to a *modus vivendi* in the second decade BC that would last for the entire term of Augustus' principate and beyond. After the period

---

[34] Cf. on this subject Hurlet 2006, 28–30.
[35] Cf. Syme 1939, 420: "For all that they [the nobiles] might flourish in the shadow of the monarchy, prosecute old feuds, construct new alliances – in short acquire a handsome share of the power and the profits. The most open political prize was the consulate."

of triumvirate, during which the distribution of the principal *honores* had been decided alone by the triumvirs, the program of restoration of the *res publica* led to the return of consular elections by the centuriate assemblies, as of 28. This return to the traditional means of designating consuls was accompanied by a renewal of electoral competition to obtain this magistracy. Even though Augustus was continuously elected to the consulship by the centuriate assemblies from 28 to 23, it was necessary as well for them to elect, each year, someone else to act as his colleague. This return to the procedure in force under the republic meant that consular elections were once again preceded each year by electoral campaigns. Given our current knowledge of the sources, we are not in a position to determine whether, besides Augustus, there were one or more candidates in the running for the second consular post. In any case, it can hardly be doubted that the status of colleague of Augustus was highly coveted within the senatorial aristocracy. Augustus' principate thus revived the principle of competition for the consulship, the essential difference from republican procedure being that the competition was now arbitrated not only by the assemblies, but also and above all by the *princeps*.[36] Indeed, the identity of the first consuls of the *res publica restituta* – M. Agrippa in 28–27 and T. Statilius Taurus in 26, both close friends of Augustus – shows that the new regime held enough sway over the designation process to have its candidate elected.

We must remember that from 28 on, the *princeps* had at his disposal the traditional powers that gave him the legal right to intervene in the choice of his colleague to the consulship. Indeed, in his capacity as consul elected without interruption between 31 and 23, he performed a central duty by presiding over the electoral assemblies held each year during the summer with the object of electing the following year's consuls, at least whenever he was in Rome (in 28 and most certainly as well in 24). In this capacity, he was sole judge of the admissibility of candidacies and was in control of the last stage of the procedure inasmuch as the president proclaimed (*renuntiare*) the candidate elected by the assemblies. When he was absent from Rome, which was more the rule than the exception during the first two decades of the new regime, he entrusted at first the presidency of the consular elections to his close colleagues – M. Agrippa in 27 and T. Statilius Taurus in 26. In addition to his legal powers, he also had at his disposal means of informal pressure, which were just as effective, in order to dissuade undesirable candidates from standing for election. But even if the

---

[36] Tac. *Ann.* 1.15.1: *nam ad eam diem* (principate of Tiberius), *etsi potissima arbitrio principis, quaedam tamen studiis tribuum fiebant.*

designation process was controlled by the *princeps*, electoral competition still played itself out in front of the assemblies under the watchful eye of the *princeps* or his close colleagues.

After the year 28, Augustus' abdication of the consulship in the summer of 23 marked a new and important stage, representing a major reform that resulted in the allocation to former praetors of not one consulship per year, as in the past, but two. As Cassius Dio notes (53.33.2), the measures of 23 were justified as much – if not more – by fear of an aristocratic reaction to an imperial monopolization of the consulship that deprived, in a very concrete manner, several senators of the right to govern consular provinces as they were by the institutional difficulties created by the continuous practice of the supreme magistracy, which it had not been customary for one man to hold for so long.[37] Competition between former praetors was all the more fierce as a result. Indeed, an examination of the consular elections subsequent to the summer of 23 shows the existence of sometimes turbulent electoral campaigns and consequently demonstrates that there could be, on occasion, more candidates than posts to fill, at least during the years 23 to 19.

The events of the years from 22 to 21 are particularly telling. In 22, amidst uprisings, Augustus was first elected once again by the assemblies to the consulship for the year 21 at the same time as M. Lollius, despite Augustus' abdication in 23 and his absence – being in Sicily at the time. However, in the beginning of the year 21, he made it known that he refused the office. In accordance with the still effective republican tradition, it was the responsibility of the sole consul, M. Lollius, to duly take office on January 1, 21, and to preside over the consular assemblies in order to elect a new colleague. We know that two candidates stood for the election to the vacant position, Q. Aemilius Lepidus and L. Silvanus (or L. Silanus), and that at the end of an electoral campaign once again noted for unrest, the former was finally elected.[38]

We encounter almost identical circumstances at the beginning of the year 19, except that one of the candidates for the consulship, M. Egnatius Rufus, was dismissed by the sole consul who had already taken up his duties, C. Sentius Saturninus, and finally executed on the grounds that he

---

[37] Cf. Cartledge 1975, 34; Bleicken 1990, 94–5; Dettenhofer 2000, 103.
[38] On the events of 22–21, cf. Cass. Dio 54.6.1–4, which leaves no doubt whatsoever as to the existence of electoral competition by his use of the verb σπουδαρχιάω, further stating that due to the unrest breaking out on the announcement of the candidacies for the consulship of Q. Aemilius Lepidus (Barbula; cf. Tansey 2008) and L. Silvanus (or L. Silanus?), Augustus refused to return to Rome and had the two candidates come to Sicily, forbidding them to be present in Rome at the time of the elections in hopes of calming the tensions. Q. Aemilius Lepidus was finally elected in his absence.

had organized a plot against Augustus, after which Q. Lucretius Vespillo was elected to the consulship, at the behest of the *princeps*.[39] We thus see that the popular assemblies had regained what had been their principal function during the republican era: choosing between members of the great Roman families continually struggling for power, but with one essential difference in that it was now only a matter of election to honors that were to all intents and purposes of a secondary status compared to the imperial powers, and that Augustus efficiently controlled the choice of consuls from afar. The new regime thus used the assemblies for assigning the traditional magistracies such as the consulship. In this way, the *princeps* displaced the field of senatorial competition from what had become the heart of political power.

We have no precise information concerning the consular elections of the years following the year 19, undoubtedly because the people had gotten used to the idea that Augustus would no longer be consul (the reform of 19 had clarified the situation on this matter). The unrest had consequently ceased, which does not mean that electoral competition disappeared in the second decade BC. Indeed, the opposite is undoubtedly true, but we have no way of knowing if more than two candidates stood each year for consular elections. Whether their number was freely fixed according to senators' ambitions or whether it was decided in advance by the new regime (i.e. as many candidates as posts to fill), the intensity of the rivalry between former praetors – be it out in the open or more hushed and behind the scenes of imperial power – was the same. The fact that the consulship was taken up by members of the imperial family (Tiberius in 13 and 7 BC, Drusus the Elder in 9 BC, Caius Caesar in AD 1 and Germanicus in AD 12) highlights in any case the interest that such a magistracy continued to exert.[40] The systematic reappearance of the suffect consulship as of 5 BC, little more than twenty years after the practice was abandoned, is another clue to the attraction that this magistracy continued to hold.

In this way, Augustus was made to increase the number of consuls, undoubtedly under pressure from the senatorial aristocracy, in order to allow a larger number of senators to hold the title of consul (even if only for a few months) and to lessen the competition aroused by access to the supreme magistracy. This measure did not bring with it advantages. It only displaced the principal problem, which was the necessity of managing this competition, as it eventually put an end to the fragile equilibrium that had

---

[39] On these events of the beginning of the year 19, cf. Cass. Dio 54.10.1–2 (cf. Cogitore 2002, 136–41).
[40] Cf. Hurlet 1997, 233–4.

been observed until then between the number of those capable of holding the consulship and the number of consular positions to be filled. Indeed, numbers of candidates for the proconsulships of Asia and Africa were to grow as time went by, whereas the fixed number of two consular provinces did not allow for more than two people capable of filling consular positions in each year.

CONCLUSIONS

The birth of the principate, which represented such a fundamental political split, was not accompanied by an upheaval in the institutional structures and among certain practices already in place at the end of the republic. An analysis of the consulship under Augustus and of the position assigned to consuls during this period shows us precisely that, in many respects, the opposite was the case, by pointing out the multiple examples of continuity between republic and empire. From a legal standpoint, if a law might occasionally affect the highest of the ordinary magistracies by conferring privileges linked to the familial status of consuls (*lex Iulia* of 18 BC) or by redefining the process by which they were elected (*lex Valeria Cornelia* of AD 5), we can say that no law directly questioned the magistracy's traditional foundations, that is, the consul's possession of *imperium militiae*, if only in theory. However, in practice, Augustus achieved the same result indirectly, by reviving a law dating from the time of Pompey forbidding a consul to leave to govern a province in the same year as his magistracy. The consulship continued to exacerbate rivalries within the aristocracy despite its depreciation given the primacy of Augustus at the head of the state; primacy accorded by the mass of powers conferred upon him.

Mutatis mutandis, this permanent situation of competition for the consulship only prolonged a practice attested under the Roman republic that Hölkeskamp has named as one of the characteristic elements of a highly competitive aristocratic political culture. In a recent essay, the German scholar studied the connections that were created in the Roman republic between consensus (on the aristocratic nature of the regime) and competition (amongst aristocrats), concepts that are often in opposition, but that he shows to be in fact complementary under the republic.[41] Under Augustus' principate, consensus and competition continued to operate, but the new political context gave them a different meaning than that which they had had under the republic.

[41] Hölkeskamp 2004b.

A new consensus slowly emerged among the principal actors of Roman political life on the necessity of establishing an extraordinary position at the head of the state to be given to one man (the *princeps*) and to his family (the *domus Augusta* or *Diuina*).[42] As for competition, we have seen that it still existed in the method of assigning the consulship under Augustus even after the regime change, the essential difference being that a phenomenon of this order was now supervised by the *princeps*. Outside of periods of crisis following usurpations and those contributing to the overthrow of the dynasty and (or) the *princeps*, competition between aristocrats thus no longer took place within the heart of political power, which was now in the hands of the *princeps*. Still, the stakes were no less important. The status of consul under Augustus continued to be a criterion of hierarchization in a society of orders that never substituted the *princep*'s favors for the office of the most important of the polyadic magistracies. If the consulship lost the political power that it had enjoyed under the republic, its social prestige was maintained (or even reinforced) by Augustus, within the framework of a program of restoration of the *res publica* that saw a return of the traditional foundations of Roman society. The resulting situation cannot be seen as one more incarnation of Syme's well-known contention that "Roman history, republican or Imperial, is the history of the governing class."[43] Rather, it would be more apt to conceive of it as a concrete application of the idea that political history can no longer be limited to an examination of institutional machinery bound by strict rules. Indeed, we have seen to what extent and how Augustus made use of existing political practices such as aristocratic competition as well as republican institutions to bring forth a radically new political situation in the misleading, but reassuring, guise of a return to tradition. The institutional continuity within which the Augustan consulship was situated and the permanence of competition for the awarding of this magistracy had a great deal to do with the Roman aristocracy's acceptance of the new regime and the social consensus as it was eventually redefined during the years from 20 to 10 BC.

---

[42] On the subject of this new consensus and its definition, cf. Flaig 1992. Whereas Dettenhofer 2000 believes that the new regime was only finally accepted by the Roman aristocracy during the last decade of Augustus' principate, it seems to me that the consensus pertaining to the new regime was established in the second decade BC. (cf. my remarks on this subject in Hurlet 2003; Hurlet 2007, 199–204).

[43] Syme 1939, 7.

Bibliography

Achard, G. 1981. *Pratique rhétorique et idéologie politique dans les discours Optimates de Cicéron.* Leiden.
Aigner Foresti, L. 1995. "La tradizione antica sul 'ver sacrum'" in M. Sordi (ed.), *Coercizione e mobilità umana nel mondo antico.* Milan. 141–7.
Alexander, M. 1990. *Trials in the Late Roman Republic, 149 BC–50 BC.* Toronto.
Alföldi, A. 1965. *Early Rome and the Latins.* Ann Arbor.
Alfonsi, L. 1960. "Sul circolo di Lutazio Catulo" in *Hommages à Léon Herrmann.* Brussels. 61–7.
Allély, A. 2004. *Lépide le triumvir.* Bordeaux.
Althoff, G. 2003. *Die Macht der Rituale: Symbolik und Herrschaft im Mittelalter.* Darmstadt.
Arangio Ruiz, V. 1957. *Storia del diritto romano*, 2nd edn. Naples.
Arnold, E.V. 1911. *Roman Stoicism.* London.
Assman, J. 1995. "Collective Memory and Cultural Memory" *New German Critique* 65: 125–33.
 2006. *Religion and Cultural Memory.* Stanford.
Astin, A.E. 1958. *The Lex Annalis before Sulla.* Brussels.
 1971. *Scipio Aemilianus.* Oxford.
 1978. *Cato the Censor.* Oxford.
 1982. "The Censorship of the Roman Republic: Frequency and Regularity" *Historia* 31: 174–87.
 1985. "Censorships in the Late Republic" *Historia* 34: 175–90.
Auliard, C. 2006. *La diplomatie romaine: l'autre instrument de la conquête. De la fondation à la fin des guerres samnites (755–290 av. J.-C.).* Rennes.
Badian, E. 1958. *Foreign Clientelae, 264–70 B.C.* Oxford.
 1962. "From the Gracchi to Sulla" *Historia* 11: 197–245.
 1964. *Studies in Greek and Roman History.* Oxford.
 1968. *Roman Imperialism in the Late Republic.* Ithaca.
 1970. "Lucius Sulla: The Deadly Reformer" in A.J. Dunston (ed.), *Essays on Roman Culture: The Todd Memorial Lectures.* Toronto and Sarasota. 35–74.
 1972. *Publicans and Sinners: Private Enterprise in the Service of the Roman Republic.* Ithaca.
 1990a. "Magistratur und Gesellschaft" in W. Eder (ed.), *Staat und Staatlichkeit in der frühen römischen Republik.* Stuttgart. 458–75.

1990b. "The Consuls, 179–49 BC" *Chiron* 20: 371–413.
Baldry, H.C. 1959. "Zeno's Ideal State" *JHS* 79: 3–15.
Balsdon, J.P.V.D. 1939. "Consular Provinces under the Late Republic I: General Considerations" *JRS* 29: 57–73.
Bandel, F. 1910. "Die Dictaturen der römischen Republik." Dissertation. Breslau.
Bandy, A.C. 1983. *Iohannes Lydus: On Powers or the Magistracies of the Roman State*. Philadelphia.
Barker, G. and Rasmussen, T. 2000. *The Etruscans*. Oxford.
Barnabei, F. 1895. "Trasacco: di una rarissima 'tessera hospitalis' con inscrizione Latina" *NSA*: 85–93.
Bates, R.L. 1986. "Rex in Senatu: A Political Biography of M. Aemilius Scaurus" *Proceedings of the American Philosophical Society* 130: 251–88.
Baudy, D. 1998. s.v. Feriae Latinae, *DNP*: 477.
Bauman, R.A. 1973a. "The Lex Valeria de Provocatione of 300 BC" *Historia* 22: 34–47.
  1973b. "The Hostis Declarations of 88 and 87 B.C." *Athenaeum* 51: 270–93.
Baviera, G. 1925. "Contributo critico alla storia della Lex XII tabularum" in *Studi in onore di Silvio Perozzi nel XL anno del suo insegnamento*. Palermo. 1–51.
Beacham, R.C. 1999. *Spectacle Entertainments of Early Imperial Rome*. New Haven.
Beard, M. 1990. "Priesthood in the Roman Republic" in M. Beard and J. North (eds.), *Pagan Priests: Religion and Power in the Ancient World*. London. 19–48.
  2007. *The Roman Triumph*. Cambridge, MA.
Beard, M., North, J. and Price, S. 1998. *Religions of Rome, 1: A History*. Cambridge.
Becher, I. 1985. "Tiberüberschwemmungen: die Interpretation von Prodigien in augusteischer Zeit" *Klio* 67: 471–9.
Beck, H. 2000. "Quintus Fabius Maximus: Musterkarriere ohne Zögern" in K.-J. Hölkeskamp and E. Stein-Hölkeskamp (eds.), *Von Romulus zu Augustus: Grosse Gestalten der römischen Republik*. Munich. 79–91.
  2002. "Interne synkrisis by Plutarch" *Hermes* 130: 467–89.
  2003. "Den Ruhm nicht teilen wollen: Fabius Pictor und die Anfänge des römischen Nobilitätsdiskurses" in U. Eigler, U. Gotter, N. Luraghi and U. Walter (eds.), *Formen römischer Geschichtsschreibung von den Anfängen bis Livius: Gattungen, Autoren, Kontexte*. Darmstadt. 73–92.
  2005. *Karriere und Hierarchie: Die römische Aristokratie und die Anfänge des cursus honorum in der mittleren Republik*. Berlin.
  2006. "Züge in die Ewigkeit: Prozessionen durch das republikanische Rom" in F. Marco, F. Pina and J. Remesal (eds.), *Repúblicas y ciudadanos: modelos de participación cívica en el mundo antiguo*. Barcelona. 131–51.
Beck, H. and Walter, U. (eds) ²2005 / 2004. *Die Frühen Römischen Historiker (FRH), I–II*. Darmstadt.
Beetham, D. 1991. *The Legitimation of Power*. Atlantic Highlands.
Behr, H. 1993. *Die Selbstdarstellung Sullas: Ein aristokratischer Politiker zwischen persönlichem Führungsanspruch und Standessolidarität*. Frankfurt.
Bell, A. 1997. "Cicero and the Spectacle of Power" *JRS* 87: 1–22.
  2004. *Spectacular Power in the Greek and Roman City*. Oxford.

Bellemore, J. 2005. "Cato's Opposition to Caesar in 59" in K. Welch and T.W. Hillard (eds.), *Roman Crossings: Theory and Practice in the Roman Republic*. Swansea. 225–58.
Beloch, K.J. 1926. *Römische Geschichte bis zum Beginn der punischen Kriege*. Berlin and Leipzig.
Bennett, H. 1923. *Cinna and His Times: A Critical and Interpretive Study of Roman History during the Period 87–84 BC*. Menasha, WI.
Béranger, J. 1953. *Recherches sur l'aspect idéologique du principat*. Basle.
Bergemann, J. 1990. *Römische Reiterstatuen: Ehrendenkmäler im öffentlichen Bereich*. Mainz.
Bergmann, B. and Kondoleon, Ch. (eds.) 1999. *The Art of Ancient Spectacle*. New Haven.
Bernardi, A. 1952. "Dagli ausiliari del rex ai magistrati della respublica" *Athenaeum* 30: 3–58.
1988. "Le XII tavole: i contenuti legislativi" in A. Momigliano and A. Schiavone (eds.), *Storia di Roma*, 1. Turin. 415–25.
Bernstein, F. 1998. *Ludi publici: Untersuchungen zur Entstehung und Entwicklung der öffentlichen Spiele im republikanischen Rom*. Stuttgart.
Berti, N. 1988. *La guerra di Cesare contro Pompeo: commento storico a Cassio Dione, libri XLI–XLII*. Milan.
Bispham, E. 2007. *From Asculum to Actium: The Municipalization of Italy from the Social War to Augustus*. Oxford.
Bleckmann, B. 2002. *Die römische Nobilität im Ersten Punischen Krieg: Untersuchungen zur aristokratischen Konkurrenz in der Republik*. Berlin.
Bleicken, J. 1955 (1968). *Das Volkstribunat der klassischen Republik*. Munich.
1959. "Ursprung und Bedeutung der Provocation" *ZRG* 76: 324–77.
1962. "Der politische Standpunkt Dios gegenüber der Monarchie: die Rede des Maecenas Buch 52, 14–40" *Hermes* 90: 444–67.
1967. "Imperium" *Der Kleine Pauly* II: 1381–3. Stuttgart.
1975. *Lex publica: Gesetz und Recht in der römischen Republik*. Berlin.
1981. "Zum Begriff der römischen Amtsgewalt. auspicium – potestas – imperium" *Nachrichten d. Akad. d. W. in Göttingen Phil.-Hist. Kl*. 9: 257–300.
1990. *Zwischen Republik und Prinzipat: zum Charakter des zweiten Triumvirats*. Göttingen.
1995. *Die Verfassung der Römischen Republik*. Paderborn.
1998. *Augustus: eine Biographie*. Berlin.
Bloch, R. 1963. *Les prodiges dans l'antiquité classique*. Paris.
Blösel, W. 2000. "Die Geschichte des Begriffes *mos maiorum* von den Anfängen bis zu Cicero" in B. Linke and M. Stemmler (eds.), *Mos maiorum: Untersuchungen zu den Formen der Identitätsstiftung und Stabilisierung in der römischen Republik*. Stuttgart. 25–97.
2003. "Die memoria der gentes als Rückgrat der kollektiven Erinnerung im republikanischen Rom" in U. Eigler, U. Gotter, N. Luraghi and U. Walter (eds.), *Formen römischer Geschichtsschreibung von den Anfängen bis Livius: Gattungen, Autoren, Kontexte*. Darmstadt. 53–72.

Bodel, J. 1999. "Death on Display: Looking at Roman Funerals" in B. Bergmann and Ch. Kondoleon (eds.), *The Art of Ancient Spectacle*. New Haven. 259–81.
Boissevain, U.P. 1895. *Cassii Dionis Cocceiani historiarum Romanarum quae supersunt*, I. Berlin.
  1901. *Cassii Dionis Cocceiani historiarum Romanarum quae supersunt*, III. Berlin.
Bona, F. 1960. "Sul concetto di 'manubiae' e sulla responsibilità del magistrato in ordine alla preda" *SDHI* 26: 105–75.
Bonnefond-Coudry, M. 1982. "Calendrier des séances et lieux de réunion du Sénat républicain: la contribution de l'épigraphie" in *Epigrafia ed ordine senatorio* I, Tituli 4. Rome. 55–71.
  1984. "La lex Gabinia sur les ambassades" in C. Nicolet (ed.), *Des ordres à Rome*. Paris. 61–99.
  1989. *Le sénat de la république romaine de la guerre d'Hannibal à Auguste*. Paris and Rome.
Boren, H.C. 1961–2. "The Sources of Cicero's Income: Some Suggestions" *CJ* 57: 17–24.
Boschung, D. 2005. "Ordo senatorius: Gliederung und Rang des Senats als Thema der römischen Kunst" in W. Eck and M. Heil (eds.), *Senatores populi Romani: Realität und mediale Repräsentation einer Führungsschicht*. Stuttgart. 97–110.
Botsford, G.W. 1909. *The Roman Assemblies*. New York.
Boulanger, A. 1960. *Cicéron: Discours* IX. Paris.
Boulogne, J. 1992. "Les questions romaines de Plutarque" *ANRW* 11.33.6: 4682–708.
Bowersock, G.W. 1969. *Greek Sophists in the Roman Empire*. Oxford.
Bradeen, D. 1959. "Roman Citizenship *per magistratum*" *CJ* 54: 221–8.
Brand, C. 1968. *Roman Military Law*. Austin and London.
Brennan, T.C. 1996. "Triumphus in Monte Albano" in W. Wallace and E.M. Harris (eds.), *Transitions to Empire: Essays in Graeco-Roman History, 360–146 B.C.* Norman, OK. 315–37.
  2000. *The Praetorship in the Roman Republic*. 2 vols. Oxford.
  2004. "Power and Process under the Roman 'Constitution'" in H. Flower (ed.), *The Cambridge Companion to the Roman Republic*. Cambridge. 31–65.
Bretone, M. 1982. *Tecniche e ideologie dei giuristi romani*. Naples.
Brind'Amour, P. 1983. *Le calendrier romain*. Ottawa.
Bringmann, K. 1985. *Die Agrarreform des Tiberius Gracchus: Legende und Wirklichkeit*. Stuttgart.
Briscoe, J. 1981. *A Commentary on Livy, Books* XXXIV–XXXVII. Oxford.
  1989. *A Commentary on Livy, Books* XXXI–XXXIII. Oxford.
Brodersen, K. 1995. *Terra cognita: Studien zur römischen Raumerfassung*. Hildesheim, Zurich and New York.
Broughton, T.R.S. 1951–86. *The Magistrates of the Roman Republic*. 3 vols. New York.
Bruhns, H., David, J.M. and Nippel, W. (eds) 1997. *Die späte römische Republik/La fin de la république romaine*. Rome.
Brunt, P.A. 1965. "Italian Aims at the Time of the Social War" *JRS* 55: 90–109.

1968. "Review of Meier 1966" *JRS* 58: 229–32.
1971. *Italian Manpower, 225 B.C.–A.D. 14*. Oxford.
1975. "Stoics and the Principate" *PBSR* 43: 7–35.
1988. *The Fall of the Roman Republic and Related Essays*. Oxford.
Brupbacher, O. 2006. "Wider das Richterkönigtum: Ein Versuch der Rekonstruktion von Aufgaben und Funktionen des Republikanischen Prätors als Iurisdiktionsmagistrat" *Ancilla Iuris*: 107–51.
Bücher, F. 2006. *Verargumentierte Geschichte: Exempla Romana im politischen Diskurs der späten römischen Republik*. Stuttgart.
Bucher, G.S. 1987 (1995). "The *Annales Maximi* in the Light of Roman Methods of Keeping Records" *AJAH* 12: 3–61.
Büchner, K. 1982. *Sallust*. Heidelberg.
Bunse, R. 1998. *Das römische Oberamt in der frühen Republik und das Problem der Konsulartribunen*. Trier.
   2001. "Die frühe Zensur und die Entstehung der Kollegialität" *Historia* 50: 145–62.
   2002a. "Entstehung und Funktion der Losung ('sortitio') unter den 'magistratus maiores' der römischen Republik" *Hermes* 130: 416–32.
   2002b. "Die klassische Prätur und die Kollegialität" *ZRG* 119: 29–43.
Burckhardt, L.A. 1988. *Politische Strategien der Optimaten in der späten römischen Republik*. Stuttgart.
Burkert, W. 1962. "Caesar und Romulus-Quirinus" *Historia* 11: 356–76.
Burrer, F. and Müller, H. (eds.) 2008. *Kriegskosten und Kriegsfinanzierung in der Antike*. Darmstadt:
Calboli, G. 1969. *Cornifici Rhetorica ad C. Herennium: introduzione, testo critico, commento a cura di Gualtiero Calboli*. Bologna.
Caltabiano, M. 1976. "Motivi polemici nella tradizione storiografica relativa a C. Flaminio" *Contr. Ist. St. Ant. Sacr. Cuore* 4: 102–17.
Cameron, A. 2004. *Greek Mythography in the Roman World*. Oxford.
Campbell, J.B. 1984. *The Emperor and the Roman Army, 31 BC–AD 235*. Oxford.
Canali de Rossi, F. 1997. *Le ambascerie dal mondo greco a Roma in età repubblicana*. Rome.
   2000. *Le ambascerie romane ad gentes in età repubblicana*. Rome.
   2005. *Le relazioni diplomatiche di Roma, 1: Dall'età regia alla conquista del primato in Italia (753–265 a.C.) con una appendice sulla più antica iscrizione greca del Lazio*. Rome.
Cape, R.W. 2002. "Cicero's Consular Speeches" in J. May (ed.), *Brill's Companion to Cicero: Oratory and Rhetoric*. Leiden, Boston and Cologne. 113–58.
Carandini, A. 1997. *La nascita di Roma: dèi, lari, eroi e uomini all'alba di una civiltà*. Turin.
Carey, S. 2003. *Pliny's Catalogue of Culture: Art and Empire in the Natural History*. Oxford.
Cartledge, P. 1975. "The Second Thoughts of Augustus on the *Res Publica* in 28/27 B.C." *Hermathena* 119: 30–40.
Cary, E. 1914. *Dio's Roman history, 1*. Cambridge, MA and London.

Cavo Chiarucci, P. 1996. "La documentazione archeologica Pre-Protostorica nell'area albana e le più recenti scoperte" in A. Pasqualini (ed.), *Alba Longa: mito, storia, archeologia: Atti dell'Incontro di studio Roma-Albano Laziale, 27–29 gennaio 1994*. Rome. 1–27.

Cecamore, C. 1993. "Il santuario di Iuppiter Latiaris sul Monte Cavo: spunti e materiali dai vecchi scavi" *Bullettino della Commisione Archeologica Comunale di Roma* XCV: 19–44.

  2006. "Nuovi spunti sul santuario di Iuppiter Latiaris attraverso la documentazione d'archivio" in A. Pasqualini (ed.), *Alba Longa: mito, storia, archeologia: Atti dell'Incontro di studio Roma-Albano Laziale, 27–29 gennaio 1994*. Rome. 49–68.

Chioffi, L. 1995. "Fornix Fabianus" *LTUR* 2: 264–6.

Chrissanthos, S.G. 2001. "Caesar and the Mutiny of 47 B.C." *JRS* 91: 63–75.

Churchill, J.B. 1999. "Ex qua quod vellent facerent: Roman Magistrates' Authority over Praeda and Manubiae" *TAPhA* 129: 85–116.

Clavel-Lévêque, M. 1984. *L'empire en jeux: espace symbolique et pratique sociale dans le monde romain*. Paris.

Coarelli, F. 1972. "Il sepolcro degli Scipioni" *DdA* 6: 36–106.

  1981. "La doppia tradizione sulla morte di Romulus" in *Gli Etruschi e Roma*. Rome. 173–88.

  1983. *Il foro romano: periodo arcaico*. Rome.

  1995a. s.v. "Fornix Scipionis" *LTUR* 2: 266–7.

  1995b. s.v. "Fornix Calpurnius" *LTUR* 2: 263.

  1996. s.v. "Porta Capena" *LTUR* 3.

Cogitore, I. 2002. *La légitimité dynastique d'Auguste à Néron à l'épreuve des conspirations*. Rome.

Coleman, K.M. 1990. "Fatal Charades: Roman Executions Staged as Mythological Enactments" *JRS* 80: 44–73.

Colonna, G. 1988. "I Latini e altri popoli del Lazio" in *Italia omnis terrarum alumna*. Milan. 409–528.

Comparette, T.L. 1906. "The Reorganization of the Municipal Administration under the Antonines" *AJP* 27: 166–83.

Cooley, A. and Cooley, M.G.L. 2004. *Pompeii: A Sourcebook*. London.

Cordier, P. 2005. *Nudités romaines: un problème d'histoire et d'anthropologie*. Paris.

Cornell, T.J. 1995. *The Beginnings of Rome: Italy From the Bronze Age to the Punic Wars (c. 1000 to 264 B.C.)*. London.

  2000. "The Lex Ovinia and the Emancipation of the Senate" in Chr. Bruun (ed.), *The Roman Middle Republic: Politics, Religion, and Historiography c. 400 to 133 B.C.* Rome. 69–89.

  2004. "Deconstructing the Samnite Wars: An Essay in Historiography" in H. Jones (ed.), *Samnium: Settlement and Cultural Change: The Proceedings of the Third E. Togo Salmon Conference on Roman Studies*. Providence, RI. 115–31.

Cotton, H. M. and Yakobson, A. 2002. "*Arcanum Imperii*: The Powers of Augustus" in G. Clark and T. Rajak (eds.), *Philosophy and Power in the Graeco-Roman World: Essays in Honour of M. Griffin*. Oxford. 193–209.

Coudry, M. 2004. "Contrôle et traitement des ambassadeurs étrangers sous la République romaine" in C. Moatti (ed.), *La mobilité des personnes en Méditerranée de l'antiquité à l'époque moderne: procédures de contrôle et documents d'identification*. Rome. 529–65.
Crawford, J. 1994. *Tullius Cicero: The Fragmentary Speeches*. Atlanta.
Crawford, M.H. 1973. "*Foedus* and *Sponsio*" *PBSR* 41: 1–7.
1974. *Roman Republican Coinage*. Cambridge.
1985. *Coinage and Money under the Roman Republic: Italy and the Mediterranean Economy*. London.
1992. *The Roman Republic*. London.
1996a. "Consular Dating Formulae in Republican Italy" *CAH*² x: 979–81.
(ed.) 1996b. *Roman Statutes*. 2 vols. London.
Crifò, G. 1976. "Ulpiano: esperienze e responsabilità del giurista" *ANRW* 2.15: 729–730.
Criniti, N. 1969. "M. Aemilius Q.F. M.N. Lepidus 'ut ignis in stipula'" in *MIL* xxx/4. Milan. 320–459.
Cristofani, M. 1986. "C. Genucius Cleusina pretore a Caere" *Archeologia nella Tuscia* II: 24–6.
Crook, J. A., Lintott, A. and Rawson, E. (eds.) 1994. *The Last Age of the Roman Republic, 146–43 B.C.* (*CAH*, IX). Cambridge.
Dahlheim, W. 1993. "Der Staatsstreich des Konsuls Sulla und die römische Italienpolitik der achtziger Jahre" in J. Bleicken (ed.), *Colloquium aus Anlaß des 80. Geburtstages von Alfred Heuß*. Kallmünz. 97–115.
Daubner, F. 2007. "Die *lex Porcia*, das Ehrendekret für Menippos von Kolophon und die römische Provinzverwaltung der 120er Jahre" *GFA* 10: 9–20.
David, J.-M. 1980. "'Eloquentia popularis' et conduites symboliques des orateurs de la fin de la république: problèmes d'efficacité" *QS* 12: 171–98.
1996. *The Roman Conquest of Italy*. Trans. A. Neville. Oxford.
2006. "Una reppublica in cantiere" *Studi Storici* 47: 365–76.
De Blois, L. 1987. *The Roman Army and Politics in the First Century B.C.* Amsterdam.
2000. "Army and Society in the Late Roman Republic: Professionalism and the Role of the Military Middle Cadre" in G. Alföldy, B. Dobson and W. Eck (eds.), *Kaiser, Heer und Gesellschaft in der Römischen Kaiserzeit: Gedenkschrift für Eric Birley*. Stuttgart. 11–31.
De Cazanove, O. 2000. "Sacrifier les bêtes, consacrer les hommes: le printemps sacré italique" in S. Verger (ed.), *Rites et espaces dans le pays celte et méditerranéen: étude comparée à partir du sanctuaire d'Acy-Romance (Ardennes, France)*. Rome. 253–77.
2005. "Mont et citadelle, temple et templum: quelques réflexions sur l'usage religieux des hauteurs dans l'Italie républicaine" *Archiv für Religionsgeschichte* 7: 62–82.
De Francisci, P. 1959. *Primordia civitatis*. Rome.
1970. *Arcana Imperii III, 1*. Rome.
Degrassi, A. 1947. *Inscriptiones Italiae* XIII, *1*. Rome.

Bibliography 343

De Libero, L. 1992. *Obstruktion: Politische Praktiken im Senat und in der Volksversammlung der ausgehenden römischen Republik (70–49 v. Chr.)*. Stuttgart.
De Ligt, L. 2004. "Poverty and Demography: The Case of the Gracchan Land Reforms" *Mnemosyne* 57: 725–57.
  2007. "The Economy: Agrarian Change during the Second Century" in N.S. Rosenstein and R. Morstein-Marx (eds.), *A Companion to the Roman Republic*. Malden and Oxford. 590–605.
De Ligt, L. and Northwood, S. (eds.) 2008. *People, Land, and Politics: Demographic Developments and the Transformation of Roman Italy 300 BC–AD 14*. Leiden and Boston.
De Martino, Fr. 1958. *Storia della costituzione romana, 1*. Naples.
  1972. "Intorno all'origine della repubblica romana e delle magistrature" *ANRW* 1.1: 217–49.
  1972–5. *Storia della costituzione romana, I–VI*, 2nd edn. Naples.
Dench, E. 2005. *Romulus' Asylum: Roman Identities from the Age of Alexander to the Age of Hadrian*. Oxford.
De Ruggiero, E. 1892. s.v. Consul, in *Dizionario Epigrafico di Antichità Romane* II: 679–862.
  1922. s.v. "Feriae (Latinae)" in *Dizionario Epigrafico di Antichità Romane* III: 53–6.
De Sanctis, G. 1956–67. *Storia dei Romani, I–III.1*. Florence.
De Sensi Sestito, G. 1974. "Il problema della *aitia* della prima guerra punica" *Archivio storico per la Sicilia orientale* 70: 7–44.
  1977. *Gerone II: un monarca ellenistico in Sicilia*. Palermo.
De Simone, C. 1975. "Il nome del Tevere: contributo per la storia delle più antiche relazione tra testi latino-italiche ed etrusche" *Studi Etruschi* 43: 119–57.
Detienne, M. and Vernant, J.P. 1979. *La cuisine du sacrifice en pays grec*. Paris.
Dettenhofer, M.H. 2000. *Herrschaft und Widerstand im augusteischen Principat: die Konkurrenz zwischen res publica und domus Augusta*. Stuttgart.
Develin, R. 1975a. "Prorogation of *Imperium* before the Hannibalic War" *Latomus* 34: 716–22.
  1975b. "*Comitia Tributa Plebis*" *Athenaeum* 53: 302–37.
De Vita, A. 1955. "Un milliarium del 252 a.C. e l'antica via Agrigento–Palermo" *Kokalos* 1: 10–21.
  1963. "Una recente nota e la datazione del miliario sicilano del console C. Aurelio Cotta" *Latomus* 22: 477–88.
De Witt, N.W. 1937. "Semantic Notes to *Ob, Optimus, Optimates*" *Language* 13: 70–3.
Diliberto, O. 1996. "L'inesauribile tematica del '*furor*'" *Labeo* 42.1: 107–16.
Di Stefano Manzella, I. 1994. "Accensi velati consulibus apparentes ad sacra" *ZPE* 101: 261–79.
Dreyer, B. and Engelmann, H. 2003. *Die Inschriften von Metropolis, 1: Die Dekrete für Apollonios*. Bonn.
Drogula, F.K. 2007. "*Imperium, Potestas*, and the *Pomerium* in the Roman Republic" *Historia* 56: 419–52.
Drucker, H.M. 1974. *The Political Uses of Ideology*. London.

Drummond, A. 1974. *The History and Reliability of the Early Fasti Consulares: With Special Reference to the So-Called Plebeian Consuls.* Oxford.
  1978. "The dictator years" *Historia* 27: 550–72.
  1989a. "Rome in the Fifth Century, I: The Social and Economic Framework" *CAH²*, VII.2: 113–71.
  1989b. "Rome in the Fifth Century, II: The Citizen Community" *CAH²*, VII.2: 172–242.
  1995. *Law, Politics and Power: Sallust and the Execution of the Catilinarian Conspirators.* Stuttgart.
Dubourdieu, A. 1989. *Les origines et le développement du culte des Pénates à Rome.* Rome.
Dubuisson, M. and Schamp, J. 2006. *Jean le Lydien: des magistratures de l'état romain.* Paris.
Ducos, M. 1984. *Les romains et la loi: recherches sur les rapports de la philosophie grecque et de la tradition romaine à la fin de la République.* Paris.
Dumézil, G. 1986. *Fêtes romaines d'été et d'automne: suivi de dix questions romaines,* 2nd edn. Paris.
Duncan-Jones, R. 1982. *The Economy of the Roman Empire: Quantitative Studies,* 2. Cambridge.
Duplá, A. 2007. "Interpretaciones de la crisis tardorrepublicana: del conflicto social a la articulación del consenso" *Studia Historica: Historia Antigua* 25: 185–201.
Dupont, F. 1985. *L'acteur-roi ou le théâtre dans la Rome antique.* Paris.
  1989 (1992). *Daily Life in Ancient Rome.* Oxford.
Dyck, A.R. 2004. *A Commentary on Cicero, De Legibus.* Ann Arbor.
Earl, D.C. 1967. *The Moral and Political Tradition of Rome.* Ithaca.
Eckstein, A.M. 1980. "Polybius on the Role of the Senate in the Crisis of 264 B.C." *GRBS* 21: 175–90.
  1987. *Senate and General: Individual Decision Making and Roman Foreign Relations, 264–194 B.C.* Berkeley.
  2007. *Mediterranean Anarchy, Interstate War, and the Rise of Rome.* Berkeley.
Eder, W. 2001. s.v. "Sacramentum" *DNP* 10: 1199–1200.
Eilers, C. 2002. *Roman Patrons of Greek Cities.* Oxford.
Eisenhut, W. 1955. s.v. "Ver sacrum" *RE II,* 15: 911–23.
  1974. s.v. "Votum" *RE* Suppl. 14: 964–73.
  1975. s.v. "Ver sacrum" in *Der Kleine Pauly:* 1181–3.
Elliott, J. 2009. "Ennius' 'Cunctator' and the History of a Gerund in the Roman Historiographical Tradition" *CQ* 59: 533–42.
Elster, M. (ed.) 2003. *Die Gesetze der mittleren römischen Republik: Text und Kommentar.* Darmstadt.
Engels, D. 2007. *Das römische Vorzeichenwesen (753–27 v. Chr.): Quellen, Terminologie, Kommentar, historische Entwicklung.* Stuttgart.
Engels, J. 2001. "Die Exempla-Reihe *de iure triumphandi*: römisch-republikanische Werte und Institutionen im frühkaiserzeitlichen Spiegel der *facta et dicta memorabilia* des Valerius Maximus" in A. Barzanò *et al.* (eds.), *Identità e*

valori: fattori di aggregazione di crisi nel' esperienza politica antica. Rome. 139–69.
Erdkamp, P. 1992. "Polybius, Livy, and the 'Fabian Strategy'" *Ancient Society* 23: 127–47.
  1998. *Hunger and the Sword: Warfare and Food Supply in Roman Republican Wars (264–30 B.C.)*. Amsterdam.
Erdmann, E. 1972. *Die Rolle des Heeres in der Zeit von Marius bis Caesar: Militärische und politische Probleme einer Berufsarmee*. Neustadt an der Aisch.
Ernout, A. and Meillet, A. 1951. *Dictionnaire étymologique de la langue latine/histoire des mots, I–II*. Paris.
Erskine, A. 1990. *The Hellenistic Stoa: Political Thought and Action*. London.
Evans, R.J. 1991. "Candidates and Competition in Consular Elections at Rome between 218 and 49 BC" *AClass* 34: 111–36.
  1994. *Gaius Marius: A Political Biography*. Pretoria.
Farney, G. 2007. *Ethnic Identity and Aristocratic Competition in Republican Rome*. Cambridge.
Farrell, J. 1986. "The Distinction between *Comitia* and *Concilium*" *Athenaeum* 74: 407–38.
Feeney, D. 2007. *Caesar's Calendar: Ancient Time and the Beginnings of History*. Berkeley and Los Angeles.
Feig Vishnia, R. 1996. *State, Society and Popular Leaders in Mid-Republican Rome, 241–167 B.C.* London.
  2007. "The Delayed Career of the 'Delayer': The Early Years of Q. Fabius Maximus Verrucosus the 'Cunctator'" *SCI* 26: 19–37.
Feldherr, A. 1998. *Spectacle and Society in Livy's History*. Berkeley.
Ferenczy, E. 1976. *From the Patrician State to the Patricio-Plebeian State*. Budapest.
Ferrary, J.-L. 1982. "Le idee politiche a Roma nell'epoca Repubblicana" in L. Firpo (ed.), *Storia delle idee politiche economiche e sociali*. Turin. 723–804.
  1984. "L'archéologie du *De Re Publica* (2.2.4–3.7.63): Cicéron entre Polybe et Platon" *JRS* 74: 87–98.
  1988. *Philhellénisme et impérialisme*. Rome.
  1995. "The statesman and the law in the political philosophy of Cicero" in A. Lacks and M. Schofield (Eds.), *Justice and Generosity: Studies in Hellenistic Social and Political Philosophy: Proceedings of the Sixth Symposium Hellenisticum*. Cambridge. 48–73.
  1997. "*Optimates* et *populares*: le problème du rôle de l'idéologie dans la politique" in H. Bruhns, J.M. David and W. Nippel (eds.), *Die späte römische Republik/La fin de la république romaine*. Rome. 221–31.
  2001. "A propos des pouvoirs d'Auguste" *CCGG* 12: 101–54.
  2007. "Les ambassadeurs grecs au Sénat romain" in J.P. Caillet and M. Sot (eds.), *L'audience rituel et cadres spatiaux dans l'antiquité et le haut Moyen Age*. Paris. 113–22.
Finley, M.I. 1983. *Politics in the Ancient World*. Cambridge.
Flach, D. 1994. *Die Gesetze der frühen römischen Republik: Text und Kommentar in Zusammenarbeit mit Stefan von der Lahr*. Darmstadt.

Flaig, E. 1992. *Den Kaiser herausfordern: die Usurpation im römischen Reich*. Frankfurt and New York.
  2003. *Ritualisierte Politik: Zeichen, Gesten und Herrschaft im Alten Rom*. Göttingen.
Flower, H. 1996. *Ancestor Masks and Aristocratic Power in Roman Culture*. Oxford.
  2000. "The Tradition of the *Spolia Opima*: M. Claudius Marcellus and Augustus" *Classical Antiquity* 19: 34–64.
  2004. "Spectacle and Political Culture in the Roman Republic" in H. Flower (ed.), *The Cambridge Companion to the Roman Republic*. Cambridge. 322–43.
  2006. "Der Leichenzug – die Ahnen kommen wieder" in E. Stein-Hölkeskamp and K.J. Hölkeskamp (eds.), *Erinnerungsorte der Antike: die Römische Welt*. Munich. 321–37, 752–3.
  2010. *Roman Republics*. Princeton.
Forsythe, G. 2005. *A Critical History of Early Rome: From Prehistory to the First Punic War*. Berkeley.
Foxhall, L. and Forbes, H.A. 1982. "*Sitometria*: The Role of Grain as a Staple Food in Classical Antiquity" *Chiron* 12: 41–90.
Frank, T. 1933. *An Economic Survey of Ancient Rome, 1: Rome and Italy of the Republic*. Baltimore.
Franklin, J.L. 1980. *Pompeii: The Electoral Programmata, Campaigns, and Politics, AD 71–79*. Rome.
Frederiksen, M. 1984. *Campania*. London.
Freyburger-Galland, M.-L. 1997. *Aspects du vocabulaire politique et institutionnel de Dion Cassius*. Paris.
Freyburger-Galland, M.-L. and Roddaz, J.M. 1991. *Dion Cassius: Histoire romaine: Livres 50 et 51*. Paris.
  1994. *Dion Cassius: Histoire romaine: Livres 48 et 49*. Paris.
Freyburger-Galland, M.-L., Hinard, F. and Cordier, P. 2002. *Dion Cassius: Histoire romaine: Livres 41 et 42*. Paris.
Frézouls, E. 1980. "Hiéron, Carthage et Rome: Polybe ou Philinos?" in M.J. Fontana, M.T. Piraino and F.P. Rizzo (eds.), *Fillias Xarin: miscellanea di studi classici in onore di Eugenio Manni, III*. Rome. 963–90.
Frier, B.W. 1999. *Libri Annales Pontificum Maximorum: The Origins of the Annalistic Tradition*. Michigan.
Frisch, P. 1980. "Zu den Elogien des Augustusforum" *ZPE* 39: 91–7.
Fronda, M.P. 2006. "Livy 9.20 and Early Roman Imperialism in Apulia" *Historia* 55: 397–417.
  2007. "Hegemony and Rivalry: The Revolt of Capua Revisited" *Phoenix* 61: 83–108.
Früchtl, A. 1912. "Die Geldgeschäfte bei Cicero." Dissertation. Erlangen.
Fuhrmann, M. 1962. "Verbera" *RE* Suppl. 9: 1590–7.
Futrell, A. 1997. *Blood in the Arena: The Spectacle of Roman Power*. Austin.
Gabba, E. 1956. *Appiano e la storia delle guerre civili*. Florence.
  (ed.) 1967. *Appiani Bellorum Civilium Liber Primus*. Florence.
  1976. *Republican Rome, the Army, and the Allies*. Trans. P.J. Cuff. Oxford.

1989. "Rome and Italy in the Second Century BC" *CAH²*, 8: 197–243.
1991. *Dionysius and "The History of Archaic Rome."* Berkeley.
Gagé, J. 1952. "Les noms des Philippiques de Cicéron: Marcius Philippus et la première guerre de Modène" *REL* 30: 66–8.
Gallia, A.B. 2007. "Reassessing the 'Cumaean Chronicle': Greek Chronology and Roman History in Dionysius of Halicarnassus" *JRS* 97: 50–67.
Garbarino, G. 1973. *Roma e la filosofia greca dalle origini alla fine del II secolo A.C.* Turin.
García Quintela, M. 2007. *Le pendu et le noyé des Monts Albains: recherches comparatives autour des mythes et rites Albains.* Brussels.
Gargola, D.J. 2006. "Mediterranean Empire (264–134)" in N. Rosenstein and R. Morstein-Marx (eds.), *A Companion to the Roman Republic*. Oxford. 147–66.
Geertz, C. 1993. *The Interpretation of Cultures: Selected Essays.* London.
Gelzer, M. 1968. *Caesar: Politician and Statesman.* Oxford.
Giangrieco Pessi, M.V. 2000. "Dalla lex Aemilia al plebiscito Ovinio: problemi e riflessioni" in F. Serrao (ed.), *Legge e società nella repubblica romana, 2*. Naples. 299–340.
Gilbert, R. 1939. "The Origin and History of the Peregrine Praetorship" *Res Judicatae* 2: 50–58.
Gildenhard, I. 2003. "The 'Annalist' Before the Annalists: Ennius and his Annales" in U. Eigler, U. Gotter, N. Luraghi and U. Walter (eds.), *Formen römischer Geschichtsschreibung von den Anfängen bis Livius: Gattungen, Autoren, Kontexte*. Darmstadt. 93–114.
 2007. *Paideia Romana: Cicero's Tusculan Disputations.* Cambridge.
Giles, P. 1887. "Emendation of Livy XLII.17 and of Appian *Maced*. XI. 7, 8" *CR* 1: 170.
Giovannini, A. 1983. *Consulare imperium.* Basle.
 1993. "Il passaggio dalle istituzioni monarchiche alle istituzioni repubblicane" in M.A. Levi (ed.), *Bilancio critico su Roma arcaica fra monarchia e repubblica: in memoria di Ferdinando Castagnoli*. Rome. 75–96.
 1999. "Les pouvoirs d'Auguste de 27 à 23 av. J.-C.: une relecture de l'ordonnance de Kymè de l'an 27 (IK 5, n. 17)" *ZPE* 124: 95–106.
Girardet, Kl. 1990. "Die Entmachtung des Konsulates im Übergang von der Republik zur Monarchie und die Rechtsgrundlagen des augusteischen Prinzipats" in W. Görler and S. Koster (eds.), *Pratum Saraviense: Festschrift für P. Steinmetz*. Stuttgart. 89–126.
 2001. "Imperia und provinciae des Pompeius 82 bis 48 v.Chr" *Chiron* 31: 153–209.
 2007. M. *Rom auf dem Weg von der Republik zum Prinzipat.* Bonn.
Gjerstad, E. 1953–73. *Early Rome*. 6 vols. Lund.
Gladigow, B. 1972. "Die sakralen Funktionen der Liktoren: zum Problem von institutioneller Macht und sakraler Präsentation" *ANRW* I.2: 295–314.
Goette, H.R. 1988. "*Mulleus – embas – calceus*: ikonographische Studien zu römischem Schuhwerk" *JdI* 103: 401–64.
Goltz, A. 2000. "*Maiestas sine viribus*: die Bedeutung der Liktoren für die Konfliktbewältigungsstrategien römischer Magistrate" in B. Linke and M. Stemmler

(eds.), *Mos maiorum: Untersuchungen zu den Formen der Identitätsstiftung und Stabilisierung in der römischen Republik*. Stuttgart. 237–67.
Goppold, U. 2007. *Politische Kommunikation in den Städten der Vormoderne*. Cologne.
Gorostidi Pi, D. 2006. "Il collegio degli aeditui e gli aediles lustrales di Tusculum: una nuova lettura di CIL XIV, 2620" *Epigraphia*: 361–76.
(forthcoming). "La epigrafia latina de la antigua ciudad de Tusculum (Lacio, Italia)." Dissertation. Saragossa.
Graeber, A. 2001. *Auctoritas patrum: Formen und Wege der Senatsherrschaft zwischen Politik und Tradition*. Berlin, Heidelberg and New York.
Grandazzi, A. 1986. "La localisation d'Albe" *MEFRA* 98, 47–90.
2006. "*Arx Albana*: Notes d'épigraphie religieuse" in J. Champeaux and M. Chassignet (eds.), *Aere perennius: Hommage à Hubert Zehnacker*. Paris, 197–212.
2008. *Alba Longa: histoire d'une légende: recherches sur l'archéologie, la religion, les traditions de l'ancien Latium, I–II*. Rome.
Granino Cecere, M.G. 2006. "Sacerdotes Cabenses e sacerdotes Albani: la documentazione epigrafica" in A. Pasqualini (ed.), *Alba Longa: mito, storia, archeologia: Atti dell'Incontro di studio Roma-Albano Laziale, 27–29 gennaio 1994*. Rome. 275–316.
Granino Cecere, M.G. and Scheid, J. 1999. "Les sacerdoces publics équestres" in *L'ordre équestre: histoire d'une aristocratie (IIe siècle av. J.-C. – IIIe. siècle ap. J.-C.), Coll. EFR* 257. Rome. 79–189.
Graver, M.R. 2002. *Cicero on the Emotions*. Chicago and London.
2007. *Stoicism and Emotions*. Chicago and London.
Griffin, M. 1989. "Philosophy, Politics and Politicians at Rome" in M. Griffin and J. Barnes (eds.), *Philosophia Togata: Essays on Philosophy and Roman Society*. Oxford. 1–37.
Gruen, E.S. 1974. *The Last Generation of the Roman Republic*. Berkeley.
1991. "The Exercise of Power in the Roman Republic" in A. Molho, K. Raaflaub and J. Emlen (eds.), *City States in Classical Antiquity and Medieval Italy*. Ann Arbor. 251–67.
1995. "The 'Fall' of the Scipios" in I. Malkin and Z. Rubinsohn (eds.), *Leaders and Masses in the Roman World: Studies in Honor of Zvi Yavetz*. Leiden. 59–90.
Gundel, H.G. 1969. s.v. Lepidus (5), *RE* 3: 577.
Gunderson, E. 1996. "The Ideology of the Arena" *Classical Antiquity* 15: 113–51.
Habinek, T. 2000. "Seneca's Renown: *Gloria, Claritudo*, and the Replication of the Roman Elite" *Classical Antiquity* 19: 264–303.
Hadot, I. 1970. "Tradition stoïcienne des idées politiques au temps des Gracques" *REL* 48: 133–79.
Halbwachs, M. 1997. *La mémoire collective*, 2nd edn. Paris.
Händel, P. 1959. s.v. Prodigium, *RE* 23.1: 2283–96.
Hanell, K. 1946. *Das altrömische eponyme Amt*. Lund.

Hantos, Th. 1997. "Rom und Veii: eine Rivalität und ihre Konsequenzen" *ACD* 32: 127–48.
Harmand, J. 1967. *L'armée et le soldat à Rome de 107 à 50 avant notre ère*. Paris.
Harris, W.V. 1965. "The Via Cassia and the Via Traiana Nova between Bolsena and Chiusi" *PBSR* 33: 113–33.
  1979. *War and Imperialism in Republican Rome, 327–70 B.C.* Oxford.
Hartfield, M. 1982. "The Roman Dictatorship: Its Character and its Evolution." Dissertation. Berkeley.
Hayne, L. 1972. "M. Lepidus (cos. 78): a reappraisal" *Historia* 21: 661–8.
Head, B. 1911. *Historia Nummorum: A Manual of Greek Numismatics*. Chicago.
Heil, M. 2005. "Sozialer Abstieg: Beredtes Schweigen?" in W. Eck and M. Heil (eds.), *Senatores populi Romani: Realität und mediale Repräsentation einer Führungsschicht*. Stuttgart. 295–312.
Hellegouarc'h, J. 1963. *Le vocabulaire latin des relations et des partis politiques sous la république*. Paris.
Hermon, E. 2001. *Habiter et partager les terres avant les Gracques*. Rome.
Heurgon, J. 1957. *Trois études sur le "ver sacrum."* Brussels.
  1967. "Magistratures romaines et étrusques" in *Les origines de la république romaine: neuf exposés suivis de discussions*. Geneva. 99–127.
  1969. *Rome et la Méditerranée occidentale jusqu'aux guerres puniques*. Paris.
Heuss, A. 1944. "Zur Entwicklung des Imperiums der römischen Oberbeamten" *ZRG* 64: 57–133.
  1982. *Gedanken und Vermutungen zur frühen römischen Regierungsgewalt*. Göttingen.
Hillard, T.W. 2005. "Res publica in theory and practice" in K. Welch and T.W. Hillard (eds.), *Roman Crossings: The Roman Republic in Theory and Practice*. Swansea. 1–48.
Hillyard, M.J. 2001. *Cincinnatus and the Citizen-Servant Ideal: The Roman Legend's Life, Times, and Legacy*. Philadelphia.
Hinard, Fr. 1985. *Sylla*. Paris.
  1999. "Dion Cassius et l'abdication de Sylla" *REA* 101: 427–32.
  2005. "Dion Cassius et les institutions de la république romaine" in L. Troiani and G. Zecchini (eds.), *La cultura storica nei primi due secoli dell'impero romano*. Rome. 261–79.
Hofmann, F. 1847 (1972). *Der römische Senat zur Zeit der Republik*. Aalen.
Hölkeskamp, K.-J. 1987. *Die Entstehung der Nobilität: Studien zur sozialen und politischen Geschichte der Römischen Republik im 4. Jhdt. v. Chr.* Stuttgart.
  1997a. "Kommentar zu J.-L. Ferrary, 'Optimates et populares'" in H. Bruhns, J.-M. David and W. Nippel (eds.), *Die späte römische Republik/La fin de la république romaine*. Rome. 232–5.
  1997b. "Zwischen 'System' und 'Geschichte': Theodor Mommsens *Staatsrecht* und die römische 'Verfassung' in Frankreich und Deutschland" in H. Bruhns, J.-M. David and W. Nippel (eds.), *Die späte römische Republik/La fin de la république romaine*. Rome. 93–111.

2000. "The Roman Republic: Government of the People, by the People, for the People?" *SCI* 19: 203–23. Reprinted in Hölkeskamp 2004a: 257–80.

2004a. *Senatus Populusque Romanus: die politische Kultur der Republik: Dimensionen und Deutungen*. Stuttgart.

2004b. *Rekonstruktionen einer Republik: die politische Kultur des antiken Roms und die Forschung der letzten Jahrzehnte*. Munich.

2006a. "Rituali e cerimonie 'alla romana': nuove prospettive sulla cultura politica dell'età repubblicana" *Studi storici* 47.2: 319–63.

2006b. "Der Triumph: 'erinnere Dich, daß Du ein Mensch bist'" in E. Stein-Hölkeskamp and K.-J. Hölkeskamp (eds.), *Erinnerungsorte der Antike: Die römische Welt*. Munich, 258–76, 745–7.

2007. "Pomp und Prozessionen: Rituale und Zeremonien in der politischen Kultur der römischen Republik" *Jahrbuch des Historischen Kollegs*: 35–72.

2008. "Hierarchie und Konsens. *Pompae* in der politischen Kultur der römischen Republik" in A.H. Arweiler and B.M. Gauly (eds.), *Machtfragen: Zur Kulturellen Repräsentation und Konstruktion von Macht in Antike, Mittelalter und Neuzeit*. Stuttgart, 79–126.

Honoré, T. 2002. *Ulpian: Pioneer of Human Rights*. Oxford.

Hopkins, K. 1978. *Conquerors and Slaves*. Cambridge.

1983. *Death and Renewal*. Cambridge.

1991. "From Violence to Blessing: Symbols and Rituals in Ancient Rome" in A. Molho, K. Raaflaub and J. Emlen (eds.), *City-States in Classical Antiquity and Medieval Italy*. Stuttgart. 479–81.

2009. "The Political Economy of the Roman Empire" in I. Morris and W. Scheidel (eds.), *The Dynamics of Ancient Empires*. Oxford. 178–204.

Hose, M. 1994. *Erneuerung der Vergangenheit: Die Historiker im Imperium Romanum von Florus bis Cassius Dio*. Stuttgart and Leipzig.

Hoyos, B.D. 1984. "Polybius' Roman *hoi polloi* in 264 B.C." *LCM* 9: 88–93.

Humbert, M. 1990. "La crise politique du ve siècle et la législation décemvirale" in *Crise et transformation des sociétés archaïques de l'Italie antique au ve siècle av. J.-C.: Actes de la table ronde organisée par l'École française de Rome et l'Unité de recherches étrusco-italiques associée au CNRS (UA 1132). Rome 19–21 novembre 1987*. Rome and Paris. 263–87.

Humm, M. 2005. *Appius Claudius Caecus: la république accomplie*. Rome.

Humphrey, J.H. 1986. *Roman Circuses: Arenas for Chariot Racing*. Berkeley.

Hunt, L. 1984. *Politics, Culture, and Class in the French Revolution*. Berkeley.

Hurlet, Fr. 1993. *La dictature de Sylla: monarchie ou magistrature républicaine? Essai d'histoire constitutionnelle*. Rome.

1997. *Les collègues du prince sous Auguste et Tibère: de la légalité républicaine à la légitimité dynastique*. Rome.

2003. "Review of Dettenhofer, *Herrschaft und Widerstand im augusteischen Principat: Die Konkurrenz zwischen res publica und domus Augusta*" *Latomus* 62: 192–5.

2006. *Le proconsul et le prince d'Auguste à Dioclétien*. Bordeaux.

2007. "Une décennie de recherches sur Auguste: bilan historiographique (1996–2006)" *Anabases* 6: 187–218.

2009. "La *Res publica restituta* et l'aristocratie augustéenne" in Fr. Hurlet and B. Mineo (eds.), *Res publica restituta: le pouvoir et ses représentations à Rome durant le principat d'Auguste*. Rennes. 9–24.
Ihne, W. 1847. *Forschungen auf dem Gebiet der römischen Verfassungsgeschichte*. Frankfurt.
1868. *Römische Geschichte*, I. Leipzig.
Itgenshorst, T. 2005. *Tota illa pompa: der Triumph in der römischen Republik*. Göttingen.
Jacques, Fr. and Scheid, J. 1990. *Rome et l'intégration de l'Empire, 44 av. J.-C. – 260 ap. J.-C.: les structures de l'empire romain*, 1. Paris.
Jal, P. 1963. *La guerre civile à Rome: étude littéraire et morale*. Paris.
Jehne, M. (ed.) 1995. *Demokratie in Rom? Die Rolle des Volkes in der Politik der römischen Republik*. Stuttgart.
2002. "Die Geltung der Provocation und die Konstruktion der römischen Republik als Freiheitsgemeinschaft" in G. Melville and H. Vorländer (eds.), *Geltungsgeschichten: Über die Stabilisierung und Legitimierung institutioneller Ordnungen*. Cologne. 55–74.
2006. "Methods, Models, and Historiography" in N. Rosenstein and R. Morstein-Marx (eds.), *A Companion to the Roman Republic*. Oxford. 3–28.
2009. "Diplomacy in Italy in the Second Century BC" in C. Eilers (ed.), *Diplomats and Diplomacy in the Roman World*. Leiden and Boston. 143–70.
Jones, C. P. 2004. "Events Surrounding the Bequest of Pergamon to Rome and the Revolt of Aristonicos: New Inscriptions from Metropolis" *JRA* 17: 469–85.
Jones, H.S. and Last, H. 1928. "The Early Republic" *CAH¹*, VII: 436–84.
Jullian, C. 1899. "Feriae Latinae" in Ch. Daremberg and E. Saglio (eds.), *Dict. Ant. Gr. Rom.* II.2. 1066–73.
Kallet-Marx, R. 1995. *Hegemony to Empire: The Development of the Roman Imperium in the East from 148 to 62 B.C.* Berkeley.
Kaster, R.A. 2002. "The Taxonomy of Patience, or When is *Patientia* Not a Virtue?" *CP* 97: 133–44.
Katz, B.R. 1975. "The First Fruits of Sulla's March" *AC* 44: 100–25.
1976. "Studies on the Period of Cinna and Sulla" *AC* 45: 497–549.
1979. "The Selection of L. Cornelius Merula" *RhM* 122: 162–6.
Keaveney, A. 1982. *Sulla: The Last Republican*. London and Canberra.
1983. "What Happened in 88?" *Eirene* 20: 53–86.
1987. *Rome and the Unification of Italy*. London.
2005a. *Sulla: The Last Republican*, 2nd edn. London and New York.
2005b. *Rome and the Unification of Italy*, 2nd edn. Exeter.
2007. *The Army in the Roman Revolution*. London and New York.
Kelly, B. 2005. "The Law that Catulus Passed" in K. Welch and T.W. Hillard (eds.), *Roman Crossings: Theory and Practice in the Roman Republic*. Swansea. 95–118.
Kienast, D. 1999. *Augustus: Prinzeps und Monarch*, 3rd edn. Darmstadt.
Klebs, E. 1893. s.v. Aemilius 72, *RE* I: 554–6.
Kloft, H. 1977. *Prorogation und außerordentliche Imperien 326–81 v.Chr.: Untersuchungen zur Verfassung der römischen Republik*. Meisenheim am Glan.

Klotz, A. 1936. "Über die Stellung des Cassius Dio unter den Quellen zur Geschichte des zweiten punischen Krieges: eine Vorarbeit zur Quellenanalyse der dritten Dekade des Livius" *RhM* n.F. 85: 68–116.
  1938. "Zu den Quellen der Archaiologia des Dionysios von Halikarnassos" *RhM* n.F. 87: 32–50.
  1952. "Studien zu Polybios" *Hermes* 80: 325–43.
Koch, B. 2006. *Philosophie als Medizin für die Seele.* Stuttgart.
Kondratieff, E. 2003. "Popular Power in Action: Tribunes of the Plebs in the Later Republic." Thesis. University of Pennsylvania.
  2004. "The Column and Coinage of C. Duilius: Innovations in Iconography in Large and Small Media in the Middle Republic" *SCI* 23: 1–39.
Konrad, C.F. 1994. *Plutarch's Sertorius: A Historical Commentary.* Chapel Hill and London.
Kornemann, E. 1915. "Zur altitalischen Verfassungsgeschichte" *Klio* 14: 190–206.
Kroll, W. 1910. "Papirius (38)" *RE* 18.3: 1024–31.
Kübler, B. 1901a. "Consul" *RE* 4: 1112–38.
  1901b. "Decemviri" *RE* 4: 2257–60.
  1923. "Sella curulis" *RE* 11.2: 1310–15.
  1926. "Lictor" *RE* 13: 507–18.
Kunkel, W. and Wittmann, R. 1995. *Staatsordnung und Staatspraxis der römischen Republik.* Munich.
Kuttner, A. 2004. "Roman Art during the Republic" in H. Flower (ed.), *The Cambridge Companion to the Roman Republic.* Cambridge. 294–321.
Kyle, D.G. 1998. *Spectacles of Death in Ancient Rome.* London.
Labruna, L. 1975. *Il console sovversivo: Marco Emilio Lepido e la sua rivolta.* Naples.
La Bua, V. 1981. "Cassio Dione: Zonara ed altre tradizioni sugli inizi della prima guerra punica" in L. Gasperini (ed.), *Scritti sul mondo antico in memoria di Fulvio Grosso.* Rome. 241–71.
Lacey, W.K. 1986. "*Patria potestas*" in B. Rawson (ed.), *The Family in Ancient Rome: New Perspectives.* Ithaca. 121–44.
Laffi, U. 1967. "Il mito di Silla" *Athenaeum* 45: 177–213, 255–77.
Lammert, F. 1937. "Tribunal (2)" *RE* 11.6.2: 2430–2.
Lana, I. 1961. *Rutilio Namaziano.* Turin.
La Penna, A. 1968. *Sallustio e la rivoluzione romana.* Milan.
Laser, G. 1997. *Populo et scaenae serviendum est: die Bedeutung der städtischen Masse in der späten römischen Republik.* Trier.
Latte, K. 1960. *Römische Religionsgeschichte.* Munich.
Lazenby, J. 1978. *Hannibal's War.* Warminster.
Lehmann, G.A. 1980. *Politische Reformvorschläge in der Krise der späten römischen Republik.* Meisenheim.
Lendon, J.E. 1997. *Empire of Honour: The Art of Government in the Roman World.* Oxford.
Lesiński, J. 2002. "Quintus Fabius Maximus Verrucosus: A Dictator in 217 BC?" in T. Derda, J. Urbanik and M. Węcowski (eds.), *ΕΥΕΡΓΕΣΙΑΣ ΧΑΡΙΝ:*

Studies Presented to Benedetto Bravo and Ewa Wipszycka by their Disciples. Warsaw. 131–58.
Letta, C. and D'Amato, S. 1975. *Epigrafia della regione Marsi.* Milan.
Leuze, O. 1914. "Aedilis lustralis" *Hermes* 49: 110–19.
Levi, M.A. 1932. *"Auspicio, imperio, ductu, felicitate" RIL* 71: 101–18.
Levick, B.M. 1982. "Sulla's March on Rome in 88 B.C." *Historia* 31: 503–8.
Lewis, R.G. 1968. "Rome's New Tribes 90–87 B.C." *Athenaeum* 46: 273–91.
Libourel, N.M. 1968. "Dio Cassius on the Early Roman republic." Dissertation. University of California.
Liebeschuetz, J.H.W.G. 1979. *Continuity and Change in Roman Religion.* Oxford.
Lincoln, B. 1986. *Myth, Cosmos, and Society: Indo-European Themes of Creation and Destruction.* London.
Linderski, J. 1986. "The Augural Law" *ANRW* 16.3: 2146–312.
 1987 (1995). "A Missing Ponticus" *AJAH* 12: 148–66.
 1990. "The Auspices and the Struggle of the Orders" in W. Eder (ed.), *Staat und Staatlichkeit in der frühen römischen Republik.* Stuttgart. 34–48.
Linke, B. and Stemmler, M. (eds.) 2000. *Mos maiorum: Untersuchungen zu den Formen der Identitätsstiftung und Stabilisierung in der römischen Republik.* Stuttgart.
Lintott, A.W. 1972. "*Provocatio*: From the Struggle of the Orders to the Principate" *ANRW* I.2: 226–67.
 1994. "Political History, 146–95 B.C." *CAH*, IX: 41–103.
 1997. "Cassius Dio and the History of the Late Republic" *ANRW* II.34.3: 2497–523.
 1999a. *Violence in Republican Rome.* Oxford.
 1999b. *The Constitution of the Roman Republic.* Oxford.
 2008. *Cicero as Evidence: A Historian's Companion.* Oxford.
Liou-Gille, B. 1996. "Naissance de la langue latine: mythe et culte de formation" *Revue Belge de Philologie et d'Histoire* 74: 73–97.
 1998. *Une lecture "religieuse" de Tite Live, I: cultes, rites, croyances de la Rome archaïque.* Paris.
 2007. "Lucius Quinctius Cincinnatus et ses quatre arpents" *Latomus* 66: 301–26.
Lippold, A. 1963. *Consules: Untersuchungen zur Geschichte des römischen Konsulates von 264 bis 201 v. Chr.* Bonn.
Lobrano, G. 1982. *Il potere dei tribuni della plebe.* Milan.
Lo Cascio, E. 1994. "The Size of the Roman Population: Beloch and the Meaning of the Augustan Census Figures" *JRS* 84: 23–40.
 2001. "Recruitment and the Size of the Roman Population from the Third to the First Century BCE" in W. Scheidel (ed.), *Debating Roman Demography.* Leiden. 111–37.
Long, A.A. and Sedley, D.N. 1987. *The Hellenistic Philosophers, I–II.* Cambridge.
Lovano, M. 2002. *The Age of Cinna: Crucible of Late Republican Rome.* Stuttgart.
Lugli, G. 1923. "La via trionfale a Monte Cavo" *MPAA*, ser. 3, 1: 251–72.
Luterbacher, F. 1904. *Der Prodigienglaube und Prodigienstil der Römer.* Burgdorf.

MacBain, B. 1982. *Prodigy and Expiation: A Study in Religion and Politics in Republican Rome*. Brussels.
Mackay, Ch.S. 2004. *Ancient Rome: A Military and Political History*. Cambridge.
Mackie, N. 1992. "Popularis Ideology and Popular Politics at Rome in the first Century" *RhM* 135: 12–39.
MacMullen, R. 1980. "Romans in Tears" *CPh* 75: 254–55.
Magdelain, A. 1947. *Auctoritas principis*. Paris.
Malavolta, M. 2006. "I ludi delle Feriae Latinae a Roma" in A. Pasqualini (ed.), *Alba Longa: mito, storia, archeologia: Atti dell'Incontro di studio Roma-Albano Laziale, 27–29 gennaio 1994*. Rome. 255–73.
Malcovati, E. 1967. *Oratorum romanorum fragmenta*. Turin.
Manuwald, B. 1979. *Cassius Dio und Augustus*. Wiesbaden.
Marco Simón, F. 1997. "*Romano sacro:* las ceremonias de noviembre y la apertura del *mundus*" in C. Schrader, V. Ramón and J. Vela (eds.), *Plutarco y la historia: Actas del v Simposio Español sobre Plutarco: Zaragoza 20–22 de junio de 1996*. Saragossa. 271–81.
  2006. "Ritual Participation and Collective Identity in the Roman Republic: *Census* and *lustrum*" in F. Marco Simón, F. Pina and J. Remesal (eds.), *Repúblicas y ciudadanos: modelos de participación cívica en el mundo antiguo: III Coloquio Internacional de Historia Antigua Universidad de Zaragoza, Zaragoza 2005*. Saragossa. 153–66.
Marinone, N. 2004. *Cronologia ciceroniana*, 2nd edn., ed. E. Malaspina. Bologna.
Marotta, V. 2000. *Ulpiano e l'impero, 1*. Naples.
Marshall, A.J. 1984. "Symbols and Showmanship in Roman Public Life: The *Fasces*" *Phoenix* 38: 120–41.
Martin, J. 1965. *Die Popularen der späten römischen Republik*. Freiburg.
  1970. "Die Provokation in der klassischen und späten Republik" *Hermes* 98: 77–86.
Martin, P. 2000. "Sur quelques thèmes de l'éloquence popularis, notamment l'invective contre la passivité du peuple" in G. Achard and M. Ledentu (eds.), *Orateur, auditeurs, lecteurs: à propos de l'éloquence romaine à la fin de la république et au début du principat*. Lyon. 27–41.
Martínez-Pinna, J. 2004. *Tusculum latina: aproximación histórica a una ciudad del antiguo Lacio (siglos VI–IV a.C.)*. Rome.
Maschi, C.A. 1976. "La conclusione della giurisprudenza classica all'età dei Severi. Iulius Paulus" *ANRW* 2.15: 667–707.
Masi Doria, C. 2000. *Spretum imperium: prassi costituzionale e momenti di crisi nei rapporti tra magistrati nella media e tarda repubblica*. Naples.
Mason, G.G. 1987. "*Senacula* and Meeting Places of the Roman Senate" *CJ* 83: 39–50.
Mattingly, H.B. 1975. "The *Consilium* of Cn. Pompeius Strabo in 89 B.C." *Athenaeum* 53: 262–6.
Maxfield, V. 1981. *The Military Decorations of the Roman Army*. Berkeley.
Maxis, E. 1911. *Die Prätoren Roms von 366–167 v. Chr.* Breslau.
Mazzarino, S. 1945. *Dalla monarchia allo stato repubblicano*. Catania.

1971. "Intorno ai rapporti fra annalistica e diritto: problemi di esegesi e di critica testuale" in *La critica del testo: Atti del secondo congresso internazionale della società italiana di storia del diritto*, 1. Florence. 441–66.
McDonnell, M. 2006a. *Roman Manliness: Virtus and the Roman Republic.* Cambridge.
    2006b. "Roman Aesthetics and the Spoils of Syracuse" in S. Dillon and K.E. Welch (eds.), *Representations of War in Ancient Rome.* Cambridge. 68–90.
McGushin, P. 1994. *Sallust, The Historiae: Translated with Introduction and Commentary.* Oxford.
Meier, Ch. 1965. "Populares" *RE* Suppl. 10: 515–650.
    1966 (1980). *Res publica amissa: eine Studie zu Verfassung und Geschichte der späten römischen Republik.* Wiesbaden.
Meister, K. 1994. "La storiografia: Flavio Giuseppe, Appiano, Arriano, Cassio Dione" in G. Cambiano, L. Canfora and D. Lanza (eds.), *Lo spazio letterario della Grecia antica, 1.3.* Rome. 117–47.
Meyer, E. 1961. *Römischer Staat und Staatsgedanke.* Zurich.
Michel, A. 2003. *Les rapports de la rhétorique et de la philosophie dans l'oeuvre de Cicéron: recherches sur les fondements philosophiques de l'art de persuader.* Louvain.
Millar, F. 1961. "Some Speeches in Cassius Dio" *MH* 18: 11–22.
    1964. *A Study of Cassius Dio.* Oxford.
    1986. "Politics, Persuasion, and the People Before the Social War (150–90 B.C.)" *JRS* 76: 1–11.
    1995. "Popular Politics at Rome" in I. Malkin and Z.W. Rubinsohn (eds.), *Leaders and Masses in the Roman World: Studies in Honour of Zvi Yavetz.* Tel Aviv. 91–113.
    1998. *The Crowd in Rome in the Late Republic.* Ann Arbor.
    2002. *Rome, the Greek World, and the East, 1: The Roman Republic and the Augustan Principate.* Chapel Hill.
    2005. "Rome in Greek Culture: Cassius Dio and Ulpian" in L. Troiani and G. Zecchini (eds.), *La cultura storica nei primi due secoli dell'impero romano.* Rome. 17–40.
Mitchell, L. 1997. *Greeks Bearing Gifts: The Public Use of Private Relationships in the Greek World, 435–323 BC.* Cambridge.
Mitchell, R.E. 1990. *Patricians and Plebeians: The Origins of the Roman State.* Ithaca.
Mitchell, T.N. 1979. *Cicero: The Ascending Years.* New Haven and London.
    1991. *Cicero: The Senior Statesman.* New Haven and London.
Molho, A., Raaflaub, K. and Emlen, J. (eds.) 1991. *City-States in Classical Antiquity and Medieval Italy.* Stuttgart.
Momigliano, A. 1967. "L'ascesa della plebe nella storia arcaica di Roma" *RSI* 79: 297–312.
Mommsen, Th. 1859. *Die Römische Chronologie bis auf Caesar.* Berlin.
    1861. "Sul *sacerdos Cabesis*" *Bull. Inst.*, 205–7.

1871. "Die neuen Fragmente der Jahrtafel des latinischen Festes" *Hermes* 5: 379–85.
1876. "Der Begriff des Pomerium" *Hermes* 10: 40–50.
1887–8. *Römisches Staatsrecht*. 3 vols. Leipzig.
1899. *Römisches Strafrecht*. Leipzig.
1902. *Römische Geschichte*. Berlin.
Mora, F. 1999. *Fasti e schemi cronologici: la riorganizzazione annalistica del passato remoto romano*. Stuttgart.
Moreau, Ph. 2003. *"Florent sub Caesare leges*: quelques remarques de technique législative à propos des lois matrimoniales d'Auguste" *RHD* 81: 461–77.
Morello, R. 2002. "Livy's Alexander Digression (9.17–19): Counterfactuals and Apologetics" *JRS* 92: 62–85.
Morley, N. 2001. "The Transformation of Italy, 225–28 B.C." *JRS* 91: 50–62.
Morstein-Marx, R. 2000. *"Res Publica Res Populi" SCI* 19: 224–33.
2004. *Mass Oratory and Political Power in the Late Roman Republic*. Cambridge and New York.
2009. "*Dignitas* and *Res Publica*: Caesar and Republican Legitimacy" in K.J. Hölkeskamp (ed.), *Eine politische Kultur (in) der Krise? Die "letzte Generation" der römischen Republik*. Munich. 115–40.
Morstein-Marx, R. and Rosenstein, N. 2006. "The Transformation of the Republic" in N. Rosenstein and R. Morstein-Marx (eds.), *A Companion to the Roman Republic*. Oxford. 625–37.
Mouritsen, H. 1998. *Italian Unification: A Study in Ancient and Modern Historiography*. London.
2001. *Plebs and Politics in the Late Roman Republic*. Cambridge.
Muir, E. 1981. *Civic Ritual in Renaissance Venice*. Princeton.
1997. *Ritual in Early Modern Europe*. Cambridge.
Müller, H. 2009a. "Die Kosten des 3. Makedonischen Krieges" *Historia* 58: 438–67.
(ed.) 2009b. *1000 & 1 Talente: Visualisierung antiker Kriegskosten: Begleitband zu einer studentischen Ausstellung*. Gutenberg.
Münscher, K. 1907. "Die Philostrate" *Philologus* Suppl. 10: 467–558.
Münzer, F. 1891. *De gente Valeria*. Berlin.
1897. s.v. "Calpurnius (28)", *RE* 3:1368–9.
1900. s.v. "Cornelius (338)" *RE* 4: 1483–5.
1910. s.v. "Fulvius (58)" *RE* 7: 241–3.
1927. s.v. "Lutatius (8)", *RE* 13: 2082–94.
1930. s.v. "Marius (15)" *RE* 14: 1811–15.
1931. s.v. "Sulpicius (64)", RE *11*, 4.1: 805.
1936. s.v. "Norbanus (5)" *RE* 17.1: 927–30.
Murphy, T. 2004. *Pliny the Elder's Natural History*. Oxford.
Naco del Hoyo, T. 2005. "*Vectigal incertum*: guerra y fiscalidad republicana en el siglo II a.C." *Klio* 87: 366–95.
Naso, A. 1986. "Un'epigrafe funeraria latina dalla necropoli etrusca di Pian della Conserva" *Epigraphica* 48: 191–8.
Niccolini, G. 1932. *Il tribunate della plebe*. Milan.

Nicolai, R. 2002. "*Unam ex tam multis orationem perscribere*: riflessioni sui discorsi nelle monografie di Sallustio" in G. Marinangeli (ed.), *Atti del primo convegno nazionale sallustinao, L'Aquila 28–9 Settembre 2001*. L'Aquila. 43–65.

Nicolet, Cl. 1976a. *Tributum: recherches sur la fiscalité directe sous la république romaine*. Bonn.

1976b. "L'idéologie du système centuriate et l'influence de la philosophie politique grecque" in *La filosofia greca ed il diritto romano: Colloquio italo-francese*. Rome. 111–37.

1980. *The World of the Citizen in Republican Rome*. Trans. P.S. Falla. Berkeley and Los Angeles.

1992. "Autour de l'*imperium*" *CCGG* 3: 163–6.

Nicols, J. 1980. "*Tabulae patronatus*: A Study of the Agreement Between Patron and Client-Community" *ANRW* 2.13: 535–61.

1999. "Sallust and the Greek Historical Tradition" in R. Mellor and L. Tritle (eds.), *Text and Tradition: Studies in Greek History and Historiography in Honor of Mortimer Chambers*. Claremont. 329–44.

Nippel, W. 1995. *Public Order in Ancient Rome*. Cambridge.

Noè, E. 1988. "Consenso politico nella Roma repubblicana" in E. Gabba (ed.), *AA.VV. Studi di storia e Storiografia antiche*. Como. 49–72.

1994. *Commento storico a Cassio Dione* LIII. Como.

North, J.A. 1990a. "Democratic Politics in Republican Rome" *Past and Present* 126: 3–21.

1990b. "Family Strategy and Priesthood in the late Republic" in J. Andreau and H. Bruhns (eds.), *Parenté et stratégies familiales dans l'antiquité romaine*. Rome. 527–43.

2006. "The Constitution of the Roman Republic" in N. Rosenstein and R. Morstein-Marx (eds.), *A Companion to the Roman Republic*. Oxford. 256–77.

Nybakken, O. 1946. "The Moral Basis of *Hospitium Privatum*" *CJ* 41: 248–53.

Oakley, S. 1993. "The Roman Conquest of Italy" in J. Rich and G. Shipley (eds.), *War and Society in the Roman World*. London. 9–37.

1997–2005. *Commentary on Livy*, Books VI–X, 4 vols. Oxford.

Ogilvie, R.M. 1961, "*Lustrum condere*" *JRS* 51: 31–9.

1965. *A Commentary on Livy. Books 1–5*. Oxford.

Orlin, E.M. 1997. *Temples, Religion and Politics in the Roman Republic*. Leiden, New York and Cologne.

Östenberg, I. 2009. *Staging the World: Spoils, Captives, and Representations in the Roman Triumphal Procession*. Oxford.

Paananen, U. 1972. *Sallust's Political-Social Terminology: Its Use and Biographical Significance*. Helsinki.

Palombi, D. 1993. s.v. Honos et Virtus, aedes, *LTUR* 3: 31–3.

Pareti, L. 1952. *Storia di Roma e del mondo romano, 1*. Turin.

Pasoli, E. 1967. *Le Historiae e le opere minori di Sallustio*. Bologna.

Pasqualini, A. 1996. "I miti albani e l'origine delle Feriae Latinae" in A. Pasquilini (ed.), *Alba Longa: mito, storia, archeologia: Atti dell'Incontro di studio Roma-Albano Laziale, 27–29 gennaio 1994*. Rome. 217–53.

Patterson, J.R. 2006. "The Relationship of the Italian Ruling Classes with Rome: Friendship, Family Relations and their Consequences" in M. Jehne and R. Pfeilschifter (eds.), *Herrschaft ohne Integration? Rom und Italien in republikanischer Zeit*. Frankfurt. 139–53.
Patterson, M.L. 1942. "Rome's Choice of Magistrates During the Hannibalic War" *TAPhA* 73: 319–40.
Pembroke, S. 1971. "Oikeiōsis" in A.A. Long (ed.), *Problems in Stoicism*. London. 114–49.
Perelli, L. 1982. *I populares dai Gracchi alla fine della repubblica*. Turin.
Perrochat, P. 1949. *Les modèles grecs de Salluste*. Paris.
Pfeilschifter, R. 2005. *Titus Quinctius Flamininus: Untersuchungen zur römischen Griechenlandpolitik*. Göttingen.
Pieri, G. 1968. *L'histoire du cens jusqu'à la fin de la république romaine*. Paris.
Pina Polo, F. 1989. *Las contiones civiles y militares en Roma*. Saragossa.
—— 1991. "Cicerón contra Clodio: el lenguaje de la invectiva" *Gerión* 9: 131–50.
—— 1996. *Contra arma verbis: Der Redner vor dem Volk in der späten römischen Republik*. Stuttgart.
Pinsent, J. 1975. *Military Tribunes and Plebeian Consuls: The Fasti from 444 V to 342 V*. Stuttgart.
Piper, D.J. 1988. "The *Ius Adipiscendae Ciuitatis Romanae per Magistratum* and its Effect on Roman-Latin Relations" *Latomus* 47: 59–68.
Pittenger, M.P. 2008. *Contested Triumphs: Politics, Pageantry, and Performance in Livy's Republican Rome*. Berkeley.
Pittia, S. 2006. "La fiabilité des fragments d'Appien sur l'histoire diplomatique et militaire de Rome aux IVe–IIIe siècles" in E. Caire and S. Pittia (eds.), *Guerre et diplomatie romaines (IVe–IIIe siècles): pour un réexamen des sources*. Aix-en-Provence. 113–35.
Pobjoy, M. 2000. "The First *Italia*" in H. Herring and K. Lomas (eds.), *The Emergence of State Identities in Italy in the First Millenium BC*. London. 187–211.
Poma, G. 1984. *Tra legislatori e tiranni: problemi storici e storiografici sull'età delle XII tavole*. Bologna.
Powell, J.G.F. (ed.) 1988. *Cicero, Cato Maior De Senectute*. Cambridge.
—— (ed.) 1995a. *Cicero The Philosopher: Twelve Papers*. Oxford.
—— 1995b. "Cicero's Translations from Greek" in J.G.F. Powell (ed.), *Cicero the Philosopher: Twelve Papers*. Oxford. 273–300.
—— 2001. "Were Cicero's Laws the Laws of Cicero's Republic?" in J. North and J.G.F. Powell (eds.), *Cicero's Republic*. London. 17–39.
Prachner, G. 1994. "Bemerkungen zu den erbeuteten signa militaria der Samnitenkriege" *Militärgeschichtliche Mitteilungen* 53: 1–32.
—— 1995. "Untersuchungen zum Verhältnis von Lösegeld-Forderungen für Kriegsgefangene im 4. und 3. Jahrhundert v. Chr., zu den Verkaufserlösen bei einer Auktion im Jahre 293 v. Chr. und Sklavenpreisen im italisch-sizilischen und griechischen Raum sowie in Ägypten" *Laverna* 6: 1–40.
Puhvel, J. 1975. "Remus and *Frater*" *History of Religions* 15: 146–57.

Purcell, N. 2003. "Becoming Historical: The Roman Case" in D. Braund and C. Gill (eds.), *History and Culture in Republican Rome*. Exeter. 12–40.
Quilici Gigli, S. 2003. "Norba: l'acropoli minore e i suoi templi" in L. Quilici and S. Quilici Gigli (eds.), *Santuari e luoghi di culti nell'Italia antica*. Rome. 289–322.
Quinn-Schofield, W.K. 1967. "*Ludi, Romani magnique varie appellati*" *Latomus* 26: 96–103.
Radin, M. 1936. "Imperium" *Studi Salvatore Riccobono*. Palermo. II: 21–45.
Radke, G. 1973. s.v. Viae publicae Romanae, *RE* 13: 1488, 1493.
  1975. s.v. Penates, in *Der Kleine Pauly* 4: 611.
  1980. "Anmerkungen zu den kultischen Maßnahmen in Rom während des Zweiten Punischen Krieges" *WJA N.F.* 6: 105–21.
Rainer, J.-M. 2006. *Römisches Staatsrecht: Republik und Prinzipat*. Darmstadt.
Rambaud, M. 1980. "Exemples de déformation historique chez Tite-Live: le Tessin, la Trébie, Trasimène" in R. Chevalier (ed.), *Colloque histoire et historiographie: Clio*. Paris. 109–26.
Rasmussen, S.W. 2003. *Public Portents in Republican Rome*. Rome.
Rathbone, D. 1993. "The Census Qualifications of the Assidui and the Prima Classis" in H. Sancisi-Weerdenberg *et al.* (eds.), *De Agricultura: In Memoriam Pieter Willem de Neeve (1945–1990)*. Amsterdam. 121–52.
Rawlings, L. 1999. "Condottieri and Clansmen: Early Italian Raiding, Warfare, and the State" in K. Hopwood (ed.), *Organised Crime in Antiquity*. London. 97–127.
Rawson, E. 1971. "Prodigy Lists and the Use of the Annales Maximi" *CQ* 21: 158–69.
  1979. "L. Cornelius Sisenna and the Early First Century B.C." *CQ* 29: 327–46.
  1985. *Intellectual Life in the Late Roman Republic*. London.
Rebuffat, R. 1982. "*Unus homo nobis cunctando restituit rem*" *REL* 60: 153–65.
Reid, J.S. 1885. *M. Tulli Ciceronis Academica*. London.
Reinhold, M. 1986. "In Praise of Cassius Dio" *AC* 55: 213–22.
  1988. *From Republic to Principate: An Historical Commentary on Cassius Dio's Roman History Books 49–52 (36–29 B.C.)*. Atlanta.
Rich, J.W. 1998. "Augustus' Parthian Honours, the Temple of Mars Ultor and the Arch in the Forum Romanum" *PBSR* 66: 71–128.
  1999. "Drusus and the Spolia Opima" *CQ* 49: 544–55.
Rich, J.W. and Williams, J.H.C. 1999. "*Leges et iura P. R. Restituit*: A New Aureus of Octavian and the Settlement of 28–27 BC" *NC*: 169–213.
Richard, J.-C. 1978. *Les origines de la plèbe romaine: essai sur la formation du dualisme patricio-plébéien*. Rome and Paris.
  1982. "*Praetor collega consulis est*: contribution à l'histoire de la préture" *RPh* 56: 19–31.
  1990. "Réflexions sur le tribunat consulaire" *MEFRA* 102: 767–99.
Richardson, J. 1986. *Hispaniae: Spain and the Development of Roman Imperialism, 218–82 BC*. Cambridge.
Ricoeur, P. 2000. *La mémoire, l'histoire, l'oubli*. Paris.

Ridley, R.T. 1980. "Fastenkritik: a stocktaking" *Athenaeum* 58: 264–98.
  1983. "*Falsi triumphi, plures consulares*" *Latomus* 43: 372–82.
  1986. "The 'Consular Tribunate': The Testimony of Livy" *Klio* 68: 444–65.
  2000. "Livy and the Hannibalic War" in C. Bruun (ed.), *The Roman Middle Republic: Politics, Religion, and Historiography, c. 400–133 BC*. Rome. 13–40.
Rieger, M. 2007. *Tribus und Stadt: die Entstehung der römischen Wahlbezirke im urbanen und mediterranen Kontext (ca. 750–450 v.Chr.)*. Göttingen.
Rilinger, R. 1976. *Der Einfluß des Wahlleiters bei den römischen Konsulwahlen von 366 bis 50 v. Chr.* Munich.
Ritter, H.-W. 1998. "Zu libertas und den Tabellargesetzen in der republikanischen Münzprägung" in P. Kneissl and V. Losemann (eds.), *Imperium Romanum: Studien zu Geschichte und Rezeption (Festschrift für Karl Christ)*. Stuttgart. 608–14.
Rivero Gracia, M.P. 2006. *Imperator populi romani: una aproximación al poder republicano*. Saragossa.
Roberts, E.S. 1881. "Inscriptions from Dodona II" *JHS* 2: 102–21.
Rocchi, M. 1989. "Kithairon et les fêtes des *Daidala*" *DHE* 15: 309–24.
Roddaz, J.-M. 1983. "De César à Auguste: l'image de la monarchie chez un historien du siècle des Sévères: réflexions sur l'oeuvre de Dion Cassius, à propos d'ouvrages récents" *REA* 85: 67–87.
  1992. "*Imperium*: nature et compétences à la fin de la république et au début de l'empire" *CCGG* 3: 189–211.
  2003. "La métamorphose: d'Octavien à Auguste" in S. Franchet d'Esperey, V. Fromentin, S. Gotteland and J.M. Roddaz (eds.), *Fondements et crises du pouvoir*. Bordeaux. 397–418.
Rodríguez Almeida, E. 2003. *Forma vrbis antiquae: le mappe marmoree di Roma tra la repubblica e Settimio Severo*. Rome.
Rodríguez Mayorgas, A. 2007. *La memoria en Roma: oralidad, escritura e historia en la república romana*. Oxford.
Rohr Vio, F. 1998. *Cassio Dione: Storia romana*, v. Milan.
Roller, M. 2001. *Constructing Autocracy: Aristocrats and Emperors in Julio-Claudian Rome*. Princeton.
  2004. "Exemplarity in Roman Culture: The Cases of Horatius Cocles and Cloelia" *CP* 99: 1–56.
Rosenberg, A. 1913. "Die Ädilität von Tusculum" in *Der Staat der alten Italiker: Untersuchungen über die ursprünliche Verfassung der Latiner, Osker und Etrusker*. Berlin. 1–15.
Rosenberger, V. 1998. *Gezähmte Götter: Das Prodigienwesen der römischen Republik*. Stuttgart.
Rosenstein, N. 1990. *Imperatores Victi: Military Defeat and Aristocratic Competition in the Middle and Late Republic*. Berkeley and Los Angeles.
  2004. *Rome at War: Farms, Families, and Death in the Middle Republic*. Chapel Hill and London.
  2006. "Aristocratic Values" in N. Rosenstein and R. Morstein-Marx (eds.), *A Companion to the Roman Republic*. Oxford. 365–82.

2008. "Aristocrats and Agriculture in the Middle and Late Republic" *JRS* 98: 1–26.
Rotondi, G. 1912 (1966). *Leges publicae populi Romani: elenco cronologico con una introduzione sull'attività legislativa dei comizi romani*. Hildesheim.
Rüpke, J. 1990. *Domi militiae: die religiöse Konstruktion des Krieges*. Stuttgart.
Ryan, F.X. 1998. *Rank and Participation in the Republican Senate*. Stuttgart.
2001. "Die Senatorenernennung gemäss dem ovinischen Gesetz" *RSA* 31: 83–91.
2003. "Die Fasten der Erstgewählten des Senates" *Hyperboreus* 9: 112–13.
Sabbatucci, D. 1954. *L'edilità romana, magistratura e sacerdozio*. Rome.
1988. *La religione di Roma antica: del calendario festivo all'ordine cosmico*. Rome.
Sacchetti, L. 1996. *Prodigi e cronaca religiosa: uno studio sulla storiografia latina arcaica*. Rome.
Saladino, V. 1970. *Der Sarkophag des Lucius Cornelius Scipio Barbatus*. Würzburg.
Saller, R.P. 1994. *Patriarchy, Property and Death in the Roman Family*. Cambridge.
Salmon, E.T. 1929. "The Pax Caudina" *JRS* 19: 12–18.
1962. "The Causes of the Social War" *Phoenix* 16: 107–19.
1967. *Samnium and the Samnites*. Cambridge.
Salomonson, J.W. 1956. "Chair, Sceptre and Wreath. Historical Aspects of their Representation on some Roman Sepulchral Monuments." Dissertation. Groningen.
Sampson, G.C. 2005. "Re-examination of the Office of the Tribunate of the Plebs in the Roman Republic (494–23 BC)." Thesis. Manchester.
Samter, E. 1909a. s.v. "Feriae Latinae" *RE* 6.2: 2213–16.
1909b. s.v. "Fasces" *RE* 6: 2002–6.
Sancho, L. 1984. *El tribunado de la plebe en la república arcaica (494–287 a.C.)*. Saragossa.
Sandberg, K. 2001. *Magistrates and Assemblies: A Study of Legislative Practice in Republican Rome*. Rome.
Santi, C. 2000. "Su alcuni aspetti dei pellegrinaggi e dei culti federali nel mondo clásico" *SMSR* 66: 217–26.
Sauer, H. 1949. s.v. "Paludamentum" *RE* 18.3: 281–6.
Sblendorio Cugusi, M.T. 1982. *M. Porci Catonis orationum reliquiae: introduzione, testo critico e commento filologico*. Turin.
Scardigli, B. 1989. *Grani Liciniani reliquiae*. Florence.
Scardigli, B. and Berardi, A.R. 1983. *Grani Liciniani: reliquiae: introduzione, commento storico e traduzione*. Florence.
Schäfer, Th. 1989. *Imperii Insignia: Sella curulis und Fasces: Zur Repräsentation römischer Magistrate*. Mainz.
Schanzer, E. 1968. "Hercules and His Load" *Review of English Studies* n. s. 19: 51–3.
Scheid, J. 1984. "La spartizione a Roma" *Studi Storici* 25: 945–56.
1985. *Religion et piété à Rome*. Paris.
1989. "Il sacerdote" in A.Giardina (ed.), *L'uomo romano*. Rome. 47–79.
1998. "Les incertitudes de la voti sponsio: observations en marge du *ver sacrum* de 217 av. J.C" in M. Humbert and Y. Thomas (eds.), *Mélanges de droit*

romain et d'histoire ancienne: hommage à la mémoire de André Magdelain. Paris. 417–25.

Scheidel, W. 2004. "Human Mobility in Roman Italy, 1: The Free Population" *JRS* 94: 1–26.

2005a. "Human Mobility in Roman Italy, 2: The Slave Population" *JRS* 95: 64–79.

2005b. "Real Slave Prices and the Relative Cost of Slave Labor in the Greco-Roman World" *Ancient Society* 35: 1–17.

2008. "The Comparative Economics of Slavery in the Greco-Roman World" in E. Dal Lago and C. Katsari (eds.), *Slave Systems Ancient and Modern.* Cambridge. 105–26.

Schiavone, A. 1992. "Il pensiero giuridico fra scienza del diritto e potere imperiale" in E. Gabba and A. Schiavone (eds.), *Storia di Roma, 11.3.* Turin. 7–84.

Schleussner, B. 1978. *Die Legaten der römischen Republik: decem legati und ständige Hilfsgesandte.* Munich.

Schlögl, R. 2004. "Vergesellschaftung unter Anwesenden: zur kommunikativen Form des Politischen in der vormodernen Stadt" in R. Schlögl (ed.), *Interaktion und Herrschaft: die Politik der frühneuzeitlichen Stadt.* Constance. 9–60.

Schmidt, W.A. 1875. "Ueber die Quellen des Zonaras" in L. Dindorf (ed.), *Ioannis Zonarae Epitome historiarum*, VI. Lipsiae, iii–lx (= *Zeitschrift für die Alterthumswissenschaft* 30–6 (1839), 238–85).

Schnurbusch, D. 2005. "Das Gastmahl römischer Aristokraten: Form und politisch-soziale Bedeutung aristokratischer Geselligkeit in der römischen Antike." Dissertation. Bielefeld.

Schofield, M. 1995. "Two Stoic Approaches to Justice" in A. Lacks and M. Schofield (eds.), *Justice and Generosity: Studies in Hellenistic Social and Political Philosophy: Proceedings of the Sixth Symposium Hellenisticum.* Cambridge. 195–205.

2000. "Epicurean and Stoic Political Thought" in C. Rowe and M. Schofield (eds.), *The History of Greek and Roman Political Thought.* Cambridge. 435–56.

Scholz, P. 2005. "Zur öffentlichen Repräsentation römischer Senatoren und Magistrate: einige Überlegungen zur (verlorenen) materiellen Kultur der republikanischen Senatsaristokratie" in T.L. Kienlin (ed.), *Die Dinge als Zeichen: Kulturelles Wissen und materielle Kultur.* Bonn. 409–31.

Schwartz, E. 1899. s.v. "Cassius (40)" *RE* 3: 1684–722.

Scullard, H.H. 1967. *The Etruscan Cities and Rome.* Baltimore.

1981. *Festivals and Ceremonies of the Roman Republic.* Ithaca.

Seager, R. 1972. "Cicero and the Word '*Popularis*'" *CQ* 2: 328–38.

1994. "Sulla" *CAH*, IX: 165–207.

Sealey, R. 1959. "Consular Tribunes Once More" *Latomus* 18: 521–30.

Sehlmeyer, M. 1999. *Stadtrömische Ehrenstatuen der republikanischen Zeit: Historizität und Kontext von Symbolen nobilitären Standesbewußtseins.* Stuttgart.

2003. "Die Anfänge der antiquarischen Literatur in Rom: Motivation und Bezug zur Historiographie bis in die Zeit von Tuditanus und Gracchanus" in U. Eigler, U. Gotter, N. Luraghi and U. Walter (eds.), *Formen römischer*

Geschichtsschreibung von den Anfängen bis Livius: Gattungen, Autoren, Kontexte. Darmstadt. 157–71.
Seibert, J. 1993. *Hannibal.* Darmstadt.
Senatore, F. 2006. *La Lega Sannitica.* Capri.
Serrao, F. 1970. *Classi, partiti e legge nella repubblica romana.* Pisa.
Serrati, J. 2000. "Garrisons and Grain: Sicily between the Punic Wars" in C.J. Smith and J. Serrati (eds.), *Sicily from Aeneas to Augustus: New Approaches to Archaeology and History.* Edinburgh. 115–33.
Sharpe, K. 1993. "Representations and Negotiations: Texts, Images, and Authority in Early Modern England" *Historical Journal* 42.3: 853–81.
Shatzman, I. 1972. "The Roman General's Authority over Booty" *Historia* 21: 177–205.
  1973. "Patricians and Plebeians: The Case of the Veturii" *CQ* 23: 65–77.
  1975. *Senatorial Wealth and Roman Politics.* Brussels.
Sherwin-White, A.N. 1973. *The Roman Citizenship*, 2nd edn. Oxford.
Siber, H. 1951. s.v. "Plebs" *RE* 21.1: 103–87.
  1952. *Römisches Verfassungsrecht in geschichtlicher Entwicklung.* Lahr.
Sklénar, R. 1998. "*La République des Signes*: Caesar, Cato and the Language of Sallustian Morality" *TAPhA* 128: 205–20.
Skutsch, O. 1985. *The Annals of Q. Ennius.* Oxford.
Smith, C.J. 2006a. "The *Origo Gentis Romanae*: Facts and Fictions" *BICS*: 97–136.
  2006b. *The Roman Clan: The Gens from Ancient Ideology to Modern Anthropology.* Cambridge.
Smith, R.E. 1958. *Service in the Post-Marian Roman Army.* Manchester.
Sordi, M. 1971. "Cassio Dione e il VII libro del *De bello Gallico* di Cesare" in *Studi di storiografia antica in memoria di Leonardo Ferrero.* Turin. 167–83.
Spannagel, M. 1999. *Exemplaria Principis: Untersuchungen zu Entstehung und Ausstattung des Augustusforums.* Heidelberg.
Staccioli, R.A. 1972. "A proposito della identificazione di Volsinii etrusca" *PP* 27: 246–52.
Stanton, G.R. 1971. "*Cunctando Restituit Rem*: The Tradition about Fabius" *Antichthon* 5: 49–56.
Staveley, E.S. 1956. "The Constitution of the Roman Republic 1940–1956" *Historia* 32: 74–122.
  1963. "The *Fasces* and *Imperium Maius*" *Historia* 12: 458–84.
Stein, C. 2007. "Qui sont les aristocrates romains à la fin de la république?" in H.-L. Fernoux and C. Stein (eds.), *Aristocratie antique: modèles et exemplarité sociale.* Dijon. 127–59.
Stein-Hölkeskamp, E. 2005. *Das römische Gastmahl: eine Kulturgeschichte.* Munich.
Stein-Hölkeskamp, E. and Hölkeskamp, K.-J. (eds.) 2006. *Erinnerungsorte der Antike: die Römische Welt.* Munich.
Stemmler, M. 2000. "*Auctoritas exempli*: zur Wechselwirkung von kanonisierten Vergangenheitsbildern und gesellschaftlicher Gegenwart in der spätrepublikanischen Rethorik" in B. Linke and M. Stemmler (eds.), *Mos*

maiorum: Untersuchungen zu den Formen der Identitätsstiftung und Stabilisierung in der römischen Republik. Stuttgart. 141–205.
Stevenson, A.J. 2004. "Gellius and the Roman Antiquarian Tradition" in L. Holford-Strevens and A. Vardi (eds.), *The Worlds of Aulus Gellius*. Oxford. 118–55.
Stewart, R. 1998. *Public Office in Early Rome: Ritual Procedure and Political Practice*. Ann Arbor.
Storchi Marino, A. 1993. "Quinqueviri mensarii: censo e debiti nel IV secolo" *Athenaeum* 81: 213–50.
Strassburger, H. 1939. s.v. "Optimates" *RE* 18.1: 773–88.
Sumi, G.S. 2002. "Impersonating the Dead: Mimes at Roman Funerals" *AJPh* 125: 559–85.
　2005. *Ceremony and Power: Performing Politics in Rome between Republic and Empire*. Ann Arbor.
Suolahti, J. 1963. *The Roman Censors: A Study on Social Structure*. Helsinki.
Syme, R. 1939 (1985). *The Roman Revolution*. Oxford.
　1964. *Sallust*. Berkeley and Cambridge.
Taldone, A. 1993. "Su *insania* e *furor* in Cicero" *BStudLat* 23: 3–19.
Tansey, P. 2008. "Q. Aemilius Lepidus (Barbula ?) cos. 21 B.C." *Historia* 57: 174–207.
Tarpin, M. 2000. "Le butin sonnant et trébuchant dans la Rome républicaine" in *Économie antique: la guerre dans les économies antiques*. Saint-Bertrand-de-Comminges.
Taylor, L.R. 1946. "The Date of the Capitoline Fasti" *CPh* 41: 1–11.
　1950. "Annals of the Roman Consulship on the Arch of Augustus" *Proceedings of the American Philosophical Society* 94: 511–16.
　1951a. "New Indications of Augustan Editing in the Capitoline Fasti" *CPh* 46: 73–80.
　1951b. "Review of *Das altrömische eponyme Amt* by K. Hanell" *AJPh* 72: 69–72.
　1966. *Roman Voting Assemblies*. Ann Arbor.
Taylor, L.R. and Broughton, T.R.S. 1949. "The Order of the Two Consuls' Names in the Yearly Lists" *MAAR* 19: 3–14.
　1968. "The Order of the Consuls' Names in Official Republican Lists" *Historia* 17: 166–72.
Teodorsson, S.-T. 1989. *A Commentary on Plutarch's Table Talks, 1 (Books 1–3)*. Göteborg.
Thomas, J.-F. 2002. *Gloria et laus: étude sémantique*. Louvain.
Thommen, L. 1989. *Das Volkstribunat der späten römischen Republik*. Stuttgart.
Thompson, R. 1957–61. *Early Roman Coinage: A Study of the Chronology*. 3 vols. Copenhagen.
Thomsen, R. 1980. *King Servius Tullius: A Historical Synthesis*. Copenhagen.
Tibiletti, G. 1953. "La politica delle colonie e città Latine nella Guerra Sociale" *RIL* 86: 45–63.
Till, R. 1970. "Die Scipionenelogien" in K. Vretska, D. Ableitinger and H. Gugel (eds.), *Festschrift Karl Vretska*. Heidelberg. 276–89.

Timpe, D. 1990. "Das Kriegsmonopol des römischen Staates" in W. Eder (ed.), *Staat und Staatlichkeit in der frühen Republik*. Stuttgart. 368–87.
Torelli, M. 2000. "C. Cenucio(s) Clousino(s) prai(fectos): la fondazione della praefectura Caeritum" in Ch. Bruun (ed.), *The Roman Middle Republic: Politics, Religion, and Historiography c. 400–133 B.C.* Rome. 141–76.
Trexler, R.C. 1980. *Public Life in Renaissance Florence*. Ithaca.
Uggeri, G. 1998. s.v. "Hirpini" *DNP* 5: 613.
Ullmann, R. 1927. *La technique des discours dans Salluste, Tite-Live et Tacite*. Oslo.
Ungern-Sternberg, J. von 1975. "Die Einführung spezieller Sitze für die Senatoren bei den Spielen (194 v.Chr.)" *Chiron* 5: 157–63.
  1986. "The Formation of the 'Annalistic Tradition': The Example of the Decemvirate" in K.A. Raaflaub (ed.), *Social Struggles in Archaic Rome: New Perspectives on the Conflict of the Orders*. Berkeley, Los Angeles and London. 77–104.
  1990. "Die Wahrnehmung des Ständekampfes in der römischen Geschichtsschreibung" in W. Eder (ed.), *Staat und Staatlichkeit in der frühen römischen Republik*. Stuttgart. 92–102.
Urso, G. 2005. *Cassio Dione e i magistrati: le origini della repubblica nei frammenti della Storia romana*. Milan.
Valditara, G. 1989. *Studi sul magister populi: dagli ausiliari militari del rex ai primi magistrati repubblicani*. Milan.
Valgiglio, E. 1957. *Silla e la crisi repubblicana*. Florence.
Vanderbroek, P.J.J. 1987. *Popular Leadership and Collective Behavior in the Late Roman Republic (ca. 80–50 B.C.)*. Amsterdam.
Vander Waerdt, P.A. 1991. "Politics and Philosophy in Stoicism" *OSAPh* 9: 185–211.
Van Leijenhorst, C.G. 1986. "Zu zwei lateinischen Amtsbezeichnungen" *MH* 43: 176–83.
Venturini, C. 1973. "'*Libertas*' e '*dominatio*' nell'opera di Sallustio e nella pubblicistica dei '*populares*'" in *Studi E. Graziani*. Pisa. 636–58.
Versnel, H.S. 1970. *Triumphus: An Enquiry into the Origin, Development and Meaning of the Roman Triumph*. Leiden.
  1980. "Historical Implications" in C.M. Stibbe, G. Colonna, C. de Simone and H.S. Versnel (eds.), *Lapis Satricanus: Archaeological, Epigraphical, Linguistic and Historical Aspects of the New Inscription from Satricum*. Rome. 95–150.
  1997. "[IUN]IEI: A New Conjecture in the Satricum Inscription" *Mededelingen van het Nederlands Instituut te Rom* 56: 177–200.
Vervaet, Fr. forthcoming. *The Principle of the Summum Imperium Auspiciumque under the Roman Republic*. Stuttgart.
Voisin, J.L. 1979. "Pendus, crucifiés, oscilla dans la Rome païenne" *Latomus* 38: 422–50.
Vrind, G. 1923. "De Cassii Dionis vocabulis quae ad ius publicum pertinent." Dissertation. Amsterdam.
Wachter, R. 1987. *Altlateinische Inschriften. Sprachliche und epigraphische Untersuchungen zu den Dokumenten bis etwa 150 v. Chr.* Bern and Frankfurt.

Wagner-Hasel, B. 1998. s.v. "Gastfreundschaft" *DNP* 4: 793–7.
Walbank, F. 1957–79. *A Historical Commentary on Polybius*. 3 vols. Oxford.
Wallace-Hadrill, A. 1997. "*Mutatio Morum*: The Idea of a Cultural Revolution" in T. Habinek (ed.), *The Roman Cultural Revolution*. Cambridge. 3–22.
Walt, S. 1997. *Der Historiker C. Licinius Macer: Einleitung, Fragmente, Kommentar*. Stuttgart.
Walter, U. 2004a. "'Ein Ebenbild des Vaters': Familiale Wiederholungen in der historiographischen Traditionsbildung der römischen Republik" *Hermes* 132: 406–25.
  2004b. *Memoria und res publica: zur Geschichtskultur im republikanischen Rom*. Frankfurt.
Waurick, G. 1975. "Kunstraub der Römer: Untersuchungen zu seinen Anfängen anhand der Inschriften" *JRGZ* 22: 1–46.
Weber, M. 1968. *Economy and Society*. Trans. Ephraim Fischoff *et al*. New York.
Weigel, R.D. 1992. *Lepidus the Tarnished Triumvir*. London and New York.
Weinrib, E.J. 1968. "The Prosecution of Roman Magistrates" *Phoenix* 22: 32–56.
Weinstock, S. 1937. s.v. "Penates" *RE* 19.1: 428.
  1971. *Divus Iulius*. Oxford.
Weische, A. 1966. *Studien zur politischen Sprache der römischen Republik*. Munich.
Weiss, E. 1937. s.v. "Tribunal (1)" *RE* 11.6.2: 2428–30.
Welch, K. 2006. "*Domi Militiaeque*: Roman Domestic Aesthetics and War Booty in the Republic" in S. Dillon and K. Welch (eds.), *Representations of War in Ancient Rome*. Cambridge. 91–161.
Werner, C. 1888. "De feriis Latinis." Dissertation. Leipzig.
Werner, R. 1963. *Der Beginn der römischen Republik: Historisch-chronologische Untersuchungen über die Anfangszeit der libera res publica*. Munich and Vienna.
Wesemberg, G. 1954. s.v. "Praetor" *RE* 22.2: 1581–605.
Weynand, R. 1935. s.v. "Marius" *RE Suppl*. VI: 1363–1425.
Whitehead, S. 2005. "Cicero's *Viri Clarissimi*" in K. Welch and T.W. Hillard (eds.), *Roman Crossings: Theory and Practice in the Roman Republic*. Swansea. 141–207.
Willems, P. 1968 (1878–85). *Le Sénat de la république romaine: sa composition et ses attributions*. 2 vols. Aalen.
Wirszubzki, Ch. 1961. "Audaces" *JRS* 51: 12–22.
  1968. *Libertas as a Political Idea during the Late Republic and the Early Principate*. Cambridge.
Wiseman, T.P. 1971. *New Men in the Roman Senate, 139 BC–AD 14*. Oxford.
  1979. *Clio's Cosmetics: Three Studies in Greco-Roman Literature*. Leicester.
  1994. "The Senate and the *Populares*, 69–60 B.C" *CAH*, IX: 327–67.
  2002. "Roman History and the Ideological Vacuum" in T.P. Wiseman (ed.), *Classics in Progress: Essays on Ancient Greece and Rome*. London. 285–310.
Wissowa, G. 1904. "Die Überlieferung über die römischen Penaten" in G. Wissowa (ed.), *Gesammelte Abhandlungen zur römischen Religions- und Stadtgeschichte*. Munich. 95–128.

1912. *Religion und Kultus der Römer*. Munich.
1915. "Die römischen staatspriestertümer Altlatinischen Gemeindekulte" *Hermes* 50: 1–32.
Wülcker, L. 1903. *Die geschichtliche Entwicklung des Prodigienswesens bei den Römern*. Leipzig.
Yakobson, A. 1992. "*Petitio et Largitio*: Popular Participation in the Centuriate Assembly of the Late Republic" *JRS* 82: 32–52.
1999. *Elections and Electioneering in Rome: A Study in the Political System of the Late Republic*. Stuttgart.
2004. "The People's Voice and the Speaker's Platform: Popular Power, Persuasion and Manipulation in the Roman Forum" *SCI* 18: 201–12.
2006a. "Il popolo romano, il sistema e l'elite: il dibattito continua" *Studi Storici* 47.2: 377–93.
2006b. "Popular Power in the Roman Republic" in N. Rosenstein and R. Morstein-Marx (eds.), *A Companion to the Roman Republic*. Oxford. 383–400.
Yates, F. A. 1974. *The Art of Memory*. Chicago.
Yavetz, Z. 1988. *Plebs and Princeps*. New Brunswick and Oxford.
Zecchini, G. 1978. *Cassio Dione e la guerra gallica di Cesare*. Milan.
1979. "Catone a Cipro (58–56 a.C.): dal dibattito politico alle polemiche storiografiche" *Aevum* 53: 78–87.
1998. "La Constitutio Antoniniana e l'universalismo politico di Roma" in L. Aigner-Foresti *et al.* (eds.), *L'ecumenismo politico nella coscienza dell'Occidente*. Rome. 349–58.
2002. "Scipione in Spagna: un approccio critico alla tradizione polibiano-liviana" in G. Urso (ed.), *Hispania terris omnibus felicior: Premesse ed esiti di un processo di integrazione: Atti del convegno internazionale, Cividale del Friuli, 27–29 settembre 2001*. Pisa. 87–103.
2006. "Presentazione" *Studi Storici* 47.2: 317.
Ziegler, K. 1972. s.v. "Zonaras" *RE* 11.10: 718–32.
Ziolkowski, A. 1992. *The Temples of Mid-Republican Rome and their Historical and Topographical Context*. Rome.
1998. "*Urbs Direpta*, or How the Romans Sacked Cities" in J. Rich and G. Shipley (eds.), *War and Society in the Roman World*. London. 69–91.

Index of persons

All dates are BC unless otherwise stated.

Acilius Glabrio, M'. (cos. 191) 102, 134, 135, 149
Aelius Tubero, Q. (historian) 29
Aemilius Lepidus, M. (cos. 187, 175; cens. 179) 235, 244, 249
Aemilius Lepidus, M. (cos. 78) 287, 288, 299, 300, 301, 302, 303, 304, 305, 306, 307, 308, 310, 311, 312, 315, 316
Aemilius Lepidus, Q. (cos. 21) 332
Aemilius Lepidus Livianus, Mam. (cos. 77) 302
Aemilius Macer 43
Aemilius Papinianus (jurist; praef. praet. AD 203–12) 42
Aemilius Paullus, L. (cos. 219, 216) 187, 196, 200, 201, 204
Aemilius Paullus, L. (cos. 182, 168) 110, 143, 144, 149, 204, 205
Aemilius (Regillus?), M. (pr. 217) 113
Aemilius Scaurus, M. (cos. 115; cens. 109) 230
Aeneas 117, 121
Albius, C. (mutinous legionary in Scipio Africanus' army in Hispania) 177
Alcibiades, son of Kleinias (Ath. politician and *strategos*) 70
Ammianus Marcellinus (historian) 207
Antiochus III 134
Antistius, C. (equestrian priest) 129
Antonius, M. (cos. 44, 34) 261, 310, 325
Antonius Merenda, Q. (tr. mil. c. p. 422) 36
Appian of Alexandreia (historian) 190, 206, 239, 260, 264, 265, 266, 267, 268, 269, 271, 272, 273, 274, 275, 277, 278, 286, 301, 302
Appuleius Saturninus, L. (tr. pl. 103, 100) 272, 282, 285, 292
Aristotle (philosopher) 313
Asconius Pedianus, Q. (commentator) 262, 286
Atilius Caiatinus, A. (cos. 258, 254; dict. 249) 72
Atilius Luscus, L. (tr. mil. c. p. 444) 29, 36
Atrius, C. (mutinous legionary in Scipio Africanus' army in Hispania) 177

Atticus: *see* Pomponius Atticus
Augustus *emperor* (C. Octavius, Octavianus) 9, 15, 22, 30, 44, 45, 125, 126, 127, 206, 207, 319, 320, 321, 322, 323, 324, 325, 326, 327, 328, 329, 330, 331, 332, 333, 334, 335
Aurelius Cotta, C. (cos. 200) 102
Aurelius Cotta, C. (cos. 75) 287
Aurelius Cotta, M. (cos. 74) 152

Bantius, L. (aristocrat of Nola, rewarded by Claudius Marcellus) 243

Caecilius Metellus Numidicus, Q. (cos. 109) 285
Caelius Rufus, M. (tr. pl. 52) 126
Caerellius, Q. (patron of C. Censorinus) 73
Caesar: *see* Iulius Caesar
Caesius, M. (friend of Cicero; from Arpinum) 248
Caligula *emperor* (C. Caesar Germanicus) 122
Callicratidas (Spartan *nauarchos* 406) 206
Calpurnius Bibulus, M. (cos. 59) 205, 206
Caracalla *emperor* (M. Aurelius Severus Antoninus; (L.) Septimius Bassianus) 43, 130
Carvilius Maximus, Sp. (cos. 293, 272) 128
Cassius Dio Cocceianus (cos. ord. AD 229; cos. suff. date uncertain; historian) 10, 24, 34, 36, 37, 38, 39, 40, 41, 42, 43, 44, 45, 46, 47, 48, 50, 51, 52, 53, 54, 55, 56, 57, 58, 59, 60, 123, 125, 190, 198, 199, 304, 310, 311, 312, 325, 326, 328, 332
Cato the Elder: *see* Porcius Cato
Catullus: *see* Valerius Catullus
Censorinus, C. (grammarian) 73, 74
Chrysippus (philosopher) 313
Cicereius, C. (pr. 173) 118
Cicero: *see* Tullius Cicero
Cincius, L. (antiquarian) 33, 38, 39
Cineas (envoy of Pyrrhus) 228

Index of persons

Claudius Caecus, Ap. (cos. 307, 296; dict. between 292 and 285) 67
Claudius Crassus Inregillensis Sabinus, Ap. (cos. 471, 451; Xvir) 55, 56, 58
Claudius Marcellus, M. (cos. 222, 214, 210, 208; cos. suff. 215) 144, 202, 241, 243
Claudius Marcellus, M. (cos. 196) 114
Claudius Marcellus, M. (cos. 51) 174, 175
Claudius Pulcher, Ap. (cos. 79) 266, 300, 303
Claudius Pulcher, P. (cos. 249) 142
Claudius Quadrigarius, Q. (historian) 87, 88, 90, 91
Cleombrotus (Spartan king 380–371) 206
Cleopatra VII 325
Clodius Pulcher, P. (tr. pl. 58) 282
Cluentius Habitus, A. (father of Cicero's client; client of Marius Babrius) 252
Cluentius Habitus, A. (client of Cicero from Larinum) 252
Coelius Antipater, L. (historian) 45
Consius Cerinthus, M. (*accensus velatus*) 129
Cornelius Cethegus, M. (cos. 204; cens. 209) 203
Cornelius Cinna, L. (cos. 87–84) 8, 14, 259, 260, 261, 262, 264, 265, 266, 267, 269, 270, 271, 273, 276, 277, 278, 286
Cornelius Cinna, L. (pr. 44) 302
Cornelius Cossus, A. (cos. 428) 30
Cornelius Lentulus, Ser. (cos. 303) 234
Cornelius Lentulus Caudinus, L. (cos. 237) 113
Cornelius Maluginensis, Ser. (cos. 393?; tr. mil. c. p. 386, 384, 382, 380, 376, 370, 368; mag. eq. 361) 30
Cornelius Mammula, A. (pr. 217) 111, 114
Cornelius Merula, L. (cos. suff. 87) 266
Cornelius Rufinus, P. (cos. 290, 277; dict. between 292 and 285) 70, 239
Cornelius Scipio Africanus, P. (cos. 205, 194; cens. 199) 93, 114, 148, 149, 175, 177, 208, 209, 227, 245, 246
Cornelius Scipio Africanus Aemilianus, P. (cos. 147, 134) 134, 150, 283, 314
Cornelius Scipio Asiaticus, L. (cos. 190) 149
Cornelius Scipio Asiaticus, L. (cos. 83) 286
Cornelius Scipio Nasica, P. (cos. 191) 102, 134
Cornelius Scipio Nasica Serapio, P. (cos. 138) 261
Cornelius Sisenna, L. (pr. 78; historian) 271, 302
Cornelius Sulla, L. (cos. 88, 80; dict. 82–80) 6, 7, 14, 88, 89, 90, 92, 100, 106, 259, 260, 261, 262, 263, 264, 271, 273, 274, 275, 276, 277, 282, 287, 289, 300, 301, 302, 303, 305, 310, 316, 317, 318, 324
Cornelius Tacitus, P.? (cos. AD 97; historian) 34, 325
Cornificius Longus, C (etymologist) 121

Curius Dentatus, M'. (cos. 290, 275, 274; cens. 272) 214, 215

Decius *emperor* (C. Messius Quintus Decius Valerinus, Imp. Caes. C. Messius Quintus Traianus Decius) 129
Diodorus Siculus (historian) 263
Diogenes of Seleucia (in Mesopotamia; philosopher) 314
Dionysius of Halicarnassus (historian) 20, 25, 34, 35, 39, 42, 55, 56, 107, 108, 109, 110, 118, 119, 121, 125, 129, 138, 216
Domitius Ulpianus (jurist, praef. praet. under Alexander Severus) 42, 43, 44
Drusus the Elder (Nero Claudius Drusus, cos. 9) 333
Duilius, C. (cos. 260) 138

Egnatius Rufus, M. (candidate for the consulship of 19) 332
Ennius, Q. (poet) 109, 110, 175, 182, 183, 184, 185, 195, 197, 205, 206
Epidius Sabinus, T. (aristocrat of Pompeii) 247

Fabius Buteo, M. (cos. 245; dict. 216) 219, 222, 223, 226
Fabius Maximus, Q. (cos. 213) 87, 90
Fabius Maximus Gurges, Q. (cos. 265) 234
Fabius Maximus Rullianus, Q. (cos. 322, 310, 308, 297, 295; dict. 315, 313(?)) 67, 70, 177, 237
Fabius Maximus Verrucosus (Cunctator), Q. (cos. 233, 228, 215, 214, 209; dict. 221?, 217) 13, 87, 90, 113, 167, 182, 183, 184, 185, 186, 187, 188, 189, 190, 191, 192, 193, 194, 195, 196, 197, 198, 199, 200, 201, 202, 203, 204, 205, 206, 207, 208, 209, 210
Fabius Pictor, Q. (historian) 5, 27, 64, 82, 108, 109
Fabius Quintilianus, M. (rhetorician) 317
Fabius Vibulanus, K. (cos. 484, 481, 479) 51, 52
Fabricius, C. (inhabitant of Aletrium) 252
Fabricius, L. (inhabitant of Aletrium) 252
Fabricius Luscinus, C. (cos. 282, 278; cens. 275) 138, 139, 142, 146, 214
Fenestella (antiquarian) 37
Festus: *see* Pompeius Festus
Flaminius, C. (cos. 223, 217) 102, 113, 116, 124, 283
Flavius Theodosius (mag. eq. (West) AD 369–75; father of Theodosius I) 207
Flavus (leader of the Roman party in Lucania; pr. in Lucania 213; *hospes* of Gracchus (cos. 213)) 237

Index of persons

Florus (*epitomator*) 70, 121, 195, 196, 197, 302, 305, 306
Fulvius Flaccus, M. (cos. 125) 284
Fulvius Flaccus, Q. (cos. 179; cens. 174) 140, 235, 249
Fulvius Nobilior, M. (cos. 189; cens. 179) 149
Furius Camillus, M. (tr. mil. c. p. 401, 398, 394, 386, 384, 381; dict. 396, 390, 389, 368–367) 64, 65, 69
Furius Fusus, Sp. (cos. 481) 51

Geganius Macerinus, M. (cos. 447, 443, 437; cens. 435) 29
Gellius, A. (antiquarian) 38, 49, 66
Genucius Augurinus, T. (cos. 451; Xvir) 55, 56
Genucius Aventinensis, L. (cos. 303) 234
Germanicus (Nero Claudius Drusus Germanicus, cos. AD 12, 18) 333
Granius Licinianus (antiquarian) 265, 305

Hannibal 140, 146, 184, 186, 187, 189, 190, 191, 192, 193, 194, 195, 196, 197, 198, 200, 203, 204, 210, 227, 235, 239, 244, 245, 246, 250
Hesiod 313
Hippias (son of Peisistratos, tyrant of Athens) 259
Hirtius, A. (cos. 43) 116
Homer 313
Horatius Pulvillus, M. (cos. 507; cos. suff. 509) 33
Horatius (Tu?)rrinus Barbatus, M. (cos. 449) 50, 123, 283
Hostilius Mancinus, C. (cos. 137) 106, 108

Iugurtha 150
Iulius Caesar, C. (cos. 59, 48, 46–44; dict. 49, 48/7, 46–44) 14, 45, 90, 125, 126, 133, 143, 147, 151, 152, 175, 205, 259, 260, 264, 269, 274, 276, 280, 282, 289, 290, 297, 302, 307, 325, 326
Iulius Caesar, C. (grandson of Augustus; cos. AD 1) 326, 333
Iulius Caesar, L. (grandson of Augustus) 326
Iulius Iullus, C. (cos. 447, 435, 434?) 29
Iulius Paulus (jurist) 43
Iulius Proculus (witness of Romulus' deification) 126
Iunius Brutus, M. (cos. 509) 4, 21, 46, 47
Iunius Brutus, M. (tr. pl. 83) 302
Iunius Brutus, M. (pr. 44) 248
Iunius Brutus, P. (pr. 190) 236
Iunius Congus Gracchanus, M. (antiquarian) 37
Iustinus (philosopher and martyr) 121

Labienus, T. (tr. pl. 63) 292
Laelius (Sapiens), C. (cos. 140) 313, 314
Latinus (king of Latium) 121
Licinius Calvus, C. (cos. 364 or 361; mag. eq. 368) 30, 31, 65
Licinius Calvus Esquilinus, P. (tr. mil. c.p. 400, 396) 36
Licinius Crassus, C. (cos. 168) 109, 110
Licinius Crassus, L. (cos. 95) 171, 270
Licinius Crassus, M. (cos. 70, 55) 133, 282, 288, 289, 290, 302
Licinius Crassus, P. (cos. 171) 173
Licinius Crassus Dives, P. (cos. 205; cens. 210) 111, 114
Licinius Dives Crassus Mucianus, P. (cos. 131) 283
Licinius Lucullus, L. (pr. 104) 236
Licinius Lucullus, L. (cos. 74) 136, 143, 144, 147, 149, 150, 151, 152, 302
Licinius Macer, C. (pr. 68?; historian) 28, 29, 30, 31, 36, 271
Licinius Macer Calvus, C. (orator; poet; son of the historian) 30
Licinius Stolo, C. (cos. 364 or 361, tr. pl. 376–367) 30, 31, 64
Livius, C. (Roman garrison commander in Tarentum during Second Punic War) 239
Livius Salinator, M. (cos. 219, 207; dict. 207) 209
Livy (Titus Livius) 3, 4, 20, 25, 27, 30, 31, 33, 34, 36, 37, 38, 39, 42, 44, 45, 49, 50, 51, 54, 55, 56, 57, 61, 62, 63, 64, 65, 67, 68, 99, 100, 101, 102, 104, 107, 108, 109, 110, 111, 112, 114, 115, 117, 122, 137, 139, 142, 143, 145, 147, 148, 149, 161, 169, 170, 173, 174, 175, 177, 178, 190, 192, 193, 194, 196, 198, 200, 202, 203, 204, 205, 212, 216, 222, 223, 232, 234, 235, 236, 237, 238, 241, 243, 244, 245, 250, 271
Lollius, M. (cos. 21) 332
Lollius Palicanus, M. (pr. 69) 282
Lucretia 4, 46
Lucretius Gallus, C. (pr. 171) 249
Lucretius Vespillo, Q: (cos. 19) 333
Lutatius Catulus, L. (cos. 242) 71, 72
Lutatius Catulus, Q. (cos. 78; cens. 65) 15, 290, 299, 300, 301, 302, 303, 304, 305, 306, 308, 310, 311, 312, 313, 315, 316, 317, 318
Lydus (antiquarian) 36, 37, 38, 55, 56

Maccius (?) Plautus, T. (poet) 138
Macrobius, Ambrosius Theodosius 37, 105, 107, 108
Manilius (astrologer; poet) 197
Manlius Capitolinus (Vulso?), M. (cos. or tr. mil. c. p. 434) 29
Manlius Capitolinus, P. (tr. mil. c. p. 379, 367; dict. suff. 368) 65

Index of persons

Manlius Cincinnatus, Cn. (cos. 480) 52
Manlius Imperiosus Torquatus, T. (cos. 347, 344, 340; dict. 353, 349, 320) 175, 177
Manlius Torquatus, T. (praef. 340; son of Imperiosus) 177
Manlius Torquatus, T. (cos. 235, 224; dict. 208) 111, 238
Manlius Vulso, Cn. (cos. 189) 137, 138, 149
Marcius Coriolanus, Cn. (Roman renegade) 259
Marcius Philippus, L. (cos. 91; cens. 86) 300, 302, 303, 305, 310, 311, 312, 313, 315, 316, 317
Marcius Philippus, Q. (cos. 186, 169; cens. 164) 235
Marcius Tremulus, Q. (cos. 306, 288)
Marius, C. (cos. 107, 104–100, 86) 8, 13, 142, 229, 259, 260, 261, 262, 263, 264, 271, 272, 273, 274, 275, 276, 280, 283, 284, 285, 286, 290, 292
Marius Babrius (Roman senator; patron of the elder Cluentius) 252
Marius Gratidianus, M. (pr. 85(?), 82(?)) 265
Mark Antony: *see* Antonius
Memmius, C. (tr. pl. 111; pr. 104 or 103) 282, 311
Menenius Agrippa Lanatus (cos. 503) 48
Metilius, M. (tr. pl. 217) 189
Minucius Rufus, M. (cos. 221; dict. 217) 186, 189, 190, 192, 193, 194, 198, 199, 200, 201, 202, 203
Minucius Rufus, M. (cos. 110) 249
Minucius Rufus, Q. (monetal. 137–134) 249
Mithridates VI Eupator 94, 150, 152, 207, 261, 263, 264, 302
Mucius Scaevola, P. (cos. 133) 20, 283
Mucius Scaevola, Q. (cos. 95) 274
Mummius, L. (cos. 146; cens. 142) 249

Nicias of Engyion (in Sicily; handed his town over to Claudius Marcellus during Second Punic War) 241, 243
Nonius Iustinus, C. (equestrian priest) 129
Nonius Vansa, C. (equestrian priest) 129
Norbanus, C. (cos. 83) 286

Octavius, Cn. (cos. 87) 264, 265, 286
Opimius, L. (cos. 121) 236, 261
Oppianicus the Elder (inhabitant of Larinum) 252
Oppianicus the Younger (inhabitant of Larinum) 252
Orosius Paulus (historian; church father) 304
Ovinius (tr. pl. before 312) 217

Pacuvius Calavius (*meddix tuticus* in Capua 216) 238
Panaetius of Rhodos (philosopher) 300, 314

Papia (wife of Oppianicus the Younger from Larinum) 252
Papirius Carbo, C. (pr. 62) 152
Papirius Carbo, Cn. (cos. 85, 84, 82) 286
Papirius Carbo, L. (cos. 85, 84, 82) 8
Papirius Cursor, L. (cos. 326, 320, 319, 315, 313; dict. 325 (Liv.) or 324 (FC), 310 (Liv.) or 309 (FC)) 70, 177, 241
Papirius Cursor, L. (cos. 293, 272) 69, 139, 143
Papirius Maso, C. (cos. 231) 118, 128
Papirius Mugillanus, L. (cos. suff. 444) 28
Paulinus of Nola (Meropius Pontius Paulinus, bishop of Nola) 121
Perseus (king of Macedonia) 143, 149, 237, 250
Philip V (king of Macedonia) 112, 149
Plato 313
Plautius (tr. pl. 70) 288
Plautus: *see* Maccius (?) Plautus
Pliny the Elder (Plinius Secundus, C.) 21, 49, 70, 73, 128, 129, 138, 203
Plutarchus of Chaironeia (philosopher) 34, 46, 53, 77, 78, 96, 189, 190, 199, 201, 203, 204, 208, 214, 243, 263, 290, 304, 305, 310, 311
Polyaenus (writer on *strategemata*) 189
Polybius (historian) 7, 10, 35, 36, 45, 97, 134, 135, 144, 189, 201, 300, 314, 317
Pompeius, Q. (cos. 141; cens. 131) 283
Pompeius Festus, Sex. (antiquarian) 4, 33, 38, 39, 217, 218
Pompeius Magnus, Cn. (cos. 70, 55, 52) 7, 8, 14, 45, 90, 94, 126, 133, 135, 136, 143, 150, 151, 207, 259, 261, 274, 280, 282, 287, 288, 289, 290, 291, 293, 294, 300, 301, 302, 303, 305, 310, 311, 313, 315, 316, 317, 330, 334
Pompeius Rufus, Q. (cos. 88) 263
Pompeius Strabo, Cn. (cos. 89) 135
Pompey: *see* Pompeius Magnus
Pomponius Atticus, T. 144, 205, 259
Pomponius, Sex. (jurist) 54
Popillius Laenas, C. (cos. 172, 158) 110
Poppeius (aristocrat of Interamna) 237
Poppeius, Q. (aristocrat of Interamna) 237
Porcius Cato, M. (cos. 195; cens. 184) 27, 35, 37, 106, 114, 139, 174, 191, 196, 212, 214, 215
Porcius Cato (Uticensis), M. (pr. 54) 281, 310
Porphyry of Tyre (philosopher) 121
Porsenna (Etruscan king) 4
Postumius Albinus, A. (cos. 242; cens. 234) 71
Postumius Albinus, L. (cos. 173) 232, 233, 235, 255
Postumius Albinus, Sp. (cos. 186) 235
Postumius Albinus Luscus, A. (cos. 180; cens. 174) 249
Postumius Tubertus, P. (cos. 505, 503) 48
Propertius, Sex. (poet) 197
Pseudo-Aurelius Victor 119

Publilius Philo, Q. (cos. 339, 327, 320, 315; dict. 339) 6, 70
Pyrrhus of Epirus 68, 70, 227, 228
Pythagoras of Samos (philosopher) 70

Quinctius Capitolinus Barbatus, T. (cos. 471, 468, 465, 446, 443, 439) 28, 29
Quinctius Cincinnatus Capitolinus, T. (tr. mil. c. p. 388, 385?, 384; dict. 380) 69, 212, 213, 214
Quinctius Flamininus, T. (cos. 198; cens. 189) 227
Quinctius Poenus Capitolinus Crispinus, T. (cos. 354, 351; dict. 361) 30
Quinctius Poenus Cincinnatus, T. (cos. 431, 428) 30
Quintilian: *see* Fabius Quintilianus

Rabirius, C. (tr. mil. (?) 89; senator) 289, 292, 295
Rammius, L. (Brundisian; assassin in the service of Perseus of Macedonia in 172 (?)) 237, 250, 252, 254
Remus 109
Romulus 34, 107, 109, 126
Roscius, Sex. (client of Cicero) 237

Sallustius Crispus, C. (historian; pr. 46) 239, 271, 280, 284, 287, 301, 305, 310, 311, 312
Saturninus: *see* Appuleius Saturninus
Scipio Africanus: *see* Cornelius Scipio Africanus
Sempronius Atratinus, L. (cos. suff. 444) 28
Sempronius Gracchus, C. (tr. pl. 123–122) 150, 174, 282, 284, 292
Sempronius Gracchus, Ti. (cos. 215, 213) 237
Sempronius Gracchus, Ti. (cos. 177, 163) 143
Sempronius Gracchus, Ti. (tr. pl. 133) 282, 283, 284, 292
Sempronius Longus, Ti. (cos. 194) 114
Sempronius Tuditanus, C. (cos. 129) 36, 38
Sempronius Tuditanus, P. (cos. 204; cens. 209) 203
Sentius Saturninus, C. (cos. 19) 332
Sertorius, Q. (pr. 83) 265, 288, 302
Servilia (stepmother of Q. Lutatius Catulus (cos. 78)) 300
Servilius Caepio, Q. (cos. 140) 300
Servilius Caepio, Q. (cos. 106) 135
Servilius Geminus, Cn. (cos. 217) 102, 113
Servilius Glaucia, C. (pr. 100) 282, 285
Servilius Rullus, P. (tr. pl. 63) 291, 293
Servilius Vatia Isauricus, P. (cos. 79; cens. 55) 300
Servius Honoratus (?), Marius or Maurus (grammarian, commentator on Virgil) 105, 107, 108, 120

Servius Tullius (king of Rome) 21
Sextius Sextinus Lateranus, L. (cos. 366; tr. pl. 376–367) 64, 65
Silius Italicus (Ti. Catius Asconius Silius Italicus, epicist) 192, 194, 196, 202
Silvanus, L. (candidate for the consulship of 21) 332
Sisenna: *see* Cornelius Sisenna
Socrates (philosopher) 70
Staiodus, T. (aristocrat of Trasacco; *hospes* of Manlius Torquatus (cos. 235, 224)) 238
Statilius Taurus, T. (cos. 26; cos. suff. 37) 331
Statius Trebius (aristocrat of Samnite town of Compsa) 244
Suedius Clemens, T. (officer in Campania under Vespasian) 247
Suetonius Tranquillus, C. (biographer; *a studiis, a bibliothecis, ab epistulis*) 151, 206, 327
Sulla: *see* Cornelius Sulla
Sulpicius Camerinus Cornutus, Ser. (cos. 500) 26
Sulpicius Camerinus Praetextatus, Q. (cos. or tr. mil. c. p. 434) 29
Sulpicius Galba Maximus, P. (cos. 211, 200; dict. 203) 102, 112
Sulpicius Peticus, C. (cos. 364, 361, 355, 353, 351; cens. 366; dict. 358) 31
Sulpicius Rufus, P. (tr. pl. 88) 261, 262, 263, 264, 271, 274, 275, 276, 282, 286

Tacitus: *see* Cornelius Tacitus
Tarquinius Collatinus, L. (cos. 509) 4, 46, 47
Tarquinius Superbus, L. (last king of Rome) 46, 119, 120, 121, 259
Terentilius Harsa, C. (tr. pl. 462) 60
Terentius Varro, C. (cos. 216) 200, 201
Terentius Varro, M. (pr. date uncertain; antiquarian) 33, 38, 196, 205, 216
Themistocles, son of Neokles (Athenian archon 493/2) 70, 259
Theodosius I. *emperor* 131
Tiberius *emperor* (Ti. Claudius Nero; Ti. Caesar Augustus) 206, 207, 333
Tigranes I (king of Armenia) 94
Trebatius Testa, C. (jurist) 37
Tuccius, M. (pr. 190) 236
Tullius Cicero, M. (cos. 63) 14, 15, 20, 26, 27, 31, 59, 72, 109, 118, 119, 121, 124, 126, 129, 144, 147, 151, 152, 174, 182, 191, 196, 205, 206, 212, 213, 214, 219, 230, 237, 248, 249, 252, 259, 261, 262, 274, 280, 281, 282, 283, 284, 285, 290, 291, 292, 293, 294, 295, 304, 305, 306, 307, 308, 309, 310, 311, 313, 314, 315, 316, 317
Tullius Cicero, Q. (pr. 62) 262
Tullius Longus, M'. (cos. 500) 26

Ulpianus: *see* Domitius Ulpianus

Valeria (fifth wife of Q. Lutatius Catulus (cos. 78)) 301
Valerius Antias (historian) 29, 45
Valerius Catullus, C. (poet) 121
Valerius Falto, Q. (cos. 239) 71, 72
Valerius Flaccus, L. (cos. 195) 114
Valerius Flaccus, L. (cos. suff. 86) 286
Valerius Maximus (rhet. and historian) 72, 106, 192, 204, 216, 265, 304
Valerius Maximus Corvus, M. (cos. 348, 346, 343, 335, 300; cos. suff. 299; dict. 342, 302 (Liv.) or 301 (FC)) 70, 241
Valerius Messala Rufus, M. (cos. 53) 38, 66
Valerius Potitus, L. (cos. 449) 50, 123, 283
Valerius Publicola, P. (cos. 508, 507, 504; cos. suff. 509) 47, 48, 171, 172, 283
Velleius Paterculus (historian) 304
Vergilius Maro, P. (poet) 105, 121
Verginius Tricostus, L. (cos. 435, 434?) 29
Verres, C. (pr. 74) 152, 174, 281, 293
Vespasian *emperor* (T. Flavius Vespasianus; Imp. Caesar Vespasianus Augustus) 247
Vibius Pansa Caetronianus, C. (cos. 43) 116
Vipsanius Agrippa, M. (cos. 37, 28, 27 BC) 21, 325, 331

Zonaras (Ioannes Zonaras, Byzantine chronicler) 36, 45, 46, 48, 51, 53, 57, 234, 239, 243

Subject index

aedile, aedileship 2, 35, 37, 81, 108, 109, 130, 248, 289, 290
aerarium 12, 135, 136, 137, 142, 149, 150, 152
aristocracy 5, 8, 12, 183, 234, 238, 242, 244, 246, 252, 253, 268, 270, 298, 300, 302, 322, 329, 330, 331, 333, 334, 335
assemblies 4, 7, 32, 34, 36, 38, 39, 65, 67, 69, 78, 83, 86, 92, 94, 114, 171, 178, 213, 230, 266, 267, 269, 270, 271, 279, 280, 285, 290, 295, 316, 318, 327, 331, 332, 333; *see also comitia centuriata; concilium plebis; contio*
assidui 137, 139, 140, 142, 148, 149, 150
auctoritas 12, 88, 220, 303, 312
auctoritas senatus 315, 316
auspices, *auspicia* 27, 36, 50, 65, 66, 72, 79, 80, 83, 91, 95, 102, 117, 125, 126, 130, 166, 173, 176, 192

banquets 77, 96, 119, 123, 225
booty 69, 70, 74, 123, 134, 135, 136, 137, 138, 139, 142, 143, 144, 145, 146, 147, 148, 149, 150, 152, 168, 209, 213, 214; *see also manubiae;* plunder

calendar 21, 100, 116, 161
Capitol, Capitolium, Capitoline temple 4, 23, 69, 98, 109, 116, 118, 125, 127, 128, 167, 168, 170, 173, 174, 209, 301
censor, censorship 2, 6, 21, 29, 35, 184, 203, 215, 217, 218, 223, 236, 249
Circus Maximus 109
comitia centuriata 4, 142, 173, 220, 269, 313
concilium plebis 64
consul, consulship: *passim*
consul suffect 28, 29, 266, 286, 325, 333
consular army 185, 234, 241, 243
consular authority 12, 232, 323
consular elections 269, 300, 305, 331, 332, 333
consular laws 11

consular tribunes 24, 28, 29, 36, 66
consular year 6, 11, 13, 98, 99, 100, 101, 103, 106, 107, 115
consulares, consulars 7, 8, 12, 13, 31, 71, 84, 183, 211, 213, 215, 222, 223, 224, 225, 226, 227, 228, 229, 230, 231, 233, 235, 238, 239, 240, 248, 249
contio 8, 163, 269, 270, 271, 279, 280, 293, 295, 296
cursus honorum 6, 63, 84, 89, 95, 165, 223, 227, 281, 284, 294

decemvirate, decemvirs 4, 10, 20, 23, 26, 34, 35, 36, 37, 39, 50, 54, 55, 56, 57, 58, 59, 102, 110, 123, 222, 291
democracy 297, 314
dictator, dictatorship 2, 11, 22, 24, 26, 30, 31, 32, 33, 34, 37, 38, 57, 64, 65, 69, 81, 87, 100, 105, 108, 110, 111, 112, 113, 125, 126, 171, 177, 178, 183, 184, 186, 187, 189, 190, 192, 193, 198, 199, 200, 203, 204, 212, 233, 234, 235, 241, 300, 301, 302, 326
domi (militiae) 4, 89, 91, 95, 173, 329

exempla virtutis, exemplum 13, 74, 176, 177, 182, 183, 184, 185, 187, 200, 206, 207, 208, 215, 226

fasces 4, 88, 90, 166, 169, 170, 171, 173, 174, 178, 180, 266, 267, 278
fasti 1, 4, 5, 19, 20, 21, 22, 23, 25, 26, 31, 32, 63, 118, 325
Fasti Antiates 22
Fasti Capitolini 9, 21, 22
Fasti Feriarum Latinarum 104, 123, 124, 126
Fasti Triumphales 22
Feriae Latinae 12, 103, 104, 107, 112, 115, 116, 117, 120, 121, 122, 123, 125, 126, 127, 129, 131
flamen Dialis 266
flamen Martialis 71

Subject index

games 11, 108, 109, 110, 111, 112, 115, 133, 134, 145, 150, 161, 180, 186, 217; *see also* ludi

historiography (ancient) 19, 25, 27, 28, 35, 68, 184, 311
historiography (modern) 7, 262, 295
honos, honores 5, 9, 71, 78, 83, 84, 85, 87, 95, 164, 278, 331
hospitium 233, 237, 238, 239, 242, 250, 251, 252, 255

imperium 2, 3, 4, 5, 6, 7, 9, 10, 11, 15, 24, 27, 33, 38, 61, 63, 66, 67, 68, 71, 74, 78, 79, 80, 81, 82, 83, 84, 85, 86, 87, 88, 89, 90, 91, 92, 93, 94, 95, 96, 108, 110, 112, 117, 125, 126, 130, 132, 152, 167, 168, 169, 171, 172, 173, 174, 175, 176, 180, 220, 232, 233, 234, 235, 236, 237, 240, 242, 266, 285, 290, 297, 303, 316, 323, 324, 328, 330, 334; *see also* consular authority
Iuppiter Latiaris 103, 116, 119, 121, 122

lectio senatus 218, 223
lex Cornelia de provinciis ordinandis 1, 7, 89, 323
lex curiata de imperio 3, 78
lex Gabinia 94, 312, 315
lex Hortensia 64, 69, 71
lex Licinia Sextia de consule plebeio 5, 64
lex Manlia 263
lex Ovinia 217, 218, 219
lex Plaetoria 73, 74
lex Pompeia de provinciis 8
lex Porcia de provinciis 92
lex Villia annalis 6, 227
lictor 4, 73, 166, 167, 169, 170, 171, 172, 173, 174, 178, 179, 180, 224, 243, 266, 323
ludi 108, 109, 110, 111, 112, 113, 115, 161, 220; *see also* games

magistracies, magistrates; *see* aedile; censor; consul; dictator; praetor; quaestor; tribune of the plebs
manubiae 12, 133, 134, 135, 136, 142, 143, 144, 145, 149, 151, 152; *see also* booty; plunder
memory 13, 131, 167
military tribunes 20, 24, 28, 29, 34, 35, 95, 177, 217, 272, 273
Mommsen 1, 13, 61, 79, 80, 89, 216, 276, 320, 321, 322, 323, 324
money 133, 134, 135, 137, 138, 139, 140, 144, 145, 146, 151, 152, 204, 242, 249, 250, 267, 308; *see also* wealth
monuments 21, 33, 95, 133, 148, 150, 167, 168, 199, 209

nobilitas, nobility 1, 5, 6, 273, 283, 284, 287, 288, 294, 296, 297, 322

optimates 14, 15, 279, 280, 281, 286, 288, 289, 290, 293, 294, 296, 299, 300, 302, 304, 306, 310, 311, 312, 313, 317

patron, patronage 73, 165, 228, 246, 247, 248, 249, 250, 252, 253
pax deorum 11, 97, 98, 100, 101, 113, 115, 116
performances 100, 129, 131, 162, 179, 181, 183, 184, 191, 193, 200, 202, 204, 208
plunder 135, 142, 143, 144, 149, 151, 152, 190, 261; *see also* booty; *manubiae*
pomerium 91, 171, 174, 323, 330
pompa circensis 109, 110
pompa funebris 164, 168, 224
pompa triumphalis 164, 174
populares 14, 279, 280, 281, 282, 283, 284, 285, 286, 287, 288, 289, 290, 291, 292, 293, 294, 296, 297, 300, 305, 306, 307
praetor, praetorship 2, 6, 7, 10, 24, 25, 32, 33, 35, 38, 39, 49, 50, 52, 54, 55, 59, 61, 62, 63, 64, 66, 67, 68, 69, 71, 72, 73, 74, 80, 81, 82, 83, 84, 85, 86, 88, 89, 93, 100, 101, 105, 108, 110, 111, 112, 113, 114, 151, 169, 178, 215, 219, 222, 227, 233, 236, 249, 323, 327, 332, 333
praetor maximus 4, 5, 20, 23, 24, 32, 33, 38, 39, 40, 49
princeps 9, 321, 322, 323, 326, 329, 331, 332, 333, 335
princeps senatus 203, 207, 230, 305
privatus 170, 171, 215, 263
processions 12, 101, 109, 118, 161, 164, 165, 167, 173, 174, 183; *see also pompa circensis; pompa funebris; pompa triumphalis; profectio*
prodigia, prodigies 11, 98, 99, 100, 101, 102, 103, 106, 111, 112, 115, 116, 125, 220, 327
profectio 173, 174; *see also pompa circensis; pompa funebris; pompa triumphalis;* processions
province, *provincia* 6, 8, 10, 13, 14, 25, 67, 68, 85, 86, 89, 92, 93, 94, 98, 100, 101, 102, 103, 106, 107, 108, 110, 111, 112, 114, 115, 118, 122, 124, 141, 150, 151, 152, 169, 174, 230, 233, 236, 263, 272, 301, 323, 330, 332, 334

quaestor, quaestorship 34, 37, 81, 137, 273, 289

sacrifices 99, 101, 102, 104, 105, 106, 107, 108, 111, 113, 117, 119, 121, 122, 123, 125, 129, 167, 192

senate: *passim*; *see also auctoritas senatus*; *senatus consultum*
senatus consultum 99, 117, 220, 281, 316
senatus consultum ultimum 8, 279, 287, 295, 303, 310
symbolic capital 164, 243, 250, 253

tessera hospitalis 238, 251, 252
tribune of the plebs 2, 5, 86, 171, 172, 189, 215, 263, 271, 272, 284, 285, 288, 291, 292

triumph, *triumphator* 26, 69, 70, 71, 72, 77, 78, 91, 93, 95, 96, 114, 118, 125, 128, 133, 134, 137, 139, 143, 144, 145, 150, 152, 173, 184, 199, 208, 209, 214, 235, 236, 241, 283

ver sacrum 11, 111, 112, 113, 114, 115, 186, 192, 193
violence 58, 262, 263, 276, 282, 303, 313, 316

wealth 71, 134, 135, 136, 137, 150, 152, 242, 243, 250, 288; *see also* money

Milton Keynes UK
Ingram Content Group UK Ltd.
UKHW022253290823
427731UK00025B/259